Edited by Michael J. Trebilcock, J. Robert S. Prichard,
Thomas J. Courchene, and John Whalley

Federalism and the
Canadian Economic Union

PUBLISHED FOR THE ONTARIO ECONOMIC COUNCIL BY
UNIVERSITY OF TORONTO PRESS
TORONTO   BUFFALO   LONDON

ISBN 0-8020-3401-2

Canadian Cataloguing in Publication Data

Main entry under title:
Federalism and the Canadian economic union

Papers presented at a conference held at the
University of Western Ontario Law School, Dec. 1981.
ISBN 0-8020-3401-2

1. Canada – Commercial policy – Congresses.
2. Interprovincial commerce – Canada – Congresses.*
3. Nontariff trade barriers – Canada – Congresses.
I. Trebilcock, Michael J.,   II. Ontario
Economic Council.

HF1479.F42   381'.5'0971   C83-098278-7

This report reflects the views of the authors and not necessarily those of the Ontario
Economic Council or of the Ontario government. The Council establishes policy
questions to be investigated and commissions research projects, but it does not
influence the conclusions or recommendations of authors. The decision to sponsor
publication of this study was based on its competence and relevance to public policy
and was made with the advice of anonymous referees expert in the area.

FEDERALISM AND THE CANADIAN ECONOMIC UNION

April , 1984

Dick

With enormous respect.

Rob.

Contents

PREFACE vii

ACKNOWLEDGMENTS xi

CONTRIBUTORS xiii

PART ONE: THEORY AND CONCEPTS 1

1
Securing the Canadian economic union: federalism and internal barriers to trade
J. Robert S. Prichard with Jamie Benedickson 3

2
Analytical perspectives on the Canadian economic union
Thomas J. Courchene 51

3
Political structure and the pursuit of economic objectives
J.R. Melvin 111

PART TWO: EVIDENCE 159

4
Induced distortions of interprovincial activity: an overview of issues
John Whalley 161

5
The impact of federal policies on interprovincial activity
John Whalley 201

6
Provincially induced barriers to trade in Canada: a survey
Michael J. Trebilcock, John Whalley, Carol Rogerson, and Ian Ness 243

PART THREE: COMPARATIVE PERSPECTIVES 353

7
Government procurement policies: GATT, the EEC, and the United States
W.C. Graham 355

8
Regulation of industrial subsidies in the EEC, the United States, and GATT
Warren F. Schwartz 394

9
Fiscal harmonization in the United States, Australia, West Germany,
Switzerland, and the EEC
Wayne R. Thirsk 424

10
Personal mobility in the United States and the EEC
John B. Laskin 456

PART FOUR: PROPOSALS AND CONCLUSIONS 499

11
Existing and proposed constitutional constraints on provincially induced
barriers to economic mobility in Canada
Michael Penny with Michael J. Trebilcock and John B. Laskin 501

12
Summary and implications
The editors 542

Preface

This book was prompted by the current controversy about barriers to trade in Canada. It is widely believed that the Canadian market is rapidly becoming highly balkanized by the spread of such barriers and that constitutional reforms are required to arrest this trend. Concern about internal barriers to trade has been spurred by a number of political developments. The publication of the federal government's policy paper entitled *Securing the Canadian Economic Union*,[1] the constitutional debates over the inclusion of mobility rights in the new Canadian Charter of Rights, and the prominence of sovereignty-association as a form of economic integration in the Quebec referendum have all focused attention on the nature and strength of the Canadian economic union. Furthermore, a number of recent studies have catalogued and generally decried the apparently increasing number of barriers to trade within Canada.[2]

This book attempts a substantial study of these issues, drawing on law, economics, and political science and including theoretical, empirical, comparative, and institutional perspectives. It is something of a collaborative effort. In 1980 the Canada-U.S. Law Institute of the University of Western Ontario and the Ontario Economic Council agreed to sponsor a major research project in which lawyers and economists would examine the myriad of issues that arise under the

1 Chrétien, *Securing the Canadian Economic Union in the Constitution: Discussion Paper Published by the Government of Canada* (Ottawa: Ministry of Supply and Services, 1980).
2 Safarian, *Ten Markets or One? Regional Barriers to Economic Activity in Canada* (Toronto: Ontario Economic Council Discussion Paper, 1980); Maxwell and Pestieau, *Economic Realities of Contemporary Confederation* (Montreal: Accent Quebec, C.D. Howe Research Institute, 1980); Trebilcock, Prichard, and Kaiser, 'Interprovincial Restrictions on the Mobility of Resources: Goods, Capital and Labour,' in Ontario Economic Council, *Intergovernmental Relations: Issues and Alternatives – 1977* (Toronto: Ontario Economic Council, 1977); *Interprovincial Economic Co-operation* (Toronto: Ontario Ministry of Industry and Tourism, 1981); John C. Pattison, 'Dividing the Power to Regulate,' in *Canadian Confederation at the Crossroads* (Vancouver: Fraser Institute, 1978).

general rubric of securing the Canadian economic union. Draft study outlines from the contributors were reviewed by all of them collectively and examined critically by a group of distinguished outside commentators. On the basis of the revised research plans drafts were prepared of the essays that compose this book.

These essays were presented in December 1981 at a conference at the University of Western Ontario Law School. Participants at that conference included specialists in the field as well as representatives of both the public and private sectors. During the conference the essays were discussed individually, and at a final session conference participants commented generally on what they believed the constitutional implications to be. The individual papers have been revised in light of the conference, and the final discussion of constitutional reforms is reflected in the concluding essay in the book.

The book consists of four parts. The first part deals with issues and concepts in the debate over interprovincial barriers to trade, identifying the key conceptual issues in this subject as a background for the empirical work and comparative case studies that follow. Though the three chapters in this part address a common set of issues, each has a distinct focus. The first chapter, by Prichard and Benedickson, addresses the issue at the heart of the entire project, that is, when considering government intervention how to distinguish barriers to trade from non-distortionary economic policies. This chapter also includes a discussion of the advantages and disadvantages of decentralization, the various constitutional and institutional mechanisms that can be used to capture the advantages of decentralization without suffering some of its more extreme costs, and varied perspectives on the sharing of powers within a federal state. The second essay, by Courchene, emphasizes the historical context of the debate over barriers to trade and the prominent role of the federal government in creating distortions within the Canadian economy. The differences between the approaches of the first two chapters and Courchene's emphasis on the role of both provincial and federal government distortions highlight some of the controversies surrounding the very definition of the problem. In the final essay in the first part, Melvin provides a more theoretical perspective on these issues, developing a model of decision-making for both unitary and federal states and demonstrating the incentives for distortionary activity in both. In doing so, Melvin confirms and demonstrates that the phenomenon of distortionary government intervention in the economy is not simply a consequence of federalism but can arise with any political structure and is in fact an artifact of the state itself.

The second part of the book is largely empirical. The number of apparent barriers to trade in Canada is large and increasing, but there has been no comprehensive attempt to measure their economic significance. The contributors to this part attempt three tasks. First, drawing on international trade theory in economics, they develop a methodology whereby it is possible to make estimates of the welfare losses associated with different types of barriers. Second, they catalogue, and make preliminary measurements of, the most prominent federally induced barriers to trade. Third, they catalogue in some detail provincially induced barriers to trade on a province-by-province basis and measure the most significant of them. The results are instructive. The barriers to trade within Canada are found to have a significant but not (at least not yet) an enormous economic impact. Furthermore, the federal government is responsible for a large proportion of the total – ironically, because the federal government has tended to be popularly associated with efforts to *reduce* barriers to trade created by the provinces. However, despite the attempts to measure the significance of the barriers examined, as the studies show this task is fraught with uncertainty and plagued by an absence of data, so that all results must be considered tentative.

The third part of the book is devoted to comparative case studies of specific barriers and the response to them in other jurisdictions, primarily the United States, the European Economic Community (EEC), and countries subscribing to the General Agreement on Trade and Tariffs (GATT). These studies describe alternative institutional arrangements that can be used to respond to various types of barriers to trade in the belief that Canadian initiatives can usefully be informed by the experiences of other communities that have faced similar problems. Limitations of space and budget made it impossible to undertake comparative studies of all the major forms of barriers, and four were chosen for detailed study. Laskin examines mobility rights in the United States, the EEC, and GATT. Graham deals with government procurement policies in the United States, the EEC, and GATT. Schwartz examines industrial subsidies from a more thoretical perspective in light of experience in the United States and the EEC. Finally, Thirsk examines fiscal harmonization, evaluating the experience in numerous jurisdictions around the world. Though not comprehensive in coverage, these comparative studies suggest what the implications of alternative institutional mechanisms might be in a Canadian context.

The fourth part of the book discusses reform options for Canada. First, Penny (with Laskin and Trebilcock) reviews the current constitutional allocation of responsibilities as it bears upon interprovincial barriers to trade and the major reform initiatives which have been proposed in recent debates. Secondly, Trebilcock, Courchene, Whalley, Prichard, and other contributors in a conclusion summarize the findings of the other contributions and review critically various options for reform. This review suggests where the margins of change may lie and which types of reform seem most likely to be politically acceptable.

In the process of making this book the contributors found that their collective discussions transformed and clarified the issues and concepts. In progressing from the issues to the evidence to the comparative case studies and then to the conclusion, we hope that the reader's experience will be a similar one.

THE EDITORS

Acknowledgments

This project was given financial support by the Ontario Economic Council and the Canada-U.S. Law Institute of the University of Western Ontario Law School. We are indebted to both organizations for making the entire project possible.

As the preface indicates, the authors derived great assistance from various experts in the field both in designing the research project and in commenting on the draft essays. These commentators were Robin Boadway, Albert Breton, Edward Safarian, Douglas Hartle, Marsha Chandler, Caroline Pestieau, Richard Bird, Thomas Wilson, Richard Simeon, Gérard Bélanger, Peter Hogg, Claude Lemelin, and David Smith. We are greatly indebted to all of them in addition to all the other conference participants who gave us the benefit of their views.

Paul Jones, a second-year law student at the University of Toronto Law School, played a major role in checking all the citations and footnotes in the volume and co-ordinating the editorial process. Verna Percival, secretary to the Law and Economics Programme at the University of Toronto, provided major secretarial support in the latter stages of the project. Gail Madill of the University of Western Ontario Law School provided similar services in the organization of the research papers and the conference. The papers were edited with great care and competence by Larry MacDonald.

Among the authors, Michael Trebilcock, director of the Law and Economics Programme at the University of Toronto Law School, assumed particular responsibilities as the project director. He, Robert Prichard, Tom Courchene, and John Whalley were responsible for co-ordinating the editorial process and preparing the manuscripts for publication and are therefore identified as the editors of the volume.

Finally, Professor Jack Quinn, previously of the University of Western Ontario Law School and now at Osgoode Hall Law School, deserves special mention.

As director of the Canada-U.S. Law Institute, he helped conceive the project, perceived its potential, and gave it his wholehearted support. While his name appears nowhere else in this book, his intellectual and administrative contributions throughout the entire project were invaluable.

Contributors

THOMAS COURCHENE is a professor of economics, specializing in monetary economics and fiscal federalism, at the University of Western Ontario and is currently chairman of the Ontario Economic Council.

WILLIAM GRAHAM is a professor of law, specializing in international trade law, at the University of Toronto.

JOHN LASKIN was, until 1983, an associate professor of law, specializing in constitutional law, at the University of Toronto and is currently practising law with the Toronto law firm of Tory, Tory, DesLauriers, and Binnington.

JAMES MELVIN is a professor of economics, specializing in international trade theory, and the immediate past chairman of the Department of Economics at the University of Western Ontario.

ROBERT PRICHARD is an associate professor of law at the University of Toronto and a member of the Law Faculty's Law and Economics Programme and is currently on leave as a visiting associate professor of law at Yale University.

WARREN SCHWARTZ is a professor of law, specializing in international trade law and law and economics, at Georgetown Law Centre, Washington DC.

WAYNE THIRSK is a professor of economics, specializing in public finance, at the University of Waterloo.

MICHAEL TREBILCOCK is a professor of law at the University of Toronto and is director of the Law Faculty's Law and Economics Programme.

JOHN WHALLEY is a professor of economics and director of the Centre for the Study of International Economic Relations at the University of Western Ontario.

CAROL ROGERSON, JAMIE BENEDICKSON, MICHAEL PENNY, and IAN NESS are recent graduates of the University of Toronto Law School. Rogerson and Bendickson are currently undertaking post-graduate studies at Harvard Law School. Penny and Ness are practising law with Toronto law firms.

PART ONE: THEORY AND CONCEPTS

1
Securing the Canadian economic union: federalism and internal barriers to trade

J. Robert S. Prichard with Jamie Benedickson

INTRODUCTION

In current debates on Canadian constitutional reform, the reconciliation of the competing claims concerning political decentralization and economic integration is widely considered to be one of the more demanding conceptual challenges. The problem is not new to Canada. In the 1930s it had been elevated to the national policy agenda with the Report of the Rowell-Sirois Royal Commission,[1] and it has remained prominent ever since. Nor is it confined to Canada. The events of American constitutional history and the repeated efforts to create and strengthen the European Economic Community (EEC) and the General Agreement on Tariffs and Trade (GATT) reflect the same pervasive issue: how to attain economic unity within a decentralized political system.

Indeed, the tension between political autonomy and economic integration is inescapable in any non-unitary political system. Only by the mutual sacrifice of independence of action can states reap the full advantages of integration because the economic advantages flow from the adoption of common, or at least co-ordinated, rather than competing policies. Furthermore, the greater the advantages sought from integration, the greater the necessary sacrifice of political autonomy, either by submission to some central authority such as a federal

We have benefited from comments by Tom Courchene, Franklin Gertler, Jim Melvin, Michael Trebilcock, John Whalley, and participants at the Federalism and the Canadian Economic Union Workshop at the University of Western Ontario. In addition, this essay draws upon research supported by the Law and Economics Program at the University of Toronto by Janet Yale presented in an unpublished paper, 'Perspectives on Political Decentralization' (1980).

1 Canada, Royal Commission on Dominion-Provincial Relations, *Report* (Ottawa: King's Printer, 3 May 1940).

government or by the adoption of mutually binding prohibitions on tariff and other policies.

Thus the challenge in a federal state is not to maximize economic integration or decentralization but rather to find the appropriate compromise between the two. 'The task which we seem to be facing today' one commentator has suggested 'is to establish a balance in which the various communities which compose the country derive significant net advantages both out of their autonomy *and* out of their common association, and, equally important, perceive themselves as deriving such advantages.'[2] However, this synthesis of the tensions in Canadian federation introduces many crucial and complex issues whose solutions are inevitably intertwined. What are 'the various communities which compose the country?' What 'net advantages' do they seek, and what disadvantages might they fear? Who will establish the 'balance,' and by what means? What advantages will be perceived so that preferences are satisfied and seen to be satisfied, and how long will it take for that to happen? These and many related questions must be addressed before one can assert with any confidence that the existing position can be improved upon. Furthermore, not all the units will hold the same views as to the proper balance.

At present there is an extensive array of interprovincial barriers to trade within Canada. Both the federal and Ontario governments have recently published position papers cataloguing the impediments to the free flow of goods, capital, and labour.[3] These papers draw upon and confirm numerous Canadian academic studies, notably those by Safarian and by Maxwell and Pestieau.[4] Such studies and the vast international literature on the subject suggest that the importance of these barriers has been growing rapidly in recent years, although the evidence is based primarily on the number of such barriers rather than on measures of their cumulative economic impact.

2 D.R. Cameron, 'The political impact of the free movement of goods, persons, services and capital on the general process of integration: the Canadian case' (unpublished mimeograph, 1979), at 5.

3 J. Chrétien, *Securing the Canadian Economic Union in the Constitution: Discussion Paper Published by the Government of Canada* (Ottawa: Ministry of Supply and Services, 1980); Ontario, Ministry of Industry and Tourism, *Interprovincial Economic Co-operation – Towards the Development of a Canadian Common Market: Proposals for Interprovincial Economic Co-operation and for the Establishment of a Canadian Domestic Market Development Agency* (Toronto: Government of Ontario, 1981).

4 A.E. Safarian, *Canadian Federalism and Economic Integration: Constitutional Study prepared for the Government of Canada* (Ottawa: Information Canada, 1974); Safarian, *Ten Markets or One? Regional Barriers to Economic Activity in Canada* (Toronto: Ontario Economic Council Discussion Paper, 1980); J. Maxwell and C. Pestieau, *Economic Realities of Contemporary Confederation* (Montreal: Accent Quebec, C.D. Howe Research Institute, 1980).

Various prescriptions are offered in response to the growth in Canada of internal barriers to trade. Some argue for greater centralization of authority to strengthen and broaden the federal government's powers over the economy. Others urge that the current constitutional prohibition on customs duties in interprovincial trade be broadened to encompass other barriers. Alternatively, some argue that mobility rights for citizens should be entrenched in the constitution in order to ensure that no government, federal or provincial, could impede individual mobility. Finally, others believe the solution to lie in intergovernmental agreements and codes of conduct like the GATT codes which should be negotiated, progressively implemented, monitored, and enforced.

While the responses vary, the concern appears to be widespread as does a belief that something can be done. However, to move from merely enumerating and describing these barriers to suggesting how it is possible through negotiation or constitutional change to do better requires a number of difficult normative judgments and the resolution of some complex issues.

This chapter tries to highlight some of these judgments and issues as an introduction to the remainder of the volume. It does not attempt to reach firm conclusions or even to adopt any particular position. Rather, it simply seeks to show that consistent arguments for change depend on resolving these issues and making these judgments. As with so many public policy questions, no change is free, few are cheap, and all will be controversial. The costs of change will not be evenly distributed, and many of the possible consequences are obscure and perhaps uncertain.

The chapter consists of four parts. The first considers the definition of barriers to interprovincial trade, arguing that to distinguish between a 'distortion' and a 'correction' of trade flows one must decide whose preferences should count in a federal state and identify what those preferences are. The second part examines the case for and against political decentralization. The third part discusses some possible institutional arrangements that maintain the primary advantages of decentralization without sacrificing the potential gains from economic integration, and it compares these institutions with simple centralization. The fourth part addresses the interdependence and overlap of the provincial and federal jurisdictions. The conclusion discusses possible reforms.

DISTORTIONS, BARRIERS AND INTERPROVINCIAL BARRIERS TO TRADE

Introduction

The potential advantages of economic integration are derived primarily from the gains from trade among the participants in the form of more efficient production, enhanced international competitiveness, and consequently higher incomes. That is, through integration the participants may reap the benefits of the theory of comparative advantage through specialization and exchange. These gains are maximized when the factors of production and the resulting goods and services are allowed to move freely among participants to locations where the highest value is put on them. Thus gains from trade should increase the gross national product or national income of each of the participants, as long as the free movement of factors is maintained.[5]

Economic integration may also allow mutual gains to all the participants through three other processes: the spreading of the risk of economic instability, which may be caused by fluctuations in international demand for specific products or by natural events; co-operation in the provision of joint services (e.g. defence, transport, communications) characterized by economies of scale; and the enhancement of international stature or bargaining power.[6] In conjunction, these processes make it possible for integration to create an economic surplus to be shared by the participants, a surplus which could not be earned by each participant acting alone. The 'surplus' is the amount by which the national income of Canada is larger than the total of the separate provincial incomes that would be achieved if the provinces functioned as independent national units. Indeed, 'if a case is to be made for a revised form of federalism, it must be based on the promise that a greater economic surplus can be created if the participants agree to establish a co-ordinated approach to development policy and interregional economic relations than if they try to start afresh on their own.'[7] As Usher has observed, in the Maxwell-Pestieau analysis 'the problem of constitutional reform is to divide that surplus among the provinces so that no province is made worse off by confederation than it would be if independent.[8]

Economic integration can vary in degree. Balassa has categorized the different stages of integration as follows: 'From its lowest to its highest forms, integration has been said to progress through the freeing of barriers to trade (trade integration), the liberalization of factor movements (factor integration),

---

5 This statement ignores a number of important qualifications in the formal statement of the gains-from-trade theorem. These include: (1) that the theorem is proved in terms of utility, not income; (2) that it depends on constant returns to scale and no distortions; and (3) that there is an appropriate redistribution of income. To the extent that these conditions are relaxed, the strength of the appeal to the theorem must be diminished.

6 *Economic Realities of Contemporary Confederation*, at 14. These gains are all subject to the qualification in note 5. The sources of potential gains also include increased efficiency of capital markets, opportunities for taking advantage of scale economies outside the public sector, elimination of monopoly power, and co-ordination of taxes and tariffs.

7 Ibid., at 15.

8 Usher, 'Book review' (1981), 14 *Canadian Journal of Economics* 535, at 536.

the harmonization of national economic policies (policy integration), and the total integration of these policies.[9] These stages of integration would be accomplished through different institutional arrangements. The basic categories are as follows:

- A *free trade area* involves the elimination of tariffs on goods moving between the member countries, while each remains free to regulate its own tariff bariers against non-members. It is thus vitally important to secure agreement concerning which goods will circulate freely within the area to avoid the problem of a low-tariff state being used by a non-member as a point of entry to the entire free trade area.
- A *customs union* is a free trade area combined with standardization of tariff barriers against non-member countries.
- A *common market*, is a customs union combined with the elimination of restrictions on the mobility of capital and labour as well as on goods.
- An *economic union* involves varying degrees of harmonization of state economic policies in order to remove discrimination arising from disparities in these policies. A combined *monetary and economic union* adds to the economic union the feature of a common currency.
- A *federal union* or *federation* is a monetary and economic union with the added feature that each member forgoes a fraction of its sovereignty which is transferred to a central government.[10]

The objective of each form of union is to gain the advantages of a surplus from economic integration. As one progresses from lower to higher stages of integration or from weaker to stronger institutional arrangements, the potential economic benefits to the total community of economic integration tend to increase while the opportunities for autonomous actions by the participants tend to decrease. There is an inevitable inverse relationship between economic

9 Balassa, 'Types of economic integration'. In F. Machlup, ed., *Economic Integration, World-wide, Regional, Sectoral* (London: Macmillan, 1976), at 17, as cited in Bernier, 'Le concept d'union économique dans la Constitution canadienne: de l'intégration commerciale a l'intégration des facteurs de production' (1979), 20 *Cahiers de Droit* 177, at 181.

10 Based on Canada, Task Force on Canadian Unity, *A Future Together: Observations and Recommendations* (Ottawa: Minister of Supply and Services, 1979), at 67 (also known as the Pépin-Roberts Report); Safarian, *Canadian Federalism*, at 2; Bernier, 'Le concept d'union économique,' at 180; R. Dehem, *On the Meaning of 'Economic Association'* (Montreal: Accent Québec, C.D. Howe Research Institute, 1978), at 5–11. These issues are discussed at greater length in Courchene's contribution to this volume.

integration and political autonomy, although the optimal arrangement in the sense of maximizing the economic surplus may fall short of a single, world-wide federation.[11]

An economic distortion is any policy which interferes with the resource allocation functions of the market, thereby preventing the free flow of capital, labour, or goods and reducing the advantages that can be gained from specialization and exchange. Thus restrictions on labour mobility, discriminatory government procurement policies, capital subsidies, and the many other forms of interprovincial barriers to trade all may reduce the overall level of national economic activity by reducing the potential gains from specialization and exchange. The net effect of these barriers in Canada is not merely a redistribution of economic activity but also a net reduction in such activity, because the barriers sacrifice various productive efficiencies.

Distortions in interprovincial trade flows are not limited to the most obvious barriers to trade such as protective occupational licensing and provincial procurement preferences. They arise similarly from incentives such as industrial location subsidies, which also cause resources to flow to other than their highest valued use. Thus a capital subsidy that causes a plant to be built in one province which, in the absence of the subsidy, would have been built in another reduces economic efficiency because it also detracts from the potential gains available through specialization and exchange. The term 'interprovincial barriers to trade' includes incentives as well.

It might seem that any form of government intervention that serves to alter the relative prices of capital, labour, and goods is a distortion and thus bad. However, such a conclusion would ignore a number of important qualifications, such as the existence of externalities, the problem of the second best, and the real limitations on the use of maximizing national output as the sole objective of public decision-making. These exceptions must now be considered.

Qualifications

1 Externalities
Many forms of government intervention may be corrections of the market mechanism, rather than distortions, and thus desirable even within the objective of maximizing national income.[12] Government intervention may be required

---

11 For example, with respect to an economic union, the literature on the notion of an optimal currency area suggests an area smaller than the world.
12 Schwartz and Harper, 'The regulation of subsidies affecting international trade' (1972), 70 *Michigan Law Review* 831.

where it is too costly to account through private transactions for external effects associated with some particular activity. Such 'corrections' may respond to costs or benefits imposed on or received by non-parties to a transaction (in the relevant circumstances, ordinarily a production transaction). Accordingly, 'the issue is not that of identifying and remedying "distortions" but rather of determining if a particular measure on balance "corrects" or "distorts" the market process, that is, whether it increases or decreases the efficiency with which resources are allocated.'[13]

The introduction of the concept of externalities to traditional analysis based on comparative advantage has the following implications:

If the value that society places on the production of a good is not, for some reason, fully reflected in market transactions, its social value is higher and the costs to society of foregone production are correspondingly lower. Under these conditions, a subsidy in the amount that non-party beneficiaries would pay if there were a functioning market for the externality can theoretically be justified as increasing efficiency. This kind of subsidy would, moreover, add to, rather than reduce the gains from trade coupled with specialization, which are predicted by the theory of comparative advantage.[14]

Schwartz and Harper, who advance this argument, refer to the case of government subsidies for research and development (R & D) expenses. If a company undertaking research, particulary basic research, is unable to capture the full value of the resulting benefits, a tendency to underinvest in R & D may be expected. A government subsidy of R & D expenses in these circumstances can therefore be viewed as an additional or compensatory return equal to the value not captured or recoverable through private transactions. As a result, national income will be enhanced, not lessened, by the subsidy program.

This argument has broad implications. Before a policy which alters or affects the interprovincial flow of goods, capital, or labour is categorized as a distortion, an analysis must be undertaken to determine whether or not the policy is more accurately characterized as a correction of the market's resource allocation functions. If the policy or intervention is responsive to an externality, it may be complementary to, rather than destructive of, the objective of maximizing the gains from economic integration.

13 Ibid., at 834.
14 Ibid., at 841.

2 The problem of second best

The second qualification to the view that any government intervention altering the relative prices of capital, labour, or goods is a distortion arises from the general theory of second best.[15] This theory holds that if a market is affected by more than one imperfection (for example, by both monopoly power and barriers to trade) one cannot be certain that the elimination of either imperfection alone will improve the overall efficiency of the market or that the addition of a further imperfection will diminish efficiency. Since one imperfection may offset the effect of another, it is never certain that reducing the number of imperfections will restore the operation of the market unless all imperfections can be eliminated. Unless all interprovincial barriers to trade are eliminated, the elimination of only one or a few could reduce national output, while the addition of a new barrier could enhance output. Any set of interprovincial barriers to trade will reduce output compared to an economy free of such barriers, but the effect of the addition or elimination of any particular barrier cannot be demonstrated by theory alone.

The implications of the theory of second best are not limited to interprovincial trade policy. It applies to any form of economic intervention in an imperfect market economy since one can never be sure that any given intervention will be welfare-enhancing. However, the consensus among economists appears to be that while the limitations inherent in the theory of second best must be recognized, they should not be allowed to paralyse policy. Rather, the theory counsels a case-by-case examination of the nature of the barrier, its prevalence, the likely offsets, and so on, before the conclusion is reached that the reduction or elimination of the barrier will improve efficiency. It also suggests that, to the extent that offsetting policies are involved, co-ordinated reductions in particular types of barriers will be essential.

3 Maximizing national output as an objective

These first two qualifications on the concept of a distortion – the problem of externalities and the theory of second best – do not challenge the appropriateness of maximizing national output as a goal. They point to two difficulties in distinguishing distortions from corrections whether or not national output is maximized. The third and fourth qualifications question that goal.

---

15 F.R. Flatters and R.S. Lipsey, 'Common ground for the Canadian common market' (Kingston: mimeo, Department of Economics, Queen's University, 1981), at 29–31; Lipsey and Lancaster, 'The general theory of second best' (1956–7), 24 *Review of Economic Studies* 11.

The use of national income or output as the benchmark against which distortions should be measured carries with it an assumption that total demand as revealed in the national marketplace accurately reflects the preferences of citizens. However, if citizens have objectives other than merely maximizing output, the benchmark must be redefined to encompass them. Thus, even policies that are clearly distortions when measured against maximizing national income may become corrections of the market economy when measured against a more broadly defined objective.

Schwartz and Harper use agricultural subsidies to illustrate this proposition.[16] Noting that subsidy programs that increase the income of persons engaged in farming are often criticized as leading to inefficiency in the allocation of resources, they argue that to describe this inefficiency as a distortion ignores the possibility that the programs are responding to social preferences broader than simply maximizing national output:

We believe, however, that these criticisms are valid only if certain assumptions are made about the objectives that the government measures are designed to accomplish. Stated within the framework of our analysis, if the government action is designed to give effect to externalities and succeeds in doing so, it is efficiency-enhancing.

There are two principal externalities to which agricultural subsidies may be responsive. First, for reasons of social preference, it may be thought desirable to keep a certain portion of the population engaged in agriculture – even if purely private competition would result in a smaller number of persons remaining in farming. Second, it may be thought desirable to maintain a level of domestic production so that the country would be self-sufficient to some degree in the event that foreign supplier countries, for political or military reasons, chose not to sell to it.

These reasons can be deplored as misguided by those who disagree with them, but there is no way in principle to reject them as less legitimate than others in defining what the particular 'demand' is within a country. It is moreover by no means unreasonable to believe that such demand exists. For it has often been pointed out that income maintenance which leaves an individual free to choose his occupation, or government payment of the retraining and relocation costs involved in a change of occupation, provide less costly ways to ameliorate the condition of those who can no longer engage in agricultural production in a truly competitive market. But the persistence of programs that have the effect of keeping people in farming and domestic production at a certain level suggests that there is at least some significant preference

16 Schwartz and Harper, 'The Regulation of Subsidies,' at 845–7.

for this result quite apart from the desire simply to increase the income of persons presently engaged in farming.[17]

Thus any interventionist policy that gives effect to the preferences of citizens which would not be realized through the market can, on this argument, more properly be described as a correction than a distoriton. There is no reason why preferences that the market meets should be given special recognition; all preferences have equal claim to validity. As Schwartz and Harper say of the preferences for keeping people on the farm or for developing national self-sufficiency in the production of food: 'the fact that the demand is not manifested in the market does not mean that it does not exist.'[18]

If this argument is accepted, as surely it must be, the difficulty of making normative judgments concerning interprovincial barriers to trade is increased dramatically. It then becomes impossible to divorce the distinction between distortions and corrections from judgments concerning the ability of governments to interpret the non-market preferences of citizens, since any policy can be defended as a correction responding to those preferences. Whether or not the defence is a valid one must turn on a judgment concerning the nature of the legislative process, the relative influence of producer and consumer interest groups, and other matters. Therefore, judgments concerning the responsiveness of the legislative process are inherent in any categorization of a policy or program as a distortion, and the validity of the categorization is no more robust than the underlying judgment.

4 The impact of multiple communities

The limitations on defining a distortion as a deviation from maximizing national income becomes even more apparent in light of the fact that Canada is composed of different political communities. For example, how significant should provincial boundaries be in defining the national objectives of economic policy? If the maintenance of provincial boundaries is judged to be a national goal, then policies supporting them, even at some cost in terms of maximizing output, are not necessarily distortionary.

In a paper on regional development objectives and strategies in a federal state, Courchene develops seven possible objective functions, each of which would

---

17 Ibid., at 846. The argument could be extended by reference to potentially offsetting effects to various subsidies provided to urban areas. See Whalley's contribution to this volume.
18 Ibid., at 847.

have different implications for defining a distortion.[19] The objectives are as follows:

1 Maximize national income
2 Maximize national income subject to the constraint that:
  – that there be a minimum level of income for all Canadians:
3 Maximize national income subject to the constraints:
  – that there be a minimum level of income for all Canadians;
  – regional income disparities be narrowed.
4 Maximize national income subject to the constraints:
  – that there be a minimum level of income for all Canadians;
  – that *provincial* income disparities be narrowed.
5 Maximize national income subject to the constraints:
  – that there be a minimum level of income for all Canadians;
  – that this income be produced (earned) in each region.
6 Maximize national income subject to the constraints:
  – that there be a minimum level of income for all Canadians;
  – that this income be produced in each region;
  – that regional production disparities be narrowed.
7 Maximize national income subject to the constraints:
  – that there be a minimum level of income for all Canadians;
  – that this income be produced in each *province*;
  – that *provincial* production disparities be narrowed

These objectives are arranged so that the level of national income will fall as one moves down the list, since the greater the regional or provincial constraints imposed by the objective, the greater is the departure required from the freedom of movement of goods, capital, and labour. If any objective in the lower portion of the list is accepted as the appropriate statement of the preferences of citizens, many policies that would be distortions in terms of maximizing national income become corrections designed to achieve the more regionally or provincially oriented objective.

How to choose among these or any other objectives is the fundamental problem of Canadian federalism because it requires not choices among strategies or policies but rather choices that reflect our simultaneous desires for

19 T. Courchene, 'Alternative regional development strategies in a federal state.' In Schramm, ed., *Regional Poverty and Change* (Ottawa: Ministry of Supply and Services, Canadian Council on Rural Development, 1976), at 192–3.

integration and autonomy, and diversity without balkanization. Simeon, in his outstanding analysis of this issue, compellingly shows the difficulty of specifying notions of optimality in a federal state.[20] No single criterion seems able to capture the complex set of concerns and values that inform our intuitive judgments of good and bad in the constitutional sense; the notion of communities, both provincial and regional, is influential but not decisive. Similarly, functional arguments concerning the effectiveness of government are important but are inseparable from the choice of the community or communities within whose boundaries public welfare is to be advanced. Democratic values such as participation, responsiveness, liberty, and equality are relevant to assessing constitutional arrangements, and the tensions among these values ensure that there is no single arrangement which is demonstrably and unambiguously superior to all others. Perhaps flexibility or adaptability is itself a criterion for designing federal structures.

The very existence in federalism of competing criteria generally confirms the elusiveness of hard answers to the question of what to do about interprovincial barriers to trade. The answers, whatever they may be, cannot on the whole be arrived at without first answering the most difficult questions of constitutional design. Recognition of this fact may help to ensure that the issue of interprovincial barriers to trade will not be relegated to technocrats for decision, but rather will remain a question immersed in political, ethical, and constitutional complexity.

Conclusion

When defining the concept of a distortion it is inadequate to say simply that it is any form of government intervention which alters the relative prices of goods, capital, or labour or which reduces national output below the level which could be achieved through complete economic integration. In view of the pejorative connotations associated with the word 'distortion,' it is fundamental to recognize that a policy is only a distortion to the extent that it leads to a departure from the otpimal result, and that the optimal result is a good deal more complex than simply maximizing national output. Thus, before one concludes that the lengthening catalogue of interprovincial barriers to trade reflects a deteriorating situation which warrants a response by constitutional or other means, it is essential that the barriers be assessed not only in terms of their impact on national income but also on the more complex array of objectives inherent in a

20 R.E. Simeon, 'Criteria for choice: a survey of the issues' (Toronto: unpublished working paper, Law and Economics Programme, Faculty of Law, University of Toronto, 7 March 1979).

federal state. This is not to say that the efficiency losses associated with some interprovincial barriers are unimportant or should be ignored; any sensible assessment of the desirability of a policy requires an appreciation of its costs. Rather, it is a counsel of caution against concluding too readily that the costs associated with the barriers are necessarily unjustified. Potential benefits may frequently exist as well.

This caution is particularly important in the absence of compelling data as to the magnitude of the efficiency losses caused by the existing array of interprovincial barriers. Based on the data presented by Whalley and Trebilcock in their contributions to this volume, the losses seem modest. Furthermore, despite the impressively long catalogue of barriers, we have little indication whether the total costs associated with these barriers have increased substantially in recent years. And even if the costs have increased, the conclusion that we are therefore less well off still depends on the choice of national objectives.

If distortions are understood this way – as departures from an optimum which is not necessarily that of maximizing national income – the task of constitutional reform becomes not one of eliminating barriers to trade but rather one of designing institutions and processes for balancing costs and benefits in a manner that is sensitive both to the potential gains from economic integration and to the advantages of diversity and autonomy. A federal system that is itself a very varied structure is of course one such institution which attempts to maintain the appropriate compromise between integration and autonomy.

THE CASE FOR AND AGAINST POLITICAL DECENTRALIZATION

Introduction
The advantages and disadvantages of centralist and decentralist options for the allocation of powers within a federal system can be usefully examined from the functionalist perspective that asks 'which level of government can most efficiently and effectively carry out any given responsibility of contemporary government? The system as a whole is evaluated in terms of its ability to respond to the needs of citizens – to provide them with the mix of public policies which they prefer.'[21] We have seen that the functional perspective does not necessarily provide a comprehensive normative standard for judging the constitutional allocation of powers, but it offers insights and helps highlight the relevant compromises. The primary concern here is the overall division of powers. A governmental system may be classified according to its degree of centralization

21 Ibid., at 9.

or decentralization. Cairns offers a general statement on the process of distributing powers or functions:

The division of jurisdictional authority is undertaken in accordance with the principle that matters of significant concern to those communities whose existence compelled the federal choice in the first place are given to provincial or state governments. The central government, by contrast, is accorded governing power over those matters on which citizens are unlikely to differ on a territorial basis, or on which they share a common interest in their effective, uniform administration from the centre.[22]

The classification of different activities as significant from a national or provincial standpoint will also vary over time.

What, then, are the advantages of centralization and decentralization of powers? At this stage our benchmark is the relative ability of alternative constitutional arrangements to maximize the satisfaction of the preferences of a majority of voters.

The analysis borrows heavily from Tiebout, who was concerned with the problem of preference revelation in the context of assessing the benefits taxes which would assure Pareto-optimal expenditures on public goods and services.[23] Tiebout emphasized the role of citizen mobility among jurisdictions as a means of encouraging the revelation of preferences. The creation of a market in jurisdictions allowed consumer-sovereignty to work in a situation in which individuals had an incentive to conceal preferences for public goods and services so as to avoid paying higher tax prices for them. While individuals would not voluntarily reveal willingness to pay, decentralization of functions and jurisdictional choice would compel them to register preferences. Thus, he conceived of a world in which the packages of public goods and services offered by each jurisdiction were fixed and known and citizen/voters merely allocated themselves to the jurisdiction that offered the desired output mix. The resulting configuration was one of homogeneity within and diversity among jurisdictions.

22 Alan C. Cairns, *From Interstate to Intrastate Federalism in Canada* (Kingston: Discussion Paper No. 5, Institute of Intergovernmental Relations, Queen's University, 1979), at 4.
23 Tiebout, 'A pure theory of local expenditures' (1956), 64 *Journal of Political Economy* 416. Tiebout's work was in part a response to Samuelson's concern with concealed preferences and public goods: see Samuelson, 'The pure theory of public expenditures' (1954), 36 *Review of Economics and Statistics* 387. While we borrow Tiebout's approach, an important difference remains. The Tieboutian approach seeks to achieve Pareto-optimal (value-maximizing) outcomes as measured by aggregate willingness to pay. Our approach, taken from the public choice literature, views the satisfaction of the preferences of a majority of voters as optimal.

The analysis below posits a notion of a political market created by the diverse jurisdictions in a federal state competing by offering different policy packages to voters, and by individuals choosing among jurisdictions as a means of indicating preferences. However, the role of decentralization in policy formation is examined not only with respect to the provision of public goods and services but also in relation to all government functions. Thus, citizen choices relate to the government policies or policy packages offered by various jurisdictions, and the policy packages offered reflect the demands and preferences of the citizens.

The advantages of decentralization
Public choice theory suggests that constitutional arrangements should be judged according to their ability to maximize the satisfaction of the preferences of a majority of voters. For a number of reasons adopting such a criterion may at first appear to suggest a bias in favour of decentralization. First, interest groups that may be minorities nationally are more likely to be majorities locally.[24] Second, and complementary to the first point, the greater the homogeneity of interests on a geographical basis, the more often minorities become majorities as decentralization increases. Third, decentralization of functions in a hierarchical way disaggregates policy packages and allows a citizen to cast different votes on different components of policy because they are vested in different levels of government in the jurisdictional hierarchy. Fourth, decentralization, by creating a diversity of jurisdictions, allows a better matching of preferences and policies because voters can choose that jurisdiction which offers the most preferred policy package.[25] That is, citizens may 'vote with their feet,' searching out the jurisdiction offering the most attractive set of policies. Simultaneously, the threat of exit by voters from a jurisdiction forces the decentralized governments to reflect the policy preferences of their existing or potential constituents as the jurisdictions compete for voters. Fifth, given the greater homogeneity of tastes as boundaries contract, decentralization reduces the likelihood of policy com-

---

24 In Scott's words: 'if a nation that is divided among majority and minority parties (or interest groups) is cut up at random into small territorial jurisdictions, the total number of citizens who must suffer as minorities from the policies of the majority will decline; that is, the number of people who are in agreement with government decisions will increase.' Scott, 'An economic approach to the federal structure.' In *Options: Proceedings of the Conference on the Future of the Canadian Federation* (Toronto: University of Toronto, 1977), at 268.

25 West and Winer, 'The individual, political tension and Canada's quest for a new constitution' (1980), 6 *Canadian Public Policy/Analyse de Politique* 3.

promises being adopted that create minimum winning coalitions but do not accurately reflect the interests of any particular interest group.

These five considerations combine to offer the primary attraction of decentralization: the capacity of smaller jurisdictions to satisfy the diverse needs, tastes, and preferences of citizens in different locations. As stated by Scott: 'ideally the outcome is that diversity among citizen's demands is satisfied by diversity among actions of small governmental units.'[26] Decentralization relaxes the presumed uniformity of centralized policy formation because local governments have an electoral incentive to respond to local majorities, whether or not the local majority position would also be favoured at the national level.

A sixth advantage of decentralization is the reduction of 'signalling' and other 'transactions costs' for expressing citizen preferences. Signalling activity includes: (1) participation in efforts to influence the actions of lobbies and large pressure groups; (2) engaging in actions to influence politicians directly; (3) joining social movements; (4) regulating one's own private economic behaviour; (5) organizing the private provision of public and non-private goods; and (7) voting or the act of giving one's support to or withholding it from a candidate of a political party or, in very special cases, a policy.[27]

While signalling and other transactions costs are discussed in greater detail below, several points are worth noting. A large number of small jurisdictions reduces the distance (in the sense of access) to local politicians, thereby lowering the costs both of registering preferences and of monitoring the behaviour of politicians. In addition, access to politicians at several levels of government provides increased opportunities for signalling preferences.

A seventh, and final, advantage of decentralization is that it may encourage or facilitate innovation in the provision of public services or policy development. For example, a comparison is sometimes made between the evolution of labour laws in Canada and those of the United States. In Canada, primary jurisdiction for the regulation of labour relations is provincial while in the United States federal jurisdiction prevails. Weiler has argued that the Canadian experience has been marked by a greater openness to experimentation and innovation, partly because the costs of an unsuccessful experimental change in small jurisdictions are much less than the cost of failure of new policy initiatives in a centralized

---

26 Scott, 'An economic approach to the federal structure,' at 267. See also Boadway and Norrie, 'Constitutional reform Canadian-style: an economic perspective' (1980), 6 *Canadian Public Policy/Analyse de Politique* 492, at 495.
27 A. Breton and A. Scott, *The Economic Constitution of Federal States* (Toronto: University of Toronto Press, 1978), at 32.

system.[28] Similarly, Breton and Scott summarize the process of innovation by smaller units with reference to the concept of 'pilot projects':

Briefly stated, the point is that smaller governmental units can try out new solutions, provide new responses, and engage in experiments that, of necessity, involve smaller populations. These smaller units introduce new policies to deal with local problems and opportunities, but by doing so they, at the same time, serve as 'pilot projects' for the rest of the country. If the experiment is unsuccessful, only a small part of the country had to endure its consequences. Consequently, at the same time that risks of large errors, implicit in large or national projects, are avoided or, more exactly, minimized, experimentation on a small scale provides an efficient way of learning.[29]

The validity of the 'pilot project' interpretation of decentralization has not gone unchallenged. Rose-Ackerman, focusing on politicians' incentives to take risks and the political uncertainty of innovation, raises a number of qualifications.[30] She assumes that although voters may tend to cluster according to certain characteristics, they are not likely to be concentrated on the basis of preference for risk-taking. She then argues that 'Politicians' choices will depend upon their knowledge of other jurisdictions' actions. If they ignore other governments, wasteful duplication can occur. If they hope to benefit from other governments' activities, few risky projects may be undertaken. Those that are carried out may be structured so that it is difficult for others to copy the results.'[31] Rose-Ackerman concludes that in light of the ambitions of politicians, the opportunities for career advancement, the prevalence of free riders, and the costs of uncertainty, the force of the 'pilot project' argument in favour of decentralization may be modest.

Nor can it be guaranteed that decentralization will in all circumstances and for all policies lead to expected advantages. For example, it is difficult to see how the satisfaction of a citizen who opposes the availability of abortions can be substantially increased by moving to a jurisdiction where abortions are prohibited. As long as abortions remain available in other jurisdictions they will

28 Weiler, 'The virtues of federalism in Canadian labour law.' In *The Direction of Labour Policy in Canada, 25th Annual Conference, 1977* (Montreal: Industrial Relations Centre, McGill University, 1977), at 58.

29 A. Breton and A. Scott, *The Design of Federations* (Montreal: Institute for Research on Public Policy, 1980), at 18. See also Lysyk, 'Reshaping Canadian federalism' (1979), 13 *University of British Columbia Law Review* 1.

30 Rose-Ackerman, 'Risk-taking and re-election: does federalism promote innovation?' (1980), 9 *Journal of Legal Studies* 593.

31 Ibid., at 594.

continue to be carried out, presumably in at least the same number as before, for it is assumed that citizens opposed to abortions are not themselves potential consumers of abortions. In fact, when critics leave the jurisdiction, its decision-making is removed from their sphere of political influence, and abortions may become more readily available to those who wish them. The numbers of abortions being performed could then actually increase – as would, presumably, the level of dissatisfaction of opponents of abortions.

While this example may be interpreted as the replacement of a compromise not accurately reflecting the interests of any group by a situation in which pro-abortionists have obtained the policy they favoured, it also forces us to confront one of the possible limitations of using the satisfaction of the majority's preferences as a benchmark for evaluating constitutional arrangements: have we actually increased the overall satisfaction of the population where the anti-abortion minority's dissatisfaction may have increased greatly while the majority voters may have each experienced a moderate increase in satisfaction? Other grounds for caution regarding the apparent advantages of decentralization include the fact that the disaggregation of policy packages between levels of government may allow consistent voting and an acknowledgment that even central governments can and do innovate by means of pilot projects so as to reduce the costs of potential error.

The factors favouring decentralization are not entirely unconstrained since otherwise the case for decentralization would involve an infinite regress. If the advantages of decentralization are ordinarily seen to lie in the realm of political responsiveness and greater refinement of preference satisfaction (the demand side), centralization is commonly regarded as offering economic advantages in fulfilling government functions (the supply side). In particular, economies of scale and spillover or externality management may be more easily achieved through centralization.[32]

The disadvantages of decentralization

The inefficiencies arising from decentralization can best be understood by analogy to the notion of 'market failure.' If the diverse jurisdictions in a federal state are viewed as competing in a market for voters, it is illuminating to predict the forms of market failure that are likely to occur since, as with all markets, there is no reason to suppose that this 'market' will be perfectly competitive. In particular, as decentralization increases, externalities and spillover effects will increase

---

32 A.E. Safarian, *Canadian Federalism and Economic Integration*, at 7–8; Scott, 'An economic approach to the federal structure,' at 267; Simeon, 'Criteria for choice: a survey of the issues,' at 13.

because some of the costs of policies can be externalized by imposing them on neighbouring jurisdictions. In addition, economies of scale in the production and provision of public goods are likely to be forgone in some cases as a result of decentralization. Finally, the costs of transactions in the jurisdictional market-place may be high to the extent that the cost of voter mobility is high and/or voters face high information costs about the policies being offered by the competing jurisdictions.

Since these three forms of market failure associated with decentralization form the foundation of the case for a central authority in a federal state, some further comment on each is warranted.

1 Externalities

Political externalities are the effects of policy decisions taken in one jurisdiction on the residents of other jurisdictions. These spillovers may take several forms. In terms of the provision of local public goods and services, spillovers are created when the span or impact of the good or service extends beyond the boundaries of the jurisdiction providing it. The existence of spillovers among communities, whether positive or negative (that is, beneficial or detrimental), implies that provision is suboptimal; in a non-technical sense, the preferences of all individuals affected by the policies are not being taken into consideration. The most obvious forms of externalities relate to local public goods such as fire and police protection, emission standards for local industry, non-excludable recreational facilities such as parks, and so on. These spillovers are characterized by their large impact on those in neighbouring jurisdictions who reside closest to the boundaries of the community whose actions generate the externality.

Political externalities are also created by provincial policies which discrimi-nate against resources and goods from outside the jurisdiction. While these restrictive or protective measures may be generally advantageous to a local interest group, the costs of the policies are being externalized to voters beyond the scope of concern of the decentralized decision-maker. Costs may be imposed on those outside the jurisdiction (or on consumer groups within it). There are two possible solutions to the problem. The one most commonly suggested is that of increasing jurisdictional size to internalize these externalities. In other words, by expanding the boundaries of the jurisdiction to include those individuals who suffer the spillover effects, the new policy will reflect their preferences. In the extreme situation this leads to a unitary state. The alternative is to ensure interjurisdictional co-ordination of policies or direct enfranchisement of affected citizens in the neighbouring jurisdiction. Both of these possibilities involve maintaining decentralized authority but compelling each jurisdiction through some institutional mechanism to consider all relevant preferences. The transactions costs entailed by these two responses to interjurisdictional spillovers are primarily the costs of government administration and co-ordination in ascertaining and meeting voter preferences.[33]

Costs of co-ordination among jurisdictions may be expected to increase with the extent of spillovers and is probably related to the number of jurisdictions affected and the magnitude of the impact experienced by each. Since the likelihood of spillovers is inversely related to community size, co-ordination costs will probably increase as jurisdictional size decreases, that is, as the number of jurisdictions increases, The relationship of administrative costs to jurisdictional size on the other hand is less clear. The decentralization of functions entails the cost of setting up more administrative units; thus the centralization response to the existence of externalities eliminates duplication of facilities. However, the reduction in the number of jurisdictions constrains the use of voter mobility to reveal preferences and requires increased investment of resources by citizens and government in non-market processes such as lobbying as alternative means of ascertaining preferences. Citizen transactions costs will be discussed in a later section; for governments, it would appear that the larger the community, the less homogeneous the tastes of its residents will be and therefore the greater the administrative expense entailed in ascertaining preferences.

2 Economies of scale
A second form of political market failure occasioned by suboptimal jurisdictional size is that of economies of scale in production which may be forgone as a result of decentralization of functions. Subsumed in this category are two problem areas, one involving inefficiences in the provision of a public service or good itself and another relating to effects on national efficiency generated by the policies in a particular jurisdiction. The latter may be viewed alternatively as an externality as discussed in the preceding pages; that is, constraints on factor and output mobility in effect reduce the size of the market, thereby impairing efficient resource allocation and restraining competition.[34]

In the provision of a public good or service it may be possible to consider economies of scale in production separately from those involved in provision.[35]

33 Breton and Scott, *Design of Federations*; Pattison, 'Dividing the power to regulate.' In *Canadian Confederation at the Crossroads* (Vancouver: The Fraser Institute, 1978).

34 Barber, 'The customs union issue.' In *Options: Proceedings of the Conference on the Future of the Canadian Federation*, (Toronto: University of Toronto, 1977), at 213; Lipsey, 'The theory of customs unions: a general survey' (1960), 70 *Economic Journal* 496.

35 This point is derived from Buchanan and Goetz, 'Efficiency limits of fiscal mobility: an assessment of the Tiebout model,' (1972), 1 *Journal of Public Economics* 25; Flatters, Henderson, and Mieszkowski, 'Public goods, efficiency, and regional fiscal equalization' (1974), 3 *Journal of Public Economics* 99.

It is only with respect to provision that economic efficiency concerns may indicate the need to interfere with decentralized responsibility: production may be centralized to take advantage of economies of scale while output or service levels are left to the choice of citizens in lower-level jurisdictions. For example, while fire protection may require equipment which is optimally produced by a small number of national or international firms, community choice may be most appropriate in determining the quantity or level of protection provided. On the other hand, where the optimal scale of service provision is large (or where large-scale production is required and production and provision decisions cannot be separated), decentralized decision-making may not be the best mechanism for satisfaction of citizen preferences.

A countervailing consideration relates to declining competitive pressure among jurisdictions as functions are centralized. The economies-of-scale concern may indicate the need for large jurisdictions; however, decentralized responsibility for policy formation may produce higher quality outcomes than would a situation in which the threat of citizen exit is not present.

3 Citizen transactions costs
A third form of political market failure relates to citizen transactions costs, that is, the cost of various potential forms of investment by citizens in obtaining the policy outcomes they prefer. In situations in which the transactions costs are high, decentralization of functions may be inappropriate since the transactions costs will reduce the likelihood that the competition among jurisdictions will be sufficiently vigorous. These transactions costs can be broadly divided into two categories: mobility and signalling. They are discussed in turn below.

With respect to individuals, the main constraint on mobility would seem to be a monetary one, that is, the relationship of income to residence in a particular community. To the extent that employment is tied to a certain location, the choice of jurisdiction is limited to an area within which access to one's work may be maintained. The scope of this restriction will depend on the nature of the occupation involved, the extent of the move required to change jurisdictions, and the existence of differences in qualifications for practice in professions or occupations across jurisdictions. On the other hand, a change of employment may not be required for certain relocation decisions, such as the movement among suburban communities with equal or virtually equivalent access to a given place of employment.

Aside from employment, immobility may also be created through residence requirements attached as conditions to the provision of social services, such as medical or pension benefits, or social or cultural ties to a particular community.[36] The selection of the mobility option is also influenced by the availability of information about alternative locations.[37]

In addition to these considerations, there must in fact exist differences in policies between jurisdictions for relocation to be an effective means of increasing satisfaction. Furthermore the range of policy options must not be too discrete: discontinuities in the choices available will also constrain the effectiveness of mobility as a mechanism for reducing discontent. While decentralization of functions may be expected to encourage diversity, an alternative view is that vigorous competition between communities constrains the ability of any one jurisdiction to diverge significantly from the policies adopted by the others.

Another set of constraints on mobility concerns the desire on the part of residents not to leave but to attempt to change the policies with which they are dissatisfied. Further, a commitment to improving a particular community as opposed to abandoning it for one in which the preferred policies are already in place, may be viewed as a form of loyalty.[38]

The notion of voter mobility as a substantial constraint on policy formation may strike some as unrealistic. No doubt in the case of individual voters the importance of mobility is greatest with respect to municipal and local decision-making. However, the owners of capital can also be seen as voters in the sense that they must decide where to locate and expand. Furthermore these voters are in many cases highly mobile. One need only reflect on American experience with the chartering of corporations. The mobility of corporations has led to substantial competition between states to attract firms through modification of the state corporations statutes.[39] Similarly, the recent history of labour law amendments in Nova Scotia in response to the threats by the Michelin Tire Company to withdraw its investments from the province provides ample evidence of both mobility and the impact of the threat of mobility.[40]

---

36 Breton and Scott, *The Economic Constitution of Federal States*; A.O. Hirschman, *Exit, Voice and Loyalty: responses to decline in firms, organizations, and states*, (Cambridge, Mass.: Harvard University Press, 1970).

37 Trebilcock, Prichard, and Kaiser, 'Interprovincial restrictions on the mobility of resources: goods, capital and labour.' In Ontario Economic Council, *Intergovernmental Relations: Issues and Alternatives – 1977* (Toronto: Ontario Economic Council, 1977), at 101.

38 Hirschman, *Exit, Voice and Loyalty.*

39 R.K. Winter, *Government and the Corporation* (Washington, D.C.: American Enterprise Institute for Public Policy Research, 1978); cf. Cary, 'Federalism and corporate law: reflections upon Delaware' (1974), 83 *Yale Law Journal* 663.

40 The Michelin story is fully explained in Langille, 'The Michelin amendment in context' (1981), 6 *Dalhousie Law Journal* 523. Weiler, in 'The virtues of federalism in Canadian labour law,' suggests that cases such as Michelin are the exception rather than the rule.

Signalling refers to any form of interest articulation such as voting, citizen involvement in decision-making by public agencies, membership in an association whose purpose is to advance the interests of a particular group, and even letters to the editor. Voting serves to indicate preferences for general policy platforms although, as mentioned previously, the existence of multiple jurisdictional levels makes possible the separation of policy issues and increased effectiveness of voting as a form of signalling activity.

The decision to invest in signalling activity presumably involves an evaluation of expected benefits and costs. The likelihood of influencing the outcome of the policy-making process depends on the individual's bargaining power compared to that of other interested parties, the availability of recognized channels of influence, and the individual's willingness to search for novel means of influence. In addition, the effectiveness of signalling is positively related to the amount of time, effort, and other resources each individual invests. This, in turn, will depend on the individual's degree of discontent with current policies or expected discontent with future policy. In other words the investment in signalling will be positively related to the nature of the issue involved: a policy decision expected to have a large impact and to be exempt from frequent review suggests a relatively large benefit from signalling activity. On the other hand, the smaller the stakes and the more numerous the decisions in a given policy area, the less advantageous is investment in signalling on any particular policy issue. In terms of influence, subject to the possibility of forming coalitions, it would appear that an individual's bargaining power would be inversely related to the number of individuals or interests in the community affected by a particular policy, the intensity of their preferences, and their corresponding commitment to signalling.

Mobility and signalling costs are clearly interdependent. The prospects for successful use of signalling will influence the mobility decision, while in turn the availability and costs of the mobility option will have an impact on the size of investment in signalling. The potential for signalling to operate as a substitute for mobility is important not only where costs associated with the latter are high but also in situations in which the various forms of market failure previously discussed suggest policy areas or functions which should be centralized. In other words, the viability of non-market mechanisms for registering preferences can alleviate concerns that higher jurisdictional levels lack sensitivity to citizen interests.

These inefficiencies of decentralization are alone sufficient to make the economic model of the costs and benefits of decentralization determinate rather than subject to infinite regress. In addition, however, the outcomes created by a highly decentralized structure of government may be uncongenial on distributive grounds as well.

4 Distribution

Even if there were no market failure in the allocative efficiency sense, the results of the decentralized structure might still be viewed as suboptimal if the distributive outcomes violated some generally accepted normative principles regarding the distribution of wealth within the overall political entity.[41] There are two complementary concerns in this respect. First, with competing jurisdictions there may be the potential for wealthier individuals (who are likely the most mobile) to group together and then provide for themselves a superior package of public goods while poorer individuals who are less flexible in terms of jurisdictional location may be left with an inferior package of public goods owing to a lack of sufficient resources to finance a more extensive public output. In other words, if the package of public goods and services offered by each jurisdiction includes the tax prices necessary to finance them, poorer individuals may not be able to 'vote' for the desired jurisdiction. Second, this tendency is compounded by the restricted potential for redistribution within a decentralized federation; the mobility of voters constrains the ability of a particular jurisdiction to impose on the wealthier individuals the obligation to pay for services which most benefit those least able to pay. While this may be viewed as a constraint on wealth redistribution, it may also be characterized as a strong form of protection for minority rights, since such rights are, at least for mobile voters, protected by the potential for exit. Where the appropriate balance lies between these two positions is unclear, but an appreciation of the competing considerations should draw careful attention to the political dynamics of any centralized redistributive instrument or institution.

Summary

This part has demonstrated both the advantages and disadvantages of political decentralization. The advantages derive primarily from increased responsiveness to citizens' preferences. The disadvantages lie in the loss of economies of scale, the potential for externalizing costs from one jurisdiction onto another, transactions costs, and distributive effects. These competing considerations indicate that the optimal political arrangement lies somewhere between extreme decentralization and a unitary state. It is also clear that the task of locating that optimal arrangement requires the balancing of complex tradeoffs.

Any shift away from decentralization intended to overcome some of the costs – for example, externalities – will necessarily come at a price in terms of lost advantages of decentralization. This fact suggests the importance of giving

---

41 Caroline Pestieau, 'The optimality limits of the Tiebout model' (unpublished mimeograph, 1976).

careful consideration to mechanisms and institutions which will ensure that as many as possible of the advantages of decentralization will be preserved while simultaneously minimizing the disadvantages.

INSTITUTIONAL RESPONSES

We have seen that while political decentralization has certain attractive implications, these attractions are constrained by a number of costs analogous to market failures. The problem of interprovincial barriers to trade can be viewed in this framework as a form of market failure arising from the independent decision-making of the provinces. This section explores various institutional mechanisms which might be used to respond to these market failures. In each case, we examine the institution in terms of its ability to maintain and preserve the advantages of decentralization while simultaneously avoiding the costs associated with the decentralization. In this way the analysis illustrates the competing tensions between autonomy and integration reflected in all the mechanisms.

The institutional mechanisms for eliminating externalities, realizing economies of scale, reducing transactions costs, and achieving an acceptable distribution of income can be thought of as lying along a continuum. The continuum extends from those institutions which interfere least with decentralized decision-making to those involving more central control, including ultimately centralization of functions.

This section is primarily a survey of the different institutional options available. A number of the options are explored in greater depth elsewhere in this volume.

Co-ordination
Co-ordination of policies among governments in a federal state may be achieved through negotiations between the executive branches of the governments involved. Often referred to as executive federalism, such arrangements provide an informal mechanism for consultation and co-operation while at the same time maintaining decentralized decision-making authority.

Co-ordination of policies is most often recommended in the context of potential responses to interjurisdictional spillovers. For example, with respect to economic stabilization programs, Maxwell and Pestieau have noted that the effectiveness of provincial fiscal policy is constrained by the leakages and spillovers among regions.[42] Not only are the provincial economies subject to

---

42 Maxwell and Pestieau, *Economic Realities of Contemporary Confederation*, at 47–55.

disturbances originating outside their boundaries, but stabilization policies may also be rendered ineffective if the corresponding efforts of neighbouring provinces are geared to economic problems of a conflicting cyclical or structural nature. Such considerations indicate the need for consultation among regions to ensure co-ordination of economic stabilization policies.

The most often mentioned institutional arrangement for ensuring federal-provincial consultation is an annual conference of first ministers. The Pépin-Roberts Task Force on Canadian Unity recommended emphasis on that mechanism.[43] In addition it recommended the formation of a committee on inter-governmental policy issues composed of the eleven ministers responsible for intergovernmental affairs (Recommendation 55) as well as a permanent intergovernmental committee of officials and experts to study policy and program duplication (Recommendation 56). Similar proposals have been made with respect to interprovincial consultation. For example, the Ontario Advisory Committee on Confederation has recommended co-operation among provinces where policies have national implications but the function is under provincial jurisdiction.[44] The Committee cites education as an example of such a policy area, given the national interest in labour mobility and a trained pool of labour for the national market, and notes the work of the Council of Ministers of Education in this regard.

Indeed, co-ordination and consultation now constitute the predominant mechanism for resolving interjurisdictional disputes. The Federal-Provincial Relations Office in 1972 prepared an inventory showing nearly five hundred organizations providing liaison between the federal and provincial governments.[45]

Co-operation between provinces serves a useful role not only in responding to interjurisdictional spillovers but also in offering some potential for realization of economies of scale in the provision of public services or goods. A good illustration of this option is the joint funding by the Maritime provinces of a single economic research organization. Clearly the resources available to each of the participating provinces for such an enterprise are more profitably spent on a joint rather than a separate venture. The pooling of resources allows for more

---

43 See for example, Task Force on Canadian Unity, *A Future Together: Observations and Recommendations*, Recommendation 54, at 129.
44 Ontario Advisory Committee on Confederation *Second Report of The Advisory Commitee on Confederation: The Federal-Provincial Distribution of Powers* (Toronto: Advisory Committee on Confederation, 1979), at 37–9.
45 R. Bastien, *Federalism and Decentralization: where do we stand?* (Ottawa: Ministry of Supply and Services, 1981), at 45.

extensive research on shared economic problems, avoids duplication of efforts, and saves administrative expenses. Similarly, the provision of police services to certain provinces by contract with the federal government and the RCMP presumably takes advantage of economies of scale in training.

The drawbacks of co-ordination as a means of eliminating political market failures relate to the consensus nature of such endeavours. The effectiveness of liaison arrangements such as intergovernmental committees is dependent upon the environment in which negotiations are conducted, specifically the relative bargaining power of the parties, and the decision rule in place. Bargaining power is in turn a function of the constitutional allocation of powers and the size of the potential gains. To begin with, there must be an incentive for both parties to reach a compromise: gains must be bilateral (e.g. the elimination of reciprocal externalities) for bargaining to produce a mutually beneficial result.[46] Furthermore, where unanimous agreement is required, the transactions costs of consensus must not outweigh the expected benefits. Strategic behaviour, such as holdouts in multijurisdictional negotiations and bilateral monopoly when only two communities must reach a compromise, may preclude the success of attempts at co-ordination and co-operation.

On the other hand it is difficult to conceive of a decision rule short of unanimity in this context. Parties are unlikely to be willing to participate on consultation committees if outcomes may be imposed. Rather, within its sphere of legislative responsibility each jurisdiction will insist on approving any co-ordinated policy objectives before being bound by them. Further, given the tradition of parliamentary sovereignty in Canada, the removal of the policy formation process from the legislative arena poses problems in terms of ensuring accountability to the electorate.

Finally, it should be noted that it may not be possible for jurisdictions to settle their differences in a mutually satisfactory way. Dehem has argued that economic associations or communities tend to fail precisely because there is no effective overriding mechanism for dispute resolution.[47] By contrast, a federal authority overcomes the need for unanimous agreement between member jurisdictions since the central government is endowed with the power to impose the majority solution, subject to constitutional protection for minority interests. In fact the very notion of a federal government implies the internalization of the bargaining processes within the central government, although, as is argued below, the effectiveness and legitimacy of brokerage among competing

46 M. Sproule-Jones, *Public Choice and Federalism in Australia and Canada*, (Canberra: Centre for Research on Federal Financial Relations, Australian National University, 1975), at 45–55.

47 Dehem, *On the Meaning of 'Economic Association.'*

parliamentary interests in reaching fair compromises is contingent upon the structure of the rules determining parliamentary representation.

Harmonization

It was suggested in the previous section that co-ordination may be an inadequate response to political market failures owing to the consensual nature of intergovernmental liaison arrangements. The term 'harmonization' refers to institutional mechanisms for achieving policy co-ordination which entail some element of federal control while at the same time maintaining provincial autonomy in other respects. The methods are directives, as used in the European Economic Community; local option legislation; and delegation.

1 Directives

An institutional response to interjurisdictional political market failures which focuses on harmonization of ends is suggested by the directives used by the European Economic Community.[48] The Commission, the EEC's administrative body, initiates policy proposals in areas in which it believes harmonization of laws is required in order to achieve the objectives of the common market, as manifested in the Treaty. These proposals must be adopted by the Council of Ministers, the EEC's political body, and may be amended by the Council to obtain consensus. The process also provides for consultation with the European Parliament and the relevant government departments of member-states. As an instrument of harmonization, the directive merits particular attention: once passed by the procedure just described, it becomes binding as to the result to be achieved but allows member-states to choose the form and method of implementation.

In the Canadian context, the use of directives might alleviate some of the barriers to trade which arise from decentralized decision-making. A binding directive issued by the federal government could constrain the outcomes but allow for provincial diversity in implementing legislation. In fact such a recommendation has been made by the Canadian Bar Association's Committee on the Constitution in its report entitled *Towards a New Canada*.[49] That Committee proposed that the federal government have the power to establish general economic objectives binding on the provinces as to 'ends' but that the provinces be left free to choose the means of attaining these objectives. Similarly, in international affairs, it was recommended that the provinces be free to pursue

---

48 This discussion is based on ibid.

49 Canadian Bar Association, Committee on the Constitution, *Towards a New Canada* (Montreal: Canadian Bar Association, 1978) at 86; Recommendation 5.

with foreign governments matters within provincial legislative competence, though provincial initiatives would have to conform to the basic orientation of federal foreign policy.[50]

The most fundamental concern with an instrument like a directive relates to the procedure for determining the policy areas requiring harmonization and the subsequent formulation of the content of the directives. In view of the significant impact of such measures on the provincial economies, it would be unrealistic to expect the provinces to agree to the introduction of these instruments into the institutional framework provided for in the constitution unless they received guarantees of participation and consultation. In fact, the Canadian Bar Association proposal included a requirement of ratification of directives by two-thirds of the members of a reconstituted Upper House, whose representatives were to be selected by the provincial governments.[51] The Committee on the Constitution further recommended annual review by both Houses of directives previously issued.[52]

The Canadian Bar Association proposal shows the complexity of the problem of interprovincial barriers to trade. In attempting to ensure substantial provincial input into the formulation of directives, the proposal implicitly recognizes that harmonization (integration) may well be costly in terms of diversity and autonomy and that the central government acting alone cannot be entrusted with the task of determining the appropriate compromises. Limiting the exercise of federal power by providing for provincial representation within the federal institutions themselves is bound to preserve some barriers to trade in the interest of other values. At the same time, by relaxing the decision rule to the point of requiring something short of unanimity, this institutional agreement would probably lead to somewhat different outcomes than mere co-ordination alone.

2 Local-option legislation

An alternative instrument of harmonization which has in fact been applied in Canada is the local-option form of federal legislation. In such legislative schemes the federal statute provides that the provinces must choose to opt in or out of the program in question. For example, this mechanism was used in the context of prohibitions on the consumption and sale of liquor as sanctioned by the decision in *Russell* v. *The Queen*.[53] While alcoholism was held to be a matter

50 Ibid., at 125; Recommendation 2.
51 Ibid., at 86; Recommendation 5.
52 Ibid.
53 (1882), 7 App. Cas. 829 (P.C.).

falling within federal legislative competence, the provinces, by means of a local option provision in the federal statute, The Canada Temperance Act,[54] were free to decide whether or not to participate in the temperance scheme.

The underlying rationale for these attempts at harmonization and co-ordination may be expressed in terms of two of the political market failures previously identified, economies of scale and externalities. The administrative costs of a single national program are likely to be less than the corresponding costs of separate provincially run services. However, the economies-of-scale constraint on decentralization of functions must be weighed against the costs of uniformity, in particular the lack of responsiveness to regional preferences in situations in which a homogeneous national policy is inappropriate.[55] Local-option legislation attempts a compromise between the two extremes of complete decentralization and centralization and provides a solution which takes advantage of economies of scale in administration. Only provinces desiring a policy divergent from the federal one need duplicate the administrative machinery necessary to implement the preferred local program.

The externalities justification for local-option legislation relates to the pursuit of inconsistent regional policies, or policies established by one jurisdiction which neutralize those of neighbouring jurisdictions.[56] As mentioned previously, this potential problem is especially significant in the context of fiscal policy, where leakages and spillovers are inevitable because of the high degree of interdependence of the provincial economies. Unlike with binding directives, however, 'opted-out' provinces are not compelled to meet specified objectives, with the result that diversity among 'ends' as well as 'means' may be expected. Such outcomes may generate externalities in the form of non-tariff barriers to mobility of goods, labour, and capital or (stated in terms of political market failure) may raise the transactions costs associated with jurisdictional choice.

3 Delegation

Co-ordinated action may also be achieved through the use of delegated authority, where one level of government is delegated those powers possessed by another jurisdictional level which are necessary to the implementation of a shared objective. In theory this delegation can be of two kinds, involving either provincial delegation of powers to the federal government or federal delegation of powers to provincial governments. The former depends on consent, of course,

---

54 *Canada Temperance Act*, 1878, s.c. 1878, c. 16.
55 Maxwell and Pestieau, *Economic Realities of Contemporary Confederation*, at 26–38. See also Bastien, *Federalism and Decentralization*, at 25–44.
56 Maxwell and Pestieau, *Economic Realities of Contemporary Confederation*, at 41–58.

and is to that extent limited in its effectiveness by the inherent weakness of a purely voluntary mechanism, as under co-ordination. The latter form of delegation is also limited in being relevant only in those cases in which the federal government has been allocated primary responsibility. Despite these limitations, both forms of delegation are potentially important in addressing interprovincial barriers to trade.

As a response to political market failures, delegation of administrative responsibility for a particular legislative scheme quite clearly enables the realization of economies of scale in administrative expenditures to the extent that it avoids duplicate organizations and facilities. These advantages are dissipated somewhat, however, if the administrative standards of the two jurisdictions are not homogeneous, as shown by the discrimination between intra- and extra-provincial carrier regulation sanctioned by the Supreme Court of Canada in the *Smith* case.[57]

In terms of externalities the use of interdelegation among the provinces can be used to ensure the elimination of spillovers on neighbouring jurisdictions but need not necessarily lead to the pursuit of free trade and the full realization of the advantages of a common market. For example, the egg marketing scheme sanctioned in *Reference re Agricultural Products Marketing Act*[58] ensured reciprocal benefits to producers at the expense of consumers through a restraint on competition, specifically the prohibition on the sale of eggs in excess of provincial quotas. Thus, interdelegation as an instrument of co-operative action may serve to inhibit the entry of goods from other jurisdictions rather than facilitate it. On the other hand, where goods are sold in national markets, delegation of regulatory responsibility to a single agency for the product in question could readily contribute to free movement through avoidance of conflicting standards. In this context harmonization could promote competition in terms of both elimination of externalities in the form of barriers to mobility and realization of scale economies in production when a uniform national standard is imposed.

Prohibitions

Various types of prohibitions on legislative and executive behaviour serve to define and constrain the bounds of permissible government activity either through some form of prior restraint or through subsequent review by another institution. These prohibitions may apply equally to all levels in the jurisdictional hierarchy. Such prohibitions constitute a potentially more extensive

---

57 *R.* v. *Smith*, [1972] s.c.r. 359.
58 *Re Agricultural Products Marketing Act, R.S.C. 1970, Farm Products Marketing Agencies Act, S.C. 1972, Farm Products Marketing Act, R.S.O. 1970* (1978), 19 N.R. 361 (S.C.C.).

response to political market failures than those surveyed to this point, because if widely drawn they can limit interprovincial barriers to trade created by *all* levels of government, including the federal government.

1 Expanded Section 121 / codes of conduct

At present the only explicit constitutional guarantee of free movement of goods is that contained in Section 121 of the BNA Act. The section provides that 'all Articles of the Growth, Produce and Manufacturer of any one of the Provinces shall, from and after the Union, be admitted free into each of the other Provinces.' Safarian has recommended that this section be expanded to include non-tariff barriers to interprovincial trade as a means of ensuring that the free flow of goods and resources is not impeded by provincial regulatory policies.[59] Expanding the scope of Section 121 would be less important if the federal power to regulate trade and commerce were more broadly interpreted so as to reach all important forms of interprovincial barriers to trade. However, it has been notoriously difficult for the courts to determine the boundary between policies aimed at regulation of intraprovincial trade and policies aimed at interprovincial or export trade.[60]

Neither an expanded Section 121 nor an expanded trade and commerce power would restrict the federal government's power to create interprovincial barriers to trade. That is, Section 121 is limited to preventing the provincial imposition of barriers, not federally induced barriers, and the trade and commerce power, as a federal power, is, by definition, not a limit on the federal government's power to create barriers.

This suggests that if the prohibition is to be effective as a constraint on all sources of interprovincial barriers, the scope of Section 121 will have to be expanded to include both federal and provincial policies that create non-tariff barriers to trade. While this would impose a substantial constraint on the growth of barriers, it could at the same time become a substantial constraint on the scope of legitimate governmental activities. Thus there would remain the need for a mechanism to identify justifiable exceptions to the requirement of non-discriminatory treatment. Clearly, restrictions on mobility on such grounds as public morality, public policy, national security, health, and safety must be accepted. However, the difficulty lies in determining, first, the grounds that

---

59 Safarian, *Canadian Federalism and Economic Integration* and Safarian, *Ten Markets or One?* See also Chrétien, *Securing the Canadian Economic Union*, at 29–31.

60 See, for example, *Attorney-General for Manitoba* v. *Manitoba Egg and Poultry Association et al.*, [1971] s.c.r. 689; *Burns Food Ltd. et al.* v. *A.G. Manitoba et al.* (1973), 40 d.l.r. (3d) 731 (s.c.c.); *Carnation Co.* v. *Quebec Agricultural Marketing Board et al.*, [1968] s.c.r. 238.

constitute a basis for legitimate intervention and, second, when the actual circumstances warrant interference on one of the approved grounds for imposing restrictions on mobility.

The question of justifiable exception could be left to judicial determination. The difficulty in this respect relates to the institutional competence of courts to adjudicate issues which will often require an assessment of complex facts and policies, secondary and tertiary economic effects, shifting incidences of burdens of taxes and other costs, and a host of competing policy considerations. This issue of competence may suggest that an alternative should be sought in the form of codes of conduct negotiated among the governments which could specify the legitimate exceptions to the general prohibition. But this solution, which would parallel to some extent the codes of conduct negotiated as part of GATT in the Tokyo round, would raise its own difficulties. First, it would be necessary to determine the decision rule which would apply to code negotiations. To the extent that it is a rule of unanimity, the problems discussed under co-ordination must be faced. To the extent that the rule requires less than unanimity, a degree of homogeneity is introduced which would begin to undermine the case for decentralization itself. Second, there must be an incentive for the governments to reach agreement.

2 Economic bill of rights

An alternative method of ensuring mobility of goods, labour, and capital is to entrench in the individual citizen or firm the right of free movement and the right to gain a livelihood and acquire property in any province.[61] Since the imposition of policies tending to generate tariff and other barriers to mobility would be inconsistent with these entrenched rights, the ability of any one jurisdiction, provincial or federal, to enact discriminatory legislation harmful to economic integration would thereby be constrained. While notionally different from the broad terms of an amended Section 121, which would be binding on both levels of government, the potential effects and difficulties would appear to be similar. The problems of justifiable exceptions and judicial competence would remain, although the solution in the form of codes of conduct may be unavailable.

Economic and mobility rights, including the recently adopted Charter of Rights, are analysed extensively in the contribution to this volume by Laskin, and the reader is referred to that essay for a full review of this instrument.

---

61 West and Winer, 'Canada's quest for a new constitution,' at 12; Sproule-Jones, *Public Choice and Federalism in Australia and Canada*, at 82; H.G. Grubel, 'Reflections on a Canadian bill of economic rights' (unpublished mimeograph, Vancouver, 1981); Chrétien, *Securing the Canadian Economic Union*, at 29–31.

3 Veto

The last type of prohibition to be examined is the veto, possessed by either level of government and operating after the passing of legislation. This instrument has not generally met with the approval of participants in the constitutional reform debate, and it is generally proposed that the federal powers of reservation and disallowance be abolished.[62] The underlying rationale for this recommendation is a concern for maintaining the balance in the division of powers between the two levels of government. It is feared that the ability to intrude after the fact may result in unwarranted interference in matters properly within provincial jurisdiction. It would seem that the instruments of harmonization operating before the passing of legislation to limit the pursuit of protectionist policies by the provinces are a more appropriate mechanism for federal supervision.

Centralization

While prohibitions as a means of responding to political market failures are directed at reserving a sphere of activity free from legislative intervention, centralization entails reallocation of legislative competence from the provincial to the federal level of government. In terms of externalities and economies of scale, it is argued that centralization of function would be expected to secure the elimination of policies which create interprovincial barriers to the free movement of goods, capital, and labour and to ensure the optimal scale of production and provision of public and private goods and services. The argument is based on the assumption that since the central government is accountable to the entire national community, the problem of externalities is eliminated because all costs are internalized. As a result, there is no incentive for the federal government to engage in 'beggar my neighbour' policies of the kind so common in a decentralized system. Furthermore, to the extent that national policies affect regions differently, compensation can be provided by the most efficient means, which would not normally be interprovincial barriers.

However, this argument is subject to qualification because it ignores the vote-maximizing calculus that federal political parties face in varying degrees according to the rules of the electoral system. This calculus requires a party to fashion policies so as to benefit marginal voters while, if possible, imposing the costs of these policies on inframarginal voters in light of the prevailing voting rules which influence the shape of these margins.[63] As Lipsey and Flatters have

---

62 Ontario, *Interprovincial Economic Co-operation – Towards the Development of a Canadian Common Market*, at 53; *A Future Together*, at 127; Recommendation 43.

63 See Trebilcock et al., *The Choice of Governing Instruments* (Ottawa: Ministry of Supply and Services, 1982); Hartle and Trebilcock, 'The choice of governing instrument' (1982), 2 *International Review of Law and Economics* 29.

argued and Canadian history demonstrates: 'a federal government can be elected and stay in power for long periods of time without any support from many significant groups in the population.'[64] A simple majority of parliamentary ridings is all that is required to form a government, and the overall majority need not include majorities from every region. Accordingly, regionally discriminatory policies may be politically attractive to the federal government, as well as to provincial governments, despite the internalization of costs. Examples of such policies abound: regional development grants, energy pricing regulation, differential unemployment insurance compensation payments, and equalization payments. Indeed, as Whalley and Trebilcock demonstrate in their contributions to this volume, the cost of these programs exceeds the total cost of the provincially induced barriers.

To evaluate the degree to which centralization is likely to reduce interprovincial barriers, we must consider whether the federal government would be more committed than provincial governments to efficiency-promoting policies, including the facilitation of the free movement of goods, capital, and labour. The answer is unclear, but a qualified yes may be warranted.

Provincial governments, being responsible only to their local constituencies, are, as has been argued above, directly susceptible to pressures favouring regionally discriminatory policies, because they have no electoral incentive to take account of the damaging effects of such policies on the residents of other regions. Lipsey and Flatters consider and discount two possible restraints on provincial government implementation of barriers.[65] The first of these is provincial recognition that the relatively limited power of their industries in national and international markets severely limits the potential gains from protectionist policies. This restraint, however, may be rendered ineffective because producer interests who are the principal beneficiaries of protectionist policies participate more effectively than consumers in government decision-making, and because local protectionist policies are intended not only to benefit existing producers but also to induce new industries, capital, and labour to enter the jurisdiction.[66]

The second potential restraint on provincial protectionism lies in the recognition by all provinces of the mutually harmful consequences of protectionism and the benefits 'from a voluntary compact whereby each province would agree to restrict their use of such policies on the condition that other provinces did likewise.' Flatters and Lipsey argue that voluntary arrangements are unlikely, however, because of the 'prisoners' dilemma': while it is mutually beneficial for

64 Flatters and Lipsey, 'Common ground for the Canadian common market,' at 14.
65 Ibid., at 15–18.
66 Ibid., at 16.

all provinces to refrain from protectionism, barriers can promote the interest of any individual province (subject to the risk of retaliation).[67]

By contrast, in a broad sense the federal government is not able to externalize costs. Federal political parties only have to maintain majority support and can do so by shifting the costs and benefits of policies within the nation. Furthermore, as a central government, Ottawa has a greater opportunity to redistribute wealth and to do so by means of a wider array of instruments than is available to the provinces, since the 'taxpayers' are less able to exit. Thus a central government is arguably less likely to resort to trade barriers to accomplish regional objectives. However, the argument for assigning redistributive functions to the central government is not beyond criticism. It rests in part on an assumed national commitment to ensuring some significant degree of equality in the level of basic public services and personal income available to each individual within the federation. The community across which redistribution is to occur may itself be a matter of contention. Moreover, preferences about the community within which redistribution is intended to occur may be seen as attempts to foster a desired sense of community identity rather than as responses to an existing feeling of community:

It is at least arguable that the sense of identity of Canadians as a whole or of residents of any particular province and the relative importance to each Canadian of those associations, may ultimately rest on narrow economic interests that may in turn be what they are as a direct consequence of the assignment of powers in a federal system. Provincial jurisdiction over the redistribution accustoms residents of the same province to working with one another and to identifying themselves with one another's needs, while at the same time loosening the social and cultural bonds between people in different provinces. If it is really true, as it is often asserted, that Canadians are a diverse people seeking a national community and a national identity, then the case for a national as opposed to provincial redistributive power becomes very strong indeed.[68]

Another argument for centralized redistributive functions might be developed on the basis of risk-spreading.[69] Since the resources and economic prospects of

---

67 Ibid., at 17.
68 D. Usher, 'How should the redistributive power of the state be divided between federal and provincial governments?' (1980), 6 *Canadian Public Policy / Analyse de politique* 16, at 26.
69 P. Leslie, *Equal to Equal: Economic Association and the Canadian Common Market* (Kingston: Discussion Paper 6, Institute of Intergovernmental Relations, Queen's University, 1979), at 18–19 and 34.

the federation's units differ from each other, their fortunes will fluctuate differently over time. At any given moment some regions will be prosperous, and they should contribute to the support of the less successful regions. This argument is easiest to make it if each unit seems likely at some stage over the long term to produce more than it needs, so that no unit will be a permanent recipient of transfers.

In addition to the previous arguments, which might support a central allocation of distributive functions, and besides the greater range of direct redistributive instruments available to the central government, it also seems that the central government would be less able than provincial governments to externalize costs to the political minority and confine benefits to the political majority. A province can use instruments that are geographically specific. For example, occupational licensing restrictions are readily made coterminous with the provincial boundary, imposing costs on outsiders and preserving benefits for residents. The federal government would appear to be less able to rely on such geographic definitions of costs and benefits and more dependent on less effective and precise instruments to create the barriers.

To the extent that these observations are accurate – that is, to the extent, that the federal government has more effective or lower-cost redistributive instruments and less effective or higher-cost instruments for creating barriers – one would predict that the federal government would be less likely to erect barriers to the free movement of goods, labour, and capital, although it may well engage in substantial redistributive activity.[70]

This argument highlights an important difference between centralization and the prohibitions discussed above. The effect of the prohibitions, if written to encompass both levels of government, could be largely to eliminate the barriers; the effect of centralization is primarily to shift the source of the barriers, although it may also reduce them somewhat.

Once a power is allocated to the central government, how the power is in fact exercised will depend on the particular design of the central government's institutions. Many objections to centralization are actually objections to the manner in which centralized authority is exercised rather than to the existence of central authority itself. Of special relevance in this respect is Lowenstein's distinction between 'interstate' and 'intrastate' federalism, particularly as it has been applied to Canada by Cairns.[71] Interstate federalism is characterized by an

---

70 A countervailing consideration may be that since both signalling and mobility costs faced by citizens tend to increase with centralization of functions, the incentives for efficiency are reduced accordingly.

71 Cairns, *From Interstate to Intrastate Federalism in Canada.*

emphasis on the division of powers whereby the central order of government is assigned responsibilities in which differences of opinion are unlikely to be organized along territorial lines and where decisions within the federal sphere may legitimately be made on the basis of national majorities. Intrastate analysis accepts the pervasiveness of territorial interests and focuses on means of accommodating such differences within the decision-making processes and institutions of the central government: 'territorial particularisms are given an outlet not only by the control of a government at the state or provincial level, but also in the key policy-making institutions of the central government.'[72]

The inventory of possible reforms suggested by the intrastate framework in Canada is extensive.[73] Proportional representation would foster greater parliamentary representation of geographically diverse regional support within the existing party structure. Leadership selection procedures could enhance regional acceptability. The federal bureaucracy could become more regionally representative in terms of recruitment practices and administrative organization. Regional or provincial responsibility might be given renewed emphasis in cabinet formation. Appointments to the Senate, the Supreme Court, and federal administrative boards might be adjusted to give greater recognition to regional claims. Indeed, Cairns has demonstrated that even within the realm of intrastate proposals there are variants whose implications are more or less decentralist, that is, more or less responsive to the claims that provincial governments make to the status of authentic regional representatives. Intrastate federalism, he writes, 'can be appreciated either as a strategy for increasing the impact of provincial governments on national politics, or as a strategy for weakening provincial governments by enhancing the capacity of Ottawa to represent territorial diversities that otherwise constitute the social base of provincial power.'[74]

The purpose of this discussion of the centralization option is not to attempt to resolve all the pressing issues of Canadian federalism but to emphasize the theme we began with: the subtlety and complexity of the issues raised by the issue of interprovincial barriers to trade. There are no straightforward answers; the prospects of satisfactorily reconciling the forces of nation-building and province-building in Canada or any federal society by means of a reallocation of powers under a new constitution must also be assessed in light of the many differing ways in which constitutional powers can actually be exercised. In other words, the level of assignment will not in itself provide a sufficient or conclusive indication of the effectiveness of the original distribution of authority through

72 Ibid., at 4.
73 Ibid., at 12.
74 Ibid., at 3.

constitutional drafting. Each institutional 'solution' carries with it a set of political dynamics that will influence its effectiveness. Furthermore, the particular design of the institution will determine its particular dynamics and thus its likely consequences. As a result, so-called solutions such as 'greater centralization' or 'an economic bill of rights' raise as many difficult questions as they answer. Any such response to interprovincial trade barriers requires the most careful scrutiny to determine by means of positive analysis its likely effects, and only then to evaluate these outcomes within the normative context of satisfying citizens' preferences.

DIVIDED JURISDICTION, OVERLAP, AND INTERDEPENDENCE

The previous analysis of centralization and decentralization concentrated on the allocation of powers to one level of government or the other and then traced the implications of that allocation. It was assumed throughout that the powers could and would be assigned to one level or the other. An alternative solution, which has a ubiquitous presence in Canadian federalism, is that of shared powers. In this arrangement, known as 'divided jurisdiction,' certain constitutional powers, rather than being assigned exclusively to the federal or provincial sphere, are, at least to some extent, jointly held by both. The pervasiveness of the phenomenon is increased by the fact that even when powers are not formally shared, there is nevertheless interaction because policies generated at different levels under different powers will often affect each other. Furthermore, many of the institutional responses discussed above would continue to place emphasis on the sharing as opposed to the exclusive division of powers. This arrangement adds an additional level of complexity to the study of federalism and its implications for securing the Canadian economic union.

Depending on one's perspective and objectives, overlap and interdependence of powers can be viewed as advantageous or disadvantageous. Our discussion of decentralization and the possible institutional responses has already suggested certain effects of overlap. This section considers those effects more explicitly and adds a number of other perspectives.

Attitudes towards the desirability of intergovernmental interdependence vary markedly from an acceptance of the existence of overlap to the view that interdependence is an unfortunate condition to be minimized or eliminated. The classic expression of the latter is found in the report of the Rowell-Sirois Royal Commission on Dominion Provincial Relations:

Both Dominion and provincial Governments are now embarked on joint administration of projects which require positive and constructive co-operation if they are to be carried out efficiently. Two separate governments, neither of which has any authority over the other, must agree on objectives, or the means of reaching them, and on the daily applicaton of these means to new situations. However, there are always a number of issues on which the interests of the Dominion and those of the separate provinces do not run side by side. These differences in interest lead to disagreements which cannot be solved by appeals to the courts because they do not involve questions of formal constitutional power at all ... Accordingly, if the co-operative projects are to be continued, the governments involved must be their own arbitrators. Arbitration conducted solely by the interested parties leads to delay and sometimes to deadlock which is ruinous to administrative efficiency. It always leads in the end to compromise. While compromise is inherent in the political process, it is rarely conducive to good administration ... Where legislative power over a particular subject matter is divided, it is ordinarily desirable that these powers should be pooled under the control of a single government in order to secure a unified effort in administration.[75]

The concerns underlying this view persist. However, the prospects for clearly delineating separate and independent spheres of authority for the federal and provincial governments appear limited. Watts in *Administration in Federal Systems* remarked: 'A supposedly ideal solution is that assumed by the traditional concept of dual federalism. This envisages the minimization of intergovernmental friction by clearly dividing the jurisdiction between governments with no overlap so that each government could operate independently within its own shpere of competence. But ... in practice it has always proved impossible to achieve such a neat division.'[76] Similarly, Sproule-Jones, after considering some criticisms of overlap and proposals to eliminate it, reached this conclusion: 'Such institutional prescriptions and conclusions are derived from assumptions about the monopoly of government and the omnicompetence of government officials in providing goods and services, assumptions which are at best unrealistic in their correspondence to the empirical world.'[77]

In assessing the merits and demerits of overlap and interdependence, four separate perspectives can be developed: accountability, competition, administration, and efficiency.

Accountability and the threat to democracy
Intergovernmental interdependence has come under criticism on the grounds that overlap reduces opportunities for ensuring political accountability, a result

75 Cited in Sproule-Jones, *Public Choice and Federalism*, at 21.
76 R.L. Watts, *Administration in Federal Systems* (London: Hutchinson, 1970), at 62.
77 Sproule-Jones, *Public Choice and Federalism*, at 28.

which is regarded as a cost of divided jurisdiction when compared with the ideal exclusivity of dual federalism. Safarian has described the federal-provincial committee system as a third level of government: 'Fundamentally, it is less accountable than other levels of government, if only because most of its proceedings are far from public view. In a parliamentary system, moreover, if agreement can be reached in such committees, it is difficult either to examine or undo them in legislatures.'[78]

To appreciate the significance of the accountability argument, it is helpful to review the assumptions on which it rests and to consider the relevance of these assumptions today. Ideally, accountability involves the possibility of direct political controls over decision-makers for actions in their spheres of responsibility and assumes meaningful connections can be identified between decisions and outcomes. Such accountability might be described as issue accountability to distinguish it from more general political controls or sanctions related to the overall performance of governments in a wide range of policy areas. Overlap makes accountability difficult to achieve, it is argued, in several ways. The sharing of power can create some confusion or uncertainty in the minds of the electorate concerning who is actually responsible for particular decisions. The tendency for much intergovernmental negotiation to be conducted in a closed manner in unfamiliar forums may also contribute to voter uncertainty. Long-term commitments involving the separation of responsibilities for financing and for spending may also make it difficult for a dissatisfied electorate to exercise its influence effectively. And frequently there is a substantial time lag between policy decisions and their consequences with room for so many intervening influences that cause and effect are not easily traced. But the latter threat to accountability is certainly not confined to fields of government activity where power is shared.

On the other hand, it is not unreasonable to suggest that some features of overlapping arrangements may have improved the environment of political accountability.[79] For example, the focus of attention and the availability of information on federal-provincial meetings or conferences at the prime ministerial level is noteworthy. Issues under consideration appear to receive more exposure than might be the case if they were being handled within one jurisdiction. Public information may be improved by the focusing of resources by both the media and the governments involved. Government participants have

78 Safarian, 'Ten Markets or One?' at 24. See also Black, *Divided Loyalties* (Montreal: McGill-Queen's University Press, 1975).
79 Smiley, *Canada in Question: Federalism in the Eighties* (Toronto: McGraw-Hill Ryerson, 1980).

sufficient resources and self-interest to make investment in analysis and informa-
worthwhile. Finally, delays which are often attributed to the complexity of
intergovernmental co-ordination may also increase opportunities for citizen
involvement in decision-making.

Competition
Another perspective on overlap, and one from which intergovernmental interdependence is seen in a favourable light, is taken by those who regard divided
jurisdiction as a potential safeguard to individual liberty. In essence, this perspective is but a variant of the general case for decentralization, which was discussed
earlier. This view – referred to here as the competitive perspective – has been best
articulated in Canada by West and Winer, presenting the Madisonian concept of
'the compound republic' as expounded recently in the American context by
Ostrom.[80]

West and Winer suggest that 'just as competition among producers prevents a
"centre of power" in the market, so competition between governments is
required to reduce the disadvantages of monopoly organization in the political
process.' Following Ostrom, they see James Madison and his Federalist col-
leagues as attempting 'to devise a system of government where rulers themselves
would be subject to an "enforceable system of constitutional law."' This
required overlapping and concurrency, an arrangement that West and Winer
consider to be multidimensional, in contrast to the unidimensional or hierarchical approach of those who seek a tidy federalism involving careful separation of
powers. Their competitive model, which involves overlap as well as a wider
dispersal of power to other jurisdictions such as municipalities, would help to
provide checks against the power of other levels: 'while the maintenance of
strong, autonomous, local governments is not a sufficient guarantee of the
citizen's rights in general, it is a practical method of protecting the citizen from
the centralized political and bureaucratic elites.'

Administration
Unlike the competitive model's focus on overlap as a safeguard of individual
freedom, the administrative perspective emphasizes the effectiveness of interdependence in meeting citizens' demands for public services. Interdependence and
government interaction may occur in the context of both federal-provincial
relations and interprovincial co-ordination.[81]

---

80 West and Winer, 'Canada's quest for a new constitution'; Ostrom, *The Political Theory of a
Compound Republic* (Blacksburg, Va.: Center of Public Choice, 1971).
81 Black, *Divided Loyalties*, at 110.

The positive features of overlap, duplication, and concurrency within this framework have been analysed from a public choice perspective.[82] Redundancy and rivalry among government agencies may actually facilitate a pattern of ordered relationships if it is assumed that 'sovereign individuals, rather than governments, must agree collectively upon the terms and conditions for providing themselves with preferred types and levels of goods and services that have varying degrees of divisibility, exclusion and choice in consumption.'[83] The contribution of overlap to this result ('the appropriate provision of goods and services in a public economy') has at least three dimensions.

First, overlap and concurrence may permit more precise registration of citizens' demands for goods and services from governments. Overlap, in other words, increases opportunities for signalling. 'By increasing the range of access points within and between governmental authorities, individuals can exploit a wider range of participatory strategies for obtaining preferred policies from collective agencies of government.'[84]

A second, and related, possibility is that overlap gives individuals more opportunities to remedy, moderate, or avoid harmful consequences resulting from the policy preferences of others: 'In the first place, fragmentation within government provides institutional means or facilities for internalizing any negative interdependencies between individuals, between individuals and organizations, and between organizations. It also provides means for seeking remedies for the consumption costs associated with the provision of collective-consumption goods and services.'[85]

The third attractive feature of overlap suggested by Sproule-Jones is a supply-side characteristic. Ongoing interjurisdicitonal interdependence provides continual opportunities for adapting and readapting the collective mechanisms for producing goods and services as citizen preferences change and technology alters economies of scale.

Ostrom reached similar conclusions based on a consideration of the limits of efficiency in large-scale bureaucratic structures. His advocacy of overlap (aside from the individual freedom rationale discussed under the competitive model) emphasizes the public administration advantages:

As long as ample overlap and fragmentation of authority exist, agencies at one level of government can take advantage of the capabilities afforded by agencies operating

---

82 Sproule-Jones, *Public Choice and Federalism*, at 29–33.
83 Ibid., at 29.
84 Ibid., at 29.
85 Ibid., at 29–30.

at other levels. If economies of scale in the production of a public good can be realized by a larger agency, smaller-sized agencies can enter into contractual arrangements to buy services from the larger agency. In such a circumstance small, local government agencies can operate as buyers' co-operatives on behalf of their constituents in arranging for the production of public services in accordance with the preferences of local inhabitants ... Overlapping jurisdictions and fragmentation of authority are thus necessary conditions for public-service industries to exist in structures other than fully integrated monopolies. Centralization need not be conceived as the converse of decentralization in the sense that we speak of centralization *versus* decentralization. In responding to problems of diverse economies of scale, elements of concurrent authority must exist simultaneously in a system of overlapping jurisdictions.[86]

Efficiency

As applied to discussion of overlap, the concept of efficiency has been given both a narrow and a broader meaning or significance. The more limited and more familiar meaning of efficiency is simply used to make the point that intergovernmental relations necessitated by divided jurisdiction are not costless. Joint decision-making consumes resources which might otherwise be available for other purposes. Overlap is also seen as a cause of friction, a problem that presumably could be avoided or reduced by a clearer separation of authority.[87] Furthermore, as Simeon has observed, there is a further dimension to these costs: 'It is also evident that the difficulties of operating the process do tend to channel the energies of the decision-makers towards a concentration on the problem of federal-provincial relations *per se* and away from evaluation of substantive policies.'[88]

More recently, Breton and Scott, using the concept of organizational costs, have commented on concurrent authority as follows:

Concurrent authority and minimum standards can be understood by reference to our model of a constituent assembly assigning functions in such a way as to minimize the use of resources for organizational purposes. These devices will be adopted whenever the costs of co-ordination activities are low enough to permit the formulation and development of contractual payment schemes that go in the direction of internalizing some of the existing interjurisdictional spillovers and externalities and of exploiting some of the interjurisdictional economies of scale ...

86 Ostrom, *Political Theory.*
87 Pattison, 'Dividing the power to regulate,' at 110.
88 Simeon, 'Criteria for choice.'

Concurrent authority means that some kind of machinery will be set up to allow both levels of government to work together on devising and implementing the policies that are encompassed by the function assigned to both levels of government ... Concurrent authority may raise the total amount of investment in co-ordination and in administration, but when it exists and is a decision by a cost-minimizing constituent assembly it must, on an overall basis, be resource-saving.[89]

The Breton and Scott position appears to involve consideration of more issues related to overlap than the other viewpoints. In addition to the claim of the competitive model that overlap may be desirable because it fosters individual freedom, the broad-efficiency argument suggests the conditions or characteristics of a policy area which might explain a preference for concurrence in some areas but not in others. As Breton and Scott acknowledge, however, it is not evident in advance how the conditions would actually apply to any specific public function. Indeed, that this is true of all the perspectives on overlap may easily be seen.

From the perspective of accountability, overlap may be costly in terms of the loss of control by the electorate and legislative decline, but it is also possible to imagine that the contribution of overlap to public information and understanding might be beneficial. The competitive model, which is also a general argument for federalism, might favour overlap where it enhances individual freedom, although the point has been made that this may inhibit the operation of government with unfortunate distributive consequences. Overlap is attractive within the public administration framework to the extent that it facilitates the responsiveness of institutions to citizen preferences and changing economies of scale, but it is viewed unfavourably if an excessive technocratic influence results in undesirable homogenization. The efficiency perspective really encompasses considerations central to the other frameworks (e.g. accountability as a signalling cost problem) and thus also offers uncertain guidelines.

Conclusion
At a minimum, this review of different perspectives on the reality of overlapping powers should have demonstrated that this kind of interdependence as such is neither good nor bad. Like central institutions under intrastate federalism, overlap and interdependence can be tailored and adapted to produce generally desirable results in terms of the complex set of value constraints which inform our federal form of government. Possibly Canadians have spent so much time and energy resisting and decrying the concept of overlap that too little effort has

89 Breton and Scott, *The Economic Constitution of Federal States*, at 85–6.

been devoted to the problem of managing interdependence. Furthermore, so long as this condition persists, it seems improbable that a satisfactory resolution of the competing claims of centralization and decentralization and the range of institutional mechanisms for resolving them will be found.

CONCLUSION

As stated at the outset the primary purpose of this chapter is to demonstrate the subtlety, elusiveness, and essential interdependence of the many issues on the constitutional agenda and in particular those concerning interprovincial trade. In particular, the issue of securing the Canadian economic union must be seen within the broader framework of federalism itself. It is not possible to make coherent arguments for change in this area without linking those arguments to the fundamental value choices inherent in federal systems of government.

The concept of a distortion in interprovincial trade flows cannot be given content independent of normative conclusions concerning the appropriate role of government intervention within a federal state. Furthermore, while political decentralization does inevitably give rise to barriers to trade, it also facilitates a range of desirable objectives in terms of satisfying the preferences of citizens. At the same time a central government faces many similar incentives to create barriers to trade. A range of insitutional arrangements is available to obtain the advantages of decentralization while avoiding its most severe costs. The variety of possible institutional responses and the Canadian policy environment suggests that overlap and interdependence will probably remain major features on the political landscape.

Interprovincial barriers are a predictable, indeed inherent, feature of federal states. At the same time, even in a unitary or centralized state, interregional barriers not dissimilar to interprovincial barriers would arise. The current Canadian situation confirms this argument: the barriers to trade within Canada are far from the exclusive preserve of provincial governments. As Courchene argues and Trebilcock and Whalley document in their contributions to this volume, the federal government itself in the exercise of its central authority is responsible for the most significant departures from and barriers to free trade (in the full sense of the word) within Canada.

This reality causes Courchene to be highly sceptical of any claims by the federal government that it possesses some unique commitment to securing the Canadian economic union and that constitutional proposals for greater centralization (e.g. expansion of the trade and power clause) would facilitate the achievement of this goal. There is, of course, some merit to this scepticism. For the federal government to make self-righteous claims while demonstrating by its actions that it too will fracture the Canadian economic union invites the response that the federal government should be judged by its deeds, not its words. Yet this view of the federal government should not be adopted whole-heartedly. The potential error in the argument that the federal government is at least as threatening as the provinces to the Canadian economic union lies in its exclusive emphasis on economic costs and benefits of government intervention and its disregard for the important distinction between interventions that distort and those that correct.

In evaluating government interventions by federal and provincial governments a fundamental difference between the two must constantly be remembered. The federal government's interventions are motivated by its perception of the vote-maximizing calculus taking into account all Canadians. Subject to the possibility of international externalities, the federal government is accountable in an electoral sense for all the costs and all the benefits imposed on all of the citizens affected by the intervention. That is not to say that the federal government will not impose disproportionate benefits on some voters in some areas of the country and disproportionate costs on others. It is clear, however, that the federal government cannot impose any of the costs of its policies on citizens to whom it is not at least potentially accountable. And it is this fact which gives an inherently different character to federal actions since provincial government interventions are not similarly constrained.

As we have seen, one source of political market failure in a decentralized state is that of externalities. Externalities arise where a province is able to impose at least a portion of the costs of its policies on persons outside the province to whom the provincial government is not even potentially accountable. To the extent that any provincial policy is motivated by this incentive – the desire to externalize costs – it is affected by a fundamental illegitimacy that does not apply, at least in theory, to federal interventions.

Provincial interventions of this kind that distort interprovincial trade must necessarily be suspect because they are difficult to defend by reference to either their substance or the political processes which generated them. In contrast, federal interventions, despite any apparent substantive defects, possess a presumptive legitimacy derived from the political process which generated them: they were adopted by the federal government acting within its constitutional authority and potentially accountable to the entire electorate.

This distinction does not mean that all decisions taken by the federal government are good simply because the federal government took them. Such a position would depend on heroic assumptions concerning the perfection of the democratic processes that underlie the federal government's authority. Even the most casual observer of Canadian politics could quickly rebut such an assumption;

the current regional disaffection with the federal government, the gross imbalances in the regional representation of the federal parties in Parliament, and the inadequacy of the Senate as a countervailing influence are but some of the most obvious inconsistencies. This argument stresses the *potential* accountability of federal actions, where the word 'potential' encompasses qualifications attributable to the current structure of federal decision-making.

The distinction between federal and provincial interventions emphasizes two points. First, simple numerical measures of the distortions introduced by the two levels of government are not comparable because the underlying policies are not necessarily comparable. Second, and more important for this chapter, the distinction suggests that different institutional responses are called for to resolve the two types of problems. To the extent that the distortions arise from externalities, intergovernmental institutions are placed in question. To the extent that distortions arise from some form of political failure in the decision-making structure of a particular level of government, intragovernmental reforms should attract attention. However, if political failure is the issue, provincial governments require scrutiny no less than the federal government.

In securing the Canadian economic union, as in all other areas of public policy, no changes are free and few are cheap. Yet it seems clear that some changes may well be cheaper than others. In particular, it would seem wiser to concentrate on those changes which leave the balance between autonomy and integration within Canada relatively stable, while fashioning both intergovernmental and intragovernmental institutional arrangements to maximize economic output within this constraint, rather than seeking changes that make a change in the balance in order to increase output. With respect to the latter, good people can disagree at the level of principle since fundamental political values are at stake. With respect to the former, disagreement is more likely to emerge over matters of strategy and implementation. These are far from easy problems, but they can at least be approached with a widely shared desire to resolve them.

2
Analytical perspectives on
the Canadian economic union

Thomas J. Courchene

The surfacing of the common market issue
The summer of 1980 will long be remembered for the flurry of activity associated with the travelling constitutional circus, more correctly referred to as the continuing Committee of Ministers on the Constitution (and more familiarly termed the 'Uke and Tuque Show' after its co-leaders Roy Romanow and Jean Chrétien). What most probably sticks in the minds of the Canadian public is the abortive week-long televised First Ministers' Conference in September 1980 which eventually led to Ottawa's initial unilateral move on the constitutional front. However, what also distinguished this round of constitutional bargaining, and what surely caught the provinces by surprise, was the federal government's introduction of the 'internal-common-market' or the 'Canadian-economic-union' issue into the negotiations. On the surface at least, this notion of protecting the Canadian domestic market from being balkanized by provincial beggar-my-neighbour policies was highly appealing to a broad range of Canadians. For some, the appeal was simply that they viewed this as a measure that would reverse the general drift of power towards the provinces. For others, the concept of ensuring an internal common market was welcomed because they viewed it as

It is a pleasure to acknowledge the very helpful comments I have received from my fellow contributors to this volume, particularly Professors Melvin, Prichard, Trebilcock, and Whalley. I wish also to thank Richard Bird, Albert Breton, Caroline Pestieau, and Edward Safarian, who participated in a most valuable round table at the inception of the project. Others who have had an influence on this paper include Marsha Chandler, Gérard Bélanger, and my graduate assistant Kevin Dowd. The usual caveat that responsibility rests with the author takes on added significance in a paper that is as policy-oriented as this one is.

an instrument which would curtail the activities of *all* government on the economic front and in this way reverse the general trend toward increased government intervention. In any event, the federal government attempted to utilize this new initiative to argue for a strengthening of either or both of Sections 91(2) of the British North America Act (the trade and commerce power) and Section 121 (which prohibits the imposition of customs duties on goods crossing provincial borders)[1] and for incorporating a series of 'economic rights' for all citizens as part of its proposed charter of rights.

To buttress its position on this issue, the federal justice minister, Jean Chrétien, published an eminently readable and superficially persuasive document, *Securing the Canadian Economic Union in the Constitution*, which defined an economic union as follows:

An economic union is an entity within which goods, services, labour, capital and enterprise can move freely, that is, without being subject to fiscal and other institutional barriers, and which is endowed with institutions capable of harmonizing the broad internal policies which affect economic development and of implementing common policies with regard to the entity's external economic relations.[2]

As its title indicated, the purpose of the document was to explore the various avenues whereby a Canadian economic union might be better secured under the constitution. To lend some perspective and persuasion, the discussion paper also focused on the degree to which the constitutions of other federations incorporated features that facilitated the development of an internal common market. With some degree of misrepresentation, the message to the reader was that, compared to the constitutions of most if not all other federations, the British North America Act lacks the means (principally because of an inadequate 'interstate commerce' clause, if I can use this term) to secure an internal common market. Bolstering this point of view was an appendix presenting a survey of actual restrictions on the interprovincial mobility of goods, services, labour, and capital within Canada. Not surprisingly, perhaps, the federal position paper concluded that there were 'compelling reasons for securing in the Constitution the basic operational rules of our economic union and for ensuring that both orders of government abide by these rules.'[3] Accordingly, the federal

---

1 Constitution Act, 1867 (formerly the British North America Act, 1867, 30–31 Vict., c. 3 (U.K.)) and *Constitution Act, 1982* as enacted by *Canada Act* 1982, c. 11 (U.K.).
2 Chrétien, *Securing the Canadian Economic Union in the Constitution: Discussion Paper Published by the Government of Canada* (Ottawa: Ministry of Supply and Services, 1980), at 1.
3 Ibid., at 29.

government outlined three possible techniques, which could be employed singly or in tandem, for accomplishing this:

(i) entrenching in the Constitution the mobility rights of citizens, as well as their right to gain a livelihood and acquire property in any province, regardless of their provinces of residence or previous residence and subject to laws of general application;

(ii) placing limitations upon the ability of governments to use their legislative and executive powers to impede economic mobility by way of general provisions, through the revision and expansion of Section 121 of the BNA Act;

(iii) broadening federal powers so that they may encompass all matters that are necessary for economic integration, thus ensuring that the relevant laws and regulations will apply uniformly throughout Canada, or that the 'test' of the public interest will be brought to bear upon derogation from uniformity.[4]

Not surprisingly, some provinces reacted strongly to these initiatives, claiming on the one hand that they embodied unacceptable intrusions into their own spheres of authority and on the other that they effectively amounted to a greater centralization of powers in Ottawa's hands. These fears were heightened by the fact that Ottawa insisted on certain derogations from an internal economic union that would allow it to initiate policies on the regional front, a loophole which the provinces perceived as allowing the federal government to do some of the very things it was attempting to prevent them from doing.

Even if the underlying motives of all participants were beyond reproach, it was nonetheless relatively easy to see self-interest in their positions. Thus what might have proceeded as a fascinating and fruitful interchange on the economic underpinnings of Canadian federalism soon deteriorated into a straightforward political struggle over the division of power where each side accused the other of promoting its own self-interest. Two examples will suffice. A charter of rights would serve to protect some basic rights and could be an important vehicle for securing an internal economic union, thereby increasing national efficiency. However, such a charter would also deflect citizen loyalty and attachment away

---

4 Ibid., Section 121 is the 'trade and commerce' clause. It reads: 'All articles of the growth, produce, or manufacture of any one of the provinces shall, from and after the union, be admitted free and freely into each of the other provinces.' This is viewed by Ottawa as applying too narrowly. One proposed broadening of this clause would have it read: 'All articles, services, and persons in any one of the provinces shall be admitted to each of the other provinces free of duties, quantitative restrictions, or charges, or measures with equivalent effect.' See Safarian, *Canadian Federalism and Economic Integration: Constitutional Study prepared for the Government of Canada* (Ottawa: Information Canada, 1974), at 99.

from provincial governments and toward the federal government. As Alan Cairns has noted:

At a more profound political level ... [the Charter] was an attempt to enhance and extend the meaning of being Canadian and thus to strengthen identificaiton with the national community on which Ottawa ultimately depends for support ... The resultant rights and freedoms were to be country-wide in scope, enforced by a national supreme court, and entrenched in a national constitution beyond the reach of fleeting legislative majorities at either level of government. *The consequence, and a very clear purpose, was to set limits to the diversities of treatment by provincial governments, and thus to strengthen Canadian as against provincial identities.* Rights 'must not be dependent on the particular place where an individual chooses to reside.'[5]

Thus the Charter of Rights, particularly in terms of the so-called economic rights, was perceived rightly or wrongly as undercutting provincial powers, and this view served to diminish considerably the range of discussion and analysis that the concept of an economic bill of rights ought to have generated.

Likewise, Ontario's support for an internal common market led to considerable controversy because that approach also seemed self-interested. Specifically, with the substantial shift of purchasing power toward the energy-producing provinces, the access of Ontario industry to contracts, particularly government-related contracts originating in the western provinces, would be greatly enhanced if provincial purchasing preferences, for example, were eliminated. But the Ontario position went further. In addition to arguing for domestic free trade, Ontario took the next step and appealed to Ottawa to implement a 'buy-Canadian' policy. This combination of free access domestically but restricted access internationally would put Ontario in an enviable position for supplying the industrial needs of the expanding west.[6] I do not wish to single out Ontario, which acted magnanimously in many other areas. For example, Ontario agreed in effect to forgo well over a billion dollars of equalization payments by accepting a retroactive provision excluding it from being a recipient under the formula. Rather, my point is that it has now become virtually impossible to separate idealism from self-interest in the debate. Principally for this reason the cutting edge of the controversy is moving away from theory and toward some

---

5 Cairns, 'Recent federalist constitutional proposals: a review essay.' (1979), 5 *Canadian Public Policy / Analysé de Politique* 348, at 354. Emphasis has been added.

6 Compounding the Ontario position still further is that this switch to a free trade approach came not too long after a decision on the part of the Ontario government to award a large contract to a Northern Ontario firm despite the fact that Bombardier of Quebec was the lowest bidder.

quantification of the costs involved. Indeed, that is the underlying rationale for the present volume.

The tax harmonization aspect

The result of this series of events has catapulted the internal common market issue onto the centre stage of policy-making. And with the fiscal arrangements coming up for revision in April 1982 another aspect of the Canadian economic union is now in the foreground, namely 'tax harmonization.' The principal vehicles relating to tax harmonization are the tax collection agreements and the common allocation formula for corporate profits.[7] Under the tax collection agreements, the federal government collects (free of charge, except for nominal fees relating to certain specific tax credits) the personal income taxes levied by all provinces except Quebec, and the corporate income taxes of all provinces except Quebec, Ontario, and Alberta. In return, the agreeing provinces have to accept the federal definition of the tax base, although some modifications of this principle have occurred for selective tax credits (such as property tax credits) offered by the provinces. On the corporate side, even though three provinces are not signatories to the agreements, they have thus far adhered to the same formula for allocating corporate profits. As will be detailed below, these provisions have given Canada a remarkably harmonized tax system in light of its decentralization.

However, problems are looming on the horizon. In terms of the personal income tax, one of the major stumbling blocks is the recent move by Quebec to introduce a provision into its tax system whereby Quebeckers who purchase new share issues of Quebec-based companies can treat a significant portion, in effect, as an RRSP for provincial income tax purposes. In my view this amounts to a significant impediment to the free mobility of capital within the nation. If all provinces followed suit there would be an incentive for residents of each province to invest principally in equities of their own province, thereby balkanizing the domestic capital market. In terms of the matter under discussion, namely tax harmonization and the tax collection agreements, this issue quickly surfaced

---

7 Originally by Section 6(1) of the Federal Provincial Fiscal Arrangements Act, S.C. 1960–61, c. 58, and now by Section 7 of the Federal-Provincial Fiscal Arrangements and Established Programs Financing Act 1977, S.C. 1976–77, c. 10, the minister of finance is empowered to conclude tax collection agreements with the provinces. The agreements are all patterned on one master text. The full text of the original agreements were published in the *Canada Gazette*, Part I, 8 September 1962, 'Supplement: Department of Finance Tax Collection Agreements Between the Government of Canada and the Governments of the Provinces.' An updated and amended version of the master text is available in 'Tax Collection Agreements,' 3 *Canada Income Tax Guide* (CCH), 71,000 ff.

into a major problem when other provinces, particularly British Columbia, wanted to follow Quebec's lead and to implement a similar program. Ottawa refused to collect such a tax for British Columbia on the ground that it would create a barrier to the free movement of capital in Canada and therefore violate the spirit of the tax collection agreements.[8] The message was clear: British Columbia could follow Quebec's lead, but only at the cost of withdrawing from the tax collection agreements and setting up its own personal income tax system.

On the corporate side, the situation has become just as delicate. Alberta has recently pulled out of the tax collection agreements and joined Ontario and Quebec in mounting its own corporate tax system. This means that over two-thirds of all corporate profits in Canada fall outside the umbrella of the agreement. Moreover, with corporation taxes playing a relatively minor role in Alberta's overall revenue picture, there is rising concern in Ottawa (probably alleviated somewhat by the recent energy agreement) that Alberta might also withdraw from the provision of the common allocation formula and use its corporate tax for 'development' purposes. This possibility was of sufficient interest to the Parliamentary Task Force on Federal-Provincial Fiscal Arrangements that it included the following revealing passage in its report:

It has been suggested to the Task Force that the federal government's present concern with tax harmony and barriers to the free flow of goods and people seems to have developed only since western provinces began to use provincial revenues for economic development purposes. There was no evident concern for tax harmony when Quebec and Ontario were permitted to run all or part of their own tax systems by staying out of the 1962 tax collection agreements – only now that Alberta has decided

8 The minister of finance, Allan MacEachen, outlined before the recent Parliamentary Task Force on Federal-Provincial Fiscal Arrangements the three general guidelines that are to be followed to determine whether a measure will be administered under the tax collection agreements: 'First, the measure must be able to be administered reasonably effectively. Second, the measure must not significantly erode or have the potential to erode the essential harmony and uniformity of the federal and provincial tax system. Third, the measure must not jeopardize the efficient functioning of the Canadian economic union by the erection of income tax barriers to normal interprovincial investment flows.' MacEachen, Department of Finance, *Federal Provincial Fiscal Arrangements in the Eighties: A Submission to the Parliamentary Task Force on the Federal Provincial Fiscal Arrangements, April 23, 1981* (Ottawa: Ministry of Supply and Services, 1981), at 54 (in 'Annex IV – Income Tax Collection Agreements). The submission without the annexes is reproduced in Canada. House of Commons. Special committee [also known as the 'Parliamentary Task Force'] on the Federal-Provincial Fiscal Arrangements. *Minutes of Proceedings and Evidence of the Special Committee on the Federal-Provincial Arrangements*, Issue No. 2 (Ottawa: Ministry of Supply and Services, 1st Session of the 32nd Parliament, 1980–81).

to collect its own corporate tax and British Columbia has indicated some interest in withdrawing from the agreements is tax harmonization seen as a major problem.'[9]

It is probably the case that the federal government must take some responsibility for any tendency on the part of the western provinces and particularly Alberta to contemplate utilizing their corporate tax system for development purposes. As I have argued elsewhere with respect to the National Energy Progam (NEP):

In effect, Ottawa [by distinguishing between Canada lands and provincial lands for corporate income treatment for the energy sector] is telling the provinces that it is up to them to provide any additional incentives in this area. Presumably they would do this via the corporate income tax route. Hence it is an incentive (and an invitation!) for the energy producing provinces to pull out of the tax collection agreements and to 'patriate' their corporate income tax systems. Alberta is in the process of doing this anyway. The problem is that any changes in the provincial corporate tax system will probably *not* be limited to the energy area. Rather, the affected provinces may well utilize their tax systems as a vehicle for provincial economic development. Not only would the common allocation formula for corporate profits likely be in jeopardy, but as well Canada may face the spectre of having ten corporate tax systems. Moreover, if corporate taxes can be used in this manner, so can personal tax systems, and the Quebec approach of offering special incentives for residents' purchases of new equity issues of Quebec-based companies may become fairly widespread. In short, Canada could be opening the door to a veritable tax jungle – a beggar-my-neighbour system which will surely embody negative economic implications for resource allocation and economic growth.

The provincial response will surely be that if Ottawa, for its own tax purposes, can discriminate on the basis of the location of economic activity, so can the provinces.[10]

In other words, on both the personal and corporate income tax fronts there is some anxiety that events may lead to an unwinding of the high degree of tax harmonization that has characterized our federation. Since the tax collection agreements are currently under study as part of the overall fiscal arrangements negotiations, this has served to heighten the interest in these matters and, more

---

9 Canada, House of Commons, Parliamentary Task Force on Federal-Provincial Fiscal Arrangements, *Fiscal Federalism in Canada* (Ottawa: Ministry of Supply and Services, 1981), at 181

10 Courchene, 'The National Energy Program and fiscal federalism: some observations.' In Watkins and Walker, eds, *Reaction: The National Energy Program* (Vancouver: The Fraser Institute, 1981), at 94–5

generally, in the internal common market issue of which tax harmonization forms an integral part.

Overview of the analysis
With this backdrop I can now proceed to outline my analysis of the interaction between federalism and the Canadian economic union. The second part of this paper focuses on what is referred to as the 'integration spectrum,' namely the various forms of economic association that run the gamut from free trade areas to economic unions and further to federalisms and unitary states. As is usual in such analyses, the focus of the discussion relates to developments in the European Common Market and what these might imply for the achievement of an internal common market within Canada. Accordingly, the third part examines in more detail the federal government's proposals for securing an internal common market in the constitution. The reader may well argue that this is putting too much emphasis on the constitutional aspects and not enough on the analytical relationship between internal common markets and federalisms. I am sympathetic to this criticism, but it also seems important to pay attention to the underlying thrust that gave rise to the present concern over the concept of an internal economic union.

The fourth part attempts to redress the imbalance by presenting what is referred to as a 'federalism continuum' or a 'decentralization-centralization spectrum.' By bringing into the analysis the 'economic theory of federalism' I attempt to establish the following points:

– There is a 'federal' aspect to all governments, where a federal aspect is defined as the ability of a subnational unit to provide public goods on a geographical basis. This would include the local governments in a unitary state.
– The more decentralized is the form of government, the more the potential exists for the subnational units to distort free trade. The more centralized the form of government, the more potential there is for the national government to distort interregional resource allocation. Hence, it is not obvious that federalism (as traditionally defined) ought to be viewed as a degenerate case of economic union (which by the way is precisely the impression that Ottawa has attempted to foster).
– In large measure, the question of the significance of the departures from an internal common market is an empirical issue. On this score, I define as a barrier, or an impediment, any policy change designed to alter the geographical allocation of the production of goods and the distribution of factors.

The fifth part devotes some attention to the implications that arise from quantification of provincial and federal barriers following from this definition of an impediment or distortion. (The quantification itself is contained in other papers in this volume.) One such implication is that the quantification estimates pay no attention at all to any social goals or priorities that may be part of the political fabric of a nation, federal or otherwise. It is essentially an exercise in the degree of conformity to the most productive geographical allocation of resources (what an economist would call geographical Pareto optimality), an approach that would be generally accepted by economists but one that would not likely sit well with political scientists, lawyers, and others interested in the economic union issue.

Are there other approaches that can incorporate social goals in assessing the significance of departures from a domestic common market? Undoubtedly there are. The sixth part of this paper attempts to formulate one such alternative in the context of Canadian federalism. Essentially it argues that the costs in terms of national output of provincially generated departures from an internal common market will depend on the overall objective function that the federal government is pursuing. This approach also presents one framework for viewing ongoing policy on the regional front.

The final part addresses the delicate issue of whether Canada's version of federalism is geared more to serving the interests of the individual provinces than to serving the interests of individual Canadians. One implication that follows from this admittedly speculative analysis is that there appears to be a need for a 'code of economic conduct' as suggested by A.E. Safarian,[11] which would guarantee Canadians some rights in the economic sphere, rights that neither level of government should be able to take away from them.

A brief conclusion pulls together the various strands of the analysis and stresses some of the more immediate implications for policy that follow from the study.

THE INTEGRATION CONTINUUM

Edward Safarian, in his influential study *Canadian Federalism and Economic Integration*, presents the following scheme for classifying the degree of economic integration:

(a) *Free trade area*, which involves the removal of customs tariffs and quantitative restrictions, such as quotas, on trade between the member countries, but with each of them retaining its own distinct barriers against non-members.

11 Safarian, *Ten Markets or One? Regional Barriers to Economic Activity in Canada* (Toronto: Ontario Economic Council Discussion Paper, 1980), at 18.

(b) *Customs union*, which in addition to (a) standardizes such barriers by member countries against non-members [i.e. adopts a common external tariff].

(c) *Common market*, which in addition to (b) removes restrictions on the movement of labour and capital between member countries.

(d) *Economic union*, which in addition to (c) involves varying degrees of harmonization of national economic policies in order to remove discrimination due to disparities in these policies.

(e) *A federal state*, which is a form of union in which the general government and the provinces or states each exercise exclusive jurisdiction in some major areas of policy and shared jurisdiction in others.

(f) *A unitary state*, wherein the general government has jurisdiction over economic and other major policies.[12]

For our purposes it is best to view this classification as a continuum through which a group of countries (say the present members of the European Economic Community) might proceed from their initial positions of separate national entities through to the final position of submerging their respective nationhoods first in a federal (or perhaps confederal) state and then in a single unitary state.

If we conceptualize this integration process as beginning with a group of countries who trade with each other, then the move to the first stage – a free trade area – will probably increase the degree of economic interdependence in the sense that trade flows within the free trade area will increase. Not much in the way of harmonization of domestic policies is called for under this arrangement, except some provisions to ensure 'deflection prohibition' (i.e. some provisions to ensure that imports from the rest of the world do not enter the free trade area through the country that has the lowest tariff for this class of imports). If there is no deflection prohibition, a free trade area becomes almost indistinguishable from a customs union. This is so because, de facto, there will be a common external tariff under such a free trade area. For each commodity the relevant external tariff will be the lowest of the individual countries' rates. The principal distinction between a customs union and a free trade area without a deflection prohibition will be the country of entry for various classes of imports. This level of integration (a customs union or a free trade area without a deflection prohibition) will involve a greater degree of integration because it will normally incorporate some provision for sharing the revenues of the common tariff (or for allocating the proceeds arising from access through a preferential country under a free trade area without a deflection prohibition). More often than not these

12 Safarian, *Canadian Federation and Economic Integration*; at 2.

funds are allocated to compensate the member countries for the 'adjustment costs' of entering into a customs union. These 'regional' allocations or transfers are likely to increase as one moves up the integration continuum.[13] It is important to keep these regional allocations in mind for what comes later since they will constitute impediments to an internal common market because they represent policy-induced measures which will influence the geographic allocation of both output and factors of production. Thus, even though moving progressively along the integration spectrum supposedly increases the size of the overall economic pie by removing internal trade barriers and harmonizing various sorts of economic policies, there is a potential offset (presumably only a partial one) to integration if any surplus arising from the customs union is allocated to specific regions rather than to, say, disadvantaged individuals no matter where they reside.

A common market carries the integration much further because the process of ensuring free movement of capital and labour among member countries involves a surrender of some elements of political sovereignty. To see this it is convenient to refer to the conditions for the European Economic Community (EEC) set out in the Treaty of Rome. These include

– abolishing all discrimination based on the nationality of workers of member countries concerning employment, remuneration and other conditions of work;
– establishing the right to settle freely, including the right to engage in any economic activity and to establish or manage companies and enterprises;
– providing for the removal of restrictions on the offering of services by insurance companies, banks, other financial institutions, wholesale and retail trades and professionals;
– removing, progressively, restrictions on the movement of capital, with some exception for agreed protective measures.[14]

A full economic union requires, in addition, the harmonization of a broad range of economic and social policies. The most important of these would be tax harmonization, an issue which has occupied much of the research on the EEC. As noted in the introduction, tax harmonization is now emerging as an important issue in Canada, and as Wayne Thirsk notes 'it is more than a little ironic that the

13 This point is emphasized by Bird, 'Regional policies in a common market.' In Shoup, ed., *Fiscal Harmonization in Common Markets – Volume 1: Theory* (New York: Columbia University Press, 1967), at 385–456.
14 Chrétien, *Securing the Canadian Economic Union*, at 12.

existing literature on harmonization owes its existence to the prospect of economic integration among European countries, while nascent Canadian interest in this matter is attributable to the prospect of increasing economic disintegration.'[15] Concerns over tax harmonization arise in the context of a common market since different tax regimes in countries can affect the movement of both goods and factors across jurisdictions, as will be emphasized later.

Economic union would call for the harmonization of other policies as well, such as expenditure policies, social policies (particularly social assistance and pension portability), and probably some aspects of macro policy. This latter is particularly the case if one goal of the economic union is to maintain relative fixity in the exchange rates of the member nations. However, if exchange rates are allowed to vary, the pressures on harmonization would appear to be lessened. What matters then for tax harmonization is that the forms of taxation and the tax bases be harmonized. Differences in tax rates across nations can to a large degree be offset by exchange rate movements. This aspect too has considerable relevance to tax harmonization in the Canadian setting since exchange rate movement among provinces is *not* an available option.

If, to continue with our hypothetical example, the member countries were to take the next step and join in a federation (or a looser confederation) the degree of integration and harmonization would increase further. Federation, arising in the staged manner in which we have been proceeding, implies a political union and a monetary union (both in terms of a common currency and a single monetary authority) as well as full harmonization for those aspects of taxes and expenditures that are allocated to the central government. To go to the next step and convert the federation into a unitary state would, abstracting from the role played by local governments,[16] complete the harmonization and integration process.

In spite of the fact that a federal system should be more integrated than a common market, it has often been said that in some spheres there are more barriers to geographical mobility within Canada than there are between the member countries of the EEC. Two implications are usually drawn from this,

---

15 Thirsk, 'Tax harmonization and its importance in the Canadian federation.' In Bird, ed., *Fiscal Dimensions of Canadian Federalism* (Toronto: Canadian Tax Foundation, 1980), at 120.

16 Frequently, too much is made of the distinction between a federation and a unitary state in terms of the potential for erecting barriers to the geographical flows of economic activity because of the failure to realize that the actions of local governments can be every bit as distorting as those enacted by state or provincial governments. This potential will play a role in the ensuing analysis.

more often implicitly than explicitly. First, unless fully protected by constitutional provisions, federations are inherently prone to the forces of economic disintegration; and second, by contrast, unitary states are models of virtue in that almost by definition they incorporate unrestricted mobility of goods, services, and factors of production. In theory, both observations are questionable; in practice it is not difficult to find unitary states where the geographical location of goods and factors is more restricted than it is in most federal nations.

However, in terms of the integration continuum, that is, of a group of countries moving progressively towards a unitary state, the possibility a federal arrangement cannot be more restrictive on the geographical movements of goods and factors than, say, a customs union. Under our scenario a federation would result in a larger economic pie than would an economic union, and it achieves this by reaping the gains from increased integration. This is so because the implicit driving force in our example is what Tony Scott refers to as the *economic deterministic* approach to federalism.[17] Our hypothetical group of nations moves stage by stage along the integration spectrum *because* the size of the aggregate economic pie is expected to increase. And it is expected to increase because of the gains from specialization and trade that accompany the creation of a larger market area initially unimpeded by tariffs, later unimpeded by barriers to factor mobility, and finally unimpeded by distortions emanating from taxes, government expenditures, and the like. The issue of whether there may be more barriers to trade in goods and factors as one moves along the spectrum does not arise: the reason there is movement is to reap the gains from a progressively freer internal market. One might even expect that the member nations, as they become more and more integrated, would rationalize their common external tariff so that over the longer term it too would be an instrument to maximize output within their geographical domain.

However, in reality this need no longer be the case. Federalisms need not, and in some cases probably will not, have fewer impediments to mobility of goods and factors than customs unions. It is even more obvious, as will be detailed below, that many unitary states will have greater internal barriers than most federalisms. What to make of such observations, however, is not so clear. The economist may be able to put a dollar figure on the costs of internal barriers to trade within Canada. Indeed, to estimate some of these costs is in large part the

---

17 To be more precise, it might be better to refer to this as an 'income deterministic' approach since the driving force underlying the scenario is to increase total income. Overall welfare, which would normally be associated with an 'economic' approach, may or may not be increased as one moves along the spectrum. Scott, 'The economic goals of federal finance.' (1964), 19 *Public Finance* 241.

rationale for this entire study. But the economist will not be able to guarantee that eliminating these barriers will make each person, let alone each province, better off. More important, it is likely that some of these 'benefits' can be achieved only by overriding the very essence of a federation, which, as elaborated later, is the ability of provinces to provide bundles of goods and services that cater to the preferences of their respective populations. This restriction is acceptable provided that the underlying rationale of the federation is to maximize overall output (the economic deterministic approach referred to earlier). There are, however, other views of why federations exist. This is not the place to enter into a prolonged discussion of competing theories of federalism. (Nor would I be able to do so!) I shall merely observe that some writers on federalism emphasize the theme, adopted from the American *Federalist* papers, that the attractivenesss of federalism 'lies in its ability to preserve and encourage individualism, by allowing like people to migrate freely, and congregate into local, provincial or other types of political jurisdictions. Here the rules of majorities will tend toward unanimity, for minorities can always emigrate to political units of similarly-inclined people.'[18] Unlike the economic determinists, these writers stress competition or rivalry between jurisdictions. Such competition is in part the antithesis of harmonization since it postulates geographically differentiated bundles of public services and quite possibly different patterns of marginal rates of substitution for factors and goods. Another way of making much the same point is to note that whereas association treaties (like the EEC's Treaty of Rome) are essentially economic documents, federal constitutions are primarily political documents.[19]

In this light, care must be exercised in basing conclusions on the existence or the quantitative significance of internal barriers to resource allocation. Distortions that could be eliminated without at the same time eroding the essence of a meaningful federal structure must be clearly distinguished from distortions which could be removed only by emasculating provincial autonomy. To detail the costs of geographical distortions that could be removed only by converting Canada into a unitary state may be a highly revealing exercise but is not a particularly relevant one since folding the federation into a unitary state is not an acceptable option for Canadians. In what follows this point will be kept in mind, although only in the sixth part will it be recognized explicitly.

In order to analyse the interaction between internal economic barriers and federalism we need to develop some aspects of the economic theory of federalism. Before doing so, however, I shall discuss further the federal government's

18 Ibid., at 245.
19 This is adopted from Lemelin, 'Dimensions of fiscal harmonization in Canada' (Ottawa: Department of Finance, mimeo, 1981).

concern that our federation has failed to secure an adequate internal common market and review its proposals for achieving this goal within the constitution.

SECURING AN ECONOMIC UNION IN THE CONSTITUTION

Mr Chrétien's position paper notes that, although the BNA Act does not contain an explicit economic definition of our federation, the following characteristics, as interpreted by the courts, can be seen to apply.

– a customs union, since provincial legislatures are prohibited from levying internal border taxes and Parliament is empowered to establish a common external tariff;
– an imperfect comon market for goods – imperfect because Section 121 does not prohibit non-tariff barriers to interprovincial trade and because judicial interpretation has limited the federal trade and commerce power;
– an imperfectly safeguarded common market for capital and enterprise, since provinces can impede the movement of some financial assets and business establishments across interprovincial borders;
– distinct and 'protectable' markets for labour and most other services.[20]

Some of these points merit elaboration. The suggestion that Canada has a customs union but also an imperfect common market for goods may appear a bit confusing. From a legal standpoint, the first point is certainly correct: the provinces are not allowed to mount tariffs against products from other provinces. However, it is well known that a combination of taxes and subsidies can duplicate any system of tariffs. What this means is that while the provinces are prohibited from levying tariffs against goods entering from other provinces, they can always duplicate the impact of a tariff by selected taxes and subsidies. For example, provincial purchasing preferences act as a tariff against out-of-province production. Moreover, Ontario's protectionist policy toward British Columbia wines (and vice versa) and indeed all provinces' safeguarding of their domestic beer markets are in effect tariffs, especially when one recalls that a quota can be viewed as a prohibitive tariff. Thus it is not even clear that Canada can be said to have a true customs union, let alone an internal common market.

One other comment is appropriate here. By and large, the foregoing features are derived not so much from what the constitution says as from the interpretation that the courts have given to the relevant clauses of the BNA Act through the years. At the turn of the century, for example, Section 91(2), the trade and commerce clause, was viewed as having much less relevance than it currently

20 Chrétien, *Securing the Canadian Economic Union*; at 1.

does. In his survey of the role of the trade and commerce power as it relates to the control of natural resources, S.I. Bushnell notes that in the 1920s the Judicial Committee of the Privy Council of the United Kingdom

reduced the specific grant of power to regulate trade and commerce [i.e. Section 91(2)] to that of an auxiliary status within the Constitution, meaning that it could only be used in aid of Dominion power found elsewhere in the Constitution. Lord Haldane termed the trade and commerce power 'merely ancillary' and in addition spoke of it as needing some paramount Dominion purpose, some exceptional situation before it could be utilized, in other words, an emergency situation.[21]

This is clearly no longer the case. The trade and commerce power has emerged over the recent years as an effective limit in its own right on provincial activities. Perhaps the most obvious recent example of this is the Supreme Court of Canada's judgment in the CIGOL case, where Saskatchewan attempted to appropriate the windfall profits arising from the increase in the domestic price of energy.[22] The majority decision argued that the precise tax levied by the province not only was an indirect tax but also impinged on interprovincial trade. This

---

21 Bushnell, 'The control of natural resources through the trade and commerce power and proprietary rights.' (1980), 6 *Canadian Public Policy / Analysé de Politique* 313, at 315. See also *Toronto Electric Commissioners* v. *Snider* [1925], A.C. 396 (P.C.) and *Re The Board of Commerce Act, 1919, and the Combines and Fair Prices Act, 1919* [1922], 1 A.C. 191 (P.C.).

22 As outlined in a recent paper by John D. Whyte, the CIGOL case can be summarized as follows:

Following the jump in oil prices in the autumn of 1973, the Government of Saskatchewan moved quickly to capture what were perceived to be the windfall profits of oil producers. By a complex set of legislation and regulations, Saskatchewan moved on three fronts. First, revenues from oil produced from lands held in freehold were subjected to a 'mineral income tax.' The tax was 100 per cent of the difference between the price received at the well-head and the statutorily defined 'basic well-head price' which was established at approximately the same level as the price per barrel received by producers prior to the oil embargo and price escalation ... Second, freehold rights in about one-half of the 40 per cent of the producing tracts in the province not held by the province as crown lands were expropriated. Third, a royalty surcharge was imposed upon oil whether it came from existing crown lands or whether it came from newly expropriated lands.

The Saskatchewan Court of Queen's Bench and the Court of Appeal upheld this scheme as a valid taxation measure. The law did not, however, survive review by the Supreme Court of Canada which, in a 7 to 2 decision, found the tax to be invalid both because it was considered to be a form of indirect taxation and because it was thought to interfere with international and interprovincial trade to such a degree that it constituted an invalid encroachment on a federal head of power [Section 91(2)].

judgment is difficult for an economist to comprehend since, almost by definition, windfall profits are in the nature of rents and any tax on rents is a *direct* tax. In addition, with the federal government setting the domestic price it is difficult to understand how the Court could view Saskatchewan's scheme as an attempt to sell the product 'at a price equivalent to what the Minister [of the Saskatchewan government] considers to be its fair value.'[23]

Be that as it may, the role attributed to the trade and commerce clause appears to be on the rise. If this trend continues, it is quite possible that some of the present provincial initiatives and in particular those that fall under the category of 'distinct and protective' outlined above, will be struck down. Thus, the description presented above of the sort of economic guarantees embodied in the BNA Act and its interpretation is not etched in stone. If the trend towards greater reliance on the trade and commerce clause continues, the degree to which an economic union is secured within the constitution will correspondingly be enhanced.

The federal position, at least as reflected in the background document, is not as negative as the elaboration of the four points above might imply. Indeed, the report adds a fifth item, namely that in spite of the existence of barriers to internal mobility Canada nonetheless has by a 'highly integrated economic union ... by virtue of *federal* jurisdiction over taxation, money and banking, interprovincial trade and commerce, transportation, agriculture, communications, weights and measures, etc.'[24] I have stressed the word 'federal' because it shows the position Ottawa has taken toward the internal common market issue. Apparently all actions that lead to the fragmentation of our domestic market are instigated by the provinces, whereas all actions that contribute to freeing the domestic market arise either from federal actions or because the constitutional authority for these areas rests with Ottawa. This is simply not the case. The issue will be dealt with in some detail below. For now, one example will suffice. Federal ministers are quick to point to the existence of the numerous provincial marketing boards as examples of impediments to the flow of goods across

---

See Whyte, 'A constitutional perspective on federal-provincial sharing of revenues from natural resources.' Forthcoming in a volume on resource issues published by the Lincoln Institute; also *Canadian Industrial Gas and Oil Ltd.* v. *Government of Saskatchewan et al.* [1978], 2 S.C.R. 545, (1978) 80 D.L.R. (3d) 449. While the thrust of Whyte's paper is on the resource area, it nonetheless provides an up-to-date review of some aspects of federal powers as they relate to interprovincial trade.

23 Whyte, 'A constitutional perspective' and *Canadian Industrial Gas, supra* note 22, 2 S.C.R., at 568; D.L.R. 464.

24 Chrétien, *Securing the Canadian Economic Union*, at 2. Emphasis added.

provincial boundaries. And they are right to do so since these boards do in fact fragment the national economy. However, what is not quite correct is to lay the blame for their existence on the provinces. As Safarian has documented, marketing boards were initially restricted by the courts to the control of intraprovincial trade only.[25] But in 1949 Ottawa passed the Agricultural Products Marketing Act which authorized the governor in council 'to grant provincial marketing boards the same powers with respect to provincial produce sold in *interprovincial* and *export* trades as the boards already exercised with respect to such produce sold in intraprovincial trade.'[26] Safarian goes on to elaborate on a fascinating further development:

Financing was a problem for these boards, as was the attempt to pool returns to producers. A provincial board can impose license fees for operating costs, but attempts by provincial boards to impose a levy on one group of producers in order to increase the return to another group have generally been considered by the courts to be an indirect tax and the granting of such power to a board by a provincial legislature to be *ultra vires*. As a result of this line of ruling, the Agricultural Products Marketing Act was amended in 1957 to provide that the Governor in Council could authorize provincial boards to impose indirect taxes and use the funds from such levies for all purposes of the board including equalization of returns.[27]

In short, under the constitution provinces do not, through their marketing boards, have the authority to regulate interprovincial movements of products. However, the federal government can, and did, extend interprovincial powers to provincial marketing boards. In light of all of this, it is far from clear that Ottawa has a right to argue that marketing boards are an example of the way in which the provinces have balkanized the domestic market since the latter can only engage in market segmentation because Ottawa has passed the enabling legislation.

In spite of this view that Ottawa's approach to the issue of internal barriers to trade ought to be more balanced as to the sources of the impediments, it is

---

25 Safarian, *Canadian Federalism and Economic Integration*, at 49–50.
26 Ibid., at 49. Emphasis added. See also Agricultural Products Marketing Act, R.S.C. 1970, c. A-7.
27 Safarian, *Canadian Federalism and Economic Integration*, at 49–50. However, in *Reference re Agricultural Products Marketing Act and two other Acts* [1978] 2 S.C.R. 1198, (1978) 84 D.L.R. (3d) 257, delegation of the authority to regulate interprovincial trade was held to be *intra vires*, but the authorization of the imposition of levies was held to be *ultra vires* to the federal government and within the provincial jurisdiction.

nonetheless the case that I am in considerable sympathy with the overall thrust of the position, namely that it is important to ensure more geographical mobility of goods and factors than currently exists. In this spirit, and in order to introduce more fully the analysis behind the notion of securing an economic union within the constitution, I turn now to Ottawa's proposed solutions to this problem.

The charter-of-rights solution
While the basic analytical arguments in favour of promoting an internal common market are economic, an important political element underpins the general issue. Citizenship itself ought to bestow some economic rights on individuals. The federal position paper makes a great deal of this argument, and perhaps with good reason because the rhetoric strikes a responsive chord even for people who would normally favour a greater degree of decentralization:

To be a citizen of Canada must be a dynamic reality rather than a static abstraction, a reality that extends beyond the realm of political and legal institutions to the vital aspects of one's material existence ... To the extent compatible with federalism, the basic equality of all citizens must apply to economic affairs, under provincial law as well as federal law. Wherever they may have been born or have chosen to reside in the country, Canadians should be free to take up residence, to acquire and hold property, and purchase their supplies in any province or territory of Canada, provided they abide by the laws of general application of that province or territory.[28]

The federal government recognizes that the pursuit of other goals may justify some restriction on the economic freedoms of Canadians, but in general 'the freest possible access to the national market should be inherent to Canadian citizenship.'[29] While the provinces found it difficult to counter the general thrust of this argument, the aspect that disturbed many of them (apart from the more general concern over a charter of rights in the first place) was that the federal government argued that this should not inhibit Ottawa from being able to enact policies that would be geared toward regional 'needs.' In other words, the federal authority would be able to enact some of the same sorts of measures that would be denied to individual provinces. Thus, what in theory would be a transfer of power and / or rights to individual Canadians from both levels of government might in practice result in a centralization of authority, or so the fear was expressed. Of concern also, as I will argue later, is that it is entirely possible that

28 Chrétien, *Securing the Canadian Economic Union*, at 2.
29 Ibid.

federal actions on the 'regional front' may do more to erode the functioning of an efficient internal common market than many of the actions taken by individual provinces.

That, however, is not the present issue. Rather, the point is that one line of argument in favour of ensuring an internal common market relates to the privileges that should attend Canadian citizenship. This rationale leads to the inclusion of 'economic freedoms,' as it were, in a charter of rights, since the arguments derive from the rights of citizenship and not from any economic benefits as such that may ensue. In terms of the three possible options outlined above for securing an economic union in the constitution (i.e. entrenching economic freedoms in a charter of rights, expanding the powers of the Canadian equivalent of the interstate commerce clause, and broadening federal powers in areas pertaining to economic integration), the first follows from a focus on the political aspect of a national economic union whereas the other two derive more from a consideration of the potential economic gains arising from greater economic integration.

Economic aspects
With the advent of the European Economic Community, Canada is in the unenviable position of having access to a domestic market that is significantly smaller than most of her trading partners. To fragment the already small Canadian market by erecting barriers to goods and factor mobility and / or by engaging in protectionist policies at the provincial level is to run a very serious risk of generating substantial inefficiency and undermining our international competitiveness. These well known costs essentially involve losses resulting from the inability to reap the gains from the division of labour and the specialization of production as the market becomes more segmented. As a first approximation to these costs, the list included in the federal discussion paper will suffice:[30]

– higher supply costs, fragmentation and stunted growth for firms, and diseconomies of scale which enhance import penetration and reduce international competitiveness of domestic production;
– diversion of trade to foreign suppliers, when fragmentation results in neither in-province nor out-of-province suppliers being able to service provincial markets on a competitive basis;
– lower incomes and fewer employment opportunities for residents of all provinces;

30 Alternatively, see Safarian, *Canadian Federalism and Economic Integration*, Part I, or any international trade textbook.

– higher burdens upon national and provincial taxpayers, due to higher cost of public procurement and lower tax yields.[31]

If the costs of balkanizing Canada's domestic market are so obvious, and perhaps so serious, one might legitimately ask why the provinces might ever engage in such a negative-sum game. One answer is that this is probably a classic case of the 'signalling' problem. Province A might be convinced not to move in the direction of protectionist policies provided that all other provinces would follow suit. Lacking such assurance, however, it may be in province A's own interest to pursue protection and to do so early rather than late. When all provinces embark on this strategy, however, the negative-sum properties of the exercise will dominate. If this was all there was to the issue, then it could easily be resolved by investing some overriding power in the hands of the central government to enforce an internal common market since, by assumption in this example, we are assuming that all provinces stand to lose in the face of complete retaliation.

But the issue is more complicated. As Melvin points out in his contribution to this volume, and as others have also emphasized, a province may be willing to embark on protectionist policies in full knowledge that the overall economic impact may be negative provided that certain specific groups, namely the groups for which the legislation was tailored, are net gainers. To pursue this would lead us too far into the literature on public choice. What can be noted, however, is that the incentive for this sort of action on the part of the provinces is heightened if the gainers are a well-identified group (and preferably marginal voters) while the costs are dispersed more or less uniformly across the population. This implies that, even if all provinces recognized that the imposition of barriers to the mobility of factors and goods (explicitly through such measures as quotas or implicitly through a system of subsidies) would lead to a fall not only in national output but as well in output in each of the provinces, it might still be in the provinces' 'interests'[32] to pursue these protectionist policies. Although this argument does not appear in the federal government's position paper, presumably it is part of the reason for its decision to use the constitution to secure an internal economic union. As noted above, this could be accomplished either by strengthening the interstate commerce clause [Section 91(2)] to apply to all goods and services or by granting the central government additional powers.

---

31 Chrétien, *Securing the Canadian Economic Union*, at 5–6.
32 The word 'interests' is meant to be defined broadly to include, for example, maximization of the possibility of success at the polls. See Melvin's contribution to this volume.

Such, then, are the federal government's reasons for and alternative approaches to securing the internal economic union in the constitution. As is frequently the case in the policy arena, the party who leads off the debate has a major effect on the way the discussion and analysis of the issue unfolds. In this case the federal government has staked out the initial criteria for defining the problem and assessing the impact and implications of the lack of an adequate internal common market. It is important now to broaden the perspective somewhat by providing a more comprehensive framework within which to approach the issue. To begin this exercise, the next part will focus on the economic theory of federalism. Only when federalism has been defined will we be ready to focus on the interaction between federalism and economic union.

INTERNAL BARRIERS AND THE ECONOMIC THEORY OF FEDERALISM

Defining federalism
Federalism is not a concept that lends itself to a very precise or well-accepted definition. For example, Kenneth G. Wheare in his classic study of federalism was able to identify only four genuinely federal systems of government, and among those four he was willing to grant Canada only 'quasi-federal' status.[33] However, I assume that most students of government would find acceptable, at least as a starting point, the view that a federation can be defined as a political system in which two levels of government exist side by side in a self-rule, shared-rule relationship with a constitution providing the basic framework in allocating the autonomous and shared powers. From the vantage point of an economist, and more particularly to assess barriers to the attainment of an internal economic union, it is useful to go beyond this and focus upon the territorial nature of the two levels of government. In this light I find Donald Smiley's introductory paragraph of his *Canada in Question: Federalism in the Eighties* particularly appealing:

A federal nation is one in which most politically salient aspects of human differentiation, identification, and conflict are related to *specific territories.* Conversely, of course, in a non-federal nation these political differentiations, identifications, and conflicts are not territorially bounded ... If gender became the most important basis for social, economic, and political demands and people identified themselves almost exclusively with members of their own sex, we would not have a federal country –

---

33 Wheare, *Federal Government* (London: Oxford University Press, 4th ed., 1963), at 18–20, cited in Oates, *Fiscal Federalism* (New York: Harcourt Brace Jovanich, 1972), at xv.

except in the unlikely and unhappy event that all or almost all the women lived in one part of it and all the men in the other. [Thus] every country has its own mix of federal and non-federal elements.[34]

Incorporating the territorial aspect into the definition of federalism allows one to introduce the concept of a 'federalism continuum' which can incorporate the extremes of confederation and the unitary state, noting that the latter may in an important sense be 'federal' in nature depending on the effect local governments have on the allocation of resources. No doubt many readers will find this view of 'federalism' quite unacceptable because it tends to ignore almost completely such important aspects of the political fabric such as constitutions and provinces. For present purposes, however, this degree of abstraction seems appropriate as a starting point for focusing on the manner in which the internal common market can be fragmented, particularly since the operating definition of a 'distortion,' or an internal barrier, in much of the analysis in later chapters is any policy-induced departure on a geographical basis from the pattern of relative prices that would otherwise prevail. These assumptions will be relaxed later in order to incorporate, to some extent at least, the role of constitutions, provinces, and the like.

Since definitions have occupied much of the attention of this part it may be useful to extend the list to confederations and unitary states, where the reader is asked to note the emphasis on 'regional' that runs throughout:

Federal government is to be distinguished from a *confederacy* in which the general government is dependent on the regional governments, and from a *unitary* system, in which the regional governments are dependent on the general government. In a confederacy, sovereignty may be said to lie with the regional governments: in a unitary system it lies with the general government; in a federation it lies with neither and is said to be divided between the two.[35]

We can now direct the emphasis of the analysis toward the notion of regional versus central government as the distinguishing feature of political entities rather than the more constraining federal-versus-unitary-state emphasis. In addition, this approach accords well with what might be termed the economist's approach to federalism.

---

34 Smiley, *Canada in Question: Federalism in the Eighties* (Toronto: McGraw-Hill Ryerson, 3rd ed., 1980), at 1. Emphasis added.
35 Livingston, 'Federal government.' In *The Encyclopedia Americana*, Vol. II (New York: The Americana Corporation, 1963), at 88.

An economic approach to federalism

1 The advantages of centralization
If we take as the appropriate role for the public sector the classification of objectives suggested by Richard Musgrave – allocative efficiency, income distribution, and economic stablization[36] – it is not difficult to make a case for centralizing some aspects of the public sector. The stabilization role suggests itself immediately. Control over the printing of money must be centralized, almost by definition. Likewise, responsibility for fiscal measures which are designed to ensure a high level of output and employment also are most efficaciously assigned to the central government. The regional economies are likely to be far more open than the national economy, so that there will be a less-than-optimal amount of stabilization supplied at the regional level because a large part of the benefits of such measures will 'leak out' to neighbouring regions. This is but a specific example of the more general propositon that where there are large spillovers to other regions a decentralized production system will lead to a less-than-optimal level of output. It is basically on these grounds that one can argue for centralized rather than regional provision of certain public goods: the externalities or spillovers that exist at the regional level can be internalized by assigning the function to the higher level of government. Economies of scale may also argue for centralizing the production of some public goods. Finally, the rationale for centralizing a substantial portion of the income distribution function in a federation might appear somewhat less persuasive. However, without going into unnecessary detail, attempts by decentralized fiscal units to pursue their own distributional objectives in the face of a highly mobile population are sure to run into serious problems.

In general, then, a system of decentralized governments would find it extremely difficult 'to stabilize their respective economies, to realize the most equitable distribution of income, and to provide efficient levels of output of those public goods that confer benefits on the members of all or several communities.'[37] Nonetheless, there also are substantial advantages accruing to decentralized decision-making.

2 The case for decentralization[38]
If all public goods are provided centrally, welfare will not be maximized if citizens have different preferences for public goods. Or, to put it more positively,

36 Musgrave, *The Theory of Public Finance: A Study in Public Economy* (New York: McGraw Hill, 1959), at 3–27.
37 Oates, *Fiscal Federalism*, at 10.
38 The arguments for and against decentralization are treated in more detail in Prichard's contribution to this volume.

a decentralized form of government offers the possibility of increasing economic welfare by providing a range of locally produced public goods that reflects the preferences of individuals in the community instead of requiring them to consume a uniform bundle of centrally provided public goods. This is the heart of the economic theory of federalism. Local units are viewed as providing alternative bundles of public services, and citizens can choose their province of residence ('voting by foot' as it were) in accordance with their preferences for these various bundles. Not surprisingly, this notion is quite appealing to market-oriented economists since it introduces into the government sphere some of the flexibility and competition that characterizes the operation of decentralized markets. For example, decentralization along these lines will likely encourage greater experimentation and innovation across jurisdictions in both the production and financing of public goods. In this sense a decentralized system 'may thus promote both static and dynamic efficiency in the provision of public goods and services.'[39]

Therefore, while the political scientist may prefer to include under the umbrella of federalism only those few countries in which there exists a constitutionally explicit scope for responsibility and authority for both levels of government, the economist's definition (or perhaps more correctly, W.E. Oates's conception of the economic definition) is far more comprehensive. This is so because these locally produced public goods can be produced by units which are 'provinces' or 'states' as well as by units which are 'local governments.' Indeed, what now frequently passes as the economic theory of federalism was initially developed in a context of an analysis of local governments, not state or provincial governments.[40] And as Oates recognizes, according to this definition 'most if not all [political] systems are federal.'[41]

To be sure, it is probably the case that where there does exist a true federalism (in the political scientist's conception) the likelihood is that the degree of responsiveness of the regional governments to local preferences will be greater. However, this need not always be so. Canada provides a good example here. Constitutionally, health and education fall under provincial jurisdiction. Yet the presence of the former shared-cost programs in hospital insurance, medicare, and post-secondary education meant, with some degree of misrepresentation, that the provinces were in effect spending 'fifty-cent dollars' on these activities provided they satisfied certain national standards. One may wish to argue that the results were desirable, but it is abundantly clear that this was an erosion of

39 Oates, *Fiscal Federalism*, at 12.
40 Tiebout, 'A pure theory of local expenditure.' (1956), 64 *Journal of Political Economy* 416.
41 Oates, *Fiscal Federalism*, at 18.

provincial autonomy – local preferences for the provision of these goods were distorted by the presence of massive subsidies from the central government. Thus, while the economist's approach to federalism abstracts from reality, so too can a focus which is geared toward the formal wording of a constitution.

The centralization-decentralization spectrum

In any event, I want to carry the analysis somewhat further by introducing Figure 1, which is a highly stylized representation of what I refer to as the 'federalism continuum.' At one extreme R, all government activity is in the hands of decentralized governments. At the other extreme, A, there exists only a central government. Neither of these polar positions exists in the real world, unless one classifies such political configurations as the Principality of Monaco as corresponding to polar extreme A. Range UU' is intended to indicate the location of unitary states along the centralization-decentralization spectrum. Not much should be read into the precise horizontal distance allocated to unitary states. Naturally, the existence of local governments implies that a unitary state must be to the left of A, and the range itself implies that there can be a considerable variance in the degree of decentralization associated with such a state.

The range associated with a federation, FF', occupies the middle ground. The overlap with both unitary states and confederations is designed to imply that on occasion the distinction between the political systems may be more a matter of degree than of substance. Finally, the range for confederations occupies the leftmost portion of the spectrum, indicating the likelihood that they will in general be characterized by more decentralized forms of government.[42]

It should be noted that this centralization-decentralization spectrum is to be interpreted as an aggregate across all functions. If our concern was a particular function, say monetary policy, there would probably be very little difference between federations and unitary states. Both would indicate that this function would be highly centralized.

As noted in Figure 1, the range allocated to federations is rather broad. Incorporated within that range and centred rather toward the decentralized end of it is the interval encompassed by BNA-BNA'. This is meant to constrain the federal options in terms of the possibilities allowed by the BNA Act. More centralized federations, such as the USA, would presumably have this interval centred to the right of that shown for Canada, and so on.

While a constitution may set the overall boundaries in the federalism continuum, other factors will determine where in the range a particular federation

---

42 If one were to make the spectrum fully general, all three ranges would overlap.

Figure 1
The centralization-decentralization spectrum

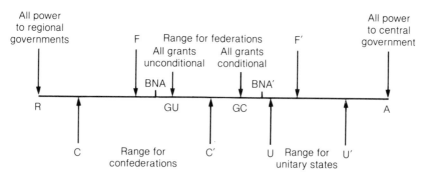

will be located. One of these factors is the nature of the intergovernmental transfers. This is especially important in Canada because Ottawa collects a proportion of total taxes larger than its expenditure needs, and vice versa for the provinces, so that some intergovernmental transfers are required.[43] Such transfers are normally classified into two broad categories – conditional and unconditional. The latter increase provincial revenues without governing how the money should be spent, thereby encouraging decentralization, while the former impinge on provincial autonomy in one way or another and therefore are more consistent with centralization. The most succinct discussion of these two types of transfers still remains that by Jacques Parizeau:

Unconditional transfers can take all kinds of shapes or forms. They can, for instance, be the result of a change in the shares that each level of government raises in a given tax field, when it has been accepted by both sides that that tax field will be shared and that the total tax burden in that field is set at a certain level. Or, they can result in the complete evacuation by the federal government of a given tax field. Or again, they can be produced by the creation of a new tax field, accepted by both authorities as

43 In the extreme, this non-coincidence of spending and revenue-raising authorities could lead by mutual agreement to a transfer of expenditure functions to Ottawa (rather than a transfer of revenues to the provinces). With some degree of misrepresentation, this is what occurred in 1940 (for unemployment insurance) and in 1951 (for old age pensions), despite the fact that in the present environment such transfers of spending authority from the provinces to Ottawa are far less likely. One should note, however, that Ontario's Treasurer, Frank Miller, has recently suggested, perhaps tongue-in-cheek, that if Ottawa continues to squeeze the provinces financially Ontario may simply give Ottawa the responsibility for hospital insurance.

being allocated permanently to the provinces. Or, they can be straight financial annual transfers from the federal budget to the provincial treasuries. And, of course, there can be a combination of all these formulas.

A conditional transfer implies that the federal authorities agree to pay for all or part of a provincial program, as long as that program, its norms, and possibly its administration, have received federal approval or are subject to federal controls.

Conditional transfers not only maintain federal control but they can also be used to expand it. Insofar as they take the shape of shared-cost programs, in other words, while the federal contribution is only a fraction of the total cost, the provincial contribution constitutes so much that cannot be allocated by provincial authorities to autonomous adventures. If the federal government opens shared-cost programs in existing fields of public expenditures, it can thus 'freeze' gradually an increasing share of provincial budgets. At the limit, provincial authorities become more or less administrative agencies of federally initiated or federally financed programs, irrespective of how the legal documents distribute formal powers between the two levels of government.

It should be pointed out that each of these two formulas is compatible with the present Canadian constitution. While one formula strengthens provincial autonomy and the second maintains federal control, both can be fitted to the same legal document.[44]

In terms of Figure 1, extensive reliance on unconditional transfers would imply a position like GU along the spectrum, whereas the other extreme, extensive reliance on conditional transfers, is represented by GC. It is not an exaggeration to assert that altering the form of intergovernmental transfers is essentially equivalent to altering the formal division of powers within the constitution. However, just as the nature of these transfers can influence the degree of centralization or decentralization, so too the formal delineation of powers set out in the constitution is likely to affect the form of interprovincial grants. Thus it is not surprising to find that transfers from Ottawa to the provinces have tended to be of the unconditional variety, compared to similar transfers between Washington and the American states because the Canadian provinces have more constitutional autonomy.

Obviously, much more could be added to the centralization-decentralization spectrum in order to make it more realistic. The essential point is that once one

---

44 Parizeau, 'Federal-provincial economic co-ordination.' In Officer and Smith, eds, *Canadian Economic Problems and Policies* (Toronto: McGraw-Hill, 1970), at 82–3. The last two paragraphs have been reversed.

incorporates into the notion of federalism the existence of geographically distinct governments it becomes fruitful to speak of a federalism continuum or a centralization-decentralization spectrum or, perhaps more appropriately still, a regional-central spectrum. This will, hopefully, allow us to gain some insight into the relationship between federalism and internal common markets.

What is a barrier?
From an economic standpoint an internal-common-market barrier or distortion can be defined as a policy measure which leads to resources being misallocated either within or between provinces or, in the economist's jargon, as a policy measure which leads to a departure from Pareto optimality.[45] In the presence of such a distortion it is always possible to reallocate resources so as to make someone in the country better off without making anyone else worse off (referred to as a Pareto improvement), or, less binding, it is always possible that the amounts accruing to the gainers from removing the distortion are such as to be able to compensate the losers with some leftover (referred to as a potential Pareto improvement). Two of the conditions for Pareto optimality are production efficiency (the marginal rate of substitution between factors should be the same in all industries) and exchange efficiency (the marginal rate of substitution between goods should be the same for all consumers).

How does federalism fare with this definition of a distortion? At first blush, perhaps not all that well. As R.A. Musgrave recognized long ago:

The very purpose of fiscal federalism ... is to permit different groups living in various states to express different preferences for public services; and this, inevitably, leads to differences in the levels of taxation and public services. The resulting differentiation in tax levels may interfere with the most efficient allocation of resources and location of industries for the region as a whole; such is the cost of political subdivision, be it on an intranational or international basis.[46]

How serious is this apparent conflict between the essence of federalism on the one hand and the existence of barriers in the form of departures from interregional pareto optimality on the other? The fact that citizens of various provinces will consume different bundles of provincially produced public goods is not a problem at all. This is clear from Melvin's contribution to this volume. After all, the market for *private* goods allows individuals to consume different bundles of

---

45 This is essentially the definition adopted by Whalley in his contribution for this volume. The remainder of this paragraph is also adapted from Whalley's analysis.
46 Musgrave, *Theory of Public Finance*, at 179–80.

commodities according to their preferences, thereby contributing to consumption efficiency. Different provision levels and mixes of public goods by the various governments serve the same purpose of allowing citizens to attain more closely their (different) desired levels of public goods. Indeed, if citizens' tastes for public goods do differ across provincial boundaries, it is only with different levels and mixes of public goods that Pareto optimality is attainable.

It is possible, however, that these different bundles of public services can, in Musgrave's sense, generate some distortions across the country. Different methods of financing a given bundle of public services could distort the relative price between public sector goods and private sector goods across provinces. Moreover, it is also likely that the work / leisure tradeoff will vary between provinces as a result of both the expenditure level and mix and the tax schemes used to finance these alternative provincial provisions of public services. It is therefore possible that the process of satisfying different citizen preferences for public services between provinces may reduce overall national output. But national efficiency criteria (defined here as maximizing national output) are not entirely meaningful for evaluating potential distortions when it comes to the provision of locally provided public goods and services in a federation.

With this in mind, I would prefer to define an impediment to an internal common market as a policy that both alters the regional allocations of goods and factors and does so in a manner that discriminates against non-residents. I realize that this wording is somewhat unsatisfactory, so that an example or two may be helpful. It seems to me that provinces have the right to reflect the preferences of their citizens in setting standards for various professions and / or trades. There is always the possibility that this could be a subterfuge for favouring local manpower. However, as long as provinces do not impose residency requirements and as long as they establish fair transfer mechanisms for training received elsewhere I would not view this as an impediment to the internal common market. The issue here is one of a lack of harmonization, not a case of discrimination against outsiders. Secondary education is also a case in point. Ontario has five years of high school, but students from provinces with only four years of high school can in many circumstances enter Ontario universities. One might be tempted to question the wisdom of this policy on Ontario's part, but I would not classify it as an impediment to the internal common market. More generally, there is no doubt that lack of harmonization in many areas can and will reduce overall output, but these are not barriers in the sense of representing discriminatory distortions in the pattern of regional relative prices. Over time, however, for most of the various categories where different standards occur it is likely that the substantial mobility of citizens combined with the increasing flows of information will lead to an increasing homogeneity of citizen preferences between provinces, which will in turn increase the degree of harmonization.

At the empirical level, as distinct from the analytical level, this modification of the definition of what constitutes a barrier or an impediment will not be very important. Most of the focus of the quantitative exercise in later chapters is on policies that would also qualify as distortions under the revised concept. In large measure this is because the empirical work does not put too much emphasis on provincial expenditure patterns or revenue-raising techniques.

So far so good. But surely the controversy over internal barriers is not related to these sorts of issues. Rather it has to do with the fact that in federal nations the provinces are autonomous in certain areas and can as a result enact legislation which generates benefits within the province at the expense of residents of other provinces. Moreover, the ability of the provinces to engage in such behaviour is enhanced by grants that are unconditional rather than conditional. Therefore, would it not be the case that barriers to internal trade and factor mobility automatically diminish as one moves to the right in Figure 1?

Is decentralization synonymous with balkanization?
The answer, I think, is not as obvious as one might expect. It seems very clear that the more decentralized is the federation and the more fiscally autonomous are the junior governments the more likely it is that they can engage in self-interest policies. But this does not necessarily imply that federal systems will have more fragmented internal markets than unitary states. For example, nothing in Canadian legislation restricts the mobility of individuals as much as the housing policy in the United Kingdom. The combination of rent controls and the associated regulations pertaining to tenancy, which are under the jurisdiction of the local authorities in the UK, inject a degree of immobility into the British economy that is far more severe than anything that exists in Canada and indeed in most federal nations. Thus, I would reject virtually out of hand the all-too-common notion that federalism and the fragmentation of the internal economic union are synonymous.

What does happen as one moves to the right in Figure 1? As pointed out in the integration continuum, the movement to greater integration is usually accompanied by increased interregional transfers, which, since they may alter relative prices on a geographical basis, fall in the category of an internal barrier. There is no hard and fast rule governing this, but it does seem to be the case. Is this also likely to hold true as one moves toward the centralization extreme in Figure 1? I think that the answer is yes, although my reasons are more intuitive than rigorous.

Before proceeding to this discussion it is instructive to enumerate the sorts of policies that would fall in the category of centrally induced barriers to an internal common market. On the taxation side, the list would include such items as regional investment tax credits and the special incentives for energy companies to explore and develop in the so-called Canada Lands as distinct from provincial lands. Examples on the expenditure side are Department of Regional Economic Expansion (DREE) payments[47] and regionally differentiated unemployment insurance payments. Equalization payments, whether arising from the formal equalization program or from the implicit equalization component embodied in, say, the established programs financing arrangements, are examples of how incentives to migrate can be influenced by intergovernmental transfers. Quotas and / or tariffs directed toward particular industries that are regionally concentrated (such as textiles) provide an example of how tariffs can affect the geographical distribution of both labour and capital. Last, but certainly not least, there is the common-market fragmentation arising from the regulatory process. The federal government's role, alluded to above, in facilitating the existence of provincial marketing boards which influence interprovincial trade is a case in point. Another is Canada's policy with respect to the domestic energy price. There is an equally varied and probably more lengthy list of distortions that arise from the exercise of provincial intitatives, but our concern here is with the actions of the central government.

Greater centralization clearly means that more and more powers fall into the hands of the central government. In a very decentralized federation the central government's role will likely be perceived as basically taking a 'hands-off' approach to the problems of regional adjustment. As more power accrues to the central government, its scope for influencing resource allocation on a regional basis increases. Of course, it need not use this power to distort resource allocation, although as mentioned above it would be difficult to find provincial barriers affecting factor mobility as strongly as the actions of British local authorities on housing. Might it be the case that, despite their additional authority, central governments will not be more prone to distort allocation the more centralized the system?

The answer is likely to be no for several reasons, all of which have to do with the regional checks and balances on central government initiatives in a federal state and the lack thereof in a unitary state. One such check to central government activity in a federation is the fact that the junior level of governments can respond with offsetting policies. Consider the activities of DREE. Ottawa restricted the availability of industry subsidies to certain designated regions. For

47 Legislation has been tabled in the House which will amalgamate programs currently under the Regional Development Incentives Act and certain programs from Industry, Trade and Commerce. The new programs (one of which will replace DREE) are expected to be announced in the fall of 1982.

their part, some of the richer provinces (which were not included in the designated areas) responded by offering roughly similar location incentives. In one
sense this compounds the distortion – a new firm will now be subsidized wherever it locates, and in the limit all new firms would be eligible. However, it does
offset the 'regional' nature of the initial incentive and in large measure negates
the original thrust of the subsidy. This sort of action on the part of the junior
governments, which by the way is enhanced when intergovernmental transfers
are unconditional, provides some check on central government activities on the
regional front in a federal state, a check that is absent in a unitary state.

It should also be noted in this context that some checks and balances keep
individual provinces from venturing too far afield with protectionist measures.
There is no piece of legislation that states that Quebec and Ontario, since they
have mounted their own corporate tax systems, must adhere to the same
formula as the rest of the provinces for allocating corporate profits across
provinces. Nor is there any formal requirement that they define corporate
income in roughly the same manner. Yet they do. And one reason for this is that
to deviate in a province-serving direction would surely be to invite retaliation
from the other governments. Another reason is that the provinces are very open
economies. Some analysts have argued that since it is not far from reality to view
capital as perfectly mobile, the cost of engaging in self-interest policies will
eventually fall on the residents of the offending province. Thus, they would
assert, there is really no such thing as a beggar-my-neighbour policy: over the
longer term the province imposing the impediment will ultimately lose. The
conclusion is that we should not be too much concerned about provincial action
vis-à-vis the fragmentation of the internal common market; if provinces are
foolish enough to enact discriminatory policies, the consequences of which they
will ultimately bear, why should Ottawa or anyone else assume a paternalistic
stance to prevent them from self-inflicted injury? The issue is not this clear-cut,
however. Although the distinction between 'competitive federalism' and
'beggar-my-neighbour federalism' may frequently be one of degree rather than
substance, I feel that the latter can exist, even in the long run. It is true that the
costs of preferential purchasing policies will mean that taxpayers in the offending province will now pay more for their government's purchases. But this may
be a cost that the province is willing to bear if it is offset even in part by a gain to
its local producers, particularly if these producers are important for electoral
purposes. If one assumes that *new* capital is perfectly mobile and that Canada is
an insignificant part of the world capital market, then preferential treatment of
capital by one province will not draw capital away from the other provinces. If,
however, one argues that the more appropriate assumption is that capital is
mobile in a *national* context, the other provinces will indeed be hurt by a policy

that subsidizes capital in any one province.[48] In any event, existing capital is much less mobile than new capital, so that there is plenty of room for provincial policies that inflict costs on in-place capital in other provinces. Finally, it seems to me that, regardless of the assumptions one makes about capital mobility, the sheer size of Alberta's Heritage Fund is such that there is the potential for long-run beggar-my-neighbour implications if these monies are directed toward attracting industry currently located outside of Alberta. The fact that this may not make economic sense and that any such industry attracted may require continued subsidization is somewhat beside the point if Alberta is willing to bear such costs. In short, beggar-my-neighbour policies can and do exist, although the open-economy nature of the provincial economies surely does serve to discourage their implementation.

To put the case more positively, there tend to exist mechanisms in federal states for sorting out interprovincial discrimination. Some of these may involve both levels of government: there are nearly one thousand federal-provincial conferences on all aspects of social and economic activity. Others are restricted to the junior level of government. One example of the manner in which interprovincial consultations can minimize the erection of barriers to mobility is the Maritime provinces' approach to university education. Rather than mounting out-of-province tuition fees, these provincial governments have in place a set of interprovincial transfers to compensate for cross-province registrations, thereby allowing citizens relatively free rein in selecting the university of their choice. Safarian has pointed out that the Interprovincial Seal Programme for the skilled trades has met with some success in encouraging common examinations and improved transfer arrangements among provincial systems, thereby enhancing the mobility of skilled tradesmen.[49]

Contributing to this general situation where Ottawa increasingly becomes a regional broker and the provinces likewise take into account the influence of their decisions on other parts of the country is the growing interdependence between the two levels of government, quite irrespective of the formal delineation of powers within the constitution.[50] As noted previously, Ottawa invaded the provincial domain by making an offer that the provinces could not refuse with respect to the provincial areas of health and higher education, thereby

---

48 These two views of the nature of the capital market will play an important role in the empirical chapters in this volume.

49 Safarian, 'Ten Markets or One?' at 19.

50 The view that the Canadian federalism is becoming dominated by the fact that both levels of government are increasingly interdependent is most effectively put forward in an excellent recent study by Bastien, *Federalism and Decentralization: Where do We Stand?* (Ottawa: Ministry of Supply and Services, 1981).

distorting provincial preferences in favour of national goals. (In passing, it should be noted that even though this represents a major interference in the system it does not qualify as a federal distortion by our definition because it does not discriminate on a *geographical* basis.) For their part the provinces are also moving in the direction of becoming more involved in matters coming under federal authority. For example, former top Ottawa bureaucrat Gordon Robertson has described the 1973 Western Economic Opportunities Conference as a 'milestone in the involvement of the provincial governments in matters wholly or exclusively within the jurisdiction of the federal government. This agenda of this meeting was almost wholly devoted to western grievances involving such matters as national transportation policies, tariffs and federal agricultural policies, and the provincial governments were confident and aggressive in assuming the role as spokesman for their respective electorates.'[51] This growing interdependence serves to condition federal policy to take account of regional concerns as well as to ensure that provincial decisions take into account some national perspectives. In our federation, much of this interaction between the two levels of government takes place in federal-provincial conferences and more generally in the exercise of what has come to be known as 'executive federalism.' Other federations have different vehicles for accomplishing much the same ends (such as a regionally elected upper chamber). The main point is that there are mechanisms in federations that at the same time constrain and co-ordinate decision-making at both levels of government and between governments of the second tier. These procedures serve to inhibit and sometimes rectify policies that would come under the umbrella of internal barriers. Needless to say they are not entirely successful. However, they do represent a set of forces that may not exist in unitary states.

The constitution as a limit to central-government-induced impediments
Much of the thrust of the public discussion on the internal common market concerns the role that the constitution can or should play in curbing provincial protectionist measures. Implicit in this discussion is the view that the more a nation resembles a unitary state, the less need there is for such constitutional guarantees to control the actions of regional governments. It is useful, however, to view this from the opposite perspective, namely that of the relationship between the constitution and the central government. In unitary states with a

51 This quotation appears in Smiley, *Canada in Question*, at 115. Robertson's paper, 'The role of interministerial conferences in the decision-making process" appears in Simeon, ed., *Confrontation and Collaboration – Intergovernmental Relations in Canada Today* (Toronto: Institute of Public Administration of Canada, 1979), at 78. The quotation is at 82.

parliamentary form of government there is sometimes no formal consitution (e.g. the United Kingdom), and in any event there are usually no meaningful constraints on the range of actions open to the central government. Yet in a federal state the constitution can be the most important mechanism for controlling the ability of the central government to interfere with the geographical allocation of resources. For example, in the Australian constitution, Section 99 prevents this very sort of discrimination by the central government: 'The Commonwealth shall not, by any law or regulation of trade, commerce, or revenue, give preference to one State or any part thereof over another State or any part thereof.' This section certainly restrains the regional initiatives available to the central government. The American constitution is not as restrictive on this issue, but there has developed a strong tradition that Washington should not interfere in regional development. In response to a recent call for federal intervention in regional problems, American Senator Daniel Moynihan reflected this ingrained tradition very well:

We must not politicize the question of relative regional growth or, for that matter, regional decline ... It would be contrary to the spirit of the constitution for the federal government to intervene in our economy to try to prevent the natural movements of capital and people from one state or region to another, if a free choice is made by those concerned. Such a restraint, surely, is imposed by the constitution on state governments by the interstate commerce clause. Certainly, the federal government should not act in a manner forbidden to the states. The founders of this nation understood that our political freedoms and national stability very much depended on our becoming a single economy with the freest possible movement of capital and labor across state and regional borders. The Supreme Court more than once has had occasion to reaffirm that commitment.[52]

The tradition in Canada is, if anything, the opposite. The federal government is very active in the regional arena. What is far more significant, however, is that Ottawa appears to envisage the whole approach to securing an internal common market as a means by which its role in the regional side can be increased. This comes out loud and clear from Mr Chrétien's position paper. Throughout the analysis there is reference to the 'economic surplus' that will be generated by eliminating interprovincial barriers to the free movement of goods and factors. No problem here. But the document then goes on to suggest that this surplus can be put to use on a regional basis in order to reduce any existing disparities

52 Moynihan, 'The politics and economics of regional growth.' (1978), 51 *The Public Interest* 3, at 7.

between provinces or regions, with the proviso that some mechanisms must be put in place so that this can occur.[53] Part of this mechanism is the entrenching, in Part II of The Constitutional Act 1982, of the authority for the federal government to legislate in the area of reducing regional disparities.[54]

This is at the same time a most intriguing and disturbing feature of the overall federal position. In effect it means that Ottawa will be able to do the very things that it wants to prevent the provinces from doing, namely to engage in policies that will alter relative prices across regions. What Ottawa does not accept or appreciate is that any such regional policies will also contribute to the fragmenting of the internal common market. Any such measures initiated by Ottawa are of course undertaken in the 'national interest.' This underlying attitude, among other things, has led Laval's Gérard Bélanger to see in the federal concern over fiscal harmonization Ottawa's desire to centralize power.[55]

Recapitulation

If one adopts an economic concept of federalism (defined as the existence of a central government and a tier of regionally based governments, which can tailor locally produced public goods to the preferences of residents) then one can speak of a federalism continuum where the difference between a formal federal state and a unitary state is one of degree rather than substance.

The provision of differentiated locally produced public goods in response to citizens' desires is efficient and welfare-maximizing. Such provision should not be viewed as a barrier to trade even though it may inhibit mobility. For example, one province may have higher standards and/or qualifications for certain occupations. This should not be viewed as a barrier to trade as long as there exist appropriate 'transfer' criteria for non-residents. Problems arise only when provinces take protectionist measures which alter the geographical pattern of market sector relative prices.

It is no doubt the case that the *potential* for fragmentation of interprovincial barriers increases where the constitution assigns larger areas of responsibility to the junior level of government. One might also expect that the potential for fragmentation increases when the intergovernmental transfers are unconditional, since this adds to the fiscal autonomy of the junior governments. However, reality may be different. It is not difficult to find unitary states where the local governments can impose very substantial impediments to factor mobility

53 For example see Chrétien, *Securing the Canadian Economic Union*, at 5.
54 See also *supra* note 1.
55 Bélanger, 'Doit-on imposer l'harmonization fiscale?' (forthcoming from the Economic Council of Canada).

(such as Britain and housing). Even in the absence of constitutional provisions ensuring a full common market, there exist checks in virtually all federal countries on the degree to which the provinces are likely to adopt protectionist measures. These come not only from the possible retaliation of other provinces but from the central government as well. Moreover, given the very open nature of most provincial economies, the longer-term costs of many of these geographical distortions will be borne by the initiating province.

In assessing the degree to which nations can be characterized as having an internal common market, one has to also take account of the likelihood that the central government will be the vehicle for fragmenting the market. On this score, it seems to me that central governments of federal nations are less likely to engage in altering interregional relative prices than are the central governments of unitary states. Once again, the issue revolves around the existence of checks and balances. Some federal nations (Australia) have provisions that restrict the ability of central governments to favour one region or state over another. Even in the absence of such constitutional provisions, the junior governments can often mount policies that can offset any central government initiatives. More generally, the very essence of sharing power in a federal nation would appear to make it difficult for either level of government to enact policies that favour or discriminate against particular regions. At the very least, there will exist forums where such actions will come under general scrutiny. These sorts of restrictions do not appear to be present in unitary states. This need not imply that central governments in unitary states will be more interventionist on the regional front; only that if they are that way inclined they have a relatively free rein to indulge themselves.

Thus, there appears to be no necessary relationship between the federalism on the one hand and the achievement of an internal common market on the other. In practice, I would not be surprised to find many unitary states where the internal common market is less secure than it is in most federations (the definition of an internal market barrier being any distortion in the geographical pattern of relative prices).

What appears intriguing about the Government of Canada's approach to this whole issue is its intent to remove the provinces' abilities to fragment the internal market while at the same time including in the constitution a provision which would allow itself to embark on the same sorts of policies. Ottawa bemoans the fact that the clauses in the Canadian constitution that might curb provincial protectionist initiatives are not as strong as those enshrined in the constitutions of other federal nations but does not stress the fact that those other federal constitutions also place restrictions on the activities of the central governments as well. Such restrictions are rejected as an unnecessary constraint on Ottawa's

ability to legislate in the national interest. Were Ottawa to succeed in its endeavours my hunch would be that the Canadian internal common market might
end up being even more balkanized than it is, because the process would remove
the existing constraints (weak as they may be on occasion) on the ability of the
federal government to legislate preferentially in favour of one or another province or region.

In summary, then, federalism should not be viewed as a degenerate case of
economic union. This does not mean that actions should not be taken that will
enhance the free movement of goods and factors across regions. What it does
mean, however, is that care should be exercised to ensure that what might be
gained by restricting provincial initiatives is not overturned by opening the door
to discriminatory actions on the part of the central government. In the Canadian
context this is probably a rather strong assertion, because the federal government seems unwilling to view many of its regional initiatives as measures that
will fragment the common market and / or firmly believes that they will contribute to both regional and national well-being. In my view both these perceptions
are wrong. Indeed, in the longer term it is quite possible that preferential
regional initiatives will not only lead to a balkanization of economic activity
within the country but as well may contribute to a lower standard of living in
both the regional and national economies. The final two parts of this section are
devoted to this issue, with the first of these also providing some further evidence
to support the claims that there need be no necessary relationship between
federalism and fragmentation of the internal common market.

Internal barriers and narrow vs broad special interest groups
In a recent study of why growth rates differ, Mancur Olson argues that one of the
distinguishing features between countries in terms of their economic growth is
whether or not they are characterized as having 'narrow' or 'encompassing'
special interest groups.[56] Specifically, the more encompassing the special interest
group (such as a labour union) the more it will be in the group's own interest to
ensure that overall national goals such as economic growth and efficient
resource allocation are taken into consideration in decision-making. A narrow
special interest group will usually not find it in its own interest to be too
concerned with the larger consequences resulting from receiving government
protection. Sweden and Britain (two unitary states) are obvious examples.
Practically all the unionized manual labourers in Sweden belong to one great
labour organization, and as a result, Olson asserts, Swedish labour leaders have
been distinguished from their counterparts in many countries by their advocacy

56 Olson, 'The political economy of comparative growth rates' (manuscript, 1979).

of growth-increasing policies such as encouragements to labour mobility and retraining rather than the subsidization of inefficient plants.[57] In Britain on the other hand many of the powerful common-interest organizations fall into the 'narrow' rather than the encompassing category and have much less concern for the effects of their actions on other parts of the economy.

Sam Brittain comes to much the same conclusion in a paper focussing on the so-called British Disease. Commenting on the difference between Britain and Sweden in economic performance, he notes: 'Sweden ... [like Britain] had a high level of social services and fiscal redistribution but [unlike Britain], until recently at least, was a model market economy. Industrial policy was geared to encouraging workers to shift as quickly as possible to the most profitable industries, and investment was guided by world markets rather than government planning.'[58]

Two implications arising from these observations are relevant to our own analysis. The first is that significant factors other than the formal political structure of nation states will probably have a bearing on whether or not a country's domestic economy will be free of internal barriers. Special interest groups will exist under any political system, and unless one is willing to argue that federations tend to be represented more by 'narrow' special interest groups this will not lead to any meaningful relationship between federalism and economic union. It is certaily true that the provinces can be viewed as special interest groups. It is also true that the province most in favour of securing interprovincial free trade is Ontario, which is no doubt the most 'encompassing' of these special interest groups. In general, however, the tendency of governments to intervene in geographical resource allocation is related as much if not more to basic factors such as the attitudes of citizens toward the role of government, the industrial and geographical distribution of economic activity, and features such as narrow vs broad special interest groups as it is to the political fabric.

The second implication concerns the role of intervention itself. Both Brittain and Olson argue that policies that stifle economic adjustment have played a contributing role in Britain's economic decline and that the maintenance of a market economy has enabled Sweden to perform very well, in spite of other similarities between the two nations. Is this likely to carry over to Canada? Specifically, is it likely that the federal government is on solid economic ground when it proposes to use the 'economic surplus' arising from removing interprovincial barriers to engage in more intervention on the regional front? Or is this

---

57 Ibid., at 53. Emphasis added.
58 Brittain, 'How British is the British sickness?' (1978), 21 *Journal of Law and Economics* 245, at 256–7.

intervention itself likely to lead to significant output costs? To this question I now turn.

Regional policy and regional disparities[59]

That there exist regional disparities across our nation is not in doubt. It should, however, be emphasized that these disparities exist principally in the sphere of market-sector incomes. Access to public goods and services does not differ nearly as much between provinces as access to market-sector goods and services.

In recent decades Canada's approach to the plight of its less favoured regions has been progressively to cushion the short-term adjustment problem by an ever-growing network of transfers to persons, business, and provinces. Ottawa moved in with increased equalization payments, industrial subsidies, infrastructure grants, regionally differentiated unemployment insurance benefits, specific tariff provisions, and so forth. That there were and are short-term benefits (and some long-run ones too) is also not in doubt. Fewer people were required to make the decision to migrate, partly because governments were now able to provide services well in excess of those that their own tax bases would permit. With more dollars flowing into the provinces, marginal business could still get by. And so on.

But there were also longer-term costs. The provinces became more and more dependent on these transfers. Government income became a substitute for market income. This has come to be known as 'transfer dependency.' Examples are plentiful.

The decision to allow self-employed fishermen to become eligible for unemployment insurance benefits in the off-season has increased Newfoundland's population and its unemployment rate and hampered the rationalization of the fishing industry. Had Ottawa also granted the same dubious privilege to self-employed Saskatchewan farmers the economic geography of that province would have been significantly altered. Saskatchewan would now have a much larger population and a significantly higher unemployment rate. Its farms would be smaller and less efficient, and the overall incentive environment would have been changed to render its economic fabric less viable. To be sure there were large costs imposed on farmers in the short run as they adjusted to altering economic circumstances. But over the longer term both Saskatchewan and Canada are better off as a result of the absence of federal intervention in the form of unemployment insurance subsidization.

---

59 This section is adopted from Courchene, 'Regions, transfers and growth' (1981), 8:1 *Canadian Business Review* 6, and 'A market perspective on regional disparities' (1981), 7 *Canadian Public Policy / Analysé de Politiques* 506.

Quebec provides another interesting case. It has the highest minimum wage on the continent, let alone in Canada. This does not make economic sense, but it exists in large measure because of the incentives embodied in the transfer system. Basically, Quebec does not bear the full economic and financial costs of such a decision. The unemployment resulting from the high minimum wage generates larger unemployment insurance benefits and federal contributions to welfare, as well as equalization payments. But this is not the end of the story. Because of its high unemployment rate, Quebec can then lobby successfully for such things as tariffs and quota protection for its textile industry. Thus, in the current regional policy environment provinces are able to export large portions of the costs of their decisions through Ottawa to the rest of Canada.

More generally, focusing on data relating to the role of government expenditure flows into the economies of the have-not regions indicates that not only are these flows very large (averaging over 70 per cent of the gross demostic product (GDP) for the Atlantic Region for 1974) but that they have been increasing.[60] Much the same is true of the current account deficits. As a percentage of GDP, those deficits for the Atlantic provinces range from 48 per cent for PEI to 27 per cent for New Brunswick, and on average they have increased substantially in recent years. These facts do not 'prove' that the regional policy initiatives have been a failure. However, I do not find them very surprising because decades of interrupting the natural adjustment processes at both the inter-regional and interprovincial levels (by enacting policies that in effect fragment the domestic market) are in my opinion bound to lead to a situation where existing disparities become entrenched and exacerbated and where provinces and regions alike are made more dependent on the system of transfers.

Therefore, while the federal government is correct in noting that the existence of provincially imposed barriers to free domestic trade serves to reduce domestic efficiency and to create a problem for the international competitiveness of Canadian industry, this same concern must be carried over to federal actions as well. To use a system of subsidies to induce a corporation to locate in a 'designated' province may well appear to reduce domestic regional disparities, but it may do so at the cost of severely undermining the longer-term ability of this industry to be competitive in an international environment. Overall, Ottawa's concern with enshrining constitutional measures to limit the actions of the provinces while at the same time ensuring the constitutional right for it to engage in essentially identical activities is both inconsistent and inappropriate. The American economist Lester Thurow recently commented on this issue:

---

60 Figures detailing this and the results in the next sentence are contained in Table 1 of Courchene, 'Regions, Transfers and Growth.'

An industrial policy designed to prop up dying industries is a route to disaster ... Productivity and real standards of living rise by getting into new high-productivity industries and getting out of old low-productivity industries. If the latter are protected, that stops labour and capital from leaving them and flowing into new industries. In addition, the bail-out funds usually come from somewhere, and they usually come out of funds that would otherwise be available for new industries. This leads to a slower growth for the sunrise industries and a lower real standard of living.

Nor does the shift result in permanently depressed regions of the country ... New England is a prosperous region because it got out of its old dying industries and into new growth industries. *If Washington had protected New England's old dying industries, the area would still be depressed.* It is correct to point out that New England went through forty years of economic pain before it made that transition, but the correct answer to this is a national policy for aiding individuals and speeding up the transition. To prop up dying industries will only prolong the pain. Whatever government does they will die in the end.[61]

ESTIMATING THE QUANTITATIVE SIGNIFICANCE OF BARRIERS TO
TRADE: SOME OBSERVATIONS

The overall thrust of the papers in this volume is to define, analyse, and subject to empirical quantification the interaction between federalism and internal economic barriers. We have now examined the background and have established a framework for the quantification that is the subject of the papers to follow. In particular, I have argued

– that there is no *necessary* relationship between federalism and the degree to which the domestic economy is fragmented. The issue boils down to an empirical question of deciding how costly to overall efficiency are the barriers that do exist.
– that the most appropriate definition for an internal barrier from an economist's vantage point is any policy measure by any level of government that distorts relative prices on a regional or geographical basis. I have modified the definition to incorporate the essence of federalism by adding that a policy action

61 Thurow, 'The productivity problem.' In Ontario Economic Council, *Policies for Stagflation: Focus on Supply. Volume 2* (Toronto: Ontario Economic Council Special Report Series, 1981), at 30–2. Thurow is not espousing a 'hands off' approach on the part of governments. Rather, he is arguing for intervention to be directed toward the sunrise industries rather than the sunset industries, in part because this is the policy adopted by governments of our trading partners.

that reflects local preferences and does not discriminate on a geographical basis should not be construed as an internal market barrier. The former is the definition that is utilized in later chapters for quantifying the significance of Canada's internal barriers. However, most of this empirical work is consistent with the modified version as well.

The quantitative analysis undertaken elsewhere in this volume finds, first, that federally induced barriers are likely to be every bit as harmful as provincially induced barriers and, second, that except for one or two cases the distortions are not very important in terms of the overall cost to the Canadian economy. How should one interpret these results?

Comments on the estimation procedure
While most economists would feel comfortable with this approach to measuring policy-induced distortions, there are, nonetheless, several problems that economists would raise (and that the authors themselves have raised) in interpreting the estimates. To non-economists, however, the problems associated with this approach to quantifying barriers probably run much deeper. In this section I want to focus on both sets of concerns in order to prepare the way for an alternative approach to viewing internal barriers in a federation.

Some of the barriers may in fact offset each other, so that it is inappropriate to view the total cost as the sum of the constituent parts. For example, suppose that the tariff distorts economic activity in a way that encourages the movements of goods and factors away from the periphery of the nation and towards the centre. Suppose too that there exists a set of intergovernmental transfers that in effect distribute money back from the centre towards the periphery. Call these 'equalization payments' if you like. In isolation, both policies represent impediments to the free flow of goods and factors on a regional basis. Yet one offsets the other. Indeed, a frequent rationale for equalization payments is that they represent a quid pro quo for the range of other policies that favour the centre. In this sense, it is inappropriate to *sum* the impacts of these two policies, as Whalley and Trebilcock are careful to note.[62]

This is but a particular example of the more general 'second-best' proposition, which in effect, states that in an economy already riddled with distortions it is not in general true that adding another distortion will diminish aggregate welfare.

Some impediments to mobility may enhance efficiency. Concerning for example the substantial resource rents which accrue to the provinces, the following

62 See their contributions to this volume.

argument can be made.[63] Individuals will choose their province of residence on the basis of an overall bundle of amenities, such as gross income, taxes, and public services. If one or more provinces derive substantial resource rents and use these revenues either to provide an enhanced bundle of public services or to reduce taxes on the existing services, then inefficient or rent-seeking migration to the resource-rich provinces may occur. This result is inefficient in the sense that workers will be willing to take lower productivity jobs in the resource provinces than the ones they are leaving because this differential will be more than offset by the resource-rent-financed public services they will receive. However, from the vantage point of the migrants this is optimal behaviour since they will be better off as a result of the move.

Yet from the national viewpoint resources will be misallocated and national output will be reduced if people migrate in order to take jobs that pay less than those they are leaving. Under these circumstances it should be possible to embark on a transfer scheme which would be classified as a Pareto improvement. This might involve greater revenue sharing between Ottawa and the resource provinces or some interprovincial revenue-sharing pool for resource revenues. Such schemes should not be classified as a 'distortion' since they are consistent with enhancing efficiency. This point is recognized in the empirical work in this volume.

Quantitative analyses may underestimate the true economic costs of internal barriers. Notwithstanding the previous two points, quantitative analyses of interprovincial barriers may underestimate the economic costs. This is so because the results must, almost of necessity, be calculated within a static framework. One looks at actual interprovincial trade flows to calculate the economic loss generated from various impediments. This is fine as far as it goes. But such an analysis neglects the dynamic efficiency losses. Because the market is fragmented firms may be of less-than-optimal size. Protection leads to complacency – firms need not be highly efficient in order to obtain contracts if governments treat them preferentially. There is less reward for innovative behaviour if non-tariff barriers prevent access to larger markets. More important still, protected firms will tend to look once again to governments if altered economic circumstances challenge the status quo. This is but another way in which the transfer-dependency syndrome impacts on the viability of the domestic economy. The world of the 1980s is going to be a very competitive one. The rewards are going to go to those nations that can with speed and efficiency allocate

63 This argument is outlined in full in Boadway and Flatters, 'The role of equalization payments in a federal system of government: a synthesis and extension of recent results.' Queen's University, Institute for Economic Research, Discussion Paper 443, 1981.

resources to the 'sunrise' industries. Protectionist measures stifle innovative entrepreneurship and in effect reward complacency, both of which augur poorly for Canada's longer-term international competitiveness. It is difficult to quantify these dynamic efficiency losses, but in my opinion they are every bit as important as the more easily quantifiable static losses.

Another issue is important here, one that in the economic literature is referred to as 'rent-seeking behaviour.' If special-interest groups realize that there are benefits to be reaped by obtaining government concessions, it will pay them to invest real resources (lobbyists, advertising, etc.) to secure these benefits. Likewise, groups will also invest time and effort to maintain any privileges that they currently have. Thus, included in the costs associated with internal barriers should be the resource costs that are spent in order to obtain or maintain such privileges. Normally, these considerations are excluded in empirical work devoted to measuring the costs of distortions.

The potential exists for the costs of protection to rise. In part, this is merely a statement about the way in which the international economy is unfolding. I have already asserted that the competitive pressures will increase in the 1980s. The tendency in such an international climate, particularly in light of the overall stagnation of world economic activity, is for countries to turn inward and intervene to prevent employment from falling. If this occurs, the short-term costs of a country not following suit can be substantial, even though most or all nations realize that this is a negative-sum game.

A second reason for rising protectionism arises from the internal environment in which Canada now finds itself. More than ever before, the financial capacities of some provinces place them in a vastly superior position to other provinces. For example, the existence of the heritage funds in the west could lead to very serious economic distortions if these pools of capital are utilized to further 'province-first' policies. The same is true if more provinces follow Quebec's lead in providing tax concessions for purchases of new share issues of provincially based companies. The result would be an unacceptable fragmentation of the internal capital market. The recent constitutional accord represents an ominous move in this very direction.[64] To allow provinces with high unemployment to engage in preferential employment policies will kindle a beggar-my-

---

64 Section 6, subsection 4, of the Canadian Charter of Rights and Freedoms of the *Constitution Act 1982* reads: 'Subsections (2) and (3) [relating to mobility rights including the right to pursue the gaining of a livelihood in any province] do not preclude any law, program, or activity that has as its object the amelioration in a province of conditions of individuals in that province who are socially or economically disadvantaged if the rate of employment in that province is below the rate of employment in Canada.'

neighbour atmosphere across provinces. No law, whether enhsrined in the constitution or not, can possibly cover anywhere near the range of alternatives that can fall under the umbrella of protectionist measures. If the present environment of interprovincial co-operation becomes soured with self-serving policies enacted by high unemployment provinces (which includes all provinces except Ontario and the prairies) this could well spell the unwinding of the quite impressive degree of integration and harmonization that the country has worked so hard to attain.

These comments obviously transcend the range of issues considered in the quantitative chapters of the study. However, one of the reasons why the internal-common-market issues has surfaced at this time is precisely because the nation is perched rather perilously at the precipice, where a further move in the direction of provincial protection might lead to a landslide of retaliatory measures. Speaking only for myself, I cannot fathom this astounding turn of events. The entire initial thrust of the federal position was to utilize the constitution to curb the growing sentiment towards protectionist measures. To turn around and in effect enshrine as a constitutional right the ability to fragment the internal common market is incomprehensible!

I shall return to this point later. I wish now to consider some other concerns relating to the approach taken to the quantification of internal barriers. These concerns amount, in effect, to a questioning of the entire rationale underlying the empirical work in this volume.

What the quantitative exercise accomplishes is to determine the degree to which a nation is adhering to the precepts of efficient resource allocation. *There is no room in the analysis for any political or social norms that may be essential to Canadian nationhood.* This is absolutely correct. The more a country departs from geographical Pareto optimality, whether the departures are a result of central or regional policy initiatives, the larger the resulting distortions will be.

But in one sense this is exactly what we want to measure – the costs of departures from Pareto optimality on a regional basis. This does not mean that all such departures are to be deplored. After all, there are also benefits for specific groups and regions that attend these distortions. Thus there is no intent on my part to argue for the elimination of all such distortions. It is nonetheless appropriate to estimate these costs not only because they represent a valuable piece of information when assessing whether, for example, equalization payments should be increased, but as well because they provide a backdrop against which one can compare the costs of higher-profile barriers such as provincial purchasing preferences and discriminatory hiring policies.

Thus, although the procedures adopted for identifying internal barriers boil down to an assessment of the degree to which market forces are allowed a free rein within the economy, this approach is probably the most appropriate economic perspective from which to assess these barriers. Any other benchmark would at the same time be less general and more arbitrary.

However, I am also concerned that the overall framework I have adopted up to now may not be particularly useful for policy purposes. I shall now try to redress this balance. What follows is a framework for assessing interprovincial barriers that incorporate the essence of federalism as well as a range of possible socioeconomic goals. At the outset it is important to emphasize that the focus of this framework is on the evaluation of internal barriers in terms of their impact on national output, whereas much of the preceding analysis in this paper has been in terms of economic welfare. As Melvin notes in his contribution to this volume, there are serious problems associated with evaluating internal barriers in terms of their impact on national income or output. In spite of this important reservation, I shall proceed, noting only that the concept of lost output arising from internal barriers appears to be the thrust of the federal government's background paper.

OBJECTIVE FUNCTIONS, INTERNAL BARRIERS, AND FEDERALISM[65]

Table 1 presents a variety of potential objective functions for the central government in a federal state. The provinces may well have their own objective functions, but we shall ignore them for the moment. The objective functions are intended to be ordered so that the constraints become ever more binding.[66] This means that the level of national output arising from sixth objective function, for example, will be less than the national output that will be generated under the second objective function.[67] The constraint set is designed so that Ottawa becomes more and more involved in the pursuit of regional and provincial goals. Indeed, this is what generates the falling national output as one moves down the various possible objective functions. Objective functions 5 and 6 look quite

65 The framework for this section follows closely that developed in an earlier paper: Courchene, 'Alternative regional development strategies in a federal state.' In Schramm, ed., *Regional Poverty and Change* (Ottawa: Ministry of Supply and Services, Canadian Council on Rural Development, 1976), at 191.

66 As a matter of fact the objective function, as reflected in the table, remains the same, i.e. to maximize national output. All that changes as one moves down the table is that the constraint set embodies differing goals. However, for the sake of convenience I will refer to these as different objective functions, thus implicitly incorporating the constraint set into the objective function.

67 Some readers might feel that a slightly different ordering is necessary in order to ensure that the constraints become progressively more binding Amen!

TABLE 1

Alternative central government objective functions

1 Maximize national output.

2 Maximize national output, subject to the constraint
    a) that there be a minimum level of income for all Canadians.

3 Maximize national output, subject to the constraints
    a) above and
    b) that regional *income* disparities be narrowed.

4 Maximize national output subject to the constraints
    a) and b) and, further,
    c) that provincial *income* disparities be narrowed.

5 Maximize national output subject to the constraints
    a) and
    d) that regional *production* disparities be reduced.

6 Maximize national output subject to the constraints
    a) and d) and, further,
    e) that provincial *production* disparities be narrowed.

similar to objective functions 3 and 4. But there is a major difference. Under either 3 or 4, Ottawa can satisfy the minimization of regional or provincial disparities by transferring income to those regions or provinces – for example, by equalization payments or even equal-per-capita funding for the established programs since this incorporates some 'implicit' equalization. There need be no distortion on the allocation front, except that which arises because of the higher tax bite to service the greater transfer flow. Not so for objective functions 5 and 6. Here the central government has to intervene in the allocative process directly in order to move production, as distinct from income, to the various provinces and regions. With some degree of misrepresentation one can make the following two observations. First, objective functions 2 through 4 involve the federal government increasingly in the direction of concerning itself with interprovincial income (equity) considerations, whereas 5 and 6 engage the central government increasingly in interprovincial production (allocative) considerations. Second, as one moves through the various objective functions the central government is increasingly engaged in the process of mounting internal barriers to the free movement of goods and factors.

Which objective function is the most appropriate? The answer to this crucial and complicated question will differ between federations depending on such things as tradition and the constitution. An economist cannot really provide the answer. What the economist can do is indicate the benefits and costs associated with the alternative objective functions. Ideally, one would like to be able to quantify the costs in terms of national output resulting from objective functions 2 through 6. Unfortunately such calculations have never been undertaken. Indeed, the attempt in this volume at quantifying federal impediments to the internal common market represents the most comprehensive estimates to date. Yet it is precisely such estimates of the amount of national output forgone for the sake of regional and provincial goals that are required for Canadians to make intelligent decisions on the objectives they wish the government to pursue.

Since this method of casting the goals of federalism in terms of objective functions is essentially equivalent to putting them in a linear programming context, it is interesting to pursue this methodology further. The solution to the 'dual' of the linear program would represent the potential increase in national income that could be attained by relaxing the respective constraints. In particular, the dual prices associated with objective function 6 would represent the increase in national income attainable by relaxing the requirement that the minimum income be 'produced' in each province. In other words, this would present the 'economic cost' of having provinces rather than regions as the political units, in the sense that one could measure the cost of moving from objective function 5 to 6. To be sure this is a delicate framework from which to view our nation's objectives. Delicate or not, one cannot escape the increasing costs associated with moving down the list of objective functions in Table 1.

There are, of course, increased benefits too as one moves from objective function 1 to 6. As a matter of fact, these benefits are even more difficult to quantify than are the costs. In part, they represent direct income benefits accruing to people and provinces. However, they also incorporate the psychic benefits accruing to all Canadians because they know that their fellow citizens may be better off, and so on.

Given the curves for total benefits and total costs (assuming that they could be measured) the economist could then construct marginal benefit and marginal cost curves and select as the appropriate objective function the one where the marginal benefits are equated with the marginal costs. Just where this intersection is likely to occur depends very much on whether Canadians are interested more in 'people' prosperity or 'place' prosperity, which is another way of describing the difference between objective functions 5 and 6, which are concerned primarily with place prosperity, and the earlier objective functions where the focus is more on people prosperity. It seems clear to me that the marginal costs in terms of lost output rise substantially from 4 to 5 and even more so from 5 to 6. Since I am basically a believer in people prosperity I would attach the largest marginal benefit to moving from 1 to 2, with marginal benefits positive thereafter but lower. Thus, from my vantage point I would think that marginal costs would clearly exceed marginal benefits for objective function 5 and probably much earlier along the spectrum. But in making this assessement I can cast only one vote in the political marketplace.

Let us now use this framework to shed some light on the relationship between federalism and internal barriers by bringing the provinces back into the analysis.

Introducing provincial policies
Consider objective function 1: the role of the central government is to ensure that its policies maximize national output. This need not imply that there will be no regional aspect to central policy. If one interprets maximum output as a longer-term goal, it may be fully consistent for the federal government to provide, say, regional infrastructure, on grounds that parallel the infant industry ('infant region') justification for the imposition of tariffs.

All of this assumes that provincial policies are also consistent with maximizing national output. But suppose the provinces are engaging in protectionist policies. What then is the role, under the first objective function, for the central government? The answer is not obvious. It depends on whether the central government takes as 'given' the provincial actions or whether it views its role as one of offsetting any distortions that may arise from them. This quandary also arises with objective functions 3 and 4 where the issue will be how the federal government interprets 'equity.' In this context, Boadway and Flatters recently discussed two views of horizontal equity that the federal government can adopt:

There are two views the federal government might take. The first, what we shall call *broad-based horizontal equity*, is that persons with the same real comprehensive income ought to be treated identically by all governments taken together, both federal and provincial. Since provincial governments violate this norm [almost by definition in terms of the choice of bundles of services they provide and how they collect revenues to finance them] the federal government must take steps to redress the differences in treatment ... The second, or *narrow-based horizontal equity*, is that the federal government need only concern itself with the equity of its own actions when deciding upon a policy. The real income levels achieved after the policies of the provincial government actions have been taken is regarded as the starting point. The federal government only insures that its own actions are equitable.[68]

One can, without doing much violence to the underlying notion, substitute 'efficiency' wherever 'horizontal equity' or 'equity' appears in the above quotation. If one adopts the narrow-based view of efficiency, then the role for the central government under the first objective function is the same whether the

68 Boadway and Flatters, 'Efficiency, equity and the allocation of resource rents in a federal state: the case of Canada.' (forthcoming in *Taxation Resources and Economic Development*).

provinces mount protectionist policies or whether they do not. If one adopts the broad-based notion of efficiency then the central government's role in maximizing national output has to take these provincially generated distortions into account. In either case, however, the central government has no policy responsibility for the regional distribution of income (earned or unearned). Interprovincial barriers will be costly to national output (even if they are offset by federal actions), and it is obviously preferable if they not exist, but they pose no serious problem since regional concerns are not part of the objective function.

Objective function 1 is clearly unsatisfactory as an overall framework for policy in the Canadian federation. It is more consistent with a confederal state where most powers lie with provincial governments, including concerns relating to income distribution, and the role for the national government is largely one of a coordinating agency and the supplier of certain national public goods.

The second objective function incorporates an income distribution constraint and could be implemented by having Ottawa embark on some sort of guaranteed income scheme, such as negative income tax. Beyond this, the central government would again only concern itself with overall output in pursuing its policies.

The third and fourth objective functions involve the federal government directly in regional policy. One type of federal policy that might satisfy objective function 4 would combine a guaranteed income scheme with an equalization program. Unlike the case for the first two objective functions there would now be some concern on the part of the central government over the policies at the provincial level that would work against narrowing these income disparities. Policies that inhibit migration or favour in-province producers could at the same time lower national output and call for more federal transfers to the poorer regions. On the other hand, one can view these objective functions as still falling well within the purview of 'people' prosperity. Ensuring a minimum level of income for all Canadians and ensuring that all Canadians have access to the average level of public services need not involve direct federal intervention on the allocative front. These goals could be achieved through the tax-transfer system (although this would of course involve generating some indirect allocative effects).

Not so for the last two objective functions. Here the central government is called upon to reallocate the production or allocation of economic activity. In other words, it has a mandate to erect barriers to the internal common market. The stance of provincial policies now becomes critical. If they are embarking on beggar-my-neighbour policies the overall cost in terms of forgone national output in achieving, say, objective function 6 could be very substantial indeed. Note that what should be of concern to the central government is not only the possibility of discriminatory policies emanating from the 'have' provinces or regions. The costs that can arise from similar policies mounted by the poorer provinces can be just as serious. Since this may not be obvious, an example or two will help. Suppose that the criterion for narrowing production disparities between provinces is the unemployment rate. The central government will intervene in the allocative process whenever a particular province's unemployment rate is deemed to be too high relative to the national level. If the provinces are fully aware of this, they can engage in policies that will have the effect of holding Ottawa to ransom.

The earlier example of Quebec's high minimum wage leading to higher unemployment in the province and in turn to increased protection (via quotas) for its beleaguered industries is a case in point. By being able to export the costs of its decisions through Ottawa to the rest of Canada, it is in effect forcing the central government's hand. This is also the case when provinces take steps to inhibit population outflows. Such a policy can arise indirectly if, as is currently the case, the province can choose the types of (federally funded) retraining courses that its citizens can attend. Happily, the federal government now appears to be moving in the direction of rectifying this policy. In a similar vein, provincial governments can enact policies that will encourage greater labour force participation by secondary workers, thereby putting upward pressure on unemployment rates. If the unemployment rate is one of the indicators of whether the federal government is going to intervene in a region, then these sorts of provincial measures can be utilized to induce further federal injections into the various regions.

The reader may feel that I am grasping at straws in order to press the point that measures enacted by the poorer provinces can create problems for an objective function like number 6 when in fact the more fundamental problem probably lies more in the direction of protectionist policies mounted by rich provinces. For example, if Ottawa decides to subsidize reallocation in certain designated regions, then comparable policies at the provincial level in non-designated provinces will frustrate this initiative and lead to a diminution of national output with the problem remaining unsolved. This of course is true. But it must be remembered that the poorer provinces can also present problems for the achievement of an objective function like number 6.

A view of current policy

It appears to me that in terms of Table 1 the federal government has opted for at least objective function 5 and probably number 6. The Constitution Act, 1982 explicitly enshrines the narrowing of regional disparities as a national goal (Part II). Moreover, it forbids low-unemployment provinces from mounting barriers to internal labour mobility.[69] Interpreted widely enough, this would imply that these provinces could not move to counter any federal initiatives on the regional front. Yet the high-unemployment provinces can, as a constitutional right, inhibit in-migration. Presumably this is viewed by the federal authorities as a step in the direction of ameliorating regional economic disparities. But as I have argued throughout, this proposition is far from obvious. In any event, what began as a process of enshrining the economic rights of citizens in the constitution has in the end enshrined the right of most provincial governments to fragment the domestic market.

Two further observations are relevant. The first is that even though the federal government appears to have adopted objective function 5 or 6, constraint (a) of the objective function has in effect been shelved. The overriding concern appears to be with place prosperity or province prosperity without ensuring that this will filter down to individual Canadians, wherever they may reside. This, I think, is not an accident but rather is a direct result of the structure of Canadian federalism. I shall treat this issue in more detail in the following section.

The second observation is that Canadians have not as yet addressed the real issue at stake here, namely, whether it is appropriate as a national goal to embark on the fragmentation of our internal market in order to achieve objective function 6. What is the opportunity cost in terms of national output of pursuing this overall goal? Who are the beneficiaries – the provinces or individual Canadians? It is highly appropriate that Ottawa resurrected the issue of the internal common market. Barriers to interprovincial trade, whether provincially or federally induced, do violate the rights of citizens and do reduce national output. However, the issue can now be clearly seen as raising fundamental questions about how Canadians perceive themselves and their governments interacting in the economic sphere.

FEDERALISM: A SYSTEM FOR PEOPLE OR FOR PROVINCES?

Elsewhere I have described federalism as a regulatory process with the federal government as the regulator and the provinces as the regulatees.[70] Such a process

---

69 Note that the group of provinces that has greater-than-average unemployment rates is not the same as the group that qualifies for equalization payments. British Columbia is not a recipient of equalization, and yet it is a high-unemployment province; and vice versa for Manitoba.

70 The ideas in this paragraph are from Courchene, 'Towards a protected society: the politicization of economic life.' (1980), 13 *Canadian Journal of Economics* 556, at 572–5.

is subject to Stigler's Law, which suggests that regulation is normally in the interest of those being regulated. What this means is that all too frequently the beneficiaries of this process are the provinces as *provinces* and not as the individuals that compose them. As long as one is talking about the 'economic rights' of citizens in the context of the Charter of Rights and Freedoms, the direction in which we ought to be moving is one which 'emphasizes the rights of Canadians, individually and in voluntary associations, against *all* levels of government.'[71] It is not at all clear that the interaction between the federal government and the provinces is serving to enhance the economic freedoms of individual Canadians. Indeed, I would argue that the opposite is true. It has always struck me as anomalous that we have a comprehensive negative income tax scheme for provinces (the equalization program) but lack a comprehensive negative income tax scheme for Canadians. Furthermore, when the courts ruled that provincial marketing boards could not interfere with interprovincial trade, the federal government passed enabling legislation to allow them to do so. This would surely run counter to any meaningful code of economic conduct designed to ensure an internal common market in goods, services, labour and capital.

More generally, entrenching economic freedoms in a charter of rights would mean that the Supreme Court would be called upon to play a much greater role than before as arbiter.[72] It has not been our tradition, until recently at least, to place great reliance on the courts for ironing out federal-provincial conflicts. Instead, Canada has engaged in what has come to be known as 'executive federalism' – conferences of executives from the federal and provincial governments. With nearly one thousand such meetings annually, this may well be Canada's 'contribution to the art of federalism.'[73] However valuable executive federalism may be in lending the needed flexibility to the BNA Act in the political sphere, this 'third level of government' has not, in my opinion, had a positive influence in the economic sphere. Just as the regulatory process is usurping the role of the marketplace in the private sector of the economy, executive federalism is usurping the role of the courts in the public sector. And without the courts to protect the basic economic rights of private sector economic agents it is entirely possible that executive federalism will lead to a further fragmentation of the Canadian economic union. Once again some examples are useful:

Section 125 of the constitution states, in effect, that the crown cannot tax the crown. What this means in practice is that factor incomes (e.g. rents, profits,

---

71 Safarian, *Ten Markets or One?*, at 18.
72 This paragraph is reproduced almost verbatim from Courchene, *Towards a Protected Society*, at 575.
73 Safarian, *Ten Markets or One?*, at 18.

interest) accruing to one level of government are not taxable by the other level. Thus energy royalties (rents), earnings of the heritage funds (interest), and profits of provincial liquor monopolies and hydro corporations are not subject to federal tax. A similar list of federal business enterprises that escape provincial tax can be noted. This is a very serious distortion in the economy because it puts public sector enterprises in a privileged position compared to comparable private sector enterprises. This sort of distortion would seem to me to be inconsistent with a full-blown constitutional provision for safeguarding the economic rights of citizens. It is not even clear that the present interpretation of the powers incorporated under Section 125 would stand up in the courts with respect to many government activities. But here is where the process of executive federalism intervenes. In the energy agreement with Saskatchewan the federal government is in practice, if not in principle, deriving some revenues that accrue to provincial crown corporations. Yet as part of the agreement, both parties agreed *not* to take the issue before the courts. Much the same was to apply in the proposed agreement with Newfoundland. Neither party was to bring the issue of control over offshore energy before the courts.

The constitution's bestowing on high-unemployment provinces the right to engage in protectionist policies is a further example of how executive federalism can restrict the economic freedoms of private sector agents.

More generally, one of the reasons why the range of economic freedoms enshrined in the constitution was limited principally to the mobility of people and not extended to the full range of goods, services, and factors of production is that the federal government insisted on derogations for itself under the rubric of regional policy, which meant that actions forbidden to the provinces would have been a constitutional right for the federal government. Political struggle on this issue continues, but what is disturbing is that constitutions from the Magna Carta onward have sought to protect the rights and liberties of citizens *against* the power of the state. As for protecting citizens' economic rights in particular and the concept of an internal economic market in general, it is hard to avoid the conclusion that when Ottawa and the provinces get together there is precious little reference to, and even less action on behalf of, any third parties who might also be privy to some of the spoils.

CONCLUSION

Examining the degree to which Canada ought to be characterized by an internal common market or an economic union is tantamount to addressing the underlying economic and even political structure of the nation. My treatment of the issue has been rather abstract and somewhat narrow. I did not even discuss some of the obvious larger issues, such as the implications for the division of powers that flow from the principle of an internal common market. For example, Wayne Thirsk argues that one necessary component of an internal common market is that 'source-based' taxes (such as corporate income taxes and resource revenues) require harmonization in order to avoid, among other things, tax-exporting across provincial boundaries.[74] His specific recommendation is that source-based taxes like the corporate income tax be centralized in federal hands. Rather, the discussion has been restricted to the range of issues raised by the federal background paper *Securing the Canadian Economic Union in the Constitution.* I have accepted the federal concern that there are substantial costs in terms of national output, both present and future, that attend these barriers. What I have not accepted is the proposal implicit in that paper to the effect that federalism is a degenerate case of economic union. Indeed, much of the analysis was directed toward the notion that centrally induced barriers to the internal market can be every bit as costly as provincially induced barriers. In other words, unitary states are not paragons of virtue when it comes to internal common markets.

The analysis then became somewhat more pragmatic. The issue of the costs of provincial barriers was raised in the context of the possible objective functions of the nation as a whole. The more the national objective function involves inter-vention to fragment the common market, the more costly were provincial policies that did the same. The major issue that arose and was left unresolved was what the nation's objective function in the economic sphere ought to be. To answer this question adequately requires, in my opinion, considerably more information than is available at present, but it is a question that must be addressed.

Finally, I noted the incredible about-turn made by Ottawa when it agreed to enshrining the right of high-unemployment provinces to fragment the internal market for labour. The federal-provincial tug-of-war over economic power seems to be restricting the economic freedoms of private sector agents.

One important remaining question is the relative degree of political legiti-macy associated with centrally induced and provincially induced barriers. Sup-pose a province enacts a preferential purchasing provision which discriminates against all out-of-province suppliers. Compare this to a federal-initiated policy which bestows roughly the same privilege on the producers in this particular province. In the former case the out-of-province producers who are hurt by this action have no official forum for mounting their point of view, and the provin-

---

74 Thirsk, 'Tax harmonization.'

cial politicians who enacted the legislation are not accountable to these suppliers. In the latter case, even if one assumes that the same costs are inflicted on these out-of-province suppliers, they do have an official forum (Parliament), and the legislators who enact the measure are accountable politically to these firms. Thus, it would appear that centrally induced barriers are much more legitimate politically than provincially induced barriers. This question is examined in detail in this volume by Robert Prichard.

If, as I have argued, the regionally based tier of governments should be able to tailor their public goods and services to the preferences of their citizens, should centrally-provided goods and services not also be tailored to the preferences of all citizens? And of course they are! Were one to make political legitimacy paramount in any analysis of internal barriers, one would be quickly driven to the conclusion that in the Canadian context there can be no federally induced barriers to internal economic activity; as I have noted above, that is one way of interpreting the thrust of the federal government's background study. This paper has essentially downplayed the legitimacy issue and concentrated on policies emanating from both levels of government and their economic effect on the free movement of goods, services, labour, and capital across provincial boundaries. Yet the concept has not been entirely neglected. For example, it was recommended that a set of economic rights for Canadians should be entrenched in the constitution to constrain the actions of all governments, because without such a provision there is precious little in the way of limiting the range of policies that the federal government can implement. Presumably Ottawa recognized this as well, and that is probably why it advocated incorporating into our constitution only those aspects of the constitutions of other countries which contained stricter restraints on the ability of junior levels of government to fragment the internal common market and omitting provisions that constrained the role of the federal government. In any event the concept of political legitimacy did not play a major role in the analysis.

In spite of all the problems and concerns dealt with above, we should not lose sight of the fact that Canada certainly has a workable internal common market. And in terms of the degree of tax harmonization our accomplishments are really quite enviable, particularly in comparison with other federations that have a decentralized tax system. While it is certainly a laudable goal to seek to improve on the status quo, it is probably more important in the current economic context to ensure that what we have accomplished over the years does not begin to unravel. In this regard, several points merit emphasis.

First, it is important that the federal government attempt to maintain the tax collection agreements essentially intact. Among the many contentious issues involved here the one that probably poses the most immediate problem is how to deal with the fact that many of the provinces want to imitate Quebec's special tax treatment for residents who purchase new shares of Quebec-based companies. If this privilege is incorporated in most or all provincial income taxes it will fragment the domestic capital market.

Second, it is important that the provinces continue to agree to abide by the current formula for allocating corporate profits of multiprovincial corporations across the various provinces. In this connection it appears to be essential for maintaining an effective internal common market that the provinces continue to adhere to a common definition of corporate income. Failure to do so will result almost inevitably in a beggar-my-neighbour struggle between provinces for corporate headquarters. Ottawa could help considerably in this process if it made some concessions relating to the differential manner in which it treats corporate writeoffs for the energy section in the so-called provincial and Canada Lands (as defined by the National Energy Program).

Third, in the current recession both levels of government will engage in interventionist policies. Frequently, however, alternative instruments could be deployed to achieve substantially the same end. Wherever possible the instrument selected should be the one that will do the least damage to the internal allocation of resources, will impose the fewest impediments to the internal economic union, and will be the easiest to remove when the existing problem has passed. This is particularly important because how policies are implemented is often as important as the policies themselves.

Fourth, it is probably important for all governments to agree on guidelines for the investment of the various heritage funds. Whenever possible these investments should accord with market principles throughout the nation. Since this would be in the best interest of all parties, it should not be too difficult to get agreement on. If these funds become a vehicle for province-first policies it bodes ill for preserving the Canadian economic union.

Fifth, there is a growing problem with respect to the differential treatment of factor incomes accruing to the public and private sectors. Section 125 of the constitution should be modified so that these incomes accruing at one level of government are subject to taxation at the other level.[75] Otherwise, private sector industries will be at a severe disadvantage across an increasingly wide range of activities, and provinces will be pushed into nationalizing or 'provincializing' an increasing number of firms.

75 For a discussion of how such a measure could also provide the basis for a revenue sharing agreement relating to energy, see Courchene, 'The National Energy Program and Fiscal Federalism.'

Finally, the federal government performed an extremely valuable service to all Canadians by highlighting the internal common market issue and by alerting everyone to the realities that accompany a fragmented internal market. While not willing to go so far as having this concept entrenched in the constitution, several provinces did embrace the notion of a 'code of economic conduct' which would lay down some general guidelines relating to ways in which the erection of internal barriers could be limited. I hope that these provinces will work to bring others into the fold and will develop a meaningful code of economic conduct that will apply to all governments and will indeed secure an economic union within Canada, since such a provision is obviously not secured in the Constitution Act.

3

Political structure and
the pursuit of economic objectives

J.R. Melvin

INTRODUCTION

The purpose of this paper is to provide a framework for the investigation of those government policies which reduce the welfare of Canadians. The underlying premise is that certain actions by federal, provincial, and lower levels of government often result in reductions in national welfare to levels below those which would otherwise have prevailed, and often seems to be attempting to achieve conflicting goals. But why would governments pursue policies which can easily be shown to reduce welfare, and why would different levels of governments be in conflict over the appropriate policies to be pursued? To put these issues in perspective this discussion concentrates attention on the reasons why one would expect governments to exist in the first place, and more particularly on why one would expect to observe more than one level of government. In order to understand the sources of policy conflicts between different levels of government it seems important to have a clear understanding of the reasons why different levels are required.

After discussing the notion of national welfare in the second section, the third and fourth sections provide a summary of the literature on the theory of government and present a simple model of the provision of public and non-private goods. The fifth section shows that a unitary state will suffice for identical tastes; the sixth section then shows that more than one level of government will be required for the efficient provisions of public goods when tastes differ. In the seventh section some preliminary comments are made on the question of the size and allocation responsibilities that would be optimal for different levels of government. The eighth section argues that optimal policies pursued by lower government levels may not be optimal from the point of view of the nation as a whole. Some specific policies in this class are briefly described.

The ninth section considers taxes as barriers to the intranational flow of goods and factors of production. In the tenth section non-optimal policies pursued by the federal government are considered; and the eleventh and twelfth sections deal with two such policies: the tariff and the federal energy policy. The final section presents a summary and some conclusions.

THE CONCEPT OF NATIONAL WELFARE

What meaning should be attached to a term like 'national welfare'? A number of definitions have been employed in a variety of economic contents, and this section compares them with a view of arriving at some consensus on how government policy can be evaluated. Welfare measures will be considered first, then some of the difficulties associated with using the level of national income as a criterion, and finally the circumstances under which one or the other will be more appropriate.

Welfare measures

Ideally, policy should be evaluated in terms of utility or welfare. All consumer analysis is based on the proposition that individuals attempt to maximize their personal utility, and the role of government should ultimately be viewed as an attempt to assist in this maximization. Unfortunately serious problems arise when one attempts to transfer the criterion of utility maximization to society, such as the ever-present aggregation problem and the difficulties with interpersonal comparisons. These are discussed below, and to facilitate such a discussion it is useful to introduce the notion of Pareto optimality. By this criterion situation A is said to be Pareto optimal if increases in the utility enjoyed by any individual can only be accomplished by reductions in the utility of someone else. Situation C is said to be Pareto superior to B if the movement from B to C increases the utility of at least one individual and does not reduce the utility of anyone else. A movement from B to C is said to be Pareto improving.

These definitions are illustrated in Figure 1, where two individuals are assumed to have utility functions defined over commodities X and Y. The contour lines of the utility functions, or the indifference curves, have their origin at O^1 for the first individual and at O^2 for the second. The locus of tangencies of these sets of indifference curves, the contract curve, is $O^1 A O^2$ and defines the set of all Pareto optimal points. By the definition above, points such as $E, A, C,$ and F are Pareto superior to B. Note that E is not Pareto superior to C, nor are any of the above-mentioned points Pareto superior to G.

Figure 1 illustrates one of the basic difficulties with the pareto criterion, namely its inability to provide a unique ranking of all allocations. Thus while E is

Figure 1

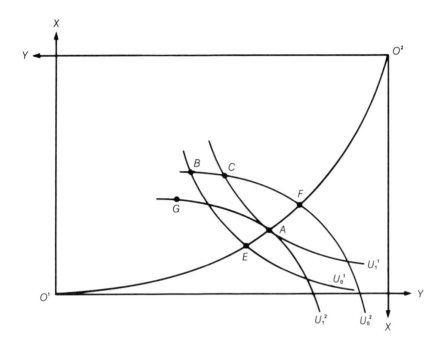

Pareto optimal and C is not, the Pareto criterion does not allow us to say that E is 'better' than C. Furthermore, while all points on the contract curve O^1AO^2 are Pareto optimal, including the situations where one or the other of the two individuals have all the available supply of X and Y (points O^1 and O^2), no comparison of any of these points is possible by the Pareto criterion.

The inability of the Pareto criterion to rank all alternatives demonstrates one of the difficulties associated with evaluating government policy. The Pareto criterion is concerned only with efficiency, while many policy measures are concerned with equity. As a simple example, suppose in Figure 1 the initial allocation is O^1, where the first individual has all the available X and Y. Suppose the government believes that income should be equally distributed among all consumers and, through taxes and subsidies, redistributes income to point C, the centre of the Edgeworth Box. Note that the Pareto criterion can make no statement about the relative merits of O^1 and C except to say that O^1 is Pareto optimal and C is not. Of course any point on AF is Pareto superior to C. The point is that if society values more equality of income, as most societies evidently do,[1] then the government may quite legitimately choose a point such as C in preference to O^1. Policy measures undertaken to change the distribution on income will *never* be Pareto improving, for they necessarily make someone worse off, but they may nevertheless be quite appropriate if they conform to society's goals.

The problems associated with the inability of the Pareto criterion to rank all alternatives could be avoided if society could be assumed to have a well-defined utility or welfare function analogous to the individualistic utility function. Two fundamentally different approaches to this problem have been taken, depending on whether a positive or normative theory of government behaviour is required. In the positive approach where interpersonal utility comparisons are not permitted, the question becomes one of when an aggregate welfare function can be assumed to exist. If one assumes that the arguments of the social welfare function are just the utilities of individuals within the society, it is well known that the conditions which permit evaluation of social welfare W are quite severe.[2] Putting aside the trivial cases where society is composed of a single individual, or where only one individual 'counts,' the social welfare function will be an unambiguous guide to community well-being only if W possesses the characteristics traditionally associated with utility functions of individuals, namely, the requirement that individual indifference curves do not cross and the condition that higher-utility contours are associated with higher levels of utility or welfare. The conditions for the existence of such community indifference curves are known to be quite restrictive. One must have the condition that all individual utility functions are homothetic and either that all individuals have identical tastes or that all individuals have a distribution of income proportional to the aggregate. While for many theoretical purposes such assumptions are quite acceptable, both sets of conditions are at variance with the characteristics of any society for which the question of the role and structure of government is of practical interest.

The conditions for the existence of community indifference curves implicitly assume that all goods consumed are private goods. It will subsequently be shown that one of the fundamental assumptions associated with the economic explanation of the existence of government is the need for the provision of public goods. If one or more of the goods entering an individual's utility functions are public goods, then the conditions for aggregation to yield well-behaved social utility

---

1 The existence of a progressive income tax is one indication that governments favour some degree of income equalization.
2 For a discussion of community indifference curves see Chipman, 'A survey of the theory of international trade: Part A, the neo-classical theory.' (1965), 33 *Econometrica* 685.

Figure 2

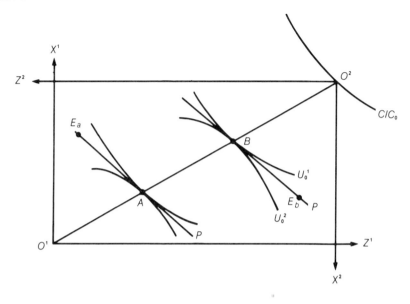

functions are even more severe. Figure 2 illustrates the conditions for the existence of community indifference curves for two individuals where the two goods X and Z are assumed to be private goods. Preferences for the first individual are measured from O^1 and preferences for the second from O^2. The conditions that utility functions are homothetic and that tastes are identical result in a contract curve which is linear and the diagonal of the box. Note that it is also assumed that the total quantity of X and Y is given and is equal to the dimensions of the box diagram.

In the situation illustrated in Figure 2, well-behaved community indifference curves can be constructed; one such curve is CIC_0. It can easily be shown that the slope of CIC_0 at O^2 must be equal to the slope of the two individual indifference curves from which the CIC was derived. Thus, for example, the common tangent to U_0^1 and U_0^2 at B is the same as the slope of CIC_0 and O^2. It is also known that for homogeneous utility functions all indifference curves have the same slope along any ray from the origin. Thus at any point along the line O^1O^2 the indifference curves for both individuals have the same slope and the community indifference curve constructed from the allocation of resources associated with point A will be identical to that associated with the point B. Thus a single CIC is associated with the infinity of points along O^1O^2.

Figure 3

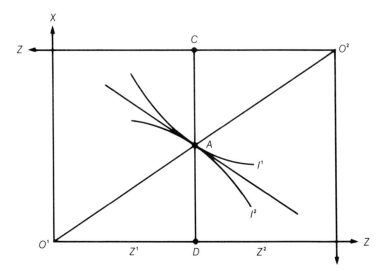

It is clear, however, that if Z is a public good the construction of a diagram such as Figure 2 is not appropriate, for now both individuals can consume the total available quantity of Z. A diagram for the public good case comparable to Figure 2 is shown as Figure 3, where now the Z dimension of the box represents twice the total available quantity of Z. Thus $O^1D = CO^2$, and both are equal to the production of Z. With identical tastes for the two consumers, the only possible equilibrium is point A on the mid-point of the contract curve O^1O^2. Note also that in Figure 2 any initial endowment of X and Z between the two individuals will lead to the same community indifference curve. Two such endowments could be E_a or E_b. In Figure 3, however, trade between the two individuals in commodity Z cannot take place, and thus the only initial endowment consistent with equilibrium is the endowment point A. Thus in a model with public goods, as well as the assumptions of homothetic and identical preferences, we must have the additional assumption that the incomes of all individuals be identical.

Of course in Figure 2 there are many other Pareto optimal distributions which are possible if we wish to drop the assumption that all individuals are in equilibrium. This would require that individuals consume more or less of the public good than they would wish to at the terms of trade indicated by the slope of the indifference curves at A. Consider point B, for example. This point is

Pareto optimal, because any movement along the line DC will make one or the other of the individuals worse off. Only movements along DC are allowed, since both individuals are required to consume the total available quantity of Z. Of course the same argument is true for all points on DC, and thus DC represents a locus of Pareto optimal points. Of all these points, however, only point A is an equilibrium, for at all other points for any single price, either one or the other individual (or both) would rather consume some other bundle. In other words, only ponit A can be sustained by a single relative price ratio.

If we do insist on full equilibrium for all consumers then the problem of not having a complete ordering is no longer a difficulty, for in the situation of Figure 3 only point A is permissible. It is also clear, of course, that the model is now completely without interest, for in a world in which all individuals have identical preferences and identical initial endowments, no interesting public finance questions arise. While it is therefore clear that we must abandon the community indifference curve construct if progress towards a theory of the structure of government is to be made, it is worth noting that if one wants to obtain a well-defined community preference relationship one must make these rather restrictive assumptions if pure public goods are present.

One can avoid the difficulties associated with the positive aspects of the Pareto approach if one is willing to drop the requirement that any welfare improvement requires that no individuals suffer reductions in utility. Indeed one of the earliest social welfare criteria, predating that of Pareto, is that of Bentham. By Bentham's criterion one simply sums all individual utility indices to form a social welfare function. Such an approach quite explicitly abandons the suggestion that utility levels among individuals are not comparable. Perhaps a more serious difficulty is that the welfare index is cardinal, and thus requires that individual utilities can actually be measured in some way. Clearly such a notion is not going to be of much help in ranking government policies.

A more recent addition to the social welfare literature is the Rawlsian, or maxi-mini, approach. Here society's objective is seen to be the maximization of the welfare of the worst-off individual in society. Although the Rawlsian model has created a good deal of interest over the last number of years, the results of the research using this approach do not seem particularly relevant to the problem at hand. It certainly does not provide a useful criterion for ranking government policies or measuring social welfare.

National income as a welfare measure
Substantial difficulties thus exist in using a welfare criterion to evaluate policy, not the least being the fact that utility cannot be measured, so that interpersonal comparisons and aggregations are difficult or impossible. In an attempt to

Figure 4

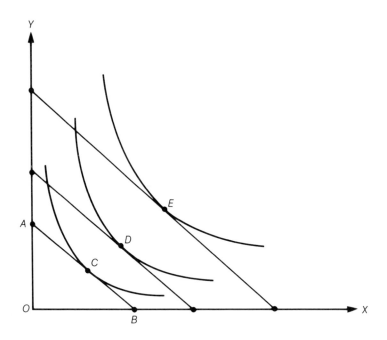

overcome these difficulties national income is often used instead. Using income as a proxy for utility is easily justified in certain circumstances, and in certain simple cases the two measures are equivalent. For example, consider a single individual with well-defined preferences and a known income who faces fixed prices for X and Y, the two commodities he consumes. In Figure 4 with budget line AB the consumer is in equilibrium at point C. Now suppose income increases so that the new equilibrium is at D. Here both utility and income are higher than at C. Furthermore, any change in income will change utility in the same direction, and thus income is a perfect proxy for utility; and of course income has the further advantage of being easily measured.

The situation shown in Figure 4 is simplified by the fact that commodity prices have been assumed fixed. Now consider Figure 5 where two individuals, Don and Frank, are at equilibrium at points D and F respectively on budget line AB. Now suppose income for both increases from, say, $100 to $120, but that there is also an increase in the price of Y and a decrease in the price of X so that the new budget constraint is A^1B^1. It is clear that while this income (and price)

Figure 5

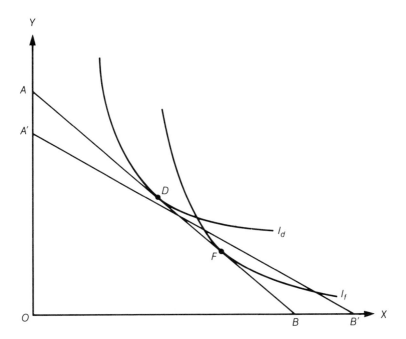

change has made Frank better off it has reduced Don's utility. Thus while money income for both has risen, real income in terms of commodities purchased has fallen for one and risen for the other. Note that there is no ambiguity here about what has happened to utility for the two individuals. The difficulty arises from the fact that money income is simply not a good proxy for utility when relative prices are changing.

Another sort of difficulty can arise if changes in national income affect different individuals differently. Assume in Figure 4 that two identical individuals with the same incomes are in equilibrium at point D. Now suppose that some government policy is introduced which shifts one individual to E and the other to C, so that aggregate income for the two has increased. There is now no ambiguity about the fact that total income has risen, but a statement about total welfare can be made only if the utility changes for the two individuals can be compared. The difficulty here is precisely the problem of the incomparability of utility discussed earlier.

In many circumstances, however, there is a way in which this difficulty can be overcome. Suppose in Figure 4 that a tax was imposed on individual E, whose income had risen, equal to the amount C had lost, and that this tax was paid as a subsidy to C. Individual C would now be back at the initial equilibrium point D and would be as well off as before. Individual E would still be in a preferred position to D, and thus with the tax and subsidy the income increase can be made Pareto superior to the original situation. Thus the income change depicted is a *potential* improvement, and an actual improvement can be generated by the appropriate distribution of income. Even in the situation of Figure 5 a small transfer of income from F and D could result in both individuals enjoying higher utilities than at the initial situation. When prices have changed, however, such a welfare improving redistribution will not always be possible.

The difficulties just described have their counterparts in general equilibrium analysis as well. Suppose, in a simple, closed, two-commodity world with X and Y both private goods, that national income is measured by prices P, assumed to be fixed. In Figure 6 the production possibility curve between X and Y is TT'. We further suppose that consumers are identical and have homogeneous preferences, so that a set of community indifference curves exists. Suppose that two policies are open to the government: the first involves taxing the consumption of commodity X leading to an equilibrium at point A; the second involves a subsidy to producers of X and results in an equilibrium at B. Because of our assumption that national income is evaluated in terms of P, it is clear that the higher level of income is achieved by the consumption tax at point A. It is equally clear, however, that social welfare, and indeed the welfare of all individuals, is higher at point B, achieved through the subsidy.

Alternatively, suppose income had been measured by the slope of the indifference curve through A and the production possibility curve at B^3. In this case the welfare measure and the income measures give the same result. As another alternative one might wish to measure the consumer (or producer) price at both A and B. These give rise to the kind of index number problem discussed in connection with Figure 5.

Another difficulty with national income measures is that some government policies which are welfare improving (or reducing) have no income effects. Consider Figure 7 where a small open economy is facing world terms of trade P. A certain level of taxes could be raised either through a common sales tax on both X and Y or through a consumer tax on commodity X. The tax on both

---

3 In general there is no reason to believe that the slope of the indifference curve at A will be equal to the slope of the production possibility curve at B. There will be a point on the production possibility curve, however, with a slope equal to A.

Figure 6

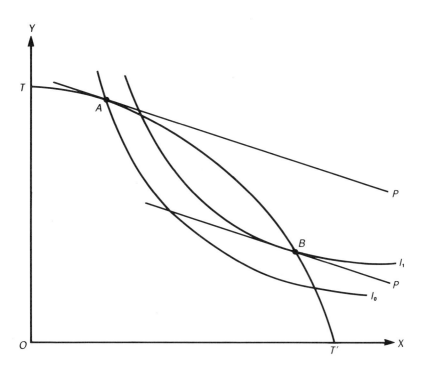

commodities would leave relative prices unchanged and would result in an equilibrium at C. A tax only on X would raise the relative price of X and result in consumption at point E. If national income is evaluated at world prices, measured national income is the same in both cases. It is clear, however, that in this simple model all consumers would have higher utility at point C under the system where the tax rate is the same for both commodities.

Finally, and perhaps most important, measured national income does not provide an appropriate measure of the welfare contributions of public goods. As a simple example, suppose the government is making a choice between an increase in the level of provision of a public good (a park for instance) and the increase in provision of some private benefit (a welfare payment to some consumer for instance), where the cost to the government is the same for either. The effect on national income will be the same whichever choice is made, but the effect on overall welfare may not be. This is a serious difficulty, for as will be argued in the next section, the existence and provision of public goods is a principal reason for the existence of different levels of government.

Figure 7

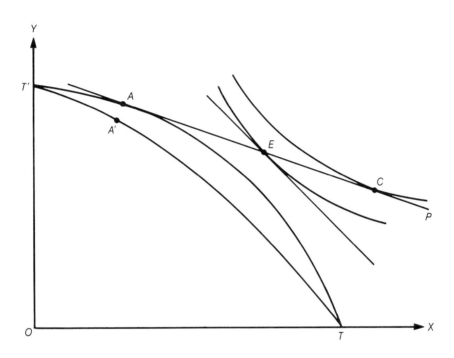

There are situations at the aggregate level which, while income changes may not make everyone better off, will be potentially welfare increasing. The clearest example of this are situations where the removal of a distortion results in an unambiguous income increase. For example it is well known that for situations in which factor market distortions exist, the locus of equilibrium production points will be shifted in towards the origin. Thus suppose a policy has resulted in a different wage rate in an industry in one region than exists elsewhere. This would have the effect of shifting the production locus in to $TA'T'$ in Figure 7. The production point would then be A' rather than A. While it is not clear how the removal of this distortion would affect the utility of all individuals, it is clear that the shift in output from A to A' could, with an appropriate redistribution of income, be used to make everyone better off.

A more familiar example of this kind of argument is the gains-from-trade theorem. It is well known that the introduction of free trade will make some individuals better off and some worse off. At the same time it can be shown that such trade has the potential of making everyone better off if there is an appropriate redistribution of income. Note that without such a redistribution, the introduction of trade cannot be said to be welfare improving.

An evaluation

All the criteria surveyed in this section for measuring national welfare and evaluating public policy have serious shortcomings. National income measures cannot always be assumed to be associated with national welfare; the conditions for the existence of community utility functions cannot be assumed in a policy model; and the Pareto criterion is too restrictive and does not permit a comparison of all alternatives. Nonetheless, if progress is to be made, evaluations must be undertaken. In many circumstances the Pareto criterion is the most useful. With the pareto criterion some situations are comparable, and policies can be evaluated in terms of whether or not the most efficient methods of achieving the policy goal have been chosen. Consider, for example, the alternatives discussed in Figure 1. While no criterion will permit a comparison of O^1 and C, the Pareto criterion will allow one to conclude that there are points Pareto superior to C, namely points A and F, and in this sense C is not optimal. Note that if C is to be maintained as an equilibrium the prices consumers face must equal the slope of their indifference curve at C, and thus a policy to establish C as an equilibrium must introduce a wedge between the prices faced by the two consumers, must in other words introduce a distortion into the economic structure. The removal of this distortion would allow consumers to move to some point on AF where both face the same prices, and where the utility of at least one individual has increased. Once a point on AF has been reached, further comparisons (with O^1 for example) cannot be made, which again simply illustrates the fact that policies to redistribute income cannot be compared in terms of the Pareto criterion.

Turning to the other situations considered above, note that the Pareto criterion does not distinguish between A and B of Figure 6, for in both situations distortions exist that cause consumer and producer prices to differ. Nor can income be used, for the results will depend on which price ratio is chosen. In Figure 7 point C is Pareto superior to E, for at E there is a distortion preventing equality between consumer and producer prices.

In situations where relative prices are unchanged, income changes are perfect proxies for welfare changes, and in such cases income increases represent potential welfare increases. Even when prices change there are some situations where income increases accurately reflect welfare increases, as was seen in Figure 5. Thus there will be many circumstances where national income will serve as an appropriate criterion for policy evaluation.

In what follows, government policy will be evaluated in terms of whether or not it creates new distortions in the economic system and whether it increases income. Policies will be judged to be welfare improving if no distortions are created (and in some cases if distortions are removed)[4] or if income is increased, and policies which create distortions or reduce income will be judged to be welfare reducing. When the income criterion is used it should be remembered that the changes have the *potential* to increase welfare. Actual welfare increases require that an appropriate redistribution of income take place. At the same time it must be borne in mind that policies pursued for the purpose of redistributing income, perhaps because the existing distribution of income and wealth is not judged to be appropriate, will not come under the purview of this criterion except insofar as they incidentally create distortions (such as a movement from O^1 to C instead of to A in Figure 1). This is as it should be, of course, for the positive approach we have adopted here cannot be used to evaluate normative issues such as the appropriate distribution of income.

THEORIES OF GOVERNMENT

It would seem important to begin an analysis of the interaction between a political structure and economic policy with a discussion of the economic explanations for the existence of government, and in particular for the federal form of government with which we are particularly concerned. One of the goals of this chapter is to identify actions of lower levels of government which, while they may be perfectly consistent with economic policy as conceived by that unit, may not be consistent with the overall goals of the federal government. Another goal will be to indentify why the federal government would pursue policies which appear to be inconsistent with an overall objective of welfare maximization. It will be argued that a possible reason for such policies is a misallocation of responsibilities among the various levels of government. To analyse these situations it is obviously important to understand why a federal system exists and what the various roles of the levels of government are perceived to be. A brief discussion of the theory of government behaviour will also be included.

There are a wide variety of non-economic theories which purport to explain the existence of governments, most of which are found in political science or philosophy. I shall make no attempt to review them here. Economic explanations for the existence of governments and models to explain their behaviour are of more recent vintage, and the area is not as well developed as many other areas

---

4 From the theory of the second best it is known that removing one distortion may not be welfare improving if other distortions remain. Of course, by the same criterion adding distortions is necessarily welfare reducing only if no other distortions exist. The problems of second-best solutions of this kind are ignored throughout the analysis.

in economics. It is clear, however, that central to all discussions of the economic explanation of the existence of governments is the existence of public goods. It is well known that public goods will not be provided at the optimal levels by the free market system, and thus if such things as national defence and law and order are to be optimally supplied, a government must take responsibility for their provision.

All would surely agree with the analysis to this point. It is when one attempts to decide on the list of goods and services to be provided by governments that disagreements arise. Arguments as to what role the government should play in the economic system develop mainly along political lines. On the far right, representing those who would minimize the role of the state, authors such as Nozick[5] would restrict the activities of the government to such things as protection against outside aggressors and the basic provision of law and order. Any additional activities by government are seen by him to be an invasion of individuals' freedoms. At the other end of the spectrum Marxist authors see a very limited role for individual decision-making and would recommend state intervention in almost all areas of economic activity. Unfortunately the contributions in this general area provide little in the way of an economic rationale for the differing views taken by widely different political positions. In subsequent sections an attempt will be made to address this issue.

To this point the analysis has not been specifically concerned with the question of when one would expect to observe a federal form of government rather than a unitary state.[6] The literature in this area has recently been surveyed and extended by Breton and Scott,[7] and no attempt will be made to duplicate their analysis here. It will, however, be useful to summarize their conclusions and to comment on their model, for as will become clear their analysis and the model to be presented in the next section are similar in motivation and have several common features, although the fundamental approaches are quite different.

Breton and Scott characterize the traditional theory of federalism as resting on three basic assumptions: (a) that more than one level of government exists and that the various levels have the provision of certain public policies assigned to them; (b) that the economy is characterized by the existence of public goods, externalities, and returns to scale; and (c) that organizational costs such as signalling, mobility, and co-ordination are assumed to be absent. Breton and Scott argue that assumptions (a) and (c) are inconsistent with each other and

5 Nozick, *Anarchy, State and Utopia* (New York: Basic Books Inc., 1974).
6 Much of the literature of federalism grew out of the pioneering work by Tiebout, 'A pure theory of local expenditures.' (1956), 64 *Journal of Political Economy*, 416.
7 Breton and Scott, *The Economic Constitution of Federal States* (Toronto: University of Toronto Press, 1978).

that even the explicit recognition of organizational costs does not provide a complete theory of the existence of a federal system.[8]

In setting up their model Breton and Scott assume that all individuals have well-behaved, concave, ordinal utility functions which are weakly separable between private and public goods. They further assume that "each citizen adds up the benefits—measured in utility units or dollar equivalents—derived from each public policy supplied by a particular government; and, that in a similar way, the costs—again in utility units or in dollars—of taxes and other payments made to that government, that is, private goods forgone, are also added up."[9] It is then assumed that each citizen can calculate the present value of these costs and benefits over some time horizon T. The difference W between the costs and the benefits is defined to be the net worth associated with government policy. Citizens are further assumed to allocate resources in order to influence the level of government activity. Individuals are assumed to invest in political participation up to the point where the rate of return for such investment is just equal to the market rate of interest. They then define a centralization coefficient and include it as an argument in the function defining investment in political participation and, after summing for all citizens, write expressions for the net benefit of government policy in terms of the market rate of interest and the centralization coefficient.

Government activity is also defined in terms of the market rate of interest and the centralization coefficient, and then reaction functions for government and the aggregation of citizens are employed to determine the equilibrium level of the centralization coefficient. This coefficient in turn will indicate the degree to which decentralization is optimal.

One of the purposes of this chapter is to present a model which would explain the existence of various levels of government and provide an explanation of how policies which may be seen to be optimal from the point of view of individual governments may nevertheless be non-optimal from the point of view of society as a whole. While Breton and Scott attempt to address at least the first of these questions, there are unfortunately a number of fundamental difficulties which prevent their discussion from being useful for our analysis. The most serious difficulty relates to the aggregation of the net wealth function of citizens to derive a community net wealth function. These net wealth functions for individuals are utility measures, and the aggregation of these utility measures must necessarily be subject to the same constraints as are inherent in any such aggregation.[10] Furthermore, because the goods involved are public goods, con-

---

8 Ibid., Chapter 4.
9 Ibid., at 53.
10 Although Breton and Scott suggest that these utilities can be measured in money terms, it is known that this is not in general legitimate.

sistent aggregation requires that all individuals have identical homogeneous preferences and identical incomes. If this is not the case then no unique community net benefit function exists, with the result that none of the reaction functions derived by Breton and Scott are well-defined.[11] Models in which all individuals are identical in every respect are not of much interest in any branch of public finance, and certainly are of no interest whatsoever in the present analysis.

Another difficulty with the Breton-Scott analysis is that, while the question is clearly a general equilibrium one, the analysis is fundamentally partial equilibrium in nature. Even in the initial stage where the benefit function is derived the authors lose sight of the fact that the assumption of weakly separable utility functions is not enough to allow them to ignore completely the private goods component of the utility function. Weak separability allows the consideration of the public good as a group as long as the level of private goods remains constant. It is clear, however, that as soon as one chooses to consume a different level of public goods, government expenditure, and thus taxation, must increase. This will reduce disposable income and would be expected to lower the demand for private goods, thereby violating the implicit assumption that the levels of consumption of private goods are unchanged. One is also struck by the fact that there is no supply side in the Breton-Scott model. Thus possible conflicts in the use of resources between the private and the public sector cannot be considered. It is clear that in an economy with full employment a decision by a government to increase the level of a public good will have quite different consequences than if there were unemployed factors of production. The model presented in this paper seeks to avoid these difficulties.

Another branch of the literature of economics relevant to the present discussion, and one closely associated with the models previously discussed, is the economic theory of government behaviour. Here the concern is with the way in which the preferences of individuals become translated into government policy, or in other words the mechanism by which society makes decisions about the economic policy to be pursued. In their summary of this issue Atkinson and Stiglitz[12] identify three major models: voting models, bureaucratic models, and interest group models. In the first type the choices between different economic policies are made by voting. In the second the public has only a limited input to actual policy-making, and the major decisions are made by the bureaucracy; here the preferences of the administration are central to policy formation. In the

---

11 In other words, the reaction functions cannot be defined independent of the levels of other variables in the model. Thus a reallocation of a fixed level of income or some other change would be expected to shift the reaction function.

12 Atkinson and Stiglitz, *Lectures on Public Economics*, (Maidenhead: McGraw Hill, 1980), Lecture 10.

third, special interest groups are seen as having a dominant role in the formation of economic policy, sometimes to the complete exclusion of non-interest-group members.[13] The Marxian models of public choice fall in this last group.

The voting model has most relevance to the present analysis. The voting assumptions to be employed, however, are very simple and will entail only that individuals vote for the political party which most closely represents their own individual preferences. In this model, because of its simplicity, many of the difficulties which have been discussed in the literature in terms of voting models, such as the issue of non-single-peakedness and the basic impossibility theorems associated with the work of Arrow,[14] will not arise.

THE BASIC MODEL

The principal goal of this chapter is to provide an economic rationale for the observed behaviour of governments in the federal structure, and to provide an explanation of why policies pursued by one level of government may be in conflict with the economic objectives of another. We want the model to be as realistic as possible; in particular we do not want to assume that all individuals have identical preferences. Indeed, it will be argued that a basic reason for different levels of government will be differences in utility functions. To construct such a model we clearly need an approach where the existence of community indifference curves is not required. In the approach developed here the government is not seen as attempting to maximize a social welfare function but rather as acting in such a way as to facilitate the maximization by consumers or family units of their individual utility functions. It is assumed that the government's main objective is to be re-elected, and that the main method of ensuring re-election is through the goodwill of a majority of the electorate. This is assumed to be best secured through policies designed to guarantee that the utility levels of individuals increase over the government's term of office.

There is now a substantial empirical literature on politico-economic models which investigates the role of economic variables in both the voting behaviour of individuals and the economic policy responses of governments to voter preferences (for a summary of this literature see Bruno Frey[15]). A variety of assumptions

13 For a comprehensive analysis of this model see Becker 'A theory of political behaviour.' (Univ. of Chicago: Working Paper WSIV-4, Oct 1981).

14 Arrow, *Social Choice and Individual Values*, (New York: John Whiley, 2nd ed., 1963).

15 Frey, 'Politico-economic models and cycles.' (1978), 9 *Journal of Public Economics*, 203. Earlier contributions would include Downs, *An Economic Theory of Democracy* (New York: Harper and Bros., 1957); Stigler, 'Micropolitics and macroeconomics.' (1973), 63(2) *American Economic Review, Papers and Proceedings* 160; Frey and Lau, 'Towards a mathematical model of government behaviour.' (1968), 28 *Zeitschrift fur National okonomie* 355.

have been made about both the arguments in the utility functions of voters and about the government's objectives. Papers by Nordhaus, MacRae, and Lindbeck assumed the government's objective was to maximize votes and that the voters were concerned only with the rate of inflation and the level of unemployment.[16] Other authors have assumed a more complete set of variables in voters' utility functions. Frey and Lau and Frey and Schneider assume that the rate of growth, the inflation rate, and the level of employment are elements of the voters' utility functions.[17] These studies also assume a more complex objective function for the government, including such things as political ideology and time until the next election. Other variables included (implicitly or explicitly) in the above studies are the time preferences of individuals and the government. Thus authors such as Lindbeck assume that voters completely discount the past performance of the government, while MacRae assumes the period since the last election is relevant. Frey and Schneider assume that the government has an infinite time horizon, while Lindbeck and Nordhaus assume that the government is only interested in the next election.

Though the results of these studies are not conclusive and some of them are open to criticism on both theoretical and empirical grounds, in general they lend strong support to the assumption employed here; namely that governments behave so as to increase the utility of voters and that voters make their selections in terms of government performances. Frey and Schneider, for example, find the rate of employment and the rate of inflation to be significant determinants of presidential popularity in the United States, and that unemployment, inflation, and the growth rate are all significant determinants of British political party election success. Fair finds that changes in real economic activity have the most important and statistically most significant effect on votes for the United States president.[18]

Unlike the politico-economic models which use aggregate functions, in the model developed below the utilities of individual consumers are considered. While it is not theoretically appropriate to include the macro variables discussed above directly in the individualistic utility functions, variables such as unemployment and the rate of growth of disposable income will affect consumer choice through the budget constraints.

16 Nordhaus, 'The political business cycle.' (1975), 42 *Review of Economic Studies* 169; MacRae, 'A political model of the business cycle.' (1977), 85 *Journal of Political Economy* 239; Lindbeck, 'Stabilization policy in open economies with endogenous politicians.' (1976), 66 (2) *American Economic Review, Papers and Proceedings* 1.
17 Frey and Schneider, 'An emprical study of politico-economic interaction in the United States.' (1978), 60 *Review of Economics and Statistics* 174; Frey and Schneider, 'A politico-economic model of the United Kingdom.' (1978), 88 *Economic Journal* 243.
18 Fair, 'The effects of economic events on votes for president.' (1978), 60 *Review of Economics and Statistics* 159.

The model can be formalized as follows. Individual i has a utility function

$$u_i = U_i (X_i, Q, Z), \qquad i = 1, ..., n, \tag{1}$$

to be maximized subject to $y_i = PX_i$. In (1), X_i represents the vector of private goods consumed by individual i, Q represents the vector of pure public goods, Z represents the vector of non-private goods, and P is the vector of commodity prices.[19] The levels of both Q and Z are assumed to be provided by the government. Y_1 is the level of personal disposable income and is equal to $Y_i (1 - t_i)$, where Y_i is the total income earned by individual i and t_i is the average tax rate paid by the ith individual.

The government sector is given by equations (2), (3), and (4):

$$T = \Sigma_i t_i y_i, \tag{2}$$

$$G = PX_g + P_q Q + P_z Z, \tag{3}$$

$$T + G. \tag{4}$$

Here T is total tax revenue and G is total government expenditure. Equation (4) represents the assumption that the government has a balanced budget. P_q and P_z represent respectively the supply prices, or costs, of the level of public and non-private goods provided to the population. The vector X_g represents the level of goods and services purchased by the government, and would include the costs of adminsitering the various programs which provide the levels of Q and Z.

The government utility function is written as

$$U_g = U_g (R, V), \tag{5}$$

where R is the probability of re-election and V is a vector which could include such variables as private gain, fame, a place in history, and the provision of good government.[20] We assume that U_g is weakly separable in R and V and that V can be assumed constant over the time period under consideration. The principal determinant of R is assumed to be the level of utilities of voters. It is assumed that all those voters whose utilities increase above some threshold level will vote for the government in power. Should a majority or plurality so vote, the government will be returned.

It is clear that the model is both interactive and complex. The government must, at least implicitly, determine the level at which to operate each public policy so as to secure a majority of votes. Furthermore, significant uncertainty

---

19 Non-private goods are defined as goods which are not pure public goods, such as defence or law and order, but which have a public-good component. Examples could be education and health services.
20 Such variables are described by Breton and Scott, *The Economic Constitution of Federal States.*

will surround the government's decision-making problem, for in general there will be many policies, a wide variety of different individual utility functions, uncertainty as to the utility threshold each voter must achieve, and uncertainty as to the nature of the utility functions of individuals. Thus in general the choice will be difficult (or impossible) to formalize. Fortunately the analysis does not require that a formal solution be provided; it is sufficient to assume that the government makes some determination of these uncertainties and provides the levels of public and non-private goods it feels are appropriate. Of course a variety of interesting questions arise in terms of matching voters and policies so as to secure a majority vote, and some of these are discussed below. Determinate answers to such questions are not central to the analysis, however.

Before proceeding it should be observed that this simple model is not meant as a complete description of an economy. It is clear, for example, that the model is not closed, for there are many more variables that equations. For the discussion here it is assumed that additional equations can be added to complete the model, and that this is indeed the case can be shown.

A UNITARY STATE

Our model of a federal state should be free from the assumption that individuals are identical with homothetic preferences. As a step in the development of this model, and to illustrate why identical preferences cannot be assumed for a federal form of government, this section uses the model formulated above to consider a situation in which individuals *do* have identical and homothetic preferences. It will be seen that in such a situation a federal form of government is not required for a stable, optimal equilibrium.

The basic model has two economic agents, individuals and the government, both of whom are concerned with the maximization of U_i. Individuals maximize U_i subject to their budget constraint. The government is concerned with maximizing U_i subject to the constraint of equation (4). It is assumed that the government takes as given that each individual will maximize U_i subject to the levels of y_i, Q, and Z provided by government. Clearly increases in the level of government activity, that is, increases in T and G, will on the one hand increase individual utilities by raising Q and / or Z and on the other hand act to reduce U_i by reducing y_i. The first question to be addressed is whether there will be a solution to this maximization problem, and whether or not such a solution, if it exists, would be expected to be unique.

Assume that Q is a pure public good, so that the level of Q provided by the government enters the utility function of all individuals. It is also assumed that all individuals are identical and have homothetic utility functions and that the level of X_g is unrelated to Q. All arguments of the utility function are assumed to show diminishing marginal utility.

It seems reasonable to suppose that at low enough levels of T and G the increases in U_i associated with increasing Q will be larger than the utility loss associated with the increases in taxation. Of course, if this were never the case it would simply mean that no public goods would be provided. With diminishing marginal utilities of all inputs it is equally clear that in the model described there will be a unique $T + G$ which maximizes U_i for all individuals. Furthermore, the existence of such a unique equilibrium will not be affected by relaxing the assumption of the independence of X_g. As long as X_g is a monotonic increasing function of Q, equilibrium will still exist and be unique.

It is interesting to note that in this model the number of individuals over whom this maximization is being carried out will be an important determinant of the equilibrium level of U_i. Since it costs no more to provide Q for more individuals, increasing the number of individuals n will reduce the per capita cost of providing Q and will therefore increase X_i. Thus one of the policy instruments for increasing the equilibrium level of U_i will be n, and governments have a clear motivation for increasing the population over whom they have jurisdiction. As shall be seen subsequently, this will be an important consideration when provincial government policies are considered.

For the case where all individuals are identical and have homothetic preferences it has been shown that not only will there be a solution to the maximization problem of each individual taken separately but also there will be a unique solution to the aggregate problem. Under the conditions given, a well-behaved community preference function exists. Dropping the assumptions of identical individuals and homogeneous preferences immediately eliminates any chance that a unique aggregate equilibrium exists. The question of interest however is whether and under what conditions *individual* utilities will be maximized. Clearly, in terms of the basic model the latter question is of most interest, for it is this question which is relevant to R, the probability of re-election, and thus to the maximization of U_g. It is clear that situations can easily be constructed where a majority of individuals cannot enjoy utility increases if all voters are required to consume the same quantities of all the components of the vectors Q and Z. This naturally leads to the consideration of the possibility of more than one level of government, thereby allowing the provision of different levels of Q and Z for different individuals.

THE FEDERAL SYSTEM

In the simple world described above with identical individuals and homothetic preferences, it is clear that a single central government can achieve full optimality as long as it is able to determine the utility function of the identical consumers. There is certainly no reason to expect a federal state to develop in such a situation, for different levels of government can accomplish nothing that a single central government cannot accomplish just as well.[21] Of course, in a world of uncertainty it is possible that the party in power will misjudge consumer preferences, which may well lead to the government's losing its mandate. There will not, however, be any incentive to change the fundamental structure of the political system.

In the model for a unitary system the assumption that all individuals are identical with homothetic preferences is crucial to the conclusions reached. Suppose now that there are two public goods, Q_1 and Q_2, and that while all individuals have the same preferences for Q_1, one group of individuals has a strong preference for Q_2, while the other group would prefer to consume none at all. A central government now faces a difficulty, for it must decide whether to provide Q_2 and, if so, at what level. Of course providing Q_2 implies that G, and therefore T, must increase. It is further assumed that the government has no method of discovering the true preferences of the voters. Then since the Q's are pure public goods, taxes will have to be collected from all individuals whether they prefer Q_2 or not. Thus, should the government decide to provide Q_2, those individuals who wish to consume none of this good will be disadvantaged, for their taxes will be increased, reducing their disposable income and thus their utility. Alternatively, if Q_2 is not provided, those individuals with a preference for this good will clearly not be in equilibrium. The provision of a level of Q_2 somewhere between zero and the level demanded by those who prefer it will leave all individuals in less than optimal situations.

If the two groups of individuals are randomly spread throughout the jurisdiction there is little the government can do except to try to satisfy the majority.[22] This will generally imply an all-or-nothing decision for Q_2. On the other hand if the two groups are regionally distributed, a central government may very well improve its chance of re-election by setting up a second tier of governments and allocating to it the responsibility both for providing Q_2 and for raising the revenues to pay for it. The federal government would continue to provide those public goods for which tastes are reasonably homogeneous throughout the nation. Note that since Q_1 is a pure public good there is still a need for a federal government. If the second-level government were to take over the responsibility for providing all public goods, and if they provided Q_1 at the same level as it was

---

21 While the discussion here is in terms of federal and provincial levels of government, exactly the same arguments apply to provincial and local levels of government.
22 Alternatives are possible if distortionary policies are permitted. This question is discussed later.

previously supplied, the per unit cost would increase, and the utilities of all individuals would fall.[23] Thus regional differences in preferences can provide a clear economic justification for a federal system.

All readers might not be persuaded that regional taste differences among consumers for pure public goods would constitute a sufficient motivation for a federal system. However, even if one were to take the position that the entire justification for a federal structure must rest on economic arguments, and such a position would be difficult to defend, additional economic arguments for a federal form of government can be provided. Two such additional arguments are the existence of unevenly distributed natural resources and the provision of non-private goods.

The effect of the existence of natural resources which are unequally endowed among regions was first considered by Buchanan and Wagner and by Buchanan and Goetz.[24] These papers assume a Ricardian production model with increasing costs in a world where two regions differ in their endowment of land and where there is a single mobile factor, labour. It is shown that if labour moves to equalize utility the richer region will, in equilibrium, be characterized by a lower land/labour ratio, a lower marginal product of labour, and a lower unit cost of the public good. The free market equilibrium will not generally be Pareto optimal.

Flatters, Henderson, and Mieszkowski have extended the analysis to examine the conditions for efficient allocation of labour between the two regions.[25] They assume a single output produced under conditions of constant returns to scale and used for public and private consumption. Individuals in each region are taxed to pay for the public good consumed (generally the taxes will differ between regions). Community preference functions are assumed for both land owners and labourers.

As well as showing that, in general, labour mobility is not sufficient to achieve a Pareto optimal distribution of labour in a free market system, the authors derive conditions under which overpopulation or underpopulation will occur. They show that the critical parameter is the price elasticity of the public good in

---

23 The increase in cost of providing Q_1 will depend on the size of the new jurisdictions. With n_i individuals in each of J subdivisions and assuming constant returns to scale, the new costs in terms of taxes collected will be n/n_j of the original cost.

24 Buchanan and Wagner, 'An efficiency basis for federal fiscal equalization,' in Margolis, ed., *The Analysis of Public Output* (New York: National Bureau of Economic Research, 1970), at 139–58; Buchanan and Goetz, 'Efficiency limits of fiscal mobility: an assessment of the Tiebout model.' (1972), 1 *Journal of Public Economics* 25.

25 Flatters, Henderson, and Mieszkowski, 'Public goods, efficiency and regional fiscal equalization.' (1974), 3 *Journal of Public Economics* 99.

terms of the private good. Unless this elasticity is unity 'free migration will be inefficient, and a federation should be set up in order to induce workers to move from the overpopulated to the underpopulated region by subsidizing those residing in the latter region and taxing those residing in the former region.'[26]

Although these papers differ from the approach employed here in a number of fundamental respects (the assumptions on preferences for example), it is nevertheless clear that resource endowment differences, even without preference differences, can provide a reason for federalism in terms of our basic model.

Another justification for a federal system arises from the existence of the non-public goods Z, which were included in the utility function of the basic model. This vector includes all those goods potentially or actually provided by governments which are not pure public goods. It would include, for example, goods which have some public characteristics, such as parks and education, as well as goods which are provided by the government because it is cost-efficient to do so, such as highways and city streets. For such goods the benefits will accrue mainly to those individuals who reside in the immediate vicinity of their provision. Because the costs and optimal quantity will depend on locale, it is well known that the appropriate jurisdiction from which to collect taxes to pay for such goods is the jurisdiction which receives the benefits. It would thus be inappropriate to finance the provision of such goods from general taxation.

Of course, this does not imply that appropriate user taxes could not be levied by the federal government. One could, for example, have a system of property taxes administered by a central government to pay for services such as education or city streets. There are almost certainly diseconomies of scale associated with such a tax scheme, however, and the optimal size of a fiscal unit to charge with the responsibility of devising and collecting property taxes is almost certainly not the federal government.[27] Efficiency in the fiscal system would therefore suggest that there be a decentralizing of power and taxing responsibility.

There are a number of interesting questions associated with the provision of non-private goods. First, there is no consensus as to what goods should necessarily be provided by the government and which should be left to the private sector. In the model there is no clear distinction between whether certain goods should be in the vector X or in the vector Z. Education has been suggested as an example of a non-private good, but there are clearly those who feel that educational

---

26 Ibid., at 106.

27 Consider, for example, the problem of devising an appropriate property tax base for the entire country. And if the desired levels of non-private goods differ from place to place, as would be expected, it would be inefficient to have such taxes collected and services provided by the federal government.

services, at least after some minimal level, should be left entirely to the individual or family. Another example is health services. The debate over whether the services of hostpials and doctors should be provided by the government or should be left to the individual can be seen as a debate about whether or not such services should be in the vector X or in the vector Z.

Such debates are easily put in the context of the maximization problem of the basic model. All governments presumably agree that the level of health enjoyed by individuals is an argument in their utility functions. Whether or not this service should be provided by the government is a question of whether or not there are 'economies' associated with the provision of such services which would result in higher utilities for individuals than would be the case if the provision of such services were left to the free market system. A government which believes that it will be able to increase the welfare of the majority of the population through the provision of health services will clearly undertake to provide such services, and will therefore regard health as a component of the vector Z. Governments which feel that the provision of such services will result in a larger reduction in the utilities achievable by individuals than would be the case for a free market system, would regard health care as a component of the vector X. Arguments for this latter position could depend on inefficiencies associated with the provision of the service itself, or on the belief that the reductions in personal disposable income associated with the taxation required to finance such services would be higher than the benefits.

There are a variety of other reasons why the decision as to whether a particular good is private or non-private has relevance for this analysis. Suppose that there is a unique assignment of all public and non-private goods to the levels of government where they can be most efficiently provided. This allocation will be determined by such factors as individual taste, economies of scale in provision, and efficiencies in the collection of user taxes. Further suppose that the relative power of levels of government is defined to be a function of the resources over which they have control. Then it is clear that the decision on which goods belong in the public sector and which belong in the private sector will be an important determinant of the relative powers of government levels. Of course the existence of a constitution which allocates responsibilities among the various levels of government can be an even more important factor. The fact that Canadian provinces have, through the BNA Act, responsibility for health and education has undoubtedly resulted in a different allocation of power than would have been the case had these responsibilities been assigned to the federal government. One also observes historical changes in the relative powers of governments due, at least in part, to the shifts in public opinion concerning which goods and services should be provided by the public sector.

There may also be significant interactions between the allocation of responsibilities for the provision of public and non-private goods and the ability of political parties to function effectively in terms of getting elected. A political party in Canada whose principal concern is with such things as education and health care would be expected to have much greater success at the provincial level where the responsibility for such activities rests than it would at the federal level. It seems possible that the New Democratic Party's lack of success at the federal level is due, at least to some extent, to the fact that many of the issues with which it has been traditionally concerned are under provincial jurisdiction. If this hypothesis is true we would expect to find a positive relationship across nations between the degree to which the constitution allocates responsibilities to the federal government and the success of parties which have an interest in providing these services.

OPTIMAL FISCAL AREAS

It has been argued that, with regional differences in preferences, because of the diseconomies associated with providing certain public and non-private goods, and because of the unequal allocation of resources, it may not be optimal to have a unitary government. In this section a few brief comments will be made on the variables which will determine the structure of a federal system. Once it has been determined that more than one level of government is required several questions naturally arise: how many levels of government should there be, what is the optimal size for a fiscal area, and what is the optimal allocation of responsibilities among the various governments? Unfortunately, definitive answers to these questions are not available, and this section will simply describe some of the variables which would have to be considered in addressing these issues. To keep the problem tractable only pure public goods will be considered.

To determine the optimal number of government levels one would first identify all the pure public goods and services which are to be provided by the public sector. One would then examine each with a view to determine whether or not they could be most efficiently provided by the federal government. Those which can be efficiently provided would be allocated to that level, and if this does not exhaust the entire list of public goods a second level of government would be defined. A similar procedure would then be used for allocating the provision of public goods to this second level, and so on until all commodities had been assigned. Such a procedure could, theoretically, determine both the number of levels of government required and the allocation of responsibility for provision of the pure public good among the various levels.

In determining whether a specific level of government is most efficient at providing a particular public good one would have to compare the efficiency of that level with all subdivisions of that jurisdiction. One difficulty with this procedure is that it seems probable that the various subdivisions which would be optimal for the provision of the range of public goods would differ. Thus, suppose we find that a particular commodity Z_1 should not be provided by the federal government because it can be more efficiently provided by a level of government one-half the size of the federal state. Suppose Z_2 is found to be most efficiently provided by a level of government one-third the size of the federal state. Given that the subdivision must be unique, it is clear that in such a case the procedure described will not succeed in allocating all commodities optimally among the various levels of government.

This introduces the second question, namely the optimal size of the subdivision. Factors determining optimal size will again include, as an important variable, the preferences of the citizens. The more well-defined are regional tastes, the more subdivisions one would expect. Another important variable will be the optimal range for which public goods can be provided. For example, suppose all citizens wish to be protected against foreign attack and also wish to have a publicly provided fire-fighting service. Suppose further that communities differ significantly in terms of dwellings. These differences could result from differences in average incomes or simply from the fact that certain kinds of building materials are associated with particular regions; in some regions the typical dwellings are made of wood and in others of stone or brick. In this model, although all individuals have the same preferences for protection from invasion and protection from fire, these two public goods would not be provided by the same level of government. The optimal range of national defence is the entire state, so that it would be provided by the federal government and paid for through general taxation. The cost of fire protection, however, would vary significantly from community to community, and thus even though preferences are identical the efficient allocation of this service would be by local government. The range of the public good to be provided will therefore be an important determinant of the size of the governing jurisdiction.

Determining jurisdictional size in this fashion, however, suffers from the same difficulty as was encountered in the discussion of the optimal number of government levels. If one is restricted to non-overlapping subdivisions in moving from one level of government to the other, then it seems almost certain that some public goods will not be provided efficiently.

Allocation of the responsibility for provision of public goods among levels of government has already been dealt with as long as there is no overlapping of jurisdiction. In practice, of course, we know that in many circumstances more than one level of government is allocated or takes responsibility for the provision of certain goods and services. Parks, for example, are provided by a variety of government levels. Such situations presumably result from the fact that many goods and services which have come to be regarded as within the public domain are not consitutionally allocated to a specific level of government, and because the various levels of government do not agree on what standard of service should be provided or on how the service should be delivered. Whether or not such joint provision of certain public goods always leads to inefficiencies is not clear. One can certainly imagine situations in which the federal government could provide a service to a certain level, allowing provincial or local governments to increase the level of provision according to provincial or local demand. On the other hand it is equally easy to think of situations where the provision of some basic service by more than one level of government will lead to inefficiencies.

As will have become clear, the above discussion has not much advanced the search for answers to the questions concerning optimal fiscal areas. Fortunately, the analysis requires only that we have a justification for different levels of government and does not depend on a complete understanding of how many levels there should be or of what their optimal size is. Thus, having looked the problem squarely in the face we move on.

THE PROVINCIAL OPTIMIZATION PROBLEM

We have established that reasonable assumptions exist which would require more than one level of government for the efficient provision of the range of public and non-private goods demanded by consumers. The purpose of this section is to analyse the behaviour of regional governments. Of particular interest will be the relationships between the optimal policies of both levels of government. It will be argued that the pursuit of perfectly sensible optimizing policies by regional governments may well be in conflict with the overall welfare goals of the federal government.[28] For simplicity we will assume only one regional level of government: in the Canadian case, provincial governments. It is with respect to these two levels of government that most conflicts are likely to arise, and in any case the arguments can be applied to additional government levels with little or no modification.

The formal maximization problem faced by provincial governments is exactly the same as that faced by the federal government as outlined in the fourth section. The principal goal of the provincial government is re-election, and the principal method of gaining re-election is through facilitating an increase in the

---

28 This analysis of distortions created by the federal government will be examined below.

utilities of a majority of the citizens in its jurisdiction. The utility functions of individuals contain as arguments private goods, public goods, and non-private goods, and individuals maximize subject to a budget constraint which depends on the tax rate. The provincial governments will provide those public goods which fall within their jurisdiction at the levels they feel will maximize the utilities of the majority of the voters. It is assumed that each provincial government raises the revenue required to provide these goods and services through taxation.[29]

Decisions on how much of certain public goods to provide will depend, among other things, on who the party in power sees as its principal constituents, or in other words on who is most likely to vote for them in the next election. Thus governments which draw heavily on support of the working class would be expected to provide public goods which benefit this group, and governments which draw support from capitalists and resource owners will gear their provision of public goods to these constituents.

The principal decision faced by any provincial government will be the determination of which goods and services should be included in the non-private sector, or in other words which goods and services can be most efficiently provided by the government and which should be left entirely in the private sector. Again this decision will depend on who the government sees itself as representing and whose vote it can most easily attract. Governments have very little interest in pursuing policies which increase the utilities of those individuals who will not vote for them in any case.

As was the case for the maximization problem described in the fourth section, the provincial government will take cognizance of the fact that any increase in the level of a public good it chooses to provide will be expected to affect consumers in two distinct ways. As long as the good being provided enters the utility function of all individuals, the increased quantity would increase the level of utility they enjoy. Because we are assuming that all government expenditure must be financed through tax collections, an increase in the level of Z would reduce the disposable income of individuals and thus reduce their utilities by reducing the quantity of private goods over which they have command. Keeping these factors in mind, governments will estimate the quantity of public goods to provide in order to increase significantly the utilities of a majority of the voting population.

We have assumed a very simple proportional tax scheme, such that all individuals would be assessed for each addition to the supply of public goods in

---

29 This analysis ignores the important role of federal grants to the provincial governments. This question is discussed elsewhere in the volume.

proportion to their incomes. If one assumes a progressive tax, then it becomes clear that the provision of additional units of public goods will be proportionately more costly to high income earners than to individuals with lower incomes. This, combined with the fact that many public or non-private goods have a distinct income orientation in terms of the benefits they provide,[30] leaves governments considerable scope in attempting to facilitate the utility maximization of their constituents. Thus one would expect left-wing governments, whose constituents would be expected to be mainly lower-income individuals, to tax the rich and provide public and non-private goods which are mainly beneficial to the poor. One would expect conservative governments with a constituency mainly made up of the more well-to-do to pursue at least some policies which would do just the opposite.

We now turn to the consideration of specific policies which provincial governments might be expected to pursue, with special reference to those policies which may be in conflict with the goals of the federal government. Three broad classes of policies can be distinguished: policies which attempt to increase the level of disposable income and/or reduce the level of unemployment, possibly at the expense of other provinces; policies which attempt to increase the population or the capital stock of the province; and policies which attempt to increase provincial welfare through the use of provincial taxes. The first two of these will be dealt with here; the next section will consider the use of tax policies as a method of increasing provincial welfare.

Because provincial governments are attempting to facilitate the welfare maximization of provincial residents, it is only natural that they would have more concern for income levels and rates of unemployment of residents of their own province than they would of residents elsewhere. It is therefore not surprising to find that provincial governments sometimes institute beggar-thy-neighbour policies. Government procurement policies which give preference to provincially produced products clearly fall in this class. Such policies attempt to transfer income and/or employment either from other provinces or from the rest of the world to their own provincial residents. Regulations which make it difficult for residents of other provinces to work in the province constitute another type of policy which falls in this class. One would also include those kinds of marketing boards which attempt to guarantee provincial markets for provincial produce and which, in one way or another, discriminate against out-of-province goods.

---

30 Support to the arts, provision of airport services, and CBC Radio provide relatively higher benefits to the well-to-do. Public medical services, city parks, and public transport subsidies benefit the poor more than the rich. National parks and education are arguable.

And certainly regulations which require that business be carried out in one of the official languages are a clear example of this type of policy.

Turning next to policies which attempt to influence the residency of factors of production, we should first note that any policy which influences income is indirectly a policy which influences factor movements. It is generally assumed that factors move in response to income differences, and thus one can encourage immigration and discourage emigration by any policy which increases factor rewards. In reality (and more in line with our basic model) it seems more appropriate to consider labour flows as responses to differences in utility levels. Thus not only will factor rewards influence migration through their effects on disposable income, but the levels of provision of public goods and the level of sales and income taxes will also be important determinants of migration. It seems clear, for example, that the large labour flows to Alberta are a result of low provincial taxes as well as high wages and salaries. And the attractions associated with living in a rich province with a bright future has probably also been an important factor.

Many policies operate on factor supply much more directly, and some of these are described below. But first I shall describe the reasons why provincial governments would be interested in pursuing policies which will affect the factor supplies, and circumstances which might make such action appropriate from the provincial point of view. As was argued earlier, where a pure public good is being produced under conditions of constant returns to scale, the average cost of providing the good will be inversely related to the number of taxpayers in the province. Thus if the government could increase the population it could then either increase the level of public goods provided without increasing the average tax or provide the same level of public policy at a lower average tax rate. In either case the population increase would be expected to increase the utility of all taxpayers. It is clear, then, that provincial governments have a strong incentive for at least maintaining their population base.

Although policies designed purely to inhibit the free mobility of factors will generally be suboptimal from the national point of view, provincial governments may sometimes feel that such policies are justified.[31] There can be little doubt that from time to time provinces, or at least regions, develop real balance of payments problems vis-à-vis the rest of Canada. Such problems are often fundamental in nature, relating to changes in the relative prices of regional resources for example. Were such changes to take place among nations a new

---

31 Recall, however, the agreement for influencing labour location in Flatters et al., 'Public goods, efficiency, and regional fiscal equalization.'

equilibrium could be achieved through adjustments of the exchange rate. In a world of fixed exchange rates, as is the case for a single country, such a mechanism is not available, and adjustments must take place through changes in real income. With factor mobility, these income changes will be reflected in factor flows, and there will be a tendency for both capital and labour to leave the regions of declining average income. The provinces quite rightly see that this population outflow will exacerbate the situation, for with a reduced population base the province will be required to increase the average tax rate, further reducing average disposable incomes. Provinces may therefore feel justified in attempting to discourage such factor flows, arguing that by so doing they are increasing total welfare. Indeed, it could be argued that one way of offsetting the real income changes associated with the kind of structural change in question would be to incresae the population base so that the reduction in real income could be compensated for by increases in the level of public goods. In any case it is certainly possible that outmigration from a province could leave the remaining population worse off because of the higher tax burden they would be required to share.

The arguments concerning migration have been in terms of population and not in terms of factor supplies. The advantages of a larger population come entirely from the demand side and are related to the average tax cost of providing the appropriate level of public goods. The factor-market effects would be expected to be in the opposite direction. For a province with a fixed resource base, outmigration of factors would be expected to raise the marginal products of the factors remaining and thus raise their real returns. Other things being equal, this will result in an increase in the utility of remaining residents, thus acting to offset the reduction associated with population loss. It seems likely, however, that the population effects are much more important than the marginal product effects. Certainly provinces act as if this were so.

There are additional reasons why the effects of factor flows may be ambiguous, and reasons to expect, in some situations at least, attempts by provincial governments to restrict factor immigration. As has already been suggested, a principal reason for labour mobility is the existence of better employment opportunities elsewhere. Such moves will be particularly attractive to the unemployed (if they can be afforded), who tend to be either young and inexperienced or unskilled or both. For provinces which already have substantial unemployment, the prospect of attracting further migrants who will have difficulty finding jobs is not an attractive one. Furthermore, such immigrants would typically not, at least in the short run, be in a high enough tax bracket to make any substantial contribution to the cost of providing public and non-private goods. This is particularly true when account is taken of the fact that provincial income taxes are quite highly progressive in contrast to the simple proportional tax assumed in the model used here. And in any case, even if a new immigrant is successful in finding a job it is generally not a new job that has just been created but rather a job which could have been taken by a long-time provincial resident.

Similar arguments do not generally apply to capital. Attracting capital is almost always seen as desirable. It is generally not perceived to be unemployed, or at least the unemployment of capital is not seen as a major social problem. An inflow of capital, usually in the form of the entry of a new firm or industry to the province or the expansion of an old one, would generally be expected to increase employment opportunities and therefore reduce unemployment. Further employment multiplier effects may occur if the new firm purchases intermediate inputs in the local provincial market. It would also generally be true that the immigration which may accompany such capital flows would either be highly skilled labour or capital owners. Such individuals would be expected to more than pay for their use of public goods through their tax contributions.

From the arguments just given it is not surprising that one finds that provincial policies designed to influence factor flows directly are usually policies to encourage capital inflows or to discourage the immigration of labour. In the former group it is easy to find examples where provincial (or municipal) governments provide subsidies for new industries, sometimes through tax relief, sometimes through the provision of industrial land at well below market costs. Other provincial policies which restrict capital mobility are favourable provincial loans to corporations, the formation of provincial revenue funds such as the Alberta Heritage Fund, and the setting up of crown corporations to control provincially based industries, as in Saskatchewan. Restrictions which provincial governments place on pension reinvestment policies can also significantly affect interprovincial capital markets. In this area Quebec is perhaps the best example.

On the labour side no difficulty is encountered in providing examples where flows have been impeded. Many professions have regulations which restrict the opportunity of out-of-province people obtaining employment, and some even impose retraining periods. Certain trades require out-of-province workers to obtain licences. A more complete description of these and other labour flow restrictions can be found in other contributions to this volume.

Most of the policies discussed in this section are, from the point of view of the nation as a whole, inefficient. They create distortions in factor markets and therefore work against the federal government's objective of increasing the welfare of the population. At the same time it is worth restating the fact that these policies may well be optimal from the point of view of individual provincial governments as long as they do not anticipate direct retaliation. And even if retaliation is expected there will be circumstances under which, for some of the larger provinces at least, the policies may still be desirable.[32]

PROVINCIAL TAXES AS A POLICY TOOL

Theoretically there is probably more scope for beggar-thy-neighbour policies associated with taxes than with other policy tools. In practice, however, because of the restrictions on provincial tax policy contained in the BNA Act and the prevailing provincial practice in collection of taxes, provincial taxes have probably not introduced substantial inefficiencies into the federal system.

The fact that taxes could be a powerful weapon for provinces to use against one another can be seen from the proposition, due to Mundell that any system of tariffs can be duplicated by a system of domestic taxes.[33] Thus at the national level a 10 per cent tariff on a particular product has exactly the same effect as a 10 per cent consumption tax combined with a 10 per cent subsidy on production. With complete freedom to impose taxes and subsidies on all commodities produced and consumed within its jursidiction, a province could construct what would amount to an elaborate tariff system against other provinces and other countries. Furthermore, it is possible to define an optimal tax structure in terms of benefits achieved through changes in the terms of trade, just as it is possible to define an optimum tariff.[34]

It can also be shown that differential commodity taxes could be an important determinant of trade. Elsewhere I have considered the effects of commodity taxes on trade flows in an international trade model.[35] The model assumes that one country imposes a tax on one of two commodities while the other country raises tax revenue through an equal tax on both. The relative price difference thus created gives rise to commodity trade. Several of the results are relevant to the present analysis. With taxes collected from consumers (as they must be in the case of provinces) there will be a tendency for the taxing jurisdiction to export the taxed good. The taxing area will suffer a welfare loss relative to the initial situation, while the other area will enjoy a welfare gain. Although factor returns

---

32 It is known from international trade literature that even when retaliatory tariffs are imposed one country may still gain relative to unrestricted trade.

33 Mundell (1960), 'The pure theory of international trade' (1960), 50 *American Economic Review* 67.

34 For a discussion of optimal tariffs see Johnson, 'Optimum tariffs and retaliation.' (1953–4), 21 *Review of Economic Studies* 142.

35 Melvin, 'Commodity taxation as a determinant of trade.' (1970), 3 *Canadian Journal of Economics* 62.

will have changed, they will not differ between the regions, so no factor flows will be generated. The implications are clear. Differential commodity taxes by themselves will be welfare reducing for the region imposing the tax and should thus be avoided.[36]

Another important consideration involves the use of taxes to improve provincial welfare. Tariffs, or a system of taxes that duplicates a tariff system, cannot be expected to increase the overall welfare of the constituency that imposes them unless they improve the terms of trade for that constituency. It is generally assumed that as a nation Canada is small and has little influence on the world terms of trade, except perhaps for a few commodities. It seems even less likely that any Canadian province has any substantial monopoly power in trade. If Canada were sufficiently isolated from the rest of the world, say by prohibitive tariffs, the larger provinces would certainly have monopoly power in the domestic market. However, Canada seems sufficiently open to prevent any substantial domestic monopoly power, and thus one must conclude that there is little scope for provinces to increase welfare through the use of tax policy.

Of course provinces (or countries) may well pursue policies designed to increase not overall welfare but the welfare of specific groups. It has been argued that governments will be expected to pursue policies which increase the welfare of potential voters, and that the specific policies adopted will depend on who those potential voters are expected to be. Any policy will raise the welfare of some group, even though it may reduce the potential welfare of the province as a whole. Governments may well pursue a wide variety of policies each designed to appeal to specific groups, with the view that the benefits each group receives are more important (or perhaps just more obvious) than the costs they must bear for policies of no benefit to them. While such an approach can only lower overall welfare, it will be perceived by voters as counterproductive only if they have a sophisticated understanding of the economic system.

Although anything possible with tariffs is also possible with taxes, such taxes must be levied at the origin rather than at the destination of the commodity. In practice, provincial commodity taxes in Canada are levied almost exclusively on the destination principle, so that the scope for tax warfare is substantially reduced. Furthermore, existing provincial commodity taxes tend to be very broad in scope and, with few exceptions, not assigned to particular commodities. Thus we typically find broadly based sales taxes which exempt certain items seen to be necessities. There is also a tendency for the same items to be exempted in different provinces, further reducing the scope for inefficiencies. It thus seems unlikely that the structure of provincial commodity taxation has resulted in any

---

36 For a general treatment of taxes and trade in an open economy see Melvin, *The Tax Structure and Canadian Trade* (Ottawa: Economic Council of Canada, 1976).

substantial amount of distortion in the Canadian economic system.

One tax for which there may be some scope for tax warfare is the corporate income tax, which can be varied between provinces. There are indications that several provinces are moving toward the reduction or elimination of the provincial corporate income tax. A system in which some provinces have a substantial corporate income tax and others have none would certainly result in incentives for the migration of capital and would also be expected to generate differences in commodity prices between provinces, resulting in changes in the interprovincial flow of commodities. I have estimated the commodity price effects of the federal corporate income tax for the Canadian economy, and these figures provide some indication of the effect that the removal of the provincial corporate tax could have.[37] I assumed full shifting of the corporate income tax to commodity prices and calculated the direct price effect from data on corporate taxes collected. This avoided problems associated with the fact that only equity capital is taxed and the fact that there are loopholes in the corporate tax structure. The price effects were calculated through the use of an input-output model.

The results indicated that the removal of the Canadian corporate income tax would, on average, reduce Canadian commodity prices by from about 3.5 to 5 per cent, depending on whether weighted or unweighted averages are used. Of more significance, however, is the range of price effects calculated. Some industries, such as agriculture, show an increase of less than 2 per cent, while others range to a high of 18 per cent for distilleries. Once again, these figures are for federal taxes only, because provincial taxes paid were subtracted for the calculations.

Estimating the provincial tax price effects to be one-quarter of those of the federal tax, one finds that several industries show price effects of approximately 2 per cent. Perhaps the most interesting from the point of view of this study is pharmaceuticals and medicine, with a calculated provincial price effect of 2.1 per cent. This finding suggests that if Alberta were to remove the provincial corporate income tax and if a pharmaceutical industry were to develop in that province, assuming all other costs the same, a 2 per cent price advantage would be enjoyed over similar products produced in Ontario or elsewhere. Whether or not such difference would be enough to affect trade flows among provinces significantly cannot be determined theoretically. What is clear, however, is that such a tax policy, by creating distortions, would result in a reduction in potential Canadian welfare. Because of the distortionary effects of the corporate income

---

37 Melvin, 'Short-run price effects of the corporate income tax and implications for international trade.' (1979), 69 *American Economic Review* 765.

tax in general, the best solution would be the elimination of *all* corporate income taxes. If this is not feasible then to have equal total tax rates everywhere is probably second-best. This result could be achieved if the federal government collected the full corporate tax from all industries and refunding some proportion to provincial governments should they request it.[38]

DISTORTIONARY FEDERAL POLICIES

The last two sections have been concerned entirely with provincial government policies which result in distortions. Of course the federal government also engages in policies which create distortions. This section suggests why a federal government may find it necessary, in terms of the maximization problem of the fourth section, to pursue such policies. The following two sections will examine two examples of federal policy which are generally seen as distortionary.

It has been argued that differences in preferences between regions would require the formation of a federal system if public goods are to be provided optimally. But suppose that the appropriate federal structure did not exist and the federal government were faced with a situation in which the demand for public goods is higher in region A than in region B.[39] Further, suppose the federal government did not have the power to tax regions or individuals differentially according to their demand characteristics. Differential taxation on the basis of income (or output for a production tax) is of course quite acceptable. The problem is whether a policy can be formulated which will, by facilitating individual maximization, increase the government's chance of re-election.

One solution would be to tax everyone and then subsidize region B. If the subsidy is paid to individuals in a lump-sum fashion, or given in the form of an unconditional grant to the appropriate regional government if such existed, then a full optimum can be achieved because no distortions need be created. The solution here is similar to that proposed by Flatters, Henderson, and Mieszkowski for the problem of uneven resource distribution.[40] In many situations, however, these solutions will be either impossible or politically not feasible. Direct lump-sum subsidies to individuals are unpopular politically, and all identifiable regions are not represented by governments. In such a case some alternative mechanism must be found to subsidize region B. Several options are available. Industries in region B may be subsidized, thereby increasing incomes; benefits such as welfare

---

38 More difficult provincial policies to counteract are policies to change the base on which the tax is calculated. This has been suggested in Alberta.

39 In general more than two regions will exist, and of course the appropriate 'region' may differ depending on the public good being considered. Two regions are assumed here for ease of exposition.

40 'Public goods, efficiency, and regional fiscal equalization.'

and unemployment insurance payments may be made easier to obtain; or commodities produced throughout the region may be subsidized. Of course all such policies create distortions and are thus inferior to lump-sum subsidies or grants. It is not clear, however, that these inefficient subsidies are worse, from a welfare point of view, than no subsidies at all or than not providing the public good to anyone.

Quite a different situation will arise when the individuals with different preferences cannot be identified regionally but are distributed throughout the population. For example consider an urban-regional dichotomization. Assume that urban residents have higher preferences for such things as live theatre, art galleries, public transit, and national parks, and that all these are seen to be public or non-private goods and thus receive federal (or provincial) subsidies. To compensate the rural sector for the taxes they have paid to provide these goods and services some subsidy system is required if the party in power is to maximize its chances of re-election. The optimal solution is to give rural residents lump-sum subsidies; but handouts are politically very unpopular, especially with the recipients. A more popular alternative would be the subsidization of rural products, through such things as agricultural price supports and marketing boards. Other methods would include capital subsidization through low-interest loans, favourable tax treatment, and a tariff policy preferential to the agricultural sector. Of course all such policies create distortions and are therefore not the most appropriate from a national welfare point of view, though they may well be so from the point of view of vote maximization.

Distortionary federal policies may also arise from attempts to redistribute income among regions or among individuals. In many cases, where income differences are reflected in individual incomes, such redistribution can be accomplished through progressive taxation. In other cases matters may not be quite so simple. For example, suppose resources are unevenly distributed and one region is resource-rich. If the rents from these resources become income for individuals, no particular problem arises, because the federal government would collect a share through income taxation and redistribute it in some fashion. But suppose, as in the Canadian case, rents from the petroleum resources accrue to provincial governments and that this income is not taxable. What options are now open if the federal government is dedicated to the redistribution of resource rents? One option is to increase real incomes of residents of the non-petroleum-producing regions by keeping the price of petroleum below world levels. Of course such a policy does create distortions. Whether the benefits of such a policy outweigh the costs depends on the alternatives available and on the welfare importance of the redistribution. The welfare benefits of redistribution programs are not being judged here.

The three examples given above of distortionary federal policies represent three quite different situations. The first problem stemmed from the fact that differences in individual tastes, while regional in nature, did not correspond to defined government jurisdictions. One theoretical solution to this problem is to redefine the provinces. In general, of course, this will be impossible, and in any case, as suggested earlier, one would not expect a single subdivision to be appropriate, because the domains of different public goods almost certainly overlap.

The second problem was associated with preference differences (or endowment differences) which are not regionally identified but are widely dispersed throughout the population. In certain circumstances, this problem can be solved by permitting individuals to move to their most preferred jurisdiction, as first suggested by Tiebout.[41] In other situations, such as the urban-rural example used above, there would appear to be no solution other than the subsidization of those individuals disadvantaged by the public good provision. If lump-sum transfers are not feasible, some second-best subsidy may be required.

The third problem arose from a difficulty in achieving the desired redistribution of income; in the case cited the difficulty was the federal government's inability to tax resource rents. The best solution to this problem, at least from the federal point of view, would be to change the constitution to allow taxation of other government levels. Whatever the solution actually chosen it will be difficult or impossible to evaluate because of the difficulty in evaluating the costs and benefits of the underlying redistribution scheme. What is clear from all three cases is that various situations exist in which rational behaviour on the part of the federal government, that is, vote-maximizing behaviour, will introduce distortions.

TARIFFS AS A DISTORTION

When one thinks of distortions introduced into the Canadian economy, tariffs come immediately to mind, for the internationally distorting effects of tariffs are well understood. In the standard analysis, however, the distortions created are not between Canadians but between Canadians and foreign trade partners. The simple two-good case is illustrated in Figure 8, where with free trade production and consumption would be at A and C_0 respectively. Under the assumption that Canada is too small to affect the world terms of trade, and assuming community indifference curves, a tariff on the import good X would move production and consumption to A and C respectively, where domestic consumers and producers both face the domestic terms of trade line P_1.[42]

---

41 'A pure theory of local expenditures.'
42 With variable terms of trade the welfare loss will be less (indeed, there may be a gain), but the argument concerning relative prices is the same.

Figure 8

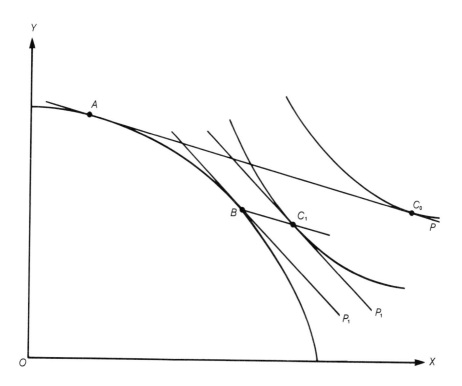

Diagrams such as Figure 8, however, do not capture the essential nature of countries such as Canada, where regions can be geographically widely separated and where transport costs form natural barriers to the interregional flow of commodities. Indeed Conlon has shown that for a significant number of commodities in both Australia and Canada transport costs are a more significant barrier to international trade than tariffs.[43] Since in Canada transport costs are often even more important for regional trade than for international trade, it seems clear that transport costs have played an important role in the development of the Canadian economy.

43 Conlon, 'International transport costs and tariffs as barriers to trade and influences on the structure and performance of Australian and Canadian manufacturing' (unpublished thesis, University of New South Wales, Australia, 1981).

The interesting question here is whether the Canadian tariff has introduced distortions between Canadians in addition to international distortions. Unfortunately the existing research on international trade is of very little assistance, because the effects of transportation costs, or spatial characteristics in general, have been almost completely ignored.[44] The inclusion of transportation costs has usually been done by means of the 'evaporation hypothesis,' which supposes that in transit some of the commodity disappears or evaporates. This is not a particularly appealing assumption, because it assumes that the capital / labour ratio of the transportation service is always exactly equal to that of the commodity being transported.

To cast some light on the interregional effects of the Canadian tariff, we may consider a simple model with two regions, East and West, where, initially with free trade, both regions trade entirely with the United States. A complication immediately arises, for while these two regions can be assumed to have disjoint commodity trade, they are in the same currency union. The significance of this is that there is no reason to assume that the two regions have individual trade balances; all that is required is that trade is balanced for the country as a whole. Not only is the question of whether an imbalance existed important for any definite conclusions, but it also seems impossible to answer because no such free trade situation has in fact existed. As a starting point, therefore, we assume that trade is initially balanced for both regions.

We assume that in the initial free trade situation the East exports manufactures and imports oil, while the West does the reverse.[45] Now suppose a tariff is imposed on all imports, a tariff high enough to eliminate all foreign trade. The question now is what the new equilibrium will look like. One thing is clear. Because all trade has been internalized, interregional trade will now be substantial, whereas at first it did not exist. Because of transport costs the welfare level for the economy as a whole will be lower. However the distribution of this welfare loss depends on the relative regional demands and supplies for imports and exports of the other region. Suppose, for example, that Eastern demand for Western oil is higher than the previous American demand, and that Western demand for Eastern manufactures is less than the previous American demand. In this case there will be a terms-of-trade change in favour of the West, which could enjoy higher welfare than in the free trade situation.

Alternatively, suppose that the new regional demands are about the same as the old American demands but that in the initial situation, when both regions

44 Conlon's study is a notable recent exception.
45 For the analysis of a similar model see Courchene and Melvin, 'Energy revenues: consequences for the rest of Canada.' (1980), 6 *Canadian Public Policy* Supplement.

faced world prices, there had been a regional balance-of-payments problem financed by income flows from the East to the West. With the tariff isolating both regions from the rest of the world, terms of trade changes will now eliminate this disequilibrium and the welfare of Eastern residents will increase.

A slightly different version of the model would have a tariff imposed only on manufactures. Now in the new equilibrium the West would export oil to the United States, the East would import oil from the United States (or Mexico), and the East would export manufactures to the West. Given the transport costs this will lower welfare in the West even if Eastern manufacturing is as efficient as American manufacturing. Welfare in the East may rise or fall.

Of course all these models are very simplistic and unrealistic. Furthermore there are many important parameters about which very little is known and on which the conclusions about the distribution of losses from the tariff will depend. With a careful choice of assumptions one can generate any result desired, and many equally realistic (or equally unrealistic) models provide quite different conclusions. The only results which seem robust over all models are the observations that the tariff has substantially increased interregional trade in Canada and that the potential welfare of the country as a whole has been reduced. It also seems clear that the tariff has resulted in an income redistribution, but the exact nature of this redistribution is unclear. There have presumably been redistributions among factors of production and among regions, but this may have been government policy, in which case it cannot be criticized on efficiency grounds. Whether the tariff introduced price distortions between regions is not clear but depends on what prices would have prevailed in autarky. If prices for commodities were identical in foreign markets in autarky, that is if both Canadian regions faced the same world prices, then the tariff introduced a distortion. If different prices prevailed initially, it is possible that no distortion was introduced by the tariff. In any case it is clear that the policy to increase interregional trade has been inefficient in that resources have been used up to overcome the transport cost barrier.

THE FEDERAL ENERGY POLICY

In several respects the analysis of recent federal energy policy is similar to the analysis of the Canadian tariff. No attempt will be made to examine all aspects of this complex question; this discussion will be confined to the effect of maintaining the Canadian price at below the world level. The policy can be seen as a tax-subsidy program whereby producers pay a tax on the world price of oil and consumers are given an equal-rate subsidy on their purchases. In practice, because the government sets the domestic price, no tax is charged on domestic sales, but a tax is levied on all foreign sales. Domestic consumers of domestic petroleum do not receive a subsidy, but domestic consumers of foreign oil do. Thus the situation is much like the tariff case; all domestic producers and consumers face the same relative prices, but a distortion has been introduced between Canadians and foreigners. Indeed the situation where petroleum would be the export good in free trade (i.e. commodity Y) is exactly the same as Figure 8.[46] The reduction in the price of Y for both producers and consumers results in a reduction in production of petroleum from A to B and an increase in consumption from C_0 to C_1. As before, overall potential welfare has been reduced.

The situation where petroleum would be imported under free trade is shown in Figure 9. When free trade production is at B and consumption at C the reduction in the domestic price of Canadian oil shifts production to B' and consumption to C'. Producers and consumers both face the domestic price P'. It is obvious that the tax-subsidy policy has reduced potential welfare below the free trade level. Furthermore the policy has resulted in a large expansion of foreign trade from vector CB to vector $C'B'$. This trade has certainly not been beneficial, however, and indeed it is clear that a higher welfare level could be achieved at A, the autarky or prohibitive-tariff situation.

The distortions associated with the National Energy program that have been described here affect all Canadians and thus are not specifically regional in nature. The question remains whether the oil pricing policy has introduced any inter-regional distortions into the Canadian economy. The answer to this question is unclear. It is certainly true that the pricing policy has resulted in a huge income transfer from Alberta to the rest of Canada, but this seems to have been the principal purpose of the policy in the first place. Thus the oil pricing policy can be seen as a method of redistributing wealth within Canada. One may or may not approve of this redistribution, just as one may approve or disapprove of any redistribution scheme, but an evaluation of redistributions is outside the scope of this analysis. If one accepts the need for such a redistribution, the question is whether it has been done efficiently, and there seem to be no obvious distortionary effects *among Canadians*. The policy will, of course, result in shifts in labour and capital between sectors of economy, but these will be in response to factor price changes associated with relative commodity price changes and cannot be seen as distortions. Again, the returns to labour and capital will change but by the same amounts everywhere (except for the effects of transportation costs, etc.), so that no distortions in factor markets are necessarily created.

46 The model is somewhat more complex than this because of the fact that petroleum is an intermediate good. For a more complete discussion see Melvin, 'Some general equilibrium consequences of Canadian oil policy' (unpublished, 1982).

Figure 9

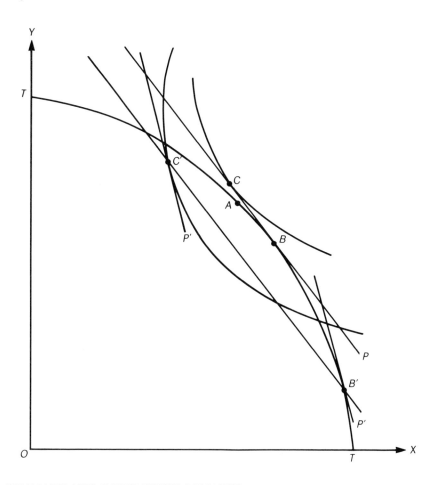

SUMMARY AND CONCLUDING REMARKS

In the Canadian economy one often observes policies being pursued by both the federal and provincial governments which can be shown to be distortionary and therefore welfare reducing. The studies in this volume have catalogued these distortions and attempted to quantify their importance. This would seem to be the logical first step in any attempt to suggest alternative policies or constitutional arrangements aimed at increasing national welfare.

To shed light on the interactions among federal and provincial policies and the reasons why they may be in conflict, an attempt was made to explain from the standpoint of economic theory why different levels of government are required and why they might pursue policies which reduce welfare. Next the various criteria proposed to evaluate government policy were reviewed.

The ultimate policy criterion is welfare or utility, but significant difficulties surround the use of utility measures for policy analysis. The problem of the incomparability of utility between individuals makes welfare judgments difficult or impossible unless all individuals are made better off (or at least no worse off) by a specific policy. Many situations are thus not comparable by utility measures. These difficulties could be overcome if a social welfare function could be defined, but the assumptions required make the concept too restrictive to be of value.

Income measures are often used as proxies for utility changes, and while this is quite appropriate in some circumstances, difficulties often arise. When prices change, income comparisons often depend on which price ratio is considered, and such comparisons may not accurately reflect welfare changes. However, where income has unambiguously increased it is usually possible to conclude that potential welfare has increased, in the sense that everyone could be made better off with an appropriate redistribution of income.

Although neither utility nor income provide completely reliable criteria for policy evaluation, in a wide range of circumstances one or the other can provide appropriate comparisons. Furthermore, some measure must be used if evaluations are to be made, and no better alternatives than welfare and income are available. In this volume both utility, in the form of consumer surplus, and national income have been employed in an attempt to measure the distortionary effects of federal and provincial policies.

The central issue addressed in this paper was not the method used to measure distortion but rather the reason one would expect to find distortionary policies in the first place. A policy that lowers welfare would presumably have been avoided if some clearly better alternative had been available. The government in question may simply not have understood the consequences of its policy, but that is not the only possible explanation. We have found reason to believe that a policy may be optimal from a provincial government's point of view and yet be welfare reducing when the entire economy is considered. If this is the case and the distortions are significant, their removal may not be easy. Persuading a government to give up a policy that from its own point of view is optimal will undoubtedly be a difficult task.

An economic role for governments is generally assumed to depend on the existence of public goods, and one explanation of the need for different levels of governments could be differences in the preferences of individuals for the public goods to be provided. With such an approach in mind it becomes clear that models which rely on the existence of social welfare functions will not be appropriate, since such welfare functions require that all individuals have identical tastes. A model is developed which does not rely on the aggregation of preferences, but views the government as acting to facilitate the utility-maximization of the households within its jurisdiction. The government is assumed to maximize the probability of re-election and does so by pursuing a policy which allows a majority of voters to enjoy utility increases. Since the government is not assumed to be attempting to maximize a social welfare function, no restrictions on individual preferences are required. This formulation of the theory of government behaviour leads naturally to a multi-level system, for if preferences for public goods are found to differ between regions, then creating lower levels of government will allow a provision of public goods which more closely approximates consumer demand and thus allow a larger number of voters to enjoy utility increases.

But while a federal system of government will generally allow a larger number of individuals to enjoy increases in utility, it is possible that some of the programs undertaken by lower levels of government may not be in the best interests of the nation as a whole. To give but one example, a provincial government may see procurement policies as a way of increasing the incomes, and therefore the utilities, of its own constituents even though such policies, by creating distortions in the economy, would be expected to lower welfare in the nation as a whole. Thus while such a policy may be optimal from the point of view of the provincial government, it will not be optimal from the point of view of the nation.

Of course not all distortions are created by provincial or lower levels of government. Many federal policies introduce distortions too. Often such policies result from voters with different preferences not being conveniently regionalized but rather distributed geographically more or less evenly, so that the formation of another level of government cannot solve the problem. One example suggested was the urban-rural dichotomy, and while methods of equalizing the benefits to these groups are clearly available, such as lump-sum subsidies, such solutions are not politically attractive. Thus a subsidy may be provided to the agricultural sector through such things as price supports and marketing boards. These create distortions, of course, but may well be seen by the government as politically the most efficient method of achieving the objective of redistribution.

This view of government policy has important implications for the question of how reforms to the present system are to be undertaken if the distortions examined in subsequent chapters prove to be significant. If a government is pursuing a policy that from its point of view is optimal, it will certainly resist change even if such change is in the best interest of the nation. Indeed, in some circumstances there may not be alternative policies which are both welfare improving and politically feasible. Of course in those circumstances where most or all provinces are pursuing similar distortionary policies a persuasive case may be made for the co-operative removal of the distortions by all. Even then, however, some jurisdictions are likely to suffer even though overall income will rise. An appropriate redistribution could allow all jurisdictions to benefit, but in practice politically feasible redistributions themselves involve distortions and are thus open to criticism.

In other contributions to this volume the various kinds of distortions which have been introduced into the Canadian economy by both the federal and provincial governments are enumerated, analysed, and quantified. When passing final judgment on these distortions it is important to consider what alternatives are available, and to keep in mind the fact that few politically feasible policies are neutral.

PART TWO: EVIDENCE

4

Induced distortions of interprovincial activity: an overview of issues

John Whalley

Although the issue of interprovincial trade barriers has always been part of the ongoing policy debate in Canada, only in the last few years has it come to centre stage. This upsurgence is partly due to the use of emotive terminology such as the 'balkanization' of Canada and the need for a Canadian 'common market.' It is also due to perceived political advantages to either federal or provincial governments from promoting the debate. As a result the discussion has significantly intensified in recent years and months.

There are several undercurrents in this debate. On the provincial side, the implicit argument seems to be that if beggar-my-neighbour trade policies exist some co-operative agreement to limit their use will improve things. On the federal side, the implicit argument is that Canada needs protection when provinces retaliate against each other's interprovincial protectionist policies. Such protection can only come from either greater centralization of power or an economic charter of rights restricting the powers of provinces.

Despite the current interest in these questions it is striking that very little empirical investigation has been done to substantiate or refute the positions taken and that there has been scarcely any analysis of the so-called barriers and

I am grateful to Jim Melvin, Wayne Thirsk, and other participants in the conference for comments on an earlier draft, and to Laurie Bland for excellent research assistance. For a general discussion of the topics in this paper, see also Chrétien, *Securing the Canadian Economic Union in the Constitution: Discussion Paper Published by the Government of Canada* (Ottawa: Ministry of Supply and Services, 1980); Ontario, Ministry of Industry and Tourism, *Interprovincial Economic Co-operation: Towards the Development of a Canadian Common Market: Proposals for Interprovincial Economic Co-operation and for the Establishment of a Canadian Domestic Market Development Agency* (Toronto: Government of Ontario, 1981); and Safarian, *Ten Markets or One? Regional Barriers to Economic Activity in Canada* (Toronto: Ontario Economic Council Discussion Paper, 1980).

how they work. Present discussions seem to rest on anecdotal evidence rather than rigorous examination of data, and terminology is used somewhat loosely so that the barriers in question are not always clearly defined. In short there is little empirical basis to the current discussion of interprovincial barriers to Canada. I know of only one summary of the major barriers[1] and no appraisal of their role or significance.

This paper focuses on distortions of interprovincial activity induced by actions of the federal and provincial governments. It attempts to clarify what is meant by the term 'distortion,' to highlight the major distortions which government policies introduce into interprovincial activity, and to provide background data on the size of interprovincial activity.

DISTORTIONS AND INTERPROVINCIAL GOODS AND FACTOR FLOWS

What is a distortion?
The concept of distortion is widely employed in international economics and in turn freely used in much of the policy debate surrounding a Canadian common market. In popular discussion, the term 'distortion' is used as a synonym for 'barrier.' A trade barrier impedes free movement of goods and factors and results in smaller trade flows between provinces than would occur in its absence. A barrier has connotations of harm since it limits the gains which would occur from increased specialization as provinces trade increasingly with each other. However, when we attempt to define the term 'distortion' more precisely than simply as an impediment to interprovincial trade, things become a little more difficult.

A distortion results from any policy if, as a result, resources are misallocated either within or between provinces. In the presence of a distortion it is always possible to reallocate resources so as to make someone in the country better off. In the vocabulary of the welfare economists, a distortion results if and only if there is a departure from the conditions required for 'Pareto optimality.'[2]

1 Pestieau, 'Whither the Canadian common market?.' In Barrett, ed., *Key Economic and Social Issues of the Early 1980s* (Ottawa: Conference Board in Canada, Canadian Study No. 62, 1980). The paper was first presented to the Round Table meeting on Key Economic and Social Issues of the Early 1980s, 16–17 October 1979.
2 The three sets of conditions usually stated are that the marginal rate of substitution between factors should be the same in all industries (production efficiency); the marginal rate of substitution between goods should be the same for all consumers (exchange efficiency); and the marginal rate of substitution between goods for all consumers should be the same as the marginal rate of substitution between goods faced by firms (overall efficiency). The classic paper by Bator. 'The simple analytics of welfare maximization' (1957), 47 *American Economic Review* 22, clearly spells out these conditions. A further reference is Boadway, *Public Sector Economics* (Boston: Little, Brown and Co. 1979).

Distortions are therefore defined by their effect on the economy, not by their characteristics as such.

Most economists use the term distortion to describe a policy that is discriminatory, in the sense that it treats participants in transactions differently. Thus, in international trade theory, the tariff is regarded as 'distortionary' simply because citizens who buy products produced domestically do not pay the tariff but citizens who buy products imported from abroad have to do so. Foreigners exporting to the country with the tariff have to cross the tariff barrier and overcome it to sell abroad, whereas if they sell domestically no tariff barrier is involved. Since goods bought from abroad are liable for the tariff, whereas goods produced domestically are not, discrimination occurs on the basis of the point of production of goods, and a distortion is created.

Discriminatory features of policy are what most economists mean when they use the term distortion. However, some policies frequently referred to as 'barriers' to interprovincial trade are not in fact distortionary because they are not discriminatory. Consider, for example, a single two-region case where one region has a domestic tax on all products bought by residents of that region. There is no distortion involved in the policy since products imported from the second region into the first are treated the same as products both produced and consumed in the first region. Although exports from the second region to the first region have to account for the tax, so that one might be inclined to argue that a trade barrier is involved, among the products sold in the first region there is no differentiation between domestic and imported products, and thus no distortion is involved.

Before discussing the concept of policy-induced distortions in the Canadian context I shall give further examples of policies that are and are not distortionary according to our use of the term.

1 Provincial government procurement policies

An issue that has attracted a substantial amount of attention in the debate on the Canadian common market is the impact of provincial government procurement policies. If a province gives a preference to local contractors when awarding government contracts, this is a clear distortion in our terms simply because discrimination exists between contractors in the province and contractors outside.

2 Different provincial sales tax rates

A provincial sales tax at a uniform rate on all products purchased in a region does not induce any significant interprovincial distortion in our terms. This is the case even if different provinces operate different sales tax rates. No distortion is involved with a uniform rate tax because there is no discrimination on the basis of point of production or consumption between products offered to a consumer. The only distortion involved in this case occurs to the extent that people who live on the border move between provinces in spending money on products. If people who live in one region drive across the border into another to spend because there are no taxes, there is some impact on interprovincial trade between the regions. While these effects are present, and potentially significant, they are not what most people have in mind when discussing barriers to trade. In practice, most provinces have exemptions on a range of goods and services which make provincial sales taxes distortionary, but their effects on interprovincial trade remain uncertain.

3 Language policies
A number of barriers to interprovincial trade naturally occur because of language, distance, and other factors. We are concerned here only with distortions that are artificially induced by policies, because they can be removed, and a policy to remove them is justified as a move towards Pareto optimality. For *natural* barriers a subsidy to 'overcome' the barrier will itself induce a distortion because the conditions for Pareto optimality will be violated.

An issue which arises in this context is the question whether language policies in Quebec or elsewhere distort interprovincial trade and free interprovincial mobility of factors. While language itself may be viewed as a natural barrier to free mobility of factors, policies which exacerbate that natural barrier provoke artificially induced distortions and therefore should be evaluated.

4 Freight rates and interprovincial trade
Under the Crow's Nest Pass Agreement, freight rates for grain and flour from the prairies to three specified locations are regulated at levels below marginal cost. The distortion of freight rates resulting is clear, since only the shipping of these commodities between specified locations qualifies for the low rate. The distortion of freight rates in turn induces a distortion in interprovincial trade flows.

Explicit and implicit distortions of interprovincial goods and factor flows
We thus define an induced distortion as any policy impact resulting in a misallocation of resource either within or between provinces. A difficulty with this definition for the purposes of the present study is that policies can be distortionary without being explicitly interprovincially so. This distinction is important since many of the policies discussed later are only implicitly interprovincially distortionary in the sense that distortions occur and affect interprovincial trade flows without the policy explicitly distorting transactions between regions.

We therefore make a distinction between policies that explicitly and implicitly lead to interprovincial distortions. Explicitly distortionary policies contain explicit provincial discrimination. Provincial government procurement policies which give a cost or other advantage to in-province contractors over out-of-province ones would be an example of this. Another example would be the regionally extended portion of unemployment insurance benefits where benefits differ depending on the provincial unemployment rate.

Implicitly distortionary policies contain discriminatory features which have significant provincial impacts without containing explicit provincial discrimination. Thus federal regulation of oil prices contains no explicit provincial discrimination, since oil is not priced according to which province produces or consumes it. The oil price ceiling is an implicit distortion, however, since the policy of differentiating between world and domestic prices has pronounced provincial consequences, with consuming provinces gaining and producing provinces losing.

Many of the issues raised in the debate on a Canadian common market focus on implicitly distortionary policies. An example is the regional impact of the tariff in Canada. A common argument is that the tariff in Canada is unfair to western provinces since manufacturing industries in Quebec and Ontario can produce manufactured products behind a tariff wall. This means that western Canada has to buy manufactured products at prices higher than world prices. Although the tariff causes significant income redistribution between central and western Canada, the tariff, itself, has no regionally discriminatory features built into it. The same tariff rates apply anywhere in Canada to any imported product. Nonetheless, the potential effects on interprovincial trade flows are marked, as are the effects on the terms of trade between western and central Canada.

Implicitly distortionary policies therefore have an important impact on the Canadian economy and significantly affect the relative income position of provinces and in turn the interprovincial trade flows between regions.

Natural barriers and artificially induced distortions
A further important distinction is that between natural barriers to interprovincial trade and artificially induced distortions. Natural barriers to interprovincial flows are perhaps self-evident; the most significant are distance and, perhaps to a lesser extent, language. These we sharply differentiate from artificially induced distortions which arise from government action. Since the latter can be changed, a meaningful policy debate can occur over whether they should be removed and what incentive structure gave rise to them in the first place.

With natural barriers the policy issues are quite different. The question is whether there should be some attempt to *offset* natural barriers through policy initiatives. Should federal or provincial government policies be designed in such a way as to offset linguistic differences, distance, and geography in so far as they impede trade? For instance, should the effects of distance be ameliorated by subsidizing transportation costs?

In the case of artificially induced distortions, there is usually a clear national gain from their removal, though it is equally clear some provinces will lose and some will gain. However, with natural barriers there is no particular reason to have positive intervention to offset their effect. Natural barriers represent a cost which society as a whole must bear, and any attempt to offset the effect of these barriers imposes additional costs that usually will not be socially justified. With artificially induced distortions, which have arisen because of pressures for protection and other concerns within provinces, those issues do not arise.

Price interventions and quantity limitations as distortions
Interventions by governments that distort relative prices are not the only source of distortions. Quantity limitations can also have significant consequences. A well-known proposition in international trade theory is the equivalence between tariffs and quotas: for any tariff it is possible to devise a quota that has exactly the same effect. Equally, for any quota there exists a corresponding tariff. Some policies (such as occupational licencing) operate as quantity limitations on flows between provinces and are induced distortions even though no direct price intervention is involved.

Distortions affecting interprovincial mobility in goods, capital, and labour
We consider both interprovincial trade in goods and free mobility of capital and labour between provinces. Capital and labour services are primary factors of production, and free mobility of them between all regions in a national economy is an essential and integral part of a move towards a common market. An offer by one province of particular incentives to attract capital would violate the conditions for Pareto optimality in resource allocation between the provinces. The same with labour mobility: if one region imposes restrictions on the mobility of labour between provinces, that too is a distortion.

Subsidies, distortions, and 'reverse barriers'
In some cases policies of provincial and federal governments can be distortionary in artificially *stimulating* flows of goods and factors between regions. For example, if provinces introduce special schemes which subsidize capital employed in small business within the province, this is an artificial stimulus to provincial investment. Instead of a barrier to interprovincial flows there is an artificial stimulus to interprovincial flows. This form of subsidy or 'reverse barrier' can be just as harmful as the policy which protects and excludes.

OVERVIEW OF MAJOR POLICY-INDUCED DISTORTIONS (FEDERAL AND PROVINCIAL)

The Canadian economy contains many distortions induced by the policies of all levels of government. We shall concentrate on the main ones. They are listed in Table 1 and briefly described. A similar list with some minor differences appears in Pestieau.[3] The policies listed in Table 1 are discussed in more detail in Chapters 5 and 6. This chapter simply reviews them and shows why they are distortionary.

Provincial government procurement policies
All ten provinces have policies that give explicit preference to in-province contractors. The nature of these preferences varies from province to province, but it usually involves a cost or other advantage given to in-province contractors on bidding for government work. Given the size of the public sector in the Canadian economy, this practice constitutes an explicit distortion which tends to limit the size of interprovincial trade.

Freight rate regulation (Crow's Nest Pass Agreement)
Transportation arrangements in Canada have evolved with a substantial degree of government intervention. The most significant government involvement involves regulation of rail freight rates. This stems from a longstanding agreement between the federal government and Canadian Pacific (CP), commonly referred to as the Crow's Nest Pass Agreement. Under this agreement the federal government gave CP a sum of money in the late nineteenth century to pay for tunnel construction. In return, CP agreed to charge below-cost freight rates on shipping certain products from the prairies to points east. This agreement has since been consolidated in various transportation acts, and regulated freight rates now prevail on Crow's Nest routes. The federal government subsidizes these rates by covering some of the losses which result. This is an explicit distortion of interprovincial trade both because of the discriminatory subsidy element from the federal government and the way this operates on particular trans-shipment routes between selected provinces. The policies are now under extensive review by the federal government.

Liquor buying and pricing policies
Most provinces operate liquor commissions which act as monopolists controlling the sale of liquor within provincial boundaries. Liquor commissions have control over buying and pricing policies, and these policies are usually exercised

---

3 'Whither the Canadian Common Market?'

TABLE 1

Summary of major induced distortions

Policy inducing distortion	Nature of distortion	Character	Level of government
Distortions of goods flows			
Provincial government procurement policies	Preference given to in-province contractors	Explicit	Provincial
Freight rate regulation (Crow's Nest Pass Agreement)	Controlled rail rates on wheat and flour from prairies	Explicit	Federal
Liquor buying and pricing policies	Buying and pricing by provincial liquor commissions give preference to in-province suppliers	Explicit	Provincial
Federal energy policies (price ceilings)	Price controls on oil and natural gas	Implicit	Federal
Marketing boards	Price setting and quotas on agricultural products	Implicit	Primarily Provincial
Tariffs, trade-restrictions and standards	'Protection' of national economy which affects interprovincial trade	Implicit/explicit	Federal and Provincial
Taxes	Limited neighbourhood effects of differential sales tax rates across provinces; effects from federal excise taxes and the manufacturers sales tax	Explicit/implicit	Federal and Provincial
Distortions of capital flows			
Provincial investment plans	Shelter from provincial taxes for in-province investors	Explicit	Provincial
Provincial heritage funds	Accumulation of provincial revenues in fund largely reinvested in province	Explicit; distortion offset by private capital markets	Provincial
Business subsidies	Grants, cheap loans for investment in provinces	Explicit	Primarily Provincial
DREE	Targeted capital financing for regional investment	Explicit	Federal
Provincial crown corporations	Provincial crown corporations free of federal taxes	Implicit	Federal and Provincial combined
Federal energy policies (exploration incentives)	Exploration incentives through cash grant program; the 'Canadianization' program.	Implicit	Federal

TABLE 1 continued

Summary of major induced distortions

Policy inducing distortion	Nature of distortion	Character	Level of government
Distortions of labour flows			
Unemployment insurance	Subsidy to 'search' which raises unemployment rate; regional features in the program	Implicit plus small explicit component	Federal
Equalization	Cash transfer to 'equalize' differences in tax bases between provinces	Explicit	Federal
Occupational licensing	Restrictions on hiring practices within provinces	Explicit	Provincial

so as to give preference to within-province products where significant in-province industries exist.

Federal energy policies (price ceilings)

The mix of energy policies in Canada is extremely complex, but a number of major structural elements are involved. In terms of distortions of trade flows, the most significant are the price controls on oil and natural gas, recently revised under the Ottawa-Alberta Oil Pricing Agreement. Oil prices are controlled below market prices; natural gas prices are also controlled. The distortion of inter-provincial trade involved is implicit rather than explicit since there is nothing in the price controls which differentiates by province. Because of the substantial regional concentration of ownership of oil in Canada, this is a very significant implicit distortion. We later examine the distortions of the national capital market which operate through exploration incentives in the energy program.

Marketing boards

All provinces have marketing boards which control the purchase and sale of agricultural products. Shoup reports that 172 marketing boards were in operation in Canada in the mid-1970s, primarily operating on a provincial level and accounting for something in the order of 25 per cent of all sales of agricultural products.[4] To the extent that marketing boards raise agricultural prices, this represents an implicit distortion of interprovincial trade.

Tariffs and trade restrictions

Federal policies that restrict international trade are frequently justified on the grounds of protecting the national economy. While there is nothing explicitly distortionary about the effect of the tariff interprovincially, many commentators have argued that it substantially changes the size and structure of interprovincial trade. An argument often made is that Ontario and Quebec are helped by the tariff. They produce import-substituted manufactured products, which they sell to western provinces and the Maritimes at a gross-of-tariff price, which is higher than the world price. Thus, so the argument goes, western provinces are forced to trade at disadvantageous terms with Ontario and Quebec compared to a situation in which tariffs and trade restrictions did not operate. The important point about these trade restrictions that they apply to manufactured products and change the relevant terms of trade between manufactured and

---

4 Shoup, 'Interregional economic barriers: the Canadian provinces.' In Ontario Economic Council, *Intergovernmental Relations: Issues and Alternatives – 1977* (Toronto: Ontario Economic Council, 1977).

non-manufactured products for interprovincial trade within Canada. This is an implicit rather than explicit distortion.

Federal and provincial taxes
Within the federal and provincial tax systems, a number of elements are subsequently cited as examples of distortions of trade flows. The most prominent are the differences in sales tax rates between provinces. As already argued, this is not in fact a major source of interprovincial distortion. A distortion only operates to the extent to which consumers move from one province to another province in order to purchase products. However, other provincially distortionary effects operate in the tax system. The most notable are the federal excise taxes on energy products, the manufacturers' sales tax, which changes the terms of trade between resource and manufacturing provinces, and differences in provincial personal and corporate tax rates, which affect factor mobility between provinces.

Provincial investment plans
In recent years provincial governments seeking to stimulate investment within the province have used explicit preferences within the provincial income tax. A widely used example is that of Quebec, which allows a deduction from provincial income taxes for investments made for in-province companies. Similar plans are now operating in other provinces. This is an explicit distortion of capital allocation between regions.

Heritage funds
In recent years Alberta has established the Heritage Fund, under which tax revenues are accumulated in a provincial investment fund. The Heritage Fund is now being copied by a number of provinces, most notably Saskatchewan. The investment policies which are adopted by these funds channel a large portion of their money into within-province investments, creating a potential distortion of the national capital market. To a large extent, however, the allocation of capital in the private market can offset interregional distortions which the Heritage fund creates; policies which target investment funds to particular regions need create no distortion if the effects are offset by reallocation elsewhere in the national capital market. This point (discussed later) also applies to provincial investment requirements in the Canada Pension Plan, which have in the past been labelled as interprovincially distortionary.

Business subsidies
In addition to provincial investment plans, both federal and provincial governments stimulate investment through a variety of policies involving grants, cheap

loans, and guarantees for investments in selected areas. Ontario offers development grants for small business, and similar policies operate in other provinces. An explicit distortion of the national capital market is introduced through these policies.

DREE

The Department of Regional Economic Expansion began in the 1960s as an explicit attempt by Ottawa to stimulate regional activity in Canada. It involves schemes of targeted capital financing for regional investment in specified projects; much of DREE expenditure goes directly to the Maritime provinces. The explicit nature of the targeting introduces elements of provincial distortion in the capital market.

Provincial crown corporations
All provinces have provincial crown corporations which control significant areas of economic activity, particularly in electrical power generation. Provincial crown corporations are in most cases free of federal taxes, so that capital invested in provincial crown corporations usually earns a different gross rate of return from capital invested elsewhere in the economy, creating an implicit distortion of the national capital market.

Federal energy policies and exploration incentives
In addition to price controls on oil and natural gas, the other major feature of federal energy policies is the exploration incentives, which currently operate through cash grant programs and previously operated through earned depletion allowances. This exploration incentive program is designed partly to offset the effect of price controls on oil and natural gas. Depending upon how one views the latter (as discussed later), an implicit distortion of the national capital market is created which has a significant interprovincial impact because of the strong regional concentration of energy activity.

Unemployment insurance
It is widely agreed by economists that unemployment insurance schemes act as subsidies to search by individuals who are seeking to change jobs, and thus tend to raise the unemployment rate. The unemployment insurance program in Canada has grown very substantially in the 1970s, the most notable changes occurring with the extensions in coverage in 1971. The program also contains a number of regional features which expand benefits for specified regions depending upon the regional unemployment rate. To the extent that certain provinces (particularly those in the Maritimes) have high unemployment rates, an implicit distortion operates because the subsidy to search operating in those provinces is

more significant than in other provinces. The implicit distortion has sharp inter-provincial effects because unemployment rates differ significantly by province.

Equalization
For many years in Canada attempts have been made to equalize the tax base of provinces through the federal budget. In the last two decades this has been enshrined in the five-year tax agreements, under which equalization calculations are made using prescribed formulas. The program involves cash transfers from the federal government to provinces reflecting a calculation of the amount of equalization for which provinces are eligible. To the extent that the equalization payments either result in a reduction in taxes in recipient provinces or an expansion in the level of provision of local public goods over those which would otherwise occur, an explicit distortion of labour flows between provinces is created.

Occupational licensing
Occupational licensing restrictions operate primarily on a provincial level and involve restrictions on the hiring practices within provinces. This question is frequently mentioned in the debate on interprovincial distortions of goods and factor flows. The distortions at issue are explicit and involve requiring either residency periods prior to hiring or a hiring preference for local workers before out-of-province workers are engaged. Instances of this are taken up in more detail later.

SIZE AND STRUCTURE OF INTERPROVINCIAL TRADE AND FACTOR FLOWS

To examine the potential significance of distortions of interprovincial trade at a broad level, we begin by asking how big interprovincial trade is in Canada and what is the scope for distortion of it. A surprising feature of work on interprovincial trade and factor flows in Canada is the relative absence of reliable data. This paper uses the latest data, much of which are unpublished, giving more broadly based estimates of interprovincial trade flows in Canada than have previously been available. Most previous work has relied heavily on data on manufacturing shipments, which gives trade only in manufactured products. Recent work by the structural analysis division of the input-output section of Statistics Canada has resulted in a set of commodity and service trade balances for Canada for 1974, which we use here.

Interprovincial trade flows
Table 2 summarizes the interprovincial trade flows in goods and goods and services between provinces in Canada in 1974. For each province we report

TABLE 2

Interprovincial trade in goods and services in 1974 ($billions)

	Imports from rest of Canada		Exports to the rest of Canada		Imbalance	
	Goods	Goods and services	Goods	Goods and services	Goods	Goods and services
Newfoundland	0.75	1.32	0.10	0.19	−0.65	−1.13
PEI	0.22	0.32	0.09	0.12	−0.13	−0.20
Nova Scotia	1.08	1.79	0.63	1.05	−0.45	−0.74
New Brunswick	0.98	1.60	0.58	0.95	−0.40	−0.65
Quebec	6.83	10.29	7.36	12.12	0.53	1.83
Ontario	7.61	11.06	10.87	18.06	3.26	7.00
Manitoba	1.64	2.50	1.19	1.78	−0.45	−0.72
Saskatchewan	1.39	2.26	1.25	1.45	−0.14	−0.81
Alberta	2.69	4.68	3.25	5.08	0.56	0.40
BC	3.14	5.17	1.15	2.16	−1.99	−3.01
Yukon/NWT	0.19	2.02	0.05	0.05	−0.14	−1.97
Total	26.52	43.01	26.52	43.01		

NOTE: Data are in 1974 producer prices. Trade in goods includes agricultural commodities, energy, metal ores, and manufacturing.
SOURCE: Unpublished commodity balances from Statistics Canada interprovincial input-output tables

imports from the rest of Canada and exports to the rest of Canada. In 1974 the total value of interprovincial trade in goods and services was around $43 billion, of which around $26 billion was trade in goods. This compares with a 1974 GNP at factor cost for Canada of approximately $120 billion. Later tables indicate that these figures are roughly comparable to the total value of trade between Canada and the rest of the world averaged over all of Canada, although significant interprovincial differences occur.

If we look at the situation within individual provinces, Table 2 clearly displays what is at stake with distortions of interprovincial trade. Approximately one-half of imports from the rest of Canada are accounted for by Ontario and Quebec, while around 65 per cent of interprovincial exports are accounted for by the same two provinces. These two provinces in combination run a surplus in trade with the rest of Canada. They specialize in export of manufactures to the rest of Canada and import raw materials and agricultural products. The largest-deficit province is British Columbia. Unlike the exports of other provinces, its exports are more heavily targeted to foreign markets than domestic markets.

TABLE 3

Relative importance of interprovincial and international trade in goods and services by province in 1974 ($ billions)

Goods	(1) Imports from rest of Canada	(2) Imports from outside Canada	(3) Exports to rest of Canada	(4) Exports to outside Canada	Combined imbalance (3+4−1−2)
Newfoundland	0.75	0.61	0.10	0.87	−0.39
PEI	0.22	0.05	0.09	0.02	−0.16
Nova Scotia	1.08	1.28	0.63	0.50	−1.23
New Brunswick	0.98	0.90	0.58	0.68	−0.62
Quebec	6.83	8.85	7.36	4.74	−3.58
Ontario	7.61	14.54	10.87	11.03	−0.25
Manitoba	1.64	0.97	1.19	0.82	−0.60
Saskatchewan	1.39	0.80	1.25	2.12	1.18
Alberta	2.69	1.87	3.25	3.34	2.03
BC	3.14	3.32	1.15	3.97	−1.34
Yukon/NWT	0.19	0.04	0.05	0.21	0.03
Total	26.52	33.23	26.52	28.30	
Goods and services					
Newfoundland	1.32	0.61	0.19	0.92	−0.82
PEI	0.32	0.05	0.12	0.02	−0.23
Nova Scotia	1.79	1.28	1.05	0.55	−1.47
New Brunswick	1.60	0.90	0.95	0.79	−0.76
Quebec	10.29	8.85	12.12	5.30	−1.72
Ontario	11.06	14.54	18.06	12.47	4.92
Manitoba	2.50	0.97	1.78	0.89	−0.80
Saskatchewan	2.26	0.80	1.45	2.17	0.56
Alberta	4.68	1.87	5.08	3.42	1.95
BC	5.17	3.32	2.16	4.37	−1.96
Yukon/NWT	2.02	0.04	0.05	0.21	−1.80
Total	43.01		43.01	31.11	

NOTE: See Table 2 note. Data on service imports from outside Canada are not reported.
SOURCE: See Table 2 source.

The Maritimes have deficits which account for approximately one-half of the value of their trade. Alberta is in small surplus in 1974 because of trade in energy products. Were later years' data available, the size of this surplus would almost certainly be considerably larger because of higher energy prices.

The relative importance of interprovincial and international trade is shown in Table 3 which reports not only imports from and exports to the rest of Canada by province, but also imports from and exports to countries outside of Canada. The combined trade balance of provinces is also reported.

Perhaps the most significant feature of the data in Table 3 is that the trade in goods between provinces is comparable in size to that of imports from and exports of goods to the rest of the world. When services are added, interprovincial trade is slightly larger than international trade. From a national point of view, therefore, a working hypothesis might be that distortions of interprovincial trade are potentially just as significant as distortions of international trade.

Another important point is the ratio of international to interprovincial trade in each province. Quebec, for instance, has a surplus in trade with the rest of Canada but a significant deficit in trade with the rest of the world. Quebec's overall 1974 trade balance (both goods and goods and services) is in deficit. Ontario has a deficit with the rest of the world, which reduces its surplus in trade with the rest of Canada to a small overall deficit on goods trade; when services are added in, Ontario still has a large overall surplus. British Columbia runs a surplus in trade with the rest of the world, as do Alberta and Saskatchewan.

A broad overview is that Quebec and Ontario run a significant surplus in interprovincial trade and a deficit in international trade, with the combined effect being a deficit in each. The international trade deficit of Ontario and Quebec is largely offset by an international surplus of the western provinces. Western provinces are in aggregate in deficit in interprovincial trade. At an international level the surpluses of the western provinces partially offset the deficits of the provinces in central and eastern Canada.

A further question is the reltive importance of trade and production within provinces. Put another way, if the focus of our study is on distortions of interprovincial trade in Canada, what is the scope for distortions of interprovincial trade compared to the total value of activity in Canada? Is interprovincial trade a small or large fraction of total activity in Canada?

Table 4 reports the value of production of goods by province in 1974 as $110 billion, and goods and services as $221 billion. Interprovincial trade runs at one-quarter and one-fifth of these two totals. Ontario, the largest province, is relatively less trade-dependent than the smaller provinces. Newfoundland, for instance, imports from other provinces the equivalent of nearly half of the total value of its own production. Not surprisingly, PEI imports more than is produced domestically. Nova Scotia and New Brunswick import goods and services to a value of more than one-third of the total value of production. In the case of Ontario, interprovincial exports represent one-fifth of the total value of internal production. Thus, larger provinces tend to have a higher proportion of internal provincial product consumed internally than smaller provinces, the implication being that trade distortions are proportionally more significant for small provinces than for large ones.

TABLE 4

Relative importance of interprovincial trade in goods and services and provincial production in 1974 ($ billions)

	Value of production in province		Imports from rest of Canada		Exports to rest of Canada	
	Goods	Goods and services	Goods	Goods and services	Goods	Goods and services
Newfoundland	1.28	2.84	0.75	1.32	0.10	0.19
PEI	0.20	0.52	0.22	0.32	0.09	0.12
Nova Scotia	2.07	4.88	1.08	1.79	0.63	1.05
New Brunswick	2.02	4.45	0.98	1.60	0.58	0.95
Quebec	26.22	53.79	6.83	10.29	7.36	12.12
Ontario	47.89	94.01	7.61	11.06	10.87	18.06
Manitoba	3.74	7.79	1.64	2.50	1.19	1.78
Saskatchewan	4.37	7.51	1.39	2.26	1.25	1.45
Alberta	10.72	21.79	2.69	4.68	3.25	5.08
BC	10.48	22.85	3.14	5.17	1.15	2.16
Yukon/NWT	0.28	0.86	0.19	2.02	0.05	0.05
Total	109.27	221.29	26.52	43.01	26.52	43.01

NOTE: See Table 2 note.
SOURCE: See Table 2 source.

This view is confirmed by Table 5 reports the markets for provincial goods and services. Each of the three largest provinces, Ontario, Quebec, and British Columbia, has more than 50 per cent of its domestically produced goods sold within the province. For Canada as a whole, Table 5 indicates that roughly half of all goods and two-thirds of all goods and services produced are sold within the province of production. Approximately one-quarter of all goods produced are shipped to other provinces, and approximately one-quarter are shipped abroad. 19 per cent of goods and services are sold to the other Canadian provinces, and 14 per cent abroad. A rough calculation would be that, of all economic activity in Canada involving production of goods and services, perhaps 15–20 per cent is 'potentially distortable' by the operation of induced interprovincial trade distortions.

Table 6 reports detailed trade statistics by commodity for 1974. In the total value of $27 billion in interprovincially traded goods, energy products account for something like 3 billion dollars in 1974. The majority of trade is accounted for by manufacturing products.

These data allow an estimate to be made of the value of interprovincial trade affected by some of the distortions outlined earlier (Table 7). These figures are

TABLE 5

Destination of production by province in 1974 (percentages of goods and services produced)

	(1) Sold within province		(2) Sold to rest of Canada		(3) Sold abroad	
	Goods	Goods and services	Goods	Goods and services	Goods	Goods and services
Newfoundland	24	61	8	7	68	32
PEI	45	75	45	22	10	3
Nova Scotia	45	67	31	22	24	11
New Brunswick	37	61	29	21	34	18
Quebec	54	68	28	22	18	10
Ontario	54	68	23	19	23	13
Manitoba	46	66	32	23	22	11
Saskatchewan	23	52	29	19	48	29
Alberta	39	61	30	23	31	16
BC	51	71	11	10	38	19
Yukon/NWT	7	71	18	5	75	24
All Canada	50	67	24	19	26	14

SOURCE: Based on unpublished commodity balances from Statistics Canada, Interprovincial input-output tables

not wholly accurate for several reasons,[5] but they at least suggest that the flows involved with these distortions are a small part of interprovincial trade.

Of the items in Table 1 not listed in Table 7, procurement is difficult to quantify in terms of trade importance but a best guess would be that it is small. Provincial government real expenditures perhaps account for less than 10 per cent of national expenditure, and since so much of it is highly labour-intensive the trade shares involved would be correspondingly smaller. In turn, not all of the interprovincial flows involved are distorted. A rough guess is that 2 per cent or less of interprovincial trade could be involved, and from what sketchy information there is the distortions look to be small in this area.

This leaves the federal tariff and the tax system (particularly the federal manufactures' sales tax) with potentially the most significant impacts on interprovincial trade since their effects are so wide-ranging. Both these policies affect

5 Examples are that Crow's Nest rates apply only to certain trans-shipment routes and that marketing boards do not control all interprovincial trade in agricultural commodities.

TABLE 6

Total interprovincial trade flows by commodity, 1974 ($ billion)

Goods		Furniture and fixtures	0.52
Grains	0.59	Pulp	0.15
Live animals	0.46		
Other agric. products	0.29	Newsprint and paper products	1.15
Forestry products	0.01	Printing, publishing, and advertising	0.40
Fishing, hunting and trapping	0.00	Primary metal products	1.78
		Fabricated metal products	1.65
Iron ores	0.13	Agricultural and industrial machinery	0.79
Other metal ores	0.44		
Coal	0.02	Motor vehicle parts	1.86
Crude mineral oils	1.51	Appliances and receivers, household	0.61
Natural gas	0.30	Other electrical products	1.45
		Cement and concrete products	0.08
Non-metallic minerals	0.07	Other non-metallic mineral products	0.30
Meat products	1.37		
Dairy products	0.41	Gasoline and fuel oil	0.75
Fish products	0.14	Other petroleum, coal, and	
Fruits and vegetables,		chemical products	1.13
miscellaneous foods	1.80	Industrial chemicals	0.66
		Fertilizers	0.03
Feeds	0.20	Pharmaceuticals	0.28
Soft drink and alcoholic beverages	0.20		
Cigarettes and tobacco	0.41	Scientific and other	
Tires, tubes, and other rubber	0.33	manufactured products	0.66
Plastic fabricated products	0.26	Electrical power	0.15
Leather and leather products	0.26	*Services*	16.44
Yarns, fabrics	2.42		
Lumber, timber, and other wood	0.71	Total	43.17

NOTE: Owing to discrepancies in data, the total in this table is inconsistent with that used in earlier tables.

TABLE 7

Approximate estimates of trade flows involved with selected interprovincial distortions in 1974
($ billions)

Distortion	Effect on		Value
Crow's Nest Pass Agreement	Grains		0.59
Liquor buying and pricing policies	Soft drink and alcoholic beverages		0.20
Federal energy policies	Natural gas	0.30	
	Gasoline and fuel oil	0.75	1.05
Marketing boards	Grains	0.59	
	Dairy products	0.41	
	Fish products	0.14	1.14

SOURCE: based on Table 6

the relative terms of trade between manufacturing and non-manufacturing in trade between Central Canada and the rest of Canada. However, these two policies operate in opposite directions, and, while not mutually cancelling, they partially offset one another.

Interprovincial labour flows

The main source of data on interprovincial labour flows used in studies of migration in Canada has been Statistics Canada data based on family allowance files. The latest data are for the census year 1978–9 and are available for adults and children, children, and family allowance families.[6] Many problems with these data are well known, the most severe being the limited coverage of family allowance (no-child households are excluded). Nonetheless, this important data source has provided the starting point for several studies of interprovincial migration patterns, and we use it as well.

Table 8 indicates that approximately 396,000 adults, or 2.4 per cent of the total adult population of 16.3 million, migrated across provincial borders in 1978–9.[7] The bottom row of Table 8 shows net in-migration by province, with

6 Canada, Statistics Canada, *International and Interprovincial migration in Canada, 1978–79* (Ottawa: Ministry of Supply and Services, Statistics Canada 91–208, 1980).
7 Data for the adult population of Canada for the census year 1978–9 are from Canada, Statistics Canada, *Estimates of population by marital status, age, and sex, Canada and provinces: 1978 final, 1979 preliminary* (Ottawa: Ministry of Supply and Services, Statistics Canada 91–203, 1981).

TABLE 8

Interprovincial migration of adults in Canada 1978-9, using family allowance records

From	To												Total out-migration
	Nfld	PEI	NS	NB	Que.	Ont.	Man.	Sask.	Alta	BC	Yukon	NWT	
Nfld	–	185	1816	838	446	5002	441	185	2285	673	9	174	12054
PEI	158	–	1258	614	174	1156	168	91	439	276	11	22	4367
NS	1452	1038	–	3464	1369	7879	712	441	2868	2428	23	142	21816
NB	699	603	3712	–	2557	6142	755	289	2111	1215	40	111	18234
Que.	531	240	1917	3943	–	37480	1505	675	6561	5200	50	168	58270
Ont.	5483	1461	9399	7401	16388	–	8572	4876	27096	20305	297	694	101972
Man.	450	88	943	612	812	8227	–	5327	10781	6865	48	413	34566
Sask.	55	111	394	232	402	3000	3507	–	11586	4970	106	253	24616
Alta	835	294	1790	1326	1799	13020	4362	9834	–	26802	515	1087	61664
BC	403	202	1799	856	1930	11223	3221	4115	15379	–	980	465	50573
Yukon	27	3	17	16	32	162	66	141	817	1290	–	118	2689
NWT	89	26	155	65	251	612	323	353	2110	660	260	–	4904
Total in-migration	10182	4251	23200	19367	26160	93903	23632	26327	92033	70684	2339	3647	395725
Net in-migration	-1872	-116	1384	1133	-32110	-8069	-10934	1711	30369	20111	-350	-1257	

SOURCE: Based on data in Canada. Statistics Canada. *International and interprovincial migration in Canada* (Ottawa: Ministry of Supply and Services, Statistics Canada 91-208, 1980), at 29.

TABLE 9

Internal and interprovincial migration of adults in Canada

From \ To	Nfld	PEI	NS	NB	Que.	Ont.	Man.	Sask.	Alta	BC	Yukon	NWT	Total out-migration
Nfld	(12 767)	169	1 988	835	466	4 743	455	167	2 345	830	34	206	12 238
PEI	135	(1 147)	1 089	601	175	883	112	52	472	263	6	24	3 812
NS	1 865	888	(17 952)	3 334	1 263	6 695	623	442	3 316	2 576	38	153	21 193
NB	656	597	3 419	(17 323)	2 220	5 066	638	302	2 309	1 285	21	105	16 618
Que.	514	223	1 914	3 013	(274 045)	37 930	1 301	590	6 394	5 713	75	216	57 883
Ont.	4 022	1 063	7 280	5 089	15 598	(317 200)	6 763	4 047	27 188	19 740	367	846	92 003
Man.	465	91	796	419	812	7 001	(30 603)	4 734	9 756	6 456	110	391	31 031
Sask.	81	78	387	187	547	2 831	3 315	(30 886)	14 860	5 057	123	266	27 732
Alta	858	355	1 792	956	1 712	11 640	3 379	7 304	(73 086)	24 726	495	962	54 179
BC	406	176	1 587	960	4 548	14 703	2 494	3 157	21 533	(112 024)	1 001	541	51 106
Yukon	36	6	22	21	41	219	55	127	682	1 554	0	407	3 170
NWT	145	21	158	78	253	769	389	350	2 156	929	288	(927)	5 536
Total in-migration	9 183	3 667	20 432	15 493	27 635	92 480	19 524	21 272	91 011	69 129	2 558	4 117	376 501
Net in-migration	−3 055	−145	−761	−1 125	−30 248	477	−11 507	−6 460	36 832	18 023	−612	−1 419	

NOTE: Numbers in parentheses denote migrations within the province and are excluded from totals.
SOURCE: Unpublished data from Statistics Canada

TABLE 10

Internal and external migration of adults by province, 1978–9

Province	(1) Out-migration to other provinces	(2) In-migration from other provinces	(3) Internal migration (within province)
Nfld	12 238	9 183	12 767
PEI	3 812	3 667	1 147
NS	21 193	20 432	17 952
NB	16 618	15 493	17 323
Que.	57 883	27 635	274 045
Ont.	92 003	92 480	317 200
Man.	31 031	19 524	30 603
Sask.	27 732	21 272	30 886
Alta	54 179	91 011	73 086
BC	51 106	69 129	112 024
Yukon	3 170	2 558	0
NWT	5 536	4 117	927
Total (All Canada)	376 501	376 501	887 960

SOURCE: Table 10

Alberta and British Columbia as the largest recipients and Quebec and Ontario as the largest losers.

An alternative source is new data compiled by Statistics Canada from tax return records. These unpublished data use a different concept of migration from that in the family allowance data and so numbers are not directly comparable. Compiled for migration between each of 265 census districts, they show migration both within provinces and across provincial boundaries. Table 9 shows a somewhat different positive picture of net migration by province. While Alberta and British Columbia remain net gainers and Quebec remains a loser in both data sets, Ontario, Nova Scotia, New Brunswick, and Saskatchewan differ significantly between the tables. Table 10 uses the data from Table 9 to show the portion of total labour migration that is internal to provinces. The fact that the internal component of migration is more than twice as large as the interprovincial component suggests that distortions of the national labour market through interprovincial impediments may not be as severe a distortion of the national economy as at first sight may appear.

Interprovincial capital flows
Data on interprovincial capital flows in Canada are virtually non-existent. Information on both stock and flow magnitudes is unavailable; the amount of

TABLE 11

Net capital inflows (+) and outflows (–) by province
($ billions)

Province	Cumulative 1961–76	1974	1975	1976
Nfld	+6.9	+0.8	+0.9	+0.9
PEI	+1.4	+0.2	+0.2	+0.1
NS	+8.9	+1.0	+1.2	+1.1
NB	+7.0	+0.9	+1.2	+1.2
Que.	+10.7	+2.2	+4.1	+4.0
Ont.	–16.3	–1.5	–0.4	–1.3
Man.	+3.1	+0.3	+0.2	+0.5
Sask.	–0.4	–0.8	–0.6	+0.1
Alta	–4.5	–2.5	–2.3	+1.6
BC	+2.4	–	+0.1	+0.1
Total	+19.2	+0.6	+4.6	+8.3

SOURCE: *Quebec's access to financial markets: A
report in the series 'Understanding Canada'* (Ottawa:
Ministry of Supply and Services 1979), at 26

capital located in particular provinces whose owners reside in other provinces is
unknown, as is the amount of investment in a province financed by savers in
other provinces. These data, which could be labelled 'interprovincial balance
sheet' and 'flow of funds' accounts, are not currently produced. However,
constructing such data is extraordinarily difficult because of the complexities of
financial intermediation involved, and their absence should perhaps not be
surprising.

Some limited data are available on net capital inflows and outflows by
province. To the extent that one views capital allocation by province as operating through a national or international market, this is all one requires to evaluate
the interprovincial distortions at work in this area. Data on bilateral flows are
not required if capital is treated as homogeneous throughout the country.

Table 11, specially produced by the Department of Finance for a federal
government publication, shows capital flows and outflows by province cumula-
tively from 1961 to 1976, and for three individual years. The positive totals
reflect inward foreign investment into Canada. The data by province indicate
that the major interprovincial net investment flows are out of Ontario and
Alberta and into Atlantic Canada and Quebec.

Beyond this single source, little information exists on interprovincial capital
flows, making evaluation of interprovincial capital distortions difficult.

METHODOLOGY FOR EVALUATING IMPACTS OF DISTORTIONS

The literature on quantifying the effects of distortions is considerable, beginning with the work of Dupuit in the nineteenth century and continuing in work by Hotelling and by Harberger.[8]

In simple terms, the impact of a distortion is to misallocate resources in the national economy. Resources are redirected to areas where their relative effectiveness is lower than the areas to which they would have been allocated had the distortion not occurred. Figure 1 shows a simple case. We consider a province which has a demand function for imports from other provinces. The demand function D is downward-sloping, reflecting the fact that as prices fall provinces tend to buy more imports from other provinces. We also assume that the province faces a supply function S from other provinces which is perfectly elastic; that means the province is a taker of prices for its imports from neighbouring provinces. No matter how much they import from neighbouring provinces, the supply price will not change; the price remains fixed irrespective of the quantity consumed. The supply function defines the price at which out-of-province sellers are willing to offer imports to the province for sale.

Suppose now that a distortion reduces the amount of interprovincial trade. For simplicity, assume that the distortion is such that sellers from out of province have to raise their price to compensate for it. In the case of an explicit tariff, a payment to the provincial government would be involved before sales could be made within the provinces. The distortion creates a difference between the price received by sellers from other provinces and the price sellers must charge to cover the costs of overcoming the trade barrier. The supply curve shifts upwards by the amount of the distortion from S to S', and the distortion reduces the quantity of imports from that which would occur in its absence. This reduction is denoted in Figure 1 as Δq.

What is the cost of the distortion? We can answer the question by seeing what would happen if we were to expand consumption by the amount Δq. The marginal benefit to the province from each extra unit of imports is approximated by the incremental area under the demand curve for the extra units. This is based on the proposition that the price that demanders are willing to pay for an additional unit provides a dollar measure of the additional benefit from that extra consumption. Thus the incremental gain from expanding imports by the

---

8 Hotelling, 'The general welfare in relation to problems of taxation and of railway and utility rates' (1938), 6 *Econometrica* 242. Harberger, 'The measurement of waste' (1964), 54 *American Economic Review: Papers and Proceedings* 58.

Figure 1
Simple partial equilibrium analysis of the welfare costs of a
goods trade distortion (no terms-of-trade effects)

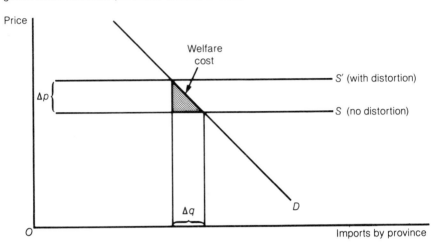

Simple Formula for Welfare Cost Calculation: Formula for calculation of welfare cost:
$C = \frac{1}{2} \Delta p \cdot \Delta q$, *where* Δp *is the price change from the distortion and* Δq *the quantity*
change. If units for q are chosen such that p (no distortion) = \$1, the distortion rate t
equals Δp. Thus $C = \frac{1}{2} t \cdot \Delta q$. But the price elasticity $E = \frac{\Delta q}{\Delta p} \cdot \frac{p}{q}$. Using $p = 1$, $\Delta p = t$,
simple substitution gives $C = \frac{1}{2} t^2 \cdot E \cdot q$, where q is the dollar measure of imports in
the no-distortion regime.

amount Δq is equal to the area under the demand curve corresponding to the
change in quantity.

What is the cost of expanding imports by the amount Δq? To allow for the
expansion of imports by Δq means that additional resources have to be devoted
to production of these goods in one of the other provinces in Canada. The
supply curve S defines the price at which additional imports will be sold and can
be thought of as representing the social value of additional resources required to
produce extra amounts of the commodities involved. Thus the area under the
supply curve represents the additional cost to the nation of expanding output by
the amount Δq. The difference between these two areas, represented by the
triangle denoted 'welfare cost,' is a measure of the national cost of restricting
trade. If trade had been allowed to take place freely without the distortion, there
would be more national welfare generated than is the case in the presence of the

distortion. Put another way, removing the distortion allows for the possibility of realizing the welfare gain represented by the shaded area in Figure 1. The area represented by the shaded portion is commonly referred to as a consumer surplus area. The loss in consumer surplus from the trade restriction is represented in Figure 1.

The same analysis also leads to a very simple formula which allows for the calculation of welfare costs. This is given below Figure 1 as one-half times the product of the price elasticity of demand times the quantity of goods consumed times the square of the distortion rate involved. In other words, we should be more concerned with large distortions of small amounts of trade than with small distortions of large amounts of trade. A further point is the importance of trade elasticities. The lower the values of the elasticities, the smaller are the welfare costs of the distortions involved. There are no existing estimates of the price elasticities of demand for traded products between provinces in Canada, a fact that qualifies the reliability of any quantification of the welfare costs involved. The best guide may be estimates of import price elasticities from international trade, although a simple transference of estimates is not strictly legitimate.

A significant further aspect of distortions is that provinces may impose them deliberately to improve the terms at which they trade with other provinces, giving rise to 'beggar-my-neighbour' policies. This feature does not appear in the analysis in Figure 1 since the province is a taker of import prices from the rest of Canada.

A simple analysis of these questions is presented in Figure 2. Here, instead of demand and supply curves, offer curves for the 'home province' and the 'foreign province' are used. The offer curve represents those combinations of imports and exports which a province is willing to offer in trade with other provinces. By constructing a price line through the origin, at any set of relative prices we can calculate what quantities of imports and exports a province is willing to trade. The intersection of the home-province offer curve and the foreign-province offer curve determines what the equilibrium interprovincial prices would be which prevail in the trade which takes place.

In addition to the offer curves in Figure 2, we can also superimpose the trade indifference curves of the home province. These trade indifference curves can be generated from the underlying indifference map of the home province. By construction, there will be an indifference curve for the home province which goes through the intersection of the home-province and foreign-province offer curves. Because the offer curve of the home province cuts the foreign-province offer curve, there must be a higher indifference curve for the home province tangent to the foreign-province offer curve. Thus, if the home province is able to shift its offer curve, as is possible with a distortion, it can achieve a higher level of

Figure 2
General equilibrium analysis of the impacts of an
explicit distortion on a province's terms of trade

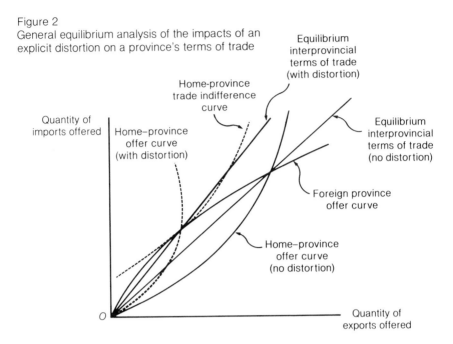

utility. By imposing a distortion, a province is able to improve its terms of trade
with the rest of Canada, and while it thereby makes other provinces worse off
they can presumably make themselves better off.

A distortion when viewed in terms of general equilibrium analysis, may be
undesirable from a national point of view but desirable provincially. If the
elasticities of the offer curves are known, it is possible to quantify the effects of
any given distortion on interprovincial terms of trade.

In addition to distortions of goods flows, we also consider distortions of
factor flows, and the methodology for the evaluation of distortions of factor
flows is presented in Figure 3. We consider two provinces and evaluate the
effects of a subsidy on the employment of a factor in one of them. We assume
that there are marginal revenue product schedules of factors which are
downward-sloping in each province and that factors are paid their marginal
product.

Factors flow between provinces such that the gross-of-subsidy return to
factors is the same in the two provinces. In the presence of a subsidy in Province
1, quantities q_1^* and q_2^* of the factors are employed in the two provinces. The
rates of return between the provinces after subsidy are different, but before
subsidy they are the same. Removal of the subsidy causes factors of production

Figure 3
Partial equilibrium analysis of the costs of factor-flow distortion

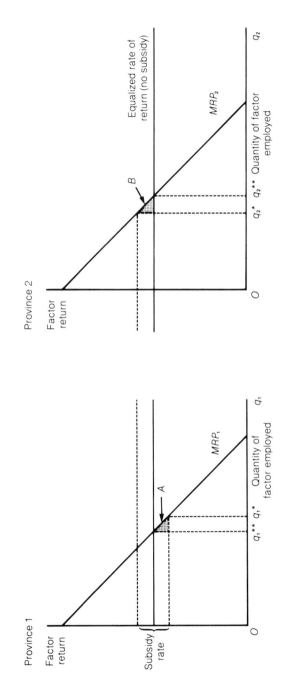

Simple formula for evaluating the cost of the distortion

Cost equals areas $A + B$. Since $\Delta q = q_2^{**} - q_2^* = q_1^* - q_1^{**}$, $A + B = \frac{1}{2} s \cdot \Delta q$, where

s is the subsidy rate. If E, the elasticity of the marginal revenue product (MRP) schedule,

is the same in each province, $A + B = \frac{1}{8} s^2 E (q_1^{**} + q_2^{**})$.

to flow from Province 1 into Province 2. This occurs until the rates of return on factors are the same, resulting in an allocation of factors between the provinces of q_1^{**} and q_2^{**}.

Figure 3 suggests a quantification of the costs of the distortion. By removing the subsidy in Province 1, factors flow from Province 1 to Province 2. The loss in output in Province 1 is the area under the marginal revenue product schedule in Province 1. The gain in production in Province 2 is the area under the marginal revenue product schedule in Province 2. Because the change in factor employments between the two provinces must be the same, by the full employment condition between the provinces we can superimpose the loss in Province 1 on top of the gain in Province 2. This gives an area which is the distortionary cost as shown in Figure 3. This area can be calculated as the sum of the area of the two triangles A and B. For the special case where the elasticity of the marginal revenue product schedule is the same in the two provinces, this produces the simple formula shown below the figure.

The analysis will change significantly, however, if Canada is modelled as a taker of factor prices on world markets. For capital market distortions this is a major issue in their appraisal and will be taken up in Chapter 5.

SOME SPECULATIVE CALCULATIONS OF THE IMPACTS OF
INTERPROVINCIAL DISTORTIONS

To place the subsequent discussion of interprovincial distortions in an overall perspective, some speculative calculations have been made using the above technique giving possible ranges for the welfare costs of these distortions. These precede the more detailed discussion of particular distortions which occurs in later chapters.

Distortions of goods flows
We first assume that a distortion rate is applied to all trade between provinces within Canada. In applying the formula developed above, the two crucial parameters are the distortion rate and the elasticity involved.

Table 12 reports some hypothetical estimates under some different assumptions. Were we, for instance, to assume that the distortion rate involved was 10 per cent, comparable perhaps to the average tariff rate applying to manufactured imports for Canada, and were we also to assume a trade elasticity of 1, a value close to those often used in international trade studies, the welfare costs involved would be approximately $0.25 billion in 1974 prices. Put another way, the welfare loss would be less than one-fifth of 1 per cent of GNP for 1974.

TABLE 12

Speculative estimates of welfare costs of goods distortions

Distortion rate (%)	Elasticity	Welfare cost (1974 $ billions)	Welfare cost (as % of 1974 GNP*)
1 *Assume same average distortion applies to all trade in goods; all provinces have the same import demand elasticity.*			
10	1	0.27	0.23
15	1	0.59	0.51
20	1	1.06	0.93
30	1	2.39	2.10
10	1/2	0.13	0.11
10	2	0.53	0.47
10	5	1.33	1.17

2 *Assume high distortion applies to a portion of trade ($1.5 billion); average distortion applies to the rest*

High	balance			
100	10	1	1.75	1.54
50	10	1	1.00	0.88
100	10	1/2	0.875	0.77
50	10	1/2	0.5	0.44

* 1974 GNP at factor cost of $113.85 billion (National Income and Expenditure Accounts, 1972–6, Statistics Canada)

Other similar calculations are reported in the first panel of Table 12 under alternative assumptions. The highest number reported is a welfare cost of 2 per cent of GNP for 1974. This involves a distortion rate on all interprovincial trade activity in Canada of 30 per cent, which would have to be considered an improbably large estimate. A working hypothesis from the first panel of calculations in Table 12 is that the potential welfare costs involved from distortions of interprovincial goods trade in Canada are quite small, perhaps in the region of one-half of 1 per cent of GNP. An important characteristic of interprovincial trade is that a relatively small proportion of interprovincial trade is explicitly distorted. Since explicit distortions do not operate on the majority of interprovincial manufacturing trade, even the numbers in the first panel of Table 12 may well be upwardly biased.

In the second panel of Table 12 are some hypothetical estimates that crudely take account of energy trade. Distortions in energy are much larger in percentage terms than distortions in other portions of interprovincial trade. The 1974 data from Table 6 report interprovincial trade in energy of around $3 billion, and if we assume a high distortion rate for energy trade and the average distortion rate for the rest of trade, the welfare costs rise significantly. Under an assumed distortion rate of 100 per cent on energy products, perhaps comparable to pre-oil pricing agreement distortion rates, a 10 per cent distortion rate on the rest of trade, and an elasticity of 1, the welfare cost to Canada of interprovincial trade distortions runs at 1.5 per cent of GNP per year. With the new oil pricing agreement this distortion rate will eventually fall as oil prices move towards 75 per cent of world prices with a corresponding reduction in the welfare costs involved. A number of features are not captured in these calculations, not the least being the terms-of-trade effects associated with particular policies and discussed in the two chapters that follow.

A further benchmark of comparison in the evaluation of the possible effects of barriers to interprovincial trade is provided by studies of the welfare costs of international trade restrictions. Since international trade barriers apply on a more general basis than interprovincial barriers, a reasonable presumption would seem to be that international distortions would have a higher welfare cost associated with them. A review of these studies might then be used to provide an alternative estimate of possible upper bounds to the welfare losses which result.

The appendix to this chapter briefly summarizes some of the major studies. As is common with economic analyses of policy issues, there is wide disagreement as to the size of the losses which may be involved. A number of studies suggest the losses involved are quite modest,[9] which might be taken as support for the position that losses from interprovincial distortions of goods flows in Canada are small.

Distortions of labour flows
In order to provide an evaluation of the welfare costs from distortions of interprovincial labour flows, the preceding methodological discussion highlights the importance of examining interprovincial distortions of the stock factor allocation by region rather than distortions of the annual flow.

Thus the key elements of a calculation of the cost of interprovincial labour market distortions are the size of the distortion, the interregional allocation of labour, and the elasticity of the marginal revenue product of labour schedules.

A stylized calculation which can be used at this stage would divide Canada into two regions – the Atlantic region and the rest. Atlantic Canada would

9 The view that the losses are large is presented in Wonnacott and Wonnacott, *Free Trade Between U.S. and Canada: The Potential Economic Effects* (Cambridge, Mass: Harvard University Press, 1967) and Wonnacott, *Canada's Trade Options* (Ottawa: Economic Council of Canada, 1975).

account for 5–7 per cent of national labour employment. If we assume an elasticity of unity for the marginal revenue product schedules and a distortion rate of 15 per cent (to be justified later), an annual welfare cost in the region of 0.06 per cent of the labour bill would result, an insignificant welfare cost. This might be in the range of 0.04 per cent of GNP. This suggests an inconsequential impact of interprovincial distortions of regional labour allocation, even smaller than distortions of goods flows.

Distortions of capital flows
The evaluation of distortions of interprovincial capital allocation is even more treacherous than that of labour misallocation by region. Limited data exist on the interprovincial allocation, and it is even more hazardous to estimate what the distorting wedges are. One argument might be that, save for energy policies, interprovincial capital market distortions are small and some supposed distortions are not distortions at all. On this basis, an educated guess could be that the annual welfare costs are unlikely to exceed those for labour distortions. A key issue in evaluating interprovincial capital market distortions, however, is the treatment of crown corporations and especially electric power utilities. In a recent paper, Jenkins has argued that substantial overutilization of capital by provincial electric power significantly misallocates capital.[10] However, it is not self-evident that such policies would cause capital to be allocated in one province rather than another; they might cause overutilization of capital in all provinces. If these distortions are included, distortions of interprovincial capital allocation become more significant.

SUMMARY OF MAIN POINTS

This chapter began with a review of the concept of a distortion, showing by example what economists mean by the term. In the context of interprovincial distortions, a distinction is made between implicitly and explicitly distortionary policies. An explicit distortion contains provisions which discriminate by province; an implicit distortion does not, but has significant interprovincial impacts.

There follows an outline of the major distortionary policies raised thus far in the debate on interprovincial distortions, and distortions of goods flows, capital flows, and labour flows between provinces are briefly outlined.

10 Jenkins, 'Public utility finance and economic waste' (unpublished mimeo, Harvard University, October 1980)

The main features of interprovincial activity in Canada are examined through currently available data. Some new data on interprovincial trade and labour migration flows are used to enlarge the picture. Around 20 per cent of all goods and services produced in Canada are sold in provinces other than where produced. Interprovincial trade is therefore slightly larger than international trade, because exports account for around 15 per cent of all goods and services produced in Canada.

A simple methodology for evaluating the welfare and other impacts of interprovincial distortions is outlined; goods and factor allocation distortions are analysed.

Finally some stylized calculations are presented of possible impacts. Annual welfare costs of interprovincial distortions may well be very small, and probably are significantly smaller than international trade distortions. A possible implication of this position is that perhaps too much concern may be currently devoted to these matters to the neglect of other more significant economic policy issues.

APPENDIX A: SUMMARY OF STUDIES OF EFFECTS OF TRADE-
DISTORTING POLICIES ON THE INTERNATIONAL ECONOMY

This appendix summarizes a number of studies which attempt to evaluate the effects of trade restrictions in the international economy. This summary is presented because of the absence of empirical studies of the impact of restrictions on interprovincial trade flows in Canada. Because international trade restrictions are broader in coverage than interprovincial trade restrictions in Canada, these studies provide an indirect route to assessing a possible upper bound for restrictive effects of interprovincial restrictions on goods flows.

A range of studies is summarized here, covering different countries, time periods and policies. Eight studies are reported on, from which it seems fair to conclude that six show trade restriction effects that, in terms of welfare, are modest to small (less than 1 per cent of GNP/year). Two of the eight studies show large welfare gains. These differences are primarily accounted for by the different methodologies used.

Table A.1 identifies the analytical framework and empirical results of these studies. A cursory glance at the results will suffice to indicate that there is no general agreement on the size of welfare gains to be enjoyed from trade liberalization. Of the papers listed here, two – Pearson and Ingram, and Wonnacott and Wonnacott – conclude that the gains from trade liberalizatin will be significant.[11] Estimates obtained by Johnson, by Baldwin, Mutti, and Richardson, by

---

11 Pearson and Ingram, 'Economics of scale, domestic divergence, and potential gains from
     economic integration in Ghana and the Ivory Coast' (1980), 88 (5) *Journal of Political*

Deardorff and Stern, and by Brown and Whalley, seem to suggest that the magnitude of such gains is insignificant.[12]

Balassa essentially calculates welfare gains and losses from an estimate of the trade creation and diversion expected to result from the setting up of the European Economic Community.[13] In addition to his own estimates, arrived at through an elasticities approach, he examines estimates put forward by several other investigators. He finds that, in general, trade creation far outweighs trade diversion. From his estimates of trade creation, he estimates a welfare gain (from formation of the European Economic Community) to be $0.7 billion in 1970, or 0.15 per cent of Community GNP. But he goes on to argue that in addition to the static gain, trade liberalization expands the market and makes possible intra-industry specialization, exploitation of economies of scale, and rationalization of production. Incorporating the gains from these features, Balassa arrives at a 'dynamic' welfare gain of 5 per cent of GNP and concludes in favour of trade liberalization in the Community.

The figures arrived at by Wonnacott and Wonnacott and Cline et al. reflect a similar approach of calculating both 'static' and 'dynamic' gains from trade liberalization.[14] Cline et al. move from static to dynamic gains on the basis of the Balassa estimates. Wonnacott and Wonnacott base their figures on the hypothesis that the tariff wall behind which Canadian industry operates has encouraged inefficiency. Removing tariffs produces a rationalization of production and a decline in the costs of production for Canadian industries. The expansion of labour market activity causes Canadian wages to increase, giving an additional

Economy 944; Wonnacott and Wonnacott, *Free Trade Between the U.S. and Canada*; Wonnacott, *Canada's Trade Options*

12 Johnson, 'The gains from freer trade with Europe: an estimate' (1958), 26(3) *Manchester School of Economic and Social Studies* 247; Baldwin, Mutti, and Richardson, 'Welfare effects on the United States of a significant multilateral tariff reduction' (1980), 10 *Journal of International Economics* 405; U.S. Congress, Senate, Committee on Finance, Subcommittee on International Trade, *An Economic Analysis of the Effects of the Tokyo Round of Multilateral Trade Negotiations on the United States and the Other Major Industrialized Countries: Multilateral Trade Negotiations Study No. 5: A report prepared at the request of the Subcommittee by A.V. Deardorff and R.M. Stern* (Washington, D.C.: Government Printing Office, 96th Congress, 1st Session, 1979); Brown and Whalley, 'General equilibrium evaluations of tariff-cutting proposals in the Tokyo Round, and comparisons with more extensive liberalization of world trade' (1980), 90 *Economic Journal* 838

13 Balassa, 'Trade creation and diversion in the European Common Market: an appraisal of the evidence.' In Balassa, ed., *European Economic Integration* (Amsterdam: North-Holland Pub. Co., 1975)

14 *Free Trade Between the U.S. and Canada; Canada's Trade Options*; Cline, Kawanabe, Kronsjo, and Williams, *Trade Negotiations in the Tokyo Round: A Quantitative Assessment* (Washington, D.C.: The Brookings Institution, 1978)

TABLE A. 1

Outline of studies of trade liberalization, with summaries of welfare effects

Study	Scope	Methodology	Estimated welfare gains
Balassa (1975)	Estimates the static and dynamic gains accruing to European common market countries as a result of its formation, taking the pre-integration period as 1953–9 and the post-integration period as 1959–65.	Using a partial equilibrium framework estimates static welfare gains by aggregating traditional consumer surplus gains and losses. Assumes zero cross-price elasticities. Dynamic gains are obtained by multiplying static annual gains by a factor of proportionality which is assumed to reflect gains from economies of scale and increased investment opportunities.	Static 0.15% GNP (1970) Dynamic 0.5% GNP
H.G. Johnson (1958)	Estimates the expected gains to U.K. from participation in the European Economic Community over the period 1957–70.	Partial equilibrium framework. Welfare gains estimated as traditional consumer surplus changes.	Present discount value of gains (10% rate) 1% of estimated GNP for 1970
Cline, et al. (1978)	Provides estimates of the welfare gains from a reduction in trade barriers across participating countries in GATT tariff reductions– U.S., Canada, Japan, EEC, Austria, Finland, Norway, and Sweden.	Partial equilibrium analysis. Static welfare gains are calculated as traditional consumer benefits from trade liberalization (cross-price elasticities = 0). Total welfare gains–to capture gains from increased competition, economies of scale, etc.	1974 Base: Static $1.7 billion/year; Dynamic $8.5 billion/year (for 'formula tariff reduction)

TABLE A.1 continued

Study	Scope	Methodology	Estimated welfare gains
Wonnacott and Wonnacott (1967, 1976)	Estimates the welfare gains accruing to Canada (and the U.S.) from elimination of tariff barriers between the two countries.	Partial equilibrium analysis estimates based on these assumptions: (1) Canada bears the burden of U.S. tariffs, (2) Canadian tariffs impose an inefficiency on Canadian industries, (3) increasing returns to scale prevail.	7-10% GNP (1967) (Major sources of gain: (1) rationalization of production and (2) increased workers' wages in southern Ontario)
Baldwin, Mutti, and Richardson (1980)	Summarizes an estimate of the impact of a 50% multi-lateral tariff reduction on U.S. trade, employment, capacity utilization, and economic welfare.	Partial equilibrium analysis. Changes in exports and imports are calculated by applying import and export elasticities to the relevant margins. Gains here are offset by the costs of displaced factors.	Gains 0.01% of present discounted value of GNP (Major source of gain is additional tariff revenue collected.)
Pearson and Ingram (1980)	Estimates the welfare gains to Ghana and the Ivory Coast from an elimination of tariffs on bilateral trade.	Partial equilibrium analysis assumes the existence of (1) domestic policies that distort prices and thus impose inefficiencies and (2) unutilized capacity in all industries.	Ghana–23-33% of GNP (28% of all gain due to 'Corden' cost reduction effects and production effects) Ivory Coast–18-20% of GNP (86% from cost reduction effects and production effects)
Deardorff and Stern (1978)	Estimates the effects on employment, exchange rates, prices, and economic welfare of both the negotiated GATT tariff reductions and the quantifiable non-tariff barriers on 18 major industrialized countries.	General equilibrium analysis assumes (1) constant returns to scale in production and (2) Cobb-Douglas utility functions, which imply cross-price elasticities are zero	Economic welfare will increase in all countries (but Switzerland) but only marginally. In the U.S. the effect is less than 0.1% of GNP.

TABLE A.1

Outline of studies of trade liberation, with summaries of welfare effects

Study	Scope	Methodology	Estimated welfare gains
Brown and Whalley (1980)	A numerical general equilibrium model of international trade is used to analyse the effects of alternative tariff-cutting formulas proposed during the Tokyo negotiations under GATT.	General equilibrium, Heckscher-Ohlin type model incorporating Armington assumption of product heterogeneity by trading area.	Aggregate welfare gains are in the region of $1.8 billion–3 billion (1973 data).

benefit to Canada from trade liberalization with the United States. Both these factors account for the large welfare gains obtained.

The paper by Baldwin, Mutti, and Richardson can be viewed as an attempt to disprove the notion that factor displacement costs attendant on any tariff reduction outweigh any gain from increased trade. After calculating net changes in trade and tariff revenues, the authors translate changes in imports and exports into changes in labour requirements by applying labour coefficients to a 1967, 367-input-output matrix of the U.S. economy. Labour days lost are calculated assuming a mean adjustment period and translated into income losses. Effects on physical capital in terms of imposed obsolescence are also calculated in a similar rough and ready manner. The major conclusion suggested is that the net impact on trade and employment of a 50 per cent tariff reduction in the United States is fairly small. The discounted present value of the net welfare gain to the United States is estimated as $1014 million (1967). While $1014 million is significant compared to 1967 GNP, the appropriate magnitude to compare this figure with is not annual GNP but the discounted present value of the stream of expected GNP in the future. On this basis, their estimates imply a small annual welfare effect of trade liberalization.

The three papers on trade liberalization in the Tokyo Round provide interesting contrasts. Cline et al. and Deardorff and Stern are more compehensive in analysing tariff reduction effects on employment, exchange rates, prices, and economic welfare. The Brown-Whalley paper is confined to trade effects and the welfare gains resulting. The Brown-Whalley and Deardorff-Stern papers use a general equilibrium, price-endogenous model, whereas Cline et al. use a partial equilibrium analysis. Brown-Whalley also provide sensitivity results for alternative import elasticity assumptions.

All three papers report insignificant ('static') gains from trade liberalization. Cline et al., as mentioned above, magnify their estimates fivefold to account for dynamic effects. Both Cline et al. and Deardorff-Stern report insignificant effects of trade liberalization on exchange rates, trade, and employment. Estimates of welfare gains by country reported by Cline and Brown-Whalley differ quite widely. While the former report major gains for the major areas of the United States, Canada, Japan, and the EEC, the latter find the EEC being the major gainer in all cases and the rest of the world being the major loser. The difference can be accounted for by the terms-of-trade effect incorporated by the Brown-Whalley price-endogenous model.

Finally, the extremely large numerical estimate of welfare gains from trade liberalization in Africa obtained by Pearson and Ingram should be mentioned. The large gains that they arrive at stem from the assumptions of economies of scale and existing distortionary domestic policies before trade integration occurs. The decline in tariffs provides, in addition to a consumer surplus gain, a 'Corden' cost reduction effect and an 'economies-of-scale' production effect, which add up to a significant impact. Thus, for example, of the 18–22 per cent of GNP welfare gain to the Ivory Coast, 22 per cent comes from cost reduction and 64 per cent from production effects.

This feature appears to be similar in all papers studied showing large gains. Each appears to make assumptions about economies-of-scale effects, market distortions, and the like, which are important in the results obtained.

5

The impact of federal policies on interprovincial activity

John Whalley

This chapter analyses in more detail the effects of some of the federal policies listed earlier on interprovincial flows of goods and factors. The federal policies appearing in Table 1 of Chapter 4 are assessed in terms of their effects on interprovincial goods flows, the national capital market, and labour flows.

With some of these policies the distortionary effects on interprovincial activity are not clear. This is because alternative models present radically different views of the distortions involved. For example, with capital market distortions policy evaluation depends partly on whether one views Canada as part of an international capital market with rates of return on capital determined abroad or as national in character and separate from world markets. Both of these views are simplifications of a more complex reality, but the choice between them can dictate one's conclusions on policy effects.

Because the microeconomics of distortions of interprovincial activity have been so little researched, much of this chapter is devoted to analytical questions. The quantification presented afterwards is of the rough and ready type found in the previous chapter.

FEDERAL POLICY EFFECTS ON INTERPROVINCIAL FLOWS OF GOODS

Table 1 of the previous chapter lists four main areas of federal policy impacts on interprovincial flows of goods: federal·energy policies, the federal tariff and other trade restrictions such as the auto pact, the federal tax system, and federal regulation of freight rates (the Crow's Nest Pass Agreement).

We shall examine the effects of each of these using simple microeconomic analysis, to which we attach some numerical calculations based on estimates.

I am grateful to Gord Lenjosek, Jim Melvin, and Wayne Thirsk for helpful comments on an earlier draft, and to Laurie Bland for excellent research assistance.

The details of these policies are sometimes complex, especially with energy policies. So as not to interrupt the flow of the discussion and not detract from the goal of broad policy appraisal, such detail has been relegated to appendices. Appendix A reviews federal energy policies; Appendix B estimates the implicit distortions of interprovincial labour allocation arising from the combination of equalization and unemployment insurance.

Federal energy policies
Over the last year federal energy policies have grown in complexity, first (and primarily) with the National Energy Program (NEP) and secondly with the recent Ottawa-Alberta Pricing Agreement and accompanying modifications to the NEP.[1] The details of these policies are extremely complex (Appendix A). In broad terms, the NEP tries to achieve a number of goals through a series of policy instruments. To evaluate their total effect these components have to be considered in combination, but we shall first consider each one separately. We begin with a 'bare bones' representation of the NEP and ask what this does to interprovincial trade flows in energy products. The 'bare bones' NEP we take to consist of two essential elements: price controls, which keep energy prices below world market prics, and subsidies to energy exploration, which aim to offset the disincentive effects of the price controls.

The level of the controlled prices were of course set by the intensive federal-provincial negotiations that led to the Ottawa-Alberta Agreement. By the end of the latest five-year agreement period, if not before, it seems reasonable to assume that domestic oil prices will be 75 per cent of world levels.[2] Different oil prices apply by date of discovery; natural gas is separately priced; and many other complications in the NEP need to be noted. Since Canada is – and likely will remain for some time – a net importer of oil, imports at world prices under the NEP are subsidized down to controlled domestic prices.[3] The oil import compensation program (OIC) dispenses these subsidies, whose size (and significance) depends on the difference between world and domestic prices.

---

1 Canada, Department of Energy, Mines and Resources, *The National Energy Program 1980* (Ottawa: Energy Mines and Resources Canada, 1980); Canada [Department of Energy, Mines and Resources], *Memorandum of Agreement between The Government of Canada and the Government of Alberta relating to Energy Pricing and Taxation, September 1, 1981* [*Ottawa: Dept. of Energy, Mines and Resources, 1981*]
2 At current OPEC prices, this would happen sometime in early 1983.
3 It is possible to go further and argue that Canada is a net importer of oil only because of the pricing policy.

Subsidies to energy exploration also involve some complex elements. The major feature is that the pre-NEP earned depletion allowances are slowly being replaced by a system of cost-shared exploration grants with the grant level depending on the extent of Canadian ownership in the company. The latter feature forms part of the 'Canadianization' element of the NEP which is discussed below under capital market effects.

The desirability or otherwise of the NEP from a *national* viewpoint is (in my opinion at least) unclear. Despite what at times seems like near-universal condemnation from academic economists, the potential national gain from the implicit transfer of rents from foreign owners of energy resources seems indisputable. The offset comes from the domestic distortions that the NEP creates, with the net national gain or loss ambiguous. An 'optimistic' evaluation for pro-NEP advocates would include federal and provincial excise taxes on energy along with the other distortions cited above as a cleverly designed composite of offsetting distortions whose major net effect is to extract rents from foreigners with little or no distortionary cost. No impacts on interprovincial trade would result under this evaluation. A 'pessimistic' evaluation would have distortions non-cancelling because of their different quantitative size, with pronounced consequences for interprovincial trade. Whatever one thinks of the NEP from a national point of view, there seems little doubt of its pronounced effect on the distribution of rents within the country; hence the inevitable political infighting. Here we are less concerned with assessing the desirability of the NEP than with appraising its effects on interprovincial flows of energy products and on the national capital market. This section examines only goods flow effects taking each NEP feature listed above in turn.

1 Price ceilings

The effects of price ceilings in current energy policies on production, imports, and interprovincial trade can be illustrated with a simple partial equilibrium demand-supply diagram. Figure 1 shows the static partial equilibrium effects of the price ceiling features of the NEP.

In this analysis we consider a national market for energy involving a single domestic price for energy. The domestic demand function for energy is downward-sloping, and the supply function of domestically produced energy S^D is upward-sloping. Canada is assumed to face a fixed world energy price P^W. The NEP involves setting a ceiling price below world prices.

The energy ceiling price produces a larger quantity of energy consumption q_4 than in the absence of the price ceiling q_3, and a smaller volume of domestic production (q_1 instead of q_2). Imports under the ceiling-price program rise from those in the absence of the ceiling.

Figure 1
Static partial equilibrium analysis of an NEP price ceiling

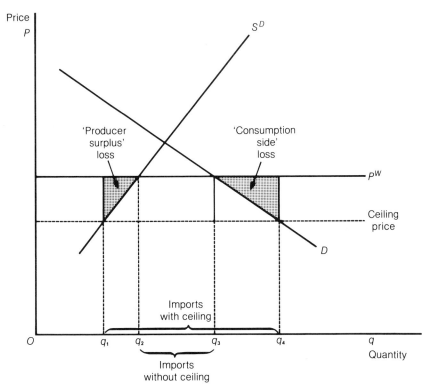

Ignoring foreign ownership for a moment, the cost of this policy to Canada is represented in Figure 1 in terms of two areas of loss. Because imports are bought at world prices and resold at the lower ceiling price, there is a welfare loss on the consumption side of the economy. Every additional barrel of oil imported has a marginal consumption valuation lower than the world price even though the higher price must be paid because of the oil import compensation program. Subsidization of imported oil results in 'overconsumption.' This results in the 'consumption side loss' in Figure 1.

On the production side the effect of the ceiling price is to cut domestic production and increase imports. Imports displace lower-cost domestic production, and a national welfare loss results on the production side. This is represented by the 'producer surplus' loss in Figure 1. The sum of the areas of producer

Figure 2
Revenue loss to resource owners from the NEP price ceiling

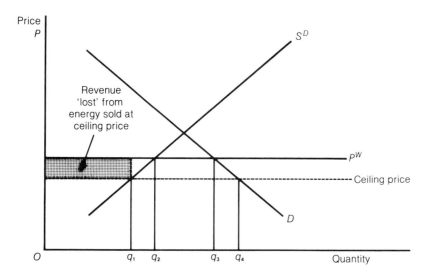

and consumer surplus loss gives the national welfare loss from the energy price ceiling.

The effects of energy price ceilings on interprovincial trade come from the same diagram. Because imports have increased and domestic production of energy has fallen, interprovincial trade falls, since energy exports by Canadian producing provinces to Canadian consuming provinces fall. However, the effect of price ceilings on interprovincial trade depends only on the elasticity of the domestic supply function and not on the elasticity of the domestic demand function for energy. This occurs because Canada is a net importer of oil. Some people believe that the domestic supply function is inelastic and, where this is so, interprovincial trade is not affected. In terms of effects on interprovincial trade, then, the key parameter is the elasticity of the domestic supply function. There seems to be no agreement on the range within which this parameter may lie, making any assessment of interprovincial trade effects difficult.

In Figure 2 we superimpose on the same diagram the revenue 'loss' to owners of energy resources from selling the smaller quantity of energy resources q_1 at the ceiling price instead of the world price. In the extreme case that existing energy resources are owned exclusively by foreigners, the revenue loss to energy owners

Figure 3
Static partial equilibrium analysis of exploration incentives

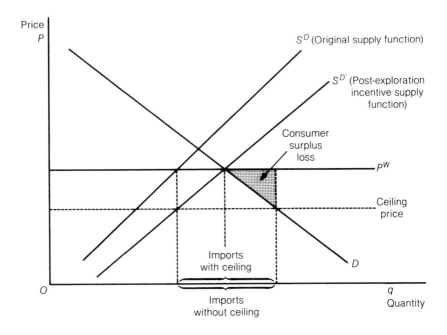

becomes a revenue saving to Canada.[4] The net gain or loss then depends on
adding the revenue saving to the consumer and producer surplus losses. In this
case if the domestic supply and demand functions are inelastic, the areas of loss
fall and the higher is the probability that the NEP is nationally gaining. A key
issue here in appraising the program's desirability from a national point of view
is the degree of foreign ownership of Canadian oil. Current estimates suggest
foreign ownership may be in the order of 75 per cent of existing proven deposits
in Canada.

2 Exploration incentives
In Figure 3 the NEP exploration incentives are also incorporated into the earlier
analysis. The major feature is that the exploration incentives act as a partial

4 A complicating factor is the presence of the corporate tax system in Canada. The corporate
   tax already extracts a portion of these rents from foreigners, and the effect of a price ceiling
   is to lower revenues to foreign owners and thus lower the taxes they pay in Canada.

offset for the distortionary effects of the price ceiling. S^D represents the original supply function as in Figure 1 in the absence of any exploration incentives. The impact of exploration incentives under cash grant or depletion programs is to shift the supply function from S^D to $S^{D'}$, denoted in Figure 2 as a post-exploration incentive supply function.

Figure 3 has been drawn so that the effect of price ceiling and exploration incentives cancel in their effects on domestic production. Domestic production is as it would be if no price ceiling or exploration incentives operate. In this case, the only loss to the economy is the consumer surplus loss, which was also depicted in Figure 1. The exact cancelling of the effects of exploration incentives and price ceiling is not guaranteed by the NEP but depends upon the particular values of the subsidies and ceilings involved; nevertheless the offsetting tendency of these distortions is clear. With sufficient exploration incentives to offset the effect of the price ceiling, interprovincial trade is unaffected by the NEP. In this case, the only consequence is the price ceiling, which increases national consumption, which in turn is met by increased imports from abroad. The volume of trade in energy products within Canada remains unchanged.

A further judicious accounting for the federal and provincial excise taxes on energy can produce that shift in the domestic demand function, referred to earlier, which leads to the exact cancellation of all distortions at the margin. In this case the only remaining effect is the lump-sum loss to owners of already discovered energy resources.

In practice many marginal distortions operate under the NEP and compound and offset each other in subtle ways. Several of these distortions are ignored in the diagrams drawn. They include special incentives to frontier exploration, price controls on natural gas, provisions for tar sands, and so on. An estimate of the overall impact of the NEP, which depends upon a complicated calculation of the offsetting features of these policies, is beyond the scope of the present study. There is reason to believe that the extent of offset in exploration incentives will be larger than the difference between ceiling and world prices under the schedule of energy prices announced in the federal-provincial oil agreement of September 1981. In some of the frontier regions substantial incentives result in a sharp rightward shift of the $S^{D'}$ function. This has the effect of artificially stimulating interprovincial trade.

Removal of all NEP distortions, both ceiling prices and exploration incentives, would result in a non-distorted situation. From a 'global' point of view this would produce the appropriate volume of interprovincial trade. It is possible through cancellation of the distortionary features of current energy policies that interprovincial trade remains largely unchanged as a result of NEP policies, although such a precise cancellation of offsetting effects is unlikely to occur. The key parameter in evaluating NEP effects on interprovincial trade seems to be the price elasticity of S^D. If this is small, NEP impacts on interprovincial trade are small.

With interprovincial energy trade running in 1974 at $1.81 billion, a price ceiling set at 75 per cent of world energy prices and an elasticity of S^D of 0.2 would decrease interprovincial trade by $0.09 billion. The associated producer loss, ignoring offsetting production incentive effects, would be $0.01 billion. These numbers seem modest in comparison to the possible effects of the federal tariff.

The federal tariff and the auto pact
While there is nothing explicitly interprovincially distortionary in the federal tariff – in the sense that the same tariff rates apply to products imported into all provinces – it may affect interprovincial trade more than any other set of policies currently in place in Canada. This occurs because the tariff provides substantial protection to domestic manufacturing industry, which is heavily concentrated in Quebec and Ontario. The prairie and Atlantic provinces, which are exporters of natural resource and agricultural items, receive little or no protection. Ontario and Quebec are thus able to sell manufacturing products at gross-of-tariff prices, whereas without tariff protection these products would have to be sold to consuming provinces on a net-of-tariff basis. The tariff differential, by providing substantial protection to these industries, makes them larger than they otherwise would be and, more important, able to sell products to western Canada at higher prices than would be possible in the absence of the tariff.

Figure 4 gives a stylized representation of the effects of the tariff on the consumption and production of manufactured goods in Canada. We assume a domestic demand function for manufactured products drawn downward sloping as the curve D_M. There is a domestic supply function of manufactured goods in Canada provided by manufacturing provinces (Ontario and Quebec), and there is also a fixed world price for manufactured goods. In the absence of the tariff the world supply function is perfectly elastic at the world price P_W. In the presence of the tariff this supply function shifts upwards by the amount of the tariff to the dotted line $P_W{}^{WT}$. In the absence of the tariff, the quantity of domestic production is q_1, and consumption is q_2, with imports into Canada the difference between q_1 and q_2. In the presence of the tariff, prices in Canada paid by consumers rise to $P_W{}^{WT}$, quantity consumed falls from q_2 to q_4, but domestic production increases from q_1 to q_3 as more expensive domestic products displace cheaper world products. There is increased production by producing provinces and increased interprovincial trade, even though there is a reduction in the consumption of manufactured goods.

Figure 4
Impact of the federal tariff on the consumption and production
of manufactured goods in Canada

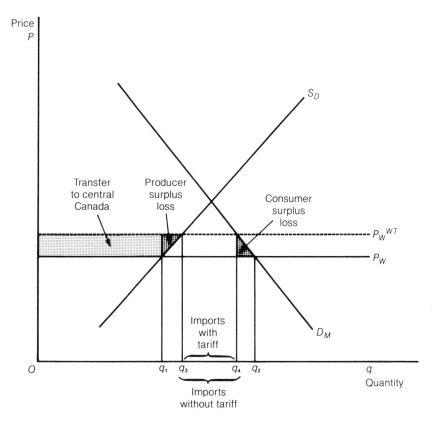

In addition to the expansion of interprovincial trade, higher prices are now paid to producing provinces than would be the case in the absence of the tariff. A transfer takes place to producing provinces denoted in the diagram by the shaded area marked 'transfer to Central Canada.' On top of this transfer there is a cost to the economy represented by the producer surplus loss and the consumer surplus loss, in the two shaded triangular areas. These losses are similar to the losses shown earlier in the analysis of the NEP. The effect of the federal tariff is to impose significant losses on consuming provinces of manufactured products in western and Atlantic Canada. A similar effect can be claimed for the protection of the auto industry in central Canada through the auto pact.[5]

These losses have been discussed by Pinchin, who calculates the effects of the tariff on provincial 'real' incomes.[6] Pinchin considers unilateral removal of the federal tariff in Canada using 1970 data under different assumptions as to the accompanying change in the exchange rate. He estimates 'net cash costs' of the tariff as forced income transfers from consumers to producers which are over and above domestic welfare losses caused by the tariff. Removal of the tariff eliminates the annual interregional transfers from regions consuming manufactured goods to regions producing them.

Pinchin's results are shown in Table 1. Both Ontario and Quebec are gainers from the tariff, with the largest absolute amount going to Ontario in the case where no exchange rate change occurs. The estimates are, however, sensitive to the assumed devaluation of the Canadian dollar which accompanies the tariff elimination. An approximate conclusion from Pinchin would be that, in income terms, Ontario and Quebec are each made better off by around 1 per cent through the operation of the federal tariff. This is approximately consistent with the data and analysis presented earlier. An average federal tariff on manufactured goods of 10 per cent (approximately current orders of magnitude) would improve central Canada's terms of trade with western Canada by the same order of magnitude. If central Canadian manufacturing exports to western Canada are around 10 per cent of provincial output (an estimate roughly consistent with the data presented in the previous chapter) this would yield the approximate Pinchin result.

The federal tax system
Most of the federal tax system has little effect on interprovincial flows of goods. The income and corporate taxes contain provisions which indirectly favour certain regions, but these features, though little explored, do not appear to be too pronounced. One can argue, for instance, that lumber industries in the west are aided by the relatively light tax treatment of housing under the federal income tax. In addition, the treatment of extractive industries under the corporate tax can be viewed as favourable, thus affecting interprovincial trade flows in energy.

---

5 For an empirical evaluation of the impact of the Auto Pact, see Moroz, 'The auto pact: a progress report; the national impact' (unpublished mimeo, Economic Council of Canada, 1978).

6 Pinchin, *The Regional Impact of the Canadian Tariff: A study prepared for the Economic Council of Canada* (Ottawa: Ministry of Supply and Services, 1979)

TABLE 1

Net interregional transfers from the federal tariff

	Gain or loss to the region from abolition of federal tariff (% of 1970 personal income)	
	Abolition without devaluation	Abolition with 10% devaluation
Atlantic	1.97	0.86
Quebec	−0.90	−0.55
Ontario	−1.11	−0.33
Prairies	2.14	−0.86
British Columbia	2.11	0.81

SOURCE: Hugh McA. Pinchin, *The Regional Impact of the Canadian Federal Tariff* (Economic Council of Canada, 1979), at 48

The one pronounced effect of the federal tax system potentially occurs through the federal manufactures' sales tax. Currently a 9 per cent tax is imposed on all manufactured goods consumed (i.e. including imports but excluding exports) in Canada; this tax alters the terms of trade between central Canada and western and Atlantic Canada. Central Canada exports manufactured goods and imports agricultural and resources products; western Canada does the opposite. The tax on the consumption of manufactured goods alters the consumption prices in each region. If substitution of locally manufactured goods is the dominant result, a deterioration in the interprovincial terms of trade against Central Canada occurs. This effect is opposite to that of the federal tariff.

The magnitude of this effect is difficult to estimate since it depends on characteristics of the regional offer curves, which are determined by interprovincial trade elasticities for which no parameter estimates are currently available. But this distortion would probably not fully offset the interprovincial trade effects of the federal tariff.

Federal transportation policies
The main issue in federal transportation policies as they affect interprovincial trade is the Crow's Nest Pass Agreement. This agreement dates back to 1897 when the Canadian Pacific Railroad received land grants and subsidies for construction of a railroad line running through the Crow's Nest Pass. The purpose of the agreement was to stimulate the economies of the prairie provinces through agriculture and to stimulate western demand for manufactured goods from Central Canada. Later, the reduced rates on westbound traffic were

eliminated, and the reduced rates on eastbound grain and flour were extended to all rail companies. These were based on the value of the transportation rates in the 1920s. Since then these freight rates have been consolidated into national transportation legislation, and government subsidies are paid direct to railroad companies to compensate them for the below-cost rates on these routes.

The freight rate question has received a large amount of attention in the discussion of interprovincial trade barriers.[7] The significance of the distortion depends upon the relative size of transportation costs and commodity costs in the agricultural products involved. For agricultural products the subsidy applies by and large to commodities exported out of Canada, and if Canada is competing on international markets this subsidy accrues directly to farmers located in the prairie provinces. They receive the world price for their products; these are the same prices they would receive in the absence of the subsidy to export, and they are able to recoup the subsidy rate directly under an assumption that the price they receive for their products through grain marketing boards is equal to the world price.

Various estimates have been made of the difference between cost-covering rates and administered freight rates from the Crow's Nest Pass Agreement.[8] They suggest that the 'Crow's rate gap,' the difference between the shipping cost to the railways and the revenues received under the Crow's Nest Rates, may be in the region of 20 per cent. However, this distortion of interprovincial trade seems of minor importance because transportation of agricultural products forms a small part of total interprovincial activity (see Table 6 of the previous chapter).

A related issue in debate on the Crow's Nest Pass Agreement is whether western producers lose from the Agreement. It is sometimes argued that with subsidized freight rates on western transportation to the East, the East can buy products from the West more cheaply than they would otherwise have been able to. In this view central Canada is the main gainer from the Crow's Nest Pass

---

7 See the discussion in Chapter 1 of Haack, Hughes, and Shapiro, *The Splintered Market: Barriers to Interprovincial Trade in Canadian Agriculture* (Ottawa: Canadian Institute for Economic Policy, 1981). See also Norrie, 'Freight rate reform and regional burden: an analysis of western freight rate proposals' (unpublished mimeo, University of Alberta, Department of Economics, April 1979).

8 See Harvey, *Christmas Turkey or Prairie Vulture? An Analysis of the Crow's Nest Pass Grain Rates* (Montreal: Institute for Research on Public Policy, 1980). See also the discussion in Martin (in collaboration with Moroz), 'Regional impact of selected non-expenditure decisions of the federal government of Canada.' In Queen's University, Institute for Intergovernmental Relations, and Economic Council of Canada, *Proceedings of the Workshop on the Political Economy of Federation: Kingston, November 8–10, 1978* (Ottawa: Ministry of Supply and Services, 1979).

Agreement since consumers rather than producers gain. In addition, the absence of subsidized freight rate's on transportation of manufactures from West to East is seen as hurting the West rather than the East.

Underlying this argument is a model in which consumers rather than producers are the gainers from transportation subsidies. Perfect competition among producers would result in a perfectly elastic provincial supply function, which would shift down by the amount of the subsidy involved and confer benefits on consumers through lower prices.

The difficulty with this analysis is that world markets partially determine prices for interprovincially traded goods. If Canada is modelled exclusively as a small, open, price-taking economy, consumer prices for interprovincially traded goods are determined by world markets, and producers are the ones who benefit from transportation subsidies. This is the implicit model used in the evaluation of these policies here.

FEDERAL POLICY EFFECTS ON THE NATIONAL CAPITAL MARKET

Federal policy effects acting through the national capital market to misallocate capital interprovincially appear to be relatively minor.[9] In this area larger distortions are caused by provincial policies.[10]

The three federal policies affecting capital flows listed in Table 1 of the previous chapter all involve elements of subsidy to capital invested in particular regions, either explicitly through DREE programs or implicitly through specific subsidies to industries heavily concentrated in targeted regions.

Regional capital subsidies, unlike distortions of interprovincial goods flows, need have no impact on capital employed in non-subsidized regions. If Canada is modelled as facing an international capital market in which the rate of return on capital is internationally determined and capital is mobile between industries and countries, all provinces in Canada are takers of rental rates on capital. In non-subsidized regions the employment of capital remains unchanged when regional subsidies are introduced. The only effect of the subsidy is 'overemployment' of capital in subsidized regions with an accompanying welfare loss. The national capital market, as such, does not exist in this model. Only the single

9 This statement should not be taken to imply that federal government policies do not have major effects on the national capital market. They clearly do. The suggestion here is that federal government policies do not have pronounced effects on the distribution of capital between provinces.

10 The effects of provincial policies are discussed more fully in the next chapter.

international capital market operates, and the impact of subsidies in one province (or industry) is so small that there are no feedback effects on other provinces. On the other hand if Canada's national capital market is viewed as either wholly or partially insulated from the international capital market, subsidies to capital employment in one region will reduce the capital employed in non-subsidized regions, the national capital market will be distorted, and the inter-provincial allocation of capital will be affected.

The key issue, therefore, is whether there is a single international capital market with internationally mobile capital or capital markets that are nationally segmented. Unfortunately, economics gives no clear guidance on this issue, and recent discussions have been sharply divided over which of these two stylized representations is more realistic. Feldstein and Horioka have provided evidence in favour of national fragmentation of capital markets, whereas an exchange between Harberger and Feldstein advances arguments on each side of this issue.[11]

The effects of these alternative assumptions are spelled out in Figure 5. In Figure 5a, with an international capital market, the subsidy to one region has no impact on capital employed in the non-subsidized region. In Figure 5b, with a nationally segmented capital market, the regional subsidy misallocates capital between the regions with overuse in the subsidized region and underuse in the non-subsidized region.

Evaluating these effects for specific policies is difficult because even if a choice between the two assumptions is made the policies at issue must be evaluated in terms of the distortionary 'wedges' which result. Calculation of these wedges at anything other than a crude level of approximation appears to be exceptionally difficult. Also, the elasticities of the marginal revenue product of capital schedules are key parameters, and no estimates of them by province seem to have been made so far.

DREE

One area of federal subsidy consists of the programs administered by the Department of Regional Economic Expansion (*DREE*). The largest portion of DREE expenditures occurs under general development agreements between DREE and nine provinces. Prince Edward Island is excluded from these agreements because it has a separate agreement with the federal government which existed

---

11 Feldstein and Horioka, 'Domestic saving and international capital flows' (1980), 90 *Economic Journal* 314. Harberger, 'Vignettes on the world capital market' (1980), 70 *American Economic Review: Papers and Proceedings* 331. Feldstein, 'Tax rules and the mismanagement of monetary policy' (1980), ibid., 182

Figure 5
Effects of regional capital subsidies under different capital market assumptions

(a) *International capital market*

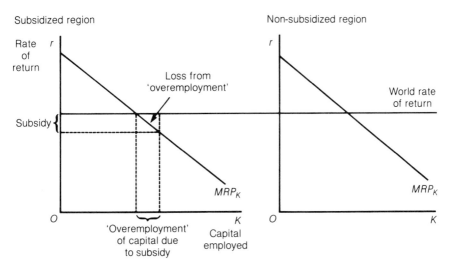

(b) *Segmented national capital market*

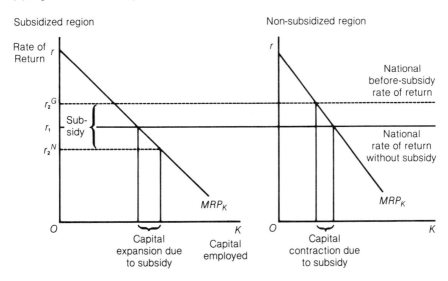

before the formation of the Department in 1969. A significant portion of DREE expenditures also goes to direct subsidization of firms under the Regional Development Incentives Program.

Under general development agreements, cost-sharing arrangements with DREE are available for various designated projects. DREE cost-shares on a graduated scale up to 90 per cent for Newfoundland projects, 80 per cent for Nova Scotia and New Brunswick, 60 per cent for Quebec, Manitoba, and Saskatchewan, and 50 per cent for Ontario, Alberta and British Columbia. Expenditures under this program were around $360 million in 1979–80, about 60 per cent of DREE's total budget.

The Regional Development Incentives Program is explicitly designed to create jobs and encourage capital investment; it provides incentive grants and loan guarantees. In 1979–80 over $100 million in expenditures were made, around 20 per cent of total DREE expenditures. The impact of this program is hard to quantify because explicit cost-share data are not available and the program operates project-by-project.

DREE also operates programs for rural areas such as prairie farm rehabilitation, the PEI comprehensive development plan, special agricultural and rural development plans, and the like.

The total disbursements under DREE are relatively modest, but they are regionally concentrated and in some cases involve high levels of cost-sharing. However, with total investment expenditures in Canada running at $59.7 billion in 1979, the overall impact of DREE expenditures of $0.5 billion is small.[12]

Federal energy policies

Taken in isolation from ceiling prices, the regional effects of exploration incentives on capital allocation become marked. If we assume that all marginal investment in oil and gas is undertaken by 75 per cent Canadian-owned companies, a 35 per cent cash grant applies, which is equivalent to a 35 per cent subsidy on the rate of return in oil and gas development. With investment in oil and gas industries of around $5 billion in 1979, this implies a marginal subsidy of $1.75 billion to oil and gas exploration. Since that excludes allowances paid to frontier regions, the actual subsidy is probably larger. A simple partial equilibrium analysis of the welfare cost of this subsidy alone would suggest a cost of $0.44 billion. However, as we have seen earlier, this distortion can be viewed as an offset to the effect of price ceilings, and its effects cannot be analysed in isolation.

12 Canada, Statistics Canada, *System of National Accounts: Financial flow accounts: Annual flows and year-end financial assets and liabilities 1961–1979* (Cat. 13–563, 1981) (Ottawa: Ministry of Supply and Services)

A further federal energy policy issue affecting the national capital market is Canadianization, the policy of achieving a designated share of national ownership by 1990. Canadianization involves a number of elements, including government-financed acquisition of foreign subsidiaries in addition to exploration incentives dependent on national ownership. With the acquisition program the interprovincial allocation of capital is not significantly affected if only a change in ownership of invested capital is involved. The effects of the incentive program have already been discussed.

FEDERAL POLICY EFFECTS ON INTERPROVINCIAL LABOUR FLOWS

The two major federal policies significantly affecting labour migration between provinces are equalization and unemployment insurance. Equalization explicitly transfers income to low income (have-not) provinces, either increasing the provision of local public goods or cutting local taxes, depending upon the decisions implemented by provincial governments. The interprovincial allocation of labour alters as labour migration decisions are modified in response to these distortions. Unemployment insurance operates as a subsidy to search activity and most heavily affects those provinces having high unemployment rates.

Equalization (unconditional transfers)[13]
The purpose of equalization is to ensure that all provinces are able to provide 'reasonably' comparable levels of public services without resorting to 'unduly' high levels of taxation. The program has concentrated on provincial revenues, being designed to ensure that no province has access to less than the all-province average of per capita revenues.

Although there were implicit equalization provisions in the 1947 and 1952 Tax Rental Agreements,[14] it is only with the 1956–57 Tax-Sharing Arrangements Acts that an explicit equalization provision covering all provinces was adopted in Canada.[15] Through a sequence of five-year agreements, the coverage of equalization has been steadily expanded. The 1967–1972 formula was based on sixteen provincial revenue sources. This provides the basis for the present formula, with some special provisions for Saskatchewan, Nova Scotia, New Brunswick, and

---

13 This section draws on the description in Courchene, 'Energy and equalization.' In Ontario Economic Council, *Energy Policies for the 1980s: An Economic Analysis* (Toronto: Ontario Economic Council Special Report, Vol. 1, 1980).
14 As authorized by *The Dominion-Provincial Tax Rental Agreements Act, 1947,* S.C. *1947*, c. 58, and the *Tax Rental Agreements Act*, 1952, S.C. 1952, c. 49, respectively.
15 *Federal-Provincial Tax-Sharing Arrangements Act*, S.C. 1956, c. 29, as amended by S.C. 1957, c. 29.

Newfoundland. In 1972, equalization was expanded to include nineteen provincial revenue sources. The 1973 revision added another revenue source. A later revision defined oil and natural gas revenues and distinguished between 'basic' and 'additional' revenues. 'Basic' referred to actual revenues in 1973–4 adjusted for volume increases, and these revenues were to be equalized in full. 'Additional' revenues over the basic 1973–4 levels would only be equalized to the extent of one-third. This was a unilateral amendment to previous equalization agreements on the part of the federal government, which abandoned full equalization.

The 1977 fiscal arrangements saw changes in the financing of the 'established' programs (hospital insurance, medicare, and other health) and in equalization.[16] Twenty-nine revenue sources were now to be included (some of the previous ones, such as taxes on alcoholic beverages, were now divided into three categories for wine, spirits, and beer). Henceforth, one-half of all energy royalties would be eligible for equalization, but this now applied to all non-renewable resources, not just energy. The proportion of total equalization arising from resource revenues of all kinds was limited to one-third.

Furthermore, for purposes of calculating the one-third ratio only, the resource entitlements of the seven 'traditional' have-not provinces would be counted even if Ontario became a have-not province. One year later Ontario was headed towards becoming a have-not province because of the importance of energy in the equalization formula. This brought about Bill C-26 (which was never passed because of the defeat of the Liberal Government in 1979) designed to reduce the total level of equalization payments which Ottawa had always paid for out of general revenues and to prevent Ontario from receiving equalization payments on the ground that its income per capita was above the national average in 1979 and in the preceding two years.

Equalization redistributes substantial amounts of income between provinces. Producing provinces contribute relatively little into equalization through taxes, so that equalization payments are made out of the general revenue of the federal government. While Ontario has qualified as a have-not province for the past three years, it has received nothing from equalization. Interprovincial redistribution is heavily slanted towards the Maritime provinces and Quebec.

Perhaps the most significant impact of equalization, however, is on labour markets. By redistributing income among provinces through unconditional transfers to provincial governments, equalization may thus produce lower tax rates in receiving provinces than otherwise would be the case. Alternatively, equalization may produce a higher level of provision of local public goods in

16 As authorized by the *Federal-Provincial Fiscal Arrangements and Established Programs Financing Act 1977*, S.C. 1976–77, c. 10.

receiving provinces than would otherwise occur. Irrespective of which, or both, of these effects occur, individual migration decisions between provinces are affected. The standard view until recently was that individuals would migrate to receiving provinces more often, or leave provinces less often, than would otherwise be the case in order to take advantage of the incentives which equalization has produced.

An important counter to this argument has recently been made by Boadway and Flatters in their discussion of interprovincial transfers in Canada.[17] They argue that the federal and the provincial tax systems induce migration because of the nature of provincial taxes. Resource taxes represent a claim on the rent accruing to owners of natural resources. Individuals who migrate into provinces such as Alberta thus share in resource rents, and migration decisions will be affected. Thus, migration decisions are distorted by the existence of resource rents. By moving money out of resource-rich provinces into resource-poor provinces, equalization tends to offset the distortionary effects of the taxation of resource rents by provinces. Viewed in isolation, equalization distorts labour markets; viewed in conjunction with taxation of resource rents, it has the desirable consequence of offsetting distortions created by provincial taxation policy.

The overall effect of equalization on labour migration in Canada is hard to ascertain. The comparative effects of alternative equalization schemes on the level of unemployment by province have not been studied. Research has indicated that equalization affects the rate of migration between provinces, but the displacement of the natural rate of unemployment by province has not yet been seriously estimated. Whether this effect is large or small is therefore difficult to say. Equalization payments per capita in some of the Maritime provinces, most notably Newfoundland, run at something like 5 per cent of provincial income, or 15 per cent of average wages in Newfoundland (Appendix B). The induced effects on migration patterns might be expected to be significant, but in the absence of any estimates of interprovincial migration elasticities they are hard to determine.

Unemployment insurance[18]
Since 1971 the unemployment insurance system has provided coverage to virtually all workers. Contributions to the unemployment insurance fund are made

17. Boadway and Flatters, 'The role of equalization in a federal system of government: a synthesis and extension of recent results' (Kingston: Queen's University Institute for Economic Research, Discussion Paper 443, 1981).

18 The discussion in this section draws on material in Canadian Tax Foundation, *The National Finances: An Analysis of the Revenues and Expenditures of the Government of Canada 1979–80* (Toronto: Canadian Tax Foundation, 1980), at 115–138, and Boadway and Kitchen, *Canadian Tax Policy* (Toronto: Canadian Tax Foundation, Canadian Tax Paper No. 63, 1980), at 214–36.

jointly by the private sector and the federal government. Private contributions involve a proportional payroll tax up to a maximum insurable earnings which is revised annually but in 1979 was $265 a week. The employer's contribution is 1.4 times the employee's contribution. Unemployment insurance contributions are tax deductible. Contributions by the federal government are determined by whether or not the unemployment insurance fund is in deficit in any year.

Payment of unemployment insurance benefits is related both to the length of time contributions have been made and the insurable earnings of the recipient while contributing to the plan. In addition, the duration of benefits may be affected by the national unemployment rate and the region of the country in which the recipient has been employed. To qualify for benefits, two criteria need to be satisfied. A minimum number of hours of work per week must have been performed or a minimum weekly earning met, and a minimum number of weeks must have been worked. All claimants on unemployment insurance are faced with a two-week waiting period before benefits begin, and the duration of benefits is determined according to a three-level benefit structure.

The weekly insurance benefit is calculated at 60 per cent of the average weekly earnings up to the maximum insurable earnings set in the year. The first level in the benefit calculation involves an initial benefit under which one benefit week is allowed for each insured week up to a maximum of twenty-five weeks in any year. The second level involves an extended benefit calculation. For those working in excess of twenty-five weeks one additional benefit week is received for every two insured weeks over twenty-five up to a maximum of thirteen. Thirdly, a regionally extended benefit portion is calculated on the basis of the regional unemployment rate in relation to a 4 per cent unemployment base across the whole country. Two additional benefit weeks can be obtained for each 0.5 per cent difference in the local unemployment rate over the 4 per cent national average, up to a maximum of thirty-two weeks, where the local unemployment rate exceeds 11.5 per cent in any region. The overall maximum number of benefit weeks is fifty, which defines a maximum benefit which can be drawn over any fifty-two-week period.

Prior to 1971, only eight weeks' contributions were necessary in any fifty-two-week period to qualify, provided thirty weeks' contributions had been made in the preceding two-year period. In 1971 an additional provision was abolished so that it was only necessary to have eight weeks' contributions in the previous fifty-two weeks or since the last receipt of payment under the program. In 1977 the qualifying period was increased to ten weeks in Atlantic provinces and Quebec but more than ten weeks elsewhere depending on the provincial unemployment rate. This qualifying period was set at fourteen weeks in Alberta, for instance, which has a low unemployment rate. In 1979 the qualifying period was lengthened further for repeaters qualifying for benefits a second or subsequent time and for new entrants and recent re-entrants to the labour force.

The unemployment insurance program creates distortions in both the national labour market and the interprovincial flow of labour. At a national level the effect of unemployment insurance (it is widely agreed among economists) is to subsidize search activity by individuals seeking new jobs as they leave existing jobs. This results in an increase in the natural rate of unemployment, a feature of unemployment insurance that has been widely studied.[19]

Two features of unemployment insurance affect interprovincial labour flows. Though in general the program is applied equally across provinces, there are some regionally specific benefits: regional fishermen's benefits and the extended benefits that reflect the level of unemployment in regions. These two features are the only characteristics of the unemployment insurance program that explicitly distort the interprovincial flow of labour across regions. However, if one argues that certain regions (such as the Maritimes), have a natural rate of unemployment higher than elsewhere, the program's major effect will be an income transfer to those regions. Alternatively, if one argues that a long-term structural readjustment is taking place in labour markets in Canada from areas of high unemployment to areas of low unemployment, particularly from the Maritimes to Alberta, then the unemployment insurance program may substantially impede flows of labour that would reduce unemployment rates.

No estimates have been made of the impact of unemployment insurance on the size of labour flows between regions; nor have the welfare costs to the national economy of this system been assessed. The presumption seems to be that the aggregate effects on the national labour market outweigh the effects on interprovincial labour flows.

IMPLICATIONS FROM THE EVALUATION OF FEDERAL POLICY EFFECTS

The federal policies identified in the previous chapter as affecting the interprovincial trade in goods and the interprovincial allocation of factors of production have been examined in more detail. A complete analysis of any of these policies is complicated by the fact that each contains details and subtleties whose consequences are impossible to quantify. The broad evaluation offered is in line with

19 See Grubel, Maki, and Sax, 'Real and insurance-induced unemployment in Canada' (1975), 8 *Canadian Journal of Economics* 174; Green and Cousineau, *Unemployment in Canada: The Impact of Unemployment Insurance* (Ottawa: Economic Council of Canada, 1976); and Lazar, 'The impact of the 1971 unemployment insurance revisions on unemployment rates: another look' (1978), 11 *Canadian Journal of Economics* 559.

the overview presented in the previous chapter 4, with the individual features of each policy drawn out more clearly.

APPENDIX A: THE NATIONAL ENERGY PROGRAM AND THE OTTAWA-ALBERTA ENERGY PRICING AND TAXATION AGREEMENT[20]

(Prepared by Gordon J. Lenjosek)

The National Energy Program (NEP) is a set of federal energy policies designed to achieve the following objectives:

– to provide revenue for the federal government to manage the Canadian economy;
– to restructure Canada's energy system to balance domestic oil supplies with domestic demand by 1990;
– to achieve an equitable sharing of energy benefits and burdens among Canadians;
– to lead to a high level of Canadian ownership and control of the energy sector;
– to expand the role of the public sector in oil and gas; and
– to ensure greater industrial benefits from energy development.

Concerned primarily with the petroleum and natural gas sectors of the economy, the NEP incorporates a system of pricing, taxation, and incentives. An estimated $16.7 billion is to be spent over the period 1980–3, with an additional $2.5 billion committed for use later in the decade.

An agreement between the federal and Alberta governments concerning the pricing and taxation of crude oil, natural gas, synthetic crude oil, and natural gas liquids produced in Alberta has recently been signed. This Ottawa-Alberta Energy Pricing and Taxation Agreement (OAPTA) began 1 September 1981 and is to remain in effect over the period ending 31 December 1986. While it modifies some of the detail of the NEP, especially with respect to the schedule of oil and natural gas prices, the basic tenets of the latter remain unaltered. The changes that do occur are included as necessary in the following survey. A summary of the NEP complete with the OAPTA modifications is provided in Table A.1.

Oil pricing policy
The federal government is committed to a single price for crude oil in Canada subject to transportation cost differences. A new price system has therefore been established that blends the costs of different oil sources into one weighted-

---

20 Much of the subsequent discussion draws heavily on the *National Energy Program 1980* and *Memorandum of Agreement*.

TABLE A. 1

The National Energy Program as revised by the Ottawa-Alberta Agreement

PRICING
Oil
– A price and price schedule have been established for conventional old oil and for new oil, i.e. conventional new oil, synthetic oil, and oil from the Canada lands.
– The conventional old oil price will not exceed 75% of world prices.
– The new oil reference price (NORP) will not exceed 100% of world price.
– A petroleum compensation charge additional to the conventional old oil price will incorporate the costs of oil import compensation and the NORP supplement into the single price that all consumers pay.
Natural Gas
– Gas will be priced at the Alberta border and subject to a fixed schedule of 50¢ annual price increases.
– Under the NEP, city gate prices were established for centres east of Alberta and are equal for the Toronto, Montreal, Quebec, and Halifax.
– Market development incentive payments will be made by the Alberta government to Ottawa to facilitate the expansion of gas markets east of Alberta.
TAXATION
– Natural gas and gas liquids tax
– Oil export tax
– Petroleum and gas revenue tax
– Incremental oil revenue tax
ENERGY INCENTIVES
– Earned depletion will be essentially phased out.
– The Petroleum Incentives Program will provide direct incentives for oil and gas exploration and development dependent on Canadian ownership and control standards being met. It is designed to replace the earned depletion and former ownership and control standards.
– A natural gas bank will provide adequate short-run cash flow to Canadian gas producers.
CANADIANIZATION
– A minimum 50% ownership of oil and gas production by 1990.
– Canadian control of a significant number of larger oil and gas firms.
– An increased government-owned share of the oil and gas sector.
OTHER FEATURES
– Energy self-sufficiency by 1990
– Updated Canada lands legislation
– Regional initiatives for western and Atlantic Canada
– Direct action programs

average price for consumers. This is accomplished through the use of the Petroleum Compensation Charge, which when added to the conventional wellhead price of oil results in the uniform price. The blended price system is to be run by the Petroleum Incentives Board.

Even though the domestic wellhead price of crude oil rose from $3.40 a barrel in 1973 to $16.75 a barrel in August 1980, it remained substantially below world oil prices. A second commitment of the federal government relates to gradual systematic increases in this price towards the international price level. A schedule has been established such that oil prices will rise significantly (to three and one-half times their August 1980 levels by 1986 under the OAPTA) yet predictably and in a manner that reflects Canadian realities. The price schedule and the blended price system are designed to foster the development of new oil supplies, encourage conservation, allow Canadian oil consumers time to adjust to the higher prices, raise revenues for the governments of Canada, and translate Canada's relative strength in oil and other energy into a competitive advantage for Canadian industry.

1 The price schedule

Conventional 'old' oil. Under the NEP the wellhead price per barrel of conventional oil rose $1.00 on 1 January and 1 July 1981 to reach $18.75. The OAPTA redefines conventional oil and establishes a new pricing schedule for it that begins 1 October 1981. A distinction is made between conventional old and conventional new oil. The former is defined as oil recovered from a pool initially discovered prior to 1 January 1981 but excludes incremental oil from pools subject to enhanced recovery schemes commencing operation after 31 December 1980. Conventional new oil is defined as oil recovered from pools initially discovered after 31 December 1980 and incremental oil from pools subject to enhanced recovery schemes and crude bitumen from experimental and non-integrated oil sands projects commencing operation after 31 December 1980.

As shown in Table A.2, the average field price per barrel of conventional old oil was to rise from $18.75 by $2.50 on 1 October 1981; by $2.25 1 January and 1 July 1982; and by $4.00 every six months to $57.75 on 1 July 1986, where it will remain to the end of the agreement. The average field price, adjusted for transportation costs to Montreal, will not exceed 75 per cent of the actual international price for oil nor the new oil reference price, explained below.

New oil. The new oil reference price (NORP) of the OAPTA applies to new oil, i.e. conventional new oil, synthetic oil from oil sands, and oil from the Canada Lands, as of 1 January 1982. Adjusted to account for transportation costs to Montreal, it is not to exceed the actual international price of oil, as shown in Table 3. There will be special phase-in price provisions for Syncrude production, which was to receive the actual international price until 30 June 1982.

The NORP replaced the oil sands reference price (OSRP), the tertiary supplement for specified incremental oil production, and a potential reference price for frontier oil contained in the NEP. These 'reference prices' were designed to make the production of some new domestic sources of oil economically feasible by being greater than conventional oil prices but less than international prices.

TABLE A. 2

Conventional 'old' oil pricing schedule ($/barrel)

	Dec 1979	Jan 1980	Aug 1980	Nov 1980	Jan 1981	July 1981	Oct[a] 1981	Jan 1982	July 1982	Jan 1983	Jan 1984	Jan 1985	Jan 1986	July 1986
Wellhead oil price	13.75	14.75	16.75	16.75	17.75	18.75	21.25	23.50	25.75	29.75	37.75	45.75	53.75	57.75
Transportation cost to Toronto	1.03	1.03	1.03	1.06	1.12	1.21	1.21	1.21	1.27	1.27	1.34	1.38	1.43	1.43
Petroleum compensation charge[b]	0.85	0.85	1.75	2.55	5.05	6.30	8.15	7.64	8.00	9.15	9.35	9.14	9.86	9.75
Canadianization levy[c]	–	–	–	–	–	1.15	1.15	1.15	1.15	–	–	–	–	–
Toronto blended price (Toronto refinery gate price)	15.63	16.63	19.53	20.36	23.92	27.41	31.76	33.50	36.17	40.17	48.44	56.27	65.04	68.93
Montreal blended price[d]	15.63	16.63	19.71	20.51	24.07	27.57	31.92	33.67	36.34	40.34	48.62	56.46	65.24	69.13
International oil price (Montreal)[e]	29.94	34.12	38.86	40.60	42.95	44.00	44.00	[47.30] est.	[50.60] est.	[54.50] est.	[61.70] est.	[68.40] est.	[75.70] est.	[79.50] est.
Wellhead oil price plus transportation costs to Montreal as a percentage of the international price (%)	49.37	46.25	46.22	44.25	44.28	45.73	51.41	52.60	53.62	57.23	63.65	69.18	73.16	74.69

a A special compensation change of $1.85 a barrel was added to the Petroleum Compensation Charge for a two-month period beginning 1 October 1981.

b A breakdown of the components of the Petroleum Compensation Charge is provided in Table A. 4.

c This levy was imposed along with the Canadianization Charge (Table A. 5) to finance the takeover of Petrofina by Petro-Canada.

d This price differs from the Toronto blended price only by an additional transportation charge ranging up to 20¢ a barrel.

e The world oil price is defined as the international price of crude laid down at Montreal.

TABLE A. 3

Conventional new, synthetic, and enhanced recovery oil pricing schedules ($/barrel)

	Dec 1979	Jan 1980	Aug 1980	Nov 1980	Jan 1981	July 1981	Jan 1982	July 1982	Jan 1983	Jan 1984	Jan 1985	Jan 1986	July 1986
Conventional wellhead new oil price	13.75	14.75	16.75	16.75	17.75	18.75	45.92	49.22	53.06	60.18	66.83	74.08	77.88
Synthetic wellhead oil price[a]	28.91	33.09	37.65	39.38	41.73	42.64	45.92	49.22	53.06	60.18	66.83	74.08	77.88
Enhanced recovery wellhead oil price	13.75	14.75	16.75	14.75	31.73	32.40	34.92	37.45	40.39	45.83	50.93	56.47	59.39
Transportation costs to Montreal	1.03	1.03	1.21	1.21	1.27	1.37	1.38	1.38	1.44	1.52	1.57	1.63	1.63
International oil price (Montreal)	29.94	34.12	38.86	40.60	42.95	44.00	[47.30] est.	[50.60] est.	[54.50] est.	[61.70] est.	[68.40] est.	[75.70] est.	[79.50] est.
Synthetic oil price as a percentage of international price[b] (%)	100	100	100	100	100	100	100	100	100	100	100	100	100

a It appears that the oil sands reference price of the NEP was never instituted. Instead, synthetic oil production continued to receive the international price at Montreal (see last row).

b These calculations also hold for the conventional wellhead new oil prices from January 1982 through July 1986.

They were primarily conditional on acceptable progress being made towards Canadian ownership objectives.

The OSRP was to be the lesser of a $38 a barrel on 1 January 1981, and escalated thereafter by the Consumer Price Index, and the international price. The tertiary supplement amounting to approximately $14 a barrel on 1 January 1981, was paid to producers using approved tertiary enhanced recovery methods in addition to the conventional wellhead oil price (see Table A.3). It was conditional on provinces at least maintaining existing fiscal incentives for tertiary production. There was also some mention of the establishment of a reference price for specified frontier oil and other domestic sources when more was known about the costs and timing of its production. In addition to the above reference prices, an incentive was offered to facilities that upgrade heavy crude oil such that the total price for upgraded heavy oil from tertiary recovery would not exceed the OSRP.

2 The blended price system

The Oil Import Compensation Program was introduced in the winter of 1973–4 along with the oil export tax. Its purpose was to control the exportation of Canadian-produced oil and gas and to subsidize consumers in eastern Canada to protect them from the full impact of imported oil price increases. Refiners processing imported oil were paid federal subsidies to reduce their costs to the same levels as refiners using Canadian oil.

The revenue from the export tax was initially shared equally between the producing provinces and the federal government. Ottawa's portion went towards subsidizing the imported oil price to eastern consumers. The tax was subsequently changed and lowered, however, and all its revenues went to the federal government to subsidize eastern imports.

Originally the export tax revenues exceeded the costs of the import subsidy. As of 1980, however, the annual import subsidy was about $20 a barrel, or approximately 53 per cent of the cost per barrel of imported oil, against which the export tax provided only a partial buffer. A gap of this magnitude is a comparatively recent phenomenon. The per-barrel difference between world and domestic prices was less than $3 in July 1978.

To promote the development and production of synthetic oil from oil sands, a subsidy was provided to domestic refiners for buying it at imported prices. This reduced their costs to the same level as those of refiners purchasing domestic conventional oil. It was financed by the federal Syncrude Levy imposed on all oil refined in Canada. The cost was passed on to oil consumers.

The NEP blended price system essentially combined a charge to finance oil import compensation and the Syncrude Levy into the Petroleum Compensation

Charge (PCC). Added to the conventional oil price, it ensures that all Canadians pay the same price for oil subject to transportation cost differences (see Tables A.2 and A.4). the burden of the imported oil price and the price of various streams of domestic oil will thus be shifted from the taxpayer to the oil consumer over time as the PCC coverage of higher-priced oil increases. The blended price was to be the lesser of 85 per cent of the international price for oil and the average price of oil in the United States under the NEP.

As shown in Table A.4, the PCC on 1 November 1980 was $2.55 a barrel, of which 95¢ went towards financing synthetic oil production while $1.60 was used to subsidize a portion of the oil import compensation costs. It was increased by $2.50 a barrel on 1 January 181 and was to rise further by the same amount on 1 January 1982 and 1983 as set out in the NEP. Instead, it was increased by $1.25 a barrel in June 1981 because of the unexpected cost increases; it had a special compensation charge of $1.85 a barrel added to it on 1 October 1981 for a two-month period; and beginning in 1982 it would be determined by an annual average estimate designed to completely finance oil import compensation and oil qualifying for the NORP but not to generate any net revenue for Ottawa as stated in the OAPTA. (The June 1981 PCC was $1.14 over the amount necessary to completely finance oil import compensation and higher-priced domestic production.) The charge was to be $7.64 a barrel on 1 January 1982.

Natural gas pricing policy
Natural gas will be priced to provide adequate incentive for its production and to offer strong encouragement for consumers to use it in preference to oil. NEP city gate prices were established for all centres east of Alberta and were equated in Toronto, Montreal, Quebec, and Halifax to ensure the financial viability of a pipeline to the Maritimes. With the exception of 1981, when a new natural gas sales tax was to be imposed, and in keeping with previous policy, gas prices were to rise 15¢ per thousand cubic feet for every $1.00 increase in the wellhead price of oil. Thus for the three-year period commencing 1 November 1980 and including the natural gas sales tax, natural gas prices were to rise 45¢ per thousand cubic feet a year.

With the signing of the OAPTA, however, natural gas destined for markets east of Alberta was to be priced at the Alberta border. The border price in effect on 1 September 1981 would increase by 25¢ per thousand cubic feet on 1 February 1982 and thereafter by 25¢ per thousand cubic feet every six months, as shown in Table A.5.

The Alberta government would also make Market Development Incentive Payments to Ottawa under the OAPTA to facilitate the expansion of gas markets in provinces east of Alberta. Amounting to a discount of 30 per cent of the

TABLE A. 4

Oil taxes ($/barrel)

	Dec 1979	Jan 1980	Aug 1980	Nov 1980	Jan 1981	July 1981	Jan 1982	July 1982	Jan 1983	Jan 1984	Jan 1985	Jan 1986	July 1986
Petroleum compensation charge													
–Synthetic oil production levy	0.85	0.85	1.75	0.95	1.22	1.09	1.26	1.32	1.63	1.71	1.71	1.67	1.66
–Enhanced oil production levy							0.01	0.01	0.04	0.07	0.08	0.08	0.06
–Conventional new oil production levy							1.65	1.73	2.39	2.95	3.55	3.95	3.91
–Import compensation levy (cost of full import compensation)	(3.50)	(3.86)	(4.40)	1.60 (4.77)	3.83 (4.55)	4.07 (4.07)	4.71 (4.71)	4.93 (4.93)	5.09 (5.09)	4.63 (4.63)	3.80 (3.80)	4.17 (4.17)	4.12 (4.12)
–Total[a]	0.85	0.85	1.75	2.55	5.05	6.30	7.64	8.00	9.15	9.35	9.14	9.86	9.75
Heavy crude oil export tax	18.00	18.66	21.40	23.11	24.58	22.04	23.07	24.12	23.96	23.08	21.73	20.98	20.78

a The June 1981 PCC was in surplus by $1.14/barrel.

TABLE A. 5

Natural gas pricing schedule ($/thousand cubic feet)

	Dec 1979	Feb 1980	Sept 1980	Nov 1980	Feb 1981	Sept 1981	Feb 1982	Aug 1982	Feb 1983	Feb 1984	Feb 1985	Feb 1986	Aug 1986
Alberta border price	1.52	1.65	1.92	1.91	1.91	1.81	2.07	2.32	2.57	3.07	3.57	4.07	4.32
Border to eastern Canada tariff	0.63	0.65	0.68	0.69	0.69	0.79	0.88	0.90	1.12	1.26	1.37	1.51	1.53
Toronto city-gate price	2.15	2.30	2.60	2.60	2.60	2.60	2.95	3.22	3.69	4.33	4.94	5.58	5.85
Natural gas tax	–	–	–	0.30	0.30	0.45	0.65	0.68	0.74	0.92	1.07	1.37	1.52
Canadianization charge[a]	–	–	–	–	–	0.15	0.15	0.15	–	–	–	–	–
Wholesale price at Toronto City Gate	2.15	2.30	2.60	2.90	2.90	3.20	3.75	4.05	4.43	5.25	6.01	6.95	7.36
Wholesale price as a percentage of the Toronto blended price for oil (%)[b]	79.82	80.26	77.25	82.66	70.35	67.75	65.00	65.00	64.00	62.89	62.00	62.00	61.96
Export price	4.04	3.99	5.21	5.30	5.23	6.77	7.10	7.42	8.20	9.04	10.16	11.28	11.93

a This charge for natural gas was imposed along with the Canadianization levy for oil (Table A. 2) to finance the takeover of Petrofina by Petro-Canada.

b The Toronto blended price for oil is found in Table A. 2.

Alberta border price on new gas sales, they would be administered by Ottawa so as to develop gas transmission and distribution utilities in new domestic eastern markets. Payments were to begin on 31 January 1982 and would be made at the end of each quarter thereafter until 31 January 1987. They would be taken from the system of revenue flowback resulting from sales of gas in the United States. Under this system, all revenues from natural gas sales, whether exported or sold domestically, are pooled, and an average price is determined. The revenues are then split up by quantity sold at the average price so that no bias remains towards the export market for natural gas.

Energy taxation
Incentives for exploration and development are to be maintained in the NEP, yet industry cash flow was to be reduced, new sources of Canadian risk capital attracted, and federal revenue increased. Further, the previous tax system gave the natural gas industry a strong orientation towards the export market through higher-priced sales opportunities (see Table A.5, bottom row). It was also unfair in that only exported oil, among exported energy types, was taxed.

To provide adequate assurance of long-term domestic supplies, export review procedures have been designed to allow exports only to the extent that they do not jeopardize Canadian needs and only then if full and fair returns are received for the energy. To prevent unfair windfall gains and simultaneously reduce the relative attractiveness of the export market and encourage substitution from imported energy supplies, a number of taxes have been proposed.

1 Natural gas and gas liquids tax
In lieu of a natural gas export tax, a natural gas and gas liquids tax (NGGLT) was introduced in the NEP. It was to be set at 30¢ per thousand cubic feet effective 1 November 1980 and increased by 15¢ per thousand cubic feet on 1 July 1981 and 1 January 1982 and 1983. All sales of natural gas, including that exported, was to be subject to the tax.

Under OAPTA, the federal government agreed to reduce the NGGLT to zero on exports of natural gas originating in an agreeing province. There would also be a refund for all ethane produced in Alberta and exported. Finally, the level of the tax on domestic sales would be set so that the wholesale price of natural gas at the Toronto city gate would be about 65 per cent of the average price of crude oil at the Toronto refinery gate (see Tables A.2 and A.5).

2 The oil export tax
The oil export tax equal to the difference between world and domestic prices, would be maintained (see Table A.4). The tax revenues were once again to be

shared equally between the two levels of government beginning 1 November 1980. Virtually all the oil now exported and therefore eligible for the tax is heavy crude oil because of a lack of refinery capacity in Canada. The exports are to be entirely phased out and the oil refined within Canada by 1986.

3 The petroleum and gas revenue tax

A new petroleum and gas revenue tax (PGRT) was imposed on net oil and gas production revenue effective 1 January 1981. It was initially set at 8 per cent of net operating revenues related to the production of oil and gas, including the income from oil and gas royalty interests. It was general in its application and not deductible for income tax purposes. Deductions for exploration and development expenditures, capital cost allowances, and interest were also not allowed. The federal government argued that where hardships resulted from the tax it would seem reasonable to expect the provinces to adjust their royalties.

Effective 1 January 1982, the rate of the PGRT would be set at 16 per cent under the OAPTA. The rate on the Alsands and Cold Lake oil projects was to be reduced to 10.67 per cent, however, until the particular project achieved payout. There would also be a new resource allowance, which in aggregate would be 25 per cent of production revenues.

4 The incremental oil revenue tax

A new incremental oil revenue tax (IORT) was introduced in the OAPTA. It came into effect 1 January 1982 at a rate of 50 per cent on incremental old oil revenues after a deduction for related crown royalties. Incremental revenue was defined as the difference between the actual revenue received by a person with an interest in production and the revenue which would have been received under the NEP price schedule. Special measures may be instituted to ensure that combined federal and provincial fiscal burdens do not result in the shutting in of production that would otherwise be economically viable.

Energy incentive system

Energy production incentives were proposed to encourage new supply development consistent with increased Canadian ownership.

1 Earned depletion

The earned depletion allowance for expenditures on conventional oil and gas development and for domestic exploration expenditures outside the Canada Lands will be eliminated and phased out respectively in the NEP. For integrated oil sands projects, enhanced recovery projects, and heavy crude oil upgraders, it will be earned at 33 1/3 per cent of qualifying expenditures net of any incentive payments and will be deductible up to a ceiling of 25 per cent of resource income. It will no longer be claimable by individuals.

Under OAPTA, earned depletion in the Canada Lands will also be phased out. It will be retained for new synthetic oil projects and for prescribed enhanced oil recovery projects. Because of the availability of the NORP and appropriate royalty regimes, the latter will only qualify in exceptional circumstances in which the incentive is necessary to ensure an adequate economic return. The NEP and OAPTA changes to the earned depletion allowance are shown in Table A.6.

2 Petroleum Incentives Program
To compensate for changes in the earned depletion allowance, provide a replacement for the former superdepletion allowance, and encourage investment by Canadian companies and individuals, the Petroleum Incentives Program (PIP) has been enacted and will be administered by the Petroleum Incentive Board. Table A.6 shows the incentive payment as a percentage of allowable expenditures each year from 1981 to 1984. The degree of Canadian ownership and control directly reflects the level of incentive to be gained. The OAPTA modifies the PIP to permit agreements under which a province could undertake to administer and fund the portion of the program that relates to activities occurring within its borders. Alberta has agreed to do so.

3 Heavy crude oil processing plants
For income tax purposes the income from heavy crude oil upgrading plants will be treated as income from a resource activity instead of manufacturing and processing and thus be eligible for the resource allowance.

4 Natural gas bank
A new crown corporation was to be established to provide firms facing a short-run cash flow problem due to the unavailability of markets with the necessary funds to finance exploration in Canada. This gas bank would purchase gas unable to be marketed by Canadian-owned and -controlled firms, enter into joint venture operations, and provide production loans. It was to begin in 1981 with a $400 million commitment from the federal government.

Canada Lands
The NEP contains updated legislation to manage these lands designed to satisfy a number of objectives:

– stiffer work requirements will be imposed to ensure active development of oil and gas rights;

TABLE A. 6

Oil and gas incentives under the National Energy Program (percentages of allowable expenditures)

	Provincial Lands				Canada Lands			
	Depletion	Incentive payments			Depletion	Incentive payments		
Canadian ownership rates:		0-50%	50-75%	75%+		0-50%	50-75%	75%+
Exploration								
1981	33-1/3	Nil	Nil	35	33-1/3	25	35	80
1982	20	Nil	10	35	33	25	45	80
1983	10	Nil	10	35	20	25	45	80
1984	Nil	Nil	15	35	10	25	50	80
Development								
1981	Nil	Nil	Nil	20	Nil	Nil	Nil	20
1982	Nil	Nil	10	20	Nil	Nil	10	20
1983	Nil	Nil	10	20	Nil	Nil	10	20
1984	Nil	Nil	10	20	Nil	Nil	10	20
Non-conventional and tertiary oil projects, and crude oil upgraders								
1981	33-1/3	Nil	Nil	20	(Not applicable)			
1982	33-1/3	Nil	10	20	(Not applicable)			
1983	33-1/3	Nil	10	20	(Not applicable)			
1984	33-1/3	Nil	10	20	(Not applicable)			

NOTE: Depletion will be earned on qualifying expenditures net of any incentive payments. The Canada Lands depletion allowance will be completely phased out in 1985 under the OAPTA. The incentive payments for the exploration of the Canada Lands across the various ownership rate categories are much larger than the corresponding exploration incentives for the Provincial Lands; the development payments for Canada, however, do not differ. Canadian-owned firms must also be Canadian-controlled to be eligible for the larger incentive payments; individual Canadians are eligible for the same payments as firms with a Canadian ownership rate of at least 75 per cent.
SOURCE: Adapted from *The National Energy Program 1980* (Ottawa: Energy Mines and Resources Canada, 1980), 40

– a 25 per cent right in every interest to be exercised by Petro-Canada or some other crown corporation and applicable to all existing interests will be reserved for the crown in the form of a carried interest convertible to a working interest at any time prior to the authorization of a production system for a particular field;
– a minimum requirement of 50 per cent Canadian ownership for production must be satisfied;

– a high level of Canadian goods and services must be employed; and
– in addition to a basic royalty of 10 per cent, a progressive incremental royalty will be established, based on the profitability of each producing field, to increase federal revenues.

Canadianization
Canadianization is a cornerstone of the NEP. Three basic goals have been set: (1) a minimum 50 per cent Canadian ownership of oil and gas production by 1990; (2) Canadian control of a significant number of the larger oil and gas firms; and (3) an increase in the share of the oil and gas sector owned by the government.

A number of features have been designed to meet these goals. The Petroleum Incentives Program dispenses payments that depend on the extent of Canadian ownership and increase with increased Canadian participation. The National Energy Board is to consider Canadian participation in the granting of export licences. The Canada Lands program requires 50 per cent ownership at the production stage. Foreign-controlled firms will continue to be ineligible for Foreign Investment Review Act purposes. Government takeovers of foreign oil subsidiaries are to occur, financed by special charges on oil and gas consumption in Canada (see Tables A.2 and A.5). Initially acquired by Petro-Canada, these assets may later form the basis for one or more new crown corporations. The Petroleum Monitoring Agency will monitor the size, financial position, and ownership of the oil companies to prevent a concentrated Canadian industry from arising in place of a concentrated foreign-owned industry.

While the problem is less severe in the non-petroleum sector of the economy, a 67 per cent Canadian ownership level will continue to be insisted on in the uranium industry. Coal liquefaction plants will also have to meet a Canadian ownership test.

Direct action programs

1 Oil substitution programs
A number of additional programs are included in the NEP designed to achieve a rapid substitution from oil to more plentiful Canadian energy sources. Oil use is to be reduced to 10 per cent in each of the residential, commerical, and industrial sectors of the economy as quickly as possible. The growth of oil consumption in the transportation sector is to be halted and eventually reversed. The measures to be taken to achieve these objectives include the following:

– New priority and additional funds to federally sponsored research and development of liquid fuel options, increased efficiency of energy use, and new energy sources, including renewable energy resources. Enertech Canada, an alternative energy corporation, will be established to focus on supporting commercial production of renewable energy and conservation technology. The Forest Industries Renewable Energy Program will be expanded to apply to organic materials other than wood. The commitment to the nuclear option will continue.

– Incentives for conversion to help households and businesses convert from oil. Conversions after 28 October 1980 were to be eligible for a grant of 50 per cent of the conversion cost up to a maximum of $800 that is not tax deductible.

– A fund to finance the conversion of federal buildings.

– A pipeline extension program with funds of up to $500 million, to be used, if required, to support both the eastern Canada system extension to provide gas to the Maritimes by 1983 and the new line to Vancouver Island.

– Market development bonuses to defray costs and thus keep prices low to ensure the rapid expansion of gas lines from the main pipeline. These are conditional on provincial commitment to the 10 per cent oil share target (below) and the agreement that the incentive be used, at least in part, to pay for system expansion rather than being passed on to existing gas consumers. Support will continue to be given to the electricity sector. Consideration is also to be given to providing financial assistance for propane distribution or storage facilities.

– Taxable grants of up to $400 a vehicle for the conversion of commercial vehicles from gasoline to propane. Support for the development of compressed natural gas as an alternative to gasoline and for the conversion of large fleets will also be provided.

– Refinery modifications to reduce the production of heavy crude oil and the construction of heavy crude oil upgrading plants, including one in Saskatchewan.

2 Conservation programs

A number of other programs in the NEP are committed to reducing the consumption of oil products as a part of a rapid improvement in the efficiency of energy use. The programs to induce conservation include the following:

– The Canadian Home Insulation Program (CHIP), which provides grants to homeowners of up to $500, with the objective of upgrading 70 per cent of Canadian homes by 1987;

– A $6 million program to support instruction for and the design and construction of energy-efficient residences;

– An enhanced conservation program to provide taxable grants of up to $800 covering 50 per cent of eligible costs and additional to the CHIP grants, applicable

in areas where neither natural gas nor reasonably priced electricity is available as an alternative to oil;
– The development of new energy-efficient residential construction standards in general and special standards for northern Canada;
– Instruction programs concerning industrial energy waste;
– Higher prices for gasoline and mandatory fuel efficiency standards for automobiles;
– A Municipal Energy Management Program proposal; and
– A fund for energy conservation through a variety of low-cost projects such as detailed studies of the conservation potential in particular industries, assistance for driver education, and the promotion of ride-sharing.

Regional initiatives
The NEP also contains a regional initiatives program to respond to the special concerns of western and Atlantic Canada.

1 Western Canada
A special fund of $4 billion has been made available to finance a series of development initiatives to be chosen jointly by both levels of government. Examples of such intitatives might include the upgrading of the western Canadian railway system and the improvement of ports. The objective of the fund is to build upon western Canada's energy and agricultural strengths a prosperous, diverse, and enduring industrial base.

2 Atlantic Canada
Because of its heavy dependence on oil, a special additional program of $400–500 million has been made available. It will aid in the shift off oil, in improving the efficiency of energy use, in holding down energy costs, and in developing regional energy options. Measures include pipeline construction, the replacement of existing oil-fired capacity for electrical generation with lower-cost alternatives, the expansion of non-oil electrical generating systems, a special emphasis on renewable energy projects, and an industrial conservation program to support part of the costs of energy efficiency improvements in industry.

Energy security
It is the intent of the NEP to eliminate oil imports by 1990. In the interim, international oil market insecurity will be countered through the following:

– collective arrangements to share large oil supply shortfalls with Canada's major industrial partners through the International Energy Agency;

TABLE B. 1

Population on 1 October 1980, labour force in 1980, and labour income in 1980 by province

	Population (thousands)	Labour force (thousands)	Labour income ($ millions)
Newfoundland	582.9	215	2 206.3
Prince Edward Island	124.0	55	454.2
Nova Scotia	855.0	362	4 178.3
New Brunswick	708.7	292	3 169.2
Quebec	6 310.8	2 922	39 610.0
Ontario	8 587.3	4 370	63 863.0
Manitoba	1 028.0	490	6 041.5
Saskatchewan	973.0	452	5 008.5
Alberta	2 113.3	1 076	15 610.9
British Columbia	2 662.0	1 282	19 952.5
Canada	24 009.6	11 516	160 094.4

SOURCE: Canada, Statistics Canada, *Quarterly Estimates of Population for Canada and the Provinces* (Cat. 91-001, 1981), *The Labour Force* (Cat. 71-001, 1980), *Estimate of Labour Income* (Cat. 72-005, 1980) (Ottawa: Ministry of Supply and Services)

– bilateral oil purchasing arrangements with selected producers;
– an emergency oil allocation system that will ensure demand restraint to the extent that is necessary and the distribution of oil within Canada on an efficient and fair basis; and
– increased oil storage.

APPENDIX B: INTERPROVINCIAL LABOUR MARKET DISTORTIONS FROM EQUALIZATION AND UNEMPLOYMENT INSURANCE

This appendix presents estimates of the implicit distortions to interprovincial labour allocation arising from equalization and unemployment insurance payments to suggest the magnitude and relative importance of these federal policies for the various provinces in Canada.

Table B.1 shows the population of Canada and the provinces on 1 October 1980, the size of the 1980 labour force, and labour income for 1980. Table B.2 deals with federal equalization payments to the provinces for 1980. Calculations of the equalization payments per capita and per member of the labour force for the seven recipient provinces, separately and as a whole, are provided. The total payment per province is then expressed as a percentage of the labour income for each. The data show that the Atlantic provinces gain most from this federal policy. It should be noted that while Ontario is eligible for payments based on the

TABLE B. 2

Equalization payments

	Nfld	PEI	NS	NB	Que.	Ont.	Man.	Sask.	Alta	BC	Seven recipient provinces	Canada
Equalization payments ($ 000)	343 842	79 053	418 943	355 595	1 574 388	(255 049)	294 817	51 517	(−2 657 808)	(−715 502)	3 118 155	3 118 155
Equalization payments per capita ($)	589.9	11.6	490.0	501.8	249.5	(29.7)	286.8	52.9	0	0	249.7	129.9
Equalization payments per labour force member ($)	1 599.3	1 437.3	1 157.3	1 217.8	538.8	(58.4)	601.7	114.0	0	0	651.2	270.8
Equalization payments as a percentage of labour income (%)	15.6	17.4	10.0	11.2	4.0	(0.4)	4.9	1.0	0	0	3.1	1.9

NOTE: Ontario is assumed to be ineligible for equalization payments. The combined population of the seven recipient provinces amounts to 10 582 400, the labour force to 4 788 000, and labour income to $60 668.0 million. Since their entitlements are negative, neither Alberta nor British Columbia qualifies for equalization payments.

SOURCE: Canadian Tax Foundation, *The National Finances, 1979-80* (Toronto, 1980)

present equalization formula, it receives nothing. Further, because of their negative entitlements, Alberta and British Columbia are not eligible for the transfer.

Table B.3 pertains to unemployment insurance payments in general and fishing benefits in particular for the provinces and Canada. The calculations are similar to those for equalization payments with an additional calculation showing the relative importance of the fishing benefit component in the total benefit payment. The Atlantic provinces, especially Prince Edward Island and Newfoundland, appear to gain the most from the federal unemployment insurance policy, as in the case of equalizatoin. The regionally specific fishing benefits also seem to favour Atlantic Canada to a significant extent.

Table B.4 uses the sum of the equalization and unemployment insurance payments to illustrate the combined degree of importance these revenue sources hold for the various provinces. The sum of the payments expressed as a percentage of labour income by province is particularly interesting. While equalling over 25 per cent of the labour income in both Newfoundland and Prince Edward Island, they amount to less than 1 per cent of the same in Alberta.

In summary, Tables B.2 to B.4 suggest that the federal policies of equalization and unemployment insurance, taken by themselves, do have the potential to significantly affect labour migration between provinces. This potential appears to be especially relevant for Atlantic Canada.

TABLE B. 3

Unemployment insurance payments

	Nfld	PEI	NS	NB	Que.	Ont.	Man.	Sask.	Alta	BC	Canada
Unemployment insurance payments ($ 000)	265 484.5	46 481.8	210 097.3	250 923.0	1 608 503.8	1 236 565.1	116 830.0	79 395.9	140 805.4	426 771.3	4 393 308.4
Unemployment insurance payments per capita ($)	455.5	374.9	245.7	354.1	254.9	144.0	113.6	81.6	66.6	160.3	183.0
Unemployment insurance payments per labour force member ($)	1 234.8	845.1	580.4	859.3	550.5	283.0	238.4	175.7	130.9	332.9	381.5
Unemployment insurance payments as a percentage of labour income (%)	12.0	10.2	5.0	7.9	4.1	1.9	1.9	1.6	0.9	2.1	2.7
Fishing benefit payment ($ 000)	33 039.3	7 243.3	16 248.1	8 585.7	7 076.3	1 204.3	612.5	58.6	7.7	8 465.0	82 571.1
Fishing benefit payment per capita (per labour force member) ($)	56.7 (157.7)	58.4 (131.7)	19.0 (44.9)	12.1 (29.4)	1.1 (2.4)	0.1 (0.3)	0.6 (1.3)	0.06 (0.1)	0.004 (0.01)	3.2 (6.6)	3.4 (7.2)
Fishing benefit payment as a percentage of UI benefits (%)	12.4	15.6	7.7	3.4	0.4	0.1	0.5	0.07	0.005	2.0	1.9

SOURCE: Canada, Statistics Canada, *Statistical Report on the Operation of the Unemployment Insurance Act* (Cat. 73-001, 1980) (Ottawa: Ministry of Supply and Services)

TABLE B. 4

Unemployment insurance and equalization payments

	Nfld	PEI	NS	NB	Que.	Ont.	Man.	Sask.	Alta	BC	Canada
Unemployment insurance payments plus equalization payments ($ 000)	609 326.5	125 534.8	629 040.3	606 518.0	3 182 891.8	1 236 565.1	411 647.0	130 912.9	140 805.4	426 771.3	7 511 463.4
Unemployment insurance plus equalization payments per capita ($)	1045.3	1012.3	735.7	855.8	504.4	144.0	400.4	134.5	66.6	160.3	312.9
Unemployment insurance plus equalization payments per labour force member ($)	2834.1	2282.4	1737.7	2077.1	1089.3	283.0	840.1	289.6	130.9	332.9	652.3
Unemployment insurance plus equalization payments as a percentage of labour income (%)	27.6	27.6	15.1	19.1	8.0	1.9	6.8	2.6	0.9	2.1	4.7

SOURCE: Tables B. 1-B. 3

6
Provincially induced barriers
to trade in Canada: a survey

Michael J. Trebilcock, John Whalley, Carol Rogerson, and Ian Ness

Provincially induced trade barriers are surveyed in three general categories: mobility of goods, personal mobility, and mobility of capital.

MOBILITY OF GOODS

We have identified six separate areas in which provincial policies or practices may restrict mobility of goods: government procurement policies, transportation regulation, agricultural policies, natural resource policies, provincial liquor policies, and retail sales taxes. The effect of each is discussed below.

Government procurement policies[1]
There is a growing tendency today for most Canadian provinces to give some form of preference to local suppliers when effecting government purchases. All ten provinces have at least some explicit guidelines that are to be followed by those making the purchases. To the extent that these guidelines are adhered to and preference is given to suppliers located within the province, this can act as a barrier to trade.

There are several major ways in which a province is able to discriminate against suppliers from another province or region. These methods include

We are grateful to Jim Melvin and conference participants for helpful comments

1 The information for this section was obtained from: Chrétien, *Securing the Canadian Economic Union in the Constitution: Discussion Paper Published by the Government of Canada* (Ottawa: Ministry of Supply and Services, 1980); Ontario Ministry of Industry and Tourism, *Interprovincial Economic Co-operation – Towards the Development of a Canadian Common Market: Proposals for Interprovincial Economic Co-operation and for the Establishment of a Canadian Domestic Market Development Agency* (Toronto: Government of Ontario, 1981); and contact with the appropriate ministry in each province.

selective or single tender instead of public tender, inadequate publicity or information on bidding opportunities (such as through maintenance of local source lists), a short time limit for submission of bids, requirements tailored to the capabilities of local producers, residence requirements for vendors, and preference margins for local suppliers. As can be seen below, a good many of these practices are utilized by some of the Canadian provinces.

In Newfoundland, the Department of Public Works and Service Act[2] requires that wherever possible products should be purchased from persons who maintain and operate businesses in the province. The policy, which is based on the 'value-added' concept, takes into consideration the value of local labour and use of local resources in each bid submitted and applies to all government-funded groups and agencies, as well as to the government itself. Also, a premium of up to 10 per cent can be paid for goods that are grown or produced in the province.

The province of New Brunswick has a more detailed program than Newfoundland in that bids are evaluated by both cost and impact upon the New Brunswick economy according to the terms of the Public Purchasing Act.[3] For any sub contracts, information must be supplied as to why the work is not being done in New Brunswick. Where there are three or more New Brunswick suppliers available, no bids will be entertained from outside the province, and even if there are no New Brunswick sources, assistance can be given to create or develop a source. All decisions affecting government purchases in New Brunswick are made by the Ministry of Supply and Services. Purchases processed by the Central Purchasing Branch total approximately $70 million annually.

For Nova Scotia, the governing legislation is the Government Purchasing Act.[4] It requires that Nova Scotia products should be purchased wherever possible and purchases should be made from persons who operate a business in Nova Scotia. As in New Brunswick, where three provincial suppliers are available bids will not be entertained from outside the province. Tenders can also be limited if, in the opinion of the Department of Government Services, Nova Scotia suppliers are reasonably competitive. There does not appear to be any explicit definition of what this means; rather the decisions are up to the discretion of the purchasing agent. As in Newfoundland, a 10 per cent premium can be paid to Nova Scotia suppliers on an ad hoc basis. The express purpose of these premiums is to support particular local industries.

2 s. Nfld. 1973, no. 30
3 S.N.B. 1974, c. P. 23.1
4 R.S.N.S. 1967, c. 120

In Prince Edward Island the policies are much less explicit than in other Maritime provinces. It has public tenders on larger contracts, but for construction contracts some unspecified preference is given to local suppliers.

In the Maritimes there is now also an agreement between PEI, New Brunswick, and Nova Scotia to favour Maritime sources. The policy is designed to ensure that 'purchasing policy supports existing local, provincial, and Maritime regional producers and encourages the establishment of new production activities.'[5] As of 12 March 1980 the provinces are to consider the province first, the maritimes second, and Canada third, based on a value-added analysis. Also, the agreement calls for standardized specifications on all provincially funded construction projects. Furthermore, if a Maritime manufacturer is not available the provinces together will support the establishment of a Maritime producer, if this is feasible.

Since 1977 Quebec has followed a policy designed to maximize the Quebec and Canadian content of goods purchased. The policy principally favours Quebec sources, however, since the lowest bid by a Quebec firm will be accepted even if it is higher than a bid from a non-Quebec firm if this promotes provincial industrial development objectives. The Order-in-Council which gave rise to this policy does not define what it meant by industrial development objectives, although it does say that Quebec goods should be favoured.[6] This policy not only covers purchases by government departments but also includes purchases by hospitals, municipalities, and school boards. For the tendering of bids, when sufficient competition exists within Quebec, as determined by the Ministry of Public Works, the bidding is limited to Quebec firms. This may be extended to the situation where there is not sufficient competition, again if this serves industrial development objectives. All tenders submitted must state the percentage of Quebec, Canadian, and foreign content that would be involved, and for contracts of over $50 000 a preference of up to 10 per cent is applied to the Quebec content of the bids. For contracts subsidized by the government, bidding is restricted to firms whose principal place of business is in the region of Quebec where the work will be done.

Ontario has no explicit preference as such for local suppliers. The Ontario government policy is to give a 10 per cent preference to Canadian and not just provincial suppliers. Preference is given to Ontario firms only when their bids

5 Excerpted from Council of Maritime Premiers, 'Regional preference in provincial purchasing policies: Minute 38–14' (unpublished, adopted 29 January 1980)
6 'Regulation respecting Government purchase contracts,' O.C. 2591–77 (1977), 109 (37) *Quebec Official Gazette* (Part 2) 4655, 10 August 1977

are competitive. However, there are exceptions to this rule; the government will exercise its discretion on occasion and buy from an Ontario firm even if the latter enters a higher bid than a non-Ontario firm. For example, in 1977 the Ontario government awarded a contract for streetcar construction to Hawker-Siddeley of Thunder Bay instead of to MLW-Bombardier of Montreal, which was the lowest bidder.

Manitoba imposes some tendering restrictions, and beginning in 1978 offered a 1 per cent premium to Manitoba firms, but only on an interim basis.

Saskatchewan has some tendering restrictions but usually will only give preference to Saskatchewan sources when all other factors are approximately equal. However, the cabinet may, in its discretion, require that for some products only Saskatchewan sources will be used. For instance, current practice dictates that only in-province sources will be used for bids on petroleum products, asphalt and emulsions, steel and concrete culverts, highway signs, and salt. The purchasing agency in Saskatchewan spends $120 million annually (this figure does not include purchases by crown corporations).

In Alberta, projects which require special permits (industrial development, forest management, or coal development) must satisfy the Ministry of Business Development and Tourism that the project is making maximum possible use of Alberta professional services and supplies. For most purchases the express policy is that preference will only be given to local suppliers where the price and quality of the goods are equal. However, in 1975–6 over 90 per cent of the goods and services bought by the Alberta government were purchased from Alberta companies.

British Columbia has a policy of paying up to a 10 per cent premium based on provincial content and may give a maximum premium of 5 per cent to non-BC Canadian suppliers. In addition, the province may take into account regional or sectoral unemployment as well as the general health of an industry instead of awarding a contract solely on a cost basis.

Despite the presence of all these provincial policies and practices which give preference to local products and producers, it must be noted that there have been proposals made to try and co-ordinate purchasing activities among the provinces so that Canadian rather than provincial content is emphasized.

The government of Ontario, with a view to increasing the amount of economic co-operation between provinces, has recently established an Office of Procurement Policy. This office is designed to make it easier for firms in all parts of Canada to bid on Ontario government contracts and to ensure that Canadian content is maximized in all contracts that are awarded. Also, Ontario has suggested that all the provinces should co-ordinate their activities so as to take advantage of their combined purchasing power, rather than having ten separate and distinct provincial policies which create barriers to trade. The federal government has been asked to convene a meeting of the ten provinces so that such co-operative arrangements can be implemented.

Although it is uncertain how much progress can be made in the area of procurement policy co-ordination, it is clear that there will always be a conflict between provincial co-operation and the industrial development of each of the provinces. As long as procurement policies are viewed by provinces as a tool by which local industry can be established or supported, barriers to the free movement of goods will continue to exist.

Transportation regulation
Since the enactment of the Motor Vehicle Transport Act (Canada)[7] in 1954 the regulation of interprovincial trucking has been undertaken by the provinces. Although the *Winner*[8] case had determined that the federal government had jurisdiction over interprovincial traffic, by this Act it effectively delegated its responsibility over the area to the provinces. Section 3 of the Act states:

(1) Where in any province a licence is by law of the province required for the operation of a local undertaking, no person shall operate an extra-provincial undertaking in the province unless he holds a licence issued under the authority of this Act.

(2) The Provincial Motor Transport Board in each province may in its discretion issue a licence to operate an extra-provincial undertaking into or through the province upon like terms and conditions as if the extra-provincial undertaking operated in the province were a local undertaking.

Thus, each province is able to control the activities of trucking firms within the province, even though a firm may conduct business beyond provincial boundaries.

There are in Canada today six areas in which there is evidence that provinces have created barriers to free trucking movement. These areas are economic regulation of the trucking industry, registration requirements, weights and dimension regulations, safety restrictions, enforcement practices, and fuel taxes.

1 Economic regulation
Every province in Canada is involved in the economic regulation of trucking at least to some extent. The usual methods of exercising this control are through

7 S.C. 1953–54, c. 59
8 *Winner* v. *S.M.T. (Eastern) Ltd.*, [1951] S.C.R. 887

TABLE 1

Trucking regulation in Canada

	Intra-provincial trucking			Extra-provincial trucking		
	Entry control	Rate approval	Rate filing	Entry control	Rate approval	Rate filing
PEI	Yes	No	Yes	Yes	No	Yes
Nfld	Yes	Yes	Yes	Yes	Yes	Yes
NS	Yes	No	Yes	Yes	No	Yes
NB	Yes	No	Yes	Yes	No	Yes
Que.	Yes	Yes	Yes	Yes	Yes	Yes
Ont.	Yes	No	Yes	Yes	No	No
Man.	Yes	Yes	Yes	Yes	No	No
Sask.	Yes	Yes	Yes	Yes	No	No
Alta	No	No	No	Yes	No	No
BC	Yes	Yes	Yes	Yes	No	No

SOURCE: Bonsor, 'The impact of regulation on for-hire highway carriers: an analysis of the cost borne by carriers in the production of regulatory decisions.' In Economic Council of Canada, ed., *Studies of Trucking Regulations: Vol III—Working Paper 3* (Ottawa: Economic Council of Canada 1980), at 8, 11

control of entry into the business, through control of rates that may be charged, or by requiring rates to be filed before they are implemented.

Table 1 shows in what manner each of the ten provinces regulates the industry. Some provinces have chosen to regulate intraprovincial trucking in a different manner from extraprovincial trucking. This situation was made possible by the decision of the Supreme Court of Canada in *Regina* v. *Smith*,[9] where different methods of control were held to be constitutional.

A major consequence of *Smith* is that provinces can now effectively create barriers to trade in trucking if they choose to do so, because they are able to apply different criteria or requirements to extraprovincial truckers than are imposed on intraprovincial truckers. A good example of this is the *Smith* case itself, where the licence issued to Smith did not allow him to haul shrubs. This stipulation was part of all interprovincial trucking licences. However, the same type of licence when issued to an intraprovincial trucker did not carry the same prohibition. The effect of this would be to allow only carriers operating within Alberta to haul shrubs.

Aside from operating conditions differing on the basis of whether trucking is inter- or intraprovincial, a further difficulty arises. The problem is that different

9 [1972] S.C.R. 359

provincial bodies do not always assign the same meaning to licence terms. Confusion arises where there are no common commodity descriptions. For instance, a household goods licence issued in Ontario includes electronic components, while a household goods licence issued in Quebec does not. The fact that there is no uniformity in licence terms means that truckers will face higher costs in transporting goods between provinces.

Although provinces could theoretically discriminate against interprovincial trucking through control of rates, there is little empirical evidence that this practice has become widespread. Instead, the existence of rate regulation poses mainly procedural concerns. For example, the fact that some provinces require different notice periods before rates become effective presents difficulties for truckers operating across provincial boundaries. There are similar difficulties with timing if the rates must also be approved.

Though the above factors can create significant impediments to trade, perhaps the largest single barrier flows from the fact that there are ten different sets of trucking regulations across Canada. A carrier wanting to transport goods from St John's to Vancouver is faced with the task of obtaining approvals from each province, since they all regulate entry into interprovincial trucking. Such a requirement may be extremely costly to satisfy. In fact, in a recent study Bonsor estimated that the cost to carriers across Canada of participating in the regulatory process was in the region of $40 million in 1978.[10] The largest component of this amount consists of the costs of obtaining the necessary licences and opposing applications by other carriers. The majority of these costs are experienced by Ontario-based carriers, not only because there are more of them but also because the regulatory process in Ontario is quite formal. Thus, the costs of compliance, especially in Ontario, are such that interprovincial carriers will experience high costs of doing business.

2 Registration requirements

Closely related to the issue of economic regulation are the registration requirements of each of the provinces. With the issuance of a licence or permit to operate, carriers must pay all the necessary registration fees, which in some instances can be quite large. The impact of these fees upon interprovincial trucking is that, in the absence of reciprocity agreements, trucks moving across provincial boundaries will be required to pay the fees and obtain licence plates from all the provinces through which movements occur. Obviously such a system will entail significant costs for the interprovincial carrier.

---

10 Bonsor, 'The impact of regulation' (see source to Table 1 above), at 58

However, on 1 April 1981 a reciprocity agreement was adopted by most of the provinces. This agreement, called the Canadian Agreement of Vehicle Registration (CAVR), came into force in all provinces except Quebec, Nova Scotia, and PEI, and it was adopted by the first two provinces on 1 April 1982. The CAVR is a type of pro-rate scheme where the registration fees are paid to one province only (the home province of the carrier) and then are distributed to the other provinces on the basis of mileage travelled within that other province. This agreement will go a long way towards reducing the burden of multiple fees, although it only covers registratoin fees. Carriers must still meet the other requirements which a province may have such as insurance premiums, operating authority fees, or fuel taxes. As with registration fees, these costs too can be non-trivial.

3 Weight and dimension regulations

A significant concern for truckers who operate interprovincially is the degree of non-uniformity which exists in the area of permissible truck weights and dimensions. In general, the prairie provinces have the lowest permissible weight levels, and the central provinces of Ontario and Quebec have the highest allowable levels. The reason for this is partly that the road beds in central Canada are of much higher quality. On the prairies the softer soil means the roads cannot withstand heavy traffic. As a result it is unlikely that uniformity can ever be achieved.

A recent conference of the Council of Ministers Responsible for Transportation and Highway Safety has suggested that increased uniformity is possible in regulations on axle spacing and weight distribution.[11] It would be much less costly for truckers if these regulations were relatively uniform across the country, and the conference decided to undertake research into this matter.

Dimensions also vary among the provinces. By and large, the prairie provinces allow longer vehicle lengths than the central provinces. As a result, interprovincial truckers will either have to change their trucks as they move between provinces or, as is more likely, make sure that the trucks they use meet the requirements of all the provinces they pass through. Both these solutions, however, involve significant costs to the carriers and ultimately to their customers.

11 Conference of the Council of Ministers Responsible for Transportation and Highway Safety. Joint Roads and Transportation Association of Canada – Canadian Conference of Motor Transport Administrators Committee. 'Report on vehicle weights and dimensions, Agenda Item 5' [unpublished document no. 860–85 / 006 prepared for the 17th Conference in Fredericton NB 27 April 1981]

4 Safety restrictions

To the extent that safety restrictions vary between provinces, it can be argued that barriers to trade are created. It is possible for a province to restrict the entry of truckers into that province by adopting safety measures that are either impossible or very costly for out-of-province carriers to meet.

In Ontario today there is a requirement that dump trucks be inspected twice a year. Similar requirements apply to buses. Recently the Ontario government proposed that this practice of periodic examination should be extended to all commercial vehicles. Resistance from out-of-province carriers caused this proposal to be shelved for the time being. However, had it been implemented, out-of-province trucks would have had to meet those requirements as well. In the absence of a reciprocity agreement between Ontario and the home jurisdiction, truckers passing through Ontario would be required to have their trucks inspected in Ontario, thereby adding to the cost of interprovincial transport.

5 Enforcement

It has sometimes been suggested that provinces enforce trucking regulations more strictly against out-of-province truckers than against intraprovincial carriers. Where this does occur, interprovincial trucks will face higher costs than provincial truckers. For example, some truckers claim that out-of-province drivers are jailed, or their trucks impounded, more frequently for alleged violations of regulations by some provincial authorities than is the case with local truckers. Also, the prairie provinces and Quebec use registration procedures as an enforcement mechanism. Before a licence plate will be issued to a trucker these provinces will check to make sure that all the local statutory requirements are met – such as safety, insurance, registration for fuel tax and sales tax, and whether the truck has a proper operating authority. Out-of-province operators often find these requirements oppressive.

6 Fuel and sales taxes

Every province in Canada except Alberta taxes diesel fuel. Because diesel fuel is such an important commodity for interprovincial trucking, it is possible for provinces to erect barriers to trade through the taxing system. Although the factors discussed below indicate that such barriers do exist within Canada today, it is unclear how significant they are.

The first way in which fuel taxes can create distortions in trade flows is simply through differences in the tax rates. All other factors equal, a trucker would prefer to purchase and consume diesel fuel in a province with a low tax rate. This would suggest that carriers would want to do more business in Alberta, which has no tax, than in, say, Ontario, which has a tax rate of 27 per cent of the price, or 7.8¢ a litre. Obviously there is a limit to the effect of such a difference since fuel tax is just one component in the total cost structure. Moreover, any distortions implied by these differences are likely to be limited to minor movements across provincial boundaries to exploit their differences and in this sense will have effects similar to those induced by differences in provincial retail sales taxes (see below).

The second method of altering trucking activities is through the actual administration of the tax. Most provinces, such as Ontario, assess the tax on the basis of fuel actually used within the province. If the trucker pays tax on the amount purchased but does not use it all in Ontario, the province will refund the excess tax paid. However, in Quebec the excess tax is not refunded; rather, it is used as a credit against any tax due in the future. The problem with this is that the credit must be used up within twelve months or it is lost. Thus, this policy can alter the buying behaviour of carriers and provide an incentive to travel more in Quebec than would otherwise be done.

As was the situation with economic regulation, a further reason why fuel taxes create barriers to interprovincial movement is the cost associated with the administration of the tax. Carriers must pay the tax in each of the provinces they travel through, and the data which must be supplied are quite detailed. For interprovincial truckers this can be an expensive process.

Despite the potential for distortions, recent initiatives suggest that perhaps this problem will be reduced in the future. For example, the Maritime provinces of Nova Scotia, New Brunswick, and PEI now have a reciprocity agreement whereby truckers purchase fuel wherever they choose within the region and the taxes are later allocated amongst them based on mileage travelled in each province. Also, to reduce administrative costs, all ten provinces now allow truckers to use the same form for calculating the tax payable. Although tax returns must still be filed in each jurisdiction, this form, called IR-1, should generate significant cost-savings for carriers.

The existence of provincial sales tax in all provinces except Alberta represents another potential source of barriers to interprovincial trucking. A barrier exists because if each province assessed a sales tax on every truck that entered, as it is legally entitled to do, there would be a disincentive for truckers to move interprovincially. For instance, a carrier in Cornwall, Ontario, who would otherwise do so, may decide not to transport goods into Quebec if he is forced to pay the 8 per cent Quebec sales tax on every truck in addition to the 7 per cent Ontario tax. In this manner the Quebec market may be too expensive for Ontario truckers to operate in, and vice versa.

Although it is a potential problem, the actual consequence of provincial sales tax on trucking may not be too great. There now exists an agreement among the provinces, called the Interprovincial Sales Tax Agreement (ISTA), whereby the provinces agree that a carrier who abides by the agreement needs only to pay the sales tax in his home jurisdiction. This amount is then distributed to other provinces according to the distance travelled by the carrier's fleet in each province.

A problem that remains occurs because many carriers travel into the United States. At the moment the ISTA does not recognize travel outside of Canada as part of its pro-rating scheme, so that a carrier who ships to the United States is technically in breach of the ISTA. Since the ISTA only applies to carriers who abide by it, this means that carriers who travel to the United States may be forced to pay the full sales tax in all provinces they travel through. Therefore, given the rules of the ISTA a carrier may have to choose between travelling to more than one province or travelling to the United States. Industry sources have told us that there are currently a significant number of carriers in Ontario who usually travel between Ontario and the United States but on occasion must also go to other provinces. Since most of their business is to the United States these carriers would most likely choose to drop the interprovincial part of their traffic. For this reason the current structure of provincial sales taxes represents a barrier to interprovincial trade.

For the most part, the difficulties that arise in interprovincial trucking occur simply because of a lack of uniformity amongst the provinces rather than because of deliberately discriminatory policies. In Canada at present one group is trying to obtain a greater degree of uniformity among the provincial regulations. This group, the Canadian Conference of Motor Transport Administrators (CCMTA), is an association of provincial and federal government administrators. One of the products of this group's activities is the CAVR, discussed above.

In addition to registration reciprocity, there are several other areas in which the CCMTA has tried to promote greater uniformity. Concurrent hearings on entry requirements by several provincial boards where routes are interprovincial in nature have been in place since 1977. Common documentation, in the form of common conditions of carriage and common categories of information required on the face of a bill of lading, as well as common requirements for information that must be carried in the cab of the truck, have been developed. Common commodity descriptions for incorporation into licence or authority grants have been initiated by the CCMTA. More uniformity has been achieved in the description of dangerous goods through the passage of Bill C-18 (federal). Complementary provincial legislation is expected to follow shortly, and a bill is now before the Ontario legislature. Amendments to the Motor Vehicle Transport Act have been agreed to. These amendments are procedural in character and would make provision for joint rather than concurrent hearings of provincial boards so that only one decision would be made at the hearings. Also, appeals from these hearings would be allowed, on questions of law, to the Federal Court of Appeal. Any regulations issued pursuant to the amendments to the Act would require the approval of both the federal cabinet and the provincial cabinets.

Thus it appears that there are important trends in Canada today towards increased uniformity in the trucking industry, thereby reducing the existing interprovincial barriers to movement. It must be realized, however, that as long as trucking regulations are set and controlled by the provinces there will always be barriers to trade. Nevertheless, through activities such as those engaged in by the CCMTA it is possible to minimize the harmful consequences of multiple sets of regulations.

Agricultural policies
A prominent way in which provinces can, and do, create interprovincial barriers to trade is through the implementation of agricultural policies which favour local products or producers. Provinces have at their disposal three basic instruments to create barriers. These are agricultural marketing boards, agricultural support programs, and restrictive product standards or regulations. As will be seen below, all of these policies are being used to some extent in Canada today.

1 Marketing boards
There are essentially two types of marketing boards within the Canadian economy (national supply management and provincial supply management boards), and both these types of marketing boards can be used to impede the free flow of goods between provinces.

National supply management marketing boards are formed pursuant to the Farm Products Marketing Agencies Act.[12] Products can be brought into the scheme if there is substantial agreement among producers, and the minister acts upon this. Once a product is within the scope of the Act the federal agency that deals with the product may delegate its authority to a provincial body. Although the federal agency allocates quotas to the provinces, it is the responsibility of the provincial body to set specific individual producer quotas. Currently, there are five products regulated on a national scale: wheat, eggs, chickens, turkeys, and industrial milk. The bodies which govern these products are respectively the Canadian Wheat Board, the Canadian Egg Marketing Agency, the Canadian

12 S.C. 1970–71–72, c. 65

Chicken Marketing Agency, the Canadian Turkey Marketing Agency, and the Canadian Dairy Commission.

Perhaps the most important consequence of a national supply management policy is that, because of its market-sharing feature, it introduces rigidity into production patterns. Quotas are initially allocated on the basis of production from an area in relation to total Canadian production over the preceding five years. These quotas will not be altered, even if costs of production change, unless the governing bodies decree that there should be a change in quota allocation. Although S.24 of the Farm Products Marketing Agencies Act requires the agency to consider the principle of comparative advantage in allocating quotas, it does not state that the agency must necessarily follow this principle. In fact, for eggs, chickens, and turkeys there is a particular emphasis on provincial self-sufficiency in production rather than on economic efficiency.[13] Because the quotas will not change unless there has been an increase in overall demand, there will be a reluctance among provincial agencies to allow more imports into their province, even if non-local producers are more cost-efficient, since they will have to give up some of their own quotas. There will be a natural tendency for provincial bodies to look after their own interests first, so in this respect quotas will not be easy to change.[14] To the extent that the principle of comparative advantage is not adhered to there will be a resulting inefficiency in the system, because efficient producers cannot produce more and potential entrants are denied entry into the market.

The provincial supply management boards can impede the interprovincial movement of goods in several ways, but the major way is in controlling where and how producers can market their products. Although many provincial agencies have become part of national schemes, there are some exceptions. The most important exception is the provincial milk marketing boards, which control the marketing of fluid milk.

13 For egg quota allocation the criteria to be considered are: the principle of comparative advantage, variations in the size of the market for eggs, failure by egg producers in any province to market the number of eggs authorized to be marketed, the feasibility of increased production, and comparative transportation costs to market areas from alternative sources of production. For chickens the criteria are any significant change in consumer demands, the ability of any province to meet its allocated production, the total market requirement within each market area, the proportion of market demand in a province that is met by production in that province, and the comparative advantage of production and marketing of chickens.
14 In fact the quota allocation for eggs, which was initially based on production from 1967 to 1971, has remained unchanged during the life of the program. Similarly, industrial milk quotas have experienced very little change from the initial allocation.

In the past in Canada there was not much interprovincial movement of fluid milk because it was perishable. Even today, despite the fact that milk can now be transported safely, there is little interprovincial trade, because provincial regulations protect the existing intraprovincial markets.

Several examples of this type of policy can be observed. For instance, the BC Milk Industry Act[15] stipulates that milk can only be sold by certified farms, and special ministerial permits are required to transport milk into the province. This policy means that Alberta dairy farmers have little hope of marketing their milk in British Columbia despite the fact that it is less expensive than BC milk.

Another example can be found in Ontario. The Ontario Milk Marketing Board, which was formed pursuant to Ontario's Milk Act,[16] regulates all aspects of milk marketing in the province. It requires all producers to be inspected by provincial inspectors before they can sell milk in any zone in Ontario, but the inspectors do not travel outside the province. The result is that under normal circumstances non-Ontario producers cannot sell milk in Ontario.

A new development within the milk industry is the introduction of UHT (ultra high temperature) milk. Though it is easily transportable, provinces treat it like regular milk: 'Current regulatory practices ensure that a major product advantage – low perishability when being transported – is not realized.'[17] Such a situation will lead to inefficiencies in the production and distribution of milk and a higher price than would otherwise prevail.

The impact of national and provincial supply management boards varies greatly between provinces. The Economic Council of Canada in a recent report[18] presented data on the share of supply-managed commodities (both federally and provincially regulated) in total farm receipts in mid-1978 across the country: British Columbia 41.7 per cent, Alberta 8.3, Saskatchewan 2.9, Manitoba 13.1, Ontario 37.7, Quebec 58.1, New Brunswick 38.1, Nova Scotia 53.8, Prince Edward Island 20.8, and Newfoundland (not available). In some provinces, particularly Quebec, Nova Scotia, and British Columbia, a significant proportion of the total farm receipts are represented by supply-managed commodities. At the other extreme provinces such as Alberta and Saskatchewan have almost no supply-managed commodities relative to total receipts. From

15 R.S.B.C. 1979, c. 258
16 R.S.O. 1980 c. 266
17 Haack, Hughes and Shapiro, *The Splintered Market: Barriers to Interprovincial Trade in Canadian Agriculture* (Ottawa: Canadian Institute for Economic Policy, 1981), at 29
18 Economic Council of Canada. *Reforming Regulation* (Ottawa: Minister of Supply and Services, 1981), at 57

this it is apparent that the effects of supply management boards will not be distributed evenly across the country. Some provinces stand to gain more than others.

Thus it is apparent that the existence of marketing boards can affect the flow of interprovincial trade. Whether by introducing rigidity into patterns of production or by imposing restrictive regulations, marketing boards serve as impediments to free trade. By restricting the amount of market integration, supply management boards result in lower overall net economic gains than would occur if full integration were allowed.

2 Agricultural support programs

Agricultural support programs also impede interprovincial trade in agricultural products. To the extent that policies differ among the provinces there will be artificial incentives to locate or maintain production in one province rather than encouraging development in another. Resources will therefore not be put to their most efficient uses.

There are two basic forms which support programs can take: direct aid and promotional support. There are many ways of implementing direct aid, but the usual ones are cash subsidies to farmers, stabilization schemes such as crop or income insurance, and assistance programs such as loan guarantees and capital grants. Such programs attempt to make the local agricultural sector more economically viable. In some instances the stated goal of the program is to make the province more self-sufficient. On the other hand promotional support programs attempt, by advertising and other marketing techniques, to differentiate local products from out-of-province products. This, it is hoped, will lead to increased consumption of local products and ultimately to a more profitable local agricultural sector.

Agricultural support programs can, and do, take many different forms. Although certainly not all them are intended to discriminate against out-of-province producers, it must be realized that any money spent on provincial agriculture will have this effect, whatever the intention of the policy-maker. The data available do not make comparisions easy, but it is clear that, where there are significant differences between provinces in the magnitude of expenditures on the different programs, distortions in the trade flow of agricultural goods and resources will be created. In examining these data three factors must be noted. First, the data on per capita expenditure may give rise to misleading inferences because of huge differences in the population of the provinces. For example, while PEI has a large expenditure per capita, the population of the province is only 124 200; when viewed in relation to the total Canadian market, PEI's expenditure of $14 million becomes insignificant and will probably have few

TABLE 2

Provincial agricultural expenditures 1980/81
(dollars)

	Total	Per capita
British Columbia	71 400 000	26.42
Alberta	102 533 000	47.61
Saskatchewan	59 294 350	60.66
Manitoba	33 891 500	32.94
Ontario	184 000 000	21.36
Quebec	319 000 000	50.35
New Brunswick	27 356 905	38.54
Prince Edward Island	14 322 000	115.96
Nova Scotia	22 784 700	38.84
Newfoundland	12 556 400	21.47

NOTE: Estimated expenditures for 1980/81 are from
provincial budget estimates and total provincial
populations are estimated as of 1 April 1981.

interprovincial effects. Secondly, these comparisions are relatively crude,
because provincial agriculture expenditures may include different things. For
instance, in some provinces rural development is included with agriculture,
while in others it is not. Thirdly, the amounts include administrative costs and
thus do not reflect net subsidies received by producers.

Yet comparisons can certainly be made between Alberta and British Columbia and between Ontario and Quebec. In both cases the populations are similar
and because of geography the agricultural products will be in competition.
Alberta clearly supports agriculture to a much higher degree than British
Columbia not only per capita but also in absolute dollars. Similarly, Quebec
spends a great deal more on agriculture than Ontario, reflecting Quebec's
numerous and varied programs for agriculture support.

British Columbia producers will thus find it very hard to market their
products in Alberta, and Ontario producers will have similar problems in
Quebec, when they are in competition with local producers. The level of support
in Quebec and Alberta ensures that local producers face a much more favourable cost structure than out-of-province producers. In this manner barriers to
trade in agricultural products can be created.

An appendix to this chapter contains a comprehensive list of agricultural
subsidy programs in place in each of the provinces. In addition, for Quebec and
the Maritimes some financial data on the magnitude of the subsidies have been
included.

3 Product standards

The third major instrument by which provinces can impede the free flow of agricultural goods is by setting standards, either for packaging or in grading schemes for the products themselves. Where it is constitutionally valid to enact such a system, a province could adopt different standards or packaging requirements, significantly increasing the cost outsiders face in doing business within the province.

Though it has been reported that, in general, packaging and labelling requirements do not form barriers to trade, some exceptions have been cited.[19] For example, Quebec requires that butter be wrapped in foil, whereas Ontario permits butter to be wrapped in transparent parchment. Since foil is more expensive, it is costly for Ontario producers to ship into Quebec when most of their production is geared to the less expensive Ontario market. Another example pertains to Quebec's language law, Bill 101. This law, which requires French to be as prominently displayed on labels as English, means that firms wanting to ship into Quebec will again face increased costs of doing business.

Where product grading systems are different between provinces it is possible for barriers to trade to be erected. Differences in product standards may inhibit out-of-province producers. In this manner the flow of trade could be reduced.

An example is the potato industry. Quebec and the Maritimes have both adopted the Canadian grading system, while Ontario has decided to implement its own grading system. The result of this situation is that Ontario No. 1 potatoes are considerably smaller and less expensive than Canada No. 1 potatoes from the other provinces. It has been suggested that this gives an advantage to Ontario potatoes in the Ontario market because consumers do not distinguish between the two types of No. 1 potatoes and often purchase the less expensive Ontario product.[20]

Even where standards are the same it is possible to impede trade flows through enforcement practices.[21] Quebec producers have complained that Ontario fruit and vegetable inspectors vary their behaviour depending on the supply situation in Ontario. Similar complaints have been voiced by Ontario producers who want to sell their produce in Manitoba. Also, in Quebec inspectors are allegedly instructed to undertake rigorous inspections when the supply of Quebec produce is sufficient to meet demand, thereby reducing the amount of competition from outside the province.

---

19 Haack et al., *The Splintered Market*, at 47
20 Ibid., at 50
21 Ibid.

In summary, provincial agricultural policies, no matter what form they may take, can serve as barriers to interprovincial trade. In a sense all the policies are substitutes for one another since they each attempt to increase the viability of provincial agricultural producers at the expense of out-of-province producers. Although the total effect of these policies is uncertain, it is clear that to the extent that they are effective the flow of trade among the provinces is distorted.

Natural resource policies[22]

Natural resource production and processing is another field in which barriers to trade have resulted from the implementation of provincial policies. Provinces have historically used several techniques to develop this sector of their economy. They have instituted taxes or royalties on resource income and, by altering the rate payable or the basis of taxation, can advance their development goals. Secondly, provinces can increase the amount of processing done in the province by imposing additional duties or requirements on the product if it is shipped out of the province in unprocessed form. Third, terms and conditions in provincial government leases of natural resources may restrict entry to local residents or impose obligations with respect to the processing of resources. Such techniques are used in one form or another in several provinces. By creating artificial incentives for resources to be developed within a province, they distort the flow of trade.

All provinces except Prince Edward Island levy some form of mining tax on income derived from mineral resources. As with any other provincial scheme, where policies differ between provinces there will be an incentive to concentrate activities in the least-taxed province. While firms are obviously tied to the location of the resources, they will certainly try to minimize, wherever possible, the scope of their activities in the more highly taxed provinces. For instance, in Saskatchewan the general tax rate is 12.5 per cent, while Manitoba has a tax rate of 18 per cent and Ontario and Quebec have progressive rates ranging from 15 to 30 per cent.

However, a simple comparision of tax rates could be misleading because there are also differences in what income is exempted from tax calculations. For example, in British Columbia under the Mineral Resource Tax Act[23] the taxable income exemption level was increased to $50 000 annually as of August 1980.

---

22 Sources for this section were Chrétien, *Securing the Canadian Economic Union*; Statistics Canada, Public Finance Division, *Principal Taxes in Canada 1978* (Ottawa: Dept of Industry Trade and Commerce, 1978)

23 R.S.B.C. 1979, c. 263, s. 2(2), as amended by the Mineral Resource Tax Amendment Act, 1980 S.B.C. 1980, c. 27, s. 1.

The exemption in Quebec under the Mining Duties Act[24] is now $250 000, and under Ontario's Mining Tax Act[25] it is also $250 000. The result is that it is very difficult, if not impossible, to determine the effect of the entire tax system on the production of natural resources.

Although they can affect patterns of production, most provincial efforts are directed towards increasing the level of processing done within the province. Provincial governments in general wish to develop secondary industries within the province instead of allowing other regions to process the resources. To the extent that they are successful in achieving this goal, provinces may cause comparative advantage to be distorted.

Processing allowances are a commonly used device to encourage processing within the province. A province will permit firms to deduct a certain percentage of the cost of processing or manufacturing assets from the income which is subject to the mining tax. For example, British Columbia permits an allowance of 8 per cent of the original cost of the processing assets. To be able to claim this allowance there is a minimum deduction of 15 per cent of residual taxable income. The maximum deduction is either 50 or 70 per cent, depending on the type of processing the taxpayer is involved in. Saskatchewan has a similar program in that there is an allowance of 8 per cent of the capital cost of depreciable assets located in Saskatchewan, with a minimum deduction of 15 per cent of net profits and a maximum deduction of 65 per cent. Ontario has a different type of program since all the assets a taxpayer owns in Canada may be subject to the processing allowance. The basic allowance is 8 per cent of the cost of the assets and, depending on the type of activity, the allowance may go up to 30 per cent of the cost. This higher figure, however, is only available for processing carried on in northern Ontario. The highest available rate for processing done outside Ontario is 20 per cent. As with the other provinces, Ontario has a minumum deduction of 15 per cent of net profits and a maximum deduction of 65 per cent. In Quebec allowances of between 8 and 15 per cent are available but only for assets located in Quebec. Newfoundland has no processing allowances as such but some deductions may be permitted for writing off plant and equipment. Nova Scotia has an allowance of 8 per cent given to operators who process their production in the province.

Another way in which provinces can affect the development of resources is through incentives for exploration and related costs. British Columbia allows

---

24 Loi des droits sur les mines, L.R.Q. 1977, c. D-15, s. 30, as amended by la Loi modifiant la Loi concernant les droits sur les mines, L.Q. 1979, c. 74, s. 2
25 R.S.O. 1980, c. 269, s. 3(1)(a)

deduction of all exploration costs from mining income provided that the expenditures are made within the province; some assistance is given to prospectors, and subsidies are available for copper smelters. Saskatchewan allows certain development costs to be deducted from income, and it has several programs designed to provide incentives for oil and gas exploration. In Manitoba recognition is given to exploration expenses since they can be deducted from income, and the province also gives investment credits whereby firms are given credit for investment against royalties otherwise payable. Like BC, Ontario allows for a deduction of 100 per cent of the exploration and development costs incurred in Ontario by Ontario mine operators. For Canadians who are not already engaged in mining activities in Ontario, cash grants or tax credits of 25 per cent of development costs are available. Ontario also has several programs which assist in the building of access roads in mining and logging areas. Quebec has programs similar to Ontario's in that prospectors and mining companies can deduct exploration costs from their profits, there are other programs designed to aid development within Quebec. In Nova Scotia there are no exploration grants as such, although such expenditures can be deducted from mining income; other programs provide technical and financial assistance to companies interested in resource development

Several provinces have also attempted to increase processing through the imposition of duties or requirements. For instance, the British Columbia Mineral Processing Act[26] requires that all BC minerals be processed, smelted, and refined in the province if there are available facilities. Under this Act the minister of mines and petroleum has the power to order that up to 50 per cent of the production of any mine in the province must be refined at a specific processing plant, smelter, or refinery.

Under the Alberta Oil and Gas Conservation Act[27] any party that purchases oil and gas within Alberta but wishes to remove it for consumption must receive permission before doing so. Permission will only be granted if the amount in question is surplus to the present and future needs of the people of the province. Such permission can be withdrawn by the cabinet in an emergency or other circumstances arising within the province.

Alterta's Petroleum Marketing Act[28] established a commission to acquire, sell, or exchange petroleum and related products or to act as a broker in such products. It can be argued that the authority of the commission would also allow

---

26 R.S.B.C. 1979, c. 261, s. 2
27 R.S.A. 1979, c. 261, s. 2
28 R.S.A. 1980, c. P-5

it to prevent the removal of petroleum from Alberta, thereby constituting an impediment to interprovincial trade in petroleum products.

In Saskatchewan the Mineral Disposition Regulations[29] stipulate that all minerals, mineral ores, and mineral-bearing substances from 'disposition areas' in the province must be treated and refined in Saskatchewan unless the minister authorizes removal. Failure to comply may mean that all rights to the disposition area would be lost.

Quebec and New Brunswick have similar policies regarding the shipment of natural resources. Both provinces stipulate that any unprocessed minerals shipped outside the province for treatment may be subject to additional duties or taxes. The effect of these policies is obviously to encourage local processing even when other locations would be more efficient.

Provincial liquor policies[30]

There are essentially three ways in which provinces can erect impediments to trade in these commodities, and all three are used in Canada today.

When marketing through the provincial liquor board, a province can discriminate against out-of-province producers by giving favourable support to local products, such as by better advertising support, advantageous positioning in liquor outlets, less stringent listing requirements, and preferential pricing policies. Secondly, a province can limit private purchases from other provinces either through a quota system or by levying taxes on such purchases. Thirdly, by having unique packaging requirements, a province may make it too costly for out-of-province products to enter the market.

In British Columbia almost all BC alcoholic beverages receive a preferential markup in price. For instance, provincial table wines are marked up by only 50 per cent (as a percentage of landed cost), whereas table wines from other Canadian provinces are marked up 110 per cent. Wines imported from other countries are also marked up 110 per cent. All non-BC products must apply for listing with the Liquor Distribution Branch, which reviews applications only twice a year. On the other hand, according to the BC Wine Policy each BC winery is granted an automatic listing and may have up to sixty-six listings on the BC market, although a listing application form must still be submitted. Similarly, a BC brewery need only advise the Liquor Distribution Branch when it wants to put a new product on the market, whereas non-BC beer must first get approval.

---

29 s. 86, O.C. 451 / 61 (1961), 57 *The Saskatchewan Gazette* 219, March 24, 1961, enacted pursuant to the Mineral Resources Act 1959 (now R.S.S. 1978, c.M-16, s. 11)

30 Sources for this section included correspondence with the provincial ministries responsible for liquor policies.

British Columbia products enjoy another advantage in promotion and distribution. In government liquor stores BC wines have access to approximately 25 per cent of the retail shelf space and are given special end aisle displays. Pamphlets promoting BC wines are displayed in the stores themselves.

The BC *Liquor Distribution Purchasing and Marketing Policy Manual* states that in order to support the BC wine industry imported wines will not be listed in a package size larger than 1 litre, and the minimum retail price is $2.75. Moreover, non-BC wines must meet specified sales quotas or be delisted. These requirements do not apply to BC wines. Since January 1980 the policy of the Liquor Distribution Branch has been to require that restaurants in the province list BC wines and feature them as house wines. This too gives the provincial producers a competitive advantage.

According to the Saskatchewan Liquor Board, a preferential markup is given to local products but the difference is only 5 per cent. Also, locally produced products are given promotional support with display cases advertising the product being permitted in the stores. Other barriers to trade can be found in some of the provincial statutes. For instance, Saskatchewan's Liquor Act[31] in Section 81(b) stipulates that a person can only legally bring in one quart of spirits, one quart of wine, and two gallons of beer from other provinces. The Liquor Exporters Taxation Act[32] can also serve to reduce the amount of inter-provincial trade in liquor products; Section 3 requires any party who wishes to export liquor out of Saskatchewan to pay an annual tax of $5000.

Manitoba appears to have few policies that could constitute impediments to trade. According to the Liquor Control Commission of that province there is no markup differential between local and out-of-province products. The only potential source of distortion is that products produced in Manitoba get automatic listing, while other products must be approved by the Commission.

In Ontario wines produced in accordance with the Liquor Control Act[33] and the Wine Content Act[34] are priced with a lower markup than out-of-province products. Ontario table wines are marked up by 58 per cent and dessert wines by 78 per cent, while other Canadian wines are marked up by 105 per cent. Moreover, brandy produced from Ontario grapes has a lower markup than other brandies.

One of the most significant advantages Ontario wines enjoy is in distribution. All wines produced outside Ontario must be listed with the Liquor Control

31 R.S.S. 1978, c. L-18
32 R.S.S. 1978, c. L-20
33 R.S.O. 1980, c. 243
34 R.S.O. 1980, c. 534

Board, while Ontario wineries may also sell through their own retail outlets. There are currently 123 such stores across the province. It has been suggested that, to be listed, out-of-province wines are quality-tested rigorously, whereas Ontario wines will be listed if they are of adequate quality for the price range.[35] Ontario wines can be distributed in a wider range of bottle sizes than non-Ontario wines. Further, distribution of Ontario wines in the high-volume liquor stores is automatic, whereas for out-of-province wines it is up to the store manager to decide whether or not the products will be carried.

The Société des Alcools du Québec (SAQ) states that local products are priced differently from out-of-province products. The situation in Quebec is different from most other provinces, in that SAQ itself is in competition with the provincial wineries because it bottles imported wines. One advantage which local products have over out-of-province products is that they can be distributed, along with SAQ bottled wine, in grocery stores. Imported wines must be sold through the liquor board. SAQ promotes only the wines it bottles itself, and all local producers must provide their own marketing support. Thus, although Quebec products do experience some advantages over out-of-province products, they do not seem as highly favoured as local products of other provinces, such as BC and Ontario. There have been complaints from other provinces, however, that the listing policy and labelling requirements of the Quebec Liquor Corporation can make it difficult for their producers to compete effectively in Quebec.

The New Brunswick Liquor Corporation has stated that in that province local products are priced differently only in the case of wine and beer; there is no special markup for spirits made in New Brunswick. Although there are no special listing requirements for out-of-province products, New Brunswick does have special instore merchandising displays to promote locally produced beer. In overall economic effect, however, these policies are not likely to have a major impact.

The Nova Scotia Liquor Commission prices all alcoholic products produced in the province below those from outside. It is not possible to retail an out-of-province product at a lower base price than Nova Scotia products have. All local products are automatically placed in self-service stores, specially marked as 'Nova Scotia Products,' and given preferential shelf space.

The Prince Edward Island Control Commission does not apply any discriminatory treatment to out-of-province products, largely because there are no breweries, wineries, or distilleries in the province to be protected.

In Newfoundland there are no distilleries or wineries, although the Newfoundland Liquor Corporation does some of its own bottling. These local

35 Haack et al., *The Splintered Market*, at 44

products are, in general, priced lower than out-of-province goods, although there are exceptions. The Corporation believes that where local products are priced lower than other goods it is the result of a different cost structure rather than a preferential markup. But the Newfoundland Liquor Corporation is involved in the promotion of local products, usually in the form of in-store displays and eye-level shelf positioning. This treatment is available for any product bottled by the Corporation itself.

Retail sales tax
A potential source of barriers to trade in the interprovincial movement of goods lies in the area of retail sales tax. Substantial differences exist between the provinces in both rates and exemptions from coverage; for instance, food, housing, and pharmaceuticals are exempted from tax in many provinces. Where differences in the retail sales tax exist between provinces, it is possible to argue that there will be an inefficient shift of resources to the area with lower taxes, especially near provincial borders.

The provincial retail sales tax rates[36] vary as follows: Newfoundland 11 per cent, PEI 10, Nova Scotia 8, New Brunswick 8, Quebec 8, Ontario 7, Manitoba 5, Saskatchewan 5, Alberta nil, and British Columbia 6 per cent. We would expect to see increased sales in provinces with very low sales tax rates and decreased sales in provinces with high tax rates. The problem, of course, is that consumers will not travel great distances to purchase goods for the sake of saving a few dollars in sales tax. We might see changes in the level of spending in areas close to provincial borders, but there will probably not be any effect beyond this.

To be realistic, the effects on consumer sales may be noticeable only in Alberta. Elsewhere movements of consumers are either restricted by geography (e.g. from Newfoundland to Nova Scotia) or tax rates vary little between bordering provinces. Thus, it is unrealistic to expect that there will be any significant effects upon the overall economy.

Evaluation of restrictions on goods mobility

1 Preferences in procurement
Preferences given to within-province contractors in bidding for provincial government contracts have often been cited as examples of barriers to interprovincial trade. The recent federal publication *Securing the Canadian Economic Union in the Constitution*, for instance, lists this item first in its description of

36 Goodman, Gurney and Perry, 'Provincial budget roundup – 1981' (1981), 29 *Canadian Tax Journal* 327

restrictions on the free movement of goods. But despite the attention given to these preferences their economic consequences remain difficult to quantify.

The publication mentioned above identifies three different techniques that can be used by provincial governments to provide preference to within-province contractors:

- tailoring performance requirements to match the capabilities of within-province firms;
- use of source lists (most provinces maintain lists of firms that are able to supply required goods and services, and information on how to be included in such a list may not be as accessible to out-of-province firms.); and
- when considering tenders in-province bids can be given preference over out-of-province bids.

Preferences of the last type are clearer than preferences of the first two types.

Evaluating the impact of provincial procurement policy on interprovincial activity is extremely difficult. From the interprovincial trade flows identified in Chapter 4 one is unable to determine what portion relates to government purchases. Presumably the fraction involved is small (perhaps less than 2 per cent), because real provincial non-transfer expenditures would be less than 10 per cent of GNP, and these expenditures are in turn heavily dominated by the wage and salary component. Perhaps 2 per cent of all expenditures on goods and services are thus accounted for by provincial governments. A similar fraction might apply to interprovincial trade involving government. Since the level of preference offered by provincial governments to in-province contractors is not known, it is difficult to determine the impacts of the preference in terms of welfare costs.[37]

2 Transport regulation

Little quantitative evidence is available on the impact of transport regulation since most studies of transport impacts on interprovincial trade have focused on federally induced impacts (especially the Crow's Nest Pass Agreement). Many of the items discussed above are of a regulatory nature, and for that reason quantifying their effects is difficult. A working hypothesis might be that many of these regulations are a 'nuisance' rather than 'substantive' and in aggregate have relatively little impact. After all, the transportation content of interprovincial trade is modest compared to the value of goods and services being transported.

37 See further Gillies, 'The impact of interprovincial trade barriers on the British Columbia economy' (Victoria: unpublished mimeo, 1980)

3 Agricultural policies

For restrictions on the mobility of goods, agricultural trade would seem to be potentially the most important area. There is some ambiguity as to the fraction of agricultural output involved, but there seems little doubt that it is large. The federal Task Force on Agriculture in 1972 suggested that there were at that time about 120 marketing boards in Canada involved in the sale of about one-quarter of the value of all farm produce sold in Canada. More recent research suggests the existence of even more boards than that exerting some degree of control over 60 per cent of farm sales.

At the national level the key boards are the Canadian Wheat Board, the Canadian chicken, turkey, and egg marketing agencies, and the Canadian Dairy Commission. The Wheat Board has powers to buy, sell, store, and transport grain within Canada. The federal chicken, turkey, and egg marketing agencies allocate production and marketing quotas for each product and monitor interprovincial trade in those products; Provincial boards, however, fix quotas and prices for individual producers. The Dairy Commission controls the production, pricing, and sale of industrial milk.

Provincial marketing boards usually control production, marketing, and pricing within the province. They cover a range of products, from milk, poultry, and pork to vegetables and tobacco. Generally speaking, they are regarded as restrictive in operation and as having major impacts on interprovincial trade in agriculture:

In British Columbia, the BC Milk Industry Act requires that there be no sale of food or fluid milk except by certified dairy farms, and that a ministerial permit is required in order to transport fluid milk into the province. These permits ... [the study's researchers were informed] are 'very difficult' to obtain. Milk prices in British Columbia, with the exception of Newfoundland, are the highest in Canada (price and production quotas are often set by the BC Milk Board). Due to the stringency of the regulations less-expensive Alberta fluid milk cannot be marketed in BC.

The Ontario Milk Marketing Board ... has an effective monopoly in the sale of raw milk in Ontario. The province is divided into regional milk distribution zones, and in order to sell milk in a zone producers must have their facilities inspected by Ontario inspectors and these inspectors do not travel outside the province.

A major retailer in Saskatchewan indicated that the retail trade was unable to import fluid milk products from other provinces because of the regulations of the Saskatchewan Milk Control Board.[38]

38 Haack et al., *The Splintered Market*, at 28–9

The overall effect of these marketing boards on interprovincial trade and agricultural products is hard to ascertain. While they appear to be restrictive – and in many cases cause price increases – potential interprovincial trade in these provinces may be small since products are in most cases close substitutes for internal products. The data in Chapter 4 indicate that perhaps 2.5 per cent of interprovincial trade may be involved, though it must be remembered that if marketing boards did not exist the share of interprovincial trade in agricultural products would likely be much higher than at present.

4 Natural resource policies
Besides their effects on energy resources (discussed in the previous chapter) natural resource policies in provinces have additional effects on interprovincial trade, particularly through the regulation of mining and control over royalty and licensing policies. Again, the effects of provincial natural resource policies are hard to quantify, although the current view seems to be that they are smaller than the effects of federal policies in this area.

5 Provincial liquor buying and pricing policies
Little data exist on the extent of provincial preferences from liquor control practices. The suspicion is that restrictive buying practices are used (at times harshly) to exclude significant amounts of out-of-province liquor, although firm data on this are not available. The data in Chapter 4 suggest that, at most, only one-half of 1 per cent of interprovincial trade is at issue in these restrictions, so that any effects may be small in proportion to total effects. Nonetheless, this area has some of the most formidable trade barriers:

The marketing and distribution of alcoholic beverages (typically wines) represents a very clear and unapologetic barrier to the interprovincial movement of these products. The primary wine producing provinces of British Columbia, Ontario and Quebec provide the most striking examples of barriers which virtually prohibit sale of out-of-province Canadian wines. Where possible, wineries are required to use local grapes exclusively. Liquor store policies, with regard to listings (brands made available within liquor stores), distribution and markups favour local products over those imported from other provinces or countries. These barriers are not subtle and are clearly protectionist.[39]

39 Ibid., at 56

6 Retail sales taxes

Retail sales taxes have already been discussed. Their major effect on interprovincial trade flows derives from the differences in tax rates not between provinces but between products within provinces. Most provinces exempt items from the retail sales tax; food, housing, and some clothing and footwear are usually tax-free. Recent estimates suggest that such exemptions may extend to as much as one-half of total consumer expenditures. Since a provincial retail sales tax leads consumers to spend more of their income on non-taxed items, this tendency, if anything, would hurt manufacturers, most of whom are located in Ontario and Quebec.

Differences in provincial sales tax rates, often owing to differing exemptions or special rates on some items, have neighbourhood spillover effects in communities close to provincial borders.

PERSONAL MOBILITY

The problem of personal mobility has several aspects. As a problem of labour mobility the issue merits concern because of the misallocation of resources among provinces that results when barriers are imposed to the movement of labour from regions of surplus occupational skills to regions of high demand. This concern has recently been voiced by the Task Force on Industrial and Regional Benefits from Major Canadian Projects, a joint labour-industry undertaking.[40] The Task Force concluded that the existence of concurrent shortages and surpluses of many occupational skills in different regions of Canada was evidence that the labour market is not at present operating efficiently.

As the Task Force has outlined, labour mobility is dependent upon the interaction of a number of factors. The primary incentive to mobility is economic, based upon the perception of enhanced career opportunities and economic gain. This initial impetus is in turn dependent upon the availability and accessibility of job market information, the lack of which may in itself be considered a barrier to labour mobility. As well, the appropriate level of training and skill development must have been attained, a requirement which may be more or less easily fulfilled, depending on provincial policies regarding education and manpower training. However, even if advantageous employment opportunities exist and are known, and the requisite skills are attained, many

---

40 Consultative Task Force on Industrial and Regional Benefits From Major Canadian Projects, Manpower Subcommittee, 'Report of the Manpower Subcommittee (unpublished working paper, 17 October 1980). This independent task force was cochaired by Shirley Carr of the Canadian Labour Congress and Robert Blair of Nova, An Alberta Corporation.

other factors are weighed in the equation determining the costs and benefits of relocation. The positive motivation to migrate may be offset by major disincentives posed by incompatible certification standards, restrictive hiring practices, loss of pension benefits, increased cost of living, and cultural and language barriers. Those aspects of barriers to labour mobility which are provincially induced or under provincial control will be examined in turn.

However, the issue of personal mobility is larger than the issue of labour mobility. Once a choice has been made to relocate, for whatever reasons (economic or non-economic, job-related or personal), guarantees of personal mobility would assure equal access to public services. The existence of residency requirements for both education and social assistance indicates that personal mobility is not currently unimpeded.

Preferential hiring practices
Several provinces have imposed local hiring restrictions upon the private sector. Such legislation appears to be especially common with respect to the development of natural resources, and in some cases the restrictions are combined with local procurement requirements for goods. For example, in Newfoundland persons granted permits or leases for exploration or exploitation under the Petroleum and Natural Gas Act are subject to subsection 124(1) of the regulations which provides: 'It is deemed to be a term of every permit or lease that a permittee or lessee shall give preference in his hiring practices to qualified residents of the province.'[41] 'Residence' is being interpreted as residence in Newfoundland for three years prior to 1978 or for a period of ten years at any time. Similarly, Nova Scotia's Bill 61, An Act Respecting Petroleum Resources,[42] which has been passed but not promulgated, provides under subsection 26(1)(f) for the enactment of regulation 'respecting the nature and extent of employment of Nova Scotians by holders of petroleum rights and others performing work authorized by a petroleum right.' In Quebec, mineral exploration permits require that employment preference be given to Quebec labourers and mining engineers.

In Saskatchewan, lease agreements entered into between the Department of Northern Development and resource firms seeking licences to operate in Saskatchewan contain a northern preference hiring clause requiring that 50 per cent of

---

41 'The Newfoundland and Labrador Petroleum Regulation, Nfld Reg. 139 / 78' (1978), 53 *Newfoundland Gazette (Part II)* 975, 10 November 1978, enacted pursuant to the Petroleum and Natural Gas Act, R.S. Nfld. 1970, c. 294
42 Petroleum Resources Act, S.N.S. 1980, c. 12. As of September 1982 this Act had not been proclaimed.

the staff be northern residents. 'Northern resident' is defined as someone who has lived in northern Saskatchewan for fifteen years at any time. Finally, in Alberta a policy statement by the Minister of Business Development and Tourism indicates a commitment to maximizing the Alberta and Canadian content of major construction projects within the province.[43] This policy has been translated into a requirement that for all projects needing Industrial Development Permits,[44] Forest Management Agreements, or Coal Development Permits the applicant agrees to 'the use wherever practicable of Alberta engineering and other professional services, as well as Alberta tradesmen and other construction personnel and materials and supplies from Alberta.'[45] In other projects not requiring such permits the government has no direct control over preferential hiring but 'urges the private sector to voluntarily adopt the policy outlined above.'

In Quebec, mobility constraints have been imposed not only in the natural resource sector but also throughout the construction industry. The Construction Industry Labour Relations Act,[46] enacted in 1968 to sort out internal problems in the Quebec construction industry, has also had the effect of imposing severe restrictions on the interprovincial mobility of workers within the industry. Regulation 5, brought into force under the Act in September 1977, established a three-tier system of construction worker classification (A-B-C) based on the number of hours worked annually and on the region of residence within Quebec.[47] Preference in employment is given on a regional basis, with the holder of the highest level certificate enjoying job priority in a region. The Act thereby imposes severe restrictions on intraprovincial mobility, but the effects on interprovincial mobility are even greater since workers who do not reside in one of the designated construction regions within Quebec are not able to get certificates and are effectively shut out from the Quebec market. The Ontario government

43 'Policy Statement by the Government of Alberta,' in Consultative Task Force on Industrial and Regional Benefits from Major Canadian Projects, Role of Government Subcommittee, 'A report to the Major Projects Task Force by the Subcommittee on the Role of Government (unpublished working paper, September 1980), at 65
44 Industrial Development Permits are required to establish a facility which will consume more than one trillion BTUs of energy annually in order to ensure that local users of Alberta energy conduct their activities beneficially.
45 'Policy Statement by the Government of Alberta'
46 Loi des relations du travail dans l'industrie de la construction, L.Q. 1968, c. 45; now L.R.Q. 1977, c. R-20
47 'Réglement numero 5: Réglement relatif au placement des salariés dans l'industrie de la construction,' A.C. 3282, Rég. 77–587 (1977), 109 (43) *Gazette Officielle du Québec (Partie 2)* 5581, 26 octobre, 1977

has estimated that 3000 eastern Ontario construction workers have thereby been barred from working on Quebec construction projects.[48] Retaliatory legislation considered by Ontario, which in the end did not materialize, raised the spectre of provincial legislatures engaged in a series of self-protective counterattacks.

Constraints upon labour mobility are also effected through policies imposed upon the public sector. Both Quebec and Nova Scotia, for example, have public service legislation giving preference to provincial residents. As well, government procurement policies often extend to services as well as to goods, thereby imposing constraints on labour mobility. The 1980 Newfoundland budget announced the introduction of a local preference policy for Newfoundland goods and *services* which would apply to all future government procurement. The Quebec government's procurement policy for goods has a counterpart for services which may also be considered as imposing barriers to labour mobility.[49] Article 12(h) of Order-in-Council 3989–78 concerning government construction contracts requires that the call for offers must specify that 'seules seront considérées les soumissions des entrepreneurs ayant leur principale place d'affaires au Québec.' Section 14(i) requires the applicant to engage only subcontractors established in Quebec. With regard to government professional service contracts, Sections 22 and 32 of Order-in-Council 3475–77 restrict the government to consideration of firms that have their principal place of business in Quebec. Similarly, Section 9 of Order-in-Council 2516–77 requires that all applicants for government concession contracts must have their principal place of business in Quebec.

Restrictive standards for entrance into occupations
The most widespread threats to the ease of labour mobility are occasioned by occupational licensing and certification requirements. Two closely inter-related problems pervade the area: lack of uniformity of standards between the provinces and lack of reciprocity (i.e. recognition of out-of-province training or experience). Special mention should be made at this point of the extra barriers these factors may impose upon the movement between provinces of immigrants who have received their training and work experience outside Canada. Because reciprocity arrangements in one province may not be recognized in another and

---

48 Ontario Ministry of Industry and Tourism, *Interprovincial Economic Co-operation, at 8*

49 The following references on procurement policy are taken from a memorandum prepared by Courtois, Clarkson, Parsons et Tétrault, Avocats for L'Honorable Marc-André Bédard, Ministre de la Justice, Gouvernement du Québec, concerning the effect on Quebec's laws and regulations of the entrenchment in the Constitution of a Charter of Rights (Montréal, 25 February 1981).

because some provinces have a more stringent set of requirements for foreign transfers than others, mobility problems may arise. As well, in Quebec most of the professional and trade societies require Canadian citizenship as a condition of admission.

In some occupations, such as skilled tradesmen, for example, the provinces themselves issue licences, and any barriers to mobility thus raised are attributable directly to them. In other cases, where licensing authority is exercised by professional organizations or municipalities, the provinces allow bodies under their jurisdiction to erect such barriers.

1 The professions
The licensing authority exercised by provincial professional associations, ostensibly for the purpose of protecting the public, has been used to create impediments for professionals desiring to move to the province. It is sometimes difficult to distinguish between requirements which are necessary in order to ensure levels of competence equivalent to those required by in-province professionals and those which are discriminatory in imposing higher requirements on residents than non-residents. Non-uniformity and lack of reciprocity affect the standards for academic training, apprenticeship periods, licensing examinations, and various non-technical requirements such as residency and citizenship. Out-of-province transfers are commonly subject to standard admissions criteria which impose upon experienced professionals the requirement of completing licensing courses and examinations and redoing their apprenticeships regardless of their experience. Often an arbitrary number of years of practice is made a pre-requisite to seeking a license.

A paper prepared for the Ontario Professional Organizations Committee on the transfer of professionals from other jurisdictions to Ontario contains a detailed comparison of the transfer requirements imposed across Canada in four leading professions: law, engineering, architecture, and accounting.[50] A summary of those parts of their findings which point to the existence of barriers to professional mobility follows. The Ontario committee concluded, on the basis of Murray's findings, that in the case of accounting, architecture, and engineering, interprovincial mobility is extremely high, though the situation in law was more problematic.[51]

50 Murray, *Transfer of Professionals From Other Jurisdictions to Ontario* (Toronto: Ontario Ministry of the Attorney-General, Professional Organizations Committee, Working Paper 12, 1978)
51 Conclusions contained in Ontario Ministry of the Attorney-General, Professional Organizations Committee, *Report of the Professional Organization Committee* (Toronto: Government of Ontario, 1980)

The legal profession. In every province only persons enrolled in the law society (admitted to the bar) and / or holding an annual certificate are entitled to practice. The qualifications required for admission typically include a law degree, a period of articling, and a bar exam administered by the provincial law society.

With regard to transfers of lawyers from other provinces, British Columbia, Alberta, Manitoba, Ontario, Quebec, New Brunswick, and Nova Scotia require that a lawyer have practised law full-time in his own province for three out of the five years immediately preceding application and then take an exam in provincial statutes (or, in the case of Alberta, take bar admission exams but not the course). Otherwise, the applicant is required to redo the articling and bar admission courses. While it is readily admitted that familiarity with provincial law is a justifiable requisite for transfer into a province, it is difficult to see how this is related to a period of practice in another province. In fact the Ontario committee recommended abolition of this arbitrary requirement and the introduction of a more flexible system of waiving all or part of the articling or bar admission courses depending on out-of-province experience. Some provinces (Alberta, New Brunswick, and Nova Scotia) do make provisions for cases where the transferee has had less practical experience by requiring a period of articling within the province, usually for less time than that required of candidates within the province fresh from law school. Sometimes, as in the case of Nova Scotia, this provision is combined with compulsory attendance at bar admission courses. In British Columbia if the applicant has practised for not less than three years, one of which must have been in the past five years, he must undertake to practice only as an employed lawyer for one year after call and attend the bar admission tutorial program. Quebec allows those without the required experience to obtain a restricted certificate to practise if they will be working for one employer and will have no contact with the public.

Saskatchewan does not require any minimum period of active practice and only demands a law degree equivalent to one obtained from the University of Saskatchewan; it thus offers a contrast to the more arbitrary requirements of the other provinces.

In terms of non-technical requirements for transfers in the legal profession, the only serious barrier seems to be created by Quebec's requirement that the applicant demonstrate a working knowledge of French and be a Canadian citizen. Ontario as well now requires Canadian citizenship or citizenship in a Commonwealth country, a requirement queried by the Professional Organizations Committee.[52]

---

52 Ibid.

With regard to lawyers from other countries substantial difficulties have existed over the years. Ontario in particular had foreign transfer requirements that were generally more restrictive than those of other provinces, demanding that even applicants licensed in other common law jurisdictions secure an approved Canadian law degree. While some advanced standing was given, the minimum requirement was a year of university and eighteen months of the articling and bar admission program. The other provinces generally require only some combination of articling and bar admission program. Manitoba has no special rules and does personal evaluations. New Brunswick and Nova Scotia apply the same requirement of practical experience as for Canadian applicants: active practice for three out of the five years immediately preceding application. A national evaluative program called the Joint Committee on Foreign Accreditation administered by the Federation of Law Societies of Canada and the Canadian law school deans has recently been set up and now evaluates the academic qualifications of all foreign applicants for entry into the practice of law in all common law provinces of Canada.[53]

Architecture. Laws in all provinces prohibit the practice of architecture and use of the professional designation without registration and / or a licence. Educational qualifications for provincial applicants usually consist of a period of university education and practical training. In addition, a licensing exam is required in Nova Scotia, New Brunswick, Quebec, Saskatchewan, and British Columbia.

For transfer of architects registered with other provincial associations, many of the provinces have essentially automatic admission if the applicant has the requisite number of years of post-graduate work experience (Nova Scotia, Alberta, Manitoba, Newfoundland) or if the province has a reciprocal agreement with other associations. Saskatchewan has a reciprocal agreement with Manitoba, and Quebec has reciprocal agreements with Manitoba and Ontario.

Some provinces, however, still impose requirements which can be viewed as discriminatory barriers. Both British Columbia and Ontario have minimum periods of post-registration practice for automatic acceptance: in the case of British Columbia, active practice for two out of the preceding five years; in the case of Ontario, active practice for three years following registration. Ontario requires appellants with less experience to supplement their experience with up to three years work experience in Ontario and to take required parts of the Registration Board Course.

British Columbia, Saskatchewan, and Quebec require provincial transferees to write professional practice exams, although BC does offer a pre-screening oral

---

53 Discussed in ibid.

exam that, if passed, exempts the applicant from the Registration Board Course. Saskatchewan, alone among the provinces, requires a one-year residency. Quebec requires fulfilment both of language requirements (i.e. proficiency in French) and citizenship requirements (i.e. Canadian citizenship or declared intent to become citizen when possible). Ontario requires Canadian citizenship or citizenship of a Commonwealth country, a requirement criticized by the Professional Organizations Committee.[54]

For architects from other countries many of the provinces rely upon the standards for a minimum syllabus developed by the Royal Architectural Institute of Canada (RAIC). Currently the Ontario Association of Architects is not fully integrated into the RAIC structure, and its list of foreign schools given qualified approval is not as extensive as that of other provinces. Quebec also has more stringent standards. With regard to the work experience requirement, many provinces accept the RAIC's standards. Some, however, require all work experience to be completed within the province (Quebec) or within Canada (Newfoundland).

Engineering. All provincial legislation on the engineering profession prohibits practice as a professional engineer unless registered and / or licensed. Generally the domestic requirements for entry are a university degree in engineering and two years of practical experience.

There seem to be few barriers to mobility in the engineering profession. The engineering profession has standardized academic and work experience requirements across the country. All provinces except British Columbia and Quebec have automatic acceptance for members of other provincial associations if they are residents of the province. Most provinces also provide for temporary licences for non-residents allowing them to work on specific projects for a limited period of time.

British Columbia still does a case-by-case review of all provincial transfer applicants' credentials. Quebec has strict language, domicile, and citizenship requirements in addition to academic and work experience requirements.

In terms of foreign transfers, two provinces, Manitoba and Saskatchewan, grant automatic membership to applicants from associations with similar objects and membership requirements (mainly in the United States and the United Kingdom). Ontario tends not to grant automatic membership in such cases but its generous policy of giving exemptions from the examinations of the Association of Professional Engineers of Ontario has much the same practical effect. Most provinces do an individual evaluation of academic credentials and work experience. Many have not followed Ontario's example of taking into

54 Ibid.

account work experience to supplement any formal academic deficiencies. As well, many provinces are more stringent than Ontario in requiring that part of the work experience be obtained in Canada or the United States.

Accounting. Since the three accounting associations are nationally-based and have common national standards, curricula, and exams, transfers between provincial associations are automatic. Some problems do arise, however, with regard to the practice of public accountancy. Ontario and most of the Maritime provinces employ a licensing system to regulate the practice of public accountancy. In Ontario, for example, in order to be licensed, public accountants must be members of the Institute of Chartered Accountants of Ontario. This means that CGAs (certified general accountants) and RIAs (registered industrial accountants) from the western provinces who can practise public accountancy in their home provinces cannot continue to do so in Ontario without taking additional university courses, enrolling in the School of Public Accountancy, and completing the Uniform Final Examination.

Quebec also employs a licensing system for public accountancy, but there are wider exemptions than in Ontario or the Maritimes, allowing CGAs from the western provinces greater scope to practise public accountancy.

With regard to foreign transfers, because the associations of CAs, CGAs, and RIAs rely on national standards in assessing and admitting foreign-trained applicants, there is little variation in the treatment such applicants will meet from province to province.

Other professions. There has been no recent study, comparable to that of the Professional Organizations Committee, which offers a comprehensive survey of transfer provisions in the other professions. A study of professional licensing prepared in 1978 by Muzondo and Pazderka contains a summary of the situation as of 1970.[55] Although some of the data may now be outdated, the findings indicate the type of barriers that can be created in the current constitutional state of affairs. Relatively few barriers were found for agriculturalists, social workers, dentists, veterinarians, chiropractors, and physiotherapists. In medicine, relatively few barriers were found to the mobility of practitioners duly qualified in other provinces, and the main difficulties pertained to the non-uniform recognition of foreign qualifications. In New Brunswick, PEI, Ontario, Manitoba, Alberta, and British Columbia the requirement of a certificate from the Medical Council of Canada means that graduates of foreign universities must take the

---

55 Muzondo and Pazderka, *Professional Licensing and Competition Policy: Effects of Licensing on Earnings and Rates-of-Return Differentials* (Ottawa: Ministry of Supply of Services, Bureau of Competition Policy Research Branch, Research Monograph 5, 1979)

Medical Council exams and often redo their internship unless they are covered by the reciprocity agreements some provinces (e.g. Ontario) have with the U.K. Quebec imposes the most stringent transfer requirements, requiring one year of residence in the province prior to admission.

As of 1970, the most severe restrictions were found in surveying and pharmacy. For the former, most provinces required surveyors duly qualified elsewhere to take a period of additional training (usually a minimum of one year) and also pass an exam. Newfoundland also required a one-year residency in the province. In Nova Scotia, New Brunswick, Quebec, Saskatchewan, and British Columbia Canadian citizenship or British subject status was required.

As for pharmacy, several provinces (Newfoundland, Nova Scotia, PEI, and New Brunswick) required the applicant to pass provincial exams and even take special courses in addition to holding the certificate of the National Pharmacy Examining Board. Ontario, Manitoba, and British Columbia admitted only those out-of-province applicants who had at least twelve months of experience in the original jurisdiction. Residence in the province prior to registration was required in Newfoundland (up to six months), Ontario (six months), Manitoba (three months), Alberta (three months), and BC (six months). The Quebec College of Pharmacy formerly admitted only students who had attended the two provincial pharmacy schools. Some of these restrictions have now been lifted. In Ontario, for example, changes were made in response to the Ontario Government's Committee on the Healing Arts. Alberta, however, still requires a three-month residency.

In terms of the total impact of restrictions on the mobility of professionals in Canada, Muzondo and Pazderka estimated that in 1970, for thirteen major professions, these restrictions cost Canadian consumers over $50 million.[56] The study does not clearly indicate whether this number captures only interprovincial restrictions on mobility or also restrictions on entry from abroad.

2 Provincial licensing of trades

Provincial governments license and certify various skilled trades and crafts. In Ontario, for example, thirty-three occupations are subject to provincial licensing.[57] More than one-third of craftsmen in production process occupations are

---

56 Ibid., at 127

57 Trebilcock, Kaiser, and prichard, 'Interprovincial restrictions on the mobility of resources: goods, capital, and labour (an illustrative survey).' In Ontario Economic Council, *Intergovernmental Relations: Issues and Alternatives 1977* (Toronto: Ontario Economic Council, 1977)

subject to some form of licensing in Canada.[58] Substantial variation exists between the provinces as to both what occupations are licensed and what the requirements for licensing or certification are. For example, motor mechanics must be licensed in Ontario though not in Manitoba. Although these differences cannot be viewed as discriminatory because they apply to all persons, whether within or outside Ontario, the pervasiveness of widely different entry standards does create impediments to the free flow of skilled personnel. As in the professions, problems of non-uniformity are often compounded by lack of reciprocity in recognition of out-of-province qualifications. In order to obtain certification and licensing in some provinces, a craftsman trained in another province is often required to return to school and requalify in the trade before pursuing employment.

The problems created by trade licensing and certification are perhaps not as great as in the professions because certification is often voluntary, provisional certificates are often granted, and the Interprovincial Seal Program is making considerable progress in fostering uniformity. Also known as the 'Red Seal Program' and co-ordinated by the Canada Employment and Immigration Commission, this program has brought about agreements between the provinces to recognize the qualifications of tradesmen in certain trades who receive their training in other provinces. Under the program, a red seal guaranteeing interprovincial mobility is issued to tradesmen who pass the Interprovincial Standards Exam. The exams may be written either by persons who have just completed apprenticeship, which is the more common situation, or by qualified tradesmen. Data provided by the Canada Employment and Immigration Commission[59] show that 13 210 seals were issued in 1980, bringing the total number of seals issued in twenty-two trades as of 31 December 1980 to 106 126, distributed among the provinces as shown in Table 3. However, the Seal Program is not a complete solution to the problem of barriers to the mobility of skilled tradesmen. The program is voluntary, and any province can opt out. Furthermore, the program is not universally applied. Only in British Columbia does it cover all twenty-two trades. As well, there are no provisions in the Red Seal program for transferring training credits for apprentices who have not finished their training. Finally, an examination of the above data reveals discrepancies in the degree of participation by the various provinces, notably Quebec. In the construction

58 Canada Employment and Immigration Commission, Policy and Program Analysis, Strategic Policy and Planning, 'Legislative / regulatory barriers to interprovincial labour mobility' (Ottawa: unpublished mimeo, 29 October 1979)
59 Unpublished data compiled on Interprovincial Standards Examinations for the period 1 January 1980 to 31 December 1980

TABLE 3

Number of seals guaranteeing interprovincial
mobility issued to craftsmen

	1980	Total
Newfoundland	532	5 287
Nova Scotia	563	5 803
Prince Edward Island	68	753
New Brunswick	732	5 224
Quebec	93	350
Ontario	2 928	33 393
Manitoba	640	613
Saskatchewan	2 194	6 325
Alberta	3 245	27 777
British Columbia	2 133	19 923
NWT & Yukon	82	678
Total	13 210	106 126

trades, for example, in 1980 Ontario granted 828 seals to electricians, while Quebec granted only 76; 353 seals went to plumbers in Ontario, and only three to plumbers in Quebec.[60] An explanation for the relatively few seals issued in Quebec lies both in the lack of publicity given the program and a less well-structured apprenticeship program, which results in a small number of trades being covered by the Seal Program. Quebec's relative lack of participation in the Seal Program, together with the fact that it has a system of compulsory certification in which provisional certificates are not granted, poses serious problems for labour mobility.

As in the professions, non-technical requirements for the acquisition of a provincial licence such as residence in the province or the imposition of higher fees may also create barriers to labour mobility. For example in Quebec under Section 38 of the Public Health Protection Act[61] persons wishing to operate a laboratory organ tissue bank, a vacation camp, or an ambulance service, to act as a funeral director, or to practice embalming, cremation, or thanatopraxy, must have resided in Quebec for at least twelve months in order to obtain a licence.[62]

---

60 Ibid.
61 Loi de la protection de la santé publique, L.R.Q. 1977, s. P-35
62 This information on Quebec is taken from Courtois et al., memorandum to Marc-André Bédard (see n. 49).

In situations where persons residing or businesses located outside a province wish to do work or provide services in the province, issues of labour mobility and capital or business mobility intersect. Barriers may be imposed in the form of regulations which either impose higher licence fees upon non-residents or in fact deny licences to non-residents. Quebec legislation contains many such examples. Regulations made under the Code de la Route refuse the issuance of a taxi-cab license to persons not resident in Quebec.[63] Similar regulations under the Insurance Act and the Travel Agents Act require Quebec residence for anyone requesting a licence.[64] Higher licence fees are imposed upon out-of-province applicants for contractors' permits and brokers' licenses by virtue of Section 35 of An Act Respecting Building Contractors' Vocational Qualifications and Sections 89 and 91 of the Licences Act respectively.[65]

3 Municipal licensing
As well as exercising licensing and certification functions themselves, the provinces also delegate licensing functions to the municipalities. By virtue of the Ontario Municipal Act, for example, the municipalities are empowered to 'license, regulate, or govern' some seventy-two trades and businesses.[66] A recent study of municipal licensing by Makuch and Bossons cites a figure of over 78 000 such licences issued annually in recent years by Metropolitan Toronto.[67] Of course municipal licensing does not directly affect interprovincial mobility, but it may affect internal mobility more generally.

Such regulation may in fact be expanding. Currently a municipality's ability to regulate a particular business or occupation depends upon specific legislative grants of regulatory power for each business. In 1978, however, the Ontario government introduced, but later withdrew for further consideration, Bill 105, which would have given the municipalities a general power to license, govern, or regulate any business.

Municipal licensing raises the problem of non-uniform regulation in different municipalities creating barriers to labour mobility. Potential problems may be eased by the existence of reciprocity agreements between municipalities. In Ontario, for example, five municipalities are party to such an agreement.

63 L.R.Q. 1977, c. C-24
64 Loi sur les assurances, L.R.Q. 1977, c. A-32; Loi des agents de voyages, L.R.Q. 1977, c. A-10.
65 Loi sur la qualification professionelle des entrepreneurs de construction, L.R.Q. 1977, c. Q-1; Loi des licences, L.R.Q. 1977, c. L-3
66 R.S.O. 1980, c. 302
67 John Bossons and S.M. Makuch, 'Municipal licensing: regulation in search of a rationale,' draft of a study prepared for the Ontario Economic Council

Makuch and Bossons found that municipal licensing generally created little interference with either entry or mobility except for taxicabs. They do, however, recommend the restriction of municipal powers to the certification of competence and reliability rather than the licensing of entry on other grounds. While municipal licensing may not impede labour mobility in a large way, it makes relocation more onerous than it need be.

Portability of employment-related benefits
Pension rights and paid-in premiums for various public insurance and compensation schemes are not easily portable or readily transferable, creating a 'lock-in' effect which may make workers reluctant to seek employment elsewhere and thereby impede labour mobility. Again, the mobility effects are not necessarily interprovincial in character but may also affect mobility between employers within a province.

With regard to public pension plans, there is now portability between the Quebec and Canada Plans. However, the other provinces have the constitutional right to establish their own plans, and there is no guarantee that the same degree of portability would continue if provincial government plans proliferated.

Lack of portability in private pension plans is one of the more important obstacles to labour mobility, not only between provinces but also between employers in the same province. As of 1978, 54 per cent of all employed, full-time paid workers were covered by private pension plans.[68] Private pension plans have basically developed with a minimum of government intervention, allowing employers a great deal of freedom to design an infinite variety of private plans making portability of the kind that exists under the Canada Pension Plan difficult if not impossible. In six of the provinces pension benefits legislation has been enacted establishing minimum standards of protection. Similar legislation has been enacted by the federal government to cover employees under federal jurisdiction. However, four provinces, New Brunswick, Newfoundland, Prince Edward Island, and British Columbia are still left with no comparable legislation. The only other constraint operating on private pensions plans is the relevant provisions of the federal Income Tax Act.

There are three aspects to the portability issue. The first is 'vesting,' which refers to the employee's right to all or part of the employer contributions made on his behalf upon termination of employment prior to retirement. The second

---

68 Statistics Canada, *Pension Plans in Canada 1978* (Ottawa: Dept of Industry Trade and Commerce, 1978), as cited in the report of the Consultative Task Force on Industrial and Regional Benefits from Major Canadian Projects (see n. 40), Appendix H, at 1

aspect, 'locking-in,' refers to a situation where the terminating employee is not allowed to withdraw either his own contributions or those paid by his employer, requiring the employee to take vested benefits in the form of a deferred pension rather than in the form of an immediate cash settlement. Finally, 'transferability' refers to the ability of the terminating employee to transfer his interest to his new employer's pension plan.

To the limited extent that regulation has been enacted which fosters portability of private pension plans, it relates to vesting provisions. The Department of National Revenue imposes the very minimal requirement that private pension plans must provide for vesting at least after the attainment of the age of 50 and twenty years of service. Provincial legislation has liberalized this to some extent. The Ontario, Quebec, Alberta, and Nova Scotia legislation provides for vesting after age 45 and ten years of service. Manitoba differs in providing for vesting after ten years of service without an age requirement. Recent amendments in Saskatchewan, which came into effect in July 1981, require vesting where years of age and service total 45. All of the provincial legislation provides for locking-in of benefits upon vesting.

Although provincial legislation establishes minimum requirements and some plans contain more liberal requirements, the existing provisions which allow generally for long vesting periods and locking-in of benefits mean that barriers to labour mobility can be and are being created. Employees moving before they satisfy the vesting limitations are forced to forfeit their employers' contributions. However, even the introduction by the provinces of more liberalized vesting requirements would only ease, but not solve, the problem of portability. Even when conditions for vesting are fulfilled, vesting in its present form does not guarantee perfect portability of pension rights. This is due to the fact that payments from the pension fund of the former employer will be based upon the employee's income at the time of employment termination and not on income at the time of retirement. Thus, the payments do not reflect general wage increases in the interim. Improved vesting requirements also do not deal with a problem faced by younger employees due to locking-in provisions. With defined-benefit plans, the method of funding used entails that during the early years of the plan membership, often up to age 45 or later, the cost of the accrued pension may be no greater than the value of the employee's contributions with interest. The money is therefore locked in with no compensating benefit from employer contributions.

Complete portability is only provided by a situation where pension rights can be carried forward from employer to employer. Such portability may be created by means of reciprocal transfer agreements between the employers. The key to such agreements is the essential homogeneity of several employers. They are commonly found among governments at the federal and provincial levels, some of the larger municipalities, crown corporations, universities, and other educational institutions. Such developments as have taken place in this area involve, not reciprocal transfer agreements strictly speaking, but multi-employer pension plans based upon collective agreements negotiated between a single local union and a group of employers or between a group of local unions in the same trade and an employers' association.

As the Ontario Royal Commission on the Status of Pensions has pointed out, it is not clear to what extent the provincial governments could legislate reciprocity unless they went the full step towards requiring uniformity in plan, terms and conditions.[69] The royal commission ended up recommending as its favoured solution to the problems of pension portability a mandatory employment pension plan identical to the CPP and fully portable up to levels related to the 'average industrial wage' at the time of retirement. Even were such a scheme instituted, it would solve only the problem of intraprovincial portability, leaving unsolved the even larger problem of portability between provinces unless all the provinces instituted such schemes combined with reciprocal transfer provisions. As its second choice the Commission restricted itself to seeking improved portability through improvement of the vesting rule by reduction of the vesting period to five years. The Commission dealt with the problem of locking-in by recommending that an employee be able to transfer out the portion of the benefit representing his own contribution to a special locked-in RRSP or to his new employer's pension plan.

Language and culture
Language differences have always had an important effect on labour mobility in Canada both by inhibiting the movement of anglophones into primarily francophone areas (i.e. Quebec) and, more important, the movement of francophones into anglophone Canada. Data from the 1976 Census show that between 1971 and 1976 intraprovincial migration was proportionately equal among the French-speaking and English-speaking population. However, only 2 per cent of

69 Report of the Royal Commission on the Status of Pensions in Ontario, 10 volumes (Toronto: Government of Ontario, 1980). Other sources in preparing this section included Canada Employment and Immigration Commission, 'Legislative / regulatory barriers'; Coward, *mercer Handbook of Canadian Pension and Welfare Plans* (Toronto: CCH Canadian Ltd., 1974); Pesando and Rea, *Public and Private Pensions in Canada: An Economic Analysis* (Toronto: Ontario Economic Council, 1977).

the French-speaking population migrated to another province, compared to 6 per cent of the English-speaking population.[70]

Language differences are built into the fabric of Canada and can be considered a 'natural' barrier to labour mobility. More concern is aroused by specific provincial legislation, in the form of Quebec's Bill 101, which consciously sets out to intensify linguistic differences between Quebec and the rest of Canada. The aspect of Bill 101 that perhaps creates the most serious barriers to mobility are the provisions regarding language of education, which may entail that children moving to Quebec be forced to continue their education in the official language other than that of their parents' choice. On the other hand, out-migration of francophones from Quebec has probably always in part been held down by the relative lack of education opportunities in French in the rest of the country.

Apart from mobility barriers related to the educational system, Bill 101 may also be affecting migration patterns in a different way, by leading to some migration out of Quebec which otherwise would not have taken place. Either because language legislation is a factor behind their companies' leaving the province, or because they would find work difficult and possibilities for advancement limited in Quebec, anglophones (most notably the young and well-educated) may have an interest in leaving Quebec.

Labour standards

The 'property and civil rights' subsection of the BNA Act gives the provinces major jurisdiction in the labour standards field. As a result, significant variation occurs among the provinces in areas such as minimum wages, hours of work, overtime rates, annual vacation and vacation pay, and notice of termination. While such differences may impose a cost on the worker moving from a province with more generous labour standards to one with less generous standards, a Canada Employment and Immigration paper has concluded that there is little evidence to suggest that their impact is a major barrier to labour mobility.[71]

Personal tax burden

As shown by a taxpayer profile developed by the *Globe and Mail* and the Canadian Tax Foundation in response to the 1981 Ontario budget, significant variations exist between the provinces in terms of the personal tax burden borne by individual taxpayers, ranging from Alberta, which imposes the lowest tax

---

70 1976 Census of Canada, 92–834, Table 1, as cited in Canada Employment and Immigration Commission, 'Legislative / regulatory barriers'

71 Canada Employment and Immigration Commission, 'Legislative / regulatory barriers'

burden, to Quebec, which imposes the highest.[72] Table 4 shows the different provincial tax burdens faced by a hypothetical taxpayer. The actual tax rates which were used in the computations in Table 4 are found in Table 5.[73]

The problem of the extent to which mere non-uniformity of tax rates introduces an element of inefficiency into the allocation of labour resources is a difficult one and will be encountered again in the section dealing with the effect of corporate taxation on capital mobility. Personal tax rates differentials may, and often do, reflect valid differences in the cost of providing public services. In this event it is difficult to argue that differential rates (reflecting differential levels of public services provided) create distortions in trade flows. Rather, they reflect diversity in preferences for public goods which citizens can realize by, in effect, voting with their feet.

Education

The educational system has an indirect impact on labour mobility but is much more relevant to the larger issue of personal mobility. As suggested earlier, differences and incompatibilities in school systems may affect labour mobility depending upon the extent to which their children's education affects parents' decisions to move to another province. Provincial variations in curriculum requirements may result in children not receiving full credit for past work and being placed back in a lower grade. Differences in the number of grades required for high school graduation create even more serious school system incompatibilities, with Grade 13 being compulsory in Ontario but only Grade 12 in most other provinces and Grade 11 in Newfoundland. On the whole, however, the conclusion reached by the Canada Employment and Immigration study on labour mobility,[74] that school system incompatibilities are usually not enough to deter parents from relocating, appears correct. Less directly related to labour mobility, but certainly an aspect of the larger issue of personal mobility, are the barriers that exist to the unencumbered movement of students seeking post-secondary education. Because of the high cost of such education some provinces have attempted to limit access to their post-secondary institutions for out-of-province students. At present, differential fees for out-of-province students do not exist, although fee differentials for foreign students may provide a precedent for this. Current restrictions take the form of quotas on out-of-province residents in specific faculties imposed either directly or indirectly through weighting procedures.

72 *Globe and Mail*, 21 May 1981, at 1
73 Goodman, Gurney, and Perry, 'Provincial budget roundup-1981,' at 351
74 'Legislative / regulatory barriers'

TABLE 4

Tax form	BC	Alta	Sask.	Man.	Ont.	Que.	NB	NS	PEI	Nfld
Income	1998	1748	2361	2452	2088	3550	2381	2384	2384	2633
Gasoline	240	–	230	235	243	252	198	212	315	315
Sales	310	–	280	280	380	420	400	400	450	550
Cigarettes	170	40	165	175	183	200	170	125	125	313
Amusements	–	–	–	–	100	100	110	110	115	–
Health premium	255	228	–	–	552	–	–	–	–	–
Car Licence	25	23	12	18	45	25	25	31	25	38
Total	2998	2039	3048	3160	3591	4547	3284	3262	3414	3849
Rebates/grants	380	200*	230	325	–	500*	–	300*	–	–
Net payout	2618	1839	2818	2835	3591	4047	3284	2962	3414	3849

* Estimates based on enriched education grants, assuming an average education tax on Ontario residential properties of $500. Alberta figure includes $70 in a natural gas rebate to residents. Newfoundland's denominational school system is largely provincially supported.

NOTE: Taxpayer earns $30 000 a year, supports a spouse and two young children, purchases 4 500 litres of gasoline, consumes $5 000 in sales-taxable goods and services, smokes 500 packets of cigarettes, spends $20 a week on amusements, drives a licensed Chevrolet Citation, and pays his own health insurance premiums.

TABLE 5

Actual tax rates used in computation for Table 4

	Personal income tax (% of federal tax)	Retail sales tax (%)	(%)	Gasoline tax (cents per litre	(%)	Tobacco tax (cents per cigarette)
Newfoundland	58.0	11	22	7.1		2.50
Prince Edward Island	52.5	10	22	7.3	n.a.	1.00
Nova Scotia	52.5	8	n.a.	4.7	n.a.	1.00
New Brunswick	52.45	8	16		34	1.36
Quebec	a	8	20	5.9	45	1.58
Ontario	46.0	7	20	5.4	36	1.46
Manitoba	54.0	5	20	5.7		1.40
Saskatchewan	52.0	5	20	5.6	n.a.	1.32
Alberta	38.5	nil	nil	nil		0.32
British Columbia	44.0	6	20	5.32		1.36

a Quebec's rates under its own schedule range from 13 to 33 per cent of taxable income, subject to tax reductions of 3 per cent of tax payable in 1981 and of 5 per cent beginning in 1982.

Out-of-province quotas appear with the greatest frequency in admissions requirements for medical schools. A survey of the policies of each of the sixteen medical schools in Canada with respect to out-of-province residents reveals that the majority express an explicit preference for provincial residents with the possibility of a limited number of positions available to non-residents.[75] The Universities of Sherbrooke and Saskatchewan have even more stringent policies that restrict admission to provincial residents. The University of Western Ontario admits out-of-province residents only in 'special circumstances,' while the Universities of Ottawa and Montreal have no stated policy. Only Queen's University specifically states that place of residence is not a criterion in the selection process. The restrictive effects of the policies described above are highlighted by data compiled by the Council of Ontario Universities showing that of the 617 registrants in Ontario medical schools in 1979–80, only fifty-six had a province of permanent residence outside Ontario.[76]

Restrictions on out-of-province students also occur in pharmacy, dentistry, veterinary medicine, occupational therapy, and physiotherapy.[77] In veterinary medicine, for example, there are two schools in Canada, one in Guelph and the other in Saskatoon. The two have divided the country into mutually exclusive territories, and the Ontario Veterinary College in Guelph only admits candidates from east of the Manitoba / Ontario border.

Indirect restrictions are placed on interprovincial student mobility through limitations imposed on non-resident students' access to financial assistance. The largely federally financed loan plan is administered separately by each province. A student who attends university outside his or her province of residence is only eligible for a loan and not a grant. In Ontario, even if residence status has been obtained, aid will not be provided unless the student has resided in Ontario for twelve months in a capacity other than attendance in a post-secondary institution. The change in the system of federal grants for post-secondary education in 1977 to one based on provincial population rather than number of students may

75 Compiled from information in Association of American Medical Colleges, *Medical School Admission Requirements, U.S. and Canada, 1979–80, 25th Edition* (Washington DC: Association of American Medical Colleges, 1978). The sixteen universities surveyed were Alberta, Calgary, BC, Manitoba, Dalhousie, McMaster, Ottawa, Queen's, Toronto, Western Ontario, Laval, McGill, Montreal, Sherbrooke, and Saskatchewan.

76 Council of Ontario Universities, Ontario Universities' Application Centre, Ontario Medical School Application Service, 'Statistical summary 1980' (Guelph: Ontario Universities' Application Centre, unpublished mimeo, 25 September 1980)

77 See information contained in Basso (ed. for the Career Information Resource Advisory Group), *Professional Schools Fact Sheets 1980–81* (Toronto: University and College Placement Association, 1980).

lead provinces to encourage universities to place more emphasis on enrolment of provincial residents.

Restrictions on access to welfare (income support) and social services
Restrictions on access to general income support schemes and social services impose extra burdens on persons who have recently relocated in another province. To take advantage of federal cost-sharing in welfare schemes provinces are required to comply with the Canada Assistance Plan, which requires that no province condition eligibility for income support on a minimum *period* of residence within the province. However, this still leaves it open to the provinces to make residence itself a condition. No uniform definition of 'residence' exists, and while Saskatchewan has defined residence as mere physical presence, other provinces, including Ontario, have not set down a definition in their statutes, thus creating a situation in which residence could be taken to involve the presence of the applicant's household and belongings. British Columbia regulations create a special category of 'transients,' implicitly distinguished from the category of 'residents,' and restrict assistance to persons falling in such category only if they do not possess assets in excess of $5. As well, the federal Canada Assistance Plan is not violated by municipal residence requirements, such as are imposed in Ontario for short-term immediate assistance under the General Welfare Assistance Act.[78]

Municipal administrative procedures may also result in discriminatory and restrictive treatment of non-residents. For example, in some cases only vouchers are made available immediately, and cash advances only paid on a monthly basis. In other cases, local addresses may be required to prove an intention of staying in the municipality.

Provincial health care plans are another area in which the federal government has attempted to curb provincial tendencies to place restrictions on migrants' access to social services. The Medical Care Act stipulates that if a provincial plan is to receive federal contributions it must provide coverage to persons while they are moving between provinces.[79] However, provisions in the Ontario plan indicate that coverage may be denied to transients. As well, restrictions are allowed on premium assistance, which in Ontario, for example, is conditioned upon one year of residence in the province. Such conditions can be imposed in health care, as well as in other social assistance programs, because the Canada Assistance Plan covers only income support programs and not other social

78 R.S.O. 1980, c. 188
79 R.S.C. 1970, c. M-8

services, leaving the provinces free to impose restrictions based on the period of residence.[80]

For social services, a survey of the Metropolitan Toronto area has been chosen to provide an indication of the prevalence of residence requirements, both provincial and municipal. Table 6 outlines the services in which such restrictions are imposed.

Evaluation of restrictions on personal mobility
To evaluate the effects of restrictions on personal mobility, two key issues arise. One is the size of the segment of the labour force affected by restrictions. The second is the severity of the restrictions, that is, the form in which they operate.

No data exist on how large an effect on the labour force these restrictions have. Much of the previous discussion suggests that the restrictions apply primarily at a professional level rather than a manual or non-manual level. That is especially the case with trades, because the Red Seal Program operates to offset the effect of mobility restrictions.

At a professional level the difficult issue is determining how severe the restrictions are; whether they are simply a nuisance or more significant and substantive. Regulations which simply require registration by incoming workers from a neighbouring province would appear to have very little effect on labour mobility. On the other hand a required period of residence can significantly hamper labour flows in the skill category involved.

MOBILITY OF CAPITAL

Barriers to the mobility of capital basically take the form of policies that either encourage or require investment within the province or impede the movement of foreign (i.e. out-of-province) capital into the province. These barriers will be examined in six contexts: controls on land ownership, restrictive investment policies, provincial financial institutions, provincial crown corporations, restrictive business policies, and tax policy.

Controls on land ownership
A province may create barriers to inflow of capital by imposing restrictions upon the holding of land by non-residents. While land itself is immobile between the provinces, restrictions on ownership can impede improvement in land use.

---

80 R.S.C. 1970, c. C-1

TABLE 6

Social services in the Metropolitan Toronto area in which residence restrictions are imposed

Program	Description	Residence Requirement
Welfare	Administered by the Dept of Social Services, Municipality of Metropolitan Toronto under the General Welfare Assistance Act and Regulations	Assistance provided for any person in need who resides in Metropolitan Toronto
Family benefits		Provided to residents of Ontario who are in need
City of Toronto Non-Profit Housing Corp.		Rent supplements available for low-income households, for which one year's residence in Metro immediately prior to making application is required
Ontario Housing Corp.	Crown corp. which provides housing on a rent-geared-to-income basis throughout Ontario	Access to housing in Metro Toronto based upon twelve continuous months residence in Metro Toronto in the past five years
Senior citizens apts & residential hotels	Apts for persons 60 years and over administered by the Metro Toronto Dept of Social Services	One year's residence in Metro prior to making application
Private senior citizens homes		A variety of residence periods exist from one year to a minimum of five years' residence in Metro.
OHIP (Ontario Health Insurance Plan)		Coverage for residents. Coverage begins on the first day of the third month following the month of joining a group or individual plan. Does not cover transients, tourists, or visitors.
'Extended Care'	Program under which OHIP covers costs of an extended care facility such as a home for the aged or a licensed nursing home	Eligibility based on twelve months residence in Ontario prior to application for admission to an extended care facility.
OHIP premium assistance		One year's residence in Ontario.
Senior Citizens Drug Benefit Card	Free drugs to senior citizens	Available to persons over 65 and receiving the Old Age Security pension or GAINS. Also eligible are citizens or landed immigrants 65 or older who have lived in Ontario for the past twelve months but do not receive the above.

SOURCE: Compiled from *Directory of Community Services in Metropolitan Toronto, 1979 edition* (Toronto: Community Information Centre of Metropolitan Toronto, 1979)

The most obvious example is Prince Edward Island's land policy. Section 3(3) of the Real Property Act states:

Unless he receives permission to do so from the Lieutenant Governor-in-Council, no person who is not a resident of the province of Prince Edward Island shall take, acquire, hold or in any other manner receive, either himself, or through a trustee corporation, or any such the like, title to any real property in the Province of Prince Edward Island the aggregate total of which exceeds 10 acres, nor to any real property in the Province the aggregate total of which has shore frontage in excess of five chains.[81]

'Resident of the province' is defined in section 3(1)(b) of the Act as 'a bona fide resident, animus and factum, of the province.' The legislation was upheld by the Supreme Court of Canada in the case of *Morgan et al.* v. *Attorney General for Prince Edward Island et al.*[82] as being in relation to property and civil rights in the province within Section 92(13) of the BNA Act.

Saskatchewan has also imposed significant restrictions on landholding. The Saskatchewan Farm Ownership Act provides that a non-resident may not have aggregate farm holdings in Saskatchewan in excess of the value of $15 000 as assessed for municipal tax purposes.[83] 'Non-resident' is defined as someone who does not reside in Saskatchewan for at least 183 days a year or, in the case of a farmer, who does not reside within twenty miles of the border of Saskatchewan for at least 183 days a year. A non-resident creditor who has acquired land by way of settlement or satisfaction of his security interest in excess of the allowable limit has two years from the date of acquisition to reduce his holdings. The Saskatchewan Farm Ownership Board, however, has the jurisdiction to extend that two-year period. The Act further provides that no non-agricultural corporation may have or acquire land holdings in excess of 160 acres in aggregate without the consent of the Saskatchewan Farm Ownership Board. A 'non-agricultural corporation' is defined as a corporation of which less than 60 per cent of all issued voting shares are owned by farmers who are resident persons or which is not primarily engaged in the business of farming.

Quebec imposes extra burdens upon non-residents purchasing agricultural land. Section 8 of the Loi sur l'acquisition des terres agricoles par des non-residents requires a person not residing in Quebec to obtain the authorization of the commission before acquiring agricultural land.[84]

81 R.S.P.E.I. 1951, c. 138, as amended by S.P.E.I. 1972, c. 40, s. 1; now section 3(3) of R.S.P.E.I. 1974, c. R-4
82 [1976] 2 S.C.R. 349; (1975), 55 D.L.R. (3d) 527
83 R.S.S. 1978, c. S-17, s. 7
84 L.Q. 1979, c. 65

The exercise of provincial authority to restrict landholding by out-of-province residents is not yet widespread, but residence requirements have been employed to restrict ownership by non-Canadians. Both Alberta and Manitoba have legislation directed at limiting foreign ownership of agricultural land. In Ontario until recently the Land Transfer Act imposed a stipulated percentage tax upon any person who tendered for registration a conveyance of land to a non-resident.[85]

Restrictive investment policies
In various ways the provinces are able to exert control over large investment funds in order to ensure that a large part of the capital remains with the province. Provincial heritage-type trust funds are the prime examples. However, provincial investment restrictions are also imposed upon pension funds and insurance funds. Various provincial investment schemes to encourage individuals and corporations to invest within the province constitute a related form of control, but they will be dealt with separately later.

1 Government investment funds
The establishment by Alberta of the Alberta Heritage Savings Trust Fund appears to have initiated a trend toward the creation of special provincial funds composed of natural resource revenues. Saskatchewan and Nova Scotia have followed suit by creating Heritage Funds, while Quebec, dealing with renewable rather than non-renewable resources, has adopted a different approach and rather than channelling revenues into a special fund has merely earmarked a certain portion of the royalties now being paid to the province by Hydro-Quebec. These funds, because of their possibly substantial size, may pose significant barriers to the free mobility of capital in the event that they are utilized to promote local industrial development by explicit or implicit subsidies at below-market rates.

The existence of these funds forms part of the larger issue of the federal-provincial allocation of natural resource revenues.[86] At the provincial level a

---

85 R.S.O. 1980, c. 231, s. 2(2). Though initially all non-resident land sales were taxed at 20 per cent (S.O. 1974, c. 8, s. 2(2)), now only sales of restricted land to non-residents are so taxed. Restricted land is defined in the Act as 'farm or agricultural land, woodlands, recreation land ... orchards' (Section 1(1)(o)).

86 Much of the following discussion is based upon papers included in 'The Alberta Heritage Savings Trust Fund: an overview of the issues' (1980), 6 *Canadian Public Policy / Analyse de Politiques: Special Supplement*. The papers of the most relevance for this discussion were Courchene and Melvin, 'Energy revenues: consequences for the rest of Canada' and 'Comment' by Scott.

secondary allocation issue arises about whether natural resource revenue should go into the general revenue fund or into special heritage-type funds. From the perspective of impediments to capital mobility, both methods of revenue utilization can operate as barriers. Generally, the flow of natural resource revenues into general provincial revenues results in lower provincial taxes and higher government expenditures. As is discussed in more detail in the section on taxation, tax rate differentials, and especially incentive-oriented tax cuts, may distort capital flows. Similar effects may be created by the diversion of resource revenues into special investment funds which place a priority on provincial investment, especially provincial development investments which yield lower than market rates of return and in effect operate either as subsidies or tariffs to protect provincial industries. Caution must be exercised, however, in using the terms 'barrier' and 'distortion.' It is not clear that the long-run effect of drawing population and investors to resource-rich provinces will necessarily be an inefficient location of resources. The concern may be, however, that the use by one or more of the provinces of tax incentives or direct forms of assistance through heritage funds to attract industry by offering below-market terms will provoke wasteful competition for new industries and capital among all the provinces.

Table 7 describes various provincial heritage funds and their investment patterns. It should be noted that with regard to the Alberta Heritage Fund, the two forms of investments which tended to provide a counterbalance to inefficient capital flows have recently been subjected to a major policy reorientation. The years 1976 to 1980 showed a strong trend toward increases in the share of the fund's assets channelled into loans to other provinces through the Canada Investment Division, to the extent that the original provisions restricting that Division to 15 per cent of the fund's assets was amended in 1980 and the ceiling raised. However, a decision to cut back on such loans has recently been announced, restricting them to $400 million in 1981, a sharp drop from the total of $600 million loaned in 1980.[87] As well, complaints that investments in marketable securities are not earning a high enough rate of return have forced the Alberta government to respond by promising to convert some of the term deposits and securities into shares of private companies.[88]

2 Pension plan funds

Geographical restrictions placed upon the investments of public pension funds can be considered barriers to the mobility of capital. The Canada Pension Plan, which constitutes the largest of these funds, operates under an arrangement

---

87 'Alberta lending will be cut back,' *Globe and Mail*, 23 July 1981
88 Ibid.

TABLE 7

Provincial heritage funds

	Alberta	Saskatchewan	Nova Scotia	Quebec
	Alberta Heritage Savings Trust Fund (est. 1976)	Saskatchewan Heritage Fund (est. 1978)	(announced in 1981 budget)	(announced in 1981 budget)
General nature	Takes 30% of province's non-renewable resource revenue annually	Collects all the non-renewable resource revenue of the province	Nova Scotia Resources Ltd, created in 1979 to manage and develop province's resource industries, to hold in trust the entire Heritage Fund	Royalty on earning of Hydro-Quebec to be paid directly into public treasury
Total assets	$7.9 billion as of 31 Dec. 1981; estimated $11 billion by March 1982	$604 million as of 31 March 1979; estimated $870 million as of March 1981		
Types of investments	Three investment divisions: – Alberta Investment Division, which considers investments to strengthen and diversify the Alberta economy while providing a reasonable rate of return. Consists mainly of debentures of crown corps but as of 1979 allowed to invest in private companies. Assets of $14.2 billion as of 31 Dec. 1980 – Capital Projects Division, which invests in projects providing long-term social and economic benefits although not yielding a return of income. Assets of $840 million as of 30 Dec. 1980	Three types of expenditures: – Current expenditures include both payment to the consolidated fund for general purposes ($308 million in 1979) and incentive payments for resource exploration development and conservation ($39.5 million in 1979). – Provincial development expenditures on capital projects contributing to long-term economic and social development of province while not yielding direct financial return ($15.9 million paid in 1979).	Funds to be used to give province equity position in all major mineral and resource activities	Funds earmarked for two types of expenditures directly related to economic development: – Private enterprise modernization programs. – Contributions to capital stock of provincial crown corps

TABLE 7 continued

Alberta	Saskatchewan	Nova Scotia	Quebec
Alberta Heritage Savings Trust Fund (est. 1976)	Saskatchewan Heritage Fund (est. 1978)	(announced in 1981 budget)	(announced in 1981 budget)
– Canada Investment Division, which makes loans at best province (normally Ontario) rates to federal or provincial governments or entities whose debt is guaranteed by those governments. Investments total $1.3 billion as of 31 Dec. 1980	– Non-budgetary transactions providing equity or loan capital to crown corps or investing in prescribed securities ($138.9 million in 1979)		
Funds not invested in any of three divisions invested in marketable securities totalling $1.3 billion as of 31 Dec. 1980			

NOTE: Data on Alberta from Alberta Heritage Savings Trust Fund, 1979 Annual Report and Quarterly Investment Report, note (a); Alberta Heritage Savings Trust Fund, 1980-81 Quarterly Investment Report for Quarter ending 31 Dec. 1980; 'Alberta lending will be cut back,' *Globe and Mail*, 23 July 1981. Data on Saskatchewan from Saskatchewan Heritage Fund, 1979 Annual Report; Saskatchewan Budget, 1980.

whereby the excess of expenditures over revenues is loaned to the provinces, in the form of provincial securities, in proportion to each province's contribution to the plan.[89] The provinces pay an interest rate equal to the rate on Government of Canada securities with a maturity of twenty years or more, which is less than the rate which would be paid on funds borrowed in the open market. This arrangement effectively constitues an interest subsidy for public bodies. Funds not taken up by the provinces are invested in federal securities.

Since the inception of the Canada Pension Plan (CPP) in 1966, contributions have consistently exceeded benefit payments and administrative expenses. The result has been a dramatic growth in the investment fund, which stood at $17.8 billion at the end of 1980. Table 8 shows the levels of provincial investment by the CPP since 1966.

British Columbia has allocated CPP funds to the BC Hydro and Power Authority, BC School Financing Authority, and the BC Hospital Authority; Alberta to the Alberta Municipal Financing Corp; Saskatchewan to the Saskatchewan Power Corporation, Saskatchewan Telecommunications, and the Saskatchewan Land Bank Commission; Manitoba to the Manitoba Water Supply Board, the Manitoba School Financing Authority, and the Manitoba Development Corporation; and Ontario to the Ontario Educational Capital Aid Corporation and the Ontario Universities Capital Aid Corporation.

The funds of the Quebec Pension Plan (QPP), as will be discussed in further detail in the section on provincial financial institutions, are held and invested by a crown corporation, the Caisse de Dépôt de Placement, with clear priority given to using these substantial funds for the economic development of the province. A major difference from the CPP is that QPP funds are invested in both the public and private sectors. As well, until recently the Caisse had been committed to investments yielding a market rate of return, its desire to earn a higher rate of return being one of the motives for its decision to drop out of the CPP. However, it has now adopted the controversial policy of offering less than market rates on loans to the government and Hydro-Quebec. The rate chosen is that used by the Alberta Heritage Trust and Savings Fund in lending to the other provinces, which is the best-province (normally Ontario) rate.

With respect to smaller pension funds, in Quebec the Government and Public Employees Retirement Plan and the Construction Industry Pension Fund are treated in the same way as the QPP funds, and invested by the Caisse de Dépôt et de Placement. Ontario has in the past few years eased some of the restrictions on these types of pension funds by allowing public pension plans to invest freely in

---

89 Information on both the CPP and QPP taken from Coward, *Mercer Handbook of Canadian Pension and Welfare Plans*

the market. For example, in 1975 the Ontario government agreed to allow the Ontario Municipal Employees Retirement Board to invest only 20 per cent of its yearly surplus in the market. The rest went into Ontario Hydro long-term securities at market rates minus dealer's fees. Since 1979, however, the Board has been free to invest the entire surplus on the market with no geographical boundaries.[90]

3 Insurance funds
Provincial jurisdiction over the operation of businesses within the province, by virtue of either Section 92(11) or Section 92 (13) of the BNA Act, gives provinces the power to impose restrictions on the investment of funds held by insurance companies. Some provinces have exercised this power in a minor way, by restricting investments in real estate to property located in the province or other places where business is done. Section 94(3) of the Alberta Insurance Act[91] for example, contains such a provision. This is to be contrasted with the comparable section in Ontario legislation, Section 388(1)(a) of the Ontario Insurance Act,[92] which allows investment in real estate 'in Canada or in any country in which the insurer is carrying on business.'

More general provisions enabling the provinces to require that insurance companies invest a certain percentage of their assets within the province also exist. Section 269 the Quebec Act Respecting Insurance provides, for example, that 'every insurer shall invest in Quebec part of its assets in the proportion determined by the regulations.'[93] To date apparently no regulations have been enacted under this section. But the issue surfaced in 1978 in the course of the Sun Life incident in Quebec. Finance Minister Jacques Parizeau stated that the government would force Sun Life to invest the $400 million in Quebec that he said had been collected in the province and invested elsewhere. The episode led, in part, to the commissioning of a massive study, *Savings in Quebec*, which appeared in September 1980. The basic thrust of the study, that a free market should obtain and government action should be focused on lifting restrictions rather than imposing them,[94] makes it uncertain whether Quebec will follow through with the imposition of stringent restrictions on the investment of insurance funds.

90 Taken from 'Policy shift revives row over caisse's role,' *Globe and Mail*, 11 April 1981
91 R.S.A. 1980, c. I-5
92 R.S.O. 1980, c. 218
93 Loi sur les assurances, L.R.Q. 1977, c. A-32
94 Québec, Ministre d'État au Développement économique, Groupe de travail sur l'épargne au québec, *L'Épargne* (Québec: Éditeur Officiel du Québec, 1980), as cited in 'Quebec savings study: the cannon that fired backwards,' *Montreal Gazette*, 9 September 1980

TABLE 8

Canada Pension Fund investments by province, fiscal years 1965/66 to 1979/80 and by month for 1980/81 ($ millions)

Period (fiscal years)	Securities of or guaranteed by											Total	Cumulative total
	Nfld	PEI	NS	NB	Que.	Ont.	Man.	Sask.	Alta	BC	Canada		
1965/66	0.7	0.1	1.2	1.0	–	20.1	2.1	1.4	3.1	5.0	0.1	34.9	34.9
1966/67	11.0	1.9	21.4	16.7	0.4	332.6	34.9	24.5	51.1	84.4	1.8	580.7	615.5
1967/68	12.0	2.3	25.2	19.3	1.9	375.9	39.4	29.7	59.2	96.6	3.8	665.3	1 280.6
1968/69	14.2	2.9	29.2	21.8	2.4	412.0	42.3	35.9	68.4	107.5	5.6	742.2	2 022.9
1969/70	15.6	3.2	31.6	24.2	3.1	445.8	47.7	40.4	77.1	117.2	4.1	809.8	2 832.7
1970/71	16.8	3.5	34.0	25.8	5.1	476.0	51.5	42.9	82.3	125.1	5.4	868.5	3 701.3
1971/72	17.6	3.6	35.7	26.8	6.6	498.3	53.7	42.7	87.1	131.2	6.5	910.0	4 611.3
1972/73	19.0	3.8	38.6	28.8	8.0	536.4	57.4	43.2	94.6	141.5	7.1	978.3	5 589.6
1973/74	21.7	4.3	43.8	32.8	8.1	606.6	64.5	47.8	108.2	161.7	7.9	1 107.4	6 697.0
1974/75	25.8	5.3	50.9	38.3	7.9	701.8	74.5	55.6	126.6	189.1	9.1	1 284.9	7 981.9
1975/76	29.4	6.0	57.3	43.2	8.0	784.1	83.4	62.6	143.4	213.9	10.2	1 441.5	9 423.4
1976/77	31.0	6.4	59.7	45.2	7.7	812.8	86.5	65.3	150.7	224.2	10.7	1 500.2	10 923.6
1977/78	33.0	6.8	62.9	48.0	7.5	851.1	91.1	69.3	162.0	237.3	11.4	1 580.3	12 504.0
1978/79	36.6	7.5	68.2	53.3	7.3	915.9	99.3	76.0	185.5	260.5	12.0	1 722.1	14 226.1
1979/80	40.1	8.3	73.9	53.8	7.1	987.9	106.8	82.3	207.5	282.6	17.7	1 868.1	16 094.2
1980/81 To date	36.2	7.7	66.5	43.8	5.6	882.6	94.9	73.9	194.1	256.4	20.8	1 682.6	17 776.7

TABLE 8 continued

Period (fiscal years)	Securities of or guaranteed by												Cumulative total
	Nfld	PEI	NS	NB	Que.	Ont.	Man.	Sask.	Alta	BC	Canada	Total	
April	5.1	1.1	9.3	7.3	0.8	123.7	13.3	10.3	26.9	35.8	1.8	235.4	16 329.6
May	5.8	1.2	10.7	–	0.9	141.7	15.2	11.8	30.9	41.1	10.3	269.7	16 599.3
June	6.6	1.4	12.2	9.6	1.1	162.3	17.4	13.6	35.6	47.1	2.3	309.2	16 908.3
July	4.2	0.9	7.7	6.1	0.7	102.7	11.0	8.6	22.6	29.8	1.4	195.5	17 104.0
Aug.	3.3	0.7	6.0	4.7	0.5	79.5	8.5	6.7	17.7	23.1	1.1	151.7	17 255.8
Sept.	3.3	0.7	6.1	4.8	0.5	80.4	8.6	6.8	17.8	23.4	1.1	153.5	17 409.2
Oct.	2.9	0.6	5.3	4.2	0.4	70.5	7.6	5.9	15.7	20.6	1.0	134.7	17 543.9
Nov.	3.4	0.7	6.3	4.9	0.5	83.1	8.9	7.0	18.5	24.2	1.3	158.8	17 702.7
Dec.	1.6	0.3	2.9	2.3	0.2	38.7	4.2	3.3	8.6	11.3	0.5	74.0	17 776.7
Total to date	360.8	73.8	700.2	522.8	86.7	9 639.9	1 029.9	793.5	1 800.7	2 634.2	134.2	17 776.7	–

SOURCE: See fn. 69.

Provincial control over financial institutions

Exclusive federal control over banking and currency make it quite clear that the provinces cannot control the movement of capital by establishing separate monetary systems, currency controls, or banks. However, constitutionally valid control over financial institutions other than banks, which includes control over near-banks, gives the provinces considerable powers in this field. The strongest threat to the free movement of capital is posed by the establishment of provincial government-controlled financial institutions that have provincial investment priorities and, as crown corporations, are also exempt from taxation (discussed below).

Provincial governments are involved in numerous industrial development and specialized loan programs, but their activities in the broader area of general banking have been limited. At various points in the earlier part of the century the governments of Newfoundland, Nova Scotia, Ontario, Manitoba, and Alberta have owned and operated near-banks. It has been surmised that the Ontario, Manitoba, and Alberta institutions have owned and operated near-banks. It has been surmised that the Ontario, Manitoba, and Alberta institutions were established to fill a gap in the private market for agricultural credit.[95] The Ontario and Alberta institutions still exist in the form of the Ontario Savings Offices and the Alberta Treasury Branches. Today the Ontario Savings Offices lend their funds exclusively to the Ontario government for general spending purposes. The Alberta Treasury Branches directly compete with other deposit-taking institutions across a wide range of deposit, lending, and financial services. While the Alberta Treasury Branches Act[96] does not explicitly require that priority be given to provincial investments Section 7 gives the minister wide discretion in the choice of investment.

The growth in recent years of feelings of economic discontent in the western provinces has been reflected in a resurgence of interest in the concept of provincially owned financial institutions as instruments of provincial economic development. At the Western Economic Opportunities Conference in June 1973 the issue was raised by the four western premiers as a solution to the generally held view that traditional financial institutions were not responsive to the needs of western economic development. A 1973 Manitoba document, *Guideline for the 70's*, shows that Manitoba has considered setting up a provincial institution modelled on the Alberta Treasury Branches system. The same document also suggests the option of 'strengthening those financial institutions which fall

95 Neufeld, *The Financial System of Canada: Its Growth and Development* (Toronto: Macmillan, 1972).
96 R.S.A. 1980, c. T-7

within provincial jurisdiction, principally credit unions, as another way of encouraging the development of a provincial financial system which would stem the drain of financial resources from Manitoba and make capital more accessible to local development."[97]

A proposal by the NDP government in British Columbia to establish a government-owned near-bank in the form of the BC Savings and Trust Corp. has come the nearest to fruition.[98] Established by legislation in May 1975 and scheduled to begin operation in 1976, BC Savings and Trust was halted in mid-stream by the defeat of the NDP government and the discontinuance of the plans. The specified objects and purposes of BC Savings and Trust, which included supporting the economic and social development of the province and ensuring maximum retention of funds within the province, give a clear indication of the extent to which this sort of institution could constitute a barrier to the mobility of capital.

Even more than the western provinces, Quebec has proved a fertile territory for provincially oriented financial institutions. The major institutions involved are the Caisses Populaires Desjardins and the Caisse de Dépôt et Placement.

The Caisses Populaires Desjardins credit union movement, which is not government-owned but merely provincially regulated, holds on deposit the largest mass of Quebec savings. There are currently 1400 individual Caisse Populaires, with current assets of about $12 billion.[99] As a provincially regulated body, the caisses are not required to hold reserves with the Bank of Canada, thus leaving large sums of money (estimated at $30 million) outside the Bank of Canada's control in matters of monetary policy.[100]

Since the Desjardins movement is owned entirely by Quebeckers, it has traditionally accepted an obligation to support the development of the Quebec economy. However, recent developments in the form of the establishment of a central deposit and loan system which will allow the caisses to become involved for the first time in substantial commercial loans, indicate a broader field of activity being opened up. Head of the Caisse Centrale, Bruno Riverin, was quoted in a *Globe and Mail* article of 24 July 1980 as indicating that in the process of becoming a more mature financial institution the caisses would not stop in Quebec but would be looking at investments anywhere, across Canada and also

97 Cited in Benson, *Provincial Government Banks: A Case Study of Regional Response to National Institutions* (Vancouver: The Fraser Institute, 1978)
98 Ibid.
99 All information on the Caisses Populaires Desjardins is taken from 'Desjardins Caisses to begin central deposit loan system in September,' *Globe and Mail*, 24 July 1980.
100 Ibid.

in the international money markets. In the future, therefore, the Caisses Populaires may pose less of a threat than they have in the past to the free movement of capital.

Unlike the Caisses Populaires, the Caisse de Dépôt et Placement (CDP) is a government institution and in fact the fifth biggest crown corporation in Canada.[101] Established in 1975 when Quebec dropped out of the Canada Pension Plan as the body which would be responsible for investing the funds of the Quebec Pension Plan, it also handles the funds of other public and para-public agencies. Its 1980 annual report indicates total net contributions in 1980 of $888.1 million, and total assets of $11.75 billion, consisting of $8.35 billion in public sector instruments and $3.40 billion in private sector investments.

At the time the CDP was established there were concerns both that the funds would be tampered with by the government for its own financing purposes and also that the province was laying the foundations for a central bank. There was never any doubt that the funds in the CDP would be used to accelerate the long-term economic development of Quebec. However, the CDP has until recently also maintained the policy of investing prudently at market rates of return and denied any special role of subsidizing either the government, municipalities, or local industries. As a result, many of the fears sparked by its creation were quieted and the CDP did not play a significant role in the government's financial and economic policy-making.

Much of this has changed in the last two years, with government attempts to create a much stronger political role for the CDP. A policy reorientation involving less than market rates on loans to the government and Hydro-Quebec, increased allocation of funds to public financing, increased investment in companies deemed strategic to the Quebec economy (e.g. Gaz Metropolitan Inc.), and a more active role in the direction of companies in which it has a substantial interest, has sparked intense controversy and resulted in the resignation of key members of the board of directors.

Provincial crown corporations
A recent study by Vining and Botterel places the total number of provincial crown corporations at 197, with Newfoundland owning 37, Quebec 33, British Columbia 27, Saskatchewan 24, Ontario 21, Alberta 18, Manitoba 13, New Brunswick and Nova Scotia 10 each, and the Yukon Northwest Territories 2

---

101 All information on the Caisse de Dépôt et Placement was taken from the following newspaper articles: 'Caisse assets rise by 20.5%,' *Globe and Mail*, 13 March 1981; 'Policy shift revives row over Caisse's role,' *Globe and Mail*, 11 April 1981; 'Rate policy change stirs Caisse controversy in Quebec,' *Globe and Mail*, 13 April 1981; 'Caisse profits and assets up in 1980,' *Globe and Mail*, 22 May 1981.

each.[102] The same authors estimate that provincial crown corporations own almost $59 billion in assets.

Several aspects of the existence and operation of crown corporations are relevant to the issue of misallocation of capital. Certain crown corporations, the various provincial development corporations being prime examples, have the stated objective of investment in, and development of, specific sectors of the provincial economy. The restrictions placed on the investment of the funds held by these types of crown corporations are discussed more fully in the section on industrial incentives.

A more pervasive aspect of crown corporations that introduces dislocations into the flow of capital is the special concessions given to crown corporations, both in obtaining financing and in tax status. Grants, loans on better than market terms, and guarantees permitting private sector borrowings against the government credit all represent explicit or implicit forms of state subsidy and give crown corporations an advantage over their private sector counterparts. As discussed earlier, provincial heritage funds are used to a significant extent to provide financing for provincial crown corporations.

1 Financing
Ontario, Quebec, Manitoba, Saskatchewan, and British Columbia have been chosen as examples to explore the level of financial assistance extended to provincial crown corporations, primarily because in each case large provincial power corporations account for the largest portion of loans and guarantees. The levels of financial assistance are shown in Table 9.

2 Tax status
As well as having advantageous access to financing, many crown corporations are exempt from paying income tax.[103] This may entail significant distortions in the allocation of capital. Section 149(1)(d) of the federal Income Tax Act,[104] which applies not only to federally imposed income tax but also to provincial corporate tax for the seven provinces (i.e. not Ontario, Quebec, or Alberta) who collect their taxes through Ottawa by means of tax collection agreements, expressly exempts from taxation:

---

102 Vining and Botterell, 'An overview of the origins, growth, size, and functions of provincial crown corporations' in Prichard, ed., *Crown Corporations in Canada: The Calculus of Instrument Choice* (Toronto: Butterworths, 1982)
103 Information on taxation is taken from Prichard, *Crown Corporations in Canada.*
104 R.S.C. 1970, c. I-5; sections 149 and 27 are cited as amended by S.C. 1970–71–72, c. 63.

TABLE 9

Levels of financial assistance to provincial crown corporations

Total loans and advances outstanding	Annual level of loans and advances	Guarantees
Ontario		
$8 billion in loans and advances to corporations, boards, and commissions, with $3.8 billion owed by Ontario Hydro.	$448 million, of which $300 million went to Ontario Hydro	Total outstanding of $7.52 billion, of which $7.50 billion were borrowings of Ontario Hydro
Quebec		
	$259 million in investments in crown corporations; $207 million in loans and advances	In 1980 Hydro-Quebec borrowed $2.1 billion which was guaranteed by the province
Manitoba		
$1.3 billion in advances to crown corporation agencies, boards, and commissions, with $908 million to Manitoba Hydro-Electric Board		$2 billion of securities guaranteed, with $1.6 billion those of Manitoba Hydro-Electric Board
$245 million invested in shares and debentures of crown corporations		$2 million in bank loans guaranteed
Saskatchewan		
$1.8 billion in loans advances to crown corporations, with $920 million to Sask. Power Corp	Annual loans of $390 million, including $21 million from Heritage Fund, of which $120 million went to Sask. Power and $29 million to Crown Investments Corp.	$1.8 million
Total investment in crown corporations of $482 million	Annual investment in crown corporations of $115 million (from Heritage Fund)	
British Columbia		
$393 million in investments in and advances to Crown corps.		Total of $7.5 billion, of which $5.1 billion were borrowings of BC Hydro

SOURCE: *Ontario:* All figures are as of March 1980 and are taken from the 1979-80 Ontario Public Accounts. With regard to loans to Ontario Hydro, the province has issued US dollar debentures on behalf of Ontario Hydro. The proceeds are advanced to Ontario Hydro in exchange for US dollar bonds with the same terms and conditions. *Quebec:* All figures are as of March 1980 and are taken from the 1980 Quebec budget. *Manitoba:* All figures are as of March 1979 and are taken from the 1979 Manitoba Public Accounts. *Saskatchewan:* All figures are as of March 1979 and are taken from the 1978-79 Saskatchewan Public Accounts. The $1.8 million guarantee figure is based on 'funded debt,' which refers to the intermediary activity of borrowing on behalf of crown corporations. As the corporations make payments on the debt, the amount of the advance is reduced accordingly. *British Columbia:* All figures are as of March 1979 and are taken from the 1979 B.C. Public Accounts.

a corporation, commission or association not less than 90% of the shares or capital of which was owned by Her Majesty in right of Canada or a province or by a Canadian municipality, or a wholly-owned Corporation subsidiary to such a corporation, commission or association.

Section 27 of the Income Tax Act negates the effect of the above provisions with respect to those crown corporations listed in Schedule D to the Financial Administration Act,[105] none of which, however, are provincial crown corporations.

In Ontario the effects of the federal Income Tax Act are duplicated by Section 49(1) of the Ontario Corporations Tax Act,[106] which exempts from taxation corporations referred to in Section 149(1)(d) of the federal Act. Section 12(10) denies the exemption of certain crown corporations as prescribed in Section 601 of Ontario Regulation 350/73, but the impact of the regulation on provincial crown corporations is minimal. In Quebec, Section 985 of the Taxation Act provides: 'A corporation, commission or association, the shares, capital or property of which are at least 90% owned by her Majesty in right of Canada or a province ... is exempt from tax.'[107] Section 192 of the same Act appears to negate Section 985 by imposing tax on any corporation 'carrying on business as an agent of her Majesty or of the government unless otherwise provided by the regulations.' However, the regulations again reverse the situation by providing: 'For the purposes of the first paragraph of section 192 of the Act, section 985 of said act applies to every Quebec or Canada Crown corporation with the exception of the following corporations ...'[108] The end result is that in Ontario and Quebec, as in the rest of Canada, all provincial crown corporations are exempt

---

105 R.S.C. 1970, c. F-10
106 R.S.O. 1980, c. 97
107 Loi sur les impôts, L.R.Q. 1977, c. I-3, s. 985 [am. 1980, c. 13, s. 100]; s. 192 [am. 1980, c. 13, s. 13]
108 'Règlement sur les impots,' Décret 1981–80 (1980), 112 (33) *Gazette officielle du Québec (Partie 2)* 3609, 25 juin 1980, art. 192R1 [am. 'Règlement modifiant de nouveau le Règlement sur les impôts,' Décret 3926–80 (1980), 112 (63) *Gazette officielle du Québec (Partie 2)* 7121, 22 décembre 1980, art. 5 (1) at 7123]. The corporations listed are the St Lawrence Seaway Authority, Atlantic Pilotage Authority, Great Lakes Pilotage Authority, Pacific Pilotage Authority, Air Canada, Federal Mortgage Exchange Corporation, National Railways (as defined in the Canadian National-Canadian Pacific Act R.S.C. 1952, c. 39), Seaway International Bridge Corporation Ltd, Eldorado Aviation Ltd, Eldorado Nuclear Ltd, Freshwater Fish Marketing Corporation, Petro-Canada, Canada Mortgage and Housing Corporation, Canada Deposit Insurance Corporation, Farm Credit Corporation, Cape Breton Development Corporation, Northern Transportation Company Ltd, Polysar Corp. ltd, Export Development Corp., Canada Broadcasting Corporation, Teleglobe Canada, and Via Rail Canada Inc.

from tax in their own province. The Quebec Act leaves open the possibility that crown corporations controlled by other provincial governments would be liable to be taxed in Quebec.

With regard to the capital tax, in three of the provinces, Ontario, Manitoba, and British Columbia, crown corporations, federal or provincial, are essentially exempt from tax. In Ontario, Section 63(1) of the Corporation Tax Act exempts from the capital tax all corporations exempt from income tax under the provisions of Section 49(1). As with the corporate income tax, certain crown corporations as prescribed by regulation are made ineligible for the exemption.[109] In British Columbia Section 20(1) of the Corporation Capital Tax Act[110] exempts from taxation all corporations exempt from income tax under Section 149(1) of the federal Income Tax Act. Subsection (2) contains the rider that the above provision does not apply to certain crown corporations designated by regulation, but again, the regulation has minimal impact on provincial crown corporations. In Manitoba, Section 13(2) of the Corporation Capital Tax Act,[111] which provides the basic exemption, mirrors the comparable BC provision. Subsection (3) goes on to provide that Subsection 2 does not apply to any crown corporation 'which in the opinion of the minister is engaged in a commercial operation.'

In the 1981 budget, which introduced major reforms in corporate taxation, Quebec, in a departure from the example of the other provinces, introduced measures requiring provincial crown corporations to pay capital tax.

Restrictive business policies
The provinces have the power to control business development and operations within a province through both financial and regulatory policies, and in so doing they can distort capital mobility either by subsidies provided to in-province businesses or by burdens and barriers placed upon the activity within the province of out-of-province businesses.

1 Financial assistance and industrial incentives
All the provinces have a variety of incentives to encourage businesses to settle or increase their activities in the province.[112] The diversity of what may be generally termed industrial subsidies is staggering, including not only the more direct and obvious forms of assistance such as grants, loans, and loan guarantees, but also

---

109 R.S.O. 1980, c. 97
110 R.S.B.C. 1979, c. 69
111 S.M. 1976, c. 68
112 At one stage in the preparation of this study an attempt was made to document the various programs; the result ran to nearly a hundred pages.

indirect forms of assistance through government provision of support services and infrastructure either across an entire industry or on a selective basis to individual businesses. Provincial government activity in the areas of business counselling and research and development, provision of transportation facilities, and development of export markets stand as typical examples of the latter. Many of the more formal assistance programs are administered by provincial departments of industry and commerce. As well, most of the provinces have created provincial development corporations which are directly responsible for encouraging business development within the province.

In some cases provincial incentive programs are underwritten in part by federal funds, through what are known as General Development Agreements (GDA). Each of the ten provinces has signed such an agreement with the federal Department of Regional Economic Expansion (DREE), with each GDA making provision for specific subsidiary agreements detailing specific programs to be cost-shared with the federal government.

While established incentive programs account for a major portion of provincial industrial subsidies, subsidies are implemented by many other routes, including the use of the tax system and also simply on an ad hoc basis, as in the case of the recent Ontario government payment to Ford Motor Co. to establish a plant in the province.

Faced with the extensiveness and diversity of such programs one finds it difficult, if not impossible, to distinguish between the various forms that subsidies take in trying to discern which are distortions or barriers and which are not.

A concise impression of the amounts of money involved is presented by Table 10, which indicates the total amounts of provincial involvement in terms of loans, investments, and loan guarantees in various sectors. A more detailed presentation of the diversity of subsidy programs and the dollar amounts involved can be found in the appendix to this chapter.

2 Regulation of companies

The extent of provincial control over corporations is not clearly defined, especially for federally incorporated companies. However, with regard to provincially incorporated companies Section 92(11) of the BNA Act confers on provinces the right to incorporate companies, and Section 92(13), which gives the provinces power over property and civil rights, allows them to regulate business within the province.

Several provinces have legislated residence requirements for directors of provincially incorporated companies. Under the Alberta Companies Act, at least half of the members of the board of directors must be resident Albertans as

TABLE 10

Percentage distribution of loans and investments by sectors (excluding indeterminate sectors) and guarantees, by province and for federal government, 1978-9

	Nfld	NS	PEI	NB	Que.	Ont.	Man.	Sask.	Alta	BC	Total provincial	Total federal	Total federal and provincial
Loans and investments (000)													
Agriculture	2 109	58 660	5 415	24 638	349 625	57 663	72 958	78 110	144 122	–	793 300	2 867 736	3 661 036
Fisheries	21 246	21 359	615	27 742	13 308	–	1 370	–	–	–	85 680	1 507	87 187
Natural resources	38 345	677	–	3 033	56 333	11 752	1 410	3 000	420 156	–	534 706	2 227	530 933
Industrial and commercial development	35 318	159 331	22 628	31 910	724 311	186 451	29 013	140 810	199 778	82 065	1 671 615	3 618 310	5 285 925
Export markets	–	–	–	–	–	–	171	183	1 029	–	1 383	2 067 417	2 068 870
Housing	49 403	73 171	10 076	67 436	548 418	722 176	13 515	10 433	574 393	249 385	2 318 406	3 318 202	5 626 608
Other sectors	1 205	–	638	297	16 842	122 781	263	381	27 513	5 397	175 262	165 241	340 503
Indeterminate sectors	–	12 794	–	–	2 411 028	450 600	22 308	71 986	1 312 228	161 254	4 442 198	–	4 442 198
Total (excl. indeterminate sectors)	207 626	313 238	39 417	155 055	1 708 837	1 100 823	118 600	232 917	1 366 991	336 847	5 580 359	12 040 710	17 621 062
Total	207 626	326 032	39 417	155 055	4 119 864	1 551 423	140 908	304 902	2 679 219	498 101	10 022 550	12 040 710	22 063 260
Guarantees outstanding (000)													
Agriculture	–	672	57	882	62 945	10 044	80	5 845	181 575	3 605	265 705	142 099	407 804
Fisheries	–	–	9	71	350	–	–	–	–	–	430	13 559	13 189
Natural resources	–	–	–	8 504	2 898	–	–	32 070	–	–	43 472	19 198	62 670
Industrial and commercial development	32 258	3 822	723	59 902	128 204	13 918	4 000	4 406	3 787	14 701	265 801	266 405	532 206
Export markets	–	–	–	–	–	–	–	–	–	–	–	1 962 863	1 962 843
Housing	–	–	138	–	–	38 580	607	1 941	1 654	–	42 920	21 363 562	21 406 402

TABLE 10 continued

	Nfld	NS	PEI	NB	Que.	Ont.	Man.	Sask.	Alta	BC	Total provincial	Total federal	Total federal and provincial
Other sectors	8 810	674	–	264	236 016	51 187	3 154	13 633	47 151	–	360 971	722 368	1 083 329
Indeterminate sectors	–	–	–	–	–	–	–	–	–	–	–	–	–
Total	41 018	5 168	1 090	69 521	430 413	113 729	7 841	57 895	234 167	18 306	979 299	24 490 054	25 469 351
Loans and investments–percentage distribution (excl. indeterminate sectors)													
Agriculture	0.1	18.7	13.7	15.9	19.4	5.2	61.3	33.5	10.5	–	14.0	23.8	20.7
Fisheries	10.2	6.8	1.6	17.9	0.7	–	1.2	–	–	–	1.5	0.0	0.5
Natural resources	18.4	0.2	–	2.0	3.1	1.1	1.2	1.3	30.7	–	9.4	0.0	3.0
Industrial and commercial development	45.9	50.8	57.4	20.6	45.3	16.9	24.7	60.4	14.7	24.4	31.2	30.0	30.4
Export markets	–	–	–	–	–	–	0.1	0.1	0.1	–	–	17.2	11.7
Housing	23.7	23.4	25.6	43.5	30.5	65.6	11.4	4.5	42.0	74.0	40.9	27.6	31.8
Other sectors	0.5	–	1.7	0.2	0.9	11.2	0.1	0.2	2.0	1.6	3.1	1.4	1.9
Indeterminate sectors													
Total	100.0	100.0	100.0	100.0	100.0	100.0	100.0	100.0	100.0	100.0	100.0	100.0	100.0

SOURCE: A. Ryba, Economic Council of Canada

well as Canadian citizens. The British Columbia Companies Act provides that at least one director must be ordinarily resident in the province.

The provinces also have some power to regulate the activity of companies incorporated in another province. All provinces except New Brunswick require extraprovincial corporations to register as a condition of doing business, but even New Brunswick requires extraprovincial companies to file annual returns. Most provinces also impose duties on these companies such as retaining an attorney resident in the province and giving notice of changes in corporate activities or structure. In practice these do not pose much of a barrier, though the provinces do have the right to refuse registration.

Reference should also be made at this point to the earlier discussion, in the context of labour mobility, of the more onerous occupational licensing requirements which are in some cases imposed upon non-residents.

3 Regulation of business combinations

There are three ways in which business combinations can be effected: sale of shares (or a takeover bid), sale of assets, and statutory amalgamation.

Provincial legislation covering corporations and securities does not significantly hinder interprovincial sales of corporate assets or takeover bids, although there have been a few recent cases where governments have blocked interprovincial takeovers. British Columbia managed to block the Canadian Pacific bid for MacMillan-Bloedel by relying on sanctions related to provincial control over timber resources. In Quebec, the government intervened to prevent a Nova Scotia firm from taking over Crédit Foncier, a Quebec-based trust company.

Interjurisdictional statutory amalgamations are more significantly hindered by provincial legislation, which makes it necessary for one of the corporations to transfer into the jurisdiction of the other before amalgamation. Ontario can be taken as an example. Section 196(1) of the Ontario Business Corporations Act provides for statutory amalgamation of corporations but only covers companies incorporated in Ontario. Interjurisdictional amalgamations require first of all the acquisition of a certificate of continuation under Section 198(1) of the Act which has the same effect as if the company were originally incorporated in Ontario.

Difficulties arise because such transfers are only possible when reciprocal legislation exists in the respective provinces. So far, only the federal government and four of the provinces have adopted such legislation.

While the barriers to business mobility created by such restrictions are not as serious as they might be if there were no other methods of merging available, their existence does lead to disadvantageous tax consequences and higher transaction costs and may retard some business combinations.

4 Securities regulation

Securities and prospectus requirements are provincially regulated, which may create barriers to the raising of capital across provincial boundaries.

A corporation wishing to raise capital in any given province is regulated by the securities legislation of that province and required to conform to its prospectus requirements. In themselves, prospectus requirements cannot be construed as a discriminatory barrier to the interprovincial flow of capital if the offer is restricted to a single province. They may become so, however, if an offer is made on a nationwide basis and the offerer is required to meet the prospectus requirements of each of the ten provincial authorities.

In practice, difficulties are alleviated by co-operation among the provinces, which have agreed upon a standard procedure for filing a prospectus. It involves the choice of a provincial jurisdiction, with the administrator of that jurisdiction assuming responsibility on behalf of each of the other provincial administrators for clearing difficulties with the issuer. However, this agreement does not have the force of law, and provincial authorities retain their discretion to accept or reject a prospectus.

The position adopted by the Quebec Securities Commission in requiring that prospectuses be filed in French in accordance with the Official Languages Act has added additonal costs and delay.

The tax system and capital mobility

The effect of many of the industrial subsidies and incentives which have been examined earlier as barriers to capital mobility can be duplicated by an appropriately chosen set of taxes. The Canadian tax system in all its various facets either affects or has the potential to affect the interprovincial mobility of all three of the factors under consideration: labour, goods, and capital. The influences are both direct and indirect, and for any given tax measure there may be several ramifications. Personal income tax, for example, is most relevant to the issue of labour mobility but has spillover effects into the area of capital mobility in situations where, as for example in Quebec, corporate investment decisions may be affected by the high personal tax rates on corporate executives. As well, personal tax credits may form part of provincial investment programs. Conversely, the corporate tax rate, which primarily influences capital mobility, also indirectly affects labour mobility in that the movement of labour is affected by job availability. The major aspects of the tax system which have been selected for discussion are corporate income tax, special investment incentive measures, capital tax, retail sales tax, and gasoline and fuel tax.

1 Corporate income tax

The corporate tax may be considered a barrier to capital mobility in situations where tax differentials between the provinces create distortions in the investment patterns that would result from an efficient allocation of resources. As with other forms of barriers to mobility, distortions may operate in several ways: by luring out-of-province capital into the province and thereby hindering movement of capital into other provinces; by ensuring that in-province capital remains in the province; by tax 'exporting,' whereby non-resident corporations pay a tax burden which exceeds the benefits derived from the province, which cheapens the cost of providing locally consumed public services, which in turn operates as a fiscal bonus to attract further resources into the province; and by penalizing companies that operate in more than one province by forms of double taxation. The eradication of such distorting tax differentials is what is entailed by the concept of tax harmonization, which was strongly advocated by the Carter Commission on Tax Reform.

Apart from the overriding question of the extent to which provincial desires to control economic and social development through their tax systems counterbalance the argument in support of the efficient allocation of resources, the question of tax barriers is also complicated by the difficulty of in fact defining when tax differentials constitute barriers.[113] Special tax credit and investment schemes which directly encourage investment in the province are fairly easily classified as impediments. The same may be said of different formulas for allocating which income will be taxed in which province, if such would result in double taxation. However, as Thirsk has pointed out, the mere existence of non-uniformity in tax rates poses a much more difficult question.[114] Uniformity of tax rates may not in itself bring about a proper allocation of goods if tax differentials in fact reflect differences either in the cost of supplying public services or the level of benefits received by the taxpayer. Thirsk therefore concludes that the focus in tax harmonization should be shifted from tax rates to the fiscal residue which consists of the difference between taxes paid and expenditure benefits received.

Despite the difficulties inherent in a theoretical analysis of tax barriers and tax harmonization, the problems are somewhat lessened in the current

---

113 The following discussion on tax harmonization is based upon Huggett, 'Tax base harmonization.' In Ontario Economic Council, *Intergovernmental Relations: Issues and Alternatives 1977* (Toronto: Ontario Economic Council, 1977); and Thirsk, 'Tax harmonization and its importance in the Canadian federation.' In Bird, ed., *Fiscal Dimensions of Canadian Federalism* (Toronto: Canadian Tax Foundation, 1980).

114 Thirsk, 'Tax harmonization,' *ibid.*

Canadian context by the existence of a high degree of tax harmony. Concern is now being directed at the possibility that this achievement is being eroded.

The high degree of uniformity and harmony in the current tax system has been largely brought about by the series of federal-provincial tax collection agreements introduced in 1962, which pertain to both corporate and personal income tax.[115] By means of these agreements each province legislates its own income tax, and the federal government in turn undertakes to administer it and collect the tax free of charge provided the province agrees to meet certain other conditions. These conditions include use of the federal tax base and acceptance of a common allocation formula based on the proportion of total salaries and wages paid in a province and proportion of gross revenue earned in a province. Provincial flexibility is allowed in the setting of rates. Under current federal-provincial fiscal arrangements the federal government makes available to the provinces a tax credit of 10 per cent of corporation income, but the provinces are left free to impose any additional percentage. Originally, a condition of the tax-collection agreements was that provincial taxes maintain the progressivity of the federal system, which meant that provincial tax could only be expressed as a single percentage of federal tax. This condition has now been relaxed, and the federal government has agreed to administer a variety of provincial tax credits and other measures. The rules used by the federal government in determining whether or not it will administer any given tax measure are that it must not erode the essential harmony and uniformity of the tax system and that it must not jeopardize the efficient functioning of the Canadian economic union by the erection of income tax barriers to normal interprovincial investment flows.

Originally only Quebec did not enter into any tax collection agreement, while Ontario entered only with regard to personal income tax and opted to continue administering its own corporate income tax. However, even though they were outside the formal tax collection agreements, both provinces still adhered to the same tax base and allocation formula as the other provinces, with the result that a high degree of tax harmony was still maintained. However, recent developments are beginning to cast doubt upon the continuance of this state of affairs.

Alberta began administering its own corporate tax in 1981, while British Columbia has given notice of its intention to withdraw from the tax collection agreement. This means that three of the country's largest provinces, which account for 75 per cent of the total corporate taxable income in Canada, will be

115 Information on current tax collection agreements is taken from sources in note 1, as well as from Department of Finance, *Federal Provincial Fiscal Arrangements in the Eighties: A Submission to the Parliamentary Task Force on the Federal Provincial Arrangements, April 23, 1981* (Ottawa: Ministry of Supply and Services, 1981).

outside the joint collection agreement and not formally bound by the harmonization rules. As well, there are growing signs of increasing variations in provincial taxes, both in rates and through special incentives to attract industry into the provinces. Provinces outside the collection agreements have the most flexibility in this regard, of course, and this fact has been the motivation for the Alberta and BC decisions to withdraw from the agreements. The other provinces who remain bound by the agreements are also feeling pressured to follow suit in order to maintain their competitive position and are seeking additional flexibility under the agreements. Concern has been voiced, both in recent Ontario and BC budgets and in a federal document submitted to the Parliamentary Task Force on Federal-Provincial Fiscal Arrangements, at the growing tax competition among the provinces and the spectre of a return to the tax jungle described by the Rowell-Sirois Commission of the late 1930s.

In terms of tax rates, budgets of the last few years have introduced many variations in corporate rates in efforts to stimulate industry within provinces. All provinces except PEI now levy a differential lower rate on small businesses that qualify for the federal small business deduction and a higher regular rate on other corporations. The lower rate for small businesses serves the same function as a subsidy. Some indication of the cost of these measures is provided by BC's estimate in its 1981 budget that the lower rate for small business would entail forgone revenue of $79.1 million in 1981 / 82. Ontario has a three-rate structure, with one rate for small business, the next for large corporations engaged in manufacturing or processing, farming, fishing, mining, or logging, and the third and highest rate for all other corporations. Quebec has introduced a dramatic series of cuts in the corporate tax rate for active businesses to be phased in over the next two years as part of its plan to spur economic development in the province. It is estimated in the 1981 Quebec budget that these cuts will represent a reduction of $434 million in tax revenue when the new system is in full force in 1983. Table 11 summarizes current provincial corporate taxes.

2 Special investment incentive tax measures

The most significant developments in taxation from the point of view of barriers to capital mobility are the various special incentive programs which have been either introduced or proposed by the various provinces. Some involve the corporate tax, but others also involve the personal income tax. The programs in place in Ontario and Quebec are detailed in Table 12.

In a position paper tabled in January 1975 the Alberta government made it clear that the reason for its withdrawal from the federal corporate tax collection agreement was its desire to use the tax system to encourage industrial

TABLE 11

Corporate income tax rates in Canada (percentages)

	Small business	Intermediate category	Basic rate for corporations
Newfoundland	12		15
Prince Edward Island			10
Nova Scotia	10		13
New Brunswick	9		14
Quebec (as of 1 July 1981)	3	13 for selected industries	13, active businesses will drop to 8 in 1982 and 5.5 in 1983
Ontario	10		14
Manitoba	11		15
Saskatchewan	10		14
Alberta	5		11
British Columbia	8		16

SOURCE: *Canadian Tax Journal*, May-June 1981

development within Alberta.[116] The paper proposed several incentive schemes. Although Alberta began collecting its own corporate tax in 1981, no change has yet been introduced in the method of determining the tax payable. The proposals put forward in the 1975 position paper may, however, give some indication of the type of policies which are being considered. They include tax deductions for Alberta residents similar to Ontario's SBDCs and Quebec SODEQs, and manufacturing and processing incentives in the form of reduced tax rates and special deductions for capital expenditures, research and development, and freight costs.

In its budget of 8 June 1979 British Columbia attempted to introduce two tax measures designed to stimulate investment in the province. Both proposals were refused by the federal government on the ground that they created barriers to the free movement of capital among the regions. As a result of this incident, BC has notified the federal government of its intention to withdraw from the tax collection agreement. The first of the controversial tax measures was a dividend tax credit which entailed a special 5 per cent dividend tax credit in respect of

116 Alberta, 'Basic objectives and terms of reference for Alberta business taxation and incentives: a position paper of the Government of Alberta based upon the recommendation of the Provincial Treasurer's Tax Advisory Committee, January 29, 1975' (Edmonton: unpublished mimeo, 1975)

TABLE 12

Tax incentives for provincial investment

Province/program	Operation	Amounts invested
Ontario Small Business Development Corporations (SBDC)	SBDCs are private corporations established for the purpose of directing funds to eligible small businesses. Investors receive a financial incentive equal to 30 per cent of money investment: for individuals in the form of a grant, for corporations in the form of a tax credit. Eligible individuals must be ordinarily resident in Ontario, and corporations must be subject to Ontario corporation tax. SBDCs can only invest in businesses of which at least 75 per cent of the shares are owned or controlled by residents and which pay 75 per cent of their salaries and wages in respect of operations in Ontario.	As of May 1981, 140 SBDCs had been registered in the province and had invested $40 million in small businesses.
Quebec 1) Corporations for the development of Quebec business firms (SODEQ)	Similar to Ontario's SBDCs. Provide tax incentives to individuals investing through a SODEQ in eligible small and medium-sized Quebec-based manufacturing companies. Incentive is in the form of a deduction of the totality of the investment in a SODEQ up to a maximum of 20 per cent of annual earnings or $15 000. Eligible investments are restricted to manufacturing firms whose production is mainly carried on in Quebec and in which voting control is held by Quebec residents.	
2) Industrial incentive funds for small and medium-sized firms	Introduced in 1977. Provides assistance to small and medium-sized manufacturing firms. Participating firms deposit amounts equal to a maximum of one-half of their income tax payable to the Quebec government and are able to withdraw from the fund sums required for the financing of a certain percentage (raised to 50 per cent in 1981) of allowable investments or expenditures. Program discontinued as of 30 June 1981.	
3) Tax abatement	Program runs from 1 April 1977 to 31 March 1981. With objective of assisting manufacturing firms outside of Montreal to modernize and expand operations, program provides for a reduction of tax payable of up to 25 per cent of an allowable investment, up to a maximum of 50 per cent of tax payable.	1981 budget estimates cost of one-year extension of program to be $2 million.

TABLE 12 continued

Province/program	Operation	Amounts invested
4) Shares deduction	In order to stimulate the supply of risk capital, the 1979 budget introduced this measure whereby Quebec residents are allowed to deduct from their taxable income the costs of net purchases of new share issues of qualifying companies, up to a maximum of 20 per cent of earnings of $15 000. Eligible companies are those having the head office or principal place of business in Quebec.	

SOURCE: This information compiled from J. Peter Johnson and Price Waterhouse, *Government Financial Assistance Programs in Canada* (Butterworths: 1980) and Philip H. Doherty et al., *Industrial Assistance Programs in Canada*, 6th ed., 1979 (CCH: 1979). See also the Ontario government publication *Ontario Small Business Development Corporations: A Guide for Businessmen and Investors*, Revised March 1981. Amount invested in Ontario SBDCs is from the Ontario Budget, May 1981. Information on the Quebec share deduction program is taken from *Provincial and Municipal Finances* (Canadian Tax Foundation, 1979).

dividends received by residents of BC from the public corporations whose head office and central management were in the province. The second provided for the establishment of venture capital corporations which would invest in innovative high-risk small businesses. Under the proposals both individuals and corporations investing in such corporations would be eligible for special tax deductions.

3 Capital taxes
Four provinces, Quebec, Ontario, Manitoba, and British Columbia, impose a capital tax on corporations, which involves a tax on the paid-up capital of corporations (Table 13). The current rates of tax are relatively low and would add the equivalent of perhaps 2 or 3 percentage points to the existing tax rates on corporate incomes. The capital tax raises the same issue as provincial variations in corporate tax rate, i.e. the extent to which mere non-uniformity of rates can be considered a barrier or distortion.

One of the most significant developments in this area is the taxation of oil refinery companies in Quebec. In addition to paying corporate income tax on their profits and capital tax they are also subject to a special 'education tax' on their capital. This tax has recently been raised from 1/3 of 1% to 2% in response to the Quebec government's belief that these companies were artificially reducing their Quebec earnings, and hence corporate tax payable in Quebec, by

TABLE 13

Provincial capital tax rates on corporations

Province	General rate	Special rates
Quebec	0.45 of 1%	– 0.9 of 1% on banks and loan and trust companies.
		– additional 2% on corporations refining oil in Quebec.
Ontario	0.3 of 1%	– 0.6 of 1% on loans and trust companies
		– 0.9 of 1% for banks
		– graduated flat fees of $50 or $100 for small companies with paid-up capital under $200 000
Manitoba	0.2 of 1%	– exemption for corporations with paid-up capital under $500 000
British Columbia	0.2 of 1%	– exemption for corporations with paid-up capital under $1 million
		– graduated tax for corporations with paid-up capital between $1 million and $1.25 million

SOURCE: *Canadian Tax Journal*, May-June 1981

forming resource companies in Alberta that sell crude oil to eastern refineries at high prices set by Ottawa.

4 Retail sales tax

The retail sales tax, based as it is on commodity sales, is immediately associated with mobility of goods. However, there are also indirect effects on labour mobility, in so far as perceived cost-of-living differences influence mobility decisions, and also on capital mobility in so far as business investment decisions are based upon price differentials of energy, production machinery, and production consumables.[117]

With regard to energy, only five provinces (Newfoundland, Quebec, Manitoba, Saskatchewan, and British Columbia) have a tax on sales of natural gas and electricity. Newfoundland, however, has a total exemption for energy used by manufacturers, while in Quebec up to 90 per cent of such energy costs are exempt.

Tax exemptions for production machinery, production consumables, and processing materials are becoming the norm, but with substantial provincial variation. Production machinery, for example, is completely exempt in five provinces: PEI, Nova Scotia, New Brunswick, Quebec, and Ontario. British

---

117 See Canadian Tax Foundation, *Provincial and Municipal Finances 1979* (Toronto: Canadian Tax Foundation, 1979).

Columbia has experimented with a one-year exemption, which ended in March 1979, for production machinery purchased by small business; as well, 50 per cent of the tax on certain drilling equipment used in the province is refundable. In Newfoundland the exemption for production equipment is limited to fish processors and the metal balls used for mineral ore processing.

The question of determining how far these variations in retail sales tax operate as distortions is an extremely thorny one, involving questions of the extent to which the exemptions for manufacturers constitute subsidies and the even more basic question of the extent to which provinces with either no sales tax or lower sales taxes are creating distortions in the mobility of labour or capital.

5 Gasoline and fuel tax

Motor fuel is subject to special taxation at the point of sale in all ten provinces, although in Alberta the base is restricted to fuel used in railway locomotives and aircraft. All provinces provide numerous exemptions, refunds, or reduced rates in respect of specific uses, many of which have to do with industrial consumption. Similar problems arise in defining a barrier in this area as with retail sales tax variations and exemptions.

Newfoundland, for example, has agreements with certain companies exempting them from gasoline and fuel taxes for their vehicles. With respect to industrial and commercial uses of motor fuel, Ontario, Nova Scotia, and New Brunswick provide a full industrial exemption. Other provinces provide varying exemptions for different purposes. Fuel used as an input in manufacturing receives preferential treatment, either in the form of an exemption or a reduced rate, in all provinces except PEI. Fuel used in stationary engines is taxed at a reduced rate in Quebec, Manitoba, Saskatchewan, and British Columbia. Fuel used in mining and drilling is exempt in most provinces, taxed at a lower rate in Quebec, Manitoba, and BC, and given no preferential treatment only in PEI.

Evaluation of restrictions on capital mobility

1 Land ownership

Controls on land ownership are not easy to evaluate. Land itself is the least mobile factor of production. However, controls on land ownership can affect land improvements. If prohibitions prevent out-of-province ownership of land, development activity may be significantly affected.

2 Provincial investment policies

With provincial investment policies the key issue is the operation of the Alberta Heritage Savings and Trust Fund and the similar funds which operate in

Saskatchewan, Nova Scotia, and Quebec (though the last three together are less than one-tenth as large as the Alberta Fund).

There has been much discussion of the impact of the Alberta Heritage Savings and Trust Fund on capital markets in Canada, and a number of different effects are involved. If the Fund simply invests money in Alberta in the most efficient projects available, there is no necessary impact on interprovincial allocation of capital because the capital market in the rest of Canada can offset the effect of Heritage Fund investment policies. If private markets guarantee the same rate of return on capital throughout all of Canada, the only consequence of requiring Heritage Fund investment in Alberta would be that private firms invest less in Alberta and invest more elsewhere to compensate for the effect of the regulations through the Funds.

The issue with the Trust fund, therefore, is whether or not the most efficient Alberta projects are selected. With the priority accorded special projects other than on a financial-rate-of-return basis, it seems clear that the most efficient projects are not necessarily being selected and potentially significant misallocation of capital in Alberta results.

3 Business subsidies

With business subsidies, again, the effects on the allocation of capital in Canada are potentially large. As has been emphasized in earlier chapters, however, an important issue is whether the captial market in Canada is segmented from the international capital market or whether a separate segmented national capital market operates. With a single international capital market operating, the only effect from business subsidies being introduced by provinces is that overinvestment occurs in those provinces, with no necessary underinvestment elsewhere because all provinces have equal access to the international capital market. With a segmented national capital market, however, the interprovincial allocation of capital will be affected.

The size of these business subsidies is a further issue, and the data presented in this chapter indicate that the aggregate level of subsidies involved is relatively small. While high subsidy rates may be involved for certain kinds of activities, in terms of total investment activity in the provinces the effects are probably modest.

4 Provincial crown corporations

Provincial crown corporations may restrict interprovincial capital mobility in two ways. First, provincial crown corporations are exempt from federal taxes, and therefore an incentive exists for provinces to 'provincialize' industrial activity in the provinces by organizing manufacturing activity into crown corporations. This is a hotly debated issue at the present time, and if further provincialization occurs the consequences for capital allocation will be significant.

A further issue concerns the operation of provincial power corporations. There is evidence of a high level of subsidy to provincial power corporations, which may result in a significant misallocation of capital in Canada. However, if all provinces simultaneously institute a subsidy system giving preference to in-province crown power corporations, although significant overinvestment in crown corporations can occur it is not clear that the interprovincial allocation of capital will be significantly affected.

APPENDIX:
PROVINCIAL INDUSTRIAL, GENERAL DEVELOPMENT, AND
AGRICULTURAL SUBSIDY AND INCENTIVE PROGRAMS

The following table represents the authors' best efforts to compile a reasonably comprehensive synopsis of provincial subsidy programs. The purpose is to convey an impression of some broad orders of financial magnitude and a sense of the range and diversity of these classes of government programs. However, data limitations and rapid rates of change in program content preclude reliance on this information to make detailed estimates of the impact of these programs on interprovincial trade. Despite these limitations, the unavailability of this information hitherto in accessible form explains why we have chosen to present it.

(NOTE: For this Table, CCH and Price-Waterhouse compilations of government assistance programs have been relied on throughout, as well as government budgetary estimates. All amounts are annual expenditures for fiscal year 1979–80 except as noted otherwise. Sources for provincial agricultural support programs are as follows: Canadian Federation of Agriculture, *Provincial Support of Agriculture: Credits, Grants, and Forgiveable Loans* (April 1981); R.D. Haacle, D.R. Hughes, and R.G. Shapiro, *The Splintered Market* (Canadian Institute for Economic Policy, 1981); provincial budget estimates; and letters from provincial governments. Since these data were prepared, both CCH and Price-Waterhouse have published more recent compilations, and the Economic Council of Canada has published a major study *Intervention and Efficiency: A Study of Government Credit and Credit Guarantees to the Private Sector* [1982].)

APPENDIX

Provincial subsidy and incentive programs

BRITISH COLUMBIA	Program	Amount
INDUSTRIAL SUBSIDIES	*Ministry of Economic Development*	Total departmental budget of $35.95 million including $21.5 million for GDA; $5.6 million for grants; $7.3 million for administration for computer and consulting charges.
	1) Trade Show Assistance Program	Grants of $0.110 million
	2) Trade Mission Program	Grants of $0.375 million
	3) Market Development Assistant Program	Grants of $0.120 million
	4) Incoming Buyer's Program	Grants of $0.035 million
	5) Technical Assistance Program	Grants of $0.150
	6) Business Enterprise Services	Advisory and informational services
	7) Management Development Service	Seminars and workshops
	BC Development Corp. (1980 Annual Report)	
	1) Business Finance Division	$27.8 million in loans & $24.2 million in loan guarantees
	2) Land Division	Total value of land held for development $47.1 million
	3) Projects Management Division	$0.257 million expended on professional services
	Science Council of BC (1980 Annual Report)	$3.5 million in grants
	BC Research Council (1980 Annual Report)	$1 million in grants
GENERAL DEVELOPMENT AGREEMENTS (GDA)	*Subsidiary agreements currently in force under the Canada-B.C. GDA*	(Program and amounts cost-shared between federal and provincial govts. Province committed total of $21.5 million in 1979-80.)
	1) Industrial Development – Industrial Infrastructure Program	Loans of $5.385 million

– Assistance to Industrial Commissions	Grants of $0.183 million
– Research and Analysis	Grants–amount unknown
– Assistance to Small Enterprise Program	Interest-free, forgiveable loans of $1.65 million
– Low-Interest Loan Assistance	Low-interest loans of $7.32 million
2) Agriculture and Rural Development Subsidiary Agreement	Grants of $1.432 million
3) Travel Industry	Loans of $4.648 million

AGRICULTURAL INCENTIVES

Ministry of Agriculture
Total estimated expenditures
1981/82
Minister and Deputy

Minister, Administration	$ 2 989 585
Field Operations	10 809 073
Economics and Marketing Services	1 348 293
Financial Services	46 458 103
Information Services	258 097
Milk Board	267 160
	$62 130 311

As of December 31, 1979 the guaranteed debt was as follows:

Farm Products Industry Improvement Act	$ 7 426 617
Agricultural Credit Act	$ 3 866 444

1) Field Crop Regulation and Inspection	50% shared costs
2) Livestock Financial Assistance	Purchase rebates
3) Agricultural Land Development	Direct loans at 4%, for 15 years
4) Primary Resource Development (to improve underdeveloped land)	Grants of up to three quarters of the capital cost
5) Grasshopper Control	Staff training, technical assistance and financial aid
6) Bee-Yard Bear Protection Program	$2.00 per hive
7) Agricultural and Rural Development Agreement	$11.304 million; 50% recovered from Canadian government

8)	Farm Products Finance	Loans, guarantees, grants—$122 000
9)	Agricultural Credit	Loan guarantees and reimbursement of interest payments; $11.719 million
10)	Co-ordinated Resource Management (to stabilize beef industry)	No figures available
11)	Coloured Gasoline Tax Act R.S.B.C. 1960 c. 63	Refund of 2 cents per gallon of gas
12)	Dishers Area Assistance Act R.S.B.C. 1960, c. 116	Loan guarantees, payment of interest on principal loans
13)	Farm Income Assurance Program	$13.663 million (1981-82 estimates)
14)	BC Food Promotion	$457 792 (1981-82 estimates)

ALBERTA	Program	Amount
INDUSTRIAL SUBSIDIES	*Dept of Economic Development* (1980/81 estimates)	(Total departmental expenditures of $13.5 million budgeted
	1) Transportation Services Branch	in 1980-81, including $11 million for economic development & international trade, $2.5 million for financing of Alberta grain terminals, and $1.2 million for financial assistance to rapeseed processing.)
	2) Strategic Planning Branch	
	3) Industry Development Branch	
	4) Trade Development Branch	
	Dept of Small Business & Tourism (1980-81 estimates)	(Total departmental expenditures of $15.2 million budgeted in 1980-81, including $9.6 million to development of tourism & small business, $4.9 million to Alberta Opportunity Corp.)
	Alberta Opportunity Corp. (1980 Annual Report)	Loans & loan guarantees of $45 million
	Alberta Treasury Branches Small Business Loans	Loans of $15 million
	Alberta Research Council (1979 Annual Report)	(Difficult to quantify value of assistance: 1979 annual report shows annual expenditure of $14.26 million, but also revenue of $15 million)

	Alberta Heritage Savings Trust Fund (1981 estimates; 1980-81 Quarterly Investment Report to quarter ended 31 Dec. 1980)	
	1) Alberta Investment Division	$559 million invested in 1979-80
	2) Capital Projects Division	(Total annual investment in economic projects unavailable but eg from 1981-82 budget include $15.9 million for rail hopper cars & $0.830 million for a food processing development centre.)
GENERAL DEVELOPMENT AGREEMENTS (GDA)	*Nutritive Processing Allowance Subsidiary Agreement*	Grants of $1.9 million
AGRICULTURAL INCENTIVES	Total estimated expenditures for 1980-81 were	$102 533 000
	Partial Breakdown: Departmental Support Services	20 306 000
	Production Assistance	34 507 000
	Marketing Assistance	8 936 000
	Rural Development Assistance	35 083 000
	1) Farmer Training	Employer reimbursed for 40-60% of costs
	2) Agricultural Service Boards	Grants-costs shared with local authorities
	3) Agricultural Societies Program	Unknown
	4) Municipal Seed Cleaning Plant	Grants for 1/3 of construction costs
	5) Native Range Improvement Program	Incentive rebate
	6) Vegetable Production Loan Program	Loans with incentive rebates
	7) Dairy Development Program	Loans with incentive rebates
	8) Specific Guaranteed Farm Loan	$16 million guaranteed (1980-81 estimates)
	9) Direct Loan Program	$36 million in loans (1980-81 estimates)
	10) Beginning Farmers Program	$75 million in loans (1980-81 estimates)

11) Disaster Assistance Program	Unknown
12) Alberta Farm Development Loan	Loans up to $75 000
13) Financial Restructuring Program	Direct loans for up to two years
14) Agribusiness Loan Guarantees	$7.2 million guaranteed (1980-81 estimates)
15) Market Garden Development	Grants of $200-$300
16) Livestock and Semen Fund	Up to $22 000 for technical and marketing assistance
17) Livestock Disaster Indemnity Program	Loss must exceed $100
18) Feeder Associations	Services and financial guarantees
19) Ewe Lamb Retention	Grants of $15/head
20) Horse Industry Branch	Technical assistance
21) Weed Control	Grants
22) Water and Sewage Systems	Technical information plus 50% of total costs
23) Agricultural Manpower	Financing for training
24) Small Farm Development	Grants, special credit for buying land
25) Farm Home Improvement Act	Guarantees 50% of loans up to $5 000
26) Agricultural Relief Advances Act	Loan guarantees and supply purchases
27) Alberta Home Mortgage Corporation Farm Home Lending Program	Loans
28) Farm Fuel Distribution Allowance	Reduction in fuel price by 2.6 cents/litre
29) Sheep Producers Incentive Rebate Program	Loans to a maximum of $75 000 plus annual incentive rebate
30) Agribusiness Loan Programs	$2.3 million in loans

SASKATCHEWAN	Program	Amount
INDUSTRIAL SUBSIDIES	*Dept of Industry & Commerce*	(Total departmental budget of $11 million in 1980-81)
	1) Small Industry Development Program	Interest-free forgiveable loans of $0.674 million
	2) Small Business Interest Abatement Program	Grants of $0.240 million
	3) Product Development Program	Grants of $0.202 million

4) Management Development Program	Grants of $0.022 million
5) Main Street Development Program	Grants of $0.700 million
6) Aid to Trade	Grants of $0.075 million
7) Business Assistance Branch	Management counselling services
8) Grant to SED Systems	Grant of $0.225 million
Dept of Northern Sask. Economic Development Advance Account (1980-81 estimates and 1980 budget)	(1980 budget increased statutory limit of loan capital account to $25 million)
Saskatchewan Economic Development Corp. (SEDCO) (1980 Annual Report)	Loans & loan guarantees of $28 million
Assistance for Inventory & Manufacturing Expansion (AIME)	Loans & loan guarantees amounts unavailable
Saskatchewan Research Council (1979 Annual Report)	(Total expenditures on industrial services of $0.551 million in 1979)
Saskatchewan Heritage Fund (1979 Annual Report, 1980-81 estimates)	(Provincial development expenditures of $49 million shown in 1980-81 estimates, including $0.844 to Interprovincial Steel & Pipe Corp., $9.6 million on highways & development roads.)
GENERAL DEVELOPMENT AGREEMENTS (GDA)	*Subsidiary agreements currently in force under the Canada-Sask. GDA*	(Programs cost-shared 60% by fed. govt and 40% by prov. govt)
	1) Qu'Appelle Valley	No figures available
	2) Interim Water Development	
	3) Mineral Exploration and Development	
	4) Northlands	
	5) Interim Forestry	
	6) Special ARDA	
	7) Iron, Steel, and Related Metals Development	
	8) Agricultural Services Centre	
	9) Interim Agricultural Development	
	10) Planning	

AGRICULTURAL INCENTIVES

Ministry of Agriculture
Total estimated expenditures for 1980-81 — $59 294 350
Partial breakdown:
Program Services — $33 137 760
Grants to local authorities and third parties — $13 156 280
Payments to or on behalf of individuals — $ 8 630 700

1) Special Crop Demonstrations — $33 868
2) Calf-Cash Advance Program — Cash advance of $74/calf
3) Ewe Lamb Retention Policy — Grants of $10/ewe
4) Freight Equalization—Sheep and Wool — Grants
5) Sheep Flock Health Policy — Refunds 75% of farm expenses
6) Assistance for Irrigation Development — $62 672
7) Water Control Projects — Engineering and technical services
8) Land Improvement — Cost paid by province
9) Land Purchase Policy (South Saskatchewan River Irrigation Project) — Price plus $15 a cultivated acre
10) Regional Development Program — Grant of up to $5 000
11) Weed Control — $155 082
12) Coyote Control — 75% of cost of poison bait program
13) Test Well Drilling — $100 390
14) Farmstart — $8.063 million in loans and $2.3 million in guarantees (1980-81 estimates)
15) Market Development Fund — Grants for 50% of costs
16) Small Farm Development — Loans, grants, counselling
17) Grants to Agricultural Organizations and Exhibitions — Grants
18) Agricultural Development and Adjustment Act — Loans
19) Family Farm Credit Act — Loans up to $25 000
20) Farmer Training — Training expenses
21) Irrigation Loans — Max. $180 000 each
22) Hog Assured Returns Program — Costs shared between province and producers on 50:50 basis

23) Agricultural Development $235 000 (1980-81 estimates)
Corporation

24) Saskatchewan Crop $5 027 590 (1980-81
Insurance Program   estimates)

25) Saskatchewan Grain $6 million (1980-81
Car Corporation   estimates)

26) Land Bank $25 million (capital)
(1981-82 estimates)

27) Insect Control Program   Purchase price

28) Cultivation Lease   Cost of development up to
Improvement Program $105/acre

29) Beef Stabilization Plan   Administrative costs plus
guarantee of the fund

30) Record of Performance (to   No figures available
evaluate stock)

31) Farm Water and Sewage $2 068 066 in technical
Program   assistance and equipment
at cost

32) Reservoir and Canal   Total cost of operation and
Maintenance   maintenance

33) Farm Business   No figures available
Management

34) Agriculture Research $25 million, to be spent over
5 years (1981-82 estimates)

MANITOBA	Program	Amount
INDUSTRIAL SUBSIDIES	*Dept of Economic Development & Tourism* (1977-78 Annual Report, 1980-81 estimates)	(Total dept budget of $50.4 million in 1980-81)
	1) Small Enterprise Development Program	Grants of $0.050 million
	2) Human Resources Mgmt Branch	Consulting services and mgmt courses
	3) Market Development Branch, Promotion Assistance Program (PAP)	Grants of $0.040 million
	4) Industrial Design Branch, Design Assistance Program (DIA)	Cost-sharing grants
	5) Technology Branch	
	6) Business Development Branch	Preparing industrial location reports for potential investors
	Product Research and Design Program	Grants & advisory assistance; no figures available

Communities Economic Development Fund	Loans & loan guarantees of $1.98 million
Manitoba Development Corp. (1980 Annual Report)	Loan guarantees of $15 million
Hydro Rate Freeze (1981 budget)	Requires statutory authority of $35.8 million in 1981-82
Manitoba Trading Corp.	Marketing support services & bridge financing
Manitoba Research Council	No figures available
Alcan Smelter	(No direct govt funding but Manitoba Hydro will have to build additional plant to supply Alcan's needs.)

GENERAL DEVELOPMENT AGREEMENTS (GDA)	*Enterprise Manitoba* (operating name of Canada/ Manitoba Industrial Development Subsidiary Agreement)	(Program amounts cost shared 60% by fed. govt & 40% by prov. govt; only figures available are over 5 year period; total of $44 million committed over 5 years details below)
	1) Industrial Development Program	($5 million)
	2) Technology Assistance Program	($16 million)
	3) Enterprise Development Centres Program	($5 million)
	4) Industrial/Commercial Promotion	($2 million)
	5) Community Industrial Infrastructure	($10 million)
	6) Small Rural Enterprises Incentives	($5 million; in 1979-80 loans of $0.564 million)

AGRICULTURAL INCENTIVES	*Ministry of Agriculture* Total estimated expenditures for 1980-81 were as follows:	
	General administration	$ 2 067 100
	Manitoba Crop Insurance Corp.	$ 2 139 200
	Manitoba Agricultural Credit Corp.	$ 1 948 600
	Agricultural Production Division	$ 7 655 700
	Regional Agricultural Extension	$ 5 088 600
	Agricultural Marketing and Development	$ 1 215 800

Canada-Manitoba Value-Added Crops Production Agreement	$ 1 363 400
Acquisition/Construction of Physical Assets	$ 8 305 000
Agricultural Land and Water Development	$ 4 108 100
Total for Agriculture	$33 891 500

1) Milk Recording and DHIA — Grants of $64 500
2) Bull Test Station — Grants of $27 100
3) Livestock Exhibits — Financial and technical assistance of $49 900
4) Artificial Insemination Technicians — Subsidies on transportation costs of $80 000
5) Veterinary District Grants — Grants of $245 900
6) Rabies Indemnity — Federal-provincial cost shared; $5 300
7) Special Veterinary Services — $2 900
8) Bear Fence Program — Grants of $100.00 per fence, $4 500
9) Horticultural Societies — Grants of $28 600
10) Weed District Grants — Grants of $204 400
11) Agricultural Societies — Grants of $578 700
12) Market Promotion — $26 500
13) Agricultural Crown Land Leasing Program — $771 100
14) Agri-Water
   – Farm Water Source Development Activity — Technical assistance and 30% of project costs– $121 100
   – Community Water Source Development — Rebate of 50% to local governments $127 500
   – Agricultural Area Water Pipeline Activity — Technical assistance and 30% of project costs– $127 500
   – Agricultural Community Water and Sewage Treatment — 30% of project costs– $69 800
15) Manitoba Water Services Board — Grants and loans–grants only $4 656 800
16) Manitoba Crop Insurance — $41 200 000 (high due to 1980 drought)
17) 1980 Drought Relief Program — $14 124 600
18) Manitoba Agricultural Credit Corporation
   – Direct Loans, Long Term — $25 223 300 (loans)

– Direct Loans, Intermediate Term	$618 700 (interest subsidy) $664 200
– Corporate, Co-operative and Partnership Loans	$405 800
– Guaranteed Farm Production Loans	$187 000
– Specific Comprehensive Guaranteed Loans	$56 300
– Stocker Program Loans	$1 049 200
19) Prairie Agricultural Machinery Institute.	20% of Operating and Capital Expenses $519 100
Community Studies Centre	$25 000
Farm Safety Council	$15 000
Farm Vacations Institute	$15 900
Women's Institute	$25 500
	(Note: all amounts for 1-19 from 1980-81 estimates)

ONTARIO	Program	Amount
INDUSTRIAL SUBSIDIES	*Ministry of Industry & Tourism*	(Total departmental expenditures of $122 million estimated for 1981-82) (1981 budget)
	1) Advisory Services Program	Computer & consulting services
	2) Program to Encourage Product & Process Innovation	Grants of $0.189 million
	3) Small Business Industry Technology Program	Grants; no figures available
	4) Product Development Management Program	Grants of $0.140 million
	5) Trade Development Branch	Trade missions, consultations, etc.
	6) Industrial Development Branch	Research, seminars, & consultation
	Ontario Development Corps. (1980 Annual Report)	Total loans & guarantees of $52.9 million
	1) Loans to Small Businesses	
	2) Venture Capital Loans	
	3) Ontario Business Incentive Program Loans	
	4) Term Loans	
	5) Export Support Program	
	6) Loan Guarantees	

7) Advisory Services for Small
   Businesses
8) Industrial Parks
   Financing Program for   Loan guarantees; figures
   Canadian Book Publishers   unavailable
   Employment Development   Grants of $23 million &
   Fund   loans of $4 million
   Ministry of the Environment,   Provision of water & sewer
   Rural Ontario Servicing   facilities for incoming &
   Program   expanding industries
   Small Business Incentives   Interest-free forgiveable
   Program   loans; no figures available
   Urban Transportation   Provincial equity of $35
   Development Corp.   million plus loan guarantees
   BILD (Board of Industrial   (1981 budget estimates ex-
   Leadership & Develop-   penditures of $150 million)
   ment) (1981 budget and
   Building Ontario in the
   Eighties)
1) Research Centres
2) High Technology Develop-
   ment Fund
3) Biotechnology
4) The IDEA Corp.
5) International Intern
   Program

GENERAL DEVELOPMENT   *Subsidiary agreements in*   (Programs cost-shared
AGREEMENTS GDA   *force under the Ontario-*   equally by fed. & prov.
                              Canada General Develop-   govts; figures unavailable)
                              ment Agreement
                              1) Northwestern Ontario
                              2) Northeastern Ontario
                              3) Single Industry Resource
                                 Communities
                              4) Community & Rural
                                 Resource Development
                              5) Forest Management

AGRICULTURAL INCENTIVES   *Ministry of Agriculture*
                              Total estimated expendi-
                              tures for 1979-80 were:
                              Ministry Administration $ 5 618 820
                              Agriculture Production   137 840 600
                              Rural Development   11 231 000

Agricultural Marketing	12 846 500
Agricultural Education and Research	29 270 200
Total	$196 807 120

1)	Agricultural Societies	Grants
2)	Plowing Associations	Grants and 50% of prize money
3)	Elite Seed Potato Program	Grants, $16 000 (1979-80 estimates)
4)	Regional Shows	Grants for prize money
5)	Foreign Exhibitions	50% of transportation and prize money
6)	Northern Ontario Livestock Transportation Assistance Policy	50% of transportation costs
7)	Livestock Improvement Program for Northern Ontario	Grants of 20% of purchase price
8)	Federal-Provincial Sheep Assistance Policy	Unknown
9)	Ram Premium Policy	Unknown
10)	Development of Agricultural Drainage and Water Resources	Grants
11)	Tile Drainage Act	Loans of 75% of cost– $29 967 700
12)	Drainage Act	Grants of 80% of costs– $4 765 665
13)	Housing for Seasonal Workers	Grants of 50% of costs
14)	Young Farmer Credit Program	Loans
15)	Northern Ontario Assistance Program	$210 000 available
16)	Farm Loans Adjustment Act	Unknown
17)	Farm Credit Corporation	Loans
18)	Community Pastures Program	Use of government land for grazing
19)	Asparagus Incentive Program	Grants of up to $500/acre
20)	Farm Productivity Incentive Program	40% of capital construction costs
21)	Farm Income Stabilization Program	$7 903 000 (1979-80 estimates)

22)	Foodland Ontario (promotion)	$2 million
23)	Crop Insurance	$11 178 100 (1979-80 estimates)

QUEBEC	Program	Amount

INDUSTRIAL SUBSIDIES

	Ministère de l'Industrie, du Commerce, et du Tourisme:	(Total departmental budget for 1980-81 of $139.2 million) (1980-81 estimates)
1)	APEX (Aide à la Promotion des Exports)	Grants of $937 million
2)	Program for the Expansion of Small/Medium-Sized innovative firms (PME-Innovative)	Loans of $14.1 million
3)	PME—Furniture Industry	Grants of $2.1 million
4)	PME—Shoe Industry	Grants of $1.3 million
5)	UNI-PME program	(Bringing university graduates into small & medium-sized businesses)
6)	Food & Agriculture Incentive Program (SDQUIA)	Equity loans of $12.2 million & loan guarantees of $2.5 million
	SDI (Société de Development Industrial du Québec) (1977-78 Annual Report)	
1)	Program A—Financial Assistance to Firms in Field of Technology	Loans of $5.8 million; grants of $56.8 million; equity investment of $4.1 million; loan guarantees of $2.2 million
2)	Program B—Financial Assistance to Manufacturing Firms of Mergers & Acquisitions	Loans of $0.600 million & grants of $6.3 million
3)	Program C—Financing for Manufacturing Firms	Loans of $14.5
4)	Program D—Financial Assistance for Exports	Loans of $0.500 million; grants of $31.2 million; & loan guarantees of $3.5 million
5)	Program E—Financing for Small Manufacturing Companies	Loans of $7 million

6) Program F—Financial Assistance for Traditional Industries	Loans of $9 million
7) SAT (Service d' Assistance Technique)	$425 million in machinery purchased from Quebec firms as a result of conditions imposed upon recipients of SDI assistance
8) Financing for Dynamic Industries	Loans of $1.2 million & grants of $1.7 million
9) Financing for the Tourist Industry	Loans of $1.4 million & grants of $0.500 million
10) Experimental Job Creation	Grants of $14 million
11) Commercial Fishing Program	Grants of $1.8 million
CRIQ (Le Centre de Recherche Industrielle du Québec) (1980 Annual Report)	(Total expenditures of $11.5 million in 1980-81 and total revenues, with $2.7 million recovered from contracted services.)
Industrial Parks Program	(Govt owns 12 parks; no figures of annual expenditures available.)
SGE *(La Société Générale du Financement)* (1980 Annual Report)	(Total equity investment as of 1980 was $94.9 million.)
Office Québécoise du Commerce Exterieur	(Support & promotional services)
SEQ (Société d'exportation du Québec) (Discussed in *Challenges For Quebec: A Statement of Economic Policy*, Government of Quebec, 1980)	(Establishment of export pools & consortia)
GENERAL DEVELOPMENT AGREEMENTS (GDA)	*Subsidiary agreements now in effect under the Canada-Quebec GDA*	(Cost-shared 60% by fed govt & 40% by prov. govt; no figures available)
1) Key Highways Networks	
2) Forestry Development	
3) Industrial Infrastructure	
4) Agricultural Development	
5) Mineral Development	
6) Establishment of St Felicien Pulp Mill	
7) Airport Industrial and Commercial Park	

8) Water Treatment Facilities
   for Montreal Area
9) Tourism Development
10) Public Infrastructure
11) Modernizing the Pulp &
    Paper Industry

AGRICULTURAL INCENTIVES

The following programs are administered by the Dept of Agriculture:
1) 'Sol plus' to promote capital base in agricultural land
2) Transportation of limestone
3) Promotion of Agricultural and food products
4) Innovating in merchandising and sorting vegetables
5) Improved preservation of fruits and vegetables
6) Rationalization of meat market
7) Compensation for slaughterhouses
8) Assistance for marketing of feeder steers
9) Marketing of fruits and vegetables by specialized refrigerating techniques
10) Aid to agricultural societies
11) Aid to milk collecting
12) Aid to cattle transport
13) Rationalization of warehousing of horticultural products
14) 'Le Lys D'or' contest to improve dairy products
15) Agricultural exhibitions
16) Seasonal agricultural work for students
17) Agricultural employment for prisoners
18) Agricultural employment for beneficiaries of social assistance
19) Transportation of workers
20) Agricultural education relief

(Total estimated expenditures of Dept of Agriculture for 1980-81 were $319 million with the following breakdowns: Planning, Research & Instruction, $20.7 million Farm Financing, $74.4 million; Farm Production Assistance, $128.5 million; Farm Insurance $16.9 million; Farm Produce Marketing, $42.6 million; Régie des marchés agricole du Québec, $1.4 million; Farm Land Mgmt, $15.5 million; and Internal Mgmt & Support $18.4 million.)

21) Modernization of rabbit farming
22) Wintering of beef cattle
23) Feed lot establishment assistance
24) Development of cow/calf operations
25) Development of lamb production
26) Trout farming
27) Upgrading quality of horses
28) Beekeeping assistance
29) Improvement of the sanitary condition of hives
30) Improvement of hog breeding
31) Analysis of milk herds in Quebec
32) Promotion of artificial insemination
33) Expansion of asparagus production
34) Introducing new products and new techniques
35) Reorganization of apple production
36) Use of unconventional fuels in greenhouses
37) Insulation of greenhouses
38) Aid to develop sugar beet production
39) Production of certified raspberry and strawberry seedlings
40) Employment of veterinarians
41) Vaccination against distemper, botulism, and infectious entinitis of the mink
42) Compensation for loss of beef, sheep, and goats
43) Compensation for loss of animals to rabies
44) Municipal roads
45) Development of fallow land

NEW BRUNSWICK	Program	Amount
INDUSTRIAL INCENTIVES	*Dept of Commerce & Development:* (1980 Annual Report, 1980-81 estimates)	(Total budget for 1980-81 was $10.6 million)
	1) Industrial Development Branch	
	2) Industry Services Division	
	3) Marketing Services Division	
	4) Management Services Division	
	5) Technical Services Division	
	6) Product Development Mgmt Group	
	7) Financial Assistance to Industry Program	Loans of $8.7 million
	8) Urban Small Industry Program	Loans of $0.600 million
	9) Small Industry Financial Assistance Program	Loans of $0.400 million
	Provincial Holdings	(Total investment portfolio of $1.2 million as of 1977.)
	NB Research and Productivity Council (1979 Annual Report)	(Total 1979 expenditures of $2.2 million, but $1.6 million recovered from contract revenue)
	Property Tax Reduction on Small Business (1980 Budget)	(Reduction of 30¢ per $100 on first $100 000 of assessment and 20¢ per $100 for next $100 000)
FISHERIES INCENTIVES	*Dept of Fisheries:* (1980-81 estimates)	(Total of $5.4 million allocated to Dept in 1980-81 budget, amounts which follow are allocations for 1980-81).
	1) Fisheries Training	($0.842 million)
	2) Financial Assistance	($1.1 million)
	3) Fish Inspection & Marketing	($0.531 million)
	4) Research & Development	($0.670 million)
	5) Engineering Services	($0.154 million)
	Fisherman's Loan Board	($1 million allocated as provision against losses of the Board in 1980-81)
	Fisheries Development Board	($12 million advanced to Board in 1980-81 budget)

GENERAL DEVELOPMENT AGREEMENTS (GDA)	*Subsidiary Agreements under the Canada-NB General Development Agreement currently in force:*	(Programs cost-shared 80% by fed. govt & 20% by prov. govt; no figures available)
	1) Forestry	
	2) Industrial Development	
	3) Kent Regional Pilot Project	
	4) Saint John & Moncton Arterial Highways Planning	
	5) Minerals & Fuel Development	
	6) Highways	
	7) Northeast New Brunswick	
	8) Development of Agricultural Resources	
	The following programs are administered by the Dept of Agriculture:	(Total est. expenditures of Dept of Agriculture for 1980-81 were $27.4 million of which $12.2 million was for loans & advances. All expenditures listed for the following programs are for (1980-81.)
	1) Pedigreed Cereal Seed Assistance	(nil)
	2) Feed Grain Transportation	($0.018 million)
	3) Seed grain treatment	(nil)
	4) Apple Industry Development	(nil)
	5) Processing Apple Transportation	(nil)
	6) Blueberry Field Recovery	(nil)
	7) Agricultural Limestone Assistance	($0.365 million)
	8) Stream Bank Protection	($0.034 million)
	9) Small Farm Improvement	($0.001 million in grants)
	10) Farm Machinery Loans	($0.008 million for losses on loan guarantees)
	11) Agricultural Pollution Control	(nil)
	12) Stand-by Electric Power	(nil)
	13) Farm Adjustment	($0.012 million in loans)
	14) Farm Credit Corporation	($0.622 million in interest subsidy)
	15) Farm Improvement Assistance	(nil)
	16) Family Farm Improvement Program	(nil)

17) Small Farm Development	(nil)
18) Rural Beautification	($0.005 million)
19) 4-H Club Program	($0.177 million in supervisory & financial assistance)
20) Livestock Incentives	($0.085 million for losses on guaranteed loans & $0.073 for grants
21) Agricultural Fairs Grants	($0.072 million in grants)
22) Cream Transportation Assistance	($0.074 million)
23) Beef Cattle Test Station Assistance	($0.005 million)
24) Beef Producers Sire Assistance	($0.043 million)
25) Sheep Test Station Assistance	(nil)
26) Transport Assistance to Sheep Producers	(nil)
27) Swine Assistance on Boars	($0.012 million)
28) Honey Bees for Pollination	($0.001 million)
29) Hog Marketing Board	($0.145 million)
30) Crop Insurance Commission	($0.513 million)
31) Hog Price Stabilization Program	($0.621 million in grants & $0.613 million in loans)

NOVA SCOTIA	Program	Amount
INDUSTRIAL INCENTIVES	*Dept of Development.* (1980-81 estimates)	(Total budget for 1980-81 is $87.2 million, including $52.6 million for GDA and $0.470 million in grants assistance)
	1) Business Advisory Services Branch	
	2) Trade Development Section	
	3) Marketing Assistance Program	
	4) Rural Industry Program	Loans of $1 million
	5) Opportunity Identification Program	Grants of $0.800 million
	6) Product Development Management Program	
	7) Municipal Property Tax Exemption	($1.9 million allocated in 1980-81 budget)

8) Provincial Employment Program	($13.1 million in 1980-81)
NS Resources Development Board	
1) Industrial Loan Program	Loans of $43 million
2) Tourism Industry Loan Program	Loans of $2 million
Opportunity Identification Program (NS Dept. of Development & DREE)	(Funding of consultants' fees for expanding firms)
Industrial Estates Ltd. (IEL) (1979 Annual Report)	
1) Small Business Financing Program	Loans of $2.5 million
2) General Development Program	(No figures available)
3) Industrial Incubation Program	(Rent subsidies of $0.100 million in 1980-81)
Power Rate Freeze (1979 Annual Report)	($10 million budgeted in 1980-81)
Small Business Development Corp. (1981 Budget)	(Anticipated lending program in 1981-82 of $15 million)

FISHERIES INCENTIVES	*Dept of Fisheries:* (1980-81 estimates)	(Total departmental budget of $14.4 million in 1980-81; figures which follow are for 1980-81).
	1) Market Development Services	($0.129 million)
	2) Seafood Shows & Promotions	($0.040 million)
	3) Technology Development- Fishing Vessels	($0.193 million)
	4) Financial Incentives—Fleet Development	($0.554 million)
	5) Technology Development— Fishing Gear	($0.152 million)
	6) Technology Development— Share Facilities	($0.292 million)
	7) Financial Incentives— Harbour Facilities	($0.486 million)
	8) Financial Incentives— Infrastructure	($0.032 million)
	9) Financial Incentives Quality	($0.817 million)
	10) Financial Incentives— Productivity	($0.483 million)

11)	Fisherman's Loan Board	($8 million subsidy through low interest rates)
12)	New Products, Processes & Promotion	($0.166 million)
13)	Quality Control	($0.050 million)
14)	Fisherman Training Outpost—Nets & Gear	($0.115 million)
15)	Fisheries Training Centre	($0.392 million)
16)	Marine Engineering Outpost Training	($0.105 million)
17)	Fisheries Training	($0.035 million)

GENERAL DEVELOPMENT
AGREEMENTS (GDA)

Subsidiary Agreements under the Canada-NS GDA are:

(Cost-shared 80% by fed. govt & 20% by prov. govt; total amount allocated in 1980-81 was $52.6 million, cf. breakdown below).

1)	Mineral Development	$0.600 million
2)	Metropolitan Halifax—Dartmouth Area Development	$13.8 million
3)	Strait of Canso Area Development	$0.684 million
4)	Agriculture Development	$7.9 million
5)	Industrial Development Planning	$1.7 million
6)	Cape Breton Development	$1 million
7)	Forestry Development	$9.5 million
8)	Tourism Development	$1.5 million
9)	Energy Conservation	$4.4 million
10)	Sysco & Supco II Rehabilitation	$10.3 million
11)	Fisheries & Small Shipyards	$1 million
12)	Panamax (Halifax Shipyards)	
13)	Michelin Tires	(total of $56 million over 7 years)

AGRICULTURAL INCENTIVES

The Dept of Agriculture administers the following programs:

(Total departmental expenditures of $22.8 million in 1980-81, including $5.4 million to the NS Farm Board. All expenditures listed for the following programs are for 1980-81.)

1) Pedigreed Seed Grain Production — ($0.006 million in grants)

2)	Tree Fruit Production	($0.121 million in subsidies)
3)	Low Bush Blueberry Land Clearing	($0.069 million in grants)
4)	Certified Seed Potato Assistance	($0.010 million in grants)
5)	Maple Syrup Production	($0.010 million in grants)
6)	Transportation Assistance for Importation of Package Bees	($0.003 million in grants)
7)	Cream Hauling Assistance	($0.048 million in grants)
8)	Production Incentive for Manufacturing Milk and Farm Separated Cream	($1.8 million in grants)
9)	Beef Production	($0.472 million in grants)
10)	Improved Sire (Beef)	($0.085 million in grants)
11)	Improved Sire (Sheep)	(Unknown)
12)	Sheep Production	($0.037 million in grants)
13)	Sheep Importation	($0.008 million in grants)
14)	Improved Sire (Swine)	(Unknown)
15)	Hog Quality Bonus	(Unknown)
16)	Breeders Guarantee (Swine)	(Unknown)
17)	Live Market Hog Transportation	($0.144 million in grants)
18)	Sheep Pasture Improvement	($0.020 million in grants)
19)	Agricultural Limestone Assistance	($0.897 million in grants)
20)	Fertilizer Assistance	($1.4 million in grants)
21)	Assistance to Purchase Lime Spreading Equipment	(nil)
22)	Manure Storage Incentive	($0.673 million in grants)
23)	Feed Facilities Incentives	($0.707 million in grants)
24)	Hog Industry Production Incentive	($0.376 million in grants)
25)	Greenhouse Industry Production Incentive	($0.076 million in grants)
26)	Bulk Bin Construction Assistance	($0.129 million in grants)
27)	Capital Grants	($0.987 million in grants)
28)	Livestock Loans Guarantee	($0.003 million in guaranteed loans)
29)	Establishment of New Farmers—Interest Forgiveness	($0.757 million in interest grants)
30)	Interest Subsidy	($0.920 million in interest subsidy)
31)	Farm Loans	(Loans in 1978 totalled $10.9 million)

32) Small Farms Development   (Unknown)
    Program
33) Exhibition Grants   ($0.065 million in grants)
34) Hog Stabilization Plan   ($1.3 million in grants)

PEI	Program	Amount
INDUSTRIAL INCENTIVES	*Dept of Industry & Commerce:* (1980-81 estimates)	(Total expenditures of $2.6 million for Tourism Branch & $3.7 million for Industry Branch in 1980-81)
	1) Counselling Assistance Program	(Grants of $0.015 million in 1980-81.)
	2) Training Programs	(Grants of $0.004 million in 1980-81)
	3) Student-in-Industry Program	(Grants of $0.015 million in 1980-81)
	4) Resource Based Special Incentive Program	($1 million allocated in 1980-81 budget)
	Market Development Centre (1979 Annual Report)	Grants of $0.080 plus marketing & research services
	Industrial Enterprises Inc. (1980-81 estimates)	Loans of $6.2 million
	PEI Lending Authority (1977-78 Annual Report, 1980-81 estimates)	(Loans of $12 million in 1980-81)
FISHERIES INCENTIVES	No data available	
GENERAL DEVELOPMENT AGREEMENTS (GDA)	*Comprehensive Development Plan:*	(Except where indicated no figures available; expenditures recorded in budgets of relevant prov. depts)
	1) Agriculture	
	2) Forestry	
	3) Fisheries	
	4) Industrial Development	
	a) Industrial Assistance Program	loans of $0.040 million
	b) Service Sector Assistance Program	loans of $0.025 million
	5) Community Development & Human Resources	
	6) Tourism & Conservation	
	7) Land Adjustment	
	8) Marketing & Product Development	
	9) Transportation	

AGRICULTURAL INCENTIVES

The Dept of Agriculture administers the following programs:

(Total departmental expenditures for 1980-81 were $14.3 million. All expenditures listed for the following programs are for 1980-81.)

1) Assistance to Livestock Exhibitors to Out of Province Exhibitions — ($0.005 million)

2) Assistance for Purchase of Cattle Breeding Stock — ($0.942 million in grants)

3) Purchase Assistance on Female Cattle Breeding Stock — ($0.015 million in grants)

4) Assistance for Bulk Tank and Milk House — ($0.107 million in grants)

5) Beef Breeders Bull Bonus — ($0.030 million in bonuses)

6) Sheep Production — ($0.013 million in grants)

7) Assistance for the Purchase of Sheep Breeding Stock — ($0.024 million in grants)

8) Swine ROP Home Test, Boar and Gilt Bonus Swine Breeding Stock — ($0.134 million in grants)

9) Registered Hatchery Assistance — ($0.001 million in grants)

10) Purchase of Brood Mares; Fox Breeding Stock and Mink Breeding Stock — ($0.212 million in grants)

11) Pedigreed Seed Grain — ($0.049 million in subsidies)

12) Assistance to Encourage Local Production of Certified Strawberry Plants — ($0.002 million in grants)

13) Limestone Incentive Policy — ($0.789 million in grants)

14) Assistance for Land Improvements — ($0.110 million in grants)

15) Assistance on the Capital Cost of Farm Buildings — ($2.6 million in grants)

16) Assistance for Equipment Purchases — ($1.8 million in grants)

17) Grain Storage — ($0.220 million in grants)

18) Small Farm Development Program — (nil in grants)

19) Land Development Corporation — ($0.015 million in land maintenance contracts)

20) Lending Authority — (nil in loans)

21) Hog Stabilization Plan — ($0.865 million in grants)

NEWFOUNDLAND	Program	Amount
INDUSTRIAL INCENTIVES	*Dept of Rural Development:* (1980-81 estimates)	
	1) Rural Development Authority Loan Program	Loans of $1.85 million
	2) Rural Development Program *Dept of Industrial Development:* (1980-81 estimates)	Grants of $0.600 million
	1) Market & Product Development Program	Grants of $0.040 million
	Nfld & Labrador Development Corp. (1980 Budget)	Loan & equity approvals of $4.6 million
	Gander Development Corp.	(Largely promotional activities)
FISHERIES INCENTIVES	*Dept of Fisheries:* (1980-81 estimates)	(Total budget for Dept in 1980-81 was $24.5 million)
	1) Fisheries Loan Board a) loan program b) bounties c) technical assistance	(Total 1980-81 budget of $13.4 million of which is loan fund)
	2) Fisheries Development (Market Research & Product Development)	(Total 1980-81 budget of $2.4 million)
	3) Incentives & Assistance Division a) Fishing Gear Supplement b) Fishing Gear Replacement c) Lobster Pot Program	(Total of $0.950 million budgeted in 1980-81)
	4) Capital Work	($8.6 million budgeted in 1980-81)
	5) Depts of Finance, Fisheries, and Industrial Development Financing Program	Grants of $0.500 million in form of interest subsidies
GENERAL DEVELOPMENT AGREEMENTS (GDA)	*Subsidiary Agreements under the Canada-Nfld GDA are:*	(Program cost-shared 90% by fed. govt & 10% by prov. govt; no figures available except where indicated)
	1) Forestry 2) Gros Morne Park Development 3) Ocean Research & Development 4) St. John's Urban Region	

	5) Highways 1976-80	
	6) Planning	
	7) Inshore Fisheries Development	
	8) Labrador Interim	
	9) Mineral Development	
	10) Tourism Development	Grants of $0.240 million
	11) Agriculture Development	
	12) Rural Development	
	13) Renewable Energy & Conservation Programs	
AGRICULTURAL INCENTIVES	The following programs are administered by the Dept of Rural, Agricultural & Northern Development:	(No figures available; form of assistance indicated)
	1) Assistance on Purchase of Beef Sires	Grants
	2) Assistance on Purchase of Purebred Dairy Sires	Grants
	3) Heifer Bonus Policy	Bonuses
	4) Calf Identification Program	Support services
	5) Swine Breeding Stations	Provision of breeding stock plus technical and supervisory assistance.
	6) Swine Production Policy	Provision of stock & information & veterinary services
	7) Weanling Pig Production Incentive Policy	Bonuses
	8) Multiplier Breeder of Minimal Disease Certified Hybrid Gilts	Provision of breeding stock.
	9) Sheep Breeding Station	Provision of breeding stock.
	10) Breeder Ewe Incentive	Bonuses
	11) Lambs Per Ewe Incentive	Bonuses
	12) Carcass Lamb Incentive	Bonuses
	13) Artificial Insemination of Cattle in Newfoundland	Grant plus information & support services
	14) Blueberry Development	Grant
	15) Seed Potato Farm	Provision of seed stock
	16) Maintenance of Equipment	All maintenance expenses
	17) Land Fertility Scheme	Limestone subsidy
	18) Bogland Development	Technical & financial assistance
	19) Farm Access Roads	Road construction
	20) Soil Surveys	Technical and advisory services

21)	Farm Development Loan Board	Low interest loans
22)	Farm Development Program	Grants
23)	Product and Market Development	Advisory & informational services
24)	Crop Insurance	Indemnity
25)	Dog Act	Regulatory
26)	Livestock Insurance Act	Indemnity
27)	Demonstration Equipment	Advisory
28)	Development Opportunities	Incentive grants
29)	Laboratory Equipment, Supplies, Facilities and Services	Advisory
30)	On-Farm Training	Cash allowances
31)	Travel and Exchange	Travel costs
32)	Farmer Training Short Courses	Travel costs
33)	Staff Training	Educational
34)	Financial Assistance to Agricultural Commodity Groups	Grants
35)	DACUM	Education Support Services
36)	Manpower & Related Research	Research
37)	Information	Advisory
38)	Western Agriculture Centre	Provision of facilities
39)	Dairy Herd Analysis Service	Advisory & support services
40)	ROP Sheep	Computerized indexing system
41)	ROP Beef	Computerized information services
42)	Farm Business Management	Counselling & advisory services
43)	Pesticide Laboratory	Provision of testing services
44)	Animal Health Veterinary Services	Provision of veterinary services
45)	Disease Control	Vaccination services
46)	Antibiotics and Drugs	Drug subsidized

PART THREE: COMPARATIVE PERSPECTIVES

7
Government procurement policies: GATT, the EEC, and the United States

W.C. Graham

INTRODUCTION

Government procurement policies have long been recognized as among the principal non-tariff barriers to trade.[1] The potential of the market governed by government procurements on a worldwide scale was estimated to be in the order of several hundred billion dollars at the time of the GATT 'Tokyo Round' negotiations.[2] As has been noted: 'In an era where some 20 to 40 percent of the gross national product of most countries passes through public budgets, discrimination against foreign products by government purchasing officials constitutes one of the most important barriers to world trade from a quantitative point of view.'[3]

Economists, espousing the merits of free trade on grounds of the most efficient allocation of labour and resources, have attacked government policies favouring local suppliers as 'inflationary, trade-restrictive, and generally contrary to a state or a nation's best interests.'[4] The barrier to the foreign supplier constitutes a form of subsidy to the domestic product, thus distorting the domestic market and interfering with the most efficient reallocation of labour and

I am very grateful for the research assistance of Craig Lövgren, a student in the Faculty of Law at the University of Toronto. The extensive case and statute references contained in the original version of the paper have been reduced for the purposes of publication and may be obtained from the author by request.

1 Robock and Simmonds, *International Business and Multinational Enterprises* (Homewood, Ill.: R.D. Irwin, 1973), at 110; Long, *Report of the Director-General of the G.A.T.T. on the Tokyo Round of Multilateral Trade Negotiations* (Geneva: 1979), at 50ff.
2 Long, *Report*, at 75.
3 Dam, *The G.A.T.T. – Law and International Economic Organization*, (Chicago: University of Chicago Press, 1973), at 199.
4 Japan Economic Institute, *An Analysis of Buy-American Practices*, (1981), at 4.

resources, which ultimately will result in the largest possible structure for that market.[5] The result is in conflict with Ricardo's principle of comparative advantage in international trade,[6] and like all forms of government protectionism decreases the satisfaction of wants.[7]

However, as Samuelson has observed, 'economic welfare is not the sole goal of life,'[8] and many justifications have been advanced for government procurement policies favouring local interests, including the encouragement of employment, the development of defence capacity, the formation and development of desirable industries (often in the area of advanced technology), the alleviation of regional disparities, the encouragement of local ownership of business, the control of inflation, and the possible influence on currency valuations.[9] To these more altruistic factors one might add a more cynical consideration: the degree to which politicians may facilitate their retaining office by returning to their constituents some part of their tax payments.

The result is that the forces favouring discriminatory procurement policies have steadfastly resisted all condemnations based upon economic theory to the point where one observer comments: 'Discrimination in favour of local products sometimes seems to be one of the basic human urges.'[10]

Discrimination by a government in favour of its nationals, or in the case of a province or state its residents, may be achieved by a variety of techniques. The most blatant are nationality or residence requirements and place-of-manufacture requirements. These may be used in turn either as a condition for participation in the government contract or as the basis for granting a cost preference, usually expressed in the form of a percentage, to local suppliers. The former practice may be said to be the equivalent of a quantitative restriction on imports and the latter the equivalent to a duty of approximately the same amount.[11]

---

5 Samuelson, *Economics* (New York: McGraw-Hill, 1973) (9th ed.), at 668ff.

6 For a discussion of Ricardo's theory see ibid., at 670, and Robock and Simmonds, *supra* note 1, at 99.

7 von Mises, *Human Action: A Treatise on Economics*, (Chicago: Henry Regnery Co., 1963), at 317.

8 Samuelson, *supra* note 5, at 693.

9 de Mestral, 'The impact of the GATT Agreement on government procurement in Canada' (unpublished), at 4; Stegeman and Acheson, 'Canadian government purchasing policy' (1972), 6 *Journal of World Trade Law* 422.

10 Jackson, *World Trade and the Law of G.A.T.T.* (Indianapolis, Kansas City, and New York: Bobbs-Merrill Co., 1969), at 274.

11 Bernier, 'Le concept d'union économique dans la Constitution canadienne: de l'intégration commerciale à l'intégration des facteurs de production' (1979), 20 *Cahiers de Droit* 177, 206; Lowinger, 'Discrimination in government procurement of foreign goods in the U.S. and Western Europe' (1976), 42 *Southern Economics Journal* 451, 457 speaks of 'implicit tariffs.'

There are more subtle forms of discrimination, such as selective or single tender instead of public tender, inadequate publicity or information on bidding opportunities, a short time limit for the submission of bids, definitions of technical requirements familiar to or answerable by local suppliers only, and a combination or variation of such techniques. The minister of justice has described several similar practices, or variations of them, employed by the provinces.[12]

If such practices have distorting effects when practised between nations, presumably they would have even less desirable consequences if employed by different elements within a single political unit that purports to constitute a single market. At least we may say that their use by the various provinces and the similarity of their techniques to those practised in other jurisdictions make a comparative study of how other forms of organizations have dealt with these issues a useful task.

Three systems have been selected representing three distinct forms of political co-operation, varying the degree of sovereignty retained by their participants: the 'international' General Agreement on Tariffs and Trade, the common market of the European Economic Community, and the economically integrated federal system of the United States.

Despite the recognition in GATT and the EEC that discriminatory practices exist and should be eliminated, they have not been curbed to the extent advocated by 'free-trade' economists. When the EEC was formed in 1958 their distorting influences on interstate trade were certainly recognized, but it was only in 1980 that the 'Supplies Directive' came into effect. Similarly, in the international field research on government procurement procedures along with other non-tariff barriers to trade commenced in the 1960s at the OECD. However, no international agreement was concluded until the Agreement on Government Procurement was adopted in the context of the Tokyo Round in 1979.[13]

In the United States, as we shall see, in spite of the existence of Constitutional provisions guaranteeing 'free trade' throughout the Union (the commerce clause and the privileges and immunities clause), state-preference statutes and practices are numerous and have survived many attacks upon their legitimacy.

By comparing these three systems we may gain a better understanding of the nature of government procurement preferences, the techniques that may be used to eliminate them, and the extent to which they have been allowed to continue as a justifiable exercise of economic power on the part of various constituent political units.

---

12 Chrétien, *Securing the Canadian Economic Union in the Constitution* (Ottawa: Ministry of Supply and Services, 1980), at 35ff. For methodology and techniques of procurement preferences generally, see Lowinger, 'Discrimination'.
13 de Mestral, 'Impact,' at 11; Pomeranz, 'Toward a new international order in government procurement,' (1979) 11 *Law and Policy in International Business* 1263.

GATT

The GATT Agreement on Government procurement (henceforth referred to as the 'Agreement') was realized as a part of the Tokyo Round along with five other codes governing non-tariff barriers. Because its implementation only commenced in January 1981, its success is not possible to evaluate. However, a review of the terms of the Agreement itself together with some commentary may cast some light on possible techniques for the resolution of similar issues in the Canadian context.

The Agreement was initialled at Geneva in April 1979 by twenty-three of the ninety-nine states participating in the Tokyo Round.[14] Signature by Canada was authorized by Order-in-Council in December 1979.[15] No legislative or regulatory change was required to implement the Agreement by the federal government because its government purchasing practices are largely administrative. Two notices setting out procedures to be followed under the Agreement have been published in the *Canada Gazette*.[16] Because the Agreement applies only to those federal agencies enumerated in its annexes, no provincial action is required, though during the course of the negotiations the provinces voluntarily gave some undertakings.[17]

The background to the negotiations and their significance to world trade have been reviewed from the Canadian and American points of view by de Mestral and Pomeranz in lengthy articles on the Agreement.[18] A few of their observations bear repeating here.

The amount of world trade in question is substantial; it is estimated that 'one-sixth of the Gross National Products of all states is derived from international trade, of which one-quarter is attributable to government purchases.'[19] In making these purchases governments have until now largely favoured their nationals, and how effective the Agreement will be in eliminating or reducing the effect of these powerful forces remains to be seen. The fact that the Agreement contains a specific timetable for its examination and revision may be taken both as a recognition that these will be difficult issues to confront and perhaps as an

---

14 (1979) 18 *International Legal Materials* 1052; *GATT, Basic Instruments and Selected Documents*, 26th Supp., at 33ff. (1979); Anthony and Hagerty, 'Cautious optimism as a guide to foreign government procurement,' (1979) 11 *Law and Policy in International Business* 1301.

15 P.C. 1979–3298, 6 Dec. 1979.

16 115 *Canada Gazette* Pt. I 316, 503.

17 'Provincial statement of intention' (Re: marketing of foreign wines), 12 April 1979.

18 de Mestral, *supra* note 9; Pomeranz, *supra* note 13; Lesguillons, 'L'accord sur les marchés publics' (1980), 6 *Droit et Pratique du Commerce International* 545.

19 de Mestral, *supra* note 9, at 2.

encouraging sign of the willingness of governments to continue their efforts. On the other hand it may also be a cynical recognition, based on previous GATT experience, that 'unwarranted optimism over a set of rules for international conduct may fade quickly in the face of self-interest.'[20]

The origins of the present Agreement are found in the work of the OECD, which, although it defined many of the issues, was unable to bring such an agreement to fruition. The process was therefore transferred to the GATT forum as part of the Tokyo Round.[21]

The Agreement consists of nine articles on the following issues: scope and coverage, national treatment and non-discrimination, special rules for developing countries, technical specifications, tendering procedures, information and review procedures, enforcement (including dispute settlement), exceptions, and finally the formalities for bringing the Agreement into effect. The provisions of the Agreement have already been described in several articles,[22] so that this paper will only review certain basic provisions.

Article I: scope and coverage
The threshold for applicability is 150 000 SDR ($190 000 U.S. approximately) with a proviso designed to prevent evasion by the splitting of contracts. It applies to 'laws, regulations, procedures and practices regarding procurement of products by the entities subject to the Agreement,' including services incidental to the supply of products, provided their value does not exceed 50 per cent of the total contract.

There is some pressure in the United States for the further reduction of the amount of this threshold.[23]

The reference to 'procedures and practices' in addition to laws and regulations and the specification of entities to which the Agreement applies evolved as a solution to disputes that surfaced during the OECD negotiations where there was a difference between the American and European negotiators as to how any such agreement would work. The Americans were concerned that the original proposals imposed a disadvantage on countries such as theirs whose discriminatory

---

20 Anthony and Hagerty, *supra* note 14, at 1303. The authors note, for example, that in the U.S. market only $12.5 billion out of a total of $90 billion in government purchases will be affected.

21 de Mestral, *supra* note 9, at 7, 8; Pomeranz, *supra* note 13, at 1272–3, 1275–9.

22 de Mestral, *supra* note 9; Lesguillons, *supra* note 18; Pomeranz, *supra* note 13; Fiaschetti, 'Technical analysis of the government procurement agreement,' (1979) 11 *Law & Policy in International Business* 1345; Anthony and Hagerty, *supra* note 20.

23 Anthony and Hagerty, *supra* note 20, at 1321.

provisions must be statutory compared to countries whose use of administrative procedures made them less easily subject to control.[24] The identification of entities to which the Agreement would apply went part way to resolving this problem. It also permitted the negotiations to resume when they had become blocked in 1976 since each party was able to estimate the value of the entities involved and so compare the value of its own list to the values of the lists put up by others.[25] For example, the Canadian list had an estimated value of approximately $1 billion in 1977–8.[26]

The entity enumeration technique also provided flexibility in the field of public utilities. These were excluded because of the European belief that they should be treated separately.[27]

The entities, specified by country in the annexes, vary from a single entry in one case (Jamaica – Jamaica Building Materials) to over three pages (United States – fifty-three entities). While Departments of Defence are generally included by the developed countries, excluded are purchases of security-sensitive items, including arms, ammunition, or military material. Only non-military defence purchases are covered by the Agreement.

Canada excluded crown corporations (such as Air Canada). This exclusion was extended to the Post Office in case it became a crown corporation; this move is now regarded by some other parties as evidence of malice aforethought by Canada.[28]

The exclusion from the list of heavy electrical equipment users (utilities) and communications equipment has caused adverse reaction in the United States whose manufacturers note that foreign suppliers have access to the American market subject only to the 6 per cent Buy-American preference whereas they themselves are virtually shut out of European and Japanese markets by purchasing practices.[29]

The exclusion of entities which make use of a particular type of equipment is only one technique used in the Agreement to retain protection for domestic industry. Other policy considerations are represented in the annexes as well,

24 Pomeranz, *supra* note 13, at 272–3, 276.
25 de Mestral, *supra* note 9.
26 Ibid., at 19.
27 Ibid.
28 From discussions with EEC officials in Brussels.
29 Anthony and Hagerty, *supra* note 14, at 1312–14. It should be noted that Japan has agreed not to discriminate against American goods for $1 billion procurement annually by Nippon Telegraph and Telephone. See Wilkey, 'International trade: government procurement of telecommunications equipment' – *Japan-U.S. Agreement on the Government Procurement Code*, Dec. 19, 1980,' (1981) 22 *Harvard International Law Journal* 464, 465.

such as Germany's reservation of the right to award contracts under special procedures in economically disadvantaged regions or the American exemption of its special programs for minority and small businesses.

The reference to specific entities rather than economic areas also allowed flexibility in meeting the constitutional limits on certain federal regimes against binding their constituent states. Thus Canadian provinces, American states, and German Länder are not covered. This is obviously an important omission; in the United States alone, state Buy-American preferences in 1979 applied to approximately $133 billion in state and local procurement.[30]

Article II: national treatment and non-discrimination

This may be described as the 'heart of the agreement,'[31] to which all other provisions, particularly those relating to 'transparency' and tendering, are really complementary. It establishes the principle of non-discrimination whereby all 'laws, regulations, procedures and practices regarding government procurement covered' by the Agreement must provide for no less favourable terms for 'foreign' suppliers than those granted to either domestic suppliers or to those from another party. The right to levy customs duties or tariffs or establish import regulations is preserved, however, by virtue of Secton 2 and would, under Article I of GATT itself, be governed by most favoured nation treatment.[32]

Article III: special treatment for developing countries

While it might at first seem that these provisions have only a marginal interest in the context of the Canadian economic union, they do illustrate the proposition that economic considerations based upon a perfect model of free trade do give way to certain types of political or social pressures, in this case the use of government procurement to favour economic development of a particular region. As such they correspond to Articles XXXVI to XXXVII of GATT itself, which were added in 1965 as recognition of the developing countries' need for differential treatment both in the tariff and non-tariff areas.[33] They are also a recognition that in the overall process of the multilateral trade negotiations of the Tokyo

30 *Analysis, supra* note 4, at 2.
31 Fiaschetti, *supra* note 22, at 1346.
32 *Ibid.*
33 Government of Canada, Office of the Deputy Prime Minister, 12 April 1979, cited in de Mestral, Castel, and Graham, eds, *International Business Transactions and Economic Relations: Cases, Notes and Materials*, (Faculties of Law, McGill, York, and Toronto Universities,) Chap 3, at 18.

Round one of the objectives must be to assure a better balance between developing and developed nations in the expanded world trade which should result from the arrangements, thus resulting in better foreign exchange earnings, diversification of exports, and an accelerated rate of growth in the developing economies.[34]

One obvious way in which special treatment may be afforded to the developing countries (or for that matter any participant) is in restricting the application of the agreement to a narrow range of specified government purchasing agencies. In addition, specific exceptions may be negotiated either by global or regional or special bilateral arrangements, upon approval of the Committee.

The Agreement also envisages the furnishing of technical assistance relating to government procurement and the establishment of information centres in the developed countries to provide information about procedures to the developing countries.

Other similar provisions suggest that the developing countries obtain benefits from the Agreement on a non-reciprocal basis; access to the developed countries' markets is assured to them while their own procurement policies may continue to recognize their particular needs.

Article IV: technical specifications
Generally, technical specifications are not to be used in such a way as to create obstacles to international trade and should refer to performance rather than design and be based on international or recognized national standards. References to specific trademarks, patents, or similar restrictions are prohibited unless accompanied by the qualification 'or equivalent.'

Article V: tendering procedures
The principle of non-discrimination set out in Article II is to be ensured by the tendering and contracting procedures which must be observed in procurement. The procedures developed fall into three categories: open, selective, or single tendering. The process is basically one of guaranteeing the 'transparency' of procedures to be followed and establishing basic rules for the conduct of bidding and the selection of suppliers.

The difference between open and selective procedures is that under the former all interested persons may tender, whereas under the latter tenders may be requested from suppliers on a list.

---

34 GATT Information Service, *G.A.T.T. Thirty Years, 1947–77: What it is, what it does*, ibid., at 11.

Non-discrimination in the qualification of suppliers, a principle of particular importance to the Canadian negotiators,[35] is to be ensured in the Agreement by adequate notice of qualifying requirements, equality of treatment respecting technical or financial capacity, and access to lists of qualified suppliers maintained by procurement entities.

Notice of proposed purchase and tender documentation is to be published as specified and must contain certain basic information set out, including the nature of the products in question, the nature of the procedures, whether open or selective, delivery date, and conditions of tender, including language, economic, financial and technical requirements, bid bonds, and terms of payment. A summary of this notice must be published in one of the official languages of GATT.

In the case of selective tendering procedures, invitations must invite tenders from as wide a group of domestic and foreign suppliers as is practicable. This may be done either by specific invitation at the time of call for tender or on the basis of pre-established lists, which are to be established in accordance with the criteria specified in the Agreement.

Rules are established relating to time limits to enable foreign and local suppliers to compete on an equal footing. Similarly, tender documentation supplied shall be sufficient to permit 'responsive tenders' from all parties.

The submission, receipt, and opening of tenders and awarding of contracts forms the subject matter of a series of provisions designed to ensure the fair treatment of all tenderers.

The award of a contract is to be made to the lowest bidder or to the tender which, on the basis of the evaluation criteria set out in the notice, is 'the most advantageous,' assuming that such tenderer is 'fully capable of undertaking the contract.' In the event of an abnormally low tender further information may be sought from the tenderer to ensure that the contract may be performed at such a price.

Single tendering, whereby suppliers may be selected without the publicity and awarding procedures that are to guarantee the application of national treatment in other cases, is restricted to five specific circumstances where open tendering would not be appropriate (works of art, purchasing of prototypes, etc.).

Finally, conditions requiring offset procurement opportunities or licensing of technology are 'not normally to be used.' These provisions are fairly vague and no doubt leave much room for manœuvre by purchasers.

It has been said that the EEC and Japan laid particular emphasis on the procedures for calling for tenders, while Canada and the United States were

---

35 de Mestral, *supra* note 9, at 11.

particularly concerned with the way in which such tenders would be handled upon receipt.[36] In the result, the Agreement ensures transparency through the whole of the process.

Article VI: information and review

The provisions of Article V designed to ensure transparency or availability of information should be read in the light of the requirements of Article VI. It requires the publication of 'Any law, regulation, judicial decision, administrative ruling of general application, and any procedure (including standard contract clauses) regarding government procurement covered by this Agreement.'

A further control of the process is provided by the right of an unsuccessful applicant for insertion in a suppliers' list to be told the reason for its failure to qualify. Similarly, an unsuccessful tenderer may obtain information on the reasons for its failure to obtain the contract, including specification of the advantages of the successful tender. This may be followed up by complaints supported by action of the government of the tenderer, if it is a Party to the Agreement.

Statistics on contracts awarded, broken down into various categories, are to be provided to the Committee on an annual basis.

Article VII: enforcement of obligations

Article VII establishes the mechanisms for the enforcement of the Agreement and the resolution of disputes arising thereunder. If bilateral consultations on problems should fail, the Agreement provides for the formation of a Committee consisting of representatives of the parties which may establish a fact-finding panel which then will report to the parties. If the dispute remains unresolved the panel will report to the Committee, which then may make appropriate recommendations and rulings.

Article VII: exceptions to the Agreement

In additon to the single tendering provisions there are also categories of contracts not covered by the Agreement at all, namely arms or war materials or any procurement indispensable for national security or defence. Further, the Agreement is not to be construed so as to prevent measures necessary to protect 'public morals, order or safety, human, animal or plant life or health, intellectual property, or relating to the products of handicapped persons, of philanthropic institutions or of prison labour.'

---

36 *Ibid.*, at 14.

Article IX: final revisions
Little purpose would be served in repeating here the provisions for ratification, withdrawal, amendments, registration, and so on. There are provisions for an annual review of the Agreement's operation by the Committee and its renegotiation in three years with a view to expanding its scope, including the possibility of its application to service contracts. Since the Agreement does not apply to heavy electrical, transportation, and telecommunications equipment, all of which are the subject of considerable government procurement, the significance of the review provisions should not be underestimated.

Conclusion
The long history of the negotiations and their complexity and difficulty testify to the powerful forces in favour of national preferences in government procurement. The success of the Agreement is certainly not assured but will depend upon the way in which it is applied. All commentators are reserving their verdict until their nationals have participated in foreign bidding procedures.

THE EUROPEAN ECONOMIC COMMUNITY

Two issues must be considered: the internal rules of the EEC designed to ensure that the freedom of establishment and the free movement of goods and services within the Community are not impeded by government procurement policies ('domestic community measures') and those measures taken by the Community to give effect to its adherence to the Agreement ('GATT measures'). Certain special measures which have been taken in respect of those states associated with the Community under the Lomé Convention[37] are beyond the scope of this paper.

Domestic Community measures
In the course of establishing, a single market, which is the goal of the Community, certain measures have been adopted to ensure that trade between the member states will not be distorted by attempts to give preferential treatment to nationals in the area of government procurement, whether in supply, public works, or service contracts. Specific measures adopted by the member states themselves in the course of this process cannot be dealt with here; nor can a

---

37 See list in 'Bibliographie sur les Marchés publics,' *Documentation Bulletin No. 25* (1980), and see also art. 121–2 of the Second Rome Convention (1979) which imposes certain conditions of bidding and the award of contracts as overseen by the European Monetary Fund; Lesguillons, *supra* note 18, at 546–7.

detailed description be given here of the government procurement policies prevailing in the individual member states or the extent to which, on a state-by-state basis, the Community rules have been successful in eliminating or reducing them. But some introductory remarks about the legal framework within which Community measures are enacted and to which they owe their force and effect may be useful to the reader.

Community decisions are enacted by way of regulation, directive, decision, and recommendation.[38] Any of these techniques may be employed in the area with which we are concerned. A regulation, which by the terms of the Treaty itself is 'directly applicable' in the member states, may be described as a 'normative act *erga omnes*,'[39] that is, analogous to federal legislation. A directive, while creating obligations binding on the member states, leaves to them the choice of form or method whereby the desired result is to be achieved within their national legislative system. Decisions are more in the nature of administrative action taken towards specific persons, companies, or member states who have violated the terms of the treaty. Recommendations have no legal force, as their name implies.

The power of the Council to enact regulations is fairly narrowly circumscribed by the Treaty,[40] so that it is by means of directives that most community measures relating to government procurement have been implemented. Decisions have also been used in a more limited way.

As a result of the jurisprudence of the Court the notion has evolved that Community legislative measures, if they impose obligations which are unconditional and sufficiently clear and complete in themselves, may have 'direct effect' within the legal systems of the member states. That is, they may be relied upon by individuals in actions before their national courts to challenge and render unenforceable inconsistent local legislation.[41] In this sense it may be said that the Court has furthered the development of a 'transnational constitution' by recognizing that sovereignty has been transferred from the member states to central organs endowed with legislative powers whose enactments are superior to inconsistent local laws and that any affected person may seek the resolution of such an

---

38 Art. 189, Treaty of Rome (1957). See Campbell, *Common Market Law* (London: Longmans Green and Co., 1969), Vol. II, at 132.

39 Easson, 'Can directives impose obligations on individuals?' (1979), 4 *European Law Review* 67.

40 Sawer and Doeker, 'The European Economic Community as a constitutionalist system' (1962), 4 *Inter-American Law Review* 217.

41 Easson, *supra* note 39.

inconsistency before any national court.[42] The importance of this notion in ensuring the interpenetration of the Community's legal system generally into that of the member states is readily apparent; we are particularly concerned here with national administrative acts as well as legislation, because it is in the former that discrimination on the basis of nationality most regularly arises in the European context.

While it may be obvious that government procurement policies represent one way in which the establishment of a common market may be impeded, no article of the Treaty established rules specifically applicable to government procurement.[43] The absence of any reference to this issue in the Treaty is eloquent witness to the importance states attach to their ability to favour their own nationals and the political pressures exerted in favour of discriminatory measures. Indeed, one of the drafters of the Treaty remarked that any express provison restricting the member states' freedom in the area of government procurement never would have been accepted by the various European parliaments ratifying the Treaty.[44]

In lieu of any specific provision there may be found throughout the Treaty certain general principles which have served as the foundation for Community legislation. Referred to in this context are Article 7 (general prohibition against discrimination on grounds of nationality), Articles 9 to 10 (free circulation of goods within the common market), Articles 30 to 33 (the elimination of quantitative restrictions or measures having an equivalent effect on intra-Community trade), Articles 52 to 54 (providing for the elimination of restrictions in the freedom of establishment), Articles 59 to 66 (abolition of restrictions in the provision of services), Article 90 (dealing with special rights granted to public undertakings), and finally, Article 100, which provides for the issuing of directives for the 'approximation' or harmonization of national differences in legal, regulatory, and administrative provisions that affect the operation of the common market.[45]

The Court has often been called upon to interpret the various relevant general provisions of the Treaty and has usually given them a most liberal interpretation. Thus, when commenting upon Article 30, it said: 'All trading rules enacted by member states which are capable of hindering, directly or indirectly, actually or

---

42 Stein, 'Lawyers, judges, and the making of a transnational constitution,' (1981) 75 *American Journal of International Law* 1.
43 Flamme, *Traité des Marchés publics*, (Bruxelles: Ets Emile Bruylant, 1969), p. 272; Turpin, 'Public Contracts in the EEC' (1972), 9 *Common Market Law Review* 411.
44 Flamme, *supra* note 43, at 272.
45 Balassa, ed., *European Economic Integration*, (Amsterdam and New York, 1975); Flamme, *supra* note 43; and Turpin, *supra* note 43.

potentially, intra-community trade are to be considered as measures having an effect equivalent to quantitative restrictions.'[46] A similar approach may be expected if the Court is called upon to decide a question involving the barriers to trade resulting from government procurement practices favouring local producers.[47]

Based upon the Treaty provisions a series of directives have been adopted designed to restrict discriminatory procurement practices undertaken by the member states. In part their enactment was rendered complex by the fact that the Community's legislative power finds its source in so many parts of the Treaty, such as those dealing with abolitions of restrictions on the freedom of establishment (Article 54) and on the freedom to supply services (Articles 59–66). As a result the first Community legislative moves in this area were contained in the general programs adopted in 1962 under the authority of Articles 63 (services) and 54 (establishment). Both these general programs, in virtually identical language, provide for the scheduled elimination of certain specified groups of conditions imposed by administrative practice that restricted the supply of goods or services by foreigners.[48]

The general programs are applicable to nationals of member states in business in the Community and to companies carrying on 'a business activity having a continuous and effective link to the economy of a member state.'[49] In addition, the general program for supply of services contains a specific provision relating to public works whereby the member states are required to allocate a portion of their public works contracts to non-nationals.[50]

The programs were completed by referring to the elimination of more subtle forms of hindrance of out-of-state participation, such as impediments to the movement of equipment required to perform services or restrictions on the transfer of funds.[51]

---

46 Case 8/74, *Procureur du Roi* v. *Dassonville*, [1974] European Court Reports 837, [1974] 2 Common Market Law Reports 436.

47 Wyatt and Dashwood, *The Substantive Law of the E.E.C.*, (London: Sweet and Maxwell, 1980), at 115. Case 13/70, *Cinzano* v. *Hauptzollamt Saarbrucken*, [1970] European Court Reports 1089, [1971] Common Market Law Reports 374, provides a very broad definition of a 'measure' within the meaning of art. 37.

48 *General Programme for the Abolition of Restrictions on Freedom to Supply Services*, [1962] *Journal Officiel des Communautés Européennes* 33. Adopted by Council 25 Oct. 1961, reproduced in Campbell, *supra* note 38, II, at 203–6; *General Programme for the Removal of Restrictions on the Freedom of Establishment*, [1962] *Journal Officiel des Communautés Européennes* 37, reproduced in Campbell, at 192–202; and see Turpin, *supra* note 43, at 412.

49 Head 1 of both Programs, *supra* note 48.

50 Services Programme, Head IV.C.(e); Campbell, *supra* note 38, at 206.

51 Ibid., Head III.B, C, D; Campbell, ibid., at 204.

Thus it may be said that in a general way, and subject to the limitations on categories to which the general programs were applicable and the timetables by which their provisions were to be implemented, the Community as early as 1962 had commenced to adopt measures which addressed themselves to the two most obvious restrictions in this area: bidding restrictions and preferences in favour of nationals. These measures were far from completely effective. Insofar as services were concerned, the real action in removing restrictions remained to be accomplished through the approximation mechanism of Article 100, partially because the establishment program had equal application to contracts for public works and supplies whereas the services program dealt only with public works.[52] Governments are more sensitive on the question of purchasing supplies in general than on that of public works.

Further measures have thus far taken the form of a series of directives addressing themselves to such problems as the freedom to provide services on public works contracts and the elimination of certain practices which had continued under the previous general program directives,[53] the co-ordination of procedures for the award of public works contracts,[54] the publication of notices for public works contracts over a certain size in the *Official Journal*,[55] and finally the co-ordination of national procedures for the award of public supply contracts.[56] The Council has also created, by decision, an advisory committee to examine problems arising from the application of the directives.[57]

The first directive, dated 26 July 1971, abolished restrictions on the freedom to provide services for public works contracts and on the award of public works contracts to contractors acting through agencies or branches.[58] It was restricted in its application to certain building and engineering activities. In addition to requiring the abolition of certain enumerated restrictions, it provided for equal treatment in aids, subsidies, forms of credit, and supply facilities.[59] It referred to

52 Flamme, *supra* note 43, at 274ff.; Turpin, *supra* note 43, at 413.
53 Council Directive 71 / 304 of 26 July 1971, [1971] *Journal Officiel des Communatés Européennes* L 185 / 1.
54 Council Directive 71 / 305 of 26 July 1971, [1971] *Journal Officiel des Communautés Européennes* L 185 / 5.
55 Council Directive 72 / 277 of 26 July 1972, [1972] *Journal Officiel des Communautés Européennes* L 175 / 12.
56 Council Directive 77 / 62 of 21 Dec. 1976, [1977] *Official Journal of the European Communities* L 13 / 1.
57 Turpin, *supra* note 43, at 424; Council Decision of 26 July 1971, [1971] *Journal Officiel des Communautés Européennes* L 185 / 15.
58 Council Directive 71 / 304, *supra* note 53.
59 For description, see Turpin, *supra* note 43, at 414.

'discriminatory technical qualifications' and applied to concessionary companies as well as to public authorities, a point of importance in Italy and France where roads are often constructed as toll roads.[60]

The second directive (the 'Public Works Directive'), of the same date, provides for the co-ordination of national procedures for the award of public works contracts of over one million units of account value and applies to building and civil engineering works but excludes contracts for transportation services or for the distribution, transmission, or transportation of water and energy.

Like the GATT Agreement, it distinguishes between 'open procedures' and 'restricted procedures,' the latter enabling the authority to determine qualified bidders. The local authorities are free to determine which procedure will apply in any given case.[61] To both of these procedures certain general minimum conditions, encouraging publicity and controlling tendering, apply. Advertising throughout the Community is to be achieved through the *Official Journal*, and the notice must contain certain information, the criteria varying between open and restrictive procedures. Common rules on participation are specified, and permissible restrictions on capacity to bid are defined.

The directive also addresses itself to the possibly discriminatory effects of technical specifications in language similar to that of Article IV of the Agreement.

The basic rule and purpose of the directive is that 'competitive procedures,' whether for open or restrictive bids, are to be ensured,[62] and the exceptions to this basic rule are fairly narrowly defined in terms somewhat more restrictive than those in the Agreement. The member states are obliged to report to the Commission on the number and total value of contracts awarded under this head.

In view of the diversity of public tendering systems prevailing throughout Europe, a complete harmonization of national systems would be an unreasonable goal; rather, the member states are to ' "adapt" their domestic procedures to the provisions of the directives.'[63]

The basic criterion for the award of a contract is the lowest price or the most economically advantageous tender, provided that the basis for establishing the latter is dealt with in the call for bids. Justification of awards to other than the lowest or economically most advantageous tender (when such is specified in the call for tenders) must be provided to the Advisory Committee.

---

60 Ibid., at 416.
61 Flamme, *supra* note 43, at 283.
62 Turpin, *supra* note 43, at 420–1.
63 Art. 2, ibid., at 419.

The third directive deals with the details of publication of notices.

The fourth directive deals with the co-ordination of national procedures for the award of public supply contracts (the 'Supplies Directive'). It closely parallels the provisions of the Public Works Directive in providing for both an open and a restrictive procedure, each governed by the notion of competitive bidding, and for the publication of notices containing certain basic information. Specified categories of persons, not based on nationality, may be excluded from bidding, as in the Public Works Directive, and an award may be made without following the procedures in certain cases (single tendering). The annexes provide a list of those public bodies covered. The criteria on which the contracting authority may base its award are virtually identical to the Public Works Directive. The threshold for the application of the directive is fixed at 140 000 units of account (approximately $190 000 U.S.).[64]

While the results achieved in Europe by these measures are impressive and exceed any comparable Canadian action,[65] they have not been achieved without considerable difficulty. The problems involved were exhaustively reviewed in the Charpentier-Clarke Report of 1974 which showed that much action in this field was required if this form of barrier to intra-Community trade was to be eliminated.[66] The Supplies Directive, which raises more delicate political problems than public works because of the amount of government procurement it covers, is a case in point. The directive was originally proposed by the Commission to the Council in 1964 (as was the public works directive). It was not passed until 1976 and yet allowed another eighteen months for the member states to make the necessary modifications to their procedures. Indeed, most of the directives required from five to seven years to complete the legislative process.

The Commission supervises the application of the directives in the member states to ensure that laws, regulations, and administrative practice conform. Italy has been taken before the European Court for failure to implement the Public Works Directive.[67] Implementing measures taken vary from state to state. The Netherlands, for example, has not formally changed its legislation or administrative practice on the grounds that the directives have direct effect and will prevail over any inconsistent Dutch provision without action on their part.

---

64 Council Directive 80 / 767 of 22 July 1980, [1980] *Official Journal of the European Communities* L 215 / 1.

65 Bernier, *supra* note 11, at 209.

66 de Mestral, *supra* note 9, at 6.

67 Case 10 / 76, *E.C. Commission* v. *Italy*, [1976] European Court Reports 1359, [1976] 2 Common Market Law Reports 699, Case 133 / 80, *E.C. Commission* v. *Italy*, [1981] European Court Reports 457, [1981] 3 Common Market Law Reports 456.

The British maintain that since no law discriminates against non-nationals, no remedial legal or regulatory action is necessary, although their preference for local contractors has often been commented upon by others.[68]

The effect of the directives remains uncertain as the Commission does not have 'at its disposal any significant data concerning its economic results in terms of the interpenetration of markets,' although it intends to collect statistics, which may be only marginally reliable.[69] No review of the way in which the directives have been implemented in the member states is yet available.

It is hoped that the advisory committee established by decision of the Council in 1971 will facilitate the process and serve as the guardian of 'fair play.'[70] And the possibility that the directives may now in some measure have direct effect may permit actions against local or other authorities in the courts of the member states by individuals whose bids have not been treated in conformity with Community provisions. This may be the greatest guarantee of their uniform application. But even here the issue is far from clear, as may be seen from a recent article in the *New Law Journal*, where the author doubts that the directives could serve as the basis for an injunction against a local council (in the United Kingdom) that carried out its tendering procedures contrary to the provisions of the directives.[71]

The application of the GATT Agreement in the EEC

Adherence of the member states to the Agreement on Government Procurement was negotiated by the Community organs as a part of its participation in the Tokyo Round. It was signed by the Community on 17 December 1979 and implemented by Directive 80/767 of 22 July 1980 (the 'GATT Directive'), coming into force within the member states as of 1 January 1981.[72] No formal recognition by the contracting parties to GATT approved of the EEC replacing the individual member states, but the substitution has been accepted in practice.[73]

The Agreement covers roughly the same issues as are covered in the EEC system by the Supplies Directive rather than the directives concerning public

---

68 Anthony and Hagerty, *supra* note 14, at 1306.
69 See Answer to Miss Quinn, Q. 460/89, Ans. Aug. 4, 1980, [1980] *Official Journal of the European Communities* C 236/25, and see also Answer to Mr Van Miert, Q. 1045.80, Ans. Oct. 21, 1980, [1980] *Official Journal of the European Communities* C 302/32.
70 Flamme, *supra* note 43, at 293–5; Turpin, *supra* note 43, at 424.
71 Gumbley, 'EEC directives and public bodies' (1980), 130 *New Law Journal* 1175, at 1176.
72 Council Directive 80/767, *supra* note 64, and Council Decision 80/271 of 10 Dec., 1979, [1980] *Official Journal of the European Communities* L 71/1.
73 Steenbergen, 'The status of GATT in community law' (1981), 15 *Journal of World Trade Law* 337.

works, so that comparisons will be restricted to the former. However, in any public works purchase in the EEC system an authority would have to apply the relevant provisions of all the directives on supplies, GATT, and Public Works, in addition to any local requirements.

There are substantial similarities between the operation of the two systems. Both allow either open or restricted procedures to be applied at the discretion of the purchasing agent, and both set out minimum procedures to be followed with a view to ensuring adequate publicity and discouraging discrimination. The GATT Agreement has been described as 'following to a remarkable extent' the principles of the EEC directives.[74] There seems to have been an interplay in the development of the two systems.[75]

The most substantial difference between the two is in the scope of their application: the EEC requirements extend to all government departments and public administrative bodies including local governments; the Agreement applies only to those entities enumerated in its annexes, though it extends to all purchases of such entities subject to certain specified exclusions. Thus a given purchase may be caught by one régime but not the other.

When compared with federal states such as the United States and Canada, whose states and provinces are not covered by the Agreement, the EEC system appears more extensive, a point remarked upon by EEC officials.[76] The same limitation within the EEC is found in Germany, for whom the List of Purchasing Entities in the GATT Directive is restricted to federal ministries. The absence of the Länder is important because they are responsible for a considerable amount of public construction.[77]

Moreover, utilities are excluded under both systems. In this sense too the drafters of the Agreement followed the European example of the EEC directives.[78]

Ironically, the Agreement goes somewhat further than the Supplies Directive in certain respects, so that when it was implemented certain modifications had to be made to the former. Otherwise suppliers from contracting parties to the Agreement would have been in a better position in respect of some purchases than suppliers from member states relying on the Supplies Directive.[79]

---

74 European Communities, *European Parliament Working Documents 1979–80*, Doc. 1–814 / 79 at 11, 19.

75 Pomeranz, *supra* note 13, at 1274–5.

76 Doc. 1–814 / 79, *supra* note 74 at 5, Lesguillons, *supra* note 18, at 551.

77 Doc. 1–814 / 79, *supra* note 74, at 19.

78 de Mestral, *supra* note 9, at 19.

79 Doc. 1–814 / 79, *supra* note 74, at 16.

The GATT Directive modifies the Supplies Directive only in respect of the enumerated entities for some purposes. Other differences may result from the structure of the two systems. For example, the Supplies Directive exempts from this application secret or security-sensitive materials, whereas the GATT Directive exempts military procurement generally, including non-sensitive materials.[80]

As a result of the overlapping of the various régimes the United Kingdom has noted that for government procurement purposes there are three categories of suppliers to which different conditions may apply:

– bodies covered by both the GATT Agreement and the Supplies Directive;
– bodies covered by the GATT Agreement but not by the Supplies Directive; and
– bodies covered by the Supplies Directive but not by the GATT Agreement.[81]

The member states have the adopted measures they deem appropriate to implement the GATT Directive. In Belgium this was subject of a royal decree,[82] in Germany of administrative dispositions,[83] in France of a decree.[84] In the other member countries it was achieved by means of a circular to interested purchasing authorities[85] because no legislative or regulatory steps were required; either no legislative provisions requiring modification existed or the Community measures were considered self-executing.[86] The different methods of adoption demonstrate the degree of national diversity allowed by the EEC system of directives.

Technical questions concerning the operation of two systems within the EEC, particularly in relation to single tendering and the responsibility for reports to unsuccessful tenders,[87] remain to be resolved.

Outstanding also are complicated legal questions arising out of the transfer of jurisdiction for GATT from the member states to the Community.[88]

---

80 As an example, see Annex I, E.E.C., Pt. II, Agreement, *supra* note 14, and ibid., U.S. Compare para. 6(1)(g), Council Directive 77/62, *supra* note 56.
81 *Notes for Guidance*, Issued by H.M. Treasury, 28 Oct. 1980, at para. 20.
82 *Arrêté royal relatif à la mise en concurrence de certains marchés publics de fournitures, Moniteur belge*, 26 May 1981.
83 Communication of Government of the Federal Republic of Germany, 15 Dec. 1980.
84 Décret No. 81–551 du 12 Mai 1981 modifiant le décret No. 79–98 du Jan. 1979; arrêté du 12 Mai, Modifiant l'arrêté du 12 Jan. 1979 (threshold for publication of procurement by local authorities in government departments).
85 Denmark: Ministry of Finance Circular, 18 Dec. 1980; Ireland: Circular of Dept of Finance, 31 Dec. 1980; Italy: Circular No. 2 of Ministry of Treasury of 26 Jan. 1981; UK: *Notes for Guidance, supra* note 81.
86 The Netherlands falls in the latter category.
87 European Parliament Working Document, *supra* note 74, at 20, 21.
88 Steenbergen, *supra* note 73, at 343–4.

Finally, neither GATT nor the EEC system are complete. The need for further negotiations under GATT is expressly recognized in the Agreement, and the lack of compliance by the member states under the Supplies Directive remains of concern within the Community itself.[89]

THE UNITED STATES

Internal

The degree to which states are free to favour local residents in their procurement policies is essentially a question of the constitutional limits on their legislative powers. The definition of these limits has largely been the responsibility of the courts. In this area of American constitutional law, as in others, judicial opinion has evolved since the early days of the republic. This evolution has been subject to all the exceptions, qualifications, and complexities that can arise in a wealth of judicial pronouncements.

The present paper is more concerned with a traditional analysis of 'law' as determined by courts. The wealth and diversity of the case law, it has been suggested, is due to the fact that procurement policies in the United States, both at the federal and at state level, are to be found in readily available legislative or regulatory enactments that clearly specify the nature and extent of the discrimination in question, thus making possible the use of the courts as a forum for an attack against such practices. This situation contrasts with that in Europe before the establishment of the EEC, where there was no legal basis for challenging the procurement policies of other states, whose policies, moreover, were in large part implemented through administrative discretion or action that tended to conceal the discrimination. The system prevailing in the United States thus encouraged American negotiators to emphasize 'transparency' when turning their hands to the fashioning of GATT.

Three provisions of the U.S. Constitution are relevant to the use of government procurement as a barrier to trade: the equal protection, the privileges and immunities, and the commerce clauses.[90] To some, these clauses are fundamental to the existence of the Union. Thus, in declaring invalid a milk-marketing law imposing minimum prices, Cardozo J. wrote:

---

89 European Working Document, *supra* note 74, at 6; in 1976 the U.S. General Accounting Office expressed the view that the Public Works Directive had had 'little impact on the procurement patterns of the countries involved.' See Anthony and Hagerty, *supra* note 14, at 1303; and see *E.C. Comm.* v. *Italy, supra* note 67.

90 Art. I, S. 8 of the Constitution provides in part as follows: 'The Congress shall have power ... (3) To regulate commerce with foreign nations, and among the several States, and with the Indian Tribes.' Art. IV, s.-s. 2(1) provides: 'The citizens of each State shall be entitled

If New York, in order to promote the economic welfare of her farmers, may guard them against competition with the cheaper prices of Vermont, the door has been opened to rivalries and reprisals that were meant to be averted by subjecting commerce between the states to the power of the nation ... The Constitution was framed under the dominion of a political philosophy less parochial in range. It was framed upon the theory that the peoples of the several states must sink or swim together, and that in the long run prosperity and salvation are in union and not division.[91]

And yet, as noted by Jackson, 'discrimination in favour of local products sometimes seems to be one of the basic human urges,'[92] and United States state practice is certainly rich in illustrations of the legislator's surrender to such primal desires in spite of the recognition of the broader interest in prosperity and salvation as guaranteed by the union.

Originally, state local procurement preferences were justified through the equation of the powers of the states with those of private persons. The result of this equation was to validate such preferences, because there were no rights limiting the scope of the states' powers.[93] Thus, the first court to consider the constitutionality of state procurement preferences said that: 'Viewed as a question of principle, we are unable to see why the state is forbidden to do what an individual certainly may do with impunity, viz. elect from whom it will purchase supplies needed in the discharge of its functions.'[94]

The equation of public and private contractual powers made the validity of government intervention turn upon its form. A government could not require private persons to limit the working hours of their employees,[95] but it could

---

to all privileges and immunities of citizens in the several States.' S. 1 of the Fourteenth Amendment (1868) provides as follows: 'All persons born or naturalized in the United States, and subject to the jurisdiction thereof, are citizens of the United States and of the State wherein they reside. No State shall make or enforce any law which shall abridge the privileges or immunities of citizens of the United States; nor shall any State deprive any person of life, liberty, or property, without due process of law; nor deny to any person within its jurisdiction the equal protection of the laws.

91 *Baldwin* v. *G.A.F. Seelig, Inc.*, 294 U.S. 511, (1935).

92 Jackson, *supra* note 10, at 274.

93 'Whatever is a privilege, rather than a right, may be made dependent upon citizenship.' *Crane* v. *People*, 214 N.Y. 154, 108 N.E. 427, 430, aff'd *sub nom. Crane* v. *New York*, 239 U.S. 195, 36 S. Ct. 85, 60 L. Ed. 218 (1–15), *per Cardozo*, J. But see *Salla* v. *Co. of Monroe*, 399 N.E. 2d 909, *cert.* den. 446 U.S. 909 (1979).

94 *Knight* v. *Barnes*, 7 N.D. 591, 75 N.W. 094, 096 (1898), *per Wallin*, J.

95 *Lochner* v. *New York*, 198 U.S. 45, (1905).

require those with whom it contracted to do so.[96] Similarly, the government could prefer state residents in the letting of procurement contracts.[97]

Another common-law category used to justify preferences on formal grounds was that of property. Thus, Virginia could prevent the residents of other states from planting oysters in her tidal waters, because she had property rights in such waters: 'Such an appropriation is in effect nothing more than a regulation of the use by the people of their common property. The right which the people of the State thus acquire comes not from their citizenship alone, but from their citizenship and property combined. It is, in fact, a property right, and not a mere privilege or immunity of citizenship.'[98] These decisions equated the contractual and proprietary powers of governments with those of private persons, and the rules for the exercise of these powers (such as procurement laws) were not 'public and general law(s) in the ordinary sense of the term.'[99] As such, they were not subject to judicial review: this exception was defined by the Supreme Court in *Truax* v. *Raich* as 'the regulation or distribution of the public domain, or of the common property or resources of the people of the state.'[100]

The analogy between the public and private contractual and proprietary powers is incomplete, since it is possible for citizens to have constitutional rights which limit public powers. Thus even before any general recognition of such limitations, Cardozo J. rejected the proposition that a state's private law power permitted racial discrimination.[101] The creation of the 'suspect classification' of race subject to 'strict scrutiny' in a famous dictum in *U.S.* v. *Carolene Products Co.* was based upon the exclusion in fact of certain groups from representation in the political process.[102] The leading case cited was *McCulloch* v. *Maryland*, in which Marshall C.J. reasoned that, since those who were neither citizens nor residents of a state could not actually be represented in a state legislature, such a legislature could not single out such persons in a discriminary way when levying taxes.[103]

The status of a non-resident thus became related to the question of the individual's constitutional right to equality of treatment as expressly guaranteed by the privileges and immunities clause. The leading case on the interpretation of

---

96 *Atkin* v. *Kansas*, 191 u.s. 207, (1903).
97 In addition to *Knight* v. *Barnes, supra* note 94, see *Ebbeson* v. *Board of Public Education in Wilmington*, 156 Atl. 286 (1931).
98 *McCready* v. *Virginia*, 94 u.s. 391, 395, 24 L. Ed. 248 (1876), *per Waite*, c.j.
99 *State ex p. Gemmill, supra* note 8, Pac. 301, *per Ailshie*, j.
100 239 u.s. 33, 40, 36 S. Ct. 7, 10, 60 L. Ed. 131 (1915), *per Hughes*, j.
101 *Crane, supra* note 93, n.e. 431.
102 304 u.s. 144, 152 note 4, (1938).
103 4 Wheat. (17 u.s.) 316, 428–30, 4 L. Ed. 579 (1819).

the privileges and immunities clause, which is the most general prohibition of discrimination upon grounds of state of residence, is *Toomer* v. *Witsell*, which involved a South Carolina statute providing for lower shrimp fishing licence fees for state residents.[104] Vinson C.J., who delivered the judgment of the Court, stated that the clause 'was designed to insure to a citizen of State A who ventures into State B the same privileges which the citizens of State B enjoy.'[105] The Court therefore determined that one of the 'privileges' was 'doing business' in State B on terms of substantial equality with the citizens of that state.[106] However, the clause creates only a relative immunity which might be affected by valid state legislation; thus it is necessary to go beyond the apparent discrimination to see whether a valid state purpose may be found. The Court explained the proprietary limb of the private-law power as a legal fiction giving expression to the proper state purpose of conservation of its natural resources.[107] The statute in question, however, was an unreasonable means for the achievement of that purpose and was therefore invalid.[108]

It is uncertain whether this erosion of the private-law power of state governments has gone so far as to eliminate the state's right to discriminate when purchasing supplies for its own use. Also, the validity of state statutes giving preferences to resident labourers in procurement remains to be tested.[109] *Hicklin* v. *Orbeck*, which held that a statute requiring 'Alaska-hire' provisions in state gas leases was invalid, might have resolved this uncertainty, but the Court, while considering the case as being an instance of the proprietary limb,[110] apparently thought that the proprietary aspect was so attenuated as to be 'colourable,' that is, seeking to give constitutional form to unconstitutional legislation.[111] Other

---

104 334 U.S. 385, 68 S. Ct. 1156, (1948).
105 Ibid., U.S. 395, S. Ct. 1162.
106 Ibid., U.S. 396, S. Ct. 1162.
107 Ibid., U.S. 402, S. Ct. 1165.
108 Ibid., U.S. 397–8, S. Ct. 1163.
109 See for instance Alaska: A.S. 36.10.010 (1962); Arizona: A.R.S., s. 34–302 (West 1974); and other state statutes. Oklahoma has a statute which provides that state resident labourers are not to be preferred in public works projects, where this would not affect the price or equality of the work; 61 Okl. St. Ann., ss. 9, 10 (West 1963). These provisions are probably valid notwithstanding their improper (protectionist) purpose, simply because such discrimination never breaches the Clause's requirement of 'substantial equality.'
110 'Rather than placing a statute completely beyond the Clause, a State's ownership of the property with which the statute is concerned is a factor – although often the crucial factor – to be considered in evaluating whether the statute's discrimination against non-citizens violates the Clause': 437 U.S. 518, 529, 98 S. Ct. 2482, 2489, (1978), *per Brennan, J.*
111 Ibid., U.S. 529–30, S. Ct. 2489–90.

state statutes concerned with the procurement of supplies and works for the state's own use are not open to any such objection. Viewed from the perspective of state power, therefore, the privileges and immunities clause would not appear to render procurement preferences invalid.

More recently the Court has come to consider the issue of the degree to which some form of discrimination is legitimate. For example, in *Baldwin* v. *Montana Fish & Game Commission*[112] the Supreme Court held to be valid Montana's higher elk hunting licence fees for non-residents. Blackmun J., who delivered the judgment of the Court, noted that 'Only with respect to those "privileges" and "immunities" bearing upon the vitality of the Nation as a single entity, must the State treat all citizens, residents and non-residents, equally.'[113] An example of the application of such an immunity was that of carrying on a business, as was considered in *Toomer* v. *Witsell*.[114]

The existence of such a 'business' immunity may explain *Hicklin* v. *Orbeck*. The application of a similar test to those statutes which give preferences to resident labourers results in their invalidity.[115] Indeed it is possible that such an immunity would have still more far-reaching consequences. Many states also have statutes giving preferences to resident contractors,[116] and these could be challenged for the same reason.

Many states also have statutes giving preferences to goods produced or manufactured in the state[117]; the privileges and immunities clause has never been used to attack such discrimination against the mobility of goods. That role has been performed by the commerce clause. While the latter grants a power to Congress, it has been interpreted since the early nineteenth century as implying a limitation of state powers as well.[118]

Since the 'Judicial Revolution of 1937,' the scope of the commerce power has increased,[119] and state powers to affect commerce have diminished:

---

112 436 U.S. 371, 98 S. Ct. 1852, (1978).
113 Ibid., U.S. 383.
114 *Supra* note 104.
115 *Mass. Council of Construction Employers, Inc.* v. *Mayor of Boston*, Mass., 425 N.E. 2d 346 (1981).
116 See for instance Alaska: A.S. 27.05.230(1) (1962) (5% preference) and other state statutes.
117 See for instance Alaska: A.S. 36.15.010 (1962) ('timber, lumber and manufactured lumber products') and other state statutes.
118 *Gibbons* v. *Ogden*, 9 Wheat. (22 U.S.) 1, 6 L. Ed. 23 (1824) contains important *dicta* by *Marshall*, C.J., but the first decision is *Smith* v. *Turner; Norris* v. *City of Boston*, commonly called *The Passenger Cases*, 7 How. (48 U.S.) 282, 12 L. Ed. (Mineola N.Y.: The Foundation Press, 1978), at 324 n. 2.
119 'The congressional authority to protect interstate commerce from burdens and obstructions is not limited to transactions which can be deemed to be an essential part of a "flow"

The opinions of the Court through the years have reflected an alertness to the evils of 'economic isolation' and protectionism, while at the same time recognizing that incidental burdens on interstate commerce may be unavoidable when a State legislates to safeguard the health and safety of its people. Thus, where simple economic protectionism is effected by state legislation, a virtually *per se* rule of invalidity has been erected.[120]

The nature and scope of the negative implication of the commerce clause parallels that of the privileges and immunities clause. In *Hughes* v. *Oklahoma*, Brennan J. explained that state legislation might affect interstate commerce only incidentally, in which case it would be valid.[121] Any more substantial effect was a 'burden,' and the onus then shifted to the state to show the proper purpose behind the burden, and that the means used were in reasonable proportion to that purpose. In the result, an Oklahoma statute forbidding the transportation of minnows out of the state was held invalid, and *Geer* v. *Connecticut*,[122] one of the principal authorities for the proposition that the private-law power was not subject to judicial review, was overruled. While the Court was willing to accept the conservation of a natural resource as a proper purpose of the statute, the means adopted invalidated it because more appropriate means were available.[123]

More recently, the Supreme Court has reconsidered the concept of a 'burden' upon interestate commerce. The result is a series of recent cases favourable to the constitutionality of statutes giving preferences to state products in government procurement.

For example, in *Hughes* v. *Alexandria Scrap Corp.*, the Court rejected the argument that a Maryland statutory bounty for auto hulks was unconstitutional by virtue of the fact that more stringent title documentation was required from non-resident scrap processors.[124] On behalf of the Court, Powell J. wrote that such a bounty was not 'the kind of action with which the Commerce Clause is concerned,' because it amounted to the state's participation in the market, whereas the clause was concerned only with the 'prohibition' or 'burdensome regulation' of the participation of others in the market[125]: 'We do not believe the

---

of interstate or foreign commerce': *National Labor Relations Board* v. *Jones and Laughlin Steel Corp.*, 301 U.S. 1, 36, 57 S. Ct. 615, 624, (1937), *per Hughes*, C.J.

120 *City of Philadelphia* v. *New Jersey*, 437 U.S. 617, 623–4, 98 S. Ct. 2531, 2535, (1978), *per Stewart*, J.

121 441 U.S. 322, 99 S. Ct. 1727, (1979).

122 161 U.S. 519, 16 S. Ct. 600, (1896).

123 *Supra* note 121, at 1737.

124 426 U.S. 794, 96 S. Ct. 2488, (1976).

125 Ibid., U.S. 805 and 806, S. Ct. 2495, 2496.

Commerce Clause was intended to require independent justification for such action.'[126]

According to the reasons of Blackmun J. (which were those of the Court) in *Reeves, Inc.* v. *Stake*, where it was held that a state-owned cement plant in South Dakota could ration its products in a time of shortage by selling only to consumers in that state, *Alexandria Scrap* had established a 'general rule ... in unmistakably broad terms' about 'the impact of the Commerce Clause on state proprietary activity'[127]: 'The basic distinction drawn in *Alexandria Scrap* between States as market participants and States as market regulators makes good sense and sound law.'[128] The 'good sense' of the distinction relates to its accommodation of the conflicting demands of federalism and economic union[129]; however, it is possible to maintain that the procurement preferences we have been discussing can be considered invalid as protectionist devices without contradicting the general principle that a state may 'prefer residents in the distribution of state-created resources.'[130] In the absence of this principle, the possibility of free riders might have prevented the state from building the cement plant in *Reeves*, but this is not the case with government procurement, which is necessarily ancillary to the provision of some other public service.

The significance of the creation of public resources suggests the further distinction which *Reeves* requires between preferences relating to natural resources (invalid) and those relating to finished goods (valid) in order to reconcile it with *Hughes* v. *Oklahoma*.[131] The validity of this distinction does not affect the narrower question we are discussing here. Both the dissenters[132] and the Court[133] in *Reeves* appeared to regard state protectionist procurement preferences as valid, and their disappearance from American state laws on purely constitutional grounds should not be relied upon.[134]

---

126 Ibid., U.S. 809, S. Ct. 2497.
127 447 U.S. 429, 100 S. Ct. 2271, 2282, 2277, 2276, (1980).
128 Ibid., S. Ct. 2277.
129 Varat, 'State "citizenship" and interstate equality,' 48 *University of Chicago Law Review* 487, 516 (1981)
130 Ibid., at 546, 548.
131 For an application of this second distinction, see *South-Central Timber Development, Inc.* v. *LeResche*, 511 F. Supp. 139 (D.Alk., 1981).
132 Ibid., S. Ct. 2284–5.
133 Ibid., S. Ct. 2277 n. 9.
134 See also *American Yearbook Co., Inc.* v. *Askew*, 339 F. Supp. 719 (M.D. Fla.), aff'd summarily, 409 U.S. 804, 93 S. Ct. 230, (1972). Summary affirmations are only Supreme Court authority for 'the precise issues presented and necessarily decided': *Mandel* v. *Bradley*, 432 U.S. 173, 176, 97 S. Ct. 2238, 2240, (1977), *per Burger*, C.J.

One of the problems with such preferences is that the first response of those being victimized by discrimination is likely to be retaliation. There are in the United States today statutes providing for reciprocal preferences for resident labourers,[135] for resident contractors,[136] and for state products.[137] Generally, these statutes allow a person or product to be granted a preference over another person or product equal to the preference the latter is granted in the other home state. None of these statutes has stopped the proliferation of such preferences, although the statute in Pennsylvania is even more stringent, as it 'forbids *any* procurement from residents of states with "absolute" preference laws. Its strict enforcement in the middle sixties is credited with the repeal of preference laws in several eastern states.'[138]

Many American states have expressly recognized the interests of taxpayers in buying cheap by requiring the procurement of goods and services from the 'lowest responsible bidder.'[139] Since the American courts have uniformly decided that the 'lowest responsible bid' requirement prevents preferences from being applied administratively,[140] American legislatures have been required to enact their preferences into law, thus resulting in the 'transparency' referred to earlier.

And transparent preferences, unlike administrative practices, can be changed as a result of the ordinary working of the political process: 'The Council of State Governments and the National Association of State Purchasing Officials have been strongly and actively opposed to preference laws for many years. They have recently been joined by the National Governors' Conference through a policy statement denouncing preference laws as anti-competitive and inefficient.'[141] The American Bar Association's Section on Public Contract Law has

---

135 Alabama: Ala. C. 1975, s. 39–3–2; Washington: R.C.W.A. 39.16.005 (West 1981 Supp.).

136 Florida: West's F.S.A., s. 287.084 (1975); Kansas: K.S.A. 75–3740a (1977); Louisiana: L.S.A.-R.S. 38: 2225 (West Cum. Supp. 1981) (but see note 143, *infra*); Maryland: An. C. 1957, art. 21, s. 8–503(a) (Cum. Supp. 1980); Minnesota: M.S.A., s. 16.365(1) (West 1977); Mississippi: Miss. C. 1972, s. 31–3–21 and –7–47; Nebraska: R.R.S. 1943 73–101.01 (1976); North Dakota: N.D. Cent. Code, s. 44–08–01 (Allen Smith 1980); Oklahoma: 61 Okl. St. Ann., s. 14, 74 Ibid., s. 85.17 (West 1965 and Cum. Supp. 1980–1); South Dakota: S.D.C.L. 5–19–3 (Allen Smith 1980); Virginia: C. 1950, s. 11–20.1 (Richie 1979).

137 Illinois: S.H.A., c. 127 s. 132.6(e) (Cum. Supp. 1980–1); Pennsylvania: 71 P.S., s. 203 (Purdon 1962) (prohibition); Wyoming: W.S. 1977, s. 9–8–307 (maximum of 5%).

138 Jordan, 'In-State Preferences in Public Contracting: States' Rights versus Economic Sectionalism' (1978) *49 Colorado Law Review* 205, 208

139 See for instance Alabama: Ala. C. 1975, ss. 39–2–6, and 41–16–27(a); and other state statutes.

140 See *American Institute for Imported Steel, Inc.* v. *Co. of Erie*, 32 App. Div. 2d 231. 302 N.Y.S. 2d 61 (1969).

141 Jordan, *supra* note 138, at 212, n. 38.

prepared a *Model Procurement Code for State and Local Governments*. Approved by the Association at Atlanta on 13 February 1979, the *Code* includes no preferences at all, except in the event of a tie bid.[142] As of 1 February 1981, seven states had wholly or partially enacted the *Model Procurement Code*,[143] and bills had been introduced into the legislatures of five more states.[144] It would appear, therefore, that the present tendency in American politics is away from state preferences.

Application of the Agreement in the United States
The restrictive effects of Buy-American legislation and the extent to which they may be attenuated by the GATT Agreement on Government Procurement must be considered under two heads, federal and state practices.

1 Federal practices
Generally, the federal system may be summarized as consisting of a 6 per cent price differential preference for domestic products, which may be raised to 12 per cent in the case of small businesses or firms located in areas of high unemployment. Defence Department procurement, for balance-of-payment reasons, may reach a 50 per cent preference in favour of domestic suppliers.[145] In addition to these preferences there are 'set asides' in favour of small and minority businesses. I am informed that under the Carter administration 40 per cent of the procurement requirements of the General Supplies Administration (GSA) was reserved to small businesses.[146]

It has been argued that the United States with these preferences 'discriminates quite severely against imports in its purchasing practices.'[147] This seems particularly true when American practices are contrasted with those of Germany, though not in comparison to France and the U.K., which are more restrictive than the United States.[148] In the end it would appear that a reduction of

---

142 American Bar Association, *The Model Procurement Code for State and Local Governments* (1979) s.-ss. 3–202(7), –203(7), and –207(5).
143 '*Model Procurement Code for State and Local Governments*,' Implementation Program: summary of legislative activity as of February 1, 1981,' 16/3 *Public Contract Newsletter* 5–6 (1981).
144 'Summary,' *supra* note 143, at 5–6; Colorado, Illinois, South Carolina, Virginia, West Virginia.
145 Cline et al., *Trade Negotiations in the Tokyo Round: A Quantitative Assessment*, (Washington: The Brookings Institution, 1978), at 189.
146 Conversations with officials in the Department of Industry, Trade and Commerce, Ottawa, June 1981.
147 Lowinger, *supra* note 11, at 455.
148 Cline, *supra* note 145.

discrimination in American government procurement would do more to liberalize access to the American market than corresponding European measures would do to improve access to the EEC.[149]

The federal government's acceptance or rejection of bids is controlled by statutes.[150] Preferences then tend to be enacted as statutes, such as the so-called Buy-American Act, first enacted as a rider to an appropriation bill in 1933.[151] Once so enacted the preferences thereby established have been rigidly applied,[152] and this may be an important part of the explanation of why the American government appears to discriminate so severely against imports in its purchasing.[153] These preferences have been estimated to have been equivalent to a tariff of between 26 and 43 per cent in 1963[154] and to have cost the government $121 million in that year.[155] A thorough consideration of the proliferation of statutes, orders, waivers, and determinations that constitute American practice is beyond the scope of this paper, but I will attempt a summary.

The Buy-American Act requires that only unmanufactured articles produced in the United States and only manufactured articles manufactured in the United States 'substantially' from American products shall be procured by the government.[156] In 1953, as a result of the Report of the (Randall) Commission on Foreign Economic Policy,[157] President Eisenhower issued an Executive Order[158]

149 Ibid., at 194.
150 Title 10, U.S.C.A., s.-s. 2305(c) (military) (West 1975); 41 U.S.C.A., s.-s. 253(b) (West 1965), en. by s.-s. 303(b) of the *Federal Property and Administrative Services Act of 1949*, Pub. L. 81–152, 63 Stat. 395 (civil). See also s. 2 of the *Office of Federal Procurement Policy Act Amendments of 1979*, 41 U.S.C.A., s. 401 (West Cum. Supp. 1981), en. by Pub. L. 96–83, 93 Stat. 648, wherein it is declared to be the policy of the Congress that goods and services be acquired at the 'lowest reasonable cost.'
151 41 U.S.C.A., ss. 10a *et seq.* (West 1965), en. by tit. III of the *Treasury and Post Office Appropriation Act, 1934*, Pub. L. 72–428, 47 Stat. 1520–1 (1933).
152 Watkins, 'Effects of the Buy-American Act on federal procurement,' (1972) 31 *Federal Bar Journal* 191, 204.
153 Lowinger, *supra* note 11, at 455. This study was based upon a comparison of the public and private sectors' import propensities.
154 '[D]epending on the commodity coverage and assumptions made about the elasticity of demand': ibid., at 457.
155 Ibid., at 459.
156 41 U.S.C.A., s. 10a (West 1965).
157 Horsch, 'Eliminating nontariff barriers to international trade: the M.T.N. Agreement on government procurement,' 12 *New York University Journal of International Law and Politics* 315, 322 (1979).
158 19 Fed. Reg. 8723, 41 U.S.C.A., p. 70 (West 1965).

which reduced the content requirement for a product to be considered American to 50 per cent of the cost of its components.[159]

The 50 per cent requirement is applied only to the end-product, that is, the item to be delivered to the government.[160] This purely functional concept of the nationality of the product results in a loophole in the Act in that there is no protection for the components of the components of the end-product.[161] For example, in *Textron, Inc. Bell Helicopter Textron Division* v. *Adams*,[162] a disappointed bidder alleged that the Coast Guard's identification of a 'system' that included helicopters, maintenance, and, training as the end-product was 'merely a ruse designed by Aérospatiale Helicopter Corp. [the successful bidder] to avoid the Buy-American Act.'[163] Out of deference on the part of the District Court and the comptroller general to decisions by the relevant department as to what constitutes the end-product,[164] this allegation was rejected. Since the helicopters were components of the end-product, the claim that they were merely to be assembled in Texas from French products was irrelevant.[165]

The problem of ascertaining the level of American or foreign content that 'triggers' the applicaton of the statute greatly complicates the position of foreign suppliers seeking to participate in larger American contracts. Often, precisely because of the administrative inconveniences it creates, American general contractors will avoid dealing with foreign suppliers. The definition of such criteria is seldom contained in the legislation but rather is in the various forms of subordinate legislation which vary from statute to statute. As a result a given contract might be considered 'American' for the purposes of one statute, but not for another.[166]

The first two of the five exceptions to the Buy-American Act show that the Act is not as restrictive as it seems. The statute itself releases departments from its requirements where their heads determine the cost of American products to be 'unreasonable' or their acquisition to be 'inconsistent with the public

---

159 See now the *Defense Acquisition Regulations* and the *Federal Procurement Regulations*, 32 C.F.R. 6–001(c), 18–506.4; 41 C.F.R. 1–6.101(d), –18.601(d).

160 32 C.F.R. 6–102.1, 18–507; 41 C.F.R. 1–6.102, –18.602–2.

161 Chierichella, 'The Buy-American Act and the use of foreign sources in federal procurements – an issues analysis,' (1977) 9 *Public Contract Law Journal* 73, 82, 84.

162 493 F. Supp. 824 (D.C., 1980).

163 Ibid., at 834, *per Green*, Dist. J.

164 Ibid., at 828–9, 831–2.

165 Ibid., at 834–5.

166 *Supra* note 146.

interest.'[167] Following the Randall Report, the preference was reduced from 25 to 6 per cent (or 10 per cent if the tariff was not considered as part of the price of the foreign product).[168] This preference remains effective today,[169] subject to two qualifications: first, since the late 1950s[170] a special preference of 12 per cent has been granted to small businesses or to those in areas of high unemployment[171]; second, since 1962[172] a special preference of 50 per cent has been granted to those contracting with the Department of Defence 'for balance of payments' reasons.'[173]

The military preference is also subject to exceptions. For example, the secretary of defense has determined that it would be 'inconsistent with the public interest' if Canadian products were subject to discrimination under the Buy-American Act.[174] (There are exceptions to this exception.) Similarly, between 1975 and 1980 the United States entered a series of reciprocal memoranda of understanding relating to military procurement whose signatories were exempted from the Act.[175]

The limited preferences generated by the 'unreasonable cost' and 'inconsistent with the public interest' exceptions are also applied only to the end-product.[176] The comptroller general has consistently interpreted this to exclude installation costs,[177] and the courts have generally deferred, notwithstanding some judicial suspicion that the effect is contrary to the statutory purpose.[178]

By its terms, the Act does not apply to 'supplies for use outside the United States.'[179] This exception is of no practical significance, since a special 50 per cent

---

167 *Supra* note 156.
168 19 Fed. Reg. 8723 41 U.S.C.A., p. 71 (West 1965).
169 41 C.F.R. 1–6.104–4(b), –18.603–1.
170 Knapp, 'The Buy-American Act: a review and assessment,' (1961) 61 *Columbia Law Review* 430, 443.
171 41 C.F.R. 1–6.104–4(b), –18.603–4.
172 Chierichella, *supra* note 161, at 107.
173 32 C.F.R. 6–104.4(b).
174 32 C.F.R. 6–501. Also, Canadian products are not subject to discrimination by N.A.S.A.: 41 C.F.R. 18–6.103–5.
175 32 C.F.R. 6–1401, –1504.1. The agreements may be found at: 32 C.F.R. 6–1406.2 to .9, –1504.1. The signatories were Belgium, Denmark, Germany, Israel, Italy, the Netherlands, Norway, Portugal, and the United Kingdom. See David B. Dempsey, 'Foreign procurement under Memoranda of Understanding and the Trade Agreements Act,' (1982) 12 *Public Contract Law Journal* 221.
176 *Supra* note 160.
177 *Allis-Chalmers Corp., Hydro-Turbine Division* v. *Friedkin*, 635 F. 2d 248, 256 (C.A. 3d Cir., 1980).
178 Ibid., at 252–3, 255, 257–8.
179 *Supra* note 156.

preference is imposed for American products in such circumstances 'for balance of payments' reasons.'[180]

Nor does the Act apply to products not available in commercial quantities in the United States.[181] Over the years, standardized lists of such products, often from tropical countries, have evolved.[182] The most important such product is petroleum. As recently as 1974 the Department of Defense bought more than 40 per cent of its petroleum abroad.[183] The money thus spent almost equalled the value of total federal procurement for which there was direct competition between foreign and domestic bidders.[184]

The American approval of the Agreement[185] may be said to constitute another exception to the Buy-American policies. By subsection 301(a) of the Trade Agreements Act of 1979, the president is empowered to waive 'the application of any law, regulation, procedure or practice regarding Government procurement' where this would result in less favourable treatment of foreign products than American products receive overseas.[186] Accordingly, any waiver for a particular state entails a presidential determination that the other state is providing reciprocity to American products or is a least developed country.[187] By subsection 3(a) of the Act, a federal statute is to prevail where it conflicts with any of the 1979 Agreements,[188] so that the Agreement may be said to create only an exception to the Buy-American Act. It certainly does not result in its amendment or repeal. Moreover, the limits to the coverage of the Agreement reviewed above must also be borne in mind.[189]

180 32 C.F.R. 6–803.1(d), 41 C.F.R. 1–6.806–1(a).

181 *Supra* note 156.

182 32 C.F.R. 6–105 (Defense); 41 C.F.R. 3–6.105 (Health and Human Services), 8–6.105 (Veterans' Administration), 9–6.105 (Energy), 12–6.105 (Transportation), 14–6.105 (Interior), 18–6.105 (NASA).

183 *Report to the Congress by the Comptroller-General of the United States: Governmental Buy-National Practices of the U.S. And Other Countries – An Assessment,* (Washington: Government Printing Office, 1976), at 20.

184 Ibid., at 12.

185 By s. 2 of the *Trade Agreements Act of 1979,* 19 U.S.C.A., s. 2503 (West 1980), Pub. L. 96–39, 93 Stat. 147.

186 19 U.S.C.A., s.-s. 2511(a) (West 1980), Pub. L. 96–39, 93 Stat. 236.

187 Ibid., s.-s. 2511(b). For a list of the designated countries, see: 41 C.F.R. 1–6.1612. This waiver expired 1 Jan. 1983.

188 Ibid., s.-s. 2504(a), 93 Stat. 148.

189 Sen. R. 96–249 (concerning Pub. L. 96–39) indicates that the Agreement bans protectionism in $12.5 billion annually worth of procurement, out of a total of $90 billion annually worth of federal procurement: [1979] *U.S.C. Congressional and Administration News* 381, 527–8.

Other forms of protectionism are indeed even more significant than the Buy-American Act. For example, since 1954 the Berry Amendment has prohibited the procurement of certain foreign products by the Department of Defense.[190] Continually expanded, the list now covers 'food, clothing, cotton, woven silk or woven silk blends, spun silk yarn for cartridge cloth, synthetic fibre or coated synthetic fibre, or wool (whether in the form of fibre or yarn or contained in fabrics, materials, or manufactured articles) or specialty metals including stainless metals including stainless steel flatware.'[191] The Department of Defense may also acquire only American-made buses[192] and must prefer American contractors for research and development.[193] Since 1964 the Tollefson Amendment to the annual appropriation Acts has required the components of the Navy's ships to be American,[194] while since 1967 the Byrnes Amendment requires the Navy's ships to be built in American shipyards.[195] No contract involving steel is to be awarded without American competition,[196] nor is there to be any foreign steel in 'the proposed MX missile system.'[197] Of course, it may be said that most of these items are covered by Article VIII of the Agreement, but there are non-military items too. American contractors are, for example, preferred for dredging the Indian Ocean.[198] In a study of 90 per cent of federal procurement in 1974, these specified prohibitions and preferences together controlled 9 per cent of the purchases studied, while the Buy-American Act controlled only 3 per cent.[199]

Prohibitions on the acquisition of particular foreign products by the civil departments are much less significant, controlling less than 1 per cent of the purchases studied.[200] Among such prohibitions are hand or measuring tools (since 1971),[201] stainless steel flatware (since 1978),[202] and twine for the U.S. Forest Service.[203]

---

190 Knapp, *supra* note 170, at 450.
191 *Department of Defense Appropriation Act, 1982*, s. 723; Pub. L. 97–114, 95 Stat. 1582 (1981).
192 Pub. L. 90–500, 82 Stat. 851, s. 404 (1968).
193 *Department of Defense Appropriation Act, 1973*, s. 744: Pub. L. 92–570, 86 Stat. 1184 (1972).
194 Watkins, *supra* note 152, at 216.
195 Ibid.
196 *Military Construction Appropriation Act, 1982*, s. 113; Pub. L. 97–106, 95 Stat. 1507 (1981).
197 *Military Construction Appropriation Act, 1981*, s. 127; Pub. L. 96–436, 94 Stat. 1867 (1980).
198 *Military Construction Appropriation Act, 1982*, s. 115. On the other hand, there is no preference for American-made 'swords and scabbards': 32 C.F.R. 6–103.2(c)(iii).
199 *Report, supra* note 183, at 4, 12.
200 Ibid., at 12.
201 *Treasury, Postal Service and General Government Appropriations Act, 1980*, s. 505; Pub. L. 96–74, 93 Stat. 573 (1979).
202 Ibid., s. 506.
203 16 U.S.C.A., s. 560a (West 1974), en. by s. 201 of the *Department of the Interior and Related Agencies Appropriation Act, 1974*, Pub. L. 93–120, 87 Stat. 442.

Probably of greater significance are the Buy-American provisions increasingly tied to various grants-in-aid and other forms of federal assistance. The passenger rail service has its own buy-American statute in subsection 305(k) of the Rail Passenger Act,[204] while S. 401 of the Surface Transportation Assistance Act of 1978,[205] S. 215 of the Federal Water Pollution Control Act,[206] and para. 106(f)(1) of the Local Public Works Capital Development and Investment Act of 1976[207] provide for preference for American products purchased with the funds made available under those statutes, usually in terms closely paralleling the Buy-American Act. While subsection 301(a) of the Trade Agreements Act of 1979[208] is of general application, Canadian officials believe the American position to be that where funds are allocated under such legislation to state (rather than federal) agencies they are not covered by the Agreement.[209]

2 State practices

At least nineteen states have Buy-American as well as, or instead of, 'Buy-State' policies.[210] Neither preference will be affected by the Agreement, because it expressly does not apply to the practices of states or provinces. State Buy-American practices are estimated to have involved approximately $133 billion in local and state procurement in 1979 alone.[211]

State procurement practices may be either absolute or preferential. The latter is more common and usually (taking the New Jersey Statute as an example) applies only when the preference is 'practical.'[212]

There are at present some twenty-six states with Buy-American restrictions,[213] all of which vary in scope and restrictiveness and may be found in a myriad of different statutes, often enacted as reactions to a local pressure groups. The State of New York has recently enacted four different pieces of

---

204 45 U.S.C.A., s.-s. 545(k) (West Cum. Supp. 1981), added by s. 10 of the *Amtrak Improvement Act of 1978*, Pub. L. 95–421, 92 Stat. 928, and am. by s. 109 of the *Amtrak Reorganization Act of 1979*, Pub. L. 96–73, 93 Stat. 539.

205 49 U.S.C.A., s. 1602 Note (West 1976), en. by Pub. L. 95–599, 92 Stat. 2756.

206 33 U.S.C.A., s. 1295 (West 1978), added by s. 39 of the *Clean Water Act of 1977*, Pub. L. 95–217, 91 Stat. 1581–2.

207 42 U.S.C.A., para. 6705(f)(1) (West Cum. Supp. 1981), added by s. 103 of the *Public Works Employment Act of 1977*, Pub. L. 95–28, 91 Stat. 116–7.

208 *Supra* note 186.

209 *Supra* note 146.

210 See for instance New York: State Finance Law, s. 174(1) (West Cum. Supp. 1980–1) (steel).

211 *Analysis, supra* note 4, at 2.

212 N.J.S.A. 52: 33–2, –3 (West 1955).

213 *Analysis, supra* note 4, Annex 4.

legislation in response to the Steel lobby,[214] considered one of the most vocal proponents of Buy-American legislation.[215]

Though the Agreement may not apply to state entities, such preferences have been challenged in the courts on two grounds: that they offend the 'domestic treatment' principle of Article III of GATT[216] or are incompatible with federal jurisdiction over international commerce.

The 'national treatment' provision of Article III has been held to invalidate inconsistent state legislation on the basis of the superior position of GATT as a 'Treaty.' For example, in *Territory* v. *Ho* it was held that Article III prevented a state from legislating to require that imported chicken wings be labelled as of 'foreign origin.'[217]

However the applicability of the notion of national treatment to government procurement is restricted by the terms of paragraph 8(a) of Article III itself, by which it does not apply to 'the procurement by governmental agencies of products purchased for governmental purposes and not with a view to commercial resale or with a view to use in the production of goods for commercial resale.'

In *Baldwin Lima Hamilton Corp.* v. *Superior Court of the State of California,*[218] the Appeals Court of California held that there would be an abuse of discretion in awarding a contract where the tender incorporated the Buy-American requirements of S.4303 of the California Government Code because that section was

214 *Supra* note 146.
215 *Analysis, supra* note 4, at 1.
216 Art. III. ss. 4 and 8 of the GATT (1947), *B.I.S.D., supra* n. 14, IV, pp. 5–6, provide in part as follows:

4. The products of the territory of any contracting party imported into the territory of any other contracting party shall be accorded treatment no less favourable than that accorded to like products of national origin in respect of all laws, regulations and requirements affecting their internal sale, offering for sale, purchase, transportation, distribution or use.

8. a) The provisions of this Article shall not apply to laws, regulations or requirements governing the procurement by governmental agencies of products purchased for governmental purposes and not with a view to commercial resale or with a view to use in the production of goods for commercial sale.
b) The provisions of this Article shall not prevent the payment of subsidies exclusively to domestic producers, including payments to domestic producers derived from the proceeds of internal taxes or charges applied consistently with the provisions of this Article, and subsidies affected through governmental purchases of domestic products. On this topic, see generally Jackson, 'The GATT in U.S. domestic law,' (1968) 66 *Michigan Law Review* 250.
217 41 Haw. 565, 26 (1958–II) I.L.R. 557 (1957).
218 208 Cal. App. 2d 803, 25 Cal. Rptr. 798 (1962).

inoperative by reason of Article III of GATT. The government-use exception of paragraph 8 of Article III was not available as a defence in the action because in this case the contract in question was for electrical equipment 'for use in the production of goods (electricity) for sale.' Similarly, in *Bethlehem Steel Corp.* v. *Board of Commissioners*,[219] another California case, it was held that S.4303 of the California Government Code was unconstitutional as an infringement of the exclusive federal power over foreign affairs.

On the other hand, in *KSB Technical Sales* v. *North Jersey District Water Supply Commission*[220] the New Jersey Court upheld the validity of a New Jersey Buy-American statute on the ground that the contract was for the purchase of equipment for the Commission which supplied water only to municipalities and therefore fell within paragraph 8(a) of Article III.

The Court also sustained the preference notwithstanding the commerce clause for the reasons reviewed earlier in this paper. Those reasons may not be definitive. In *Reeves*, the Supreme Court expressly refrained from deciding the validity of state Buy-American practices.[221] An argument may be made that federal power over foreign commerce is greater than over interstate commerce, since with the former 'federal uniformity is essential.'[222]

It would thus appear that state Buy-American or local preference statutes may be successfully challenged under Article III of GATT, but only where they are being applied to state purchases which are for commercial resale or for use in the production of goods for commercial resale. In such a situation a foreign supplier may be in a better position than his American competitor to challenge the application of a local state preference statute to him.

CONCLUSION

Each of the three models considered embodies the principle that the restrictive effect of government procurement preferences on the free flow of goods is economically undesirable. Each represents a different approach to the resolution of this problem, the techniques being employed varying to some extent because of the institutional framework within which the action must be taken.

In the United States, in spite of constitutional provisions relating to privileges and immunities, equal protection, and federal competence over interstate

---

219 276 Cal. App. 2d 221, 80 Cal. Rptr. 800 (1969).
220 75 N.J. 272, 381 A. 2d 774 (1977), app. dsm'd. on consent, 435 U.S. 982, 98 S. Ct. 1635 (1978).
221 *Supra* note 127, S. Ct. 2277 n. 9.
222 *Japan Line, Ltd.* v. *Co. of Los Angeles*, 441 U.S. 434, 446, 448, 99 S. Ct. 1813, 1820, 1821, (1979).

commerce, the states retain a certain measure of freedom to discriminate in favour of their residents when purchasing goods and services as long as no 'burden' is placed on interstate commerce and Article III of GATT is not violated. Federal jurisdiction over interstate commerce, even liberally interpreted, still leaves room for such practices. Does the American experience suggest that some degree of local government procurement preference is tolerable even within a highly integrated 'common market'?

In Europe, the mechanics of achieving economic integration in the EEC is provided through the operation of diverse articles of the Treaty of Rome. These have been used as the foundation for legislation to harmonize throughout Europe those procurement procedures which are seen as restricting the achievement of a single market, which is hardly surprising since the Treaty was designed precisely to eliminate all barriers to trade between member states. As a result we see in Europe today a determined 'legislative' assault on such practices by the central authorities (which, it must be recognized, are the representatives of the member states, acting unanimously). In contrast, in the United States there are no federal statutes attacking state practices; such efforts are directed instead towards voluntary compliance, as in the case of the American Bar Association's model procurement code.

GATT in turn has recognized explicitly, specifying those sectors to which it applies, that its members are reluctant to surrender their right to discriminate in favour of their nationals and will only do so when provided with something in return. Even this general principle is qualified by the recognition that such practices may be justifiable when used by developing countries to further their economic growth.

Some basic patterns emerge that may be relevant to Canada:

– Some form of local discrimination in government procurement is tolerated in all systems, depending on different policy considerations. Elimination of regional disparities is one obvious justificaiton, the right of local residents to use their own resources as they see fit (within limits) is another.
– General constitutional provisions of the American kind or like the trade and commerce clause of the BNA Act do not settle this issue. Further, for the reasons just mentioned, any outright blanket constitutional prohibition is probably unrealizable.
– Federal legislation of the EEC type is not possible in the present Canadian constitutional context. If local procurement preferences are to be curtailed by agreement between the provinces, this will probably only be done by identifying the compensating benefits for all parties and by indicating, as in the GATT Agreement those departments or types of procurement to which the rules will apply.

– 'Transparency' is essential. If contracts are to be awarded by cabinet or by some other administrative process the participants must be informed of the criteria on which their bids are judged. If a preference is to be given, it should be clearly specified by statute.

The selection of a method of limiting government procurement preferences in Canada (if indeed they need to be limited within the context of interprovincial trade) will be a complex and difficult process. Governments at all levels are most reluctant to surrender this significant right.

8

Regulation of industrial subsidies in the EEC, the United States, and GATT

Warren F. Schwartz

INTRODUCTION

The three governmental structures studied in this paper all exercise some measure of control over taxing and spending decisions by political units which have substantial autonomous authority. Three possible effects of these decisions made by the individual jurisdictions have been advanced as reasons justifying control over them by a single governmental authority: (1) the conferring of a benefit (either providing something of value or collecting less tax or some other charge than otherwise would be the case) can influence the decision of a firm in choosing a location for production facilities; (2) the conferring of the benefit can cause a firm to produce additional units of a particular output and sell them at a lower price, thus 'injuring' rival firms located outside the jurisdiction conferring the benefit; and (3) the competition between political units can lead to the conferring of 'excessive' benefits on private firms.

In the United States there is no set of legal regulations which deal explicitly with any of these effects. The theoretical and political debate, however, focuses on the consequences of state taxing and spending measures determining the location of production facilities (the 'sunbelt' versus the 'frostbelt') and the possibility of 'excessive' generosity to the private sector resulting from the

I would like to thank Abigail Freidman for her research assistance. I have benefited greatly from the comments of participants in this symposium. In addition, Charles Goetz and Steven Salop offered valuable suggestions. I also interviewed a number of members of the staff of the Commission of the European Economic Community responsible for administering the provisions of the EEC Treaty relating to state subsidies. Their views were extremely informative. In accordance with the understanding I had with the Commission personnel I do not attribute any comments to particular people.

competition between the states to attract industry.[1] What is curious about the American situation is that state competition to attract industry (and more subtly to retain existing industry and to maximize the output of plants located within its borders) is vitally affected by a number of federal provisions that are not explicitly addressed to this process at all. Consequently there is no articulated federal position on the appropriate limits which should be placed upon the rivalry among the states.

A set of provisions of the General Agreement on Tariffs and Trade (GATT) deal explicitly with subsidies granted by the member countries.[2] In addition, a comprehensive agreement implementing these provisions has recently been concluded as part of the Tokyo Round of international negotiations conducted under the auspices of GATT.[3] The basic difficulty with the GATT regulation of subsidies, however, is that subsidization may be an effective means of furthering legitimate objectives, by increasing the returns to activities that create social benefits not fully taken into account in private transactions. This possibility is dealt with only obliquely and incompletely in the text of GATT and the implementing agreements.[4] As a result, GATT regulatory efforts focus on the second question stated above, the effect of subsidization in conferring a competitive advantage on recipient firms. The legal issue is framed as whether the subsidization has caused the requisite 'injury' to rival firms that would justify either the invocation of remedies under GATT or national measures, subject to GATT limitations, in the form of countervailing duties.

Regulation by the European Economic Community (EEC) is the most inclusive of the three regulatory systems considered and the most explicit in articulating the arguments justifying restricting the taxing and spending activities of the member states. Unlike the United States, the EEC limits subsidies by member states explicitly as contrary to the overall community interest. And, in contrast

1 See e.g. *Regional Growth, Interstate Tax Competition* (Washington; Advisory Commission on Intergovernmental Relations, 1981); *Intergovernmental Perspective, Frostbelt and Sunbelt Convergence over Time* (Washington: Advisory Commission on Intergovernmental Relations, 1978); Vaughan, *State Taxation and Economic Development* (Washington: Council of State Planning Agencies 1979) Chap. 6.

2 General Agreement on Tariffs and Trade (GATT), *Basic Instruments and Selected Documents*, Volume III, November 1958. Article VI (Antidumping and Countervailing Duties) and Article XVI (Subsidies).

3 'Agreement on Interpretation and Application of Articles VI, XVI and XXIII of the General Agreement on Tariffs and Trade.' *GATT Doc MTN / NTM / W 236*, reprinted in 'Agreements Reached in the Tokyo Round of Multilateral Trade Negotiations.' 96th Congress, 1st Session, *HSE Document 96–153*, Part 1, at 259 (19 June 1979). This will be referred to as 'Subsidy Agreement.'

4 See text at note 40 below.

with GATT, the EEC considers and evaluates the possible beneficial effects of subsidization. Moreover, in implementing its regulatory system, the EEC is interested not only in the impact of the practice on rival firms but also in the effect on locational decisions and the 'overbidding' to attract investment which may lead to 'unnecessarily' large transfers to the private sector.

Accordingly, I will begin with the EEC, then turn to the United States. I offer some tentative explanations of why regulation in the former should be more explicit and articulated than in the latter. I then consider the international regulation of subsidies by GATT. In conclusion I outline the kind of inquiry a country like Canada should conduct in deciding whether to adopt any of the regulatory features discussed or variants of them which might be devised.

THE EEC

Introduction
Articles 92 through 94 of the Treaty of the European Economic Community[5] regulating 'Aids Granted by States' are placed within a group of provisions designed to ensure appropriate competition among firms within the common market. The basic conception is that just as private conduct, such as the formation of a cartel,[6] can impair the competitive process, so too can intervention by one of the member states in support of a particular firm.

The basic provision reads:

Save as otherwise provided in this Treaty, any aid granted by a Member State or through State resources in any form whatsoever which distorts or threatens to distort competition by favouring certain undertakings or the production of certain goods shall, in so far as it affects trade between Member States, be incompatible with the common market.[7]

Three aspects of this provision should be emphasized. First, the formulation 'any aid granted by a Member State or through State resources in any form whatsoever' is extremely inclusive. Secondly, the phrase 'which distorts or

---

5 The text of the Treaty of the European Economic Community can be found in; Peaslee, *International Governmental Organizations, Constitutional Documents*, Rev. 3rd, ed., prepared by Peaslee Xydis (The Hague: Martinus Nijoff, 1974) Part I, at 457–543. The Treaty Establishing The European Economic Community, Rome, 25 March 1957, as amended April 8, 1965, April 22, 1970, and January 22, 1972; and *Encyclopedia of European Community Law* (London: Sweet & Maxwell, n.d.) Vol. C (6 parts).

6 Article 85, supra note 5; *Common Market Reporter* (CCH), #2005, 2031, and 2051.

7 Article 92, supra note 5; *Common Market Reporter* (CCH) #2921.

threatens to distort competition' contains the essence of a prohibitory rationale which could be extremely far-reaching. Finally, the requirement that the grant of aid 'affects trade between Member States' appears to narrow the rationale underlying the broad definition of aid and the open-ended 'distorts or threatens to distort competition' formulation. One effect of this limitation is clear. If state assistance permits firms within the community to gain export business at the expense of firms located outside the community the aid is not prohibited. Indeed, it would also appear that aid that allowed a community firm to make a sale within the community at the expense of an outside firm would also not be prohibited. An important ambiguity of the formulation is whether the effects on the choice of location and that of reducing costs and thus lowering price and increasing output are embraced in equal degree within the concept of 'affect[ing] trade between Member States.'

There are two groups of exceptions to the general prohibition of state assistance. The first group is declared to be compatible with the common market.[8] This includes 'aid having a social character, granted to individual consumers' provided that there is no discrimination based on the origin of the product, 'aid to make good the damage caused by natural disasters or other exceptional circumstances,' and aid to Berlin 'to compensate for the economic disadvantages' caused by the division of Germany. The second group of exceptions,[9] which '*may* be considered to be compatible with the common market,' constitute the principal concern of the enforcement authority. These exceptions are:

(a) Aid to promote the economic development of areas where the standard of living is abnormally low or where there is serious underemployment;

(b) Aid to promote the execution of an important project of common European interest or to remedy a serious disturbance in the economy of a Member State;

(c) Aid to faciliate the development of certain economic activities or of certain economic areas where such aid does not adversely affect trading conditions to an extent contrary to the common interest.

This text is, of course, ambiguous in a number of respects. Most fundamentally, the formulation 'may be considered to be compatible with the common market' suggests some form of balancing between the community interest in 'undistorted' competition and the interest of each of the member states in

8 Ibid., para 2.
9 Ibid., para 3, emphasis added.

accomplishing the various purposes acknowledged by the exceptions. These purposes are, however, stated with great generality. Moreover, the text offers no standard by which potential exceptions are to be evaluated. Nor does it make it clear the extent to which the community's enforcement effort is to defer to member states' evaluations of the empirical magnitude or normative importance of the various effects of a subsidy. What is plain, however, is that for the prohibition on the grant of state aid to have a substantial impact, both evaluation and enforcement must to a significant degree be within the power of the community authorities. Either total freedom in defining the reconciliation of community and national interest or total deference to national evaluation would render the prohibition wholly ineffective. The regulatory effort discussed below constitutes in large measure an attempt by the Commission (the principal community enforcement agency) to avoid having either of these problems substantially nullify the ban on state aid. Accomplishing this purpose, in the face of the intense political pressures within the member countries for aid prohibited by the treaty has been a task of formidable difficulty.

The prohibition of state assistance is primarily enforced by the Commission of the European Economic Community. The members of the Commission, although each designated by a member state, are community officials who are not responsible to their national governments.[10]

The chief enforcement provisions read as follows:

2. If, after giving notice to the parties concerned to submit their comments, the Commission finds that aid granted by a State or through State resources is not compatible with the common market having regard to Article 92, or that such aid is being misused, it shall decide that the State concerned shall abolish or alter such aid within a period of time to be determined by the Commission ...

3. The Commission shall be informed, in sufficient time to enable it to submit its comments, of any plans to grant or alter aid. If it considers that any such plan is not compatible with the common market having regard to Article 92, it shall without delay initiate the procedure provided for in paragraph 2. The Member State concerned shall not put its proposed measures into effect until this procedure has resulted in a final decision.[11]

There are a number of important features of Commission enforcement activity. First, the Commission is unwilling to take the initiative to suggest that a

---

10 Article 157, supra note 5; *Common Market Reporter* (CCH) #4481.
11 Article 93, supra note 5; *Common Market Reporter* (CCH) #2931.

member state adopt any measures granting aid.[12] It pointedly limits its activities to reacting to measures which the member states have introduced or contemplate introducing. At the same time, however, the requirement that the member states inform the Commission of contemplated aid 'in sufficient time to enable it to submit its comments' means that the Commission is notified of draft legislation prior to its enactment by the member state. The Commission thus has an opportunity to influence the legislative processes in the Member State by its comments backed by the threat of causing at least a substantial delay in the implementation of the measure and in the extreme a prohibition of the legislation. Commission officials thus have substantial potential influence in the domestic political processes in member states. It is very difficult to assess the importance of this influence. It is clear that the Commission has in a significant number of cases secured voluntary changes in proposed legislation. And Commission decisions invalidating national measures have also been rendered with considerable frequency. Moreover, the general directives issued by the Commission,[13] discussed below, also limit the freedom of the member states. At the same time, however, the Commission is sensitive to the political support the various national measures may command. The framing of general directives and the review of particular cases are obviously viewed as practical exercises which must take account of the domestic context in which the aid is enacted. The interesting question then is the real effect of possible Commission action on the political process in the member states. To what extent is the enactment of national legislation prevented by its anticipated delay or nullification by community authorities?

Commission regulation is not limited to approving national measures as they are submitted. It also takes the form of directives which specify criteria governing various types of aid. These directives are of three kinds. First, a set of directives controls the grant of regional assistance. Secondly, there are various directives relating to aid to particular industries, such as steel, shipbuilding, and textiles, where the intensity of government assistance is very great. The final body of directives relates to general forms of assistance, that is, those which focus neither

---

12 Commission of the European Economic Community, *First Report on Competition Policy* (Brussels and Luxembourg: European Economic Community, 1972), at 115, pt 137. [The principal sources of information about Commission enforcement of the prohibition on state aids are the annual reports on competition policy issued by the Commission, starting in 1972. These will be cited by report number, page, and point number, i.e. *1st Competition Report*, at 115, pt 137.]

13 Technically a Directive requires the concurrence of the Council. Article 94, supra note 5: *Common Market Reporter* (CCH) #2961. Sometime the Commission adopts a general policy and informs the Council without having a Directive issued. I will not distinguish between these two forms.

on a particular region nor a particular industry but which may nevertheless have a substantial influence on the location or production decisions of the firm.

The use of these three types of directives mirrors the more general conception underlying commission enforcement activity: that each of these forms of aid presents a distinct set of issues. In general, regional assistance raises the issue of how to assimilate the notion of supporting development in a particular area within a general conception of community-wide efficiency. In the case of aid to particular industries, the argument is that the 'restructuring' (the prevailing euphemism for contraction) of an industry by market forces will either not be efficient or will lead to intolerable 'social' consequences. As a result, although the long-term goal of community-wide efficiency is to be maintained, short-term intervention is justified to improve the process of adjustment to basic changes in the economic environment. The Commission's role is conceived to be that of reconciling these short-term and long-term goals. In the case of general assistance, the basic issue, conceding the desirability of the national goal generally to increase investment and employment, is whether the means employed in the particular case leads to a 'distortion' of competition within the community.

Regional aids

As indicated above, the language of the Treaty provides no clear guidance as to how community and national interest are to be accommodated in the process of regulating the grant of subsidies by member states. This difficulty is, of course, present in the case of regional grants allowed by the Treaty on the grounds mentioned earlier.[14] Such grants 'may be considered to be compatible with the common market,' language indicating that adverse effects from assistance are possible and must be considered. What is not clear is how the diverse effects of aid are to be taken into account.

The Commission has understandably not explained how particular aspects of Commission policy were formulated. Moreover, it is difficult to infer the controlling rationale from the regulation itself. Nevertheless, the provisions which have been adopted and the guarded language of the Commission in its discussions of them do suggest a number of possible arguments that may have been influential in the Commission's decisions.

The regulatory solution

The basic solution adopted by the Commission is to divide the Community into four areas depending on the economic conditions specified in the Treaty, that is, per capita income and the amount of unemployment.[15]

14 Article 92, para 3, supra note 5.
15 'Communication of the Commission on Regional Aid Systems.' [1979], *O.J. Evr. Comm.*
C / 31 /9; *8th Competition Report*, at 109, pts 151–6.

In doing this the Commission has had to face an issue not resolved in the Treaty that continues to divide the members of the community. There are substantial economic disparities between the member states. Moreover, the level of economic development in the poorest regions within the community is very far below the community average. Thus, there is a tension between focusing regional development assistance on the poorest regions, which are primarily located in the poorest countries, and using development aid to reduce disparities within individual countries. The choice of absolute levels and the relative positions assigned the various regions represent a compromise in which both of these approaches are employed.[16]

In the first, poorest, area the ceiling on aid is set at '75 per cent net grant equivalent of initial investment' or 13 000 EUA [European Units of Account] per job created by the initial investment.' In the second group the ceiling is set at 30 per cent net grant equivalent, or 5000 EUA per job created, provided that the 'job creating' grant does not exceed 40 per cent of the initial investment. In the third group the ceiling is set at 25 per cent net grant, or 4500 EUA per job created, but not to exceed 30 per cent net grant equivalent. For the final group, which comprises the major part of the Community, the ceiling is set at 20 per cent net grant equivalent, or 3500 EUA per job created, not to exceed 25 per cent of the initial investment.

This basic solution is implemented by a number of provisions designed to facilitate enforcement of Commission policy. These include a requirement for prior notification of proposed aid schemes, a method for measuring assistance such as loan guarantees and tax concessions which do not involve explicit payments, a definition of investment qualifying for assistance, and the specification of a number of issues on which the Commission contemplates further action. The most important of the latter are the appropriate regulation of grants not conditional on investment or job creation, which the Commission characterizes as 'operating aids' and to which it expresses 'reservations in principle,' revision of the applicable ceilings on aids assistance, and formulation of a means of evaluating the impact of regional grants on particular industries.

The rationale for Commission policy
The Commission must have some conception of the costs and benefits it is to evaluate. There is, however, no explicit articulation of the theory on which it proceeds. But it is possible to infer from the actions taken, and from the discussions in Commission documents, the various factors which shape Commission policy and together determine the controlling standard.

16 The competition for ascendancy between the national and community perspective for measuring the need for regional aid was emphasized by a number of Commission personnel in my coversations with them.

1 Benefits

An elegant theory for assessing the benefits created by regional grants would have to be based on the positive externalities generated by investments. Although the Treaty does not speak in terms of externalities, the underlying assumptions seem to be that the allocation of investment by market forces would be suboptimal and the situation can be improved by government intervention in the form of positive investment incentives. This idea is, in principle, perfectly consonant with economic theory. If the value of an investment to a region exceeds the revenue that can be secured by selling the products made by the plant, then it is appropriate to subsidize the activity to take account of the value not reflected in private market transactions. The benefit is external in the sense that it is not taken into account in the private transactions which lead to its creation. Thus, in the absence of a subsidy, too few of such benefits will be produced. External benefits can be produced by an investment in a variety of ways. If valuable information 'spills over' to people dealing with the firm and the firm cannot capture the value of this information, then an external benefit equal to the value of the information is created. The value of an investment resulting from economies of scale or complementarities in related industries may not be entirely captured by the firm making the investment.

External benefits of this kind may exist without regard to any redistributional objectives. It is clear, however, that regional policy in the Community does embrace redistributional concerns as well. These are, however, not wholly divorced from notions of efficiency, at least as broadly conceived. To begin with, even if the purpose of regional policy is simply to redistribute wealth to people located in a region, some form of government intervention like a subsidy is required. People could not express their preferences for redistributing wealth to the region simply by buying goods emanating from the region, because the fact that non-purchasers could not be precluded from enjoying the benefits of the transfer as well might lead to 'too little' demand for goods purchased to implement the desired redistribution.

Beyond this simple case, persons located either in or outside the region might have a variety of reasons for wishing to promote regional development. One important alternative to regional development is the migration of factors, most importantly people, to the more prosperous regions. But there may be a desire to spare migrants the personal costs of dislocation, particularly when there are important cultural differences between the old and new locations. And the incoming population may impose costs on the residents (at least as the latter view it) of the more prosperous region. Moreover, capital market imperfections may impair the process of geographic adaptation.

I cannot sort out all of these effects and determine with confidence their relative importance in shaping regional policy within the Community. It is clear, however, that regional policy to the extent it redistributes wealth to people in poor regions and affects the location of plants may produce results which are desired by people outside the region. Moreover, these effects cannot in principle be secured in an appropriate quantity through private transactions. Thus, there may be substantial external benefits available through appropriate subsidization as one feature of regional policy.

There is no real dispute about either the existence of external benefits or the desirability of their inclusion in any conception of efficient location of industry. The problem is to quantify the benefits of investment with sufficient assurance to frame appropriate policy. It is often impossible even to determine afterwards which of the consequences of investment were the benefits sought by the intervention to assist it. Determining the magnitude of these consequences and the value placed on them by the relevant population are matters of formidable difficulty.

2 The Commission's approach

The way in which the Commission has approached this basic problem is extremely informative in determining what can really be accomplished by a regulatory mechanism that constrains subsidization by autonomous political units. The fundamental decision that the Commission has made is that the magnitude of regional assistance should vary with the poverty of the area, defined to include its position both within the member state and as compared to the community average. This policy is implemented by the setting of ceilings on subsidies, by refusing to let the member states grant assistance to relatively prosperous areas within the designated regions even though they are below the prescribed ceilings, and by authorizing derogations from the ceilings for areas which are experiencing severe economic problems.

Because the empirical magnitudes of the effects produced by regional subsidizations and the normative importance to be assigned to these effects are difficult, if not impossible, to determine, the Commission really had no choice but to accept a very rough measure of the external benefits created by state assistance. In effect it is postulated that benefits vary systematically with the poverty of the region.

Such a conception is not, of course, a sound theoretical means for measuring benefits. Indeed, extreme and persistent unemployment and low per capita income are strong evidence that the region is a poor location for industry. It may be, as in the case of the steel industry, that changes in various aspects of the costs of production, such as freight charges for raw materials or finished products, dictate that over time plants should be relocated. The real question, then, is not whether the region is poor but rather whether the conditions causing the poverty can be ameliorated by government intervention, in particular by subsidies to private firms.

Understandably, however, the Commission has been reluctant to exert too much pressure on politically sensitive decisions made in the member states to continue to try to improve economic conditions in depressed areas. It has consequently avoided facing directly the question of the efficacy of the national regional program. Other aspects of community policy partially mitigate any undesirable consequences which may flow from the Commission's failure to scrutinize more closely the national programs for regional subsidization. Community regulation does increase the mobility of factors so that long-term geographic adjustment to basic changes in demand or supply characteristics for an industry is facilitated. And, to the extent that regional problems can be addressed by public sector investment in social intrastructure, effects to pursue this policy alternative are carried on by the European Development Fund.[17]

But the point remains that the Commission only attempts to assure rough proportionality between regional poverty and the level of subsidization. If one views subsidization as primarily redistributional, this approach is essentially valid. If subsidization is viewed as designed to achieve economic development, the approach omits any real examination of the contribution that private investment can make to the development of the region.

Despite its essential limitations, this approach, and various policies to implement it which have been adopted by the Commission, may have an important bearing on the magnitude and content of subsidization by the member states. I now turn to these consequences of the Commission's regulatory efforts.

3 The Commission as manager of a buyers' cartel

The Commission's approach does permit it to accomplish one important purpose. If the various countries compete for investment, each will be willing to pay a subsidy equal to the marginal external benefits produced by the marginal investment. It is true, of course, that the process of evaluating benefits which determines the amount each country is willing to pay is a political one involving all the difficulties of aggregating individual preferences into an overall social calculation. But whatever may be the 'imperfection' of the political processes, they do show the willingness of each country to pay a subsidy to induce investment in each location.

The Commission's regulatory effort described above can be viewed as altering the subsidies each country is permitted to offer to conform to the standard of relative poverty as formulated by the Commission. If we postulate a schedule of subsidies thus emerging from the domestic political process and being

17 For a review of recent activities of the Fund see Commission of the *European Regional Development Funds, Sixth Annual Report* Luxembourg: EEC, 1981)

amended by the Commission, we can see that the outcome for the member states as a whole can be improved by constraining the level of subsidization.

This is so because the member states are competing for investments in depressed regions. As in all competitive processes, the price offered for an investment will be equal to the value of the marginal benefit produced by the investment. In our analysis this has been determined in the first instance by the member states and then revised by the Commission. The supply of investments by firms will also depend on marginal calculations, with the 'cost' of locating in a particular area being determined fundamentally by the forgone value of locating in the next most favoured area.

If the supply curve of investments in the community is upward-sloping, that is, if it takes a larger subsidy to induce each additional investment, the outcome for the Community as a whole can be improved by constraining the level of subsidization. The reason for this is straightforward. As the price of an invest-ment is bid up in response to the competition of other buyers, a higher price must be paid for all investments, including those which could have been obtained at the lower price.[18] If competition can be constrained, the saving in inframarginal transfers, that is, in transfers that were unnecessary to secure the investments, may exceed the loss resulting from the decrease in the number of investments made.

In the extreme cause, a vertical supply curve (completely inelastic), this result is wholly unambiguous. If the number of investments will not change as a higher subsidy is offered, the amount paid as subsidies can be reduced and nothing will be lost. However, if the curve does have some elasticity, the saving in payments has to be compared with the value of the reduction in investments.

Similar analysis applies if the Community is viewed as comprising several groups of locations where the areas within a group are viewed as perfect substitutes for investment purposes and areas within one group as substitutes, but not perfect substitutes, for areas in the other groups. From this perspective (again assuming an upward-sloping supply curve for each group) an increase in the subsidy offered in one group will not only increase the price which will have to be paid for all investments in the group but also cause a shift in the supply curves for the other groups offering substitute locations. This is so because as a higher and higher price prevails in one group, any given payment in another group will induce a smaller number of investments, or, stated differently, it will take a larger payment to induce the same number of investments. Viewed from a slightly different perspective, what this means is that increased subsidization in one group does not necessarily increase investment in the Community but

18 I put price discrimination aside.

merely shifts it from one location to the other. Thus from the Community perspective the value of the investment is the difference between the benefits it produces in the location chosen because of the additional payment and the benefits which would have been produced in the location which would have been chosen if the level of subsidization in the region selected had not been increased. The amount paid, in the absence of some constraint on the individual decisions of the member states, will, however, be the full value of the benefits in the location selected. Thus this analysis suggests a second, related, way in which constraints on the level of subsidization may produce benefits for the community as a whole.[19]

Except under extreme assumptions, some amount of investment must be forgone to achieve the available savings in subsidy payments. Thus for this strategy to be employed it is necessary to place a value on the benefits which would have been produced by the investment so that they may be traded off against reduced subsidy payments. This issue, of course, reintroduces all the problems of evaluating benefits of this kind discussed above. It is also unclear which countries will realize the benefits from lower payments and which will bear the costs in the form of fewer investments. Agreement in valuing forgone benefits and satisfaction with the distribution of cost and benefit among participants are nevertheless essential if a policy of constraining individual subsidization in the interest of maximizing the welfare of the group is to be pursued.

The cost side of this calculation also raises serious conceptual issues. The subsidy payments, the costs which can be reduced by controlling competition among the member states, are 'mere' transfers, whereas the benefits produced by subsidization may represent real welfare gains. Arguably, then, these costs should be ignored and only the benefits considered.

There are two responses to this argument. First, if the recipients of the transfers are foreigners there is a community loss. Secondly, the competition to secure these transfers may itself entail a waste of resources that diminishes community-wide welfare. It is difficult to know the extent to which the value of these transfers is competed away in efforts to lobby for subsidies and to establish entitlements within existing programs. What can be said, however, is that substantial expenditures are made for the purpose of obtaining subsidies. thus real gains from reducing the magnitude of these expenditures are available by constraining the level of subsidization.

It is not clear whether and to what extent the Commission views itself as manager of a buyers' cartel. There does seem to be a widely held view that the

19 I am indebted to Steven Salop for suggesting this analysis.

competition among the member states for investment in depressed regions will lead to excessive subsidization. But this view is not expressly limited to the economic theory discussed above. The general notion is expressed as a desire to prevent 'outbidding' by the member states.[20]

The nature of the 'outbidding' to be avoided is not spelled out in the official documents. Moreover, the term is also applied to another basic concern of the Commission: that the rich countries will bid much more than the poor countries for an investment of equal value from a Community perspective.[21]

For the Commission to respond to this concern is consistent with the notion of reducing transfers by restraining the level of subsidization. Even if it were accepted that the relative level of subsidization would be affected by the relative wealth of the country, rich and poor countries alike could be made better off by restraining the absolute level of subsidization. Of course, to the extent that a Community-wide perspective is imposed on the rich countries the Commission more directly constrains outbidding of this kind.

The fact that the national perspective must to some extent be accepted may have frustrated the effort to reduce subsidization to an appropriate level from a Community point of view.[22] If the absolute level were set low enough, some regions where subsidization is now permitted would have to be allowed no subsidization (or indeed be required to pay a negative subsidy) in order to maintain their relative position. While it would be true in theory that these areas would be better off since their position would remain unchanged compared to that of the poorer areas and they would realize a saving in the amounts paid as subsidies, this proposition may be difficult to communicate to an electorate wishing to assist a region that is viewed as poor from the national perspective. Understandably, the reaction is likely to be that a reduction in the level of subsidization will mean fewer investments and consequently less assistance for the depressed region. And of course a policy appropriate from the overall community perspective will not necessarily be equally beneficial for all member states. Apparently these difficulties have helped limit the Commission's effort to reduce the overall level of subsidization.

20 See 'Communication', supra note 15, pt 5. The discussion of outbidding does sometimes include a conception quite similar to the monopsony theory. In our conversations Commission personnel in response to my questions indicated they thought the supply of investments for the community as a whole was very inelastic.

21 See Director General for Research and Development, *Impact of the Competition Policy Provisions (Articles 92, 93) on Regional Policy in a Community Context* (Brussels and Luxembourg: European Economic Community, 1977), at 5.

22 This explanation was advanced by a member of the Commission staff.

Operating aids

As indicated above, the Directive with respect to regional aid provides that the ceilings for subsidies are to be in terms of a portion of the investment or in relation to the number of jobs created. The Directive expresses 'reservations in principle' about other types of aid which defray a portion of a firm's costs of manufacture, 'operating aids' in the terms employed by the Commission. The Commission has also induced countries to alter regional assistance programs to remove or reduce 'operating aids.'[23]

There appear to be four reasons underlying the Commissoin's opposition to assistance of this kind. First, operating aids are thought not to produce external benefits since they do not create new investment nor additional jobs. Second, operating aids may permit inefficient plants to continue in business indefinitely. Third, operating aids, since they represent payments which are not expressly limited to investment or job creation, lack 'transparency,' so that it is difficult to determine if they are having these results. Finally, operating aids which reduce a firm's costs will give the recipient firms a competitive advantage over their rivals.

Upon analysis these objections reveal basic contradictions in the Commission's policy toward regional subsidization. Its first concern is that if a firm's operating expenses are subsidized there is no assurance that additional investment and jobs are produced. But a subsidy to replace existing plant as it wears out (included in the conception of an operating aid) can just as much increase investment over time as can a payment to defray a portion of new investment. And payments to reduce material or labour costs can cause a firm to increase its output at a given plant and thus provide more jobs. By the same token, a payment to defray a portion of new investment may not increase the amount of investment at all, certainly not necessarily by the full amount of the subsidy. The effect of a subsidy on investment and production decisions is an empirical question depending on how the payment affects the relative returns to alternative activities available to the firm. Fundamentally the same problem exists in evaluating the type of subsidies viewed favourably by the Commission and the 'operating aids' about which it expresses 'reservations in principle.'

It is also true that the Commission's concern for inefficiency resulting from the payment of operating aids applies equally well to the subsidies it favours. These inefficiencies are of two types. First, the investment subsidies favoured by the Commission will not ensure the plant is located where costs are lowest. This is the precise counterpart to the fact that in the case of operating subsidies

---

23 *10th Competition Report*, at 115, pt 164; at 122, pt 175 (elimination of operating aids in British regional program following extended discussions with Commission personnel).

production will not occur where costs are lowest. Second, the choice of technology will be affected by investment subsidies, which will induce greater expenditures for those elements of the production process whose costs are partially covered by the subsidy, again just as operating subsidies reduce the costliness of employing particular inputs or producing a particular output.

The emphasis on the question of transparency masks a more fundamental difficulty. It is true that an operating subsidy may not be directly limited to investment or production decisions so that its effect is not obvious. But in the case of investment subsidies the apparent link may be illusory. The fact that the payment will occur and the investment will be made does not mean that the investment will occur *because* the payment was made. The question, of course, is what the firm would have done in the absence of the subsidy. If the underlying purpose of the transparency requirement is to assure that the member states are paying the 'right' price for investment, this cannot be achieved by simply banning operating aids and assuming that the entire investment is 'purchased' by an investment subsidy. The more difficult issue of the actual effect of the subsidy will have to be faced.

The Commission's final concern, the impact of the subsidy on rivals, is also equally applicable to investment subsidies and operating aids. It is true that an investment subsidy may serve primarily to shift the location of a plant, but if the subsidy is to matter it must more than offset the additional costs associated with the less preferred location. And, conceivably, without the subsidy the additional capacity might not come into being in any location. Moreover, if the subsidy induces a particular choice of technology this may result in lower variable costs than would obtain in a plant selected without regard to the availability of an investment subsidy. For any of these reasons an investment subsidy may lead a firm to produce a greater output and charge lower prices than would be the case in the absence of the subsidy. Similar effects may be produced by an operating subsidy which directly lower a firm's variable costs. How important these effects are is again an empirical question which can not be resolved by the simple dichotomy between investment subsidies and operating aids.

The impact of subsidization on rival farms

The question of how to deal with the impact of subsidization on rival firms is more general than the issue of regulating operating aids. As indicated above, the text of Article 92 refers to an aid which 'distorts or threatens to distort competition' and 'affects trade between member states.' One of the exceptions to the prohibition, that relating to 'aid to facilitate the development of certain activities or of certain economic areas,' stipulates that the 'aid does not adversely affect trading conditions to an extent contrary to the common interest.'

Presumably these considerations are to play a part in the Commission's decision on whether a subsidy is 'compatible with the common market.'

There is, however, no coherent theory for the Commission to apply. To begin with it is faced with a dilemma. Presumably, it does not wish to favour assistance that has no effect on investment or production decisions since subsidies of this type involve a waste of community resources. On the other hand, if investment or production decisions are affected, an adverse impact on rival firms is an inescapable consequence. And, as indicated above, there will in any event be considerable uncertainty as to what these various effects are. But even if the Commission knew what the beneficial effects of the subsidization were and the magnitude of the competitive consequences to rival firms, it would have no basis for deciding whether and to what degree the benefits outweigh the harm done. There is, if you will, no normative theory to define the measure of protection to which rivals are entitled.

I believe that because of these empirical and normative uncertainties the protection of rival firms has not played an important part in Commission policy with respect to regional subsidization. Nor could it play an important part unless a coherent theory of protection could be devised and implemented. I believe that developing such a theory raises questions as general as the right to compensation of groups adversely affected by changes in the law which are beneficial from the point of view of the enacting jurisdiction as a whole. If a theory focusing on the interests of rival firms adversely affected by subsidization is to provide the basis for regulation constraining the grant of subsidies there is no way to avoid dealing with those difficult and far-reaching questions.[24]

Regulation of aid to specific industries
In the case of Commission regulation of member state assistance to particular industries such as shipbuilding, steel, and textiles, a parallel but somewhat different set of considerations shape Community policy. Here the external benefits justifying government intervention derive not from influencing locational choices but rather from 'improving' the process of adaptation to long-run changes in the basic cost and demand factors that define the appropriate level of activity of the industry in question. In all the industries involved in Commission regulation of national subsidies, the contraction of demand and the emergence of rivals with lower costs from outside the Community have substantially reduced production.

Commission regulation of state assistance to these declining industries is based on two theories justifying government intervention. The first rationale is

---

24 These issues are explored in Quinn and Trebilcock, 'Compensation, transition costs and regulatory change.' (1982), 32 *U of T. Law Journal* 117.

that the process of adaptation to these adverse changes can somehow be made more efficient by government intervention. Efficiency in this context refers to such technological changes as introducing more advanced production processes, merging firms, abandoning facilities which constitute excess capacity, and retraining workers. The basic idea is that these adaptive responses cannot be left to private initiative. The word used to describe improvements in these processes achieved through government intervention is 'restructuring.'

The second ground for government intervention is that the social consequences associated with the contraction of these industries should simply not be tolerated. Various initiatives are thus introduced to slow the process of adjustment, to provide compensation, and to facilitate adjustment to alternative uses for material and human resources.

While the Commission accepts the legitimacy of these arguments it also attempts to shape national policies so that they will not frustrate the long-term objective of creating an industry that is essentially self-sufficient. The Directive on aid to shipbuilding demonstrates how the Commission attempts to do this.[25] First, in contrast with its regulation of regional subsidies, investment subsidies are discouraged in order to avoid creating still further excess capacity in the industry. Second, the Commission tries to prevent subsidization from enabling the industry in one member state from greatly increasing its share of the market. To the latter end the Commission seeks to limit the amount of aid granted by referring to two criteria: the first is the magnitude of the decline of a member state's industry, or, in the words of the Commission, 'the acuteness of the crisis in the Member State concerned'; the second criterion is the 'equitable' market share to be enjoyed by each member state's firms. The basic idea is that the aid scheme should not materially alter historical market shares.

The final aspect of Commission policy is the requirement that the grant of aid be 'linked to the attainment of industrial restructuring objectives with a view to making the industry competitive and able to operate without aid or intervention.' This requirement presumably is tantamount to an assurance that in the long term firms will be allowed to capture the market shares appropriate to their efficiency compared to that of their rivals inside or outside the community.

It is not clear how severe in practice this crucial aspect of Commission policy really is. The Commission does block member state aid schemes which do not include restructuring programs.[26] But it is difficult to determine the content of

25 [1978], *O.J. Evr. Comm.* L98 / 19 (4 April 1978) on aid to shipbuilding.

26 The directive on shipbuilding states, concerning 'crisis aid and intervention,' that 'such aid and interaction shall be progressively reduced; it shall be granted only if linked to the attainment of industrial restructuring objectives with a view to making the industry competitive and able to operate without aid or intervention.' On the enforcement of this requirement, see *9th Competition Report*, pts 157 and 158.

the restructuring programs which are approved or how effectively these programs are implemented in the member states. Restructuring implies far-reaching and costly steps such as abandoning production facilities, merging firms, investing in new capital equipment, and discharging large numbers of employees. It is precisely because some of the consequences of these actions were thought to be 'intolerable' that aid was often introduced in the first place. Thus the question of framing appropriate government responses to these serious problems is simply shifted to the process of formulating and implementing the restructuring plans. How the Community requirement that these restructuring plans be integrated into the national programs for granting subsidies actually affects the member states is extremely difficult to say. It is not clear from the Commission's published discussion of its efforts to regulate aid schemes of this kind how intensively the Commission reviews the restructuring proposals submitted by the member states or monitors their actual implementation.[27]

An intensive review of these plans would be extraordinarily difficult. At bottom the question is the ability of any government to outperform the private sector in adapting to fundamental changes in cost or demand. Nor is it obvious why the Commission is superior to the member states in making the requisite judgments. Moreover, if the Commission really could predict what an efficient Community-wide industry would look like, implementation of its conception would no doubt be resisted by those segments of the existing industry that would be excluded. On the other hand an individual member state would probably be inclined to include its own firms within its conception of an efficient Community industry.

Although the criteria of historical market share and relative need may limit some industrial subsidies in the short run, the real test of the Commission's influence will lie in its effort to shape national plans to conform to what it conceives to be the overall community interest. As indicated above, this process is complicated by the fact that the entire issue of government intervention to facilitate adaptation to basic changes is itself so complex. Moreover, if the effects of change on persons with specialized investment in human or physical capital are also to be considered, the regulatory process becomes even more difficult.

A final speculation about Community regulation of industrial subsidies can be offered. I have considered the possibility that the Commission was acting as a cartel manager for the member states. Might there not also be some role for the Commission as cartel manager for aids to specific industries?

---

27 Commission personnel varied in their characterization of the intensity of the review. It was asserted to me that the Commission does not simply 'rubber stamp' the actions of the member states. On the other hand the political sensitivity of these questions does lead to considerable restraint in rejecting the plans or the means employed to enforce them.

Although the analysis is less straightforward, I think the answer is yes. By subsidizing the operating costs of declining industries the member states permit them to charge lower prices and sell more output. However, if the demand for the products of the Community industry as a whole is inelastic at the price which the products would command if the firms were competing (with the aid of the subsidy), increases in price would result in less than proportional decreases in the quantity supplied. Whether this would be so would depend primarily on how quickly outside suppliers could expand output and undercut Community firms if their prices were raised. This is of course a simple restatement of the proposition that if the firms had some market power and could collude they could increase profits by reducing output and raising price.

The calculations of the member states are somewhat different. With the rise in price and reduction in output induced by lowering the level of subsidization they do not lose the revenue that the additional output would have produced but rather the external benefits associated with the output. If the reduction in benefits is less than the saving in subsidy payments, the result is a net gain for the Community as a whole.

This calculation would depend on how the right to a subsidy was defined. If, for example, a subsidy sufficient to reduce unit costs to some predetermined amount was paid and the industry supply curve were positively sloped, a reduction in output would mean that the amount paid as subsidy per unit would also be less. However, even if the industry supply curve were horizontal or the subsidy level fixed independent of cost, it would remain true that the more inelastic the Community-wide industry demand the less each dollar of price reduction by the industry 'purchased' through subsidization yields in increased output. Thus, there may be gains available from reducing the level of subsidization if the value of the marginal benefits were less than the cost resulting from the increase in inframarginal payments.

It would appear that these gains could be realized by a central authority's reducing the level of subsidization below the point which would result from unrestrained competition among the member states. There is no indication that this possibility has had any influence on the development of Commission policy. But the general point seems important if the issue is whether central control should be exercised over competition among jurisdictions to pay subsidies. It would appear that this competition impinges on the efficacy of the subsidization process in a variety of ways. In my opinion it is in these effects that the justification for central control is to be found. Whether, in light of all the problems encountered in exercising such control and the magnitude of the gains which can be realized, it is worthwhile to have regulation of this kind is a question of considerable complexity. But I believe it is the right question.

General aid schemes

The Commission's reaction to specific applications of general aid schemes which have a substantial impact on investment decisions is extremely severe. The Commission appears to be unwilling to conduct an extensive inquiry to determine how the measure in question 'affects trade between Member States' or 'distorts or threatens to distort competition.' Nor is it eager to find that a general measure satisfies one of the criteria prescribed by Article 92(3) as justification for a state aid.

The *Philip Morris* case,[28] recently decided by the EEC Court of Justice, affirms Commission policy in this regard. The aid in question represented slightly more than 3 per cent of the cost of an investment to expand and modernize one cigarette plant in the Netherlands so that all production, previously conducted at the plant and another plant located elsewhere in the Netherlands, could be concentrated at the single location. The plant, as expanded, would have a capacity 40 per cent greater than the two existing plants. It was anticipated that actual production would increase by 13 per cent. The Netherlands accounted for 36 per cent of intra-Community exports in the period immediately preceding the expansion, and Philip Morris accounted for approximately one-half of this total. The area in which the expanded plant was located had relatively high unemployment and low per capita income judged by national standards.

Sorting out the actual effects of the state aid either in terms of its competitive impact or the benefits it generated would have been a process of considerable complexity. It is not obvious that a payment of approximately 3 per cent of the cost of expanding and modernizing the plant made any difference whatever in Philip Morris's decision to undertake the investment. It would also be difficult to determine whether in the absence of the aid Philip Morris (or another firm) might have expanded its capacity elsewhere in the common market and the investment in the Netherlands not been made. And the impact on rival firms in the common market would depend on what investment would have occurred in the absence of the payment.

The Commission and the Court (despite explicit arguments by Philip Morris) displayed no inclination to explore these complexities. The materiality of the aid to the investment decision of Philip Morris was essentially assumed. The issue of competitive impact was dealt with by simply holding that a non-trivial expansion of a non-trivial firm might have had the requisite competitive impact. And, in so holding, no standard as to how great that impact must be was articulated by the Court.

28 Case 730 / 79 (1980) (1.C.J.) (Unofficial) affrm. [1980] 1 *C.M.L.R.* 453. See also *10th Competition Report*, pts 158 and 214–17.

On the issue of justification the Court was influenced by the fact that the government of the Netherlands did not urge that justification under Article 93 could be established. But it did consider Philip Morris's contention that the aid was justified. In so doing it rejected the justification based upon the depressed condition of the area judged from a national perspective, holding instead that Community standards are controlling. It also summarily rejected the claim that the aid 'facilitated the development of certain activities' on the grounds that 'market conditions in the cigarette manufacturing industry seem apt, without state intervention, to ensure a normal development' and that in any event the aid would 'adversely affect trading conditions to an extent contrary to the common interest.'

The Court opinion manifests an obvious concern that a general aid scheme can frustrate its policies with respect to regional aid and aid to specific industries. In the case of regional aid, as discussed above, areas are carefully assigned relative positions in the common market. In the case of aid to specific industries the Commission tries to restrain the level of subsidization and encourage 're-structuring.' A system of general aid which is not formulated in response to these criteria but which in particular applications impinges on the Commission's regional policy or on its policy with respect to aid to particular industries presents the Commission with a potentially awkward regulatory problem. The Commission has in effect sought to avoid this difficulty by ruling that a general subsidy which may have a substantial impact on locational decisions or on the success of particular firms in an industry is impermissible. If a country wishes to intervene and produce these effects it should employ regional aid or assistance which focuses on a particular industry so that the Commission can deal with these measures within the framework of its regulation of assistance designed to achieve these objectives.

THE UNITED STATES

The most obvious difference in the regulation of subsidies between the United States and the EEC is that explicit provisions governing the grant of subsidies by the states, similar to Articles 92 through 94 of the EEC Treaty, simply do not exist in the United States. No constitutional provision, statute, or body of case law constrains the rivalry among the states to attract industry by referring to an articulated standard of overall benefit to be derived from limitations imposed by the federal government.

One is thus placed in the curious position of explaining the absence of a regulatory system. At the same time, moreover, a number of provisions defining the consequences to individuals and firms in terms of liability for federal tax of actions taken by the states to influence locational decisions establish the essential parameters within which state rivalry can occur. None of these federal provisions, however, purport to limit state action on grounds of national interest. Thus in trying to explain relevant federal regulation one is faced with the dual difficulty of explaining the absence of regulation of the kind found in the EEC and determining whether the various effects produced by existing regulation are the result of some coherent, albeit unexpressed, conception of the appropriate limits of state rivalry.

I will attempt to do this by assuming that the rationales for control by the central government developed in the EEC are equally applicable in principle in the United States. The question then becomes whether differences in circumstances account for the differences in regulation.

The absence of explicit regulation of subsidization

One theory advanced above is that a group of jurisdictions can improve the net benefits of subsidization by agreeing to limit competition between each other. The benefits of successful collaboration depend essentially on the elasticity of supply of investments for the area as a whole covered by the agreement. If reductions in what would be the competitive price paid to induce investment produce a large diminution in the quantity of investment (with, of course, a corresponding reduction in external benefits) as compared to the saving in inframarginal payments, the monopsony strategy has little to offer. If on the other hand large savings in inframarginal payments can be achieved with relatively little decrease in investment, the strategy can be effective.

One possible explanation thus suggested by economic theory for the differences regulation observed between the EEC and the United States is that the elasticity of supply is less in the EEC, so that large inframarginal gains can be secured with modest losses in investment. I have no idea, however, what the elasticity of supply in the two jurisdictions is. The supply curve of investments does appear to be determined essentially by two factors: the relative attractiveness of alternative locations in terms of production costs and the level of subsidization prevailing in the alternative areas. If, for example, the EEC encountered less intense competition in the payment of subsidies from areas which were close substitutes as locations for investments, it could presumably lower its level of subsidization without experiencing a severe loss of investment.

Whether the elasticity of supply in the two areas does vary as monopsony theory would predict is a question I am unable to answer. Of course, if this were so, one could not conclude that this factor accounts to a significant degree for the difference in regulation unless two other issues were resolved. First, even as a matter of economic theory the elasticity of supply is only one factor bearing on the likelihood that monopsony pricing will occur. The other basic dimension, which I discuss later, is the ability to organize the cartel and enforce it in the face of the conflicting interests of the participants and the strong incentives for 'cheating.' More fundamentally, it is a giant leap to conclude, since monopsony pricing could produce greater economic benefits in one jurisdiction than the other, that this fact has indeed been decisive in the regulation adopted. It does seem plausible, nevertheless, that this factor may have had some influence in both jurisdictions, even if it was not consciously considered by the participants in the political process.

What is curious about the American situation is that the nature of the competition among the states as it is described by the commentators would seem to suggest that real gains from the practice of monopsony pricing are available. The conventional learning is that explicit subsidies to affect locational decisions have little impact.[29] The argument is that a large number of other factors affect these choices and swamp the subsidies in importance. Moreover, it is urged that a state has great difficulty in following an effective policy of subsidization. The revenue forgone or payment made must lead either to a greater tax somewhere else or a reduction in state-provided benefits. These adverse consequences may, however, ultimately be borne directly or indirectly by the firms which are the intended beneficiaries of the subsidization. For example, if corporate income taxes are reduced as an inducement to investment and personal income tax increased to make up the revenue loss, firms may have to bear a share of the increased personal income tax in the form of higher wages. Or if state benefits, such as subsidized higher education, are decreased, again a wage premium to compensate for this loss may be necessary in order to attract an employee who can secure employment in a state offering a more generous subsidy to higher education.

Complexities of this kind do make it difficult to assess the effect of explicit subsidies designed to influence a firm's locational choice. However, because the effects of the subsidy arrangements are unclear and so many factors enter the firms' decision, it urged that many payments must be made to firms which would have located in the particular area anyway. This explanation depends on the states' systematically making mistakes in assessing the impact of explicit subsidy schemes. It is equally plausible to argue that while all the complicating factors indicated are no doubt relevant, the question still remains whether an explicit subsidy can affect decision-making at the margin, taking all the complications as given. The persistent conduct of the states in offering these subsidies suggests that they believe that there is a significant effect.

29 Vaughan, *State Taxation and Economic Development*, at 99.

Moreover, all the evidence adduced of firms which 'would have located in the state anyway' can be explained without reference to a theory of systematic mistakes. If the supply curve of investments in the states is upward-sloping, then inframarginal firms do receive payments in excess of those required to induce them to locate in the state if the payment is raised to the level at which the subsidy to the marginal firm equals the external benefits generated by the marginal investment. But if small marginal gains are being purchased at large inframarginal costs, then suppression of competition between states offering identical or close substitutes can be beneficial, for all the reasons discussed with respect to EEC regulation. That this may be so gains some support from the frequent assertion, albeit without reference to any identifiable theory, that there is 'excessive' competition between the states.

In one respect the implementation of a buyers' cartel for the states as purchasers of investment would be more difficult in the United States than in the EEC. There are simply more jurisdictions in the United States, so that the costs of organizing the cartel, detecting 'cheating,' and punishing violators would be correspondingly higher. How great this difference is and whether in light of the complications I have discussed it has had any role in inhibiting the introduction of regulation like that employed in the EEC are questions I simply cannot answer.

It may also be that the subsidization phenomenon is simply less important in the United States than in the EEC.[30] Fundamentally, subsidization, whether of a depressed area or a declining industry (the most important kinds), is an alternative to factors moving to alternative uses. If factors are more mobile, geographically and between industries, the political pressure to provide subsidies should be correspondingly less intense. In the United States, where cultural, technological, and legal barriers to factor mobility are less important then they are in the EEC, subsidization would be expected to play a less important role. Moreover, in light of the larger number of states and the relatively greater importance of the central government, a much greater proportion of subsidization is provided at the federal level. Consequently, the conflict between areas in the common market which is explicitly regulated by the articles of the Treaty is in the United States worked out in the legislative process at the federal level. For all these reasons, then, state subsidization in the United States appears to be a less important phenomenon than subsidization by the member states in the EEC.

The final puzzle in explaining American regulation of state subsidization is the extent to which federal provisions that in fact do substantially restrain state competition, but without that as an express purpose, may nevertheless be explicable, in part at least, by the impact they have on the actions of the states in

---

30 This point was suggested by Wayne Thirsk.

competing for investment. The most significant limitations on the rivalry between the states to attract investment consist of the treatment as a matter of federal tax law of subsidies in the form of payments or forgiveness of state taxation. With few exceptions, subsidy payments constitute income (or reduce the basis of capital investment)[31] for purposes of federal tax liability. Since state taxes are deductible from income in determining the federal tax liability, forgiveness of a state tax increases the federal tax liability above what it would have been if the state tax had been paid.

Curiously, there are no significant cases in which a state subsidy is not treated as income for federal purposes or in which a state may forgive state taxes without increasing the federal tax liability. If such a system did exist a state could use its own taxing and spending power while getting 'full value' in external benefits generated. But although this cannot be done, the states are allowed the more extreme possibility of granting exemptions from federal taxes on the interest on certain bonds issued for the benefit of private firms, thus providing those firms with financing at subsidized rates.

The extent to which the federal government should authorize the states to engage in subsidization of this kind is a highly controversial issue.[32] But the arguments relate to points such as the 'excessive' use of these devices because they are costless to the states. This controversy is, moreover, part of the more general questions of whether, to what extent, and in what manner the federal government should subsidize borrowing by the states.

The debate does not take the form of urging that these issues should be resolved so as to achieve overall state subsidization of private industry at some level which is desirable from the perspective of maximizing net benefits to the country as a whole. Moreover, the controversy about the desirability of state subsidization does not focus on these federal fiscal relationships as institutional conditions which could or should be adjusted to come closer to the desired result for the country as a whole. Yet at the same time the discussion of state rivalry in attracting industry does emphasize the importance of the interaction between state taxing and spending and federal tax liability in defining the means of competition available to the state. Moreover, the predominant effect of these provisions (allowing forgiveness of federal tax is, of course, the principal exception) is materially to reduce the level of state subsidization from what it would be if there were no partially offsetting federal tax consequences.

31 See Bittker, *Federal Taxation of Income, Estates and Gifts* (Boston: Warren Graham & Lamont Inc., 1981), #16.4
32 See Congressional Budget Office, *Small Issue Industrial Revenue Bonds* (Washington: Congressional Budget Office, 1981).

One is left therefore with a positive puzzle. There is no indication that either the inclusion of subsidy receipts in income for federal tax purposes or the deductibility of state taxes in computing federal tax liability was adopted as means of restraining state subsidization. Yet these are the effects produced. Indeed these are the only important federal limitations on state subsidization that I have been able to find.

It does not seem possible to link these restrictions to any coherent theory for restricting state subsidization. All one can really say is that there may be good reasons similar to these which exist in the EEC for limiting rivalry among the states in granting subsidies. The federal state interaction I have described should lead to less subsidization than alternative federal arrangements which could be established. Conceivably, therefore, the effect of reducing the level of subsidization has played some role in shaping the basic federal structure.

GATT

GATT regulation of subsidies has two essential features. First, the unilateral imposition of countervailing duties by importing countries, designed to neutralize the effects of subsidies granted in the country from which the goods originate, is limited by Article VI of GATT.[33] Secondly, remedies for countries whose commercial interests are harmed by subsidization in other countries are provided within the framework of the GATT administrative organization.[34]

The substantive provisions of the Agreement with respect to subsidies concluded during the Tokyo Round of trade negotiations divides subsidies into export subsidies and all other forms. The parties agree 'not to use export subsidies in a manner inconsistent with the provisions of this Agreement.'[35] With respect to other forms of subsidy, agreement is reached only to 'seek to avoid causing through the use of any subsidy: (a) injury to the domestic industry of another signatory; (b) nullification or impairment of the benefits accruing ... to another signatory under the General Agreement or (c) serious prejudice to the interests of another signatory.'[36]

The language employed for export subsidies, 'in a manner inconsistent with this agreement,' is given content by two subsequent provisions. The parties agree that they 'shall not grant export subsidies on products other than certain

---

33 Part I of the Subsidy Agreement relates to this aspect of GATT regulation. For a discussion of these provisions of the Subsidy Agreement and their impact on domestic law, see Barcelo, 'Subsidies, countervailing duties and antidumping after the Tokyo Round.' *Institute for Research on Public Policy* (forthcoming 1982).

34 The Subsidy Agreement provides for consultation (Article 12), conciliation, dispute settlement, and the authorization of 'countermeasures' (Article 13).

35 Subsidy Agreement, Article 8.2.

36 Ibid., Article 8.3.

primary products.'[37] As to the 'primary products,' principally agricultural products, the parties agree not to grant export subsidies if the effect is that 'the signatory granting such subsidy ... [obtains] more than an equitable share of world trade.'[38]

The ambivalent attitude towards subsidies other than export subsidies reflected in the 'seek to avoid' formulation and the qualification even of this obligation to cases of injury or nullification and impairment of benefits accruing under GATT is further manifested in the provision dealing directly with subsidies of this kind. The provision begins with an acknowledgment that 'subsidies other than export subsidies are widely used as instruments for the promotion of social and economic policy objectives.'[39] Moreover, it recites a number of such objectives in terms which closely resemble the grounds specified as justifications for national assistance in the EEC Treaty.[40] At the same time, however, the provision acknowledges that subsidies to achieve these objectives 'may cause or threaten to cause serious injury to a domestic industry of another signatory' (or impair benefits under the Agreement).[41] Signatories are therefore called upon in framing domestic measures 'in addition to evaluating the essential internal objective to be achieved ... [to] weigh, as far as practicable, taking account of the nature of the particular case, possible adverse effects on trade.'[42]

The effect of Articles VI and XVI and the Agreement implementing them is much less fundamental than the provisions of the EEC Treaty. With respect to countervailing duties, the sharp distinction between export subsidies and production subsidies drawn in the Agreement is not explicitly incorporated in the

---

37 Ibid., Article 9.1.
38 Ibid., Article 10.
39 Ibid., Article 11.1.
40 These objectives are as follows:

  – the elimination of industrial, economic, and social disadvantages of specific regions;
  – to facilitate the restructuring, under socially acceptable conditions, of certain sectors, especially where this has become necessary by reason of changes in trade and economic policies, including international agreements resulting in lower barriers to trade;
  – generally to sustain employment and to encourage retraining and change in employment;
  – to encourage research and development programs, especially in the field of high-technology industries;
  – the implementation of economic programmes and policies to promote the economic and social development of developing countries;
  – redeployment of industry in order to avoid congestion and environmental problems.

41 Ibid., Article 11.2.
42 Ibid.

provisions limiting the imposition of countervailing duties or in the domestic laws which control the levy of these duties. As a result, the justifications for production subsidies are not given any effect in defining permissible practices. Consequently, the legality of the subsidy and the magnitude of the countervailing duty are determined exclusively by the definition of 'subsidy' and the 'injury' requirement contained in the domestic legislation.

The distinction between these two types of subsidies may be relevant in implementing the remedies provided within GATT itself. The Agreement contemplates a process of consultation and conciliation between the country providing the subsidy and the country allegedly injured by it. Presumably in this process the possible justifications for the subsidy will be one of the issues examined. However, if this process is not successful, a determination that the subsidy violates GATT may be made and retaliation by the injured country authorized. In this determination the various justifications recited in the Agreement may play some role. Although the principal focus is on the 'injury' or impairment issue, conceivably some discretion may exist to vary the interpretation of this requirement with the magnitude of justification for the measure. It is also possible that the 'seek to avoid' language could be construed to permit a subsidy which does cause 'injury' or impair benefits if the subsidy is sufficiently beneficial.

The consultation and conciliation process does provide a forum for attempting to co-ordinate the subsidization policies of the member countries to achieve objectives like those sought by the Commission in its implementation of the EEC Treaty. However, the difficulties of doing this seem to be very great. To begin with, as noted above, the relevance of possible justification for a subsidy, if agreement is not reached, is unclear. But, more fundamentally, in view of the large number of GATT signatories, the complexities involved in assessing the competition between them in trying to influence locational decisions; and the problems of formulating and implementing a program which takes these interdependencies into account, controls 'cheating,' and assures an acceptable distribution of benefits derived from constraining the level of subsidization, it appears unlikely that any regulatory solution approaching the comprehensiveness of EEC regulation will emerge.

CONCLUSION

The basic substantive question for Canada, in deciding whether to adopt some means for limiting the grant of subsidies by the individual provinces, is whether competition between the provinces creates costs which are not justified by the benefits produced for the country as a whole. In simple terms, the central issue is whether the subsidization principally determines the location of industry within Canada or increases the total amount of investment which occurs. With respect to subsidization designed to support specific industries, although the issues may be more subtle the ultimate question is the same: are there interdependencies between the policies pursued, so that gains are available for the country as a whole by constraining the competition between the provinces?

If the answers to these questions suggest that national control may be beneficial, formidable issues remain concerning the design of an appropriate institution to implement the requisite co-ordination of provincial policies. It is clear that the institution will require a strong, unambiguous, substantive mandate in order to resist the intense political pressures for subsidization in the individual provinces. As a related matter, the personnel of the institution will have to command considerable respect. This will require that they be perceived as being free of commitment to any particular area or interest group, technically competent, and not subject to the control of the government in power.

At the same time the personnel of the agency will have to be extremely flexible and sensitive to the social forces creating the political pressure for subsidization. The substantive mandate can only provide a framework for negotiations and a threat of sanctions reserved for the extreme case in which a province substantially disregards the co-operative rationale which underlies the national regulation. The model then is of an agency flexibly implementing a policy which seeks to realize the gains of co-operation, not of a court passing upon alleged violations of a legal code specifying in detail the subsidization which can permissibly be undertaken by the provinces.

Whether the conditions which would make a solution of this kind beneficial exist and whether an institution which can realize the potential gains can be fashioned are obviously questions of considerable difficulty. I believe, however, that these are the questions that should be addressed.

9

Fiscal harmonization in
the United States, Australia,
West Germany, Switzerland, and the EEC

Wayne R. Thirsk

An inherent conflict exists in federal countries between the national desire for fiscal uniformity and the subfederal goal of financial autonomy. Attempts to balance these competing objectives have produced a range of policies collectively referred to as fiscal harmonization. The need for compromise between these objectives in the mature federations of Australia, West Germany, Canada, the United States, and Switzerland has elicited a diverse set of choices from the highly centralized system in Australia to the extraordinarily decentralized system in Switzerland.

It is unlikely that much could be learned by expanding the size of this sample, since other federations are either similar in nature or very immature and therefore subject to a unique set of problems. Through a comparative approach the present paper seeks to promote a better understanding of the range of policy options available to Canada and the possible future consequences of each.

We begin by examining the different dimensions of economic efficiency that are affected by a particular choice of fiscal arrangement. This overview is followed by a brief examination of how the harmonization problem has been handled among the countries forming the European Economic Community and a description of the measures adopted in Australia, West Germany, the United States, and Switzerland to achieve fiscal harmony. The main concern is with federal measures intended to offset subfederal fiscal barriers to economic integration, and Canada's current position within the range of options represented by these federations is discussed. An effort is made to explain why different countries have made different choices. The importance of a system of equalization payments as an instrument of fiscal harmonization is considered, as are the

I wish to acknowledge the helpful remarks received from John Whalley, Michael Trebilcock, Tom Courchene, and Jim Melvin in revising this paper. Any errors that remain are my own.

adjustment mechanisms that can provide for continuous fiscal harmonizatin under conditions of changing economic circumstances. Finally, the relevance of international experience for Canada's policy choices is considered. Two major conclusions emerge. First, probably more attention should be paid in Canada to the U.S. model, since it is in the direction of this particular model that Canada seems to be drifting. Secondly, weighing the pros and cons of policy alternatives, provides the basis only for a qualitative assessment of what is currently in Canada's best interest. Such an evaluation, however, is no substitute for the quantitative analysis which is so sorely needed to guide policy choices in this area.

FISCAL HARMONIZATION AND ECONOMIC EFFICIENCY

The essence of a federal system is that no level of government can dictate policy to another. Within broad constitutional constraints, different levels of government in a federal system compete for revenue sources on the tax side of public sector budgets and for public approval on the expenditure side. Subfederal units of government ordinarily seek the highest possible degree of expenditure and taxation discretion. In pursuit of this fiscal freedom, however, some subfederal tax and expenditure policies may be considered or adopted which are inimical to national welfare. The task of fiscal harmonization is to secure fiscal arrangements between different levels of government that will enhance economic efficiency in the country. This task is complicated by the fact that economic efficiency has many different facets and is influenced by public policy in many complex ways.[1]

Efficient resource allocation within the private sector
A requirement for efficiency in production is that all employers of capital and of any given type of labour face the same cost conditions for these resources throughout the economy. If the costs of capital and labour vary according to the geographic location of a producer, then (ignoring locational preferences of workers) there will be an inefficient spatial pattern of economic activity in a

---

1 Although this paper is concerned with the efficiency effects of different intergovernmental fiscal relationships, that does not mean there is little or no scope for fiscal co-ordination in the pursuit of the income distribution and stabilization functions of the public sector. In these areas it could, and sometimes does, happen that subfederal units of government take actions which effectively thwart the intentions of the federal government. These issues, however, deserve a separate examination. In Canada, for example, the federal government ordinarily co-operates with provincial governments if they wish to employ tax credits or surcharges to adjust the distribution of tax liabilities determined by the federal tax system.

country. Spatially variable factor costs will arise whenever different jurisdictions in a federation impose non-uniform rates of taxation on factor use, as in the case of either a payroll tax or a corporate income tax.[2] Non-uniformity in jurisdictional tax mixes can similarly result in inefficiency; for example, if one jurisdiction relies more heavily on personal income than corporate income taxes in financing its expenditures, while another jurisdiction does the opposite, the lower cost of labour in one jurisdiction (the one that places less emphasis on personal income taxation) will be offset by the higher cost of capital in that particular fiscal unit. To the extent that these offsetting influences on total costs of production tend to cancel each other, it will be factor proportions rather than factor locations, that will be inefficiently chosen because of the disparate tax structures. Origin-based commodity taxes, such as an excise tax or a value-added tax, have a similar capacity to distort the locational choices of capital and labour.

The requirement of geographically uniform factor prices as a condition for economic efficiency is really a special case of a more general consideration. This requirement is broader in that it takes into account what is happening on the expenditure side as well as the tax side of public sector budgets and recognizes that differential expenditure benefits have the same potential as differential taxes for distorting the use of resources. Unless the fiscal residual (the difference between expenditure benefits received and tax burdens borne) is the same for mobile factors in every jurisdiction of a federal system, the activities of the public sector in the federation will produce an inefficient distribution of resources within the private sector.[3] In the earlier discussion concerning the desirability of a common set of factor prices everywhere in the economy, it was implicitly assumed that expenditure benefits were also uniform throughout the economy. Where they are not, the conditions of the special case must be abandoned in favour of the more comprehensive criterion.

A further requirement for economic efficiency is that consumers in all geographic areas of a federation confront the same structure of relative commodity

---

2 In a spatial setting transport costs naturally segment product markets and could therefore permit some small tax disparities to occur which would not provoke any reallocation of resources.

3 When first introduced, the concept of a common fiscal residual was used to examine the requirements for attaining horizontal equity (the equal treatment of equals) in a federal system. Now it is more frequently viewed as a condition for the achievement of economic efficiency. It is also an exact requirement for the realization of the efficiency goal only if tastes are uniform and private and public sector services are extremely close substitutes in consumption. Otherwise, a variable rather than uniform fiscal residual is needed to ensure economic efficiency.

prices in the marketplace (net of any transportation costs). This condition will not be satisfied if destination-based commodity or sales taxes vary according to jurisdiction in a federal country. Jurisdictional differences in user charges and in residential property tax bills that finance public education will also contribute to an inefficient pattern of consumption. Moreover, selective commodity taxes, even if they were imposed at uniform rates in a federal system, would induce an inefficient allocation of resources within the private sector by driving a wedge between the prices paid by consumers and those received by producers.

An efficient division of resources between the private and public sectors

Since the seminal articles by Samuelson on the optimum size of the public sector, economists have accepted that efficiency requires the public sector to be expanded until the sum of the value of the marginal benefits of its various activities is equal to the marginal costs of supplying them.[4] Because of the intractable problem of inducing people to reveal honestly the nature of their preferences for public goods, democratic economies rely upon a variety of voting mechanisms to deliver the right amount and type of public goods that people desire.

To the extent that people miscalculate the tax costs of providing public goods, perhaps because many taxes are not highly visible, and also misperceive the nature of the benefits that are provided by public goods, an inefficient allocation of resources between the private and public sectors of the economy will occur. Various imperfections in electoral representation will produce a similar misallocation of resources. In a federal system the pressures of tax competition between different subfederal units may result in either the partial or total destruction of some tax bases that are available to them. In the absence of a co-operative solution to this problem, the erosion of a jurisdiction's tax base may prevent it from supplying an efficient level of public goods to its jurisdictional constituents.

An efficient allocation of resources in the public sector

The Samuelson condition for an efficient size of the public sector can be applied to all the expenditure activities of both a particular jurisdiction and all the

---

4 See Samuelson, 'The pure theory of public expenditures' (1954), 36 *Review of Economics and Statistics* 387. If there are j jurisdictions in a federation and i public sector activities and MRS and MRT denote respectively marginal rates of substitution and transformation between public and private sector goods, the Samuelson criterion requires that

$$\sum_i \sum_j \mathrm{MRS}_{ij} = \sum_i \sum_j \mathrm{MRT}_{ij}.$$

jurisdictions together that constitute a federation.[5] If it were successfully applied in this fashion, the pattern, as well as the overall size of public spending, would be optimal. In a federal system if subfederal expenditures spill over and benefit residents of other jurisdictions, expenditures are apt to be inefficiently small. Conversely, if some of the taxes levied by a subfederal jurisdiction spill over and burden residents of other jurisdictions, expenditure levels are likely to be inefficiently large.[6] Moreover, if an expenditure activity of the federal government is valued more highly in some jurisdictions than in others, the uniform provision of such a federal service will be inefficient. If instead of central direction of expenditure levels, there is central collection of taxes and a subsequent redistribution of funds to lower level governments, an inefficient overexpansion of subfederal government spending may occur because the costs of taxation may not be properly taken into account. If there is a diversity of tastes within a federation, the goal of subfederal expenditure autonomy takes on an important efficiency dimension and should not be considered a separate, non-economic objective.

Efficiency in tax administration
Another consideration in designing a federal system of taxation is the minimization of the resource costs that are involved in operating that system. These costs consist both of the public sector costs incurred in tax collection and the private sector costs incurred in complying with the tax laws. If each separate jurisdiction is in charge of its own tax system, and each system diverges from all the others, there will be considerable duplication in the collection of taxes and a heavy burden on taxpayers to conform to a multiplicity of competing tax systems. The substantial economies of scale enjoyed with a single tax administration invariably provide some impetus towards either the centralization of taxation or a high degree of co-operation in administering separate tax systems.

Fiscal efficiency
Every conceivable division of taxation powers and expenditure obligations between different levels of government in a federal system will affect each of

---

5 In terms of the previous notation the efficiency requirement in this case is that

$$\sum_j \text{MRS}_i = \sum_j \text{MRT}_i,$$

for all j, where the summation is over all individuals in the jth jurisdiction.

6 There have been few empirical studies of the extent to which tax exporting occurs in the Canadian economy. A recent attempt to determine the degree of non-residential property tax exporting is Ballantine and Thirsk, *Taxation Without Representation: The Consequences of Taxing Non-residential Property* (Ottawa: Canada Mortgage and Housing Corporation, 1982).

these dimensions of economic efficiency. The question is which particular set of fiscal arrangements will minimize the efficiency costs of the public sector's operation, or, more modestly, what changes in existing fiscal arrangements offer, or promise, an improvement in economic efficiency.

It has been suggested that the fundamental problem in a federal system is that efforts to achieve financial autonomy by subfederal governments may induce them to resort to inefficient methods of taxation. Finding more efficient methods of taxation may be one way out of the dilemma. Alternatively, it may be desirable to restrict the emergence of distorting tax differentials and thus the scope for expenditure variation, if the tax distortions that result can be shown to be significant. These restrictions can be justified on the grounds of economic efficiency if the increase in tax efficiency that is secured more than outweighs any loss in expenditure efficiency that may be incurred. How can this be done? The range of policy choices open to a country runs from tax separation to tax sharing, and includes a variety of methods of tax co-ordination, such as joint audits, the adoption of a common base, the use of tax supplements, and also tax deductions and tax credits. Measures to co-ordinate expenditures might also be included. All the countries surveyed below have employed one or more of these harmonization devices at different times.

THE EEC: ITS MEMBER STATES

The goal of the European Economic Community is to provide an institutional structure which will secure the unimpeded movement of persons, goods, services, and capital. In other words, the target is to reach agreement on measures which will achieve a single, or common, market for labour, commodities, and funds. In pursuit of this objective, the guiding consideration for the discussion and decision-making on fiscal harmonization has always been the principle of fair competition.

It has been readily accepted by individual members that some expenditures and most taxation policies should be designed so that they do not distort the pattern of intra-Community trade and the allocation of the Community's capital and labour resources. With the dismantling of the system of internal tariffs it was widely recognized that indirect tax systems could effectively replace the tariff policies that were being discarded. The item of first priority on the Community's agenda for fiscal harmonization was therefore the adoption of a trade-neutral system of commodity taxation. At the time of the formation of the Community, members were eploying a bewildering array of turnover taxes that could not be easily harmonized. A simple solution to this difficulty would have been for each member to replace its turnover tax with a destination-based sales tax. With this type of sales tax regime, imports would have automatically faced the same rate of taxation as domestically produced products, and exports would have been automatically exempt from taxation. Instead the EEC chose as its future target a system of origin-based value-added taxes because they promised eventually to eliminate the need for fiscal frontiers, they were a logical progression from the earlier system of turnover taxes, and some countries were extremely suspicious of the practical effects of a system of export rebates and compensatory import levies.[7] The combined result of these various factors was the sacrifice of more tax autonomy by individual members than would have occurred under a destination approach.

The EEC sought to harmonize the structure of commodity taxation first, and the rate of taxation only much later. At the moment the value-added tax found within the EEC is one of the consumption variety and is levied on a destination-basis since the coverage of the tax or its base, and also the rate structure, vary from one country to the next. Border tax adjustments, the rebate of tax paid on exports, and the imposition of a comparable levy on imports, are used to convert the origin basis of the value-added tax into a destination-based levy. Most member countries have from one to three different VAT rates, Italy being the exception with eight rates. The current view within the Community is that only with the greater integration of the individual economies and the accompanying transfer of sovereignty to the Community from the member states will it be necessary to go further and harmonize the individual tax rates. The processes of tax harmonization and economic integration are thus seen as inseparable. The EEC has already fashioned a common tariff policy in external trade, agriculture, and transport and is seeking common policies in energy, regional policy, and the environment. Until the pressure of closer economic ties makes the need for greater commodity tax harmonization more evident to policy-makers, the Community is content to give top priority to harmonizing the excise taxation of tobacco products and alcoholic beverages.[8] These items are currently taxed according to a destination principle. Some recent progress has been made in agreeing on a common rate of excise taxation for cigarettes. Apart from these excises, however, as long as the value-added tax rates differ among members,

---

7 An excellent discussion of the background to harmonization within the EEC is by Dosser and Han, *Taxes in the EEC and Britain: The Problem of Harmonization* (London: Chatham House and PEP, 1968).
8 The problems of harmonizing excise tax rates within the EEC are reviewed in Commission of the European Communities, 'Report to the Council on the scope for convergence of tax systems in the Community (adopted 26 march 1980),' *Bulletin of the European Communities: Supplement 1 / 80* (Luxembourg: Office for Official Publications of the European Communities, 1980), at 27–46 and 55–60.

frontier checks on intra-Community trade flows will continue to be required. It is felt that agreement on a standard list of taxable goods and services, as well as agreement on a common number of tax rates, will be difficult to realize because each member relies on a multi-rate system for income distribution purposes.

Progress towards the harmonization of direct taxes has occurred at a much slower pace. Personal taxes on labour incomes have been accorded a low priority for harmonization since differential taxes on largely immobile labour are not viewed as a determinant of the price of trade goods. Moreover, if other kinds of taxes are to be harmonized, variations in personal income taxes must be tolerated if different countries are to have some scope in choosing the appropriate size of the public sector. Harmonization of corporate income taxation is of more immediate concern. In the long run differential taxation of corporate, or more generally business, incomes will be reflected in the pattern of relative product prices and create distortions both in the pattern of international trade and in the allocation of capital among countries. Corporate income taxes resemble origin-based selective value-added taxes in their relative price effects on commodities and, if administratively feasible, should be given the same border tax treatment as any selective excise tax. Proposals for the future harmonization of corporate taxation consist of two progressive steps. First, some agreement on nominal tax rates and a uniform method of taxation will be attempted. This will be followed by an effort to make effective rates of taxation more uniform. It is recognized therefore that uniform nominal tax rates are harmonizing only to the extent that measures which affect effective tax rates are also uniform. Thus, for example, a common schedule of depreciation rates is envisaged, along with guidelines which would restrict the use of depreciation allowances as a tax incentive instrument.

On the expenditure side of the budget, it is recognized that differences in transfer payments – in particular, social security benefits – will play an important role in determining locational choices once the free mobility of labour is achieved. Plans for establishing a common social security fund are likely to evolve as the barriers to intra-Community labour migration are reduced and eventually eliminated. But this effort at expenditure co-ordination, like the one to harmonize corporate taxation, will not bear much fruit in the immediate future.

OTHER FEDERATIONS

Australia
Australia has experimented with a variety of different approaches to fiscal harmonization, though as in most other countries, only on the tax side of the public ledger. In the earliest years of the Australian federation the main sources

of public revenue – customs and excise duties – were shared between the Commonwealth and the states. In order to remove internal barriers to commodity trade, the various states ceded their powers to levy customs duties and excise taxes to the Commonwealth in return for a share of the Commonwealth proceeds from these revenue sources. This system of tax-sharing proved to be too rigid and was soon replaced by the Commonwealth provision of per capita grants to the States. These grants were inadequate to meet the expenditure needs of the states. During World War I and its aftermath the states, therefore, along with the Commonwealth, began to cultivate new direct tax sources of revenue. Although the constitution had reserved the field of indirect taxation to the Commonwealth,[9] it permitted states to impose other kinds of taxes as long as they did not discriminate between states or parts of states. By the end of World War I overlapping state and Commonwealth taxes existed in the personal income and estate tax fields. In addition, local governments had moved into the area of land taxation.

The Australian High Court subsequently interpreted the prohibition on state use of indirect taxes to include all forms of sales taxation, even those levied on a destination basis.[10] In the areas of direct taxation the problems of tax competition and vertical co-ordination stood out as contentious issues. Despite numerous proposals for reform, the death duty field has had a chaotic history.[11] Pressures to harmonize Commonwealth and state income taxes produced an agreement in the 1920s to rely upon a single tax return and a process of joint collection. Proposals to introduce a common tax structure having uniform definitions of income and uniform tax rates never went beyond the stage of intergovernmental discussion.

The ongoing debate over the appropriate Commonwealth and state tax

---

9 The Australian Constitution, S. 90 gave the commonwealth government exclusive power to impose 'duties of custom and excise.'

10 This has been done in a series of decisions that extend the meaning of 'excise' duties. See *Commonwealth Oil Refineries* v. *South Australia* (1926), 38 C.L.R. 408 (High Ct), *John Fairfax and Sons Ltd.* v. *New South Wales* (1926), 39 C.L.R. 139 (High Ct), and *Attorney General (New South Wales)* v. *Homebush Flour Mills Ltd.* (1937), 56 C.L.R. 390 (High Ct). For further discussion see Lumb and Ryan, *The Constitution of the Commonwealth of Australia Annotated, Second Edition* (Sydney: Butterworths, 1977), at 297–302.

11 Prest, 'Tax arrangements and intergovernmental transfers' (1977), 7 *Publius: The Journal of Federalism* 53, at 58

structure was interrupted by the exigencies of World War II. To finance its much higher level of wartime expenditures the Commonwealth needed to impose much higher rates of income tax. However, such a move would have resulted in unreasonably high tax burdens in states that already resorted to high income tax rates. Constitutionally the Commonwealth was barred from imposing a discriminatory set of federal tax rates that would equalize the combined weight of federal and state income taxation.[12] The way out of this impasse was to persuade the states to vacate the income tax field on the understanding that they would be compensated for their loss of revenue by the Commonwealth. The result was the uniform income tax legislation of 1942, which brought the era of overlapping taxation to a close and ushered in the new system of tax separation.[13] The Commonwealth became the sole recipient of the revenues from customs and excise duties, sales taxes, and income taxes. States continued to share land taxes with local authorities and to impose succession duties alongside the federal estate tax.

In Australia states perform many of the functions that are the responsibilities of local government in other federal countries. For example, the provision of police services, education, housing, and many public utilities are the responsibilities of the states in Australia.[14] The Australian states were stripped of their main revenue sources just a few years before the rapid growth in their expenditure demands at the end of World War II. To a minor extent the enormous gap between revenue needs and reveue capacity, referred to as vertical fiscal imbalance, has been met by the steady transfer of some taxing powers from the Commonwealth to the states. The Commonwealth abandoned the land and entertainment tax fields to the states in 1953, but the revenue impact was

12 Australian Constitution, S. 51, cl. (ii)

13 In the *Uniform Tax Case No. 1 (South Australia et al. v. The Commonwealth* (1942), 65 C.L.R. 373) the High Court of Australia upheld the constitutional validity of four Commonwealth Acts that made the Commonwealth the sole effective authority in the income tax field. The four Acts were the States Grants (Income Tax Reimbursement) Act 1942, No. 20; the Income Tax (Wartime Arrangements) Act 1942, No. 21; the Income Tax Assessment Act 1942, No. 22; and the Income Tax Act 1942, No. 23. The states again challenged the States Grants Act and the Assessment Act in 1957 (*State of Victoria et al.* v. *The Commonwealth* (1957), 99 C.L.R. 575 (High Court of Australia)), but the limited success in respect of the Assessment Act was not sufficient to induce the states to re-enter the income tax field.

14 The Australian Constitution, S. 107, reserves for the states all powers not specifically given to the federal government.

negligible. A more generous transfer occurred in 1971 when the payroll tax was made available to the states by the Commonwealth. It is now the largest single source of tax revenue for the states. State lotteries have also developed since the 1950s as a fresh source of revenue.

Nonetheless, state tax revenues in the early 1970s paid for only about 40 per cent of total state expenditures. The remainder of state expenditures was financed by an extensive and elaborate system of transfer payments from the Commonwealth to the States. From the time the uniform income tax legislation came into effect until 1954, states received tax reimbursement grants as compensation for the revenue which they had sacrificed. The size of the grant was initially set at the level of average state tax collections in the years 1939–40 and 1940–1. After the War the grant was put on a formula basis with the increase in its size determined by the rate of growth of population, average wages per employee, and, after 1959, a so-called betterment or economic growth factor. After 1959 these unconditional payments were referred to as financial assistance grants and continued to be administered by the Commonwealth Grants Commission. The Commission had acted to tailor the distribution of grants among states to reflect interstate variation in school age population as well as population density. Thus these grants had a strong element of equalization in them and tended to address both horizontal and vertical fiscal imbalances in the Australian federal system. The grants more closely resemble the U.S. system of revenue-sharing than the Canadian system of equalization in that they are paid out to all states rather than to just a few. However, there is in addition to the large financial assistance and the relatively minor special assistance payments made to all states the provision of special grants to the three states of Queensland, South Australia, and Tasmania which are recognized as having higher-than-normal fiscal needs. These are pure equalization grants. Finally, a recent development in Australia has been the rapid growth of special purpose payments, or conditional grants, to help cover the operating costs of state-operated health and educational programs. While a number of states have actively sought this aid, others view it as a disruption of state budgetary priorities and a drain on state revenues since aid of this type serves to increase the demand for capital works that will ultimately provoke higher operating costs.

From the previous remarks it is clear that Australia has achieved a relatively high degree of fiscal harmonization. Almost all this co-ordination, however, has been confined to taxes. Interstate tax differentials are unimportant mainly because state taxation has not been allowed to develop. Even in the cases where the states have access to their own revenue sources, they have tended to act in unison. For example, whenever states have raised their payroll tax rates, they have so far acted in concert. There is some concern, however, that this aspect of fiscal harmonization may also produce poor decisions on the expenditure side of the budget. It is possible, for example, that state dependence on financial assistance grants may have induced an overexpansion in the size of the public sector in Australia. In other federal countries overexpansion is probably less likely to occur because states or provinces use their own revenue sources to finance marginal spending. However, a unique feature in the Australian situation is the existence of the Australian Loan Council, which, unlike in the United States or Canada, co-ordinates federal and state borrowing or capital expenditures in the interests of economic stabilization.

Whether in response to state demands for greater fiscal autonomy or from Commonwealth recognition of the need for greater state access to their own sources of revenue, a new form of fiscal federalism emerged from three premiers' conferences in 1976. Under the agreement that was reached, a system of personal income tax sharing replaced the financial assistance grants beginning in 1976–7: 33.6 per cent of the personal income tax yield was to be allotted to the various states according to the pattern of financial assistance grants paid to them in 1975–6.[15] Local authorities were also to share in this tax at the rate of 1.52 per cent. Under the second stage of this agreement, starting in 1977–8 states were permitted to piggyback onto the federal personal income tax in order to permit them to finance extra expenditures or to reduce reliance on other forms of taxation. No state has so far taken advantage of this tax option. In order to preserve the stabilization capacity of the federal government, countercyclical surcharges imposed by the Commonwealth were excluded from the sharing arrangement. In this new fiscal environment the Commonwealth Grants Commission will continue to recommend whether or not special grants should be awarded to fiscally weaker states applying for financial assistance.

West Germany

Eleven states, including the city states of Hamburg, Bremen and West Berlin, comprise the Federation of West Germany. The fiscal activities of these states (Länder) are closely co-ordinated with those of the federal government (Bund). The Constitutional Assembly of 1948 created a new fiscal system in which tax rates and tax structures were to be uniform throughout the Federation. This desire for fiscal uniformity was apparently motivated by the twin policy objectives of achieving uniform living standards across the country and avoiding the effects of interstate tax competition and the consequent need to provide substantial federal subsidies or grants to states whose tax revenues lagged behind their

15 Hunter, 'Intergovernmental fiscal adjustment in Australia: a review of recent developments in the light of experience in Canada and West Germany' (1980), 38 *Finanzarchiv* 424

expenditures. Thus the federal government was granted the power to pre-empt any tax field. However, yields from all income taxes and the value-added tax were to be shared with the states. This system of tax-sharing is West Germany's compromise between the need for fiscal uniformity and the opposing need for state financial autonomy. Interestingly enough, state control over tax rates and tax structures has never been viewed as an indispensable part of state fiscal autonomy.[16]

As shown in Table 1, the states were entitled to receive one-half of all income taxes net of any local share and in 1971 30 per cent of the proceeds of the value-added tax. Since 1969 municipalities have also shared in the income tax to the extent of 14 per cent of the total yield. These participation ratios can be adjusted biennially. In 1972–3 the state share of the value-added tax was raised to 35 per cent to offset larger state deficits but was later reduced to 32.5 per cent in 1978 when child care expenditure responsibilities were shifted to the federal government. It is the share of this tax rather than that of the income taxes which is normally and routinely adjusted to meet the financial needs of the states. The nature and extent of these needs is in turn determined by the expenditure decisions taken by several joint state and federal planning boards. This system of joint tasks arising from a 1969 constitutional amendment has resulted in a unique form of fiscal co-operation.[17] Federal and state expenditures are co-ordinated in the construction of institutes of higher education, the improvement of regional and agricultural economic structures, and coastal protection, all of which were formerly the exclusive responsibility of states.

The interstate distribution of income tax revenue is decided on the basis of derivation: that is, revenues are returned to the states in which they were originally collected by the federal government according to the predetermined sharing agreement. However, the interstate distribution of the value-added tax is made on the basis of population rather than derivation and therefore contains

16 Hunter, *Revenue Sharing in the Federal Republic of Germany* (Canberra: Centre for Research on Federal Financial Relations Research Monograph 2, The Australian National University, 1973). See also Spahn, 'The German model of horizontal federal decentralization.' In Spahn, ed., *Principles of federal policy co-ordination in the Federal Republic of Germany: basic issues and annotated legislation* (Canberra Centre for Research on Federal Financial Relations Research Monograph 25, The Australian National University, 1978) and Zimmerman, 'Fiscal federalism in the Federal Republic of Germany' (mimeo, 1980).

17 'Gesetz zur Änderung des Grundgesetzes vom 12 Mai 1969,' *Federal Law Gazette I*, at 359. For a discussion of Article 91a in English see Spahn, 'The German model,' at 121–8. For the full constitution in English see Flanz, 'Basic law for the Federal Republic of Germany' (1974). In Blaustein and Flanz, eds, *Constitutions of the Countries of the World*, Binder VI (Dobbs Ferry, New York: Ocean Publications, looseleaf)

TABLE 1

Tax-sharing in West Germany (1970-1)

Tax	Share (%)		
	Federal	State	Municipal
Wages and assessed income	43	43	14
Non-assessed tax on yields	50	50	–
Corporate income tax	50	50	–
Value-added tax	70	30	–
Trade tax	20	20	60

SOURCE: Hunter, *Revenue Sharing in The Federal Republic of Germany* (Canberra: Centre for Research on Federal Financial Relations Research Monograph No. 2, The Australian National University, 1973), at 43

an element of equalization. In addition to these revenues from shared tax sources, states enjoy the exclusive occupation of the tax fields relating to levies on motor vehicles, wealth, and inheritance, excise taxes on beer and gambling, and taxes on land acquisition. These revenue sources together account for approximately one-fifth of total state taxes. Federal grants and loans constitute less than 15 per cent of state income. Most of the federal grants are of the conditional variety and are used to finance the undertaking of the joint tasks. To maintain unrestricted internal trade, all excise taxes except for those on beer have been assigned to the federal government.

Another novel feature of German federalism is a system of equalization payments which results in a flow of fiscal transfers directly from states with above-average fiscal capacity to states with below-average fiscal capacity. The amount of these interstate transfers is determined by a simple formula which compares actual with average state revenues, and the federal government is not involved in this redistribution of tax revenue except insofar as it monitors compliance with the rules of the equalization law. Since the sharing of the value-added tax contains an implicit redistribution of tax revenues among the states and the states' share of this tax source is increasing steadily, the need for further fiscal equalization is diminishing. The fiscal transfers now taking place under the equalization scheme account for only about 4.5 per cent of total state tax revenues.

The United States

The U.S. Constitution imposes remarkably few constraints on that country's fiscal structure. It is totally silent about which expenditures should be undertaken by any given level of government and also about the forms of taxation that should be employed. Nonetheless, it does provide for some restrictions on the kinds of taxes that are available to federal and state governments. Under the Interstate Commerce Clause, for example, states must refrain from levying import duties or export taxes, although various kinds of export subsidies are not similarly proscribed.[18] Under the Interstate Privileges and Immunities Clause and the Equal Protection Clause, discrimination against out-of-state citizens is prohibited.[19] Moreover, while taxes on business profits by various states are permitted, the total tax base is supposed to be allocated among them on a reasonable basis. For its part, the federal government faces the restriction that taxes must apply uniformly across the country[20]; for example, federal excise tax rates cannot vary geographically.

There is a reasonably high degree of tax separation in the U.S. fiscal structure (Table 2). Customs duties are lodged exclusively with the federal government, the property tax nearly so with local government, and general sales taxes are employed exclusively by state and municipal governments, with state governments having a near monopoly over this particular source of revenue. Corporate and individual income taxes are shared primarily between the federal and state governments, though by far the largest share of each tax is enjoyed by the federal government. Only in the area of excise taxation, in particular, sumptuary taxation, is there anywhere near an equal division of revenues between the federal and state levels of government. As a rough generalization, the federal

18 U.S. Constitution, Art. I, S. 8, cl.3. Although the Commerce Clause is framed as a grant to Congress of the power to regulate interstate and foreign commerce, it has long been interpreted as restricting state taxing powers, see *Boston Stock Exchange et al.* v. *State Tax Commission et al.*, 97 S. Ct 599, at 606–7 (1977).

19 A series of Supreme Court decisions involving the Commerce Clause (*supra*, note 18), the Interstate Privileges and Immunities Clause (U.S. Constitution, Art. IV, S. 2, cl.1), and the Equal Protection Clause (U.S. Constitution, amend. XIV, S. 1 (1868)) have created a set of effective barriers to any significant overtaxation of outsiders by the states. Emphasis has been on the use of the interstate privileges and immunities clause, see *Ward* v. *Maryland*, 79 U.S. (12 Wall.) 418, at 429 (Sup. Ct 1871). *Toomer* v. *Witsell*, 334 U.S. 385, at 396 (Sup. Ct 1948), and *Mullaney* v. *Anderson*, 342 U.S. 415, at 417–19 (Sup. Ct 1952). For further discussion see Hellerstein, 'State tax discrimination against out-of-staters' (1977), 30 *National Tax Journal* 113.

20 U.S. Constitution, Art. 1, S. 8, cl. 1

TABLE 2

Distribution of tax revenue by source and level of
government in the United States, 1976-7

Tax	Distribution (%)		
	Federal	State	Local
Customs duties	100	0	0
Property tax	0	4	96
Corporate income tax	86	14	0
Individual income tax	84	14	2
Motor vehicle licenses	0	93	7
General sales taxes	0	85	15
Alcoholic beverage excise	70	28	2
Tobacco excise	40	58	2
Motor fuel excise	35	64	1
Public utility excise	40	34	26
Other excises	31	60	9
Death and gift taxes	80	20	–
All other taxes	18	59	23

SOURCE: Break, *Financing Government in a Federal
System* (Washington DC: The Brookings Institution,
1980), at 32

government relies primarily on income taxes, the state governments on consumption taxes, and the local governments on wealth taxes.

What Table 2 does not reveal is the considerable degree of interstate diversity in taxation. Five states, Nevada, South Dakota, Texas, Washington, and Wyoming, have neither personal nor corporate income taxes; Florida, Pennsylvania, and Tennessee have no personal income tax. However, a number of large cities apply their own local income tax, which frequently takes the form of a payroll tax since non-labour income is difficult to determine for these small jurisdictions. Most states apply progressive rates which range from 2 to 8 per cent of taxable income. Corporate income tax rates are often graduated as well, with the average rate varying between about 5 and 10 per cent. Also, in 1978, there were forty-six states which levied a general retail sales tax, with rates between 2 and 7 per cent. Moreover, local sales taxes were in place in thirty states in that year.

In view of the considerable overlapping of federal and state taxes on income, it is not surprising that a number of measures have been tried to secure a reasonable degree of vertical tax co-ordination.[21] There is fairly widespread

21 The situation in the United States is clearly described in Break, *Financing Government in a
Federal System* (Washington DC: The Brookings Institution, 1980).

co-ordination of tax administration in that currently forty-three income tax states have reached an agreement with the federal government on the exchange of information and tax data. The use of similar tax bases also facilitates tax administration and eases the burden of tax compliance. Three states currently make their individual income tax a percentage of the federal tax; eight states employ the same federal definition of taxable income; while a further twenty-one rely on the federal determination of adjusted gross income. The exemption of government interest income from taxation by other levels of government hinders, or at least seriously complicates, the adoption of tax supplements as the form in which the state individual income tax is imposed. On the side of corporate taxation, thirty-three states conform very closely to the federal definition of taxable income for the state corporate income tax. Under the Federal-State Tax Collection Act of 1972 the federal government offered to administer the taxes levied by state and local governments, all of which were free to set their own tax rate on a common tax base.[22] To the extent that this offer is taken up by the states, it promises to reduce compliance cost for taxpayers and is likely to result in some economies of scale in tax collection. A disadvantage of this option from a state viewpoint is that whenever federal income taxes decline for whatever reason, state income tax revenues will be likewise reduced.[23]

An important co-ordination device in the United States is the federal tax deduction and tax credit, both of which help to ease, although not erase, the problem of interstate tax competition. If an individual taxpayer itemizes his deductions, as about 31 per cent of them did in 1975, almost all state and local taxes are deductible under the federal income tax. State corporate income taxes on the other hand are deductible under the federal corporate income tax. By allowing for an automatic federal tax offset to any state tax increase, these measures enhance the fiscal independence of some federal units by mitigating the allocative impact of state and local tax differentials.

While it is true that these deductions give rise to the phenomenon of tax exporting, in that part of any state or local tax burden falls on taxpayers in other parts of the country and therefore encourages a larger volume of state and local expenditure, this result can be rationalized on the grounds that most kinds of state and local spending generate some amount of geographic spillover. Tax credits may be considered an alternative to deductions but differ from the latter

---

22 86 Stat. 936. Title 2

23 In Canada this problem is avoided by the operation of the Provincial Tax Revenue Guarantee Program, the purpose of which is to encourage the continuation of a uniform tax system. Under this program any provincial revenue losses in excess of 1 per cent of federal basic tax that result from changes in federal policy will be reimbursed by the federal government.

in that the amount of tax relief they provide is independent of the income status of the taxpayer. At present the federal government allows a tax credit against comparable federal taxes for state estate taxes and for payroll taxes which finance the unemployment insurance system. The estate tax credit is intended to reduce the interstate competition for wealthy taxpayers,[24] while the payroll tax credit represents an attempt to induce state adoption of unemployment insurance programs.[25]

Examples of horizontal tax co-ordination can also be found in the U.S. fiscal system. In the sales tax field most states provide a credit for sales tax which has been paid in another state. Credits also serve to harmonize state income taxes. Most states tax individuals on the basis of both source and residence, and double taxation is avoided through reciprocal provisions that allow credit for tax paid to another state. Much less success has been achieved in co-ordinating the system of state corporate income taxes. The basic problems in this area concern 'nexus' (the conditions under which a corporation is taxable in a given state) and 'allocation' (the division of a corporation's multistate income among competing state claims). In 1959 a decision of the U.S. Supreme Court supported the right of a state to tax the profits of a multistate corporation.[26] The same year Congress legislated a nexus criterion that prevented a state from applying its corporate income tax to a company whose only activity in the state consisted of the solicitation of orders.[27] An offshoot of this legislation was the Willis Committee Report, which investigated the effects of the state corporate income tax and set down recommendations for federal legislation in this area.[28] The Report underlined the large degree of non-uniformity in state laws, the frequent instances of non-enforcement by the states and failure to comply by business, the arbitrary distribution of tax burdens in which corporations doing business in a single state might be either over- or undertaxed, and the way in which states had structured

24 Introduced in the Revenue Act of 1926, S. 302, 44(2) Stat. 50. The effect has been greatly reduced because the credit ceiling is tied to federal liabilities computed at 1926 tax rates.
25 Introduced in Title IX of the Social Security Act 1935, 49(1) Stat. 639. For further discussion of this and the estate tax credit see Maxwell, *Tax Credits and Intergovernmental Fiscal Relations* (Washington DC: The Brookings Institution, 1962).
26 *Northwestern States Portland Cement Co.* v. *Minnesota*, 358 U.S. 450 (1959)
27 Public Law 86–272, 73 Stat. 555 (1959), 15 U.S.C., S. 381–4 (1970 ed.).
28 U.S. Congress, House of Representatives Committee on the Judiciary, Special Subcommittee on State Taxation of Interstate Commerce, *State Taxation of Interstate Commerce: Report-Pursuant to Public Law 86–272 as amended* (Washington, D.C.: Government Printing Office, Vols 1 and 2, 88th Congress, 2nd Session, House Report 88–1480, June 15, 1964; vol. 3, 89th Congress, 1st Session, House Report 89–565, June 30 1964; Vol. 4, 89th Congress, 1st Session, House Report 89–952, Sept. 2, 1965). The Subcommittee was chaired by Edwin E. Willis of Louisiana.

their system of taxation to create a more hospitable tax climate for resident firms than for non-resident firms.

The problems posed by the diversity of state tax laws and the spectre of interstate tax competition have induced a number of states to search for a co-operative approach to greater tax uniformity. In 1957 a state conference of tax commissioners drew up a model law for the state corporate income tax, referred to as the Uniform Division of Income for Tax Purposes Act (UDITPA).[29] Currently, twenty-five of the forty-six states levying corporate income taxes have structured their corporate income tax systems to conform with this model law. A further step in this direction was taken in 1967 with the formation of the Multi-State Tax Commission whose goal has been to establish greater uniformity in the taxation of interstate business. This voluntary association of states currently has nineteen members and twelve associates, who, although they have not adopted the uniform regulations laid down in the multistate tax compact, nonetheless take part in the Commission's deliberations and meetings.

Outside the framework established by the Multi-State Tax Commission, substantial diversity is encountered in tax rates, the definition of taxable income, and the use of apportionment formulas. State corporate income taxes are based on the concept of territoriality, the notion that the tax base should include the flow of net corporate income which originates within the taxing jurisdiction. Ideally, this concept could be implemented through the adoption of separate accounting for each of the units of a multistate enterprise. However, the accounting problems incurred in assigning fixed costs of production and in treating internal transactions that are subject to transfer price manipulation by the firm make this choice administratively not feasible. Instead of separate accounting practices, states employ apportionment formulas to divide the income of multistate companies between various jurisdictions.

If all states resorted to the same apportionment formula the amounts of taxable income assigned to different jurisdictions would add up to the total net income of the multistate enterprise. In fact, however, states tend to rely upon the use of hopelessly divergent formulas when they do not adhere to the Multi-State Tax Compact.[30] A typical apportionment formula calculates the company's

29 National Conference of Commissioners on Uniform State Laws, 'The Uniform Division of Income for Tax Purpose Act,' 7A *U.L.A.* 91 (1978)

30 The Multistate Tax Compact was developed in 1967 under the aegis of the Council of State Governments, in part at least to offset the severe criticism levelled by the Willis Committee (see note 28) against the widespread diversity in state tax formulas, and it incorporates UDITPA (see note 29) into Article IV of the Compact. The Compact is reprinted as an appendix to White, 'Note: the constutionality of the multistate tax compact' (1976), 29 *Vanderbilt Law Review* 453, at 470, and is also available with the Regulations in 'Multi-state tax compact,' 1 *State Tax Guide: All States 2nd Edition* (CCH) 351, 352 (Oct. 1980). Despite its failure

taxable income as a weighted average of the state's share of the firm's payroll and property, plus the share of the firm's total sales that are attributable to consumers of the taxing state. Unfortunately, the choice of factors, their definitions, and the relative weight applied to each varies from one state to another. If a formula incorporates a destination-based sales factor, it increases significantly the number of companies liable for taxation in more than one state, and it may also understate total taxable profit if some of the corporation's net income is assigned to states that do not have sufficient nexus, unless, as is sometimes the case, throwback rules exist to reassign this understated net income to the state of origin.

Although the adoption of a two-factor formula based on property and payrolls would simplify the determination of nexus and reduce compliance costs considerably, there is no incentive for a single state to move in this direction, and in fact there is a strong incentive to move in just the opposite direction. It is easily seen that shifting from an origin-based to a destination-based sales factor is equivalent to a state currency depreciation. Taxes imposed on the sales made by non-resident firms will be higher and taxes levied on resident firms selling outside the state lower as a result of such a shift. For example, Iowa has recently introduced a single-factor destination sales formula, which exposes out-of-state companies to a much higher rate than that which faces manufacturers producing within the state and selling to other states. Similarly, a number of so called 'snowbelt' states, such as New York, Massachusetts, and Wisconsin, have recently altered their apportionment formula to give a double weight to the sales factor in an effort to combat the shift of industry and jobs to the so-called sunbelt states.

California is unique among the states in applying a method of taxation known as unitary combination. The foreign-country business activities of firms closely affiliated with California-based firms are deemed to be part of a unitary business, and their factors are combined before the formula is applied to apportion the income of the unitary business. Most states employ separate accounting and treat intercorporate dividends as income accruing to the recipient corporation, which is to be divided by formula among the states. Under unitary combination, these dividends are netted out and do not require special treatment. A number of states attribute interfirm dividends to the state of commercial domicile of the recipient firm and thereby exclude this income flow from the apportionment formula.

---

to get Congressional approval after numerous attempts to fulfil the requirements of Art. I, S. 10. cl. 3, of the Constitution, it was upheld in *United States Steel Corp* v. *Multistate Tax Commission*, 434 U.S. 452 (Sup. Ct 1977) as not tending to increase the political power of the states.

The inclusion of foreign-source income in state apportionment formulas has elicited concern from many quarters. In principle, if the purpose of apportionment is to approximate the flow of net corporate income originating in a state, foreign-source income should be excluded from the apportionment formula. Corporations are adamant in calling for restrictions on unitary combination that limit its scope to the 'water's edge,' and foreign governments have expressed their objections to the passage of state tax laws which contravene and contradict international tax treaties. Under unitary combination the anomalous result can occur in which foreign source income is apportioned to a state in which the firm experienced business losses. A recent example of controversy in this context is Vermont's successful attempt to tax the foreign-source dividends received by the Mobil Corporation.[31] Even more anomalous is the fact that these dividends were included in Mobil's apportionable income without benefit of combination.

Unlike many other federations, the United States has not relied on an extensive system of intergovernmental grants to harmonize the tax structures of some federal units. Almost all the federal grants flowing to the state and local governments are conditional and designed to stimulate greater expenditure levels on the part of the latter. A modest concession to the principle of unconditional federal financing was made in 1972 with the introduction of the U.S. revenue-sharing program. Under this scheme every state received a share of federally raised funds, which was determined on the basis of a weighted average of the state's population and tax effort and the inverse of the level of per capita income in the state. By law, one-third of this transfer may be retained by the states, while the other two-thirds must be passed through to local governments within the state. Although it represents an interesting departure from previous practices, the contribution of this program to the achievement of greater tax harmonization is slight since these revenue transfers represent only about 6 per cent of all state tax revenues. Regardless of its relatively small impact, however, revenue-sharing may be more important for what it represents than for what it does. Proponents of revenue-sharing intended it to allow state and local governments to meet their rapidly growing expenditure needs without having to resort to taxes that were felt to be inferior to federal taxes.

Switzerland

Switzerland is a curious mixture of tax separation and tax competition. The federal government maintains a virtual monopoly in the field of indirect taxation. According to the Constitution, all customs duties and excise levies are

---

31 *Mobil Oil Corp.* v. *Commissioner of Taxes of Vermont*, 100 S. Ct 1223 (1980)

reserved to it.[32] In the direct tax field there is a bewildering degree of overlapping since both the federal government and the cantons tax personal income and net worth in addition to business profit, capital, and capital gains. This particular assignment of revenue sources is, by and large, the result of historical accident. According to the Swiss Constitution of 1874 the cantons were permitted to use any form of taxation that was not reserved by the federal government.[33] Since only the levying of customs duties was constitutionally set aside for the federal government, the direct tax field in effect was assigned to the cantons by default. Cantonal units of governments have been permitted an unusual degree of constitutional freedom in cultivating their own tax systems. A novel facet of the Swiss fiscal system is that any change in tax legislation must be submitted to a referendum.[34] In 1958 a referendum limited the contours of federal direct taxes with respect to the definition of the tax base and the level and duration of these taxes.[35] Every subsequent effort to remove these restrictions on federal financial powers has been defeated. Until that time the use of federal direct taxes had been confined to limited periods during national emergencies. In addition to customs duties, the indirect taxes imposed by the federal government consist of a single-stage turnover tax (a de facto wholesale tax) and several kinds of sumptuary taxes.[36]

Direct taxation is the major source of diversity and competition within the Swiss federation. A residence criterion is employed to allocate the personal income tax base among the various cantons.[37] The federal tax on personal

32 *Bundesverfassung der Schweizerischen Eidgenossenschaft* (vom 29 Mai 1874), Art. 28, 29, and 30. English and German texts are printed in Hughes, *The Federal Constitution of Switzerland* (Oxford: Clarendon Press, 1954). A more recent English text is available in Flanz and Klein, 'Switzerland: the federal constitution of the Swiss Confederation' (1982). In Blaustein and Flanz, eds, *Constitutions*, Binder xv.

33 Ibid., Art. 3. Though it does not specifically mention taxation, Art. 3 states that 'the Cantons are sovereign in so far as their sovereignty is not limited by the Federal Constitution, and, as such, they exercise all rights which are not transferred to the federal power.'

34 Ibid., Art. 118–23

35 From time to time additional articles of temporary duration are added to the Constitution after having been accepted in a referendum. The 1958 provisions are contained in the 'Über-gangsbestimmungen' (Transitory Provisions), Art. 8, *Bundesverfassung*. See also Dafflon, *Federal Finance in Theory and Practice with Special Reference to Switzerland* (Bern: Paul Haupt, 1977), at 82–3. These provisions as amended (see Seigenthaler, 'Switzerland: recent constitutional amendments' (1982). In Flanz and Klein, 'Switzerland') remain in force as of March 1982.

36 *Bundesverfassung*, Art. 41 as amended. See also Bieri, *Fiscal Federalsim in Switzerland* (Canberra: Centre for Research on Federal Financial Relations Research Monograph 26, The Australian National University, 1979), at 50.

37 *Bundesverfassung*, Art. 46.

income has generous exemptions and deductions and therefore tends to burden only middle- and upper-income groups in the economy. Separate communal taxes on personal income and net worth normally take the form of a tax supplement or surcharge on the cantonal tax that is applied. Not counting the communes, there are twenty-six independent taxing authorities in Switzerland, a situation which gives rise to fairly large income tax differentials between and within the cantons. According to Bieri, these differentials have fostered a climate of tax competition among the cantons, one effect of which has been a continuous effort to shift some expenditure burdens to the federal government. Tax competition has apparently made it difficult for the cantons to take full advantage of their traditional tax bases.[38]

For the corporate income tax levied both by the cantons and the federal government, the location of the company's head office, or the site of effective management, is used as the criterion to determine nexus. In lieu of some apportionment formula, the courts in Switzerland decide on a case-by-case basis the intercantonal division of the tax base for multicantonal firms. Although cantonal corporate tax burdens vary a great deal, it is felt that because they represent only a small element in total cost they may not be a significant factor in distorting the locational decisions made by firms.

The federal government distributes both conditional and unconditional grants to the cantons (Table 3). Approximately 10 per cent of total federal revenue is shared with the cantons on an unconditional basis. As shown in Table 3, a number of different income and excise taxes are shared between the federal and cantonal governments. Although some portion of each of these shared sources of revenue is distributed on the basis of origin, a significant fraction of each source is allocated on the basis of population or below-average fiscal capacity and therefore contains a large element of fiscal equalization.[39] Moreover, the size of the federal conditional grants made to the cantons also depends in part on their financial strength. Because of their emphasis on equalization, federal grants of both types alleviate the disparities in intercantonal tax rates. Since 1977 tax harmonization has been assisted by a movement towards formal harmonization, the adoption of common tax bases and unified collection procedures between the cantons and the federal government.[40] It was felt that only a small sacrifice of fiscal autonomy was required to obtain

38 Bieri, *Fiscal Federalism*
39 *Bundesverfassung*, Art. 42 ter. See also Bieri, *Fiscal Federalism*, at 57
40 Art. 42 quinques, providing for the harmonization of direct taxes was adopted as an amendment to the Constitution in the referendum of 12 June 1977. See Siegenthaler, 'Switzerland'.

TABLE 3

Tax-sharing in Switzerland (1976)

Federal tax	Percentage shared with cantons	Basis of sharing formula
Military service exemption	20	Origin
Anticipatory (dividends)	10	One-half on population; one-half to fiscally weak cantons
Distilled liquor	50	Population
Stamp duties	20	Population
Federal defence (income)	30	One-quarter on origin basis, the other five percentage points to fiscally weak cantons

SOURCE: Duss and Bird, 'Switzerland's tax jungle,' (1979) 27 *Canadian Tax Journal* 46, at 53-4

significant administrative and compliance economies. The next stage of harmonization, the adoption of common tax rates referred to by Duss and Bird as material harmonization, makes sense only if it has been preceded by formal harmonization.[41] Even if this next stage is never reached, it is noteworthy that discussion of tax reform in Switzerland frequently recommends a system of tax supplements like that in Canada.

CANADA COMPARED TO OTHER FEDERATIONS

Table 4 presents a typology of alternative approaches to tax harmonization that have been observed in different federal systems. The main features of each approach are assessed in terms of their contribution to vertical and horizontal tax co-ordination, the achievement of financial autonomy on the part of subfederal units, and their ability to realize scale economies in tax administration. The most centralized approaches to tax harmonization are represented by the policy choices of Australia and West Germany. All the harmonization advantages of Australian tax separation are also present in the West German system of tax sharing. The tax-sharing approach, however, offers the additional advantage that states will not be denied access to sufficient revenue sources to finance their expenditure needs. It is not too surprising, then, to discover that Australia has

41 Duss and Bird, 'Switzerland's tax jungle' (1979), 27 *Canadian Tax Journal* 46, at 64–6

TABLE 4

Different approaches to tax harmonization

			Tax overlapping		
Main features	Tax separation (Australia)	Tax sharing (West Germany)	(Canada)	(United States)	'Tax jungle' (Switzerland)
State tax base conformity	Yes	Yes	Yes†	Very little	None
State tax rate uniformity	Yes	Yes	No	No	No
State tax revenues more or less match expenditures	No	Yes	Yes	Yes	Yes
Equalizing grants made by the federal government	Yes	No*	Yes	Yes	Yes
Single tax administration and collection	Yes	Yes	Yes†	No	No

* Revenues are redistributed by formula directly from rich to poor states.

† Ontario and Quebec conform closely with respect to corporate income taxes. Quebec's tax base for the individual income tax diverges from the rest of the country.

recently abandoned tax separation in favour of a scheme of tax sharing. Since World War II, Canada has passed through separate stages of tax separation and tax sharing and is currently in a stage of concurrent taxation in which there is considerable tax overlapping between federal and subfederal units of governments.

Concurrent taxation characterizes the fiscal systems of both Canada and the United States. Although each Canadian province and American state has the power to determine its own tax rates, there is still a considerably greater degree of tax harmonization in Canada than in the United States.[42] Apart from a few exceptions, there is considerable tax base conformity across the provinces in Canada because of the unifying influence of the tax collection agreements negotiated since 1962. Since then nine of the ten provinces have accepted the federal definition of taxable income by applying their own tax rates to the amount of federal taxes payable. This system of provincial tax supplements allows the federal tax collection apparatus to serve as a provincial tax collector

42 For a more detailed description of the process of tax harmonization in Canada see Thirsk, 'Tax harmonization in Canada' in George F. Break, ed., *State and Local Finance in the 80s* (Madison: University of Wisconsin Press, 1983).

and is supported by a revenue-protection guarantee which preserves provincial tax revenues against legislative changes in federal taxation. Eight of the ten provinces also allow the federal government to collect their own corporate income taxes using the same definition of income and a common set of allocation rules for apportioning the income of multiprovincial companies. Each province sets whatever rate of taxation it considers to be appropriate. Although recent American legislation has enabled the states to adopt the Canadian model of tax supplements,[43] the more common co-ordinating device employed in that country is either the federal tax deduction or the federal tax credit for state taxes paid. Concurrent taxation also exists in Switzerland, which with the most decentralized tax system of all the ones surveyed has been described as a tax jungle.[44] Despite the impressive absence of tax co-ordination, however, steps have been recently taken to achieve the formal harmonization of tax bases between the cantons and the federal government. When these measures are in place, the fiscal system in Switzerland will bear a much closer resemblance to that of Canada. In summary, Canada's approach to tax harmonization is a middle-of-the-road one, in which it has sought to escape the rigidities of more centralized approaches and the dangers of more decentralized ones. In fact, changes are being introduced into the U.S. and Swiss fiscal systems which will more closely align them with Canada's current approach.

Different attitudes towards tax competition
An important but neglected factor in explaining international differences in the approach to fiscal harmonization is the extent to which there are similar preferences for the provision of public services. The more homogeneous are views of the appropriate size of the public sector, the smaller will be the loss of expenditure efficiency from adopting more centralized approaches to fiscal harmonization. In this situation most of the gains from fiscal harmonization will occur on the tax side of the public sector budget. Hunter, for instance, claims that the lack of major cultural or linguistic differences among the various Australian states has led to a widespread consensus on both the level and pattern of public services that should prevail in every part of the federation.[45] Hunter also notes that in the case of the West German federation a high priority is attached to the achievement of uniform living standards in all parts of the country.[46] Similar levels of public sector spending have been viewed as an integral part of the process by

43 Federal-State Tax Collection Act of 1972, 86 Stat. 936. Title 2
44 Duss and Bird, 'Switzerland's tax jungle'
45 Hunter, 'Intergovernmental fiscal adjustment,' at 427
46 Hunter, *Revenue Sharing*, at 18–21

which uniform living standards may be attained. Given this emphasis on uniform government spending, governments have paid more attention to the inefficiencies of non-uniform tax rates and the possible destruction of subfederal tax bases which could occur as a result of tax competition. In Canada as well as Switzerland, distinct cultural and linguistic groups exist which probably contribute to greater diversity in expectations for the public sector and make it worthwhile to tolerate the economic inefficiency arising from non-uniform tax rates. Similarly, the United States has always laid great store on the virtues and benefits of subfederal expenditure autonomy and has therefore been unwilling to sacrifice this flexibility for the sake of greater tax uniformity.

In countries that have not attempted to control tax competition, such as the United States and Switzerland, there is a deep-seated belief that the process of tax competition itself will prevent tax rates in one jurisdiction from diverging very far from the levels set in other jurisdictions. In this sense, tax competition itself is viewed as a force leading towards the achievement of uniform tax rates. However, in this view of the matter, subfederal units can compete with one another only by reducing the level of their tax rates, so that there is an inherent bias under tax competition towards the attainment of uniformity at a relatively low average rate of taxation. In the extreme, all the subfederal units will be induced to reduce their tax rates to zero, and as a result of tax competition these units will be forced to relinquish their access to these particular tax bases. An example of this kind can be found in the recent experience of Canada in the area of estate taxation and succession duties. After the federal abandonment of the estate tax field in 1972, the provincial governments, instead of moving in to occupy the tax room created for them, went in the opposite direction and abandoned their succession duties one after the other. Prior to 1972, Canada was one of the few developed countries that did not impose taxation of capital gains. With the introduction of capital gains taxation the federal government withdrew from the taxation of estates since any unrealized capital gains at the time of death were to be considered deemed for taxation purposes. Now Canada is one of the few countries in the world which does not levy some kind of tax on either the transfer or the receipt of wealth at death.

Tax competition will naturally compel a high degree of tax rate uniformity but will be undesirable, the international evidence suggests, if it also undermines the development and growth of subfederal tax bases. Tax competition will also be undesirable if, as seems likely to be the case, it applies only to particular industries such as manufacturing. From a national perspective tax competition would cause wide diversity in industry tax rates and be an unintentionally harmful incentive to misallocate capital resources between industries.

The importance of equalization as an instrument of harmonization
As shown in Table 4, all the federations examined here rely on equalization schemes that involve the use of a formula to determine the size of federal unconditional transfers to financially weak subfederal units. There is substantial diversity, nonetheless, in the choice of formula and in the extent to which variations in fiscal capacity are offset. In Canada, the equalization payments are intended to bring every province up to the national average figure for fiscal capacity. Since these payments account for approximately one-half of the own-revenues of some of the Atlantic provinces, they clearly serve to suppress the appearance of higher tax rates in these areas. It is still true, however, that personal and corporate tax rates are consistently higher in the poorer provinces.

While the role of equalization payments in assisting the less wealthy provinces to provide public services at tax rates close to the national average is widely understood, it is less well known that the system of equalization contains a set of incentives that modify and curtail the pressures towards tax competition. The following notation is introduced to aid the explanation of this indirect equalization effect: Let E_{ij} be the equalization payment made to the jth province from the ith tax source, TR_i the total revenue from the ith tax source, B_{ij} the size of the ith tax base in the jth province, B_{ic} the size of the national tax base for the ith tax source, P_j the population in the jth province, P_c the national population, t_{ij} the tax rate on the ith tax base in the province j, and t_{ic} the national average tax rate. Then:

$$t_{ic} = TR_i / B_{ic};$$
$$TR_i = \sum_{j}^{10} t_{ij} B_{ij}.$$

Under the current approach to equalization in Canada

$$E_{ij} = TR_i \cdot (P_j / P_c - B_{ij} / B_{ic}),$$

where the expression in brackets, if it is positive, indicating that a province has a proportionately larger population than its share of the ith tax base, is a measure of the deficiency in the province's fiscal capacity. Assuming a deficiency exists initially and letting Δ denote a small change in a variable to which it is attached, a province which increases its tax rate will, if population adjustments are ignored, experience a revenue change equal to:

$$\Delta R_{ij} = T_{ij}\Delta B_{ij} + \Delta t_{ij} (B_{ij} + \Delta B_{ij}). \tag{1}$$

If the elasticity of the base with respect to the tax rate is less than one, revenues will increase. Otherwise revenues will decline. However, there will always be an offsetting gain in the equalization entitlement of the province approximately equal to

$$\Delta E_{ij} \cong - \mathrm{TR}i\,(\Delta B_{ij} \,/\, B_{ic}) \cong - t_{ic}\Delta B_{ij}. \tag{2}$$

The net change in fiscal resources for the province ΔNFR is thus

$$\Delta R_{ij} + \Delta E_{ij} = (t_{ij} - t_{ic})\,\Delta B_{ij} + \Delta t_{ij}\,(B_{ij} + \Delta B_{ij}). \tag{3}$$

Since $\Delta B_{ij} < 0$ for a tax increase and $(B_{ij} + \Delta B_{ij}) \le 0$, it follows that if a province increases its tax rate there will be an unambiguous increment in total resources only if the provincial rate is initially smaller than average. The incentive to raise rates only when they are below the average rate occurs becase a province will gain more in equalization payments than it might lose in tax collected. Conversely, if a province reduces its tax rate it can gain resources only if its rate is larger than the national average since in this case it would receive more in tax revenues than it lost through equalization. In this manner, equalization is seen to provide an indirect encouragement for the adoption of uniform tax rates as well as directly making it possible.

Unfortunately, there is a basic asymmetry in the equalization arrangement since there is no comparable pressure limiting tax competition on the part of rich provinces that are ineligible for equalization assistance. An interprovincial revenue-sharing scheme, along the lines of that found in West Germany, has the merit that if a province uses fiscal incentives to attract more tax base from other jurisdictions it must automatically pay compensation to the losing governments. A scheme could be devised so that the required compensation exactly offset any revenue gain.

Federal and subfederal adjustment mechanisms
There are widespread differences in international behaviour regarding the manner in which fiscal agreements are reached between the federal and subfederal governments. In Australia the states individually and collectively petition the federal government for favourable fiscal changes, but there is no formal process that allows for continuous adjustment between the federal and state governments. According to Hunter, a major defect of the new Australian tax-sharing arrangement is that it fails to establish methods for changing the

state share in accordance with changing economic conditions.[47] In West Germany on the other hand states are able to bargain periodically with the federal government for an appropriate share of the value-added tax. In Canada an even greater degree of flexibility exists. Since the end of World War II fiscal arrangements between the provinces and federal governments are renegotiated every five years in recognition of the fact that no permanent settlement is possible because of the impossibility of accurately forecasting fiscal needs and problems. In the United States on the other hand there is a virtual absence of any institutional structure for co-operative decision-making between the federal government and the states. In fact the federal government has recently tended to ignore state pleas for financial assistance and instead to provide aid directly to local governments.

IMPLICATIONS FOR CANADA'S FUTURE

Judged on the basis of what other countries are doing or are attempting to do, Canada's current fiscal arrangement, embodied in the Tax Collection Agreement,[48] must be considered very close to optimal. The fiscal systems in other federations appear to be converging towards the model provided by Canada. The most centralized federation, Australia, is moving towards the system of tax-sharing found in West Germany, a system which existed in Canada prior to 1962. On the other hand the more decentralized fiscal systems found in the United States and Switzerland appear in recent years to have established a momentum which will carry them closer to the Canadian style of fiscal harmonization.

Though the current Canadian fiscal arrangement compares favourably with those in other countries, political momentum in the direction of further decentralization may make its retention impossible. If the status quo is rejected, the choice for Canada appears to be either to move backwards in time and revert to the tax-sharing model of West Germany or to go towards further decentralization of the fiscal system in the direction of the American model. If a closer alignment to the American model occurs, Tables 5 and 6 provide some tax base and tax rate comparisons between the two countries that may reveal a glimpse of the future. Compared to American states, Canadian provinces currently rely

47 Hunter, 'Intergovernmental fiscal adjustments,' at 434
48 *Federal-Provincial Fiscal Arrangements and Established Programs Financing Act 1977*, S.C. 1976–77, c. 10 as amended. The agreement is due for renegotiation in 1982.

TABLE 5

A comparison of provincial and state tax structures (1977)

Tax source	Provincial and state sources of tax revenue		Provincial and State Share of a given tax source	
	Canada	United States	Canada	United States
Personal income, estate and gift	26.7	16.1	40.5	16.3
Corporate income	6.2	5.2	29.3	16.0
Indirect taxes	50.2	67.5	67.7	85.8
Social security taxes	5.0	1.2	28.9	2.1
Other	12.0	10.1	88.7	90.0
Total, all sources	100	100	52.1	36.4

SOURCE: Canada, Department of Finance, *The Tax Systems of Canada and the United States: A study comparing the levels of taxation on individuals and businesses in the two countries* (Ottawa: Tax Analysis and Commodity Tax Division, Department of Finance, 1978), at 13

TABLE 6

Structure of nominal corporate tax rates in Canadian provinces and American states

	Canada	United States
Range of rates (%)	10–15	0–12
Average rate (unweighted)	13.3	6.3
Standard deviation	1.73	3.27
Coefficient of variation	0.13	0.52

SOURCE: See source for Table 5; also 'Corporate Income Taxes: Table of Rates,' 1 *State Tax Guide: All States 2nd Edition*, (CCH), at 1031 (April 1982).

much more heavily on personal income taxes and less on sales taxes. The greater dependence of American states on sales taxes seems to reflect both the absence of a federal sales tax and the fear that resort to income taxation will impair economic development within the state. Table 6 indicates that the rate of corporate taxation is both significantly higher and more uniform in Canada than in the United States. Average corporate tax rates in the United States are about 6 per cent compared to 13 per cent in Canada, although the variance in tax rates among the provinces in Canada is noticeably less than that among American states. Moreover, since state corporate income taxes are deductible under the federal corporate income tax, the effective rate of state taxation may be as much as halved as a result of their deductibility.

If the forces of decentralization make Canada follow in the footsteps of the United States, it would be worthwhile considering how the American co-ordination techniques, essentially the tax deduction and the tax credit, could be adapted to the Canadian context. For example, the nationwide benefits of a tax credit are diminished when numerous varieties of the same tax are accepted for crediting. A federal credit for a provincial corporate income or personal income tax that would be permitted only if a province adhered closely to a federal definition of taxable income would be likely to induce a great deal of tax co-ordination. Alternatively, the federal government might allow credit for provincial personal income taxes but not for corporate income taxes in order to persuade the provinces to employ the residence-based personal income tax rather than the source-based corporate income tax. If such a step was felt to be unduly coercive, the federal government might instead allow a generous credit for provincial corporate income taxes, in order to reduce the significance of interprovincial tax rate differentials and thereby limit the ability of the provincial corporate income tax to distort the allocation of resources. On the other hand, it might be argued that in some cases deductions are preferable to credits because they would grant more relief to more mobile high-income taxpayers in the economy and would therefore be more successful in limiting allocative distortions. These are only a small sample of some of the fiscal issues that may deserve more attention in the future.

It should be stressed that a comparison of policies, each having a distinct set of advantages and disadvantages, does not necessarily lead to a clear-cut public policy. Much of the hard quantitative evidence that is necessary to guide policy choices in this area is simply unavailable. Finding more efficient means to secure a given level of subfederal fiscal autonomy or determining whether a loss in expenditure efficiency is less than any gain in tax efficiency as a result of a particular harmonization technique requires careful empirical assessment. Without it, choice in these matters is more likely to be influenced by the eloquence of the argument than by its substance.

10
Personal mobility in
the United States and the EEC

John B. Laskin

In the United States and the European Economic Community a variety of actual or potential barriers exist to personal mobility between the member states of the larger economic and political unit. This paper surveys the mechanisms that have been employed to limit those barriers. Though extravagant claims have on occasion been made for the scope of personal mobility,[1] the primary concern of the paper is with freedom of movement between jurisdictions to pursue economic activity. Accordingly, it generally does not address restrictions on recreational travel; nor does it deal with mobility within a state or member state or with the position of non-citizens of the United States or of those who are not nationals of a member state of the European Community. Though the aim of the paper is largely descriptive, it concludes with an attempt to extract from the American and European Community experience some guidance for Canadian approaches to the problem.

THE UNITED STATES

Introduction
Given the importance which Americans have apparently always ascribed to freedom of movement and to freedom from discrimination by state governments against citizens of other states,[2] it is somewhat surprising that the United

---

I am grateful for the research assistance of Susan Zimmerman, a student in the Faculty of Law at the University of Toronto.
1 See for example Houseman, *The Right of Mobility* (Port Washington: Kennikat Press, 1979), at 10–20.
2 See for example Chafee, *Three Human Rights in the Constitution of 1787* (Lawrence: University of Kansas Press, 1956), at 187.

States Constitution is not more explicit in the protection it provides against barriers to movement and interstate discrimination. Its predecessor, the Articles of Confederation, did specifically recognize the freedom to move across state lines and to engage in commercial activity in any state on the same terms as its residents; Article IV provided in part as follows:

The better to secure and perpetuate mutual friendship and intercourse among the people of the different states in this union, the free inhabitants of each of these states, paupers, vagabonds and fugitives from justice excepted, shall be entitled to all the privileges and immunities of free citizens in the several states; and the people of each state shall have free ingress and regress to and from any other state, and shall enjoy therein all the privileges of trade and commerce, subject to the same duties, impositions, and restrictions, as the inhabitants thereof respectively.

Some portions of Article IV were in fact carried forward into the Constitution, and can be regarded as embraced in the interstate privileges and immunities[3] and commerce[4] clauses. Others, however, were not, and whatever the reason the result has been a 'queer uncertainty'[5] as to the constitutional source of protections against barriers to mobility, and a variety of judicial approaches to the problem. The discussion of the American position therefore begins with an examination of the major constitutional sources[6] which the United States Supreme Court has drawn upon in elaborating guarantees of personal mobility, and then proceeds with a catalogue of the barriers which the courts have found impermissible.

Constitutional sources of constraints on state barriers to personal mobility

1 The interstate privileges and immunities clause
The Supreme Court has described the primary purpose of Article IV, S. 2, of the Constitution, which provides that '[t]he Citizens of each State shall be entitled to all the Privileges and Immunities of the Citizens in the several States,' as one of '[helping] to fuse into one Nation a collection of independent, sovereign States.'[7]

---

3 *U.S. Const.*, Art. IV, S. 2, cl. 1. See text accompanying notes 7–38 below.
4 *U.S. Const.*, Art. I, S. 8, cl. 3. See text accompanying notes 39–48 below.
5 Chafee, Three Human Rights, at 188
6 The paper does not deal with all the possible sources which have been identified. See for example, Baker, 'A strict scrutiny of the right to travel' (1975), 22 *U.C.L.A. Law Review* 1129, at 1140–41, listing six distinct sources for the right to travel alone.
7 *Toomer* v. *Witsell*, 334 U.S. 385, at 395 (1948)

Like that of many other constitutional provisions, judicial interpretation of the interstate privileges and immunities clause has been less than consistent, but it continues as one of the principal protections against discrimination on the basis of state citizenship or residence.

The early view of the scope of the protection which the clause provides was laid down in 1823 in *Corfield* v. *Coryell*.[8] In the course of denying the right of non-citizens of New Jersey to gather oysters in the waters of the state, Justice Bushrod Washington, sitting as a circuit justice, confined the privileges and immunities referred to in Article IV to those 'which are, in their nature, fundamental; which belong, as of right, to the citizens of all free governments.'[9] While declining to list them exhaustively, he included among them

[t]he right of a citizen of one state to pass through, or to reside in any other state, for purposes of trade, agriculture, professional pursuits, or otherwise; to claim the benefit of the writ of habeas corpus; to institute and maintain actions of any kind in the courts of the state; to take, hold, and dispose of property, either real or personal; and an exemption from higher taxes or impositions than are paid by the other citizens of the state.[10]

The *Corfield* position, which has been identified with the doctrine that, under the Constitution, government power is inherently limited by certain natural rights,[11] would have accorded to state citizens a set of substantive rights and not simply a right to equal treatment. But in *Paul* v. *Virginia*,[12] the Supreme Court apparently rejected the fundamental rights interpretation of the privileges and immunities clause in favour of an equal rights interpretation; the object of the clause, the Court held, was 'to place the citizens of each State upon the same footing with citizens of other States, so far as the advantages resulting from citizenship in those States are concerned,' and to '[inhibit] discriminating legislation against them by other States.'[13]

The Court has made it clear, however, that the protection which Article IV provides is not absolute; it does not forbid all distinctions drawn by states between its citizens and citizens of other states.[14] But despite the longstanding

---

8 6 Fed. Cas. 546 (C.C.E.D. Pa. 1823), (3,230)

9 Ibid., at 551

10 Ibid., at 552

11 Tribe, *American Constitutional Law* (Mineola: Foundation Press, 1978), at 405–6

12 75 U.S. (8 Wall.) 168 (1869)

13 Ibid., at 180. The Court also held in *Paul* that corporations could not claim the protection of the clause.

14 *Blake* v. *McClung*, 172 U.S. 239 (1898)

recognition of the need to accommodate the interstate equality principle with the demands of local obligation and the special problems which non-residents may create for state policies,[15] the development of criteria to separate allowable from forbidden distinctions has not proved an easy task.[16] For a time, the Court exempted from the reach of the privileges and immunities clause exercises of state power which it could classify as proprietary rather than regulatory in character. In *McCready* v. *Virginai*,[17] for example, it upheld a state law prohibiting non-citizens from planting oysters in state tidelands. The state owned the beds of its tidewaters as common property, and the Constitution did not, the Court asserted, invest the citizens of one state with any interest in the common property of another. It was Virginia citizens, 'and they alone, [who] owned the property to be sold or used, and they alone had the power to dispose of it as they saw fit.'[18]

In *Toomer* v. *Witsell*,[19] the Court discounted the ownership theory as 'but a fiction expressive in legal shorthand of the importance to its people that a State have power to preserve and regulate the exploitation of an important resource'[20] and observed that there was 'no necessary conflict between that vital policy consideration and the constitutional command that the State exercise that power...so as not to discriminate without reason against citizens of other States.'[21] The more recent opinion in *Hicklin* v. *Orbeck*[22] indicated continuing ambivalence as to the role which the proprietary-regulatory distinction should play. On the one hand the Court expressly denied that 'the fact that a state owns a resource of itself, completely removes a law concerning that resource from the prohibitions of the Privileges and Immunities Clause'[23]; on the other hand state ownership was 'a factor – although often the crucial factor – to be considered in evaluating whether the statute's discrimination violates the Clause.'[24]

Apart from the specific qualification on the Clause's applicability where a state's proprietary interests are in issue, the Court has also attempted to elaborate more general standards for assessing a state's differential treatment of

---

15 Tribe, *American Constitutional Law*, at 407
16 Varat, 'State "citizenship" and interstate equality' (1981), 48 *University of Chicago Law Review* 487, at 490–1
17 94 U.S. 391 (1876)
18 Ibid., at 396
19 *Supra* note 7
20 Ibid., at 402
21 Ibid.
22 437 U.S. 518 (1978)
23 Ibid., at 528
24 Ibid., at 529

citizens and non-citizens. There has been some progress from the initial position that distinctions 'which cannot reasonably be characterized as hostile to the fundamental rights of citizens of other states'[25] would survive Article IV scrutiny. In *Toomer* v. *Witsell*,[26] the Court set out a test consistent with its view that the privileges and immunities clause was adopted 'to outlaw classifications based on non-citizenship unless there is something to indicate that non-citizens constitute a peculiar source of the evil at which the statute is aimed.'[27] Discriminations would be struck down where there was 'no substantial reason' for the discrimination beyond the fact that those against whom it was aimed were citizens of other states. But where it was animated by valid independent reasons, and where the degree of discrimination was closely related to those reasons, disparity of treatment would be permissible. Applying that test to a South Carolina statute imposing a licence fee on non-resident owners of shrimp boats of an amount one hundred times that imposed on residents, the Court held that it would have been permissible to charge non-residents a differential to compensate the state for additional enforcement costs which they might create or for conservation measures otherwise supported only by state taxpayers. Here, however, there was no 'reasonable relationship between the danger represented by non-citizens, as a class, and the severe discrimination practised upon them.'[28]

The Court has not always equated state residency classifications with state citizenship classifications of the kind reviewable under Article IV. It is now clear, however, that the terms 'citizen' and 'resident' are ' "essentially interchangeable" ... for purposes of analysis of most cases under the Privileges and Immunities Clause.'[29]

If *Toomer* 'dramatically shifted the focus of review ... from categorizing fundamental rights of state citizenship to analysing state justifications for maintaining the challenged discriminatory burdens,'[30] there has been a substantial reversal of the shift with the Supreme Court's decision in *Baldwin* v. *Fish and Game Commission*.[31] In *Baldwin*, the Court was called upon to review the licensing scheme enacted by Montana to regulate elk hunting, under which non-residents

---

25 *Blake* v. *McClung, supra* note 14, at 256

26 *Supra* note 7

27 Ibid., at 396

28 Ibid., at 399

29 *Hicklin* v. *Orbeck, supra* note 22, at 524 n. 8 (quoting *Austin* v. *New Hampshire*, 420 U.S. 656, at 662 n. 8 (1975)). Under *U.S. Const.* amend. XIV, S. 1, '[a]ll persons born or naturalized in the United States ... are citizens of the United States and of the State wherein they reside.'

30 Tribe, *American Constitutional Law*, at 410

31 435 U.S. 371 (1978)

were required to pay a license fee at least 7½ times the fee required of residents. In rejecting a constitutional challenge to the scheme, Blackmun J. held that the non-residents' interest in access to elk hunting 'simply [did] not fall within the purview of the Privileges and Immunities Clause.'[32] Only with respect to 'basic and essential activities, interference with which would frustrate the purposes of the formation of the Union,' must states 'treat residents and non-residents without unnecessary distinctions.'[33] As a sport and not a means of livelihood, elk hunting was not such activity; whatever rights or activities might be 'fundamental,' elk hunting was not among them.[34]

The Court thus appears to have largely returned to the view of the clause first laid down in *Corfield* v. *Coryell*. Where a state differentiates with respect to rights or activities which are fundamental, the 'substantial reason' test of *Toomer* v. *Witsell* will apply. However, where the differentiation is with respect to a non-fundamental right or activity, it will 'not fall within the purview' of Article IV. Apart from adverting to *Corfield*, Blackmun J. expressly declined in *Baldwin* to elaborate the content of the two categories. But in view of his reference to activities whose restriction 'would frustrate the purposes of the formation of the Union,'[35] and to those which are 'basic to the maintenance or well-being of the Union,'[36] the distinction seems to depend not only on the importance of the activity to the individual but also on the consequences of its restriction for the country as a whole.[37]

One final limitation should be mentioned at this juncture on the protection which Article IV provides. That is that like most other constitutional guarantees of rights, the interstate privileges and immunities clause is subject to a state action requirement; it does not reach differential treatment at the hands of individuals.[38]

2 The commerce clause

The commerce clause of Article I, S. 8, of the Constitution, which confers on Congress the power to 'regulate commerce ... among the several states,' also operates by implication to prohibit state regulation which unduly burdens

---

32 Ibid., at 388
33 Ibid., at 387
34 Ibid., at 388
35 Ibid.
36 Ibid., at 387
37 For criticism of the fundamental / non-fundamental distinction see Varat, 'State "citizenship" and interstate equality,' at 509–16
38 *United States* v. *Wheeler*, 254 U.S. 281 (1920)

commerce.[39] In determining whether burdens imposed by state laws are undue, the Supreme Court has, since the mid-1930s, employed a balancing approach which attempts to reconcile the desirability of permitting diverse responses to local needs with the undesirability of restricting the free flow of commerce.[40] Laws will violate the commerce clause if their effects on commerce outweigh the local interests which they promote.[41]

In *Edwards* v. *California*,[42] the Supreme Court confirmed that the interstate movement of persons could be regarded as 'commerce' within the meaning of the commerce clause, and relied on the clause in striking down a California statute making it an offence to bring or assist in bringing into the state any indigent person who was not a state resident.[43] The Court declared itself 'not unmindful' of the 'grave and perplexing social and economic dislocation' which the statute was aimed at alleviating, but held the burden which it imposed on interstate commerce to be impermissibly 'intended and immediate.'[44]

Because of the more recent judicial recognition of a constitutional right to travel independent of the commerce clause,[45] there have been very few occasions since *Edwards* on which the courts have found it necessary to rely on the clause in striking down state-imposed barriers to personal mobility. In its power-conferring capacity, however, it has proved and could prove of some significance. In *United States* v. *Guest*,[46] the Supreme Court held that the federal commerce power authorized Congress 'to legislate for the protection of individuals from violations of civil rights that impinge on their free movement in interstate commerce'[47] and accordingly upheld an indictment under federal law for conspiracy to deprive individuals of their right to travel freely to and from Georgia. *Guest* indicates that the commerce clause could provide a source for

---

39 *Breard* v. *City of Alexandria*, 341 U.S. 622, at 634–5 (1950)
40 Tribe, *American Constitutional Law*, at 325
41 See for example *Pike* v. *Bruce Church, Inc.*, 397 U.S. 137 (1970)
42 314 U.S. 160 (1941)
43 Though the decision was unanimous, only five members of the Court took the commerce clause approach. Douglas J, joined by two others, took the view that rather than be classed with 'the movement of cattle, fruit, steel and coal,' the right to move freely across state lines was a privilege of national citizenship protected by *U.S. Const.* amend. XIV, S. 1, prohibiting states from abridging 'the privileges or immunities of citizens of the United States': Ibid., at 177–8. Jackson J was of the same view, stating that 'the migration of a human being ... [does] not fit easily into my notions as to what is commerce': ibid., at 182.
44 Ibid., at 173, 174
45 See text accompanying notes 49–77 below.
46 383 U.S. 745 (1966)
47 Ibid., at 759

general federal legislative protection against individual and even state[48] discrimination against non-residents which can be characterized as interfering with the
movement of persons in interstate commerce.

3 The right to travel and the equal protection clause

Although there had been some prior indications of a judicial willingness to infer
a right of interstate travel not dependent on any particular constitutional provision,[49] the decision of the Supreme Court in *Shapiro* v. *Thompson*[50] was the first
express vindication of the right against restrictions imposed by both state and
federal legislation. The case arose when two states and the District of Columbia
denied welfare assistance to residents who could not meet a statutory eligibility
requirement of residence within the jurisdiction for a period of at least one year.
A number of justifications for the waiting period were put forward: that it
protected public welfare programs against a drain on their resources caused by
an influx of indigent newcomers to the jurisdiction; that it facilitated the planning of the welfare budget; that it provided an objective test of residency; that it
reduced the likelihood of fraudulent receipt of welfare from more than one
source; that it encouraged early entry of new residents into the labour force; and
that it apportioned the provision of public services on the basis of contribution
to the community through taxes.

The Court held none of the justifications to be sufficiently substantial to
render the requirement constitutional. The first justification, that of deterring
the in-migration of indigents, was simply constitutionally impermissible as
inconsistent with the right which all citizens possessed 'to travel throughout the
length and breadth of our land uninhibited by statutes, rules or regulations
which unreasonably burden or restrict this movement.'[51] The Court had 'no
occasion to ascribe the source of this right to travel interstate to a particular
constitutional provision'; it was one required, instead, by 'the nature of our
Federal Union and our constitutional concepts of personal liberty.'[52]

The last justification, that of apportioning public services according to past
contribution, could logically apply to all state services, and was prohibited in the

---

48 But cf. *National League of Cities* v. *Usery*, 426 U.S. 833, at 852 (1976), holding that Congress
may not, under the commerce clause, reach into the 'integral operations' of state governments.
For a discussion of the legislative potential to protect the position of non-residents of a state,
see Varat, 'State "citizenship" and interstate equality,' at 564–8.
49 See for example *United States* v. *Guest, supra* note 46.
50 394 U.S. 618 (1969)
51 Ibid., at 629
52 Ibid., at 629, 630

case of the state legislation by the equal protection clause of the fourteenth amendment, under which no state may 'deny to any person within its jurisdiction the equal protection of the laws.' As for the remainder, they did not appear to provide even a rational basis for the uniform enforcement of the waiting period, and thus likely could not meet the standard ordinarily applied to legislative classifications under the equal protection clause. But in moving from state to state or to the District of Columbia, those denied welfare had exercised a 'fundamental' constitutional right, and since the waiting period served 'to penalize the exercise of that right,' 'its constitutionality must be judged by the stricter standard of whether it [promoted] a *compelling* state interest.'[53] That standard was clearly one which the state-imposed waiting periods could not meet. The same strict standard applied to the District of Columbia waiting period stipulated by federal law, under the fifth amendment guarantee against deprivation by Congress of 'life, liberty, or property, without due process of law'; while that provision contained no equal protection clause, it had been held to prohibit 'unjustifiable' discrimination.[54]

The Court thus relied in *Shapiro* both on the right to travel itself and, perhaps unnecessarily, on the equal protection clause (or the due process clause) as well.[55] It did not express a general view on the constitutionality of either waiting periods or simple requirements of residence within the jurisdiction in contexts other than welfare; in fact, it specifically refrained from doing so, stating that some such requirements might 'not be penalties upon the exercise of the constitutional right to interstate travel.'[56] Despite the manner in which it described the right – as that of 'interstate travel' – it seemed less concerned with travel for travel's sake than with travel motivated by the desire 'to migrate, resettle, find a new job, and start a new life.'[57] Its opinion also appeared to emphasize the particularly harsh consequences for those migrating interstate of denials of welfare assistance.[58] As will be seen below, however, the *Shapiro* analysis has been applied to a variety of durational residence requirements in a variety of contexts. There has also been some elaboration by the Court of what the analysis

---

53 Ibid., at 634 (emphasis in original)
54 Ibid., at 642
55 Several commentators have pointed out that if travel is truly a fundamental right, state interferences with the right should be impermissible without regard to the equal protection clause. See for example Loewy, 'A different and more viable theory of equal protection' (1978), 57 *North Carolina Law Review* 1, at 36.
56 *Shapiro, supra* note 50, at 638 n. 21
57 Ibid., at 629
58 Ibid., at 627, 629

requires and, more recently, some apparent narrowing of the circumstances to which it may apply.

In *Dunn* v. *Blumstein*,[59] the Court struck down a Tennessee statute conditioning the ability to register to vote on prior residence within the state and within the county for one year and three months respectively. The state had argued that the strict compelling state interest standard applied in *Shapiro* should not apply, in the absence of evidence that the waiting period for voting actually deterred interstate travel. According to the Court, this was a 'fundamental misunderstanding of the law.'[60] It was not their actual deterrent effect, but rather the penalty they exacted from those who had recently exercised their right to interstate travel, which dictated the invalidity of durational residence laws that could not be shown by the state to be necessary to promote a compelling governmental interest. Though phrased in terms which could apply to any such laws, the Court's opinion did refer to the right to vote as 'basic.'[61]

In *Memorial Hospital* v. *Maricopa County*,[62] the court focused more specifically on the importance of the benefit denied recent arrivals in holding invalid an Arizona statute which established one year's residence in a county as a prerequisite to receiving non-emergency hospitalization or medical care at the county's expense. Its view of *Shapiro* was that the Court there had 'found denial of the basic "necessities of life" to be a penalty' on those who had exercised their right of interstate migration. 'Whatever the ultimate parameters of the *Shapiro* penalty analysis,' medical care was 'as much "a basic necessity of life" to an indigent as welfare assistance.'[63] In language not dissimilar from the 'basic and essential activities' standard employed in a different context in *Baldwin*,[64] it went on to speak of the right of interstate travel as 'insuring new residents the same right to vital government benefits and privileges in the States to which they migrate as are enjoyed by other residents.'[65]

Less than twelve months after *Maricopa County*, the Supreme Court took a very different approach to the validity of a durational residence requirement in *Sosna* v. *Iowa*,[66] where the statute in issue required that a petitioner for divorce be a resident of the state for the year preceding the filing of the petition. For the

---

59 405 U.S. 330 (1972)
60 Ibid., at 339
61 Ibid., at 342
62 415 U.S. 250 (1974)
63 Ibid., at 259
64 See text accompanying notes 33–7 above.
65 *Supra* note 62, at 261
66 419 U.S. 393 (1975)

majority of the Court, the case was unlike *Shapiro, Dunn,* and *Maricopa County.* In those cases, in its view, the states had attempted to justify the residence requirements on the basis of budgetary considerations or administrative convenience, and the requirements 'irretrievably foreclosed' new arrivals from part of the benefit or right they were seeking.[67] The divorce restriction, however, merely delayed and did not deny access to state courts. Moreover, it could be justified by the state on weightier grounds. Domestic relations had 'long been regarded as a virtually exclusive province of the States,'[68] and given the impact of divorce proceedings on marital status, property rights, and custody, the state could impose a durational residence requirement to ensure that the party seeking to initiate the proceedings had a 'modicum of attachment to the State.'[69] Iowa could also 'quite reasonably decide that it [did] not wish to become a divorce mill' and had an interest 'both in avoiding officious intermeddling in matters in which another State has a paramount interest, and in minimizing the susceptibility of its own decrees to collateral attack' on the basis that domicile was lacking when the decree was granted.[70] The Court never quite concluded, however, that the state's interests were 'compelling' within the meaning of the standard applied in the three previous cases. It appeared, in fact, to apply a different and much weaker standard of review. The one-year residence requirement, it said, could 'reasonably be justified'; it '[effectuated] state substantive policy.'[71]

The *Sosna* decision has left right-to-travel jurisprudence in some uncertainty. It is now even less clear when durational residency requirements will be subjected to compelling-state-interest scrutiny – a standard rarely if ever met – and when some more lenient standard will be applied. It may well be that the Court's difficulty in articulating consistent doctrine in this area, just as in its application of the interstate privileges and immunities clause, reflects the difficulty of the accommodation between rights of personal mobility and the other interests, correlated with jurisdictional boundaries, which are inevitably present when legislative authority is territorially divided.[72]

Even before *Sosna,* the Court had always been careful to distinguish between durational residence requirements of the kind it struck down in *Shapiro, Dunn,* and *Maricopa County,* and the less onerous requirement that an individual

---

67 Ibid., at 406
68 Ibid., at 404
69 Ibid., at 407
70 Ibid. Despite the 'full faith and credit' clause of *U.S. Const.* Art. IV, S. 1, decrees of divorce rendered in one state are susceptible to collateral attack in other states on the basis of lack of domicile: see for example *Williams* v. *North Carolina,* 325 U.S. 226 (1945)
71 Ibid., at 406, 408
72 See text accompanying notes 272–81 below.

simply be a bona fide resident of the state before obtaining certain benefits or privileges. In *McCarthy* v. *Philadelphia Civil Service Commission*,[73] the Court acted on the distinction in dismissing as without support in the case law a challenge based on the right to travel brought by an out-of-state resident to a municipal regulation requiring city employees to be city residents. Though the Court seemed to suggest that no requirement of simple residence could ever offend the right to travel, it did observe that 'a public agency's relationship with its own employees ... [might] justify greater control than over the citizenry at large.'[74] Durational residence requirements for public employment have, however, been struck down on a number of occasions in the lower courts on right-to-travel grounds,[75] and, as will be seen below,[76] laws which impose non-durational residence requirements for employment (whether private or public) or penalize non-residents who work in the state may be subject to review under the privileges and immunities clause.

Finally, it should be mentioned that the linkage of the right to travel with the fourteenth amendment arms Congress with a legislative power to prohibit state infringements of the right.[77] This authority has been sparingly used – its principal exercise has been in the context of voting rights –[78] but it does exist as an alternative to enforcement of the right in the courts.

Impermissible barriers to personal mobility

1 Physical mobility
The right of any American to enter, remain in, and leave any state is clearly protected against state prohibitions, despite the absence from the Constitution of the explicit recognition of the right which was present in the Articles of Confederation. However far the 'right to travel' enunciated by the Supreme Court in *Shapiro* v. *Thompson* extends, it certainly encompasses a right against state laws designed to 'fence out'[79] non-residents of the state. Prior to *Shapiro*, in *Edwards* v. *California*,[80] the Court had unanimously struck down a state statute

---

73 424 U.S. 645 (1976)
74 Ibid., at 647 n. 6
75 The cases are collected in Lee, 'Durational residence requirements for public employment' (1979), 67 *California Law Review* 387, at 388–9 nn. 155–18.
76 See text accompanying notes 87–107 below.
77 *U.S. Const.* amend. XIV, S. 5: 'The Congress shall have power to enforce, by appropriate legislation, the provisions of this article.'
78 See text accompanying note 143 below.
79 *Shapiro, supra* note 50, at 631
80 *Supra* note 42

forbidding its own residents from bringing indigents resident elsewhere into the state. While five justices were content to rely upon commerce clause analysis, which generally subjects state-imposed burdens only to a balancing standard of review, the remaining four placed the right in issue on the higher plane of a 'right to move freely from State to State' or 'to enter any state of the Union, either for temporary sojourn or for the establishment of permanent residence.'[81] This was an affirmative right of national citizenship, enforceable against the states under the privileges and immunities clause of the fourteenth amendment, which provides that '[n]o State shall make or enforce any law which shall abridge the privileges or immunities of citizens of the United States.'

As for exit from a state, the Court in 1867 held invalid a state-imposed tax on each railroad or stagecoach passenger leaving Nevada.[82] While the precise ground on which it relied was a rather strained one – that every citizen had the right, free of state obstruction, 'to come to the seat of government to assert any claim he may have upon that government, or to transact any business he may have with it'[83] – it indicated more broadly that the principle of the case could be found in the dissent of Taney CJ in the *Passenger Cases*.[84] There he said:

For all the great purposes for which the Federal government was formed we are one people with one common country. We are all citizens of the United States, and as members of the same community must have the right to pass and repass through every part of it without interruption, as freely as in our own States.[85]

The Court has held, however, that tolls and other charges levied by states on interstate travellers to help defray costs of public transportation facilities do not offend this principle.[86]

2 Work

From its first interpretation in *Corfield* v. *Coryell*,[87] the interstate privileges and immunities clause of Article IV of the Constitution has been construed as conferring the right 'to travel to another State for purposes of employment free

---

81 See note 43 above.
82 *Crandall* v. *Nevada*, 73 U.S. (6 Wall.) 35
83 Ibid., at 44
84 48 U.S. (7 How.) 283 (1849)
85 Ibid., at 492
86 See for instance *Evansville-Vanderburgh Airport Authority District* v. *Delta Airlines Inc.*, 405 U.S. 707 (1972)
87 *Supra* note 8

from discriminatory restrictions in favour of state residents imposed by the other State.'[88] The Supreme Court's most recent application of that right came in 1978 in *Hicklin* v. *Orbeck*,[89] a case which indicates the extent to which it could conceivably be qualified.

In *Hicklin*, the Court had under consideration an Alaska statute, known as 'Alaska Hire,' which prescribed that all oil and gas leases, easements, or right-of-way permits for oil or gas pipelines and unitization agreements to which the state was a party contain a provision 'requiring the employment of qualified Alaska residents' in preference to non-residents. In addition, under the regulations adopted to implement the Act, non-residents were to be laid off before any resident, provided a qualified resident was available to fill the position. The statute recited the state's 'uniquely high unemployment', and in the Supreme Court it was justified by the state as a means to alleviate that problem. The state also asserted its ownership of the oil and gas resources as exempting the restrictions which the statute imposed from the reach of Article IV.

The Court rejected the latter contention on the basis that there was little real connection between the state's ownership interest and much of the employment subject to Alaska Hire.[90] It applied to the statute the standard of review set out in *Toomer* v. *Witsell*[91]: since it discriminated against citizens of other states, it would be invalid unless non-citizens were 'a peculiar source of the evil' against which the statute was aimed, and unless the difference in treatment which it prescribed bore a substantial relationship to that evil. According to the Court, Alaska Hire met neither element of the *Toomer* standard. On the evidence, Alaska's unemployment problem was the result not of an influx of non-residents but of the lack of training and geographic isolation of Alaskans – particularly Eskimos and Indians – themselves. Moreover, assuming that were not the case, the across-the-board preference for all state residents, highly skilled as well as unskilled, was insufficiently related to aiding the unemployed.[92] The Court was careful not even to accept the premise that a state might validly seek to alleviate its unemployment problem by requiring private employers to discriminate against non-residents, or to give preference only to unemployed residents or to residents enrolled in job-training programs. In the end, however, it did leave those possibilities open.[93]

88 *Hicklin* v. *Orbeck, supra* note 22, at 525
89 Ibid.
90 Ibid., at 529
91 *Supra* note 7, at 396, 398
92 *Supra* note 22, at 526, 527–8
93 Ibid., at 528
94 See for example *Ward* v. *Maryland*, 79 U.S. (12 Wall.) 418 (1871) (merchant's licenses).

In addition to hiring restrictions and licensing requirements[94] which directly limit non-residents' ability to work once they enter the state, the Supreme Court has also found invalid under Article IV state taxing statutes which impose special burdens on non-residents working in the state but continuing to reside outside it. In *Travis* v. *Yale & Towne Manufacturing Co.*,[95] it struck down a New York taxing scheme which, while it taxed both residents and non-residents on their income from employment in the state, denied to the latter the exemptions made available to the former. In *Austin* v. *New Hampshire*,[96] a state which did not tax its residents' income earned within the state imposed a 'Commuters Income Tax' on non-residents working there. Though the non-residents might be credited by their own states with the payment of the tax, the Court held that it offended the rule of 'substantial equality of treatment for the citizens of the taxing state and non-resident taxpayers' established by the privileges and immunities clause.[97] Non-residents were not represented in the legislature which imposed the tax,[98] and to leave them to the protection of their own state legislature would invite the kind of interstate retaliation the clause was adopted to prevent.[99]

Whether the same strictures apply to limitations on public as well as private employment is not yet clearly established. Durational residence requirements or preferences for public employment have generally been struck down in lower courts as infringements on the right to travel,[100] though a durational residence preference for police employment has been upheld as relating to job performance and promoting a compelling state interest in police effectiveness.[101]

In *McCarthy* v. *Philadelphia Civil Service Commission*[102] the Supreme Court refused to apply the compelling-state-interest test, dictated by the right to travel, to a city requirement not of durational but of actual and continuing residence for members of its police and fire departments, even where the right was invoked by a non-resident of the state. The Court instead upheld the requirement as 'not irrational' under the lesser standard ordinarily applied under the fourteenth

---

95 252 U.S. 60 (1920)
96 420 U.S. 656 (1975)
97 Ibid., at 665
98 The non-representation of non-residents in a state's legislative process has been regarded as one of the principal factors leading to the inclusion in the Constitution of the privileges and immunities clause: see for instance Simson, 'Discrimination against nonresidents and the privileges and immunities clause of Article IV' (1979), 128 *University of Pennsylvania Law Review* 379, at 384–5.
99 *Supra* note 96 at 662, 667.
100 Lee, 'Durational residence requirements'
101 *Town of Milton* v. *Civil Service Comm'n*, 312 N.E. 2d 188 (Mass. 1974)
102 *Supra* note 73

amendment, and indicated that there may in general be a stronger state interest in regulating public than private employment.

McCarthy's implications, however, are uncertain. The taxing cases suggest that states do not have unlimited authority to prejudice those who wish to work in the state but continue to reside elsewhere; there the protection was found not in the right to travel, which may be limited to travel 'with intent to settle and abide,'[103] but in the privileges and immunities clause of Article IV, whose 'core concern ... is the treatment received within the state by the citizens of other states.'[104] Nor does the dictum in *McCarthy* appear to exempt all public-sector-related employment restrictions from Article IV review.[105] In *Hicklin* there was some connection, though attenuated as the Court found it, between public ownership and the employment subject to restriction. After *Hicklin*, in *Salla* v. *County of Monroe*,[106] the New York Court of Appeals applied the privileges and immunities clause in holding invalid a state statute mandating preferential employment of citizens of the state on public works projects. Perhaps the most that can now be said about discrimination in public employment is that, as the *Hicklin* Court said with respect to state proprietary interests generally, the nature of the employment is 'a factor ... to be considered in evaluating ... the statute's discrimination.'[107]

3 Professions

Like the right to pursue a trade, the right to engage in 'professional pursuits' was included among the fundamental rights held in *Corfield* to come within the purview of Article IV.[108] But despite the scope of the protection since accorded to employment and the blurring of the line which once clearly separated the professions from other occupations,[109] state-imposed restrictions on the ability of non-residents to qualify for the practice of a profession in the state have, for the most part, survived judicial scrutiny.

103 *Maricopa County, supra* note 62, at 255
104 Varat, 'State "citizenship" and interstate equality,' at 499
105 Were that the case, aliens would be in a more favoured position than residents of other states, since the Supreme Court has held that resident aliens have a right to be considered with other residents of the state for certain jobs: *Sugarman* v. *Dougall*, 413 U.S. 634 (1973); ibid., at 524–5.
106 399 N.E. 2d 909 (1979)
107 *Supra* note 22, at 529
108 *Supra* note 8, at 552
109 Note 'A constitutional analysis of state bar residency requirements under the interstate privileges and immunities clause of Article IV' (1979), 92 *Harvard Law Review* 1464, at 1470.

In the late nineteenth century a number of state courts upheld state statutes discriminating against non-resident physicians, expressing as they did a special solicitude for the need to regulate the medical profession.[110] Today, residence requirements for admission to the practice of law, whether durational – requiring residence in the state for a fixed period prior to application, examination, or admission – or simple – requiring residence only at the relevant time – are imposed by virtually every state.[111] While the appellate courts of several states have held such requirements invalid as offending the privileges and immunities clause,[112] those cases have been exceptions to the general position. The Supreme Court has never considered such a case under Article IV; in *Rose* v. *Bondurant*,[113] however, it summarily affirmed a lower court decision upholding a six-month durational residence requirement which had been challenged under *Shapiro* v. *Thompson*. Whether it could be persuaded to a different view of the right-to-travel issue after *Sosna* is highly doubtful. But the privileges and immunities dimension of the question remains open, and if the perception of residence requirements as anti-competitive devices gains judicial acceptance there may also be room for invalidating the requirements on commerce-clause grounds.[114] In cases where the requirements have been sustained, they have been regarded as promoting familiarity with local law, facilitating professional discipline, the administration of justice, and the administration of admission procedures, and providing an opportunity to monitor prospective lawyers' personal qualities.[115]

4 Ownership of property

Though restrictions on the ability of non-residents to acquire property in the state might not interfere with their capacity to move to the state 'to settle and abide' – once in the state they would be classified as residents – they could certainly interfere with travel to the state for business or recreational purposes.[116] The Articles of Conferation prohibited such restrictions before the adoption of the Constitution, and the privileges and immunities clause of Article IV has always been interpreted to the same effect. *Corfield*'s list of fundamental privileges, for example, included 'the right to acquire and possess property of every kind,'[117] and in *Paul* v. *Virginia* the Supreme Court stated that the clause

110 See the cases collected ibid., at 1469–70.
111 Ibid., at 1461
112 See *Sheley* v. *Alaska Bar Ass'n*, 620 P. 2d 640 (Alas. 1980).
113 409 U.S. 1020 (1972), *aff'g* 339 F. Supp. 257 (D.C. N.M. 1972)
114 Note *supra* note 109, at 1473.
115 Ibid., at 1480; Simson, 'Discrimination against nonresidents,' at 390
116 Cf. *Morgan* v. *A.G. P.E.I.*, [1976] 2 S.C.R. 349.
117 *Supra* note 8, at 551
118 *Supra* note 12, at 180

insured non-citizens 'in other states the same freedom possessed by the citizens of those states in the acquisition and enjoyment of property.'[118] In *Blake* v. *McClung*[119] the Court applied that principle in holding invalid a state statute which granted resident creditors a priority over non-resident creditors in the distribution of the assets of insolvent corporations.

5 Social and medical assistance

Two Supreme Court decisions already referred to, *Shapiro* v. *Thompson*[120] and *Memorial Hospital* v. *Maricopa County*,[121] have established that states may not set up barriers to personal mobility by prescribing a period of residence in the state as a condition for new arrivals' entitlement to welfare assistance and to medical services, among other 'vital government benefits and privileges,'[122] on the same terms as other residents. *Shapiro* has been applied in subsequent lower court decisions to durational residence requirements for a variety of other forms of public assistance, including veterans'[123] and old age benefits.[124]

In *Doe* v. *Bolton*[125] the Court took up an issue it had expressly reserved in *Shapiro* and *Maricopa County*: the validity of a non-durational residence requirement, not merely presence in the jurisdiction but also intention to stay, as a prerequisite for receiving medical care. Challenged in *Doe* was a Georgia statute which, among other things, permitted abortions only where the patient was a resident of the state. Though the basis of the attack was the right to travel, the Court relied on Article IV in holding the requirement unconstitutional. 'Just as the Privileges and Immunities Clause ... protects persons who enter other States to ply their trade,' it stated, 'so must it protect persons who enter Georgia seeking the medical services that are available there.'[126] It 'could not approve' the result of a contrary holding: that 'a State could limit to its own residents the general medical care available within its borders.'[127]

Despite speaking in such apparently categorical language, the Court did proceed to measure the requirement, using the standard set out in *Toomer* v.

---

119 *Supra* note 14
120 *Supra* note 50
121 *Supra* note 62
122 Ibid., at 261
123 *Barnes* v. *Board of Trustees*, 369 F. Supp. 1327 (D.C. W.D. Mich. 1973)
124 *Sheard* v. *Department of Social Welfare*, 310 F. Supp. 544 (D.C. N.D. Iowa 1969)
125 410 U.S. 179 (1973)
126 Ibid., at 200
127 Ibid.

Witsell,[128] against the justifications profferred by the state. Since the statute applied to private hospitals and privately retained physicians as well as those provided by the state, it could not be justified by the policy of preserving state-supported medical facilities for those who had supported them through taxes; and since there was no evidence that Georgia hospitals were fully utilized in caring for residents of the state, keeping facilities available for Georgia residents could provide no justification either.[129] But assuming those conditions were met, the opinion implies that a residence requirement would stand. In *Maricopa County*, moreover, the Court seemed to speak favourably of a non-durational residence requirement as a means of limiting the use of county-provided medical facilities to bona fide residents of the county.[130] Here too, then, there appears some uncertainty, though bona fide residence requirements for social assistance and medical care would presumably not deter or penalize those travelling interstate 'with intent to settle and abide.'

6 Education

In *Shapiro* v. *Thompson* the Supreme Court included residence requirements related to tuition among those which might continue to be valid as promoting compelling state interests or not penalizing the right of interstate travel.[131] Prior to *Shapiro* lower courts, applying a standard of reasonableness, had upheld both the right of a state to charge non-residents higher tuition than residents[132] and the right to fix a condition of one year's bona fide residence for entitlement to the lower rate.[133] Developments since *Shapiro* have confirmed the Supreme Court's then tentative view as to the continuing validity of such requirements.

On two occasions the Court has summarily affirmed decisions of lower courts, holding that, despite *Shapiro*, durational residence requirements need not even be subjected to compelling state interest review.[134] In neither decision was the court prepared to equate higher education with welfare as a 'basic necessity of life' whose denial to recent arrivals – or increased cost in the case of tuition – would deter or penalize interstate travel.[135] In both, the residence

---

128 *Supra* note 7
129 *Supra* note 125, at 200
130 *Supra* note 62, at 267
131 *Supra* note 50, at 638 n. 21
132 *Clarke* v. *Redeker*, 259 F. Supp. 117 (D.C. S.D. Iowa 1966)
133 *Bryan* v. *Regents of Univ. of Cal*, 205 P. 1071 (Cal. 1922)
134 *Starns* v. *Malkerson*, 401 U.S. 985 (1971), *aff'g* 326 F. Supp. 234 (D.C. Minn. 1970); *Sturgis* v. *Washington*, 414 U.S. 1057, *aff'g* 368 F. Supp. 38 (D.C. W.D. Wash.)
135 In both cases the court referred to the fact that despite the differential tuition, substantial numbers of non-residents were attending state universities: *Starns*, ibid., at 237; *Sturgis*, ibid., at 40.

requirements were upheld as a reasonable means of distributing the costs of higher education equitably between those who had and those who had not recently contributed to the state through tax payments or other expenditures.

At least superficially, that rationale appears inconsistent with the Supreme Court's statement in *Shapiro* that the equal protection clause prohibits states from apportioning state services – schools were specifically referred to – according to the past contributions of its citizens.[136] The two were apparently reconciled, however, in *Vlandis* v. *Kline*,[137] where the Court both repeated its statement in *Shapiro*[138] and recognized the legitimate state interest in 'protecting and preserving the quality of its colleges and universities and the right of its own bona fide residents to attend such institutions on a preferential tuition basis.'[139] A reasonable durational residence requirement, the Court suggested, was permissible as one element in the assessment of bona fide residence.[140] But once a student established bona fide residence, the state would presumably than be prohibited from charging him a higher tuition based on his lack of long-term contribution to the state. What the Court struck down in *Vlandis* was a statute that determined students' resident or non-resident status by reference to their address at the time of application for admission and, by providing that status as initially determined should continue throughout the period of attendance, precluded students from establishing bona fide residence, and thus entitlement to a lower rate of tuition, while attending university. It was contrary to the guarantee of due process, the Court held, for the state both to profess concern with residence in fixing tuition rates and to deny an individual, by means of a permanent and irrebuttable presumption of non-residence, the opportunity to demonstrate his status as a bona fide resident of the state.[141]

7 Political participation

As the Supreme Court recognized in *Dunn* v. *Blumstein*,[142] residence requirements which limit the participation of new arrivals to the state in the political process may penalize interstate mobility. In *Dunn*, as has already been discussed, the Court held invalid on that ground – as well as the ground that it unduly restricted the fundamental right to vote – a state statute setting up a requirement of one year's residence in the state and three months' within the county for

---

136 *Supra* note 50, at 632–3
137 412 u.s. 441 (1973)
138 Ibid., at 450 n. 6
139 Ibid., at 453
140 Ibid., at 452
141 Ibid.
142 *Supra* note 59

entitlement to register to vote in state elections. The requirement, in the Court's view, could not be said to be necessary to promote the state's interest in preventing voter fraud and assessing bona fide residence. Earlier, in *Oregon* v. *Mitchell*,[143] the Court had affirmed the power of Congress, acting under its constitutional authority to enforce the fourteenth amendment, to prohibit the disqualification of voters in presidential elections for non-compliance with state-imposed durational residence requirements, and to compel the states to permit to vote in presidential elections all 'duly qualified residents' of the state who applied to do so at least thirty days before the election. Since *Dunn*, the Court has twice given its sanction to fifty-day durational residence requirements for voting in state elections on the basis that the period had been shown to be necessary to enable state officials to prepare accurate voter lists.[144]

Unlike unduly long durational residence requirements, requirements that voters be bona fide residents of the relevant political subdivision are constitutionally permissible. As the Court observed in *Dunn*, requirements of the latter type 'may be necessary to preserve the basic conception of a political community.'[145] Durational residence requirements for candidacy for public office have also been upheld, as ensuring that the office holder is familiar with the jurisdiction he is to govern, and as giving the electorate an adequate opportunity to evaluate the candidate's character.[146]

THE EUROPEAN ECONOMIC COMMUNITY

Introduction

In the legal framework of the European Economic Community[147] a variety of explicit constraints on barriers to personal mobility serve to facilitate the achievement of a common market in labour and in the provision of services. The abolition between member states of obstacles to freedom of personal movement and the prohibition of discrimination are two of the principles set out in the Treaty establishing the community,[148] and these principles are given effect by Treaty articles relating to the free movement of workers,[149] the right of establishment,[150]

143 400 U.S. 112 (1970).
144 *Marston* v. *Lewis*, 410 U.S. 679 (1973); *Burns* v. *Fortson*, 410 U.S. 686 (1973)
145 *Supra* note 59, at 344
146 *Chimento* v. *Stark*, 353 F. Supp. 1211 (D.C. N.H. 1973)
147 For a summary of the constitutional structure of the European Economic Community, see the contribution to this volume by Graham. The Community legislation referred to hereinafter may be found, except where otherwise indicated, in *Encyclopedia of European Community Law* (London: Sweet & Maxwell, n.d.), Vol. C.; and Peaslee, *International Governmental Organizations, Constitutional Documents*, Rev. 3rd ed. (The Hague: Martinus Nijhoff, 1974) Part I, 457–543.
148 Arts. 3(c), 7
149 Arts. 48–51. See text accompanying notes 158–211 below.
150 Arts. 52–8. See text accompanying notes 212–58 below.

and the freedom to provide services.[151]

Though primarily a means to an economic end,[152] Community constraints on barriers to personal mobility are also animated by broader concerns about European social and political integration and the fundamental rights of individuals.[153] These concerns find reflection not only in the Treaty itself[154] and in the Community legislation which implements it,[155] but also in their judicial interpretation.[156] Community law leaves far less to judicial inference than the analogous provisions of the Constitution of the United States; the Court of Justice of the European Communities, together with the courts of the member states,[157] has, however, played an important role in its elaboration and application, as the discussion which follows will indicate.

The free movement of workers

1 The scope of the right of free movement
In Article 48 the treaty provides that '[f]reedom of movement for workers shall be secured within the Community by the end of the transitional period at the latest,'[158] and follows that general requirement with a statement of what freedom of movement entails. Under Article 48(2) it is the abolition of 'discrimination based on nationality between workers of the Member States as regards employment, remuneration and other conditions of work and employment'; and under Article 48(3) it is the right, subject to limitations justified by considerations of public policy, public security, or public health, to accept offers of employment, to move freely within the territory of a member state in order to do so, to stay in a member state for the purpose of employment, and to remain there after the employment is terminated, subject to implementing regulations. Article 49

---

151 Arts. 59–66. See text accompanying notes 259–69 below.
152 The free movement prescribed by EEC Treaty Art. 48, for example, is that of 'workers' and not of 'persons.'
153 Wyatt and Dashwood, *The Substantive Law of the EEC* (London: Sweet & Maxwell, 1980), at 126. For criticism of the narrowly economic focus of the implementation of personal mobility, see Durand, 'European Citizenship' (1979), 4 *European Law Review* 3.
154 See Art. 2, referring to 'closer relations between the States belonging to it' as one of the goals of the common market.
155 See text accompanying notes 161–2 and 206 below.
156 See text accompanying notes 207–8 below.
157 It is the task of the Court of Justice to provide member states with a uniform interpretation of the Treaty. Under Treaty Art. 177, courts of member states may, and in certain circumstances must, refer questions of the interpretation of the Treaty and Community legislation to the Court of Justice for a 'preliminary ruling.' They then decide the merits of the case based on the Court's interpretation.
158 The transitional period was fixed by Art. 8(1) at twelve years. It expired with respect to the original member states in 1969.

authorizes the Council of the European Communities to legislate to achieve the aims of Article 48, and the Council has done this by issuing Regulation 1612 / 68 with respect to equality of job opportunity and conditions of employment and Directive 68 / 360 with respect to entry into and residence in member states.[159]

Though Article 48 confers rights only on workers who are nationals of one of the member states,[160] the implementing legislation applies to their families as well, on the ground that free movement 'is a basic right of workers and their families.'[161] Family members are defined to include not only the worker's spouse and their descendants who are under 21 or are dependents but also any dependant relative in the ascending line.[162] Article 10(1) of the Regulation accords to family members within that definition the right to make their home with a worker who is employed in another member state, and in addition obliges member states to 'facilitate the admission' of relatives outside the definition who are dependants or who lived with the worker in his country of origin.

Under the terms of the directive, visas need not be obtained by workers and their families as a condition of exit from their country of origin[163] or entry into another member state for the purpose of employment. An identity card or passport is all that is required, and the state of entry must issue residents permits as evidence of the right to reamain.[164] Permits must be valid for at least five years and are automatically renewable,[165] though in certain cases of short-term employment a permit may be issued only for the duration of the job.[166] A valid permit may not be withdrawn solely because the worker is involuntarily unemployed or is temporarily incapacitated from working.[167] It appears, moreover, that despite the language of Article 48, which refers to free movement as entailing the right 'to accept offers of employment actually made,' the directive applies equally where a worker does not yet have a firm job offer but is merely looking for work; in *State* v. *Royer*[168] the European Court spoke of the right to enter and reside 'to look for or pursue an occupation.'[169] Where a worker

---

159 These enactments constitute the third stage in the implementation of the right of free movement. For a brief discussion of the gradual implementation of the right, see Séché, 'Free movement of workers under Community law' (1977), 14 *Common Market Law Review* 385, at 386.

160 There is some scope for interpretation of the term 'worker.' See *R.* v. *Secchi*, [1975] 1 C.M.L.R. 383 (Eng. Mag.), holding that an 'itinerant vagrant' who had done only casual work was not protected by Article 48.

161 Reg. 1612 / 68, preamble. [1968] *J.O. Eur. Comm.* L257 / 2; [1968] *O.J. Eur. Comm.* 475.

162 Ibid., Art. 10(1)

163 Dir, 68 / 360, Art. 2. [1968] *J.O. Eur. Comm.* L257 / 13

164 Ibid., Art. 4

165 Ibid., Art. 6

166 Ibid.

167 Ibid., Art. 7

168 [1976] 2 C.M.L.R. 619

permanently ceases work in a state other than his state of origin, he and his family are also entitled to remain there if the cessation is due to his reaching the retirement age or becoming permanently incapacitated, providing he has worked and lived in the country for periods which are prescribed.[170]

According to the preamble to Regulation 1612/68, freedom of movement requires that equal treatment 'be guaranteed in fact and in law with respect to everything connected with the actual pursuit of a wage-earning activity.' The regulation goes on to specify in considerable detail the conditions of equal treatment. Nationals of any member state, regardless of their place of residence, are granted 'the right to accept and to exercise a wage-earning occupation' in another member state with the same priority as its nationals.[171] Express prohibitions are set out against legislative and regulatory provisions and against administrative provisions and practices of member states which either explicitly restrict the employment of non-nationals or prescribe conditions, purportedly neutral, whose primary purpose or effect is to turn non-nationals away from available positions.[172] Job quotas are also prohibited,[173] as are medical and vocational standards and other requirements based on nationality that are not applied to prospective employees who are nationals of the state in which the job is located.[174]

Equality of treatment is prescribed not only in access to but in the exercise of employment. Under Article 7 of the regulation, nationals and non-nationals must not be treated differently with respect to employment and working conditions, including pay, discharge, and reinstatement or re-employment in the event of unemployment. The same social and tax advantages[175] and access to vocational training or retraining must also be made available. Article 7 extends to treatment at the hands of individual employers as well as at the hands of the state; it concludes by providing that '[a]ny terms of a collective or individual contract or other collective agreement relating to access to employment, employment, pay, and other working conditions and conditions for discharge are automatically null and void in so far as they provide or permit discriminatory conditions for workers who are nationals of other Member States.'

169 Ibid., at 639
170 Reg. 1251/70. [1970] *J.O. Eur. Comm.* L142/24
171 Reg. 1612/68, Art. 1, *supra* note 161. The same right is accorded to members of their families: Art. 11.
172 Ibid., Art. 3(1). The provision is stated not to apply to 'conditions relating to linguistic requirements arising out of the special nature of the position.'
173 Ibid., Art. 4(1)
174 Ibid., Art. 6(1)
175 In *Fiorini* v. *S.N.C.F.*, [1976] 1 C.M.L.R. 573 (E.C.J.), the Court held that the phrase 'the same social and tax advantages' should be interpreted broadly to include even those advantages not attached to a contract of employment; it encompassed, in the Court's view, reduced rate privileges for large families on a national railway.

The regulation also recognizes the importance of equal access to union participation and to housing in its provisions with respect to the exercise of employment.
Union membership and rights are subject to the non-discrimination principle,[176]
and non-national workers are entitled to 'all the rights and privileges of national
workers with regard to housing,'[177] including the right of home ownership and
access to public housing. The final area in which equality of treatment is mandated
is children's educational opportunities; children of non-nationals who are or have
been employed in a member state must be allowed to attend general education,
apprenticeship, and vocational training classes on the same basis as children of
nationals.[178]

In interpreting the equality of treatment provisions, the European Court has
been conscientious in applying their prohibitions to indirect as well as direct
discrimination. In the *Ugliola* case,[179] for example, the Court was asked to
consider whether Article 7 of Regulation 1612/68 required that military service
in a worker's country of origin be taken into account under a law of the country
of employment which provided that a period of compulsory service in that
country's military counted towards seniority on the job. It was a German statute
which gave rise to the issue, and the German government took the position that
it did not discriminate on the basis of nationality: non-Germans who served in
the German army would benefit from its provisions, while Germans serving
elsewhere would not. The Court accepted the counterargument by the advocate
general that, in practice, differentiation on any basis other than nationality
would be unlikely to occur. The Treaty, it held, 'does not permit member
states ... to derogate from the equality of treatment and protection for all
workers in the community ... by indirectly introducing a discrimination in
favour of their own nationals based on military service.'[180]

2 The public policy exception

As has already been pointed out, Article 48(3) of the Treaty renders certain
elements of freedom of movement – the right to accept job offers in another
member state, to move freely within that state, and to remain there for the
purpose of and after employment – 'subject to limitations justified on grounds of
public policy, public security or public health.' A Council directive forbids the
improper use of the exception for economic ends,[181] and there is no provision in

176 Ibid., Art. 8(1)
177 Ibid., Art. 9
178 Ibid., Art. 12. In *Casagrande* v. *Landeshauptstadt München*, [1974] 2 C.M.L.R. 423 (E.C.J.), this
provision was held to extend to entitle the child of an Italian worker to a scholarship like
any Bavarian child.
179 *Würtembergische Milchverwerkung-Südmilch* v. *Ugiola*, [1970] C.M.L.R. 194 (E.C.J.)
180 Ibid., at 202
181 Dir. 64/221, Art. 2(2). [1964] *J.O. Eur. Comm.* 850; [1963–4] *O.J. Eur. Comm.* 117

the Treaty or elsewhere for workers' mobility rights to be suspended to relieve pressure on areas of high unemployment.[182] The directive further provides that its application must be based exclusively on the personal conduct of the individual concerned.[183] Prior criminal convictions may not themselves justify restrictions on freedom of movement,[184] and procedural safeguards, including notice of the grounds of public policy on which the state relies and a right of appeal, must be afforded.[185]

The judicial interpretation of the public policy exception illustrates the tension, manifested by the very existence of the exception, between the Community interest in promoting freedom of movement and that of the member states in preserving their own standards of national security and public order. In *Van Duyn* v. *Home Office*,[186] the first case in which the European Court was called on to interpret the exception, the Court held that while the exception must, as a derogation from the fundamental principle of free movement, be strictly construed and be subject in its application to the control of Community institutions, '[n]evertheless the particular circumstances justifying recourse to the concept of public policy may vary from one country to another.' It was therefore 'necessary ... to allow the competent national authorities an area of discretion within the limits imposed by the Treaty.'[187] Under this position the British government, having taken the view that Scientology was socially harmful, was permitted to exclude from the country a Dutch national who had been offered employment with the college of the Church of Scientology.

The approach taken in *Van Duyn* – that of member state's discretion subject to Community judicial review – has been followed in a number of subsequent cases, though the Court has made clearer the nature of the justification which is

---

182 Art. 49(d) of the Treaty does caution that while machinery should be set up 'to bring offers of employment into touch with applications for employment' – the machinery is the European Co-ordination Bureau for Matching Job Offers and Applications, established by the Commission – it should also 'facilitate the achievement of a balance between supply and demand in the employment market in such a way as to avoid serious threats to the standard of living and level of employment in the various regions and industries.'

183 Dir. 64 / 221, Art. 3(1) *supra* note 181. It follows that an individual may not be deported as a general deterrent to others: *Bonsignore* v. *Oberstadtsdirektor der Stadt Koln*, [1975] 1 C.M.L.R. 472 (E.C.J.).

184 Ibid., Art. 3(2).

185 Ibid., Art. 6. Notice need not be given where to do so would be contrary to the interests of the state.

186 [1975] 1 C.M.L.R. 1 (E.C.J.)

187 Ibid., at 17. For criticism of this approach as unduly deferential to member states and subversive of European union, see Singer, 'Free movement of workers in the European Community: the public policy exception' (1977), 29 *Stanford Law Review* 1283.

required to support state-imposed limitations. In *Rutili* v. *Minister of the Interior*,[188] it stated that restrictions may not be imposed on the freedom of movement of a non-national 'unless his presence or conduct constitutes a genuine and sufficiently serious threat to public policy'[189] and described the exception as but a specific manifestation of the general principle set out in the European Convention on Human Rights and Fundamental Freedoms: that rights may be restricted in the interests of national security or public safety only to the extent necessary for the protection of those interests in a democratic society.[190] In *Regina* v. *Bouchereau*,[191] the Court added another element to the burden of justification; the 'genuine and sufficiently serious threat to the requirements of public policy' must, it said, affect 'one of the fundamental interests of society.'[192] Based on that interpretation, the English court which had to consider whether Bouchereau should be deported after his conviction on drug offences came to the conclusion that deportation could not be ordered consistent with the Treaty.[193]

3 The public service exception

Article 48(4) of the Treaty provides another indication that the free movement of workers cannot be absolute. In providing that '[t]he provisions of this Article shall not apply to employment in the public service,' it recognizes that public service positions may 'presume on the part of those occupying them the existence of a special relationship of allegiance to the State and reciprocity of rights and duties which form the foundation of the bond of nationality.'[194]

The Court has held, however, that not every position in the public service of a member state comes within the ambit of the exception. Its scope must be determined in light of the overall object of Article 48, particularly since in many member states government employees have been assigned economic and social

---

188 [1976] 1 C.M.L.R. 140 (E.C.J.)
189 Ibid., at 155
190 Ibid. The principle that rights should be restricted no more than is necessary is known in Community jurisprudence as 'proportionality': see Wyatt and Dashwood, *The Substantive Law of the EEC*, at 152–3. The underlying idea is very similar to that underlying 'compelling state interest' review in the United States, as illustrated in *Shapiro* v. *Thompson*, *supra* note 50.
191 (1977), 15 C.M.L.R. 214 (E.C.J.)
192 Ibid., at 221
193 An account of the decision appears in Usher, 'How fundamental is public policy?' [1977] 2 *European Law Review* 499, at 452.
194 *Re Public Employees Commission* v. *Belgium*, [1981] 2 CMLR 413 (E.C.J.)

roles which fall outside the typical functions of the public service. Accordingly, the Court will not defer to member states' own definitions of who is a public servant in interpreting Article 48(4); the Court's classification 'depends on whether or not the posts in question are typical of the specific activities of the public service in so far as the exercise of powers conferred by public law and responsibility for safeguarding the general interests of the State are vested in it.'[195]

4 Social security

The provisions of the Treaty recognize expressly what the United States Supreme Court observed in another context in *Shapiro* v. *Thompson*: that the 'territorial limitations of ... social security systems are capable of constituting an obstacle to the free movement of workers.'[196] Article 51 requires the Council 'to adopt such measures in the field of social security as are necessary to provide freedom of movement for workers' and in particular to ensure the aggregation of benefit qualification periods completed under the laws of any member state and the payment of benefits to persons resident in any member state.

The measures which have been adopted aim at the co-ordination of the various national social security systems rather than the development of a separate Community system.[197] Sickness and maternity benefits, disability benefits, old-age benefits, survivors' benefits, workers' compensation, death grants, and family benefits are subject to the co-ordination measures.[198] Discrimination against non-nationals in the payment of benefits is prohibited,[199] and member states are also generally precluded from reducing or refusing to pay benefits where a person otherwise eligible has moved to another member state.[200] Member states must take into account qualification periods completed under the legislation of another member state as if they were completed under their own[201]; aggregation thus ensures a continuous contribution record for those who work in a number of states.[202] The paying state is generally entitled to

---

195 Ibid., at 434
196 Wyatt, 'The social security rights of migrant workers and their families' (1977), 14 *Common Market Law Review* 411, at 411
197 Some commentators have described this feature of the Community's social security system as a 'weakness': see Lasok, *The Law of the Economy in the European Communities* (London: Butterworths, 1980), at 137.
198 Reg. 1408 / 71, Art. 4. [1971] *J.O. Eur. Comm.* L149 / 2; [1971] *O.J. Eur. Comm.* 416
199 Ibid., Art. 3(1)
200 Ibid., Art. 10(1)
201 Ibid., Arts. 18, 38, 45, 64, 67, 72
202 Wyatt, 'Social security rights of migrant workers,' at 413.

proportional reimbursement from other states in which the recipient has completed a qualifying period.[203] In order that the application of the social security schemes of more than one state does not lead to cumulation of benefits beyond those to which nationals of the paying state would be entitled, provisions have also been adopted to prevent overlapping benefits.[204] These have led to a rather complex case law whose treatment lies outside the scope of this discussion.[205]

Article 2 of the social security regulation provides for its application to 'workers who are or have been subject to the legislation of one or more Member States and who are nationals of one of the member states ... also to the members of their families and their survivors.'[206] The inclusion of workers' families and survivors is consistent with other implementing legislation on freedom of movement, but both judicial interpretation and legislative definition have extended the coverage of the regulation beyond those who would be regarded as workers for other purposes of the Treaty.

In *Hessische Knappschaft* v. *Maison Singer*,[207] the Court interpreted the predecessor to the present regulation to apply to a German national vacationing in France. He was killed in a motorcycle accident, and after the German social insurance institution paid benefits to his dependant it sued the owner of the other vehicle under a right of subrogation granted by the regulation. The Court was then asked to consider whether the regulation could apply to any worker affiliated to a social security system of a member state, even if he was not a migrant worker and the event giving rise to the benefits was unconnected with his work. The Court answered in the affirmative:

Since the establishment of as complete as possible a freedom of movement of labour is among the 'foundations' of the Community, it is the ultimate goal of Article 51 and, therefore, governs the exercise of the power it confers upon the Council. It would not be in keeping with such a concept to limit the idea of 'worker' to migrant workers strictly speaking or to travel connected with their employment ... [T]he system adopted ... which consists in removing, as much as possible, the territorial limitations for applying the various social security systems, is quite in keeping with the objectives of Article 51 of the Treaty.[208]

---

203 Reg. 1408 / 71, Art. 63, *supra* note 198
204 Ibid., Arts. 12, 46
205 For a brief treatment of the case law, see Lasok, *The Law of the Economy*, at 133–5.
206 Reg. 1408 / 71, Art. 2, *supra* note 198
207 [1966] C.M.L.R. 82 (E.C.J.)
208 Ibid., at 94

The legislative definition of worker, for its part, now includes all nationals of member states insured under social security schemes for employed persons, whether or not they are workers under the ordinary law of employment.[209] Thus in *Brack* v. *Insurance Officer*,[210] the Court held that a British national who had been self-employed for seventeen years but had continued to contribute to the insurance scheme to which he had contributed while employed was entitled to the protection of the regulation. The social security regulation may therefore apply, depending on the circumstances, not only to workers whose right of free movement derives from Article 48 but also to persons whose mobility rights arise from Treaty provisions relating to the right of establishment and the freedom to provide services.[211]

The right of establishment

1 The scope of the right

Article 52 of the Treaty requires the progressive abolition, in the course of the transitional period, of restrictions on the freedom of establishment of nationals of member states in the territories of other member states. The Article states that freedom of establishment includes 'the right to take up and pursue activities as self-employed persons and to set up and manage undertakings'; more generally, it connotes the right to settle in a member state in order to pursue economic activities in a capacity other than as an employed person.[212] 'To be established means to set up, unhindered, a territorial base from which the activity would be carried out. The idea combines, therefore, mobility with the elimination of obstacles.'[213]

The Treaty also sets out a framework within which the abolition of restrictions is to be carried out.[214] The Council is charged with the drawing up and implementation of a general program[215] and instructed, among other things, to accord 'priority treatment to activities where freedom of establishment makes a particularly valuable contribution to the development of production and

---

209 Reg. 1408 / 71, Art. 1, *supra* note 198
210 [1976] 2 C.M.L.R. 592 (E.C.J.).
211 Wyatt and Dashwood, *The Substantive Law of the EEC*, at 159
212 Ibid., at 182. By Art. 58 the freedom of establishment also extends to corporations incorporated under the law of a member state and having their head office or principal place of business in a member state. The position of corporations is outside the scope of this discussion.
213 Lasok, *The Law of the Economy*, at 137
214 Treaty Art. 54
215 Ibid., Art. 54(1)

trade,'[216] to ensure that workers employed in other member states have the right to remain there to become self-employed,[217] and to provide 'for the mutual recognition of diplomas, certificates and other evidence of formal qualifications.'[218] Member states are also expressly prohibited from introducing new restrictions on the right of establishment.[219]

The general program, adopted in 1961,[220] provided for the elimination of barriers to entry and residence by non-nationals which impaired their access to and exercise of non-wage-earning activities,[221] and the self-employed now enjoy with respect to entry into and residence in other member states rights almost identical with those accorded to workers under Article 48[222]; the details need not be considered.[223] There are also comparable safeguards with respect to discriminatory treatment. The general program stipulated the elimination of differential treatment based on nationality provided by or resulting from the laws, regulations, or administrative practices of member states to the extent that such differential treatment prohibited or impaired non-nationals' access to non-wage-earning activities.[224] Particularly to be eliminated were measures requiring foreigners to possess special authorization or documents, imposing on them more onerous taxes or charges, or restricting their participation in social security programs.[225] Discrimination against non-nationals in the exercise of economic activities was also to be eliminated; among the practices specifically disfavoured were those limiting opportunities to enter into contracts, to acquire and transfer property, to borrow, to sue and be sued, and to be affiliated with professional organizations.[226] The general program concluded with a timetable setting out, for various classes of economic activities, the periods within which the elimination of restrictions on freedom of establishment should be carried out.[227]

---

216 Ibid., Art. 54(3)(a)
217 Ibid., Art. 54(3)(d)
218 Ibid., Art. 57
219 Ibid., Art. 53
220 [1962] *J.O. Eur. Comm.* 36 (English translation *Common Market Reporter* (CCH) 1335). The legal status of a general program, which constitutes neither a regulation nor a directive, is discussed in Wyatt and Dashwood, *The Substantive Law of the EEC*, at 183 n. 10
221 [1962] *J.O. Eur. Comm.* 36, Title II
222 Dir. 73 / 148, [1973] *O.J. Eur. Comm.* L172 / 14
223 For discussion, see Wyatt and Dashwood, *The Substantive Law of the EEC*, at 183–4.
224 *Supra* note 220, Title III(A)
225 Ibid., Title III(A), para. 2(b) (e) (i)
226 Ibid., Title III(A), para. 3(a) (d) (f) (h) (i)
227 Ibid., Title IV

Within the transitional period a large number of detailed directives were issued to implement the general program in a variety of areas, including wholesale trade,[228] mining and quarrying,[229] manufacturing,[230] agriculture,[231] and the film industry.[232] The directives usually contained not only prohibitions against certain classes of restrictions but also specific prohibitions aimed at particular restrictions in the individual member states.[233]

Directives had not been issued for every area of economic activity when the transitional period expired; but in *Reyners* v. *Belgian State*,[234] the Court of Justice held that on the expiry of the period, Article 52 had become directly effective to confer on individuals rights against member states even in the absence of implementing legislation, which had in fact become superfluous.[235] The case arose when a Dutch national was denied membership in the Belgian bar under a statutory requirement of Belgian nationality. The Court held that though no directive had been issued abolishing restrictions in the legal profession, discrimination in access to the profession on grounds of nationality was prohibited by the provision of the Treaty itself.[236] Since the decision in *Reyners*, the Commission has taken the view that the adoption of directives to implement the abolition of restrictions on establishment is no longer necessary.[237]

The Court of Justice has stated that with respect to entry into and residence in member states and the prohibition of discrimination on the ground of nationality, Articles 48, 52, and 59 of the Treaty are 'based on the same principles.'[238] This observation has been borne out in the Court's approach to discrimination against non-nationals in the access to and exercise of activities which come within the ambit of freedom of establishment; just as in the case of workers, indirect as well as direct discrimination is prohibited.

228 Dir. 64 / 223. [1964] *J.O. Eur. Comm.* 863; [1963–4] *O.J. Eur. Comm.* 123
229 Dir. 64 / 429. [1964] *J.O. Eur. Comm.* 1880; [1963–4] *O.J. Eur. Comm.* 155
230 Dir. 64 / 429, ibid.
231 Dir. 65 / 1. [1965] *J.O. Eur. Comm.* 1; [1965–6] *O.J. Eur. Comm.* 3
232 Dir. 65 / 264. [1965] *J.O. Eur. Comm.* 1437; [1965–6] *O.J. Eur. Comm.* 62. This and the other directives implement not only the freedom of establishment but also the freedom to provide services discussed in text accompanying notes 259–69 below.
233 See for instance Dir. 64 / 429, Art. 4(2) *supra* note 229.
234 [1974] 2 C.M.L.R. 305 (E.C.J.)
235 Ibid., at 327
236 Ibid.
237 Wyatt and Dashwood, *The Substantive Law of the EEC*, at 188. However, directives facilitating the effective exercise of the freedom, such as those providing for mutual recognition of qualifications, have continued to be issued. See text accompanying notes 246–58 below.
238 *Royer, supra* note 168, at 636

In *Thieffry* v. *Paris Bar Council*,[239] for example, a Belgian advocate with a Belgian doctorate in law sought registration for a period of practical training at the Paris bar. From the University of Paris he had obtained recognition of his degree as the equivalent of a French degree and a qualifying certificate for the profession of advocate. However, he was refused registration on the ground that he did not possess a French law degree as required under French law. The Court held that Article 52 should be interpreted as prohibiting both overt and disguised discrimination, and that the requirement could constitute disguised discrimination against non-nationals in the exercise of professional activity. The national authorities administering professions were obliged, the Court stated, to consider whether the recognition of foreign qualifications for academic purposes could also constitute valid evidence of a professional qualification.[240]

2 Exceptions to the right of establishment

The Treaty sets out two exceptions to the right of establishment. Under Article 55 it is not to apply to activities which in a member state 'are connected, even occasionally, with the exercise of official authority.' Under Article 56 it does not apply to any 'special treatment for foreign nationals on grounds of public policy, public security on public health.'

The latter exception is spelled out in the same directive as applies to the analogous exception in Article 48(3), and its content is therefore the same.[241] The Court has held that the official-authority exception, too, should be strictly construed, 'having regard to the fundamental character of freedom of establishment.'[242] In *Reyners* it was argued that the whole profession of advocate was exempt from the right of establishment under Article 55 on the ground that the profession was intimately connected with the public administration of justice.[243] The Court limited the exception to particular activities connected directly and specifically with the exercise of official authority; it could encompass an entire profession only where those activities could not be separated out.[244] It observed that most activities of advocates, such as consultation and representation in court, were insufficiently connected with the exercise of official authority to justify member states' restricting them to their own nationals.[245]

239 [1977] 2 c.m.l.r. 373 (e.c.j.)
240 Ibid., at 403–4
241 Dir. 64 / 221, *supra* note 181. See text accompanying notes 181–93 above.
242 *Reyners, supra* note 234, at 328
243 Ibid.
244 Ibid., at 329
245 Ibid., at 329–30

3 Mutual recognition and co-ordination of qualifications

The Treaty acknowledges that genuine freedom of establishment 'is conditional upon the harmonization of the national rules governing professional qualifications and the admission to professional bodies which by and large enjoy a certain degree of autonomy and conduct their affairs according to their own professional codes.'[246] Article 57(1) provides that, '[i]n order to make it easier for persons to take up and pursue activities as self-employed persons, the Council shall ... issue directives for the mutual recognition of diplomas, certificates and other evidence of formal qualifications.' Under Article 57(2) there are also to be directives 'for the coordination of the provisions laid down by law, regulation or administrative action in Member States concerning the taking up and pursuit of activities as self-employed persons.' The Court of Justice has described Article 57 as 'directed towards reconciling freedom of establishment with the application of national professional rules justified by the general good.'[247]

Progress under Article 57 in ensuring freedom of establishment for professionals has been described as predictably slow,[248] the prediction resting on an assessment of the procedural and substantive complications involved in harmonization and of resistance by professional and governmental interests.[249] Despite these difficulties, the first implementing directives, those relating to medical diplomas[250] and qualifications,[251] have since been followed by similar directives relating to nurses,[252] dentists,[253] and veterinarians.[254] The directives specify which qualifications in which member states are entitled to mutual recognition and also deal in detail with such matters as the minimum content of the program of study leading to a diploma and the use of academic titles.

Directives have not yet been adopted with respect to the qualifications of lawyers,[255] though Community legislation does exist to facilitate their exercise of

---

246 Lasok, *The Law of the Economy*, at 141

247 *Thieffry, supra* note 239, at 403

248 Wyatt and Dashwood, *The Substantive Law of the EEC*, at 193

249 Orzack, 'Educators, practitioners and politicians in the European Common Market' (1980), 9 *Higher Education* 307, at 320

250 Dir. 75 / 362. [1975] *O.J. Eur. Comm.* L167 / 1

251 Dir. 75 / 363. [1975] *O.J. Eur. Comm.* L169 / 14

252 Dir. 77 / 452, 77 / 453. [1977] *O.J. Eur. Comm.* L176 / 1, [1977] *O.J. Eur. Comm.* L176 / 8

253 Dir. 78 / 686, 78 / 687. [1978] *O.J. Eur. Comm.* L233 / 1, [1978] *O.J. Eur. Comm.* L233 / 10

254 Dir. 78 / 1026, 78 / 1927. [1978] *O.J. Eur. Comm.* L362 / 1, [1978] *O.J. Eur. Comm.* 362 / 7. There is also a directive (Dir. 77–796. [1977] *O.J. Eur. Comm.* L334 / 37) with respect to the qualifications of goods haulage operators and road passenger transport operators.

255 For an account of some of the difficulties in harmonization peculiar to the legal profession, see Bronkhorst, 'Lawyers' freedom under the new directive,' [1977] 2 *European Law Review* 224, at 224–6; Edwards, 'The provision of services by lawyers' (1977), 22 *Journal of the Law Society of Scotland* 188, at 188–90.

the right to provide services conferred by Article 59.[256] The Court held in *Thieffry*,[257] however, that even in the absence of directives under Article 57 the non-recognition of foreign diplomas may constitute discrimination prohibited by Article 52. But without express provisions for mutual recognition, recognition of foreign qualifications will not be automatic.[258]

The freedom to provide services

In Article 59 the Treaty requires the progressive abolition, within the transitional period, of 'restrictions on freedom to provide services ... in respect of nationals of Member States who are established in a State of the Community other than that of the person for whom the services are intended.' Article 60 provides that services come within the ambit of the Treaty where they are normally provided for remuneration, and defines them to include, in particular, industrial, commercial, and professional activities, as well as activities of craftsmen.

The Treaty provisions relating to freedom to provide service thus encompass the same activities as those protected by the right of establishment; which set of provisions will apply will depend on the extent to which a non-national engaged in non-wage-earning activity has become permanently integrated into the economy of another member state, or instead is merely pursuing the activity on a temporary basis.[259] Article 60 suggests the distinction, in stipulating that '[w]ithout prejudice to the provisions of the Chapter relating to the right of establishment, the person providing a service may, in order to do so, temporarily pursue his activity in the State where the service is provided, under the same conditions as are imposed by that State on its own nationals.' In any event it is fair to say that Articles 48, 52, and 59, with limited exceptions, constitute 'an integrated whole embracing all economic activities, whether carried on by the employed or the self-employed, regardless of the stage of production, distribution or provision of services concerned, and irrespective of the place of business of a supplier undertaking relative to that of its customers.'[260]

As befits the relationship between the freedom of establishment and the freedom to provide services, the Community's legal regime applying to the latter

---

256 See text accompanying notes 259–69 below.
257 *Supra* note 239
258 Cf. *Ministère Public* v. *Auer*, [1979] 2 C.M.L.R. 373 (E.C.J.)
259 Wyatt and Dashwood, *The Substantive Law of the EEC*, at 182
260 Ibid., at 185. Art. 61 provides that freedom to provide services in the transport field is to be governed by the transport provisions of the Treaty, and that the liberalization of banking and insurance services connected with capital mobility should be tied to the liberalization of restrictions on the movement of capital.

either parallels, or is in fact the same as, that which applies to the former. Entry and residence are governed by the same directive[261]; the Treaty expressly provides for the same exceptions[262]; the general program required by the Treaty with respect to the abolition of restrictions on the freedom to provide services was cast in terms very similar to those of the program on the freedom of establishment[263]; and many of the implementing directives were adopted to implement both sets of provisions.[264] However, some problems are unique to the freedom to provide services. The problem of residence requirements is one; it does not arise with respect to the right of establishment, because a person's exercise of that right entails residence in a member state other than that of his nationality. The Court of Justice has held that to condition the ability to provide services in a member state on habitual residence there will generally offend Article 59, but that if no other less restrictive measures will be effective, residence requirements may be imposed to prevent non-residents from providing services in the state while flouting the professional rules which would apply to them if they resided there.[265]

Article 58, which deals with the mutual recognition and harmonization of qualifications in the context of establishment, is also stated to apply equally to the provision of services,[266] and the directives which have so far been issued on professional qualifications apply in the latter context as well.[267] As has already been mentioned, there has not yet been legislation for the mutual recognition and harmonization of qualifications in the legal profession, though a directive 'to facilitate the effective exercise by lawyers of freedom to provide services' was adopted in 1977.[268] The directive generally makes it possible for a lawyer established in one member state to pursue in any other member state the activities carried out by its lawyers, including representing clients in legal proceedings and before public authorities.[269]

---

261 Dir. 73 / 148, [1973] *O.J. Eur. Comm.* L172 / 14; see text accompanying notes 222–3 above.

262 Treaty Art. 66

263 [1962] *J.O. Eur. Comm.* 32 (English translation *Common Market Reporter* (CCH) 1545). For discussion of the general program with respect to the freedom of establishment, see text accompanying notes 220–7 above.

264 See text accompanying notes 228–33 above.

265 *Coenen* v. *Sociaal-Economische Raad*, [1976] 1 C.M.L.R. 30 (E.C.J.)

266 Treaty Art. 66

267 See text accompanying notes 250–4 above.

268 Dir. 77 / 249. [1977] *O.J. Eur. Comm.* L78 / 17

269 Under Art. 1(1) of the directive, member states may preserve for their own lawyers certain estates work and real estate conveyancing activities. For discussion of the directive, see Bronkhorst, 'Lawyers' freedom' and Edwards, 'The provision of services.'

IMPLICATIONS FOR CANADA

Though the experience of one country or continent can never simply be extrapolated to the circumstances of another, there are nonetheless some lessons to be drawn for Canada from the manner in which the United States and the European Economic Community have dealt with the problem of barriers to personal mobility. These lessons relate both to the nature of the problem and to the choice of a legal means to deal with it, and they may be even more acute now that the new Canadian Charter of Rights and Freedoms includes, in Section 6, provisions with respect to mobility rights.[270]

What the survey set out above indicates, if nothing else, is the complexity of the task of eliminating interjurisdictional barriers. It is not merely a matter of removing overt restrictions on local labour markets[271]; the potential for direct and indirect obstacles to freedom of movement exists across virtually the complete range of public policies which emanate from the governments of countries, provinces, and states. Welfare rules, property laws, tax laws, rules of professional conduct, voting rules – these are just examples of settings in which conditions may be laid down whose effect, regardless of their purpose, may be effectively to deter or penalize mobility between jurisdictions.

The fact that such conditions have been and are being laid down affords strong evidence that even where it is a widely shared value, the priority of personal mobility can never be absolute. Explicit provisions in the Treaty Establishing the European Economic Community indicate the nature of the tradeoffs thought necessary despite an otherwise firm commitment to the abolition of obstacles to freedom of personal movement. The public policy exception[272] arises only in extreme cases, but the discretion which its judicial interpretation leaves to individual member states suggests that inherent in the continuing existence of jurisdictional boundaries is an element of choice exercisable by each jurisdiction, and exercisable in a way which may adversely affect the position of those who are 'non-members' of the state.[273] In other words, the complete elimination of barriers to mobility – something which has occurred in

---

270 Constitution Act, 1982, ss. 1–34
271 That this is so was demonstrated in the Canadian context in Trebilcock et al., 'Restrictions on the interprovincial mobility of resources: goods, capital, and labour,' in *Issues and Alternatives 1977: Intergovernmental Relations* (Toronto: Ontario Economic Council, 1977) 101, at 112–18
272 Treaty Arts. 48(3), 56
273 See text accompanying notes 181–93 above.

neither the United States nor the European Community – involves the substitution of a larger for a smaller political community. The Treaty's official authority and public service exceptions[274] also demonstrate the possibility of conflict between the personal economic right of mobility between jurisdictions and the collective political interests of each jurisdiction. Apart from the explicit exceptions, the European Court of Justice has also on occasion been prepared to recognize the primacy of other interests, such as the interest in effective professional discipline.[275]

American courts, deprived of the guidance which explicit exceptions can supply, have struggled to articulate an appropriate balance between rights of personal mobility and the competing interests of the states. The compelling-state-interest standard gives presumptive priority to the former, but it has not been universally applied. On the one hand some activities and state services are insufficiently 'basic' or 'fundamental' – such as higher education[276] and recreational activity,[277] both arguably outside the economic sphere as strictly construed; on the other hand some state interests are overwhelmingly significant – in control over family relations, in the integrity of judicial processes,[278] in the qualifications of high public office,[279] and, depending on circumstances, in proprietary control of state resources.[280]

The underlying rationale for the distinctions the Supreme Court has drawn is often quite difficult to discern. In its commerce clause jurisprudence generally it is simply a restatement of the balance: in a federal system the states must be given the freedom to adopt policies which respond to local needs, but not to the extent of undue interference with the free flow of commerce between states.[281] A similar balancing process appears to underlie the right to travel, while on differential treatment of non-residents the judicial view seems to be that, prima facie, a state should be free to limit the 'benefits generated by a state program to those who fund the state treasury and whom the State was created to serve.'[282] The 'prima

---

274 Treaty Arts. 48(4), 55. See text accompanying notes 194–5 and 242–5 above.

275 See text accompanying note 264 above.

276 See text accompanying notes 131–41 above.

277 See text accompanying notes 31–7. above.

278 See text accompanying notes 66–71 above.

279 See text accompanying note 146 above.

280 See text accompanying notes 17–24 above.

281 See text accompanying notes 40–1 above.

282 *Reeves, Inc.* v. *Stake*, 447 U.S. 429, at 442 (1980). For support of this rationale see Varat, 'State "citizenship" and interstate equality,' at 529.

facie,' of course, is a substantial begging of the question. But what the proposition does show is the competing concepts of community inherent in the tension between the aspiration of interjurisdictional mobility and the urge by residents of particular jurisdictions to redistribute the wealth which they generate only among themselves.

If the balance cannot be further articulated in the abstract, and if the nature of the tradeoffs cannot be further illuminated except in concrete applications, then the question of which institutional arrangements can best deal with claims of personal mobility assumes even greater importance. In the United States and the European Economic Community there are two models which differ markedly in the specificity of the legal standards employed and the institutions which bear primary responsibility for administering them. The Americans have relied on broad constitutional guarantees, which, while supplemented to some degree by a power of Congressional enforcement, leave the applications and the tradeoffs largely to the courts. In Europe the Treaty – which acts as a supranational constitution – sets out both basic, relatively specific guarantees and a framework for legislative implementation; the courts' role, while important, is much smaller than in the United States.

In Canada the choice has been made to pursue neither of these models. There would have been attractions and difficulties in both of them. The European experience demonstrates that genuine implementation of mobility guarantees may require detailed prescriptions of a kind that courts, with a limited remedial capacity,[283] are ordinarily unable to provide. There is a profound difference, for example, between the blunt judicial instrument of a case like *Shapiro* v. *Thompson*,[284] simply striking down state welfare rules as incompatible with the right to travel, and the precise legislative instrument of the Council regulation on social security, giving positive effect to the right of free movement by co-ordinating the social security systems of the individual member states.[285]

---

283 Particularly in Canada. Compare the remedial directions given in *Brown* v. *Board of Educ.*, 349 U.S. 294 (1955), with the absence of any equivalent directions in *A.G. Man.* v. *Forest*, [1979] 2 S.C.R. 1032. The American position has evolved substantially since *Brown*: see generally Chayes, 'The role of the judge in public law litigation' (1976), 89 *Harvard Law Review* 1281. However, the Canadian Charter of Rights and Freedoms will arm Canadian courts with authority of the kind which their American counterparts have simply assumed; S. 24(1) permits the granting of 'such remedy as the court considers appropriate and just in the circumstances.'

284 *Supra* note 50.

285 Reg. 1408 / 71 [1971] *J.O. Eur. Comm.* L149 / 2; [1971] *O.J. Eur. Comm.* 416. See text accompanying notes 196–211 above.

An institutional arrangement which included a capacity for legislative implementation would therefore have had much to recommend it. But since personal mobility implicates so many areas of public policy, and since implementing legislation must itself balance the achievement of freedom of movement against other interests of the individual jurisdictions, the legislative capacity must be exercised by a legislature in which the individual jurisdictions have confidence and in which they are represented. Those conditions obtain in the European Community and, though the representation is indirect, in the United States.[286] Notoriously they do not obtain in Canada, though they could if any of the many current proposals for replacing the Senate with a second chamber representative of the provinces should ever come to fruition.[287]

The judicial enforcement mechanism, by contrast, was already in place, but apart from the lack of remedial flexibility there would have been other concerns about leaving the courts to play as unconstrained a role in Canada as in the United States.[288] First would have been the democratic concern, which again arises because of the pervasiveness of the problem of personal mobility and the inevitable tradeoffs in its implementation. Courts charged with administering guarantees of freedom of movement become substantial contributors to the making of public policy,[289] particularly where the guarantees are left relatively open-ended.[290]

---

286 See generally Choper, *Judicial Review and the National Political Process* (Chicago: University of Chicago Press, 1980), at 171–259; Wechsler, 'The political safeguards of federalism: the role of the states in the composition and selection of the national government' (1954), 54 *Columbia Law Review* 543.

287 See Task Force on Canadian Unity, *A Future Together* (Ottawa: Ministry of Supply and Services, 1979), at 96–9. The federal proposal for protecting the Canadian economic union discussed in advance of the September 1980 Federal-Provincial Conference of First Ministers on the Constitution would have permitted a reconstituted second chamber to validate laws struck down by the courts as unduly impeding mobility on the ground that they nonetheless represented desirable public policy: see 'Federal-Provincial Conference of First Ministers on the Constitution,' 8–12 September 1980, Document 800–14 / 061.

288 A very broad role for the courts was in fact contemplated by the 1980 federal proposal, ibid., which would have prohibited, subject to certain exceptions, both the federal and provincial governments from 'by law or practice [discriminating] in a manner that unduly impedes the operation of the Canadian economic union on the basis [among others] of the province or territory of residence or former residence of a person.'

289 Provincial governments have seen this quite clearly. See for instance Government of Saskatchewan, *The Future of Canada: A Saskatchewan Perspective* (Regina, 1980), at 4.

290 A general treatment of the democratic concern with judicial enforcement of constitutional guarantees is beyond the scope of this discussion. For a recent analysis see Smiley, *The Canadian Charter of Rights and Freedoms* (Toronto: Ontario Economic Council, 1981).

A second, more specific concern about primary judicial responsibility for enforcement could justifiably have been based upon Canadian courts' past performance in administering existing constitutional provisions with respect to economic regulation.[291] It is arguable that, like their counterparts in the United States, these provisions require a balancing of the national interest in the free flow of interprovincial trade and commerce against provincial interests in the control of local economic activity.[292] Though the Supreme Court of Canada may accept this view, and though it may on occasion have itself engaged in balancing, it has never felt comfortable articulating this form of reasoning and has instead adopted a more conclusory – at least on the surface – categorization approach.[293] This approach, coupled with the Court's apparent difficulty in gauging economic effects,[294] would not have inspired confidence in the judicial administration of broad mobility guarantees which – to repeat a point already made – inevitably require a balancing of interests. There was also, of course, the Court's past performance under the Canadian Bill of Rights,[295] whose restrictions on unequal treatment, it has generally held, give way to any assertion of a legislative objective within Parliament's constitutional authority.[296]

While establishing the courts as the ultimate enforcement mechanism, the new Charter's mobility rights provisions include qualifications and stipulations which fix substantial limits on the scope for judicial ordering of the priority between mobility and other values. The relevant portions of Section 6 of the Charter state:

291 Constitution Act, 1867, Ss. 91(2) ('trade and commerce'), 92(13) ('property and civil rights'), 92(16) ('matters of a merely local or private nature')
292 See Whyte and Lederman, *Canadian Constitutional Law* (2d ed. Toronto: Butterworths, 1977), at 8–55.
293 For an example of the criticism of the Court on this ground, see Leigh and Whyte, 'Two recent cases concerning the validity of commodity marketing legislation' (1974), 24 U. *University of Toronto Law Journal* 411.
294 See *Canadian Industrial Gas & Oil Ltd.* v. *Gov't of Sask.*, [1978] 2 S.C.R. 545; Pauss-Jenssen, 'Resource taxation and the Supreme Court of Canada: the CIGOL case' (1979), 5 *Canadian Public Policy* 45.
295 R.S.C. 1970, App. III
296 See *MacKay* v. *The Queen*, [1980] 2 S.C.R. 370. It has been commented that, in general, past experience with the Canadian Bill of Rights 'has not ... been successful, not simply because the courts have almost invariably failed to find violations of the Bill, but, more importantly, because their reasons for doing so have often been insensitive to the purposes and demands of a Bill of Rights': Laskin, 'The Canadian constitutional proposals,' [1981] Public Law 340, at 346. In administering the few existing constitutional guarantees the Supreme Court has, however, adopted a more purposive approach: see *A. G. Que.* v. *Blaikie*, [1979] 2 S.C.R. 1016.

6.(2) Every citizen of Canada and every person who has the status of a permanent resident of Canada has the right

(a) to move to and take up residence in any province; and

(b) to pursue the gaining of a livelihood in any province.

(3) The rights specified in subsection (2) are subject to

(a) any laws or practices of general application in force in a province other than those that discriminate among persons primarily on the basis of province of present or previous residence; and

(b) any laws providing for reasonable residency requirements as a qualification for the receipt of publicly provided social services.

(4) Subsections (2) and (3) do not preclude any law, program or activity that has as its object the amelioration in a province of conditions of individuals in that province who are socially or economically disadvantaged if the rate of employment in that province is below the rate of employment in Canada.

Subsection (4) makes a choice, one which has not been made in either the European Community or the United States,[297] against mobility and in favour of economic protectionism by jurisdictions with more than average unemployment; they would usually comprise most of the provinces. Subsection (3)(b) may also result in less protection for mobility than obtains in the United States,[298] though what residence requirements are 'reasonable' will have to be decided. In any event, there is certainly no constitutional impetus for harmonization of social services between jurisdictions, as is the case in the European Community,[299] beyond that already provided by statute.[300] It also remains to be seen whether the content of the right conferred by Subsection (2)(b) will be as limited as that of the protection against exclusion from provincial labour markets which the courts have in the past been prepared to recognize as implicit in the federal-provincial division of powers. What case law there is suggests that any provincial restrictions are permissible, short of complete deprivation of the opportunity of gaining a livelihood in the province.[301]

---

297 See text accompanying notes 42–4, 89–93 and 181–2 above.

298 See text accompanying notes 120–30 above.

299 See text accompanying notes 196–205 above.

300 Federal-Provincial Fiscal Arrangements and Established Programs Financing Act, 1977, s.c. 1976–77, C. 10, S. 17(1).

301 See the contribution to this volume by Penny, Trebilcock, and Laskin. For a more detailed treatment of S. 6 see Laskin, 'Mobility rights under the Charter' (1982), 4 *Supreme Court Law Review* 89.

But even with the relatively narrow framework of Section 6, there will still be difficult questions for the courts to address. Where Subection (4) does not operate they will, in the first place, be called on to decide which laws or practices – a term which should encompass indirect as well as direct discrimination – do in fact discriminate primarily on the basis of residence within the meaning of Subsection (3)(a). As Canadian judges are coming to hold, not every difference is a discrimination, but only a difference adopted without sufficient justification.[302] The issue thus arises as to what will justify the differential treatment of non-residents – the very issue which American courts have had to grapple with. Nor can the issue be evaded by deciding that in this context every difference should be regarded as a discrimination. It is simply moved to another plane, since the rights conferred by Section 6, like those granted by the Charter's other provisions, are not absolute; they are subject, by Section 1, 'to such reasonable limitations prescribed by law as can be demonstrably justified in a free and democratic society.'

It should be apparent that there is, perhaps unfortunately, no ready-made, coherent body of doctrine which Canadian courts can import from the United States or Europe to provide easy answers to the questions of justification which the Charter's mobility rights provisions will therefore present. American and European law is certainly suggestive of the kinds of justifications which may be persuasive, but it could never be more than that, since the values of Canadian federalism are different from those of American federalism or of European integration, and in the end the choice is between mobility and other values. Further attention to the costs imposed by barriers to personal mobility and making those costs known to the judicial decision-makers can at least help reduce the extent to which that choice is one between imponderables.

302 *MacKay* v. *The Queen, supra* note 296, at 406–7 per McIntyre J

PART FOUR: PROPOSALS AND CONCLUSIONS

11

Existing and proposed constitutional constraints on provincially induced barriers to economic mobility in Canada

Michael Penny with Michael J. Trebilcock and John B. Laskin

CONSTRAINTS UNDER THE BNA ACT

Introduction

The structure of governmental authority established by the British North America Act[1] has deeply affected the Canadian economic union. The provinces have sometimes adopted legislative and regulatory schemes that impede, or might tend to impede, the free movement of goods, capital, labour, or services across provincial boundaries. Constitutional law imposes constraints upon such provincially induced barriers to economic mobility through the federal-provincial division of powers and through restrictions which operate against both levels of government. The first part of this paper examines those constraints. The second part of the paper discusses changes in this area effected by the new Constitution Act.

In the economic climate of 1867 government intervention in commercial affairs was comparatively limited. Government revenues in British North America came largely from customs and excise taxes and, in the Canadas where municipal government had become more sophisticated, from taxes upon land. Prior to Confederation each colony maintained its own customs duties on imported manufactured goods. Income taxes and most other forms of direct taxation (except taxes upon land) were considered to be unacceptable politically and so were little utilized.

The major economic concerns of the day were the underdeveloped state of British North America's economy and the closely related problem of inadequate transportation and communications facilities. Transport and communication

---

1 1867, 30–31 Vict. c.3. (now renamed the Constitution Act, 1867 by the Constitution Act, 1982, S. 53(1)) as enacted by the Canada Act 1982 (U.K.) c. 11 and proclaimed in force 17 April 1982.

constituted the largest single category of government expenditure in the colonies before 1867.

The authors of Confederation, in creating the political and economic union of Canada, generally assigned broad economic powers to the central government while reserving social, cultural, and more local matters to the provinces.[2] Since provincial responsibilities such as education and social welfare were at that time generally less costly than federal responsibilities such as transportation and communications in support of economic development, the provinces received jurisdiction over what were viewed as the less lucrative means of raising revenues (direct taxation, BNA Act S. 92(2)). To compensate for the loss of power to levy customs and excise duties – forms of indirect taxation competent only to Parliament under S. 91(3) – the provinces were to receive substantial subsidies from the federal government. As early as 1869 the adequacy of these compensatory transfers became sufficiently contentious to threaten the existence of the new-born union.[3]

The trade and commerce power, S. 91(2), given to the central government, was also intended to be part of an overall scheme to avoid the conflicting provincial economic policies and barriers to trade then common.[4] There was a manifest concern in the speeches of the founding fathers that the recently ended American Civil War was at least in part the consequence of an improper balance of power between the states and the central government.[5]

In 1878 the newly established Supreme Court of Canada, hearing its first constitutional case,[6] had to consider the meaning and ambit of the federal power over trade and commerce. The chief justice made it plain that strong central powers had been assigned to avoid the difficulties of the American republic.[7] In that case, not one of six judges doubted that even wholly intraprovincial enterprises were embraced by the federal power over trade and commerce.[8]

---

2 Abel, 'The neglected logic of 91 and 92' (1969), 19 *University of Toronto Law Journal* 487

3 Bastien, *Federalism and Decentralization* (Ottawa: Ministry of Supply and Services, 1981), at 2

4 Scott, 'Centralization and decentralization in Canada federalism' (1951), 29 *Canadian Bar Review* 1094

5 J.A. Macdonald, speaking to the Conference of Delegates from the Provinces meeting in Quebec City, 11 October 1864, as quoted in Pope, ed., *Confederation: Being a series of hitherto unpublished documents bearing on the British North America Act* (Toronto: Carswell, 1895), at 54–9

6 *Severn* v. *The Queen* (1878), 2 S.C.R. 70

7 Ibid., at 87

8 Smith, *The Commerce Power in Canada and the United States* (Toronto: Butterworths, 1963)

Most explicitly, S. 121 created a blanket prohibition on fiscal barriers to the interprovincial movement of goods by requiring that 'All articles of the Growth, Produce, or Manufacture of any one of the Provinces shall from and after the Union, be admitted free into each of the other Provinces.' It is notable that what is now S. 121 did not appear until the fourth draft of the constitutional document, perhaps because the free movement of goods between provinces was taken for granted as inherent in the proposed federation. Whatever the reason, it is clear that a common market was the intended result.[9]

Goods

1 S. 121, BNA Act

S. 121 prohibits fiscal barriers to the movement of goods between provinces but is clearly less than a guarantee of economic union.[10] 'Articles of Growth, Produce, or Manufacture' seems to limit S. 121 to goods, since there is no mention of labour, services, or capital. The section seems to apply only to the goods 'of any one of the Provinces' and thus technically allows barriers to goods imported from abroad, although such barriers would seem to invade federal authority over international trade conferred by S. 91(2). The use of the words 'admitted free' suggests a limitation on fiscal barriers rather than on regulatory impediments generally. Finally, S. 121 requires that goods be admitted 'into' each of the other provinces, which again, technically, leaves open the possibility of barriers to the mobility of goods moving 'out of' any of the provinces – although again it is difficult to imagine provincially induced barriers that would not violate other provisions of the Act as either regulation of interprovincial or international trade or indirect taxation. In a common market members maintain common barriers against the external world and prohibit not only tariff barriers between members but restrictions on the movement of labour and capital as well. The absence of the latter characteristic makes S. 121 the statement of a customs union rather than a common market.[11]

S. 121 has generated little case law. The early jurisprudence interpreted the provision narrowly. In *Gold Seal Ltd.* v. *Attorney General of Alberta*,[12] a federal law prohibiting the import of liquor into any province where its sale was

9 La Forest, *The Allocation of Taxing Power under the Canadian Constitution: Second Edition* (Toronto: Canadian Tax Foundation, Canadian Tax Paper No. 65, 1981)
10 Safarian, *Canadian Federalism and Economic Integration: Constitutional Study Prepared for the Government of Canada* (Ottawa: Information Canada, 1974), at 20
11 Ibid., at 2
12 (1921), 62 S.C.R. 424

forbidden by provincial law was upheld. 'Admitted free' was held to mean 'without any tax or duty imposed as a condition of their admission.'

A slightly different point was raised in *Atlantic Smoke Shops Ltd.* v. *Conlon.*[13] In that case tobacco already imported into New Brunswick was subject to a tax which equalled local sales tax. In the view of Viscount Simon LC the tax was not levied on the goods as a condition of entry but was imposed directly upon the consumer. Thus it did not violate S. 121 as interpreted in the *Gold Seal* case.

A more recent case, *Murphy* v. *CPR*,[14] dealt with a challenge to a provision of the Canada Wheat Board Act[15] that prohibited unlicensed individuals from shipping grain from one province to another. The majority of the Supreme Court of Canada applied the *Gold Seal* principle. Since nothing in the Canada Wheat Board Act imposed a tax or duty on the crossing of a provincial boundary, there was no violation of S. 121.

The judgment of Rand J, however, involved a significant departure from the past interpretation of S. 121 in *Gold Seal* and *Atlantic Smoke Shops*. In his view, 'free, in S. 121, means without impediment related to the traversing of a provincial boundary,' and the aim of S. 121 was to prohibit any regulation of trade which is 'designed to place fetters upon or raise impediments to or otherwise restrict or limit the free flow of commerce across the Dominion as if provincial boundaries did not exist.'[16] Notwithstanding this considerably wider interpretation of S. 121, Rand J was also concerned with preserving federal ability to equalize the effects of market fluctuations between provinces. The Canada Wheat Board Act in effect created a producer queue for the orderly flow of wheat across Canada. Section 121, he said, prohibits the regulation of trade 'that in its essence and purpose is related to a provincial boundary.' What it does not do, he went on to say, is to extend to each producer in any province 'an individual right to ship freely regardless of his place in that order.'

The expanded view of S. 121 received the support of Laskin CJC in *Reference re Agricultural Products Marketing Act*.[17] His judgment shared the view of Rand J that S. 121 does not prohibit federal regulation of marketing which 'attempts to establish an equitable basis for the flow of trade.' The chief justice suggested that what is prohibited is 'regulation directed against or in favour of any Province.'

Traditionally, then, S. 121 has been interpreted as restricted to prohibiting fiscal barriers to the movement of goods across provincial boundaries. The

---

13 [1943] A.C. 550
14 [1958] S.C.R. 626
15 R.S.C. 1952, C. 44, S. 16
16 *Supra* note 14, at 642
17 [1978] 2 S.C.R. 1198; (1978), 84 D.L.R. (3d) 257

decision of Rand J in the *Murphy* case substituted the terms 'fetters' and 'impediments' for the older language of 'taxes' and 'custom duties' and referred to the free flow of 'commerce' rather than 'articles,' 'goods,' or 'products.' The extent to which this shift in language heralds a new and wider ambit for the effective application of S. 121 is still uncertain. The introduction by Laskin CJC of the concept of 'punitive regulation directed against or in favour of any Province' poses similar uncertainties. Does this mean, for example, that any such punitive regulation, whether customs duty or not, will constitute a violation of S. 121?

Aside from the question of which kinds of regulatory instruments are caught by S. 121 and which kinds are not, there has also been a shift in recent jurisprudence from the traditional view that 'the meaning of S. 121 cannot vary accordingly as it is applied to dominion or provincial legislation.'[18] This shift may reflect the concern that any change in the interpretation of S. 121 that tends to expand the prohibition to include non-fiscal instruments must leave room for a federal presence in regulating the flow of trade interprovincially and internationally, especially in the context of regional equalization. It may also stem from the assessment that regulations enacted by a national legislature are less likely to reflect the parochial preferences against which S. 121 is aimed than those enacted by provinces.

2 Trade and commerce

Provincial legislative authority in the field of trade and commerce extends to the regulation of commercial activity *within* the province by virtue of S. 92(13), while the federal power, 'regulation of trade and commerce,' is restricted to interprovincial or international matters.[19] Provincial laws may nevertheless be upheld even though they have 'indirect' effects upon interprovincial trade. Thus in *Carnation Co. Ltd.* v. *Quebec Agricultural Marketing Board*[20] provincial regulation of milk prices, even though it had the effect of raising the price paid by out-of-province consumers, was upheld because the extraprovincial effect was merely incidental to the valid provincial purpose of regulating transactions which took place entirely within the province.

---

18 *Atlantic Smoke Shops* v. *Conlon*, *supra* note 13, at 569; compare Laskin CJC in *Reference re Agricultural Products Marketing Act, supra* note 17, at 1267: 'what may amount to a tariff or customs duty under a provincial regulatory statute may not have that character at all under a federal regulatory statute.'

19 *The King* v. *Eastern Terminal Elevator Co.*, [1925] S.C.R. 434; *Canadian Federation of Agriculture* v. *Attorney-General of Quebec*, [1951] A.C. 179

20 [1968] S.C.R. 238

The establishment of provincial marketing boards has led to numerous constitutional challenges because the regulation of natural products to be effective must be applied not only to local produce but also to produce originating outside the province. Such provincial schemes have been struck down, for example in the *Manitoba Egg* case,[21] because they aim directly at the interprovincial flow of produce rather than merely 'affecting' such trade. One distinction between the *Carnation* and *Manitoba Egg* cases is simply that in the former the provincial regulations concerned a strictly intraprovincial transaction – the sale of milk from producer to distributor, whereas in *Manitoba Egg* the regulations sought to control the marketing of natural products produced outside the province. While this difference can be characterized as one between the regulation of production (a provincial matter) and the regulation of marketing (which, if goods moved between provinces, would be a federal matter), the judgments in the *Manitoba Egg* case also manifest a practical concern that regulations which protect local producers against the products of producers outside the province create a barrier to the mobility of a commodity between provinces. In a more recent decision a co-operative scheme created by interlocking federal and provincial legislation for the marketing of natural produce was upheld by the Supreme Court even though it employed provincial borders as the dividing line for where goods may move and where they may not.[22]

The federal trade and commerce power has also been interpreted to restrict provincial legislative activity in contexts other than natural products. Oil produced for export markets was the subject of provincial legislation in *Canadian Industrial Gas and Oil Ltd.* v. *Government of Saskatchewan*.[23] In that portion of the decision relating to the trade and commerce power Martland J (for the majority) held that 'Provincial legislative authority does not extend to fixing the price to be charged or received in respect of the sale of goods in the export market.' Whereas in *Carnation* the price was set as part of the production process before the product entered the interprovincial trade flow, here the Saskatchewan oil was produced for export and immediately upon extraction entered the flow of interprovincial or international commerce. *Central Canada Potash* v. *Government of Saskatchewan*[24] came to the same result concerning a prorationing and price stabilization scheme for potash.

---

21 *Attorney-General of Manitoba* v. *Manitoba Egg and Poultry Association*, [1971] S.C.R. 689
22 *Reference re Agricultural Products Marketing Act, supra* note 17
23 [1978] 2 S.C.R. 545; (1977), 80 D.L.R. (3d) 449
24 [1979] 1 S.C.R. 42; (1978), 88 D.L.R. (3d) 609

3 Provincial ownership

S. 92(5) assigns to the provinces the exclusive power to make laws in relation to 'the Management and Sale of Public Lands belonging to the Province.' S. 109 preserves provincial ownership of 'all Lands, Mines, Minerals and Royalties' belonging to the provinces at the time of Confederation, and S. 117 reserves to the provinces 'all their respective Public Property not otherwise disposed of in this Act.' Finally, S. 125 provides that 'no Lands or Property belonging to Canada or any Province shall be liable to Taxation.' This complex set of provisions, coupled with the division of authority over taxation and trade and commerce, creates unique constitutional problems in the context of the Canadian economic union.

The provinces have the power to regulate private natural resource production in the province if the legislation is, in pith and substance (that is, the matter with which it is fundamentally concerned), conservation and management,[25] though *Central Canada Potash*[26] made it clear that such legislation will be ultra vires where it is directed to regulating price in the export market.[27] But the Court in *Central Canada Potash* explicitly restricted its focus to the case of 'legislative and statutory authority directed to the proprietary rights of others.' This implies that in the case of legislation directed to the regulation of property belonging to the province the constitutional outcomes might be different. In fact, there is some indication in the case law that the authority of the provinces over natural resources may be stronger if the provincial crown owns those resources than if they are owned privately.

An early case decided by the Ontario Court of Appeal, *Smylie* v. *the Queen*,[28] held that provincial legislation imposing as a condition in timber leases that logs, although bound for export, be processed in Canada was valid as falling within S. 92(5). In the view of the Court the province had the same proprietary and contractual rights with respect to crown lands as any owner, and the legislature thus could stipulate whatever terms of the lease it wished. It has been commented that this analysis is unconvincing, because it suggests that the rights accruing to the province as owner extend to the regulation of international

---

25 *Spooner Oils* v. *Turner Valley Gas Conservation Board*, [1933] S.C.R. 629
26 *Supra* note 24
27 Also held invalid have been a provincial tax on export of unprocessed cut timber (*Attorney-General for B.C.* v. *McDonald Murphy Lumber Co.*, [1930] A.C. 357) and tax rebates to producers of iron ore who process before export (*Texada Mines* v. *Attorney-General of B.C.*, [1960] S.C.R. 713).
28 (1900), 27 O.A.R. 172

trade.[29] This was not the suggestion in *Attorney General for Canada* v. *Attorneys General for Ontario, Quebec and Nova Scotia*,[30] where the provincial right as owner to dispose of fisheries was recognized, but only if in conformity with federal legislation authorized by S. 91(12).

The *Smylie* rationale did not assist the government of Saskatchewan in the *CIGOL* case,[31] where most of the producing property was owned by the province. Nothing in the reasons for judgment of the Court suggests that the division of powers to tax or to regulate prices in export markets is affected by provincial ownership.

CIGOL and *Central Canada Potash* cast some doubt upon an Alberta legislative scheme[32] that asserts sovereignty over petroleum resources in the province, because it is now unclear whether legislation concerning provincially owned lands will be struck down if found to be, in pith and substance, regulation of interprovincial or international trade. One radical aspect of the Alberta scheme is the way in which non-royalty shares of oil are kept within the ambit of 92(5). This is accomplished by providing that the lease with the private producer may be unilaterally amended by legislation. Thus legislation requiring that all non-royalty oil production be delivered to the Alberta Petroleum Marketing Commission, while functionally appearing to be a regulation applying to the 'post-extraction' stage, is by unilateral amendment of the lease transformed into part of the original conveyance and so kept within 92(5). On one interpretation of *Smylie*, this would enable the province, as owner, to determine matters normally falling outside provincial jurisdiction.

With respect to regulation of Alberta's own royalty share another constitutional uncertainty develops. Control of post-extraction oil by the Commission may still be open to challenge on the basis that, once extracted, the oil is no longer 'public land,' thereby terminating the basis in 92(5) for regulation of 'the management and sale' thereof.

A final complication turns on the provisions of S. 125, which states: 'No Lands or Property belonging to Canada or any Province shall be liable to

---

29 Bushnell, 'Comment: constitutional law-proprietary rights and the control of natural resources' (1980), 58 *Canadian Bar Review* 157

30 *(Ontario Fisheries Case)*, [1898] A.C. 700

31 *Supra* note 23

32 *Mines and Minerals Act*, R.S.A. 1980, C. M-15; *Oil and Gas Conservation Act*, R.S.A. 1980. C. O-5; *Petroleum Marketing Act*, R.S.A. 1980. C. P-5. This legislation was first enacted during a special session of the Alberta legislature commencing in December 1973; see Thring, 'Alberta, oil and the Constitution' (1970), 17 *Alberta Law Review* 69, at 71, n. 8.

taxation.' The *Johnny Walker*[33] case raised the question of the liability of British Columbia to pay a federal customs duty on Scotch owned by the province and imported for sale in liquor outlets. The Privy Council held that S. 125 did not prohibit the federal duty, apparently on the ground that the customs duty was not simply a tax but had the additional purpose, embraced by S. 92(2), of regulating international trade and commerce.

This had been the leading case on the tax immunity of the province as owner until the *Alberta Gas* case.[34] In that case the Alberta Court of Appeal considered the effect of S. 125 upon a federal export tax on provincially owned natural gas. The Court held that this tax was solely to raise revenue and had no other regulatory purpose competent to Parliament. The fact that the revenues were to be used to fund the federal national energy program did not change the nature of the levy from one belonging to the S. 91(3) class of subjects (taxation) to one properly within the S. 91(2) class of subjects (trade and commerce).

It was argued by the attorney general for Canada that S. 125 in using the words 'belonging to...any Province' did not include property acquired by commercial activity as distinct from property acquired by conventional government operations. The Court found no basis for such a distinction in the BNA Act and took notice of the fact that many modern economies are characterized by extensive government involvement in commerce.

Finally, it was contended that the S. 125 immunity was applicable only with respect to 'property,' not persons or transactions, and that since the tax is levied upon export *transactions* it should not be caught by S. 125. This argument was rejected in favour of the view that the immunity from tax was applicable not only to the 'property' of the province but to the 'province' with respect to all its property. The simple expedient of taxing transactions rather than property (differing little in effect) could not be used to avoid the 'plain purpose' of S. 125. The result was that the federal tax was found to be ultra vires the federal Parliament. On appeal to the Supreme Court of Canada this decision was affirmed [(1982) 42 N.R. 361 (Laskin CJC, McIntyre and Lamer JJ dissenting)].

4 Product standards
Provincial authority over matters falling within property and civil rights undoubtedly includes the right to legislate regarding standards of quality and

---

33 *Attorney-General of B.C.* v. *Attorney-General of Canada*, [1924] A.C. 222
34 *Reference re Questions set out in O.C. 1079 / 80, Concerning Tax Proposed by Parliament of Canada on Exported Natural Gas*, [1981] 3 W.W.R. 408

commercial dealings for the protection of the consumer within the province.[35] Such legislative authority extends both to goods produced in the province and to those sold in the province since local production and contracts of sale are matters which fall within property and civil rights. While product standards could create significant barriers to the mobility of goods, it is also likely that provincial legislation deemed, in pith and substance, to erect such barriers (for example, product standards 'aimed at' restricting the entry of goods from outside the province[36]) would be struck down.

Of course the grey areas are what give rise to difficulties, as demonstrated by several recent cases in which provincial authority over product standards has predominated notwithstanding a significant federal interest.

In *McNeil* v. *Nova Scotia Board of Censors*[37] the censorship of film by a provincially constituted Board was challenged as an intrusion upon the federal criminal law power (S. 91(27)). The majority of the Supreme Court was impressed by the local nature of the exhibition and distribution of film and held accordingly that film censorship was merely part of the regulation of that business and was within provincial legislative competence. A further constitutional basis for provincial censorship was found in S. 92(16) because what is and what is not acceptable for public consumption on moral grounds, the Court found, was a matter of a 'local and private nature in the Province.'

In *Attorney General of Quebec* v. *Kellogg's Co. of Canada*[38] the question facing the Court was whether a Quebec regulation prohibiting the use of cartoons in children's advertising (pursuant to Quebec's Consumer Protection Act[39]) violated exclusive federal authority over broadcasting[40] insofar as the prohibition extended to television broadcasting. The *Capital Cities* case[41] had decided that federal authority extended to content regulation over television broadcasting, and the Quebec Court of Appeal in *Kellogg's* held that the cartoon ban was an

---

35 *Attorney-General of Quebec* v. *Kellogg's Co. of Canada*, [1978] 2 s.c.r. 211; (1978), 83 d.l.r. (3d) 314
36 *Crickard* v. *Attorney-General of B.C.* (1958), 14 d.l.r. (2d) 58; 25 w.w.r. 485 (B.C. Sup. Ct.) mentioned in Chrétien, *Securing the Canadian Economic Union: Discussion Paper Published by the Government of Canada* (Ottawa: Ministry of Supply and Services, 1980), at 20. A provincial law requiring that eggs from out of province be stamped in heavy ink with their place of origin was declared invalid.
37 [1978] 2 s.c.r. 662; (1978), 84 d.l.r. (3d) 1
38 *Supra* note 35
39 *Loi de la protection du consommateur*, l.q. 1971, C. 74, S. 116
40 *In re Regulation and Control of Radio Communication in Canada*, [1932] a.c. 304; *Capital Cities Communications Inc.*, v. *C.R.T.C.*, [1978] 2 s.c.r. 141, (1978), 81 d.l.r. (3d) 609
41 *Supra* note 40

attempt to control the content of broadcasting. The Supreme Court, speaking through Martland J, held that the Quebec Consumer Protection Act and its attendant regulations was merely a regulation of the conduct of a commercial enterprise. Its effect upon the use, by Kellogg's, of television advertising was merely incidental to this valid provincial purpose within the principle enunciated in *Carnation Co. Ltd.* v. *Quebec Agricultural Marketing Board.*[42]

Federal attempts to establish a national standard for products sold under the name 'light beer' were successfully challenged in *Labatt Breweries of Canada Ltd.* v. *Attorney General for Canada.*[43] The majority held that federal attempts under the Food and Drugs Act[44] to prescribe a 'legal recipe' for the production of light beer (containing between 1.2 and 2.5 per cent alcohol by volume) were without constitutional foundation since the legislation 'was not concerned with the control and guidance of the flow of articles of commerce through the distribution channels, but rather with the production and local sale of the specified products of the brewing industry.'[45]

Estey J also held that federal legislation could not be supported under the 'general regulation of trade' component of S. 91(2)[46] unless the legislation were to deal with industry and commerce at large in some 'sweeping, general sense.' Since 'light beer' regulations affected the production stage of a single industry and were unconcerned with any aspect of extraprovincial distribution, they did not meet this test. *Labatt Breweries* and the recent *Dominion Stores*[47] case demonstrate the federal constitutional inability to regulate product standards unless the legislation can be shown to relate to the flow of trade internationally or between provinces.[48]

5 Transportation and communications

S. 92(10) assigns the regulation of local works and undertakings to the provinces other than:

42 *Supra* note 20
43 [1980] 1 S.C.R. 914; (1979), 110 D.L.R. (3d) 594
44 R.S.C. 1970, C.F-27
45 *Supra* note 43, at 938 (S.C.R.); 622 (D.L.R.)
46 *In Citizens Insurance Co.* v. *Parsons* (1881), 7 A.C. 96 the Privy Council at 113 suggested that S. 91(2) conferred not only authority to regulate interprovincial and international trade, but also power to engage in 'general regulation of trade affecting the whole dominion.'
47 *Dominion Stores Ltd.* v. *The Queen*, [1980] 1 S.C.R. 844; (1979), 106 D.L.R. (3d) 581, holding unconstitutional the application of federally prescribed grade names in local trade.
48 For a careful analysis of these cases, see MacPherson, 'Economic regulation and the British North America Act: Labatt Breweries and other constitutional imbroglios' (1980–81), 5 *Canadian Business Law Journal* 172.

(a) Lines of Steam or other Ships, Railways, Canals, Telegraphs, and other Works and Undertakings Connecting the Province with any other or others of the Provinces, or extending beyond the Limits of the Province;

(b) Lines of steam ships between the Province and any British or Foreign country;

(c) Such works as although wholly situate within the Province are before or after their execution declared by the Parliament of Canada to be for the general advantage of Canada for the advantage of two or more of the provinces.

S. 92(10)(a) therefore catches both transportation and communication enterprises which cross provincial boundaries. In both areas too the courts have declined to sever jurisdiction over any undertakings which contain both local and interprovincial components.[49] As long as there cannot be said to be two distinct enterprises, one within the province and one of a connecting character, it is sufficient, to come within the S. 92(10)(a) exception, if the connecting aspects of the undertaking are 'continuous and regular.'[50] Air transport and radio / television 'on-air' broadcasting are two matters which have fallen within the exclusive legislative authority of Parliament, not by virtue of 92(10)(a) but because they go beyond local or private concerns sufficiently to come within the 'peace, order and good government' clause, S. 91.[51] In these cases, therefore, there is no need to demonstrate a continuous and regular connecting undertaking in order for federal authority to be sustained.

In *Winner*[52] the province of New Brunswick tried to assert regulatory authority over a United States – Nova Scotia bus line operating through New Brunswick. The province wished to protect local transport companies from competition on the more lucrative routes as a means of subsidizing service to less profitable areas. The Privy Council held, however, that because Winner conducted a single undertaking of a connecting nature even local traffic on his buses was beyond the reach of provincial legislation. Though the provinces have full authority over roads within their borders, their legislation 'will be invalid if a Dominion company is sterilized in all its functions and activities or its status and essential capacities are impaired in a substantial degree.'[53]

---

49 *Toronto* v. *Bell Telephone Co.*, [1905] A.C. 52; *Attorney-General of Ontario* v. *Winner*, [1954] A.C. 541

50 *Re Tank Truck Transport*, [1960] O.R. 497 at 508 (Ont. H.C.)

51 *Re Regulation and Control of Aeronautics in Canada*, [1932] A.C. 54; *Johannesson* v. *West St. Paul*, [1952] 1 S.C.R. 292; *Re Regulation and Control of Radio Communication in Canada*, supra note 40.

52 *Supra* note 49

53 Ibid., at 578

Transportation is an area in which substantial distortion to formal constitutional 'compartments' has occurred through the process of interdelegation; the implicit constitutional prohibition against legislative interdelegation[54] has been successfully evaded by the delegation of regulatory power to subordinate provincial agencies. Following *Winner*, Parliament transferred to provincial highway transport boards, which were already regulating local transportation undertakings under provincial legislation, the power to regulate interprovincial traffic as well.[55] Interprovincial carriers now have to meet the regulatory requirements of each province in which they intend to conduct business. Recently, in *R. v. Smith*,[56] provincial regulations that applied different sets of standards to interprovincial and intraprovincial carriers were upheld on the basis that the federal delegation of power authorized the province to impose any restriction on interprovincial enterprises that it could have placed upon wholly local ones. This decision has been criticized on the basis that the Court in *Smith* failed to look to the fundamental limitation of the original interdelegation principle, that is, that any provincial administrative board must act under legislation which has validity independent of any delegation of powers.[57] In *Smith* the validity of provincial legislation regulating extraprovincial carriers could only arise by virtue of the federal delegation of powers, which thereby actually enlarged provincial authority.

One effect of *Smith* is to affirm the validity of discriminatory practices in the transport industry since extraprovincial carriers may be subject to different and possibly more stringent conditions in their operating certificates. More generally, provincial regulation of transport has meant different rate structures, different subsidy and reallocative schemes, and different technical standards such as allowable axle loads from province to province. These differences in turn significantly increase the cost and complexity of engaging in the transport business interprovincially, giving intraprovincial operations a competitive advantage.

The regulation of communications, as noted above, has been constitutionally split so that legislative control over broadcasting to radio and television receivers by electromagnetic waves has been assigned exclusively to Parliament,[58]

---

54 *Attorney-General of Nova Scotia* v. *Attorney General of Canada* (Nova Scotia interdelegation), [1951] s.c.r. 31

55 Under the Motor Vehicle Transport Act, r.s.c. 1970, c. M-14, s. 3(1), extraprovincial carriers must obtain a licence from each province in which they operate.

56 [1972] s.c.r. 359

57 Hogg, *Constitutional Law of Canada* (Toronto: Carswell, 1977), at 231–2

58 *Radio Reference, supra* note 40

while authority over other communications undertakings depends upon S. 92(10).

The most recent problem area involves regulation of cable television. In both *Re Capital Cities Communications Inc.* v. *Canadian Radio-Television Commission*[59] and *Re Public Service Board, Dionne and Attorney-General for Canada,*[60] a majority of the Supreme Court held that transmission by cable of programming originating from television broadcasting constituted a single undertaking assigned to the exclusive legislative authority of the federal government. The Court held further that authority to regulate television broadcasting extended to the power to regulate content as well as technical processes.[61] The Court was careful to distinguish this case from the cable distribution of broadcast signals in which a cable distribution enterprise limited its operations 'to programmes locally produced by them for transmission over their lines to their local subscribers.'[62]

Pigeon J, in a dissenting judgment in *Dionne*, found the argument of the provincial attorney general more persuasive. S. 92(10) primarily assigns local undertakings to the provinces. The basis for federal authority over broadcasting, he reasoned, is simply that electromagnetic waves cannot be confined to the province. As a technical matter the cable system is severable from the broadcasting system. Since the absence of 'air wave' broadcasting is the distinctive feature of cable transmission, he concluded, jurisdiction over cable falls more appropriately under provincial authority.

The differing views on the characterization of technical processes make it clear that as the integration of multidimensional communications systems increases in sophistication and complexity the regulation of those systems will become a fertile source of constitutional dispute. What remains unclear is the extent to which provincial regulation of technical processes and program content may lead to barriers to the mobility of media programming.[63]

---

59 *Supra* note 40
60 [1978] 2 s.c.r. 191; (1978), 83 d.l.r. (3d) 178
61 *Capital Cities, supra* note 40, at 162 (s.c.r.); 623 (d.l.r.) *per* Laskin, cjc: 'Programme content regulation is inseparable from regulating the undertaking through which programmes are received and sent on as part of the total enterprise.'
62 *Supra* note 60, at 197 (s.c.r.); 181 (d.l.r.)
63 *Cf. Attorney-General of Quebec* v. *Kellogg's Co. of Canada, supra* note 35; text accompanying notes 38–40 *supra*.

Capital
1 Institutions of finance

S. 91 in subsections (14) through (21) assigns to the Parliament of Canada legislative powers necessary to the establishment of a single currency and banking system as well as other basic monetary and commercial institutions. In *Reference re Alberta Statutes*[64] the Supreme Court considered a package of provincial legislation designed to transform Alberta's economy into a social credit system. Duff CJC concluded that the essence of this legislative plan was 'the substitution generally in internal commerce of Alberta credit for bank credit and legal tender as the circulating medium.'[65] The Court held the legislation ultra vires as relating to 'Banking and Incorporation of Banks,' (S. 91(15)), 'Currency' (S. 91(14)), and 'Regulation of Trade and Commerce' (S. 91(2)).

The generally expansive ambit of this decision has recently been questioned by the Supreme Court in *Re Canadian Pioneer Management Co. and Labour Relations Board of Saskatchewan*.[66] In this case the Court had to decide which of the federal or provincial labour boards had jurisdiction to certify the formation of a union by employees of a trust company. The major issue turned on the question of whether a trust company fell within the class of subject assigned to the federal government by 91(15), 'Banking and Incorporation of Banks.'

Beetz J undertook a historical review of the judicial interpretation of the word 'banking,' involving functional, economic, and legal analyses. Chartered banks, he observed, carried on many functions not traditionally within the purview of 'banking', while 'near banks' carried on just as many functions in areas that at different times have been considered 'banking.' Beetz J was persuaded by the provincial argument that 'banking,' in the constitutional context, ought to receive a formal interpretation; thus the decision of the majority was to restrict federal authority over banking to those 'financial activities carried out by an institution that operates under the nomenclature and terms of incorporation which clearly identify it as having the distinctive institutional character of a bank.'[67] This formal interpretation of 'banking' was apparently favoured by Beetz J because it tended to preserve the integrity of the constitutional distribution of powers in face of the changing functions of banks over time. Its result has been to recognize a substantial provincial role in the regulation of financial institutions.

---

64 [1938] S.C.R. 100
65 Ibid., at 113
66 [1980] 1 S.C.R. 433; (1980), 107 D.L.R. (3d) 1
67 Ibid., at 465 (S.C.R.); 24 (D.L.R.) quoting from the factum of the attorney general of New Brunswick

2 Competition policy

Competition policy in Canada has historically been given effect through federal legislation based on the criminal law powers in S. 91(27). Early anti-combines laws were restricted to the prohibition of combinations designed to restrict competition. These laws were intended to be nothing other than criminal laws, as witnessed by the fact that the locus of anti-combines legislation from 1892 until 1919 was the Criminal Code. In *Re Board of Commerce Act*[68] an ambitious new scheme of competition regulation that established an administrative board with the power to make cease and desist orders and placed restrictions on hoarding and undue profits was found to be unconstitutional. The Privy Council rejected federal attempts to bring the legislation under trade and commerce or peace, order, and good government. The new regulatory scheme also overstepped the traditional boundaries of criminal law. The account of criminal law powers in *Re Board of Commerce* has since been recognized as unduly restrictive. In *Proprietary Articles Trade Association* v. *Attorney General of Canada*[69] the Privy Council held that 'if Parliament genuinely determines that [certain] commercial activities ... are to be suppressed in the public interest, their Lordships see no reason why Parliament should not make them crimes.'[70]

It has been suggested that competition legislation more appropriately belongs under the head of trade and commerce, and that reliance on the criminal law power has tended to produce anti-combines legislation lacking flexibility in procedural and remedial aspects.[71] The major stumbling-block to a uniform competition policy founded on the federal trade and commerce power is that provincial authority over property and civil rights usually precludes federal regulation of commercial activity which is not conducted interprovincially. The advantage of the criminal law power as a basis for competition legislation is the wide jurisdiction it confers on Parliament to act in areas which might be ultra vires under another head of federal power.

Recent amendments to the Combines Investigation Act[72] have expanded the powers of the Restrictive Trade Practices Commission to include the capacity to make prohibitory orders and have introduced the additional remedy of a civil action in damages for losses suffered due to a breach of the statute. These amendments attempt to overcome some of the inadequacies of past anti-combines law but in doing so overstep the traditional boundaries of what has

68 [1922] 1 A.C. 191
69 [1931] A.C. 310
70 Ibid., at 323–4
71 Safarian, *Canadian Federalism*; Hogg, *Constitutional Law*
72 R.S.C. 1970, C. C-23 as amended by S.C. 1974–75–76, C. 76

been termed 'criminal law,' raising the question of their constitutional validity. For example, legislation vesting an administrative board with the power to make prohibitory orders was struck down in the *Board of Commerce* case.[73] However, legislation authorizing the courts to make orders prohibiting the continuation of illegal commercial activities has been found acceptable as coming within criminal law.[74]

In *R.* v. *Hoffman-LaRoche*[75] the Ontario Court of Appeal held that the Combines Investigation Act was constitutionally supportable, not only under the criminal law power but also under both the residuary clause of S. 91 (peace, order, and good government) and under S. 91(2). The case concerned the power of the attorney general of Canada to institute and conduct proceedings under the Act rather than the validity of the new amendments. Nevertheless a strong implication of the result is that these amendments, freed from the rigidity of criminal law form, would be constitutionally valid. Recent trial decisions have come to opposing results, typified by *Henuset Bros. Ltd.* v. *Syncrude Canada Ltd.*[76] and *Rocois Construction Inc.* v. *Quebec Ready Mix Inc.*[77] In *Henuset Bros.* Rowbotham J concluded that the civil remedy in 31.1 of the Combines Investigation Act was an integral part of a scheme for the general regulation of trade across Canada. It was, he held, more than the statutory enactment of a common law remedy and was not the sole enforcement mechanism of the Act.

In *Rocois Construction*, Marceau J of the Federal Court held that federal authority over trade and commerce did not extend to the regulation of wholly intraprovincial enterprises. Because the civil action in his view stood apart as an independent remedy, it suffered the same fatal defect as the Trade Marks Act[78] in *MacDonald* v. *Vapour Canada*[79]: it was not a form of regulation at all, because it lacked the requisite public supervision in the form of continuous monitoring by a regulatory agency. The judges in *Henuset Bros.* and *Rocois Construction* agreed that competition regulation was not supportable under peace, order, and good government, being neither a subject of temporary legislation to meet an emergency nor a new class of subject not contemplated in 1867.[80] The judges also agreed[81] that there was no rational connection between the right to sue for

73 *Supra* note 68
74 *Goodyear Tire and Rubber Co.* v. *The Queen*, [1956] S.C.R. 303
75 (1981), 33 O.R. (2d) 694
76 [1980] 6 W.W.R. 218 (Alta. Q.B.)
77 (1980), 105 D.L.R. (3d) 15 (Fed. T.D.)
78 R.S.C. 1970, C. T-10
79 [1977] 2 S.C.R. 134; (1976), 66 D.L.R. (3d) 1
80 Contra, *R.* v. *Hoffman La Roche Ltd.*, *supra* note 75
81 As did the judge in *Seiko Time Canada Ltd.* v. *Consumers Distributors Co. Ltd.* (1980), 29 O.R. (2d) 221 (H.C.J.); *aff'd* on different grounds (1981), 34 O.R. (2d) 481 (C.A.)

damages and penal sanctions under the criminal law power, so that that the civil remedy was not supportable under S. 91(27) of the BNA Act.[82]

The strength of the arguments concerning the distribution of powers over competition regulation and the constitutional validity of these recent amendments to the Combines Investigation Act will remain uncertain until reviewed by the Supreme Court.[83] In any case, there seems to be general agreement that regulatory measures in aid of competition must be uniform and national in scope if they are to be effective.[84] Differing standards of regulation of competition may have implications for the reduced mobility of capital within Canada by creating incentives to conduct business or investment in provinces with less stringent competition regulations. An equally important though less speculative problem is that of conflicting laws.

A potential conflict arises when provincial legislation, or actions authorized under provincial legislation, are inconsistent with federal prohibitions against anti-competitive practices. Such a problem may occur, for example, in the context of a marketing scheme. *Reference re Farm Products Marketing Act*[85] is best known as a turning point in judicial interpretation of the trade and commerce power. A secondary issue in that case was the conflict between the provincial scheme and federal competition offences. For the Board to engage in an activity validly authorized by a provincial legislature, the Court held, could not be an offence against the federal statue. In other words, an Act authorized by provincial legislation is deemed not to be 'to the detriment of the public' solely by virtue of its legislative authorization. Thus a conflict between the two enactments is eliminated, and the question of federal paramountcy does not arise.

The *Canadian Breweries*[86] case proceeded on the basis that provincial legislation regulating anti-competitive practices was constitutionally valid. Thus the question for determination by the court was not whether the province could remove the sale of beer from market competition but to what extent it had done so. Only if Canadian Breweries were responsible for limiting competition in areas not already restricted by provincial legislation could it be convicted of

---

82 In *R.* v. *Zelensky*, [1978] 2 S.C.R. 940; 3 W.W.R. 693, the validity of a restitutionary remedy was upheld because it was available at the discretion of the court as an integral part of the sentencing process.
83 For competing views see Grange, *The Constitutionality of Federal Intervention in the Market Place – The Competition Case* (Montreal: C.D. Howe Research Institute Commentary Series, 1975) and Hogg and Glover, 'The constitutionality of the new competition bill' (1975–76), 1 *Canadian Business Law Journal* 197.
84 Hogg, *Constitutional Law*, at 281; Safarian, *Canadian Federalism*
85 [1957] S.C.R. 198
86 *R.* v. *Canadian Breweries*, [1960] O.R. 601 (H.C.J.)

federal competition offences. McRuer J reiterated the concern in *Reference re Farm Products Marketing Act* that provincially authorized commissions must be assumed to have exercised their power in the public interest and therefore cannot be in violation of the Combines Investigation Act. Only in a situation of a 'substantial monopoly,' where provincial regulations might be rendered ineffective, could the Combines Investigation Act 'catch' activities already under provincial regulation.

Most recently in the *Jabour* case,[87] Seaton J.A. for the BC Court of Appeal stated: 'I conclude that the combines legislation simply does not apply to regulatory schemes validly established by provincial legislation. Such schemes are not prohibited by the Act. The conduct of those who make the regulations is not made an offence. Compliance with such rules is not made a crime.'[88]

It seems now that the concept of the 'exemption' or 'immunity' of provincial regulation from competition legislation is firmly established.[89] Whether this is a matter of statutory interpretation (provincial legislation must be in the public interest and therefore is not 'undue' restriction of competition) or a matter of constitutional law (immunity against the application of either federal paramountcy or necessarily incidental doctrines) is less clear, and the decisions in the 'regulated industry' cases largely rely on a combination of both approaches.

3 Securities

S. 92(13) has been viewed as empowering the provinces to regulate all securities transactions within the province, and while the criminal law power in 91(27) gives Parliament some presence in this field it is restricted to the punishment of fraudulent dealings and the like. Provincial authority to regulate the issue of shares extends to federally incorporated companies as well,[90] as long as such regulation does not sterilize the activities of the company.[91] Thus a company

---

87 *Law Society of British Columbia and McCallum* v. *Attorney-General of Canada*; *Jabour* v. *Law Society of British Columbia*, [1981] 2 W.W.R. 159 (B.C.C.A.). The decision of the BC Court of Appeal has been upheld by the Supreme Court of Canada, (1982) 43 N.R. 463, at 494, where Estey J, for the full court, concluded: 'So long as the *CIA*, or at least Part V, is styled as a criminal prohibition, proceedings in its implementation and enforcement will require a demonstration of some conduct contrary to the public interest. It is this element of the federal legislation that these cases [the 'regulated industry' cases] all conclude can be negated by the authority extended by a valid provincial regulatory authority.'

88 Ibid., at 185

89 For an exhaustive analysis see Milligan, 'Federal competition law and provincial regulation' (unpublished LL.M. Thesis, University of Toronto, Faculty of Law, 1979).

90 *Lymburn* v. *Mayland*, [1932] A.C. 318

91 *Attorney-General of Manitoba* v. *Attorney-General of Canada*, [1929] A.C. 260

wishing to issue shares nationally must meet the regulatory requirements of each province in which such shares are to be sold. Provincial authority also extends to the creation of offences under their securities legislation, notwithstanding the existence of comparable provisions in the Criminal Code.[92] Regulation by the province is not impaired even when certain aspects of a securities transaction take place extraprovincially. In *R. v. W. McKenzie Securities*,[93] Manitoba securities law was held applicable to a Toronto broker who had solicited business from Manitoba residents by mail and telegraph. Manitoba law applied, it was held, because the solicitation took place in Manitoba. In *Gregory and Co. Inc. v. Quebec Securities Commission*[94] an order was upheld requiring a Quebec dealer to cease the publication of advertising which, although published in Quebec and advertising for sale only shares transferable in Quebec, was sent exclusively to subscribers outside the province. In neither case was the constitutional issue raised, although Cartright J in *Gregory and Co.* questioned whether the provincial Act authorized the regulation of this type of business. What clearly concerned him was the interprovincial character of the undertaking and the ambit of the federal trade and commerce power.[95]

The enforcement of provincial Acts and the issuance of orders by regulatory bodies has created some problems in the national market since, though shares may be issued nationally (or internationally), the application of provincial regulation must be restricted to the regulating province. Thus, for example, a cease-trading order in British Columbia does not preclude trading in Ontario. This has a distorting effect, and could result in substantial losses (or gains) where a cease-trading order causes the supply of shares to dry up in one jurisdiction, forcing up the price where the shares are still traded. Such a situation has led one judge to comment on the drastic results which follow from lack of a federal regulatory agency with authority over securities trading.[96]

There has been some suggestion that securities may involve a double aspect and so be an area of concurrent jurisdiction.[97] This, for example, is certainly true in the area of penalties and sanctions.[98] Since the federal government has a

92 *Multiple Access Ltd.* v. *McCutcheon* not yet reported, Aug. 9, 1982 (S.C.C.), *rev'g* (1977) 16 O.R. (2d) 93 (Ont H.C.); *rev'g* (1978), 86 D.L.R. (3d) 160 (Ont. C.A.).
93 (1966), 56 D.L.R. (2d) 56 (Man. C.A.)
94 [1961] S.C.R. 584
95 Anisman and Hogg, 'Constitutional aspects of federal securities regulation.' In Canada, Dept of Consumer and Corporate Affairs, *Proposals for a Securities Market Law for Canada: Volume 3 – Background Papers* (Ottawa: Ministry of Supply and Services, 1979), at 135
96 Anderson J in *Black* v. *Doherty McCuaig Ltd.*, [1974] 4 W.W.R. 342 (B.C.S.C.) at 344
97 Abel, *Laskin's Canadian Constitutional Law* (Toronto: Carswell, 4th ed., 1975), at 359–61; Hogg, *Constitutional Law*, at 313
98 *Multiple Access Ltd.* v. *McCutcheon, supra* note 92

minor legislative presence in the securities field, this issue remains largely unresolved, although an argument for federal intervention based on the interprovincial character of certain kinds of securities activity clearly can be made within existing constitutional law. The increasing integration of the securities market in Canada has led to a growing concern over the lack of comprehensive securities regulation. This has resulted in proposals for substantial changes in the character of securities regulation in Canada.[99]

4 Incorporation of companies

Incorporation of companies with provincial objects has been assigned to provincial authority in S. 92(11) of the BNA Act. A comparable provision was not made in S. 91, however, and regulation of companies with 'federal' objects had to be judicially assigned to Parliament as falling within the residual powers in the opening of S. 91. The early cases decided that provincial incorporation could confer upon a company the capacity to carry on business outside the province, but that such capacity was contingent upon recognition (express or implied) by the host, non-incorporating jurisdiction.[100] The position of federally incorporated companies is different only in the fact that they are entitled to legal status in all provinces.[101] Their activities are also subject to regulation by otherwise valid provincial legislation, as long as the legislation does not 'deprive a Dominion company of its status and powers.'[102] Thus a federally incorporated company wishing to raise capital by sale of shares may be required to issue them through a provincially licensed agent[103] or may be pre-empted altogether by a provincially run monopoly, such as, for example, over automobile insurance.[104] In all cases the determining concept is whether the 'functions and activities of a company were sterilized or its status and essential capacities impaired in a substantial degree.'[105]

People

1 Mobility

The BNA Act is virtually silent on the subject of protecting personal mobility, and few judicial pronouncements are extant. Though Canadians do enjoy a high

---

99 For a survey of these proposals, see 'Securities' in the second part of this paper.

100 *Bonanza Creek Gold Mining Co.* v. *The King*, [1916] 1 A.C. 566

101 *John Deere Plow Co.* v. *Wharton*, [1915] A.C. 330

102 Ibid., at 341. See also *Morgan* v. *Attorney-General of P.E.I.*, [1976] 2 S.C.R. 349; (1975), 55 D.L.R. (3d) 527

103 *Lymburn* v. *Mayland, supra* note 90

104 *Canadian Indemnity Co.* v. *Attorney General of B.C.*, [1977] 2 S.C.R. 504; [1976], 5 W.W.R. 748

105 *Lymburn* v. *Mayland, supra* note 90, at 325

degree of mobility between provinces, that is less the result of constitutional imperative than of the policies chosen by provinces.

The *locus classicus* of the protection of personal mobility is said to be found in the dictum of Rand J when, speaking in *Winner*, he said, 'a province cannot prevent a Canadian from entering it except, conceivably, in temporary circumstances, for some local reason as, for example, health.'[106] This assertion was based on his view that Parliament had exclusive authority over citizenship (usually said to arise out of S. 91(25), 'Naturalization and Aliens'). Rand J distinguished 'incidents' of citizenship from 'necessary elements' of citizenship; he held that the right of a Canadian to enter any province was a necessary element of citizenship and the restriction of that right was therefore ultra vires a provincial legislature. This foundation for personal mobility seems somewhat ephemeral in light of the fact that, for Rand J, the right of a citizen to vote was merely an 'incident' of the status of citizenship and therefore could be taken away by provincial legislation.[107] Nevertheless, the bare right of a Canadian to enter and remain in any province seems to be well established.[108]

2 Work

Since matters pertaining to labour generally fall within provincial jurisdiction,[109] there is considerable potential for provincial regulation of labour markets to limit personal mobility. That the authority to do so is limited is suggested by *Union Collery Co.* v. *Bryden*,[110] where the Privy Council held ultra vires a provincial statute prohibiting the employment of ethnic Chinese in BC mines. Its real purpose, according to the Board, was not the regulation of the mines, a valid provincial matter, but the deprivation of the rights of Chinese aliens – 'to prohibit their continued residence in the province since it prohibited their earning their living in that province.' The legislation therefore contravened federal authority over aliens under S. 91(25).

The Supreme Court has stated that the rights of other Canadians can be no less than those of aliens,[111] and it follows that provincial legislation which completely excludes residents of other provinces from the labour market is beyond

---

106 *Winner* v. *S.M.T. (Eastern) Ltd.*, [1951] s.c.r. 887, at 920; [1951] 4 d.l.r. 529 at 559
107 *Cunningham* v. *Tomey Homma*, [1903] a.c. 151, where oriental naturalized Canadians were denied the electoral franchise in British Columbia.
108 Laskin cjc in *Morgan*, *supra* note 102, at 358 (s.c.r.) and 533 (d.l.r.)
109 British North America Act, S. 92(13) (property and civil rights) *Toronto Electric Commissioners* v. *Snider*, [1925] a.c. 396
110 [1899] a.c. 580
111 *Morgan, supra* note 102. The Court also cast doubt upon the privy council's characterization of the bc statute in the *Union Colliery* case.

provincial authority. However, legislation implementing only a restriction rather than a complete prohibition on non-residents' ability to work is probably constitutional. In *Morgan* v. *Attorney General of Prince Edward Island*,[112] the Supreme Court drew an analogy between the position of non-residents and that of federally incorporated companies, subject to all laws enacted for a valid provincial purpose except those which 'sterilize their general capacity.' Legislation such as that restricting who may work on Quebec construction projects, giving provincial residents a preference in hiring for jobs on oil rigs in Newfoundland, or fixing strict standards for access to certain professions appears to come well within constitutionally acceptable limits.

3 Ownership of land

While provincial borders may not be strictly closed to the movement of individuals, the Supreme Court has recently upheld legislation restricting ownership of land within a province by non-residents.[113] The Court reasoned that because ownership of land was not a central feature of citizenship but had to do with a matter coming within property and civil rights in the province, the legislation was intra vires the provinces. The Court noted, moreover, that absentee ownership was a matter of legitimate provincial concern.

4 Language

S. 133 of the BNA Act provides that English or French may be used by anyone in Parliament and in the Quebec Legislature. Bilingual guarantees extend to 'Records and Journals,' the 'printing and publishing' of Acts (including 'enactment' itself[114]), and the 'Pleading or Process' issuing from any court of Canada and Quebec (including administrative tribunals).[115]

In every other respect constitutional jurisdiction over language appears simply to follow the ordinary federal-provincial division of powers.[116] Thus S. 133 does not 'freeze' any particular status of English or French except to set a minimum standard for bilingual guarantees. Provinces can stipulate the language of their own public service (S. 92(1)), much of the working environment (S. 92(13) and (16)), and education within their borders (S. 93).

112 *Supra* note 102
113 Ibid.
114 *Attorney-General of Quebec* v. *Blaikie*, [1981] 1 S.C.R. 312; (1980), 101 D.L.R. (3d) 394
115 Ibid.
116 *Jones* v. *Attorney-General of New Brunswick*, [1975] 2 S.C.R. 182; Hogg, 'Constitutional power over language.' In Law Society of Upper Canada, Special Lectures, 1978, *The Constitution and the Future of Canada* (Toronto: Richard DeBoo, 1978), at 229

The federal government, likewise, would seem to be limited in its control over language to those areas which are under federal jurisdiction, such as the federal civil service and federal courts. Thus language regulations may constitutionally exist as a practical barrier to mobility between the provinces.

CONSTITUTIONAL REFORM: RECENT AND PROPOSED CONSTRAINTS

Introduction

The federal-provincial tensions of recent years have spawned a variety of studies and proposals for constitutional reform. Some of the leading proposals which would affect the regulation of the economy are surveyed below, including those now entrenched in the Constitution Act.

Goods

1 Customs union and S. 121

S. 121, as we have seen, is an incomplete guarantee of economic mobility within Canada. The report of the Canadian Bar Association's Committee on the Constitution, entitled *Towards a New Canada*,[117] recommended adoption of an expanded S. 121 which would guarantee the free movement of goods capital, people, and services in Canada. The new provision, in their view, should prohibit not only tariff barriers but also quantitative restrictions and other provisions having an equivalent effect and should limit both Parliament and the provincial legislatures. In the view of the majority of the committee, the Courts would allow sufficient leeway to enable federal legislation to depart from this principle where necessary to achieve other national objectives such as regional equalization.[118] A minority considered it worthwhile to provide specifically for federal interference in the national market, subject to the approval of a reconstituted upper house.

Where the legitimate exercise of provincial authority (such as regulation of trades and professions for the protection of the public) might create obstacles to free movement, it would be 'for the courts to determine whether a measure constituted a legitimate exercise of constitutional power or an impermissible interference with the national market.'[119] The Bar Association's committee essentially shared the view of Safarian[120] on S. 121, although Safarian's proposal

---

117 Canadian Bar Association, Committee on the Constitution, *Towards a New Canada* (Montreal: Canadian Bar Association, 1978)
118 Ibid., at 88
119 Ibid., at 89
120 Safarian, *Canadian Federalism*

contained explicit provisions to preserve the federal capacity to regulate the economy by restricting mobility where necessary.

The report of the Task Force on Canadian Unity recommended a similarly expanded S. 121 which would contain explicit reference to the prohibition of preferential purchasing by provincial governments except where necessary to alleviate 'acute economic hardship.'[121] Even so, the authors felt, such practices should be agreed to by the other provinces in order to be constitutionally supportable.

Provincial proposals have largely supported the constitutional protection of a national market. The Ontario Advisory Committee on Confederation[122] recommended entrenchment of freedom of movement for goods, services, people, and capital, limited by provincial ability to legislate with incidental effects upon such mobility. The Quebec Liberal Party's 'Beige Paper'[123] reached a similar conclusion, pointing out that the European Economic Community prohibited more barriers to economic mobility than are currently prohibited in Canada. The Beige Paper stated that mobility guarantees nevertheless ought to be subject to non-discriminatory provincial legislation of general application in such areas as investment practices of provincially regulated bodies (insurance companies, for example) and professional organizations. Such provincial legislation would 'incidentally affect' rather than be 'directed at' internal economic mobility.

The most radical proposal to date, the Quebec White Paper,[124] while proposing Quebec nationhood, also proposed significant economic ties with Canada. These would include free movement of goods and people in the sense that there would be no customs duties and no police control at the border. Under sovereignty-association there would also be some attempt at harmonizing the external trade policies of Canada and Quebec vis-à-vis other nations. These limitations on Quebec and Canadian sovereignty would be minimal, however, since only fiscal barriers to the movement of goods would be prohibited and only the formal right to enter and leave Quebec without a passport would be preserved.

One of the most recent proposals for constitutional reform was brought before the Continuing Committee of Ministers on the Constitution on 9 July

121 Canada, Task Force on Canadian Unity, *A Future Together: Observations and Recommendations* (Ottawa: Ministry of Supply and Services, 1979). The task force was co-chaired by Jean-Luc Pépin and John P. Robarts.
122 Ontario Adivsory Committee on Confederation, *Second Report: The Federal-Provincial Distribution of Powers* (Toronto: Advisory Committee on Confederation, 1979)
123 Liberal Party, Quebec, Constitutional Committee, *A New Canadian Federation* (Montreal: Quebec Liberal Party, 1980)
124 Québec, Conseil exécutif, *Québec-Canada: A New Deal: The Québec government proposal for a new partnership between equals: Sovereignty-association* (Quebec: Éditeur Officiel, 1979)

1980. In an explicit attempt to entrench in the Constitution operational rules for a Canadian economic union, the federal government suggested (i) entrenchment of mobility rights, (ii) limiting the use of legislative and economic power which might impede economic mobility, and (iii) expanding federal powers where necessary to achieve economic integration. The new Section 121 that the federal government proposed read as follows:

121 (1) Neither Canada nor a province shall by law or practice discriminate in a manner that unduly impedes the operation of the Canadian economic union, directly or indirectly, on the basis of the province or territory of residence or former residence of a person, on the basis of the province or territory of origin or destination of goods, services or capital or on the basis of the province or territory into which or from which goods, services or capital are imported or exported.

(2) Nothing in subsection (1) renders invalid a law of Parliament or of a legislature enacted in the interests of public safety, order, health or morals.

(3) Nothing in subsection (1) renders invalid a law of Parliament enacted pursuant to the principles of equalization and regional development to which Parliament and the legislatures are committed or declared by Parliament to be in an overriding national obligation undertaken by Canada.

(4) Nothing in subsection (2) or (3) renders valid a law of Parliament or a legislature that impedes the admission free into any province of goods, services or capital originating in or imported into any other province or territory.

This provision established the very broad principle of prohibiting any discrimination based on provincial boundaries which unduly impedes economic union. Both Parliament and provincial legislatures would be subject to this principle with the two exceptions contained in 121 (2) and (3). Subsection (4) preserved the old S. 121 'free admission' concept in any event and extended it beyond goods to encompass services and capital.

The proposed S. 121 raised numerous questions and uncertainties. For example, it referred to 'unduly' impeding the operation of the economic union. What constituted an 'undue' impediment would likely be a matter of great debate, given the interpretation that word had received in the context of anti-combines legislation.[125] The exceptions in subsections (2) and (3) would create loopholes of indeterminate magnitude. The federal government's notes on the redrafted

---

125 For example, following the analysis in R. v. *Canadian Breweries, supra* note 86, provincial legislation could never be in violation of S. 121, because such legislation, by virtue of having been enacted by a democratically elected assembly, is, by definition, not an 'undue impediment.'

S. 121 asserted the possibility of affirmative action programs. It is unclear whether affirmative action constitutes discrimination under existing law.[126] Would provinces have the right to enact such programs? Would affirmative action programs, for example concerning an economically depressed region, not embody the very concept of economic protectionism at which the new Section 121 would ostensibly be aimed?

The response of the Saskatchewan government on the proposed new S. 121 is also worth noting.[127] In commenting on barriers to economic mobility in Canada, the Saskatchewan Discussion Paper of July 1980 stated: 'The bulk of the impediments are purposefully created by both orders of government in the pursuit of other social and economic objectives that are seen by political leaders to have a higher priority. They are, quite simply, considered acts by responsible governments.' The discussion paper went on to indicate that the federal proposal would leave untouched the major instruments for creating obstacles to economic mobility – national tariff and transportation policies and personal and corporate tax rates. The paper further stated: 'the richest provinces have the greatest capacity to use such instruments to attract business away from other provinces. The only defence available to a small province may be to take action which creates barriers to protect their competitive positions within the economic union – and these would be struck down instantly by the proposed Section 121.'

While most reform proposals seem to adhere to the concept of an enlarged national market, it is clear that the position taken by Saskatchewan challenges the very priority assigned to the protection of the 'national market,' which is assumed by most other reform proposals. Disagreement on such a fundamental principle makes unanimity on an expanded S. 121 impossible and raises basic doubts about the assumption that constitutional reform ought to strengthen the concept of Canada as an economic union.

2 Trade and commerce

S. 91(2) is an ongoing source of difficulty because after 115 years there is still no certainty as to the limits of federal authority to regulate trade and commerce. In

---

126 *Cf. Re. Athabasca Tribal Council and Amoco Canada Petroleum Co. Ltd.*, [1981] 1 s.c.r. 699; (1981), 124 d.l.r. (3d) 1, where the Court suggested that it does not.

127 Saskatchewan, 'Powers over the economy: securing the Canadian economic union in the Constitution: Discussion Paper submitted by the Government of Saskatchewan,' Document No. 830–83 / 003 in Continuing Committee of Ministers on the Constitution, *List of Public Documents / Liste des documents publics* (Ottawa: Canadian Government Intergovernmental Conference Secretariat, 1980). The paper was prepared for a meeting held in Vancouver, 22–4 July 1980.

1972 the Special Joint Committee of the Senate and the House of Commons[128] recommended that the federal trade and commerce power be clarified so that Parliament would have exclusive authority over trade with other countries and between provinces. Its authority would include the regulation of a product where the principal market was outside the province of production; trade throughout the country conducted via transactions which ignore provincial boundaries; all aspects of international trade; and the instrumentalities of trade and commerce (meaning those operations which, while discrete enterprises, are functionally necessary to the conduct of some broader activity, such as grain elevators as part of the national and international wheat trade).

Safarian concluded that attempts to distinguish two trade networks in Canada (the intra- and the interprovincial) have led to the attenuation of federal power to regulate the national economy.[129] He noted that the significant effects of a transaction or activity completed within a province may *not* be intraprovincial, but he disagreed with the Special Joint Committee that the destination of a product produced within the province constitutes an appropriate basis for asserting federal jurisdiction; such a criterion in his view, would limit significantly the present provincial power over 'local' production. Rather, he suggested, the problem ought to be resolved by giving substance to federal authority over 'the general regulation of trade.' To maintain the integrity of the assignment of provincial powers, the 'general regulation' power might be made exercisable only upon declaration by Parliament, as is now the case with its power under 92(10)(c).

The Constitutional Committee of the Canadian Bar Association[130] adopted aspects of both these approaches. The division of powers, it urged, should be based on a functional analysis – who is best suited to regulate a given activity? Regulatory competence would generally depend on whether the enterprise took place wholly within the province, a position which would restrict provincial interference in the national economy. To achieve a minimum of uniformity in the regulation of commercial activity, Parliament should have a declaratory power. The present provincial distrust of the declaratory power could be overcome by having its exercise subject to approval of a reconstituted upper house (that is, one whose members would be appointed by and serve at the pleasure of the governments of the provinces).

---

128 Special Joint Committee of the Senate and of the House of Commons on the Constitution of Canada, *Final Report* (Ottawa: Queen's Printer for Canada; 4th Session, 28th Parliament, 1972). The committee was chaired jointly by Senator G.L. Molgat and Mark Mac-Guigan, MP
129 *Canadian Federalism*
130 *Towards a New Canada*

The chief concern of provincial proposals for reform of the trade and commerce power is the potential for federal intrusion into exclusive provincial jurisdiction over natural resources. The proposals of the Alberta government started with the assertion that in 1867 provincial ownership of resources was meant to be comprehensive.[131] Trade and commerce was not intended to be interpreted so as to render ineffective provincial authority over natural resources. Since recent court decisions have created uncertainty, the government of Alberta recommended a reaffirmation and strengthening of exclusive provincial authority in this area.

The Ontario Advisory Committee on Confederation recommended greater opportunity for consultation between the federal and provincial governments.[132] While its position on natural resources was more moderate than Alberta's – it accepted that provincial control over natural resources should be subject to the federal primacy over international and interprovincial trade – it agreed with Alberta in recommending constitutional provisions allowing for a provincial presence in the field of foreign trade. Ontario's Select Committee on Constitutional Reform would have made interprovincial and international trade areas of concurrent jurisdiction, with federal paramountcy only where 'necessary to serve a compelling national interest.'[133]

The Quebec Liberals' Beige Paper would make allowance for federal regulations relating to the 'standardization' of products destined for export, but would have federal authority over foreign investment subject to provincial jurisdiction over land use, natural resources, and industrial planning.[134] These are obviously the major areas to which foreign investment is directed, and so the assertion of provincial powers here seems quite substantial.

Section 50 of the Constitution Act expands exclusive provincial authority to make laws in relation to certain natural resources to include regulation of export of primary production to another part of Canada.[135] This power to make laws in relation to the export of forest, hydro, and non-renewable resources would be subject to the limitation that such laws 'may not authorize or provide for discrimination in prices or in supplies exported to another part of Canada.'

131 Alberta, *Harmony in Diversity: A New Federalism for Canada-Alberta Government Position Paper on Constitutional Change* (Edmonton: Government of Alberta, 1978)
132 *Second Report*
133 Ontario Select Committee on Constitutional Reform, *Report of the Select Committee on Constitutional Reform* (Toronto: Queen's Printer, 1980)
134 *A New Canadian Federation*
135 Now cited as the Constitution Act, 1982

The amendment goes on to provide that all federal powers over interprovincial trade should continue to exist and that where provincial and federal laws conflict the federal law should prevail to the extent of the conflict.

Among the federal proposals placed before the Continuing Committee of Ministers on the Constitution in summer 1980 was an amended S. 91(2) which attempted to clarify and broaden the federal trade and commerce power. Under that amendment the provision would read:

91 (2) The regulation of trade and commerce in goods, services and capital.

(2.1) The regulation of competition throughout Canada and the establishment of product standards applicable throughout Canada where such regulation or such standards are reasonably necessary for the operation of the Canadian economic union.

3 Taxation

As the Pépin-Robarts Report pointed out, the allocation of taxation powers may fall into three general categories.[136] First, powers may be assigned a priori in a founding document. This is what Sections 91(3) and 92(2) of the BNA Act attempt to do. The problem with this approach is that the allocations may subsequently be rendered outdated by changing social and economic conditions. A second approach would be to award taxation powers only to the central government so that provincial fiscal needs are met entirely by substantial transfers. This method of raising government revenues is generally considered inappropriate in the Canadian context because it deviates from the principle of accountability (since the government that spends the tax is not the government that collects it).

The Task Force favoured the third option, which is to grant all modes of taxation to both orders of government. Several reasons were put forward to support this view. First, the growth of provincial expenditures requires access to a wider range of revenue-raising instruments. Taxation of course is also frequently utilized as an instrument of economic regulation for purposes other than the raising of revenues. In light of substantial provincial government involvement in economic matters, the use of taxation for such purposes should be open to the provinces. Thirdly, the complexities of the modern economy have rendered obsolete the distinction between direct and indirect taxation. In any event, the view of the Task Force was that provinces essentially already tax as they wish by the careful drafting of taxation statutes or the use of alternative taxing instruments.

136 *A Future Together*

Despite its support for conferring on the provinces the power to levy indirect taxes, the report of the Task Force stipulated (p. 92) that this power in provincial hands must be limited to exclude the power to levy customs and excise taxes or any tax whose impact would fall upon anyone outside the province.

An expanded provincial power to tax, including the preceding limitations, is a feature of the majority of recent proposals for constitutional reform. Even the most radical recommendations for provincial autonomy, while asserting a provincial right to use any mode of taxation, accept the need for prohibitions against fiscal barriers to economic mobility.[137] Thus under 'sovereignty-association' there would be no customs duties on goods moving between Quebec and Canada.

While there is considerable agreement that the power of indirect taxation, if allowed to provincial legislatures, ought not to become a means by which provinces could tax the import of goods from other provinces, there is less agreement on the question of territorial limitations on the impact of tax legislation. As we have seen, proposals for reform from the Task Force on Canadian Unity, the Canadian Bar Association, and the Special Joint Committee all explicitly recommended that provincial power to levy indirect taxes should be limited so that the tax would not fall on residents of another province. Proposals for constitutional reform originating with the provinces are typically silent on this issue,[138] probably more from a wish to preserve flexibility in provincial taxation measures than from a desire to tax non-residents.

The pervasive concern for the integrity of provincial control over natural resources clearly has implications for the taxing powers of both federal and provincial governments. In *Harmony in Diversity* the Alberta government pointed out that the federal policy which disallows the deductibility of provincial royalties for federal corporate income taxation is a challenge to provincial primacy over natural resources. Provincial primacy, in the view of the Alberta government, clearly includes a limitation on the federal power to raise revenues by 'any Mode or System of Taxation.'[139] On the other side, the Constitution Act[140] assigns to the provinces in a new S. 92A(4) the power to levy indirect taxes

---

137 See Quebec's proposals on sovereignty-association: *Québec-Canada*.

138 For example, Alberta, *Harmony in Diversity*; but an exception is Ontario Advisory Committee, *Second Report*.

139 See, however, the Beige Paper, *A New Canadian Federation*, which while affirming provincial authority over natural resources recognizes the right of the federal government to impose export taxes and taxes upon all commercial activity, including natural resources.

140 *Supra* note 135

in respect of primary production from non-renewable natural resources, forest products, and electrical energy whether or not such production is exported from the province. The subsection goes on to prohibit provincial laws which differentiate between production exported to another part of Canada and production not exported from the province. This addition to S. 92 is considerably more limited in scope than the majority of constitutional reform proposals referred to above because the provinces' power to levy indirect taxation does not extend throughout the resource sector and applies only to primary production. At least one provincial premier has criticized the language as grossly inadequate on this basis.[141]

4 Transportation and communications

Transportation. While most recent constitutional studies do not propose substantial changes to the assignment of legislative authority over transportation (based on 92(10), 'undertakings connecting the Province with any other') the Beige Paper[142] and the Alberta government study both recommended provincial involvement in road and rail transportation. The Quebec study noted that despite substantial delegation of authority in the road transport field, uncertainty frequently occurs in peripheral areas: for example, whether a labour dispute within a transportation undertaking is subject to provincial or federal labour legislation if the undertaking is within federal jurisdiction but its administration has been delegated to the province.

The Beige Paper recommended placing road transport fully within provincial jurisdiction and suggests that uniformity can be achieved by provincial co-ordination of the regulatory agencies. The study further noted that while there is a need for central authority over air transport, appointments to the Canadian Transport Commission and matters such as the siting and construction of airports should take more account of regional interests and priorities.

The government of Alberta has cited transportation as a key tool in regional economic development. In the view of the authors of *Harmony in Diversity*, inequities in rail transport have always been an obstacle to western economic development. The report therefore recommended concurrent power in the realm of transportation.

Communications. In a large country like Canada, subdivided regionally, culturally, and linguistically, modern communications are of great significance to

141 Peter Lougheed, premier of Alberta, stated that the federal offer 'to entrench provincial jurisdiction over resources does nothing significant for Alberta and may result in fewer rights than the province already has.' (quoted in the *Globe and Mail*, 23 October 1980, at 8).
142 *A New Canadian Federation*

national unity and to the creation and flourishing of a national identity. The national interest must also compete with enormous demand for popular foreign (American) programming in radio, television, and film. At the same time the significance of communications gives rise to a substantial provincial interest in their regulation. A further complication is the desire of both federal and provincial governments not merely to regulate but also to provide communication services themselves. For example, federal authority over radio and television communication has resulted in the exclusion of provinces as licensed operators in these fields except where educational programming is involved.

The Canadian Bar Association Report[143] attempted to resolve these complex questions by assigning concurrent power over broadcasting and cable transmission while reserving federal paramountcy in order to encourage a strong national system. Matters relating to the technical infrastructure (such as assignment of broadcast frequencies) would be the exclusive domain of Parliament. In telephone communication the report recommended assigning all intraprovincial aspects to the provinces, thus separating intra- from interprovincial functions, a step which the courts have not been willing to take.[144]

Several other recent proposals involve substantially similar assignments of legislative powers. The provincial concern is with program content, particularly in cable television because it does not involve the use of broadcast frequencies at all. The report of the Ontario Advisory Committee on Confederation recommended changes which would allow both the federal and provincial governments to own and operate radio and television broadcasting systems.

The Quebec Liberal Party's Beige Paper is notable because it would deny jurisdiction over the content of programming transmitted by electronic media to either level of government. It reasoned that control over broadcast programming, like cinematography or the written press, is essentially a matter of fundamental rights (freedom of thought, opinion, speech, and the press) and as such ought to be beyond the competence of any government to control. The Beige Paper also contained provisions for an entrenched charter of fundamental rights and freedoms.

The Beige Paper, however, was in agreement with the Bar Association's Report in recommending an end to exclusive federal authority over Bell Canada and BC Telephone because their services were essentially local. Federal regulatory authority, the paper recommended, should be restricted to interprovincial and international telephone service.

143 *Towards a New Canada*
144 *Supra* note 49

Capital

As previously noted, most reform proposals recommend a redrafted S. 121 that would include provisions for the free movement of capital between provinces. The proposals also raise a variety of secondary matters important to the movement of capital. The report of the Alberta government, for example, recommended a limitation on federal spending power because this power, by allowing Parliament to fund projects in areas in which it cannot legislate, effectively distorts provincial priorities and programs. The Report of the Task Force on Canadian Unity emphasized the need to limit current provincial regulations on corporate mergers and ownership of land which create barriers to the mobility of capital.

1 Financial institutions

The Bar Association's Report recommended that the fundamental aspects of the monetary system should continue to be regulated by the central government. Thus, where provincial financial institutions are concerned, it is a matter of some importance to define those matters which are central to the integrity of the system, since such matters would be regulated by Parliament and not by provincial legislatures. The report suggested that such matters as deposit insurance (because the collapse of a provincial financial institution could undermine confidence in other Canadian financial institutions) and foreign ownership of provincial financial institutions should fall within the legislative power of Parliament. Of the reform studies examined, only the Quebec White Paper did not recognize the need for central control of fundamental monetary matters. Nevertheless, 'sovereignty-association' is based on the unity of customs tariffs and a single currency, although federally regulated monetary institutions would be replaced, as between Quebec and Canada, by joint monetary institutions.

The Ontario Advisory Committee on Confederation recommended that provincial financial institutions be regulated provincially except in their interprovincial and international aspects and in operations which constitute part of the national banking system. The Special Joint Committee of the Senate and the House of Commons recommended that where provincially incorporated institutions conduct business in more than one province, national standards ought to apply. The Beige Paper recommended no change in this area or in securities regulation, merely noting that the present ambiguities restricting provincial control over trust companies should be removed.

2 Competition

The consensus among reform proposals is that regulation of anti-competitive practices ought to fall within the authority of the central government, although this power ought to be limited so that it does not nullify valid provincial activity in areas such as the regulation of professions, labour relations (e.g. unions), and consumer protection.[145]

The Special Joint Committee of the Senate and the House of Commons recommended that legislative authority over matters of competition policy be concurrent on the ground that assigning exclusive power to Parliament would be too radical a change in the division of powers. Under concurrency, federal authority would be restricted to circumstances in which provincial control was ineffective. Since 1972 there has been more general acceptance of the need for a dominant federal presence in competition regulation as long as certain provincial powers do not become subordinate to federal law. Provincial regulations such as those listed above, however, are potential sources of provincially induced non-tariff barriers.[146]

Subsequent proposals of the federal government to the Continuing Committee of Ministers on the Constitution included an amended S. 91(2) which would make competition an explicit part of the federal trade and commerce power.[147]

3 Securities

Recommendations for reform in the assignment of regulatory authority over securities are more divergent than those respecting competition policy.

One view is that securities regulation has largely to do with contracts for the sale of property interests and consumer protection, both areas clearly within provincial authority. Regulation of securities does not, in this view, interfere with the movement of capital, but merely enables a more efficient exercise of choice by the investor.[148]

Another view holds that a national market requires uniform standards. Thus, either by exclusive[149] or concurrent authority[150] the federal government should have primary responsibility for securities regulation. According to the Special Joint Committee, uniform standards would result in more protection for the investor and thus less outflow of capital to the United States. In 1964 the Royal

---

145 See *Second Report, Towards a New Canada*, and *A New Canadian Federation*.

146 See, for example, *R. v. Canadian Breweries, supra* note 86, and *Law Society of British Columbia, supra* note 87.

147 Canada, 'Powers over the economy: options submitted for consideration by the Government of Canada to safeguard the Canadian economic union in the constitution.' Document No. 830–83 / 007 in Continuing Committee of Ministers on the Constitution, *List of Public Documents / Liste des documents publics* (Ottawa: Canadian Government Intergovernmental Conference Secretariat, 1980)

148 *Towards a New Canada, A New Canadian Federation*, and *Second Report*

149 The view taken by a minority of the Constitution Committee of the Canadian Bar Association, *Towards a New Canada*.

150 Special Joint Committee, *Final Report*

Commission on Banking and Finance made recommendations for federal supervision of the securities market. These recommendations were pursued in greater depth in the recent study, *Proposals for a Securities Market Law in Canada*, conducted by the federal Department of Consumer and Corporate Affairs.[151] Among reasons cited for greater federal involvement in securities were (1) that new techniques in automation and computerized transactions allow instant trading on a national (and international) scale; (2) that new issues are almost always national in scope; (3) that the 'big provinces' already effectively set the standards for everyone and federal regulations would merely tidy up the process (the point being that no chaotic upheavals in the market would result should securities fall within federal authority); and (4) that investors have always ignored provincial and international boundaries, as have the perpetrators of fraud who capitalize on differing jurisdictions and regulatory systems. The predominant view, however, seems to be that securities should remain basically within the authority of the provincial legislature with some room for a federal presence where interprovincial or international transactions are concerned.

4 Incorporation of companies

The Quebec Liberals' Beige Paper presented the most substantial proposals for change in the area of jurisdiction over incorporation. In the view of the authors, incorporation pertains to juridical status and thus is essentially a question of private law (capacity to contract, to do business, to sue, and to be sued). Thus, they concluded, a province should have the authority to incorporate all companies wishing to conduct business within the province with the exception of companies engaging in activities which fall within federal jurisdictin such as air travel or interprovincial transportation. This authority would be subject to a constitutional guarantee that a provincial or federal company could do business in any province as long as it adhered to local laws of general application. According to one view, the Quebec Liberal Party's proposal would constitute a change in constitutional law because the basis for the distinction between federal and provincial companies is at present territorial (do they do business in more than one province?) rather than functional (are they involved in enterprises that fall within the federal or provincial jurisdiction?).[152] The Beige Paper recommended a functional test as a basis for this distinction.

People

The constitutional and economic aspects of personal mobility have not received a great deal of detailed attention. As noted above, most proposals for the

---

151 *Supra* note 95
152 Hogg, *Constitutional Law*, at 349–51

redrafting of S. 121 would include prohibitions against barriers to the mobility of people as well as goods, services, and capital. The extent to which personal mobility should be protected, however, is a matter of considerable disagreement. The Task Force on Canadian Unity found provincial legislation restricting the purchase of land by 'non-residents' objectionable to principles of Canadian economic union. Accordingly the report recommended an outright prohibition, constitutionally entrenched, of discrimination based on province of past or present residence (such as that embodied in the legislation challenged, but upheld by the Supreme Court of Canada, in *Morgan* v. *Attorney General of P.E.I.*).[153] Provincial regulation of professional standards was, in the view of the Task Force, also a cause for concern. The report recommended the standardization of professional requirements across the country so that regional standards could not (intentionally or unintentionally) become barriers to mobility.

The Beige Paper also recommended constitutional guarantees prohibiting legislation discriminating between people on the basis of province of permanent residence. Likewise, the Canadian Bar Association Report, because the protection available under federal authority over 'citizenship' is so unclear, recommended provisions providing that all manpower may move freely throughout the country.

The difficulty with these proposals arises out of the obvious provincial interest in protecting the local economy and local workers and other legitimate provincial concerns such as the concern over absentee landowners which animated the legislation considered in *Morgan*. Thus, the mobility rights first proposed in The Constitutional Amendment Bill (Bill C-60) in 1978 and put forward more recently in the Canadian Charter of Rights and Freedoms were, from the point of view of the provincial governments, one of the most controversial issues in the partriation / amendment debate.

More generally, it is clear that entrenched rights constitute substantial intrusions into the legislative authority of both Parliament and provincial legislatures. In a memorandum prepared for the Quebec government, the extent of the impact of an entrenched Charter on Quebec law was documented.[154] The catalogue of over fifty provincial laws which might become questionable under an entrenched Charter extended from film censorship (provincial power upheld in *McNeil* v. *Nova Scotia Board of Censors*[155]) to provincial strict liability offences (e.g., in liquor licensing), and from education and language laws to

153 *Supra* note 102
154 Memorandum from Courtois, Clarkson, Parsons et Tétrault, Avocats to L'Honorable Marc-André Bédard, Ministre de la Justice, Gouvernement du Québec (le 25 février 1981), unpublished
155 *Supra* note 37

professional standards and government subsidies. The main purpose of the memorandum was to show that the proposed Charter would redistribute regulatory authority from the provincial legislature to the judiciary. The memorandum also highlighted provincially induced barriers to mobility whose validity was well established under existing constitutional law and indicated why constitutional changes to eliminate such barriers might be repugnant to provincial governments. Thus, despite provincial agreement with the objective of facilitating personal mobility, provinces have been unwilling to accept the concomitant loss of legislative power.

These provincial concerns have been reflected in the final version of the Canadian Charter of Rights and Freedoms, whose mobility rights provision now would not apply to affirmative action programs in favour of the socially or economically disadvantaged in high unemployment provinces, and would both permit the imposition of residence requirements for social services and, unlike the 1978 Bill, provide no protection to non-residents seeking to acquire property.

The provision is as follows:

6 (1) Every citizen of Canada has the right to enter, remain in and leave Canada.

(2) Every citizen of Canada and every person who has the status of a permanent resident of Canada has the right

(a) to move to and take up residence in any province; and

(b) to pursue the gaining of a livelihood in any province.

(3) The rights in subsection (2) are subject to

(a) any laws or practices of a general application in force in a province other than those that discriminate among persons primarily on the basis of province of present or previous residence; and

(b) any laws providing for reasonable residency requirements as a qualification for the receipt of publicly provided social services.

(4) Subsection (2) and (3) do not preclude any law, program or activity that has as its object the amelioration in a province of conditions of individuals in that province who are socially or economically disadvantaged if the rate of employment in that province is below the rate of employment in Canada.

The right to mobility conferred by S. 6 is now so qualified that it will probably not significantly constrain the provinces' ability to impose barriers to labour mobility.[156]

---

156 For recent Charter cases see: *Re Federal Republic of Germany and Rauca* (1982), 38 o.r. (2d) 705 (Ont. H.C.), now affirmed by Ont. C.A. (extradition a prima facie infringement of s. 6(1) but a reasonable limitation demonstrably justified within s. 1); *Re Skapinker and Law*

The potential for provincially induced barriers to mobility arising out of provincial enactment of language laws is restricted slightly by the terms of the Charter, Ss. 16–23. Specifically S. 23(1) entrenches the right of any citizen of Canada, whose first language (or primary school instruction) is that of the English or French linguistic minority of their province of residence, to have their children receive primary and secondary school instruction in that language. This is a limited guarantee in several important respects. First, this right is one of those which applies only to a citizen of Canada. Second, it is a right which devolves only on those whose first language is, or who received their primary school instruction (in Canada) in, English or French. Finally, S. 23(3)(a) provides that the S. 23(1) right applies only where numbers of children of entitled citizens warrant expenditure of public funds. S. 23(3)(b) extends the right to include separate minority language educational facilities – again where numbers warrant. Although it may be hard to imagine a threshold which gives legal effect to the phrase 'wherever the number of children is sufficient to warrant,' S. 24(1) seems to contemplate the possibility by providing, generally, that a court may, upon application, order any remedy considered appropriate and just in the circumstances where a right has been denied or infringed. Minority language education rights entrenched in S. 23 of the Charter, while clearly drawn to cover a narrow instance, do preclude, in that specific aspect, provincial barriers to mobility through enactment of exclusionary language education laws (note that S. 23 is not subject to the S. 33 'override' provision).

Institutional reform

Many of the proposals for constitutional reform of jurisdiction over economic matters raise the collateral issue of second chamber reform. In many quarters there is a perceived failure of the institutions of federalism to adequately provide for provincial involvement in national economic policy-making. Provinces often feel that their own economic goals and priorities are frustrated or distorted by disharmonious or simply dominant federal policies (via the spending power, for

---

Society of Upper Canada (1983) 40 O.R. (2d) 481 (Ont. C.A.) (The rights to pursue the gaining of a livelihood and to move to and take up residence in any province are separate and distinct); *Malartic Hygrade Goldmines (Quebec) Ltd.* v. *The Queen in Right of Quebec* (23 Sept. 1982) 16 A.C.W.S. (2d) 498 (Que. S.C.) (provincial law prohibiting occasional practice in Quebec by a member of the Bar in another province upheld as a law of general application not discriminating primarily on basis of province of residence within S. 6(3)); *Black et al.* v. *Law Society of Alberta* [1983] 3 W.W.R. 7 (Alta. Q.B.) (interlocutory injunctions granted to restrain enforcement of law society rule prohibiting a member of the Alberta Bar, resident and practising in Alberta, from entering into partnership with anyone not an active member ordinarily resident in Alberta on the basis that the rule arguably discriminates among persons primarily on the basis of province of residence).

example). Provinces want to participate in the making of national economic policy. One instrument of that involvement is seen to be a restructuring of the Senate to provide more explicitly for regional representation. The two major issues are: the composition of a restructured Senate and its powers. Recent proposals cover the spectrum from provincial to federal predominance.

1 Composition

The 1978 Liberal government proposal (Bill C-60) envisaged a House of the Federation whose membership would be composed half of federal appointees and half of provincial appointees. The 50 / 50 concept formed the basis of the Joint Committee proposal in 1973 as well. Conversely, British Columbia, Quebec, and the Canada West Foundation all proposed that membership to the Senate be made up only of provincial delegations. The Task Force on Canadian Unity recommended non-voting involvement by the federal cabinet.[157]

While appointment of members suffers some disability in terms of political legitimacy, virtually all the proposals, with the exception of that of the Canada West Foundation,[158] have favoured appointment over election of members to a reconstituted Senate. As pointed out in the Canadian Bar Association study, membership by election would merely tend to make the upper house a pale reflection of the Commons, perpetuating existing division and enclaves.

What interests should be represented? It is a complex question whether the upper house should embody only strict provincial representation or reflect regional, cultural, and linguistic interests as well. Various schemes, such as those worked out by the Ontario Advisory Committee and the Canadian Bar Association, [159] have come up with a weighted distribution taking into account provincial and regional factors, population, language, and culture.

Another facet of the issue is the degree to which the members would be under the direct 'political' control of the appointing province. The Quebec Liberals' Beige Paper, for example, explicitly insisted that delegates in the second chamber would represent only the policies of their provincial governments.

2 Powers

What should be the exact extent of Senate powers in the law-making process? The extremes are represented here by the 1978 Liberal proposal (Bill C-60), in which the Senate could only delay passage of legislation, and the British Columbia proposals, in which the Senate would have an absolute veto regarding laws of

157 *A Future Together*
158 Canada West Foundation, *Regional Representation* (Calgary: 1981)
159 *Second Report* and *Towards a New Canada*

provincial importance.[160] The Canadian Bar Association study concluded that since the division of powers already gave extensive power to the provinces, any form of absolute veto, without provision for a Commons override, would tilt the balance of power too far in favour of the provinces.

Over what bills would a reformed Senate exercise jurisdiction? Once having settled the question of the nature of the power a reformed Senate would have, one has to decide what legislation may be subjected to that power. Most proposals have contemplated divided jurisdiction so that only legislation of importance to the provinces would come before the Senate. Divided jurisdiction in turn raises a threshold problem. When are matters of sufficient provincial importance to necessitate Senate approval, and who will decide? The Task Force on Canadian Unity proposed that bills be classified into three categories: bills competent to the central government alone, bills subject to Commons paramountcy, and bills subject to second chamber paramountcy.[161] A permanent committee would be established to preside over classification. Similarly, the Beige Paper proposed a power of ratification over federal proposals affecting the 'fundamental equilibrium of the federation' in which a joint committee of the House and the 'federal Council' would make the preliminary determination.

Second chamber reform along the lines outlined above, by increasing provincial involvement in central policy-making, might well impair federal initiatives in formulating economic policies. On the other hand an argument can be made that the integration of regional representation into central institutions will tend to make those members more attuned to the 'big picture.' This in turn could tend to decrease the identification of provincial interests with economic barriers.

Two points should be made in conclusion. First, the major (although not the only) question in the debate over a reformed upper house is provincial involvement in regulating the national economy. Constitutional reform might find more appropriate means to this end by looking at the prior issue of provincial involvement in the policy process rather than law-making. Second, the diversity of starting points on Senate reform, with current provincial attitudes, and the amending formula of the Constitution Act, combine to suggest that early reforms on this matter are not likely.[162]

---

160 'Paper No. 3, Reform of the Canadian Senate.' In British Columbia Executive Council, *British Columbia's Constitutional Proposals: Presented to the First Minister's Conference on the Constitution October, 1978* (Victoria: Queen's Printer for British Columbia, 1978), at 42

161 *A Future Together*

162 The amending formula requires, by S. 42(1)(b), the approval of Parliament and two-thirds of the provinces with at least 50 per cent of the population for an amendment relating to the powers of the Senate and the method of selecting senators.

12
Summary and implications

The editors

INTRODUCTION

Since the foregoing analyses were committed to paper in summer 1981 the press of economic events has proceeded relentlessly onward. The Canadian Constitution has been patriated and, as noted by Courchene, has enshrined the right of certain provinces to 'fragment' the internal economic union with respect to the mobility of labour. Moreover, the economic climate has also changed dramatically. The struggle against inflation by the United States, particularly the effect of very high American interest rates, has contributed to a marked slowdown in economic activity across the Western world. In turn, this has led to a heightened concern that protectionist or beggar-my-neighbour policies will come to be widely used to combat unemployment over the shorter term. Though it is natural to evaluate any analysis in light of current economic conditions, the papers in this volume are really directed toward the longer term. Whatever policy options may be applicable in a temporary recession, the options considered here address the longer-term issues of the costs and benefits of securing an internal common market within the Canadian federation.

THEORY AND CONCEPTS

This volume seeks to do two things:

– to assess the quantitative significance of internal barriers to trade in the Canadian federation both absolutely and compared to those extant in other federations,
– assuming that there is a need to ensure greater internal mobility of goods and factors, to isolate and evaluate the various channels, constitutional and otherwise, through which desired measures can be effected.

In Part 1, Prichard, Courchene, and Melvin paint the conceptual and institutional backdrop within which this analysis can proceed. Among the underlying issues addressed are the following: What is the definition of a barrier to trade within a common market? Why would governments introduce such distortions when it can be shown that overall national welfare will be reduced and indeed the overall welfare of the geographical entity introducing the distortion can often be shown to fall? Does the very essence of a federal system imply a fracturing of the internal economic union? Put somewhat differently, is decentralization likely to lead eventually to balkanization? Or do as many internal barriers exist in unitary states as in federal states? The contributions in Part 1 grapple with fundamental issues of this sort.

The question of how to ascertain whether the removal of a given 'distortion' might increase overall welfare is addressed by Melvin. His analysis is not comforting. For example, the removal of some impediments both increases national income and reduces welfare (as an economist understands these terms). In other words, there is no unique way of defining a distortion, let alone of measuring the effect of its removal. Furthermore, efficiency of resource allocation is only one goal of overall policy; another is to secure a desirable distribution of income, and the two are often in conflict. As Melvin puts it: 'when passing judgment on these distortions it is important to consider what alternatives are available and to keep in mind that few politically feasible policies are neutral.'

The questions of how to define a distortion and how to measure its consequences preoccupy many of the papers in the volume. Prichard's introductory essay argues that an appreciation of this issue is fundamental to an understanding of the entire question of securing the Canadian economic union. The conventional economic approach has been to define a policy as distorting if it results in resources being allocated either within or between provinces in such a way as to reduce potential national real income or potential real GNP. That is the definition employed in the empirical studies in Part 2. But as Melvin, Courchene, and Prichard all argue, such a definition is far from value-free.

Melvin also attempts to provide a theoretical answer to the question why governments pursue policies that can easily be shown to reduce overall welfare. To do this, he formulates a model of multi-level governments. The essence of the model is that the existence of different types of public goods and the assumption of nonuniform preferences of citizens provides the rationale for a multi-level structure of government (i.e. federalism). However, on the assumption that governments maximize the possibility of being re-elected, he argues that multi-level governments can also generate policies that, while optimal for one level of government, are non-optimal for society as a whole. Courchene takes this point further, arguing that lower-tier governments might enact policies that will clearly lower the overall output of their *own* jurisdiction as well as national output, but which may still be 'optimal' because the benefits (which are less than the costs) are directed to an important group of marginal voters. These conclusions too are not comforting for anyone trying to measure and assess the extent of internal barriers. Presuming that the provinces have a right to try to ensure that the optimal bundle of taxes and services is provided to their citizens, the relevant issue may not be whether one policy or another is distorting but rather, given that the government wants to achieve a certain goal, which policy offers the best way to accomplish this goal. Obviously the difficulty with the 'optimal policy instrument' approach is that, in the limit, there is no such thing as a distortion. This issue occupied a good deal of the Conference discussion.

Prichard and Courchene, though dwelling at some length on the issues dealt with by Melvin, carry the analysis further into the current policy arena. Prichard has much to say about the economic and political advantages and disadvantages of decentralization. He argues that there is a compromise between the capacity of smaller jurisdictions to satisfy the diverse needs, tastes, and preferences of citizens in different locations and the likelihood that decentralization entails a loss of economies of scale, the creation of externalities in the form of beggar-my-neighbour policies, and potentially adverse distributional consequences. This compromise has led to a search for institutional arrangements within the federal system that allow for regional differences in policies while constraining at least the most significant diseconomies they might cause.

Courchene concentrates on what he refers to as the 'federalism continuum' – the notion that there are federal aspects to all modern forms of government, unitary states included. He then considers whether there are likely to be more mechanisms for bringing about harmonization of internal policies in a formally federal nation than in a unitary state. Prichard's paper identifies in detail these various constitutional and institutional co-ordinating mechanisms.

Implicit in Courchene's analysis are two rather contentious arguments. First, the federal government, he says, appears to believe that junior-level governments tend to adopt province-first policies that, almost by definition, will fragment the internal economic union, whereas policies adopted by Ottawa, undertaken in the 'national' interest, again almost by definition cannot be viewed as impediments to the internal common market. Courchene objects that internal markets are fragmented in unitary states too, that current national economic policies probably harm the free flow of goods and factors within Canada more than provincial measures do, and that Ottawa wants to place constitutional limits on provincial powers, citing practices in other federal states, while avoiding equivalent limits on its own powers.

Prichard does not agree. If a provincial Act is inimical to out-of-province residents, he points out, there is no official forum in which the latter can respond, and the provincial politicians who enacted this legislation are not politically accountable to them. However, if federal legislation sought to accomplish the same purpose, the out-of-province suppliers could register their complaints in Parliament, and the legislators who enacted the measures would be politically accountable to all those affected by the policy.

This line of argument can lead to the proposition that the federal government, by definition, cannot 'distort' the internal market whatever it does. The question whether federal legislation has an inherent legitimacy denied to provincial legislation on the ground that only the former is based on decisions by legislators accountable to all those affected by them was considered a crucial one in our discussions. Depending on the answer to it the barriers to economic union and the reform proposals might, or might not, be extended to include federal as well as provincial powers. It was suggested that for some provincial protectionist measures, such as those that discriminate against out-of-province suppliers in favour of local suppliers at the cost of higher prices to local residents, these local consumers adversely affected by the measures can be viewed as political surrogates for the out-of-province producers. The discussion left the matter unresolved.

There are in fact two different and competing conceptions of the nature of the problem in much of the debate concerning distortions in internal trade flows. On one hand the 'beggar-my-neighbour' conception views spillover and externality costs caused by interjurisdictional and intergovernmental clashes as the essence of the problem. On the other hand many of the policies cited as distortions, particularly federal policies, cannot readily be so interpreted within this conception since both the benefits and the costs are largely confined to the jurisdiction adopting the policy. In these cases the notion of spillovers and externalities between jurisdictions may lose much of its relevance, and policies can be interpreted as distortions only on the basis of a conception of political failure within the jurisdiction. That is, in the absence of spillovers, the term 'distortion' must refer to some imbalance of costs and benefits within a jurisdiction, and any such imbalance must be traced to the incentives in the jurisdiction's decision-making processes that enable some groups to impose costs on others while appropriating an undue share of benefits. These competing conceptions of the problem entail different implications for institutional reform, discussed by Prichard. Not all distortions are caused by the division of powers between levels of government and between provinces. Some can be attributed to internal political failures of a given jurisdiction and so would not necessarily be affected by constitutional reform altering the division of powers.

A second area of controversy is Courchene's conception of beggar-my-neighbour policies. He argues that advantages arise from competitive federalism (in which provinces offering alternative bundles of public services and taxes) but that at some point as competition grows the line is crossed between competitive and destructive (beggar-my-neighbour) federalism. A few Conference participants argued that they did not believe that a destructive policy could be meaningfully defined, particularly over the longer term, since in virtually all cases the province that would lose by any protectionist policy was the one that enacted the restrictive measures (it was agreed that this depends on price elasticities of provincial import demand functions, for which no estimates exist). In that case placing curbs on provincial activities smacks of paternalism – protecting provinces from their own mistakes. If the process of fragmentation ever became too costly the provinces would realize the errors of their ways and would find some mechanism for harmonizing and co-ordinating behaviour across provinces. This point of view would also lead in the limit to the proposition that internal barriers to mobility are essentially a non-issue.

A related issue addressed by Prichard is that of shared powers and divided jurisdiction and the resulting overlap, interdependence, co-ordination, and conflict. This issue is not a new one in discussions of Canadian federalism, but as with the concept of distortion its implications depend on one's point of view. Prichard examines the question of the overlapping constitutional powers from a variety of vantage points – accountability, competition, administration, and function – arguing that from different perspectives the phenomenon takes on different complexions. Overlap is in itself neither good nor bad, neither desirable nor undesirable. To associate overlapping powers with barriers to trade and conclude that the overlap should therefore be reduced or eliminated is in Prichard's view unacceptable.

Courchene examines the internal common market issue in the context of a series of alternative objectives for overall Canadian policy. He stresses that estimates of the costs of internal barriers cannot be viewed in isolation from the objectives of national and regional policy. A given set of provincial protectionist measures will be more costly if the central government is actively attempting to ensure an 'appropriate' distribution of economic activity across the provinces and offsetting any effects of provincial barriers than if Ottawa seeks to be only a passive co-ordinator and a supplier of national public goods.

Not surprisingly, more problems are posed in the first part of this volume than can be readily answered by resort to quantification. That is inevitable in view of the current state of the available data and the inherent analytical difficulties attending such questions as the concept of a distortion, the notion of aggregate welfare, and the political implications of centralization and decentralization.

We now turn to the heart of the study – an attempt to get some general estimates of the costs of selected policies that tend to fragment Canada's internal economic union.

EVIDENCE

In three papers in the second part of the volume, Trebilcock, Whalley, and their coauthors evaluate the significance of interprovincial barriers to mobility of goods, capital, and labour (barriers to 'interprovincial activity' for short) at both federal and provincial levels. The first of the three papers provides an overview of these barriers, along with some discussion of methodological issues and some rough estimates of their effects. The second discusses federal barriers to mobility; the third discusses provincial barriers.

The overview chapter begins with a working definition of a distortion. Any policy is 'distortionary' if it results in resources being allocated either within or between provinces in such a way as to reduce potential national real income. Using this definition, distortions are defined by their impact on the economy rather than by their policy characteristics.

A distinction is made between natural barriers to interprovincial activity and artificially induced distortions. With natural barriers, such as language and distance, it is not obvious that any positive policy to reduce them is in order on purely economic grounds. On the other hand with artificially induced distortions, which are policy-created, policy intervention is appropriate on economic grounds.

A further important distinction is made between explicit and implicit distortions of interprovincial mobility. An 'explicit' distortion is based on a stated discrimination on the basis of province. A clear example would be a provincial government procurement policy giving explicit preference to in-province contractors in bidding on provincial government contracts. An 'implicit' distortion refers to significant effects on interprovincial activity arising from a policy that has no stated interprovincial discrimination. Implicit distortions have been said to arise, for instance, with the federal tariff and energy policies. The Maritimes and western provinces often argue that the protection afforded by the tariff primarily benefits manufacturers located in central Canada and increases the sale of their products in the other provinces. To the extent that this argument is true, Canadian tariff policy, by artificially stimulating interprovincial trade, substantially alters interprovincial activity. Similarly, the regulation of energy prices, by forcing energy-producing provinces to sell to Canada below world market prices, is said to benefit the energy-consuming provinces. Neither of these policies contains provisions discriminating by province, so they are classified as implicitly distorting.

On the basis of these distinctions the first paper in the second part summarizes the major artificially induced distortions in Canada. These are broken down into distortions of interprovincial flows of goods, capital, and labour. The following policies are highlighted as distorting goods flows: provincial government procurement policies, the regulation of freight rates under the Crow's Nest Pass Agreement, provincial liquor buying and pricing policies, federal energy policies, the operations of agricultural marketing boards, the federal tariff, and the auto pact. A final issue concerns the effects of both federal and provincial taxes.

The following are highlighted as causing distortions of capital flows: provincial investment plans, (identified as tax shelters), the Heritage Funds in Alberta and Saskatchewan, provincial business subsidies, DREE operations, the role of provincial crown corporations, and the exploration-incentive features of federal energy policies.

Highlighted as distorting interprovincial labour flows are the following: equalization grants, occupational licensing schemes, and the unemployment insurance program.

The size and nature of interprovincial activity are estimated. One of the most surprising features of the debate on interprovincial trade in Canada has been the relative absence of data. Until the last year or so, primary reliance has been placed on data on manufacturing shipments only, which give an incomplete picture. New data have been obtained from Statistics Canada that give some idea as to the size of interprovincial flows of goods. Data on interprovincial activity in capital and labour markets are even more limited.

Data for 1974 suggest that *interprovincial* trade flows in goods and services in Canada were then about $43 billion. This compares with *international* trade flows for Canada of about $33 billion. Generally speaking, for both goods and services interprovincial trade is more important than international trade, but for goods alone interprovincial and international trade are about the same.

The relative significance of interprovincial and international trade flows by province is examined, and some striking features emerge. British Columbia, for instance, is much more dependent on international than on interprovincial trade. The opposite is true for Quebec and Ontario. About two-thirds of all economic activity in Canada involves transactions which do not cross either international or interprovincial boundaries. About 20 per cent of activity crosses interprovincial boundaries only and does not cross international borders. The remaining 15 per cent involves international transactions. The fraction of total activity that is local to a province increases with the size of the province.

Data are reported on interprovincial trade by product. This enables some estimates to be made of the fraction of interprovincial trade which falls within the major distorted categories, which are identified in the summary of major distortions. Out of total interprovincial trade $43 billion in 1974, only some $3 billion of trade activity falls within those categories listed as containing major discriminatory policies. It thus seems that the significance of interprovincial barriers to trade in Canada may have been overplayed in recent public policy debates. However, to the extent that interprovincial barriers to trade have reduced the size of interprovincial trade flows, the amount of the resulting flows would underestimate the total effect.

Regarding distortions of capital flows, a recurrent theme is the question whether the capital market is national or international. If Canada is assumed to be part of a freely functioning international capital market, any barrier or artificial stimulus to capital flows would change the amount of capital that would go into a given province; but capital allocation in all other provinces would be unaffected. On the other hand if the capital market is national, increasing the capital inflow to one province would draw capital away from other provinces.

Recent Statistics Canada labour flow data presented in the overview paper indicate substantial amounts of interprovincial migration occurring in Canada. As with capital flow data, however, problems of interpretation make conclusions difficult.

In evaluating policy effects the concept of the welfare cost of trade-distorting policies using traditional partial equilibrium analysis was discussed. This is in the spirit of the Harberger-Hotelling approach to the calculation of the welfare cost of distortions, focusing on 'triangle' measures of welfare costs.

A number of methodological points are made. The most important is that whether or not a distortion exists often depends on the model used. For instance, with certain policies it is possible to argue that under one implicit model of the economy no distortion need operate, whereas under another model a significant distortion occurs. Nonetheless the calculations are done on the basis of explicit estimates of the possible impacts of these policies. The partial-equilibrium nature of the procedures and the effects of price endogeneity of interprovincial terms of trade are *not* taken into account in the estimates.

With these caveats, some speculative estimates of the potential distortionary costs of the various barriers to interprovincial activity are presented. In terms of goods flows, a 10 per cent distortion is taken as roughly the order of magnitude involved with tariff policies in international trade. Under these assumptions the annual costs of distortions (federal and provincial) of interprovincial trade flows in Canada come to significantly less than 1 per cent of GNP annually.

Some alternative estimates are made assuming large distortions for selected items of interprovincial activity (most notably energy), but the welfare cost estimates do not rise very substantially. The welfare cost estimates produced for distortions of capital and labour are smaller than for goods flows distortions. Though especially speculative, they are less than 0.05 per cent of GNP annually.

These estimates imply that too much significance may be attached to the issue of interprovincial barriers to trade in current policy debates in Canada. This conclusion is supported by the observation that the potential losses from distorting the *spatial* allocation of resources in Canada are small compared to the potential losses from other kinds of distortions. Distortions through the tax system, for instance, can significantly affect the commodity mix of items produced or the supply of factors of production in the economy with more serious consequences than spatial misallocation. Perhaps policy analysis in Canada should focus less on interprovincial barriers to trade than on other policy areas. However, the estimates underlying these conclusions are essentially static in nature, and the efficiency losses associated with spatially distorting policies may be significantly larger if viewed in a dynamic framework, that is, in light of the historic, cumulative consequences of reduced rates of innovation, rent-seeking, retaliatory costs, and so on.

Trebilcock and Whalley go on to examine federal and provincial policies and their distortionary impact on interprovincial trade. In the case of federally induced goods distortions, Whalley notes that there has been little recent discussion of the microeconomic distortionary effects of Canadian energy policies. He suggests that federal energy price ceilings substantially reduce interprovincial trade flows. In addition to the welfare costs involved, a transfer takes place from energy-producing to energy-consuming provinces by denying the former the right to sell energy at world prices. Energy is thus a key policy area, and clearly a federal one. Another important federal policy area concerns the tariff, which as we have seen substantially changes the terms of trade between Central Canada and the rest of Canada from what would prevail in a no-tariff regime.

Whalley suggests that little in the federal tax structure is explicitly interprovincially distortionary, although the manufacturers' sales tax may partially offset some features of the federal tariff. Regulation of freight rates under the Crow's Nest Pass Agreement does not seem to affect interprovincial trade very much.

As for capital market distortions, the exploration incentives under the National Energy Program partially offset the effect of price ceilings and therefore have to be considered along with the goods distortions involved. DREE activity is small in total, although the small amounts are highly concentrated in certain localities.

To review distortions in labour mobility, equalization and unemployment insurance programs are evaluated. Their effects are found to be small but significant. Defending equalization, it can be argued that it offsets the incentive for individuals to migrate to provinces with substantial amounts of resource rents.

The main distortionary provincial polices are as follows: for goods distortions government procurement policies, agricultural marketing boards, and sales taxes; for capital distortions business subsidies, heritage fund activity, and provincial tax systems; for labour distortions occupational licensing.

Government procurement policies have attracted the most attention in government documents on interprovincial barriers to trade in Canada. Trebilcock and Whalley stress how limited the data are on these issues. A rough estimate of the size of interprovincial flows potentially involved with government procurement suggests that this distortion is relatively modest in impact.

A large fraction of agricultural trade is governed by marketing boards; though some of them are federal, a significant amount of provincial activity is also involved. Recent estimates have suggested that as much as 60 per cent of agricultural trade between provinces in Canada comes under the governance of agricultural marketing boards. The effect of these boards on trade is difficult to quantify since some of them substantially raise prices while others have less impact. A particularly important issue in agriculture is the role of standards and inspection practices. A number of anecdotes are cited, but it is not known whether they represent the 'tip of the iceberg' or merely indicate a few nuisance provisions that interprovincial traders find it necessary to circumvent.

Sales taxes can affect goods flows mainly through the consequences of differentials between provincial rates. The different tax rates themselves do not constitute a barrier to interprovincial trade. The interprovincial effect occurs when people living on the borders of one province migrate to another province to spend money at lower tax rates. With large provinces the effects involved are small. However, differential rates or exemption structures that favour local producers may operate as implicit subsidies and do have the potential for distortion.

With capital flows, subsidies are discussed. The main difficulty is in obtaining information. A detailed catalogue of these subsidies is provided. However, with subsidies and guarantees a large fraction of the activity involved (more so at the federal level) concerns housing, and at the business level the numbers involved appear to be modest.

Capital flows are also affected by the operation of the Heritage Funds in Alberta and Saskatchewan and perhaps the caisses populaires in Quebec. It is often suggested that the Alberta Heritage Fund significantly distorts interprovincial allocation of capital. But the argument depends not only on the international versus national capital market issue already raised but also on the rules that are followed in allocating the resources of the Heritage Fund. If the rule is that all monies invested in the Fund are to be invested in Alberta projects, the private capital market may offset the impact of Heritage Fund allocations. If private markets ensure that the marginal product of capital is equalized across all provinces and if all the money in the Heritage fund is invested in Alberta, the private capital market elsewhere in Canada would ensure that the rate of return on capital in all provinces was the same. The net effect of the Heritage Fund on the interprovincial allocation of capital would then be zero since the private capital market would 'undo' the effect of the Heritage fund 'preference.' Differences in interprovincial corporate tax rates are at present fairly small, and thus so are the effects on capital allocation.

The effect on labour allocation of occupational licensing is examined, and much information on current regulatory practices is presented. The impression gained is that in many cases the restrictions on labour mobility are small. Sometimes other policies, such as the 'red seal' program, offset these restrictions. Furthermore, only a small fraction of the labour market is affected by occupational licensing. In general, occupational licensing scarcely influences interprovincial labour flows.

The main implication of the empirical evidence evaluated in this part of the book is that the overall impact of interprovincial barriers to interprovincial flows of goods, capital, and labour seems to have been exaggerated. A second conclusion is that by the definition of distortions adopted here the main distortionary policies appear to be federal rather than provincial, and within federal policies the major distortions arise in policy areas which have not attracted much attention because they are not explicitly interprovincially distortionary. In particular, energy policies and the tariff stand out as worthy of more detailed study.

COMPARATIVE PERSPECTIVES[1]

The four papers presented in the third part of this volume compare jurisdictional and institutional experiences in government procurement policies, industrial subsidies, fiscal harmonization, and personal mobility. The United States, the EEC, and GATT provide the chief points of reference. Each of the papers attempts to indicate what the implications or lessons for Canada (if any) may be.

Graham reviews the restraints on government procurement policies in GATT, the EEC, and the United States. As might be expected, the legal restraints

---

1 Since the studies in this volume were completed, a new and very useful review of comparative perspectives in economic mobility has been published by the federal government: John A. Hayes, *Economic Mobility in Canada: A Comparative Study* (Ottawa: Canadian Government Publishing Centre, 1982).

preventing a state from engaging in this form of discrimination are strongest in the American constitution and weakest in the GATT procedures, with the EEC lying somewhere between.

No system outlaws all discriminatin in government procurement. In the United States, where one would have expected to find the most rigorous suppression of this type of activity, one finds instead that the Constitution and the federal power over interstate trade and commerce leave to the states a considerable measure of freedom to discriminate in favour of their residents when exercising proprietary rather than regulatory functions. However, this freedom is circumscribed by two important limitations: the exercise of this right may not place a burden on interstate commerce, nor may it interfere with American international obligations, at the moment particularly Article III of GATT.

In the EEC the technique for reducing and restricting discriminatory purchasing practices is 'legislative' rather than 'constitutional' in form. The Treaty of Rome makes no specific reference to procurement policies. Because the Treaty was designed precisely to eliminate internal barriers to the free movement of goods and services, it is not surprising that the EEC organs have come to use the powers given them by the Treaty to enact Community measures addressed to this issue. The time taken and difficulties encountered by the EEC in achieving an even modest success in this field indicates how entrenched these practices are. The desire by member states to continue to favour their citizens may be understandable in the context of the present economic climate where equivalent measures are current everywhere, but they represent in many cases the antithesis of the founding principles of the community.

In the Tokyo Round of negotiations, GATT finally attempted to address this issue. The difficulties attending the negotiation of this code, together with the limited scope of its application, are eloquent testimony to the reluctance of states to surrender their freedom of action in this domain.

To translate these three experiences into the Canadian context is no simple task. They are perhaps more useful as analogies than as models. They do at least provide some examples of possible solutions. The EEC example of legislation of a federal and institutional type does not seem especially appropriate to the present Canadian political context; nor are there serious constitutional constraints in current Canadian law as in the United States (unless the Tokyo Round as 'externalized' previously intraprovincial trade so that Art. 91(2) of the BNA Act may commence to have a life hitherto denied it). In the absence of such 'centralist' checks the preferred course may be an agreement between various provinces, in which case the example of GATT seems the most appropriate, both in the type of problems involved in arriving at any such agreement and in the mechanisms that may be feasible for reducing future discriminatory practices.

Schwartz examines restraints on the use of industrial subsidies that may distort trade flows in the United States, the EEC, and GATT. In light of the possibility that a subsidy may enhance efficiency or accomplish desired distributional objectives, he assumes that any form of government support cannot be regarded as an undesirable 'distortion' without inquiry into its underlying purposes. At the same time, the nature of the political process is such that even identification, let alone quantification, of the external benefits and desired distributional effects is a hopeless task. Consequently, the evaluation of the relevant effects by the enacting jurisdiction must be largely taken as given.

The gains from regulation by some central authority derive from the interdependencies in the demands for investment by the local jurisdictions. By co-ordinating their policies (like a monopsonist), the overall level of subsidization can be constrained, with some loss of investment of course but with a net gain to the group of jurisdictions if the savings in payments is greater than the value of the decrease in investment. Achieving co-ordination of this kind, however, is extremely difficult since all the usual problems of 'cheating' are exacerbated in the political context in which the 'true' demand for investment in each jurisdiction is obscured and alternative means of attracting investment may be employed.

The most elaborate system of regulation, which in part at least seems designed to achieve co-ordination of this kind, is found in the EEC. Based on the experience in the EEC and the theoretical difficulties of achieving the desired co-operative solution, to pursue a policy of this kind an institution must be created with a clear mandate, highly respected personnel free of regional or interest-group bias, and flexibility to find politically acceptable means of discharging its responsibilities. This is a tall order. Whether it is worth attempting in Canada depends essentially on the magnitude of the gains achievable for Canada as a whole through co-ordination and the likely success in actually realizing these gains, given the conflicts of interest between the provinces and various economic groups and the political environment in which these conflicts must be resolved.

Thirsk examines and compares the diversity of approaches that various mature federations have adopted in striving to obtain an acceptable degree of fiscal harmonization. As a distinct economic objective, fiscal harmonization encompasses a wide range of tax and expenditure arrangements that co-ordinate the fiscal activities of the central and lower levels of government in a federation. All efforts at co-ordination involve a difficult compromise between fiscal uniformity, seen as desirable on grounds of economic efficiency, and fiscal freedom, often viewed as significant in its own right but which may also be related to efficiency concerns.

Historically, Canada has experimented with a number of solutions to this dilemma. In the 1930s it tried the formally unco-ordinated approach that currently characterizes the fiscal system found in Switzerland and to some extent the United States, and found it wanting. Giving the fullest scope possible for the pursuit of fiscal freedom, according to the Rowell-Sirois Commission, made the Canadian economy less able to achieve both economic efficiency and equity. Going to the other extreme, the federal pre-emption of the direct tax fields constitutionally allocated to the provinces was also considered to be a poor choice once the second world war was concluded. Since then Canadian fiscal practice has evolved from the Australian model of tax centralization towards the West German tax-sharing model and from there to the present method of direct tax base sharing. Since 1962, when the system of shared direct tax bases was introduced, each province has enjoyed the ability to impose its own tax rate on a tax base that is nationally uniform and to have the resulting revenue collected by the federal government.

In the opinion of many, including Thirsk, Canada's current approach offers the most satisfactory compromise between a permissive fiscal system and the need to constrain the fiscal choices of provincial governments for efficiency reasons. This conclusion draws considerable support from the observation that other countries, both those that are fiscally more centralized (Australia and West German) and those that are more decentralized (Switzerland and the United States), are either introducing or planning to introduce measures that will result in fiscal systems bearing a close resemblance to Canada's. While this international convergence towards the Canadian model is not proof that present practice is optimal, combined with Canada's historical experience it suggests that whatever is best cannot be far from what is now in place. However, the momentum of current political trends favouring further fiscal decentralization may carry Canada towards a model like that in the United States. In the latter the tax credit and the tax deduction have played important roles as co-ordinating devices, so it may be useful for Canadian social scientists to study how these techniques might be successfully transplanted to Canada.

Strikingly, all the federations studied rely on intergovernmental grants as one method of equalizing fiscal circumstances across geographic regions and suppressing the emergence of significant interjurisdictional tax differentials. Moreover, equalization payments may contribute indirectly to the realization of uniform tax rates by diluting the incentive any jurisdiction has in departing from the average rate of tax in a federation. The problem of fiscal harmonization would be made much more difficult without a scheme of equalization payments.

Finally, Thirsk indicates a strong correlation between a country's cultural homogeneity and its willingness to tilt the balance in favour of fiscal uniformity over fiscal autonomy. Federations with more centralized and uniform fiscal systems are apt to be those where racial, linguistic, and regional divisions are less important. Conversely, higher priority is accorded to fiscal autonomy in federations such as Switzerland where there are distinct regional and cultural groupings.

Laskin reviews experiences in the United States and the EEC with respect to constraints on barriers to personal mobility. American jurisprudence under the Privileges and Immunities Clause, the Commerce Clause, and the Equal Protection and Due Process Clauses bears on such issues of personal mobility as restrictions on physical mobility, restrictions or special imposts on out-of-state residents working in a state, restrictions on professionals seeking to relocate in a state, restrictions on ownership of property by out-of-state residents, residence and related restrictions on access to state social and medical assistance and educational facilities, residence and related restrictions on the right to vote or seek political office in a state, residence restrictions in state divorce laws, and restrictions on rights of out-of-state residents to exploit natural resources (especially those publicly owned) within a state. The case law on many of these issues is uncertain and confused. The underlying rationales for the distinctions that the U.S. Supreme Court has drawn have often been difficult to discern, revealing, Laskin argues, the complexity of the task of eliminating interjurisdictional barriers. It is not merely a matter of removing overt restrictions on local labour markets. The potential for direct and induced obstacles to freedom of movement exists across virtually the complete range of public policies: welfare rules, tax laws, property laws, voting rules, and so on.

In the EEC the Treaty of Rome contains detailed articles relating to the free movement of workers, the right of establishment, and the freedom to provide services. The Council of the EEC has issued complementary legislation and directives on equality of job opportunity, conditions of employment, and entry into and residence in member states. Directives respecting co-ordination of qualifications for social security benefit programs across member countries and entry into various businesses, trades, and professions have also been promulgated. Exceptions are made to these various mobility rights, for example on grounds of 'public policy' and 'public service employment,' although these have been narrowly interpreted both in directives and by the European Court. However, the fact that exceptions are provided suggests, as in American experience, that the priority of personal mobility can never be absolute – the complete elimination of all barriers to mobility involves the substitution of a larger for a smaller political community.

The detailed legislative prescriptions of the extent and limits of mobility rights by politically accountable bodies within the EEC, with less reliance on the judiciary operating under an open-textured mandate, has obvious attractions, and these attractions increase when it comes to effective implementation. The question this leaves open, Laskin argues, is whether in a Canadian context political structures exist or can be devised which have the acceptability and legitimacy to impose these detailed norms on the provinces (and probably on the federal government as well).

PROPOSALS AND CONCLUSIONS

As the essays make clear, there are no easy or obvious ways to restructure Canadian constitutional or institutional arrangements to enhance the integrity of the Canadian economic union. The research contained in this volume does not allow us to specify in detail appropriate constitutional responses to the problems facing the Canadian economic union. However, in developing detailed institutional reforms, several propositions should be carefully considered in light of our studies:

1. To identify policies emanating from either level of government that distort internal trade or resource flows, even measured against a conventional economic objective of maximizing national income, is an immensely difficult task. Whether a given policy creates distortions or, if it does, whether they are countervailed by other policies will often raise highly problematic issues. Thus, even within a conventional economic framework, in choosing policy instruments to reduce distortions the target of the exercise will usually not be technically well defined and readily measured. This fact has important implications for institutional choice and design.

2. Once the objective of maximizing national income is dropped as the touchstone and citizen preferences are acknowledged for other goals such as redistribution, provision of public goods, and cultural reinforcement, it becomes even more difficult to determine what policies will enhance economic or social welfare.

3. Decentralization of government functions possesses many attractive social, political, and economic properties. If these characteristics are valued by citizens, compromises are inevitable between avoiding spillovers and allowing decentralized decision-making. In other words, removing all barriers to, or distortions of, internal trade flows cannot be an absolute and over-riding objective in federalism. In a federal state the analysis must necessarily focus on the tradeoffs.

4. While centralization of ogvernment functions also possesses many desirable social, political, and economic properties, and may avoid the spillovers caused by provincial policies, even a unitary government in its choice of policies

will reflect citizen preferences that range much more broadly than simply maximizing national income. In fact, it is difficult to predict that central or unitary governments will be less prone to distort internal trade flows than lower levels of government. The evidence presented in this book suggests the opposite.

5. Questions then arise as to whether there is a qualitative difference between provincially induced and federally induced distortions (however defined). As we saw earlier, one line of argument is that because the federal government is potentially accountable to both winners and losers from its policies (i.e. costs cannot as easily be externalized to voters to whom the government is not accountable), distortionary federal policies are in this sense more politically legitimate than distortionary provincial policies, which may externalize the costs to voters in other jurisdictions. A countervailing argument is that this distinction is much too sharp. Political factors such as strong regional imbalances in federal party support mean that federal governments may not design policies to maximize net social welfare however defined. Furthermore, provinces can very rarely externalize fully or even substantially the costs of their policies. The most commonly cited provincial distortionary policies force consumers, taxpayers, and other interests within the province to bear a large part of the costs, and such opposing local interests must be taken into account by the provincial government in its political calculus. Besides, provincial legislators have an incentive to avoid measures that may provoke retaliation, direct or indirect, from other provinces, which ultimately could lead to internal political repercussions.

6. On the evidence, neither provincially induced nor federally induced barriers to trade in Canada seem, for the most part, to involve large economic costs. Therefore they do not yet present a strong case for a radical reordering of Canadian federalism. If the magnitudes involved in present distortionary policies were larger than they now appear to be, their importance would still be debatable because the economic concept of a distortion (i.e. a policy that reduces potential national real income or potential real GNP) reflects a very limited concept of social welfare. Therefore, any recommendations based on economic criteria, to be accepted, would require further support from non-economic considerations not addressed in this volume, such as their ability to enhance public perceptions of political legitimacy or to reduce the potential for national divisiveness and regional factionalism.

7. Because the tradeoffs between centralization and decentralization and between the maximization of national income and other social objectives are so intricate and value-laden, much caution is needed in assigning a central institutional role to the courts in policing barriers to trade within the Canadian economic union. The bodies of judicial experience reviewed by Laskin and Penny do not warrant confidence in entrusting to courts the task of making

complex and decisive social and political compromises. Thus, proposals to broaden the federal government's trade and commerce power, to broaden the prohibition on internal tariffs in Section 121 to include non-tariff barriers to trade in capital and services as well as goods, and the enactment of a constitutionally enshrined economic bill of rights would all seem open to question on this ground.

8. If the essence of the problem is perceived as some form of internal *political* failure at either the federal or provincial level, which causes the benefits of distortionary policies to be weighted more heavily than the costs, prescriptions directed to political structures and processes at that level seem more appropriate than assigning to courts the task of correcting for this failure.

9. With respect to provincially induced barriers to trade, it might be argued that the bearers of the costs of distortionary policies are typically widely diffused local interests such as consumers or the general body of taxpayers who lack the concentrated stakes to register effective political influence and in this sense cannot be regarded as reasonable political proxies for those interests outside the jurisdiction that may also stand to be prejudiced by these policies. If this is the form that political failure takes at the provincial level, the thrust of policy prescriptions presumably might be to confront provincial politicians more squarely with the costs of their policies in making their political calculus. While both Prichard and Penny review a host of possible constitutional and institutional reforms designed to constrain interprovincial barriers to trade, a couple of broad options seem worthy of further exploration. First, stronger incentives might be given to provincial governments to negotiate bilateral or multilateral agreements with other provinces (similar to the non-tariff barrier codes negotiated within GATT) on the types and levels of trade barriers between them. One possibility might be a substantially broadened Section 121 prohibition on tariff and non-tariff barriers to the internal movement of goods, services, and capital (policed only in a contingent way by the courts), with explicit 'gateways' out of the prohibition allowing for bilateral or multilateral agreements between provinces where discriminatory or distortionary policies are accepted by the parties on a negotiated basis (hence the internalization of political consequences).

Another option might be to attempt to internalize the political consequences of provincial distortionary policies through a reformed federal Upper House, reconstituted to represent the provinces and armed with directive powers (similar to the Council of the EEC) which could be invoked to constrain provincial policies that unacceptably distort the internal common market. Supporting administrative machinery would be needed, and the composition of the new House and its decision-rule applicable to directives would obviously be matters of considerable political delicacy.

10. With respect to federally induced barriers to trade, if the political failure that promotes distortionary policies is a persistent regional imbalance in party support, this problem should be attacked directly. Again, Prichard and Penny review a number of reform proposals. One broad option would be to adopt a form of proportional representation in the election of the Lower House, so that all major parties have significant representation from all major regions of the country and are thus forced to take account of (internalize) more fully than at present both the benefits and costs of potentially distortionary policies, especially when the benefits and costs are regionally differentiated. Another broad option is to restructure the Senate as essentially a House of the Provinces, comprised wholly or largely of provincial representatives, and invest it with power to delay or even block federal legislation that involves a distortion of benefits and costs across provinces that is not acceptable to all (or most) of the provinces affected. Again, this might force a greater political internalization of the costs and benefits of proposed policies in the political calculus of federal politicians. How precisely such an Upper House might be structured, what powers it would have, what rules would govern its decisions, whether its resolutions would be subject to an over-ride by the Commons, and, if so, the rules governing the over-ride power, all raise difficult, but not insoluble, problems.

11. Both lines of options sketched for constraining provincially induced and federally induced barriers to trade assume that the source of a barrier can be readily identified and attributed to one or other level of government. However, in many cases the increasing and unavoidable overlapping of levels of jurisdiction in complex governmental functions makes prescriptions predicated on mutually exclusive areas of jurisdiction incomplete. If 'executive federalism' in its present form is thought to have some undesirable features in dealing with overlapping functions, especially in terms of attenuated political accountability, a strengthened role for a reformed Upper House may have the added virtue of providing an integrated parliamentary forum for debate and resolution of some areas of conflict and tension in federal-provincial relations.

The general train of analysis outlined in these closing comments suggests that what began as essentially an economic problem – how to define and constrain barriers to trade within the Canadian economic union – has become redefined as a political problem – how to render both levels of government more sensitive to, and politically accountable for, the full consequences (benefits *and* costs) of their policies. This in turn is ultimately a legal and institutional problem – how to design constitutional or institutional arrangements that may enhance this objective without necessarily upsetting the broad balance to which the Canadian federal system aspires among the diverse advantages of centralization and decentralization.